TASK	AS NEEDED	DAILY	WEEKLY	MONTHLY	CHAPTER
DATA PROTECTION					
System backups		●			17
Restore lost/deleted/corrupted/archived files	●				17
Check file server UPS				●	15
Review file server "hot-fix" statistics				●	15
Test backup/restore procedures				●	15, 17
NETWORK MAINTENANCE					
Troubleshoot network problems	●				7, 12, 19
Review file server error log			●		15
Monitor network performance			●		12, 15, 19
Increase network performance			●		12, 18, 19
Review network maintenance procedures				●	12
Expanding network services	●				12, 20
Add new nodes	●				5, 7, 12
Establish connectivity with other networks	●				12, 20
Assessing new software and hardware				●	12
Technology updates (self-education)			●		12
Network documentation (software/hardware)	●				12

INTRODUCING NETWORK PRESS™

You *can* judge a book by its cover.

Welcome to Network Press™, the new and expanded successor to **Sybex's** acclaimed **Novell Press**® book series. If you liked our Novell Press books, you'll be impressed by the improvements we've made in the books that replace them. With **Network Press**, you'll find the same quality from a truly independent and unbiased viewpoint. You'll also find full coverage of not only Novell, but Microsoft and other network environments.

Building on a 20-year history of technical and publishing excellence, **Network Press**™ is dedicated to providing you with the fullest range and depth of networking information available today. You'll find the same commitment to quality, contents, and timeliness that you have come to expect from Novell Press books by Sybex. All previously released Novell Press titles remain available from Sybex.

> **Network Press** books continue to offer you:
> - winning certification test preparation strategies
> - respected authors you know and trust
> - all new titles in a wide variety of topics
> - completely updated editions of familiar best-sellers
> - distinctive new covers
>
> Our leadership approach guarantees your ongoing success in managing every aspect of your network's software and hardware.

Look for these **Network Press** titles, available now at your local bookstore:

The CNE Study Guide, Second Edition, by David James Clarke IV
    (Revised and updated edition of *Novell's CNE Study Guide*)
The Network Press Dictionary of Networking, by Peter Dyson
    (Revised and updated edition of *Novell's Dictionary of Networking*)
The Complete Guide to NetWare 4.1, by James E. Gaskin
Managing an Inherited NetWare Network, by Michael J. Miller
The CNE Update to NetWare 4.1, by Michael Moncur

For more information about Network Press, please contact:

 Network Press
2021 Challenger Drive
Alameda, CA 94501
Tel: (510) 523-8233/(800) 227-2346
Fax: (510) 523-2373/Email: info@sybex.com

NOVELL'S® GUIDE TO
NetWare® 3.12
NETWORKS

CHERYL CURRID AND COMPANY

Novell Press, San Jose

PUBLISHER: Peter Jerram
EDITOR-IN-CHIEF: Dr. R.S. Langer
SERIES EDITOR: David Kolodney
ACQUISITIONS EDITOR: Dianne King
PROGRAM MANAGER: Rosalie Kearsley
DEVELOPMENTAL EDITOR: David Kolodney
EDITOR: Guy Hart-Davis
TECHNICAL EDITORS: John T. McCann, William J. Harding
NOVELL TECHNICAL ADVISOR: Kelley Lindberg
BOOK DESIGNER: Helen Bruno
PRODUCTION ARTIST: Lisa Jaffe
SCREEN GRAPHICS: John Corrigan
LINE ART: Cuong Le
DESKTOP-PUBLISHING SPECIALIST: Helen Bruno
PROOFREADERS/PRODUCTION ASSISTANTS: David Silva and Janet MacEachern
INDEXER: Ted Laux
COVER DESIGNER: Archer Design
LOGO DESIGN: Jennifer Gill
COVER PHOTOGRAPHER: Nicholas Pazloff

Screen reproductions produced with Collage Plus.

Collage Plus is a trademark of Inner Media Inc.

SYBEX is a registered trademark of SYBEX Inc.

Novell Press and the Novell Press logo are trademarks of Novell, Inc.

TRADEMARKS: SYBEX and Novell have attempted throughout this book to distinguish proprietary trademarks from descriptive terms by following the capitalization style used by the manufacturer.

Every effort has been made to supply complete and accurate information. However, neither SYBEX nor Novell assumes any responsibility for its use, nor for any infringement of the intellectual property rights of third parties which would result from such use.

Library of Congress Card Number: 93-60632
ISBN: 0-7821-1093-2

Manufactured in the United States of America

To Ray, Tray, and Justy.

C.C.

To Beckie, my greatest source of understanding and support, and to Russ Puckett, a good friend and one of the most inspiring men I know.

T.C.

To Sue, for the continuous encouragement; to Traci, for a sympathetic ear to bend; and to my dog, KAD, for not forgetting who I am.

J.P.

Acknowledgments

Currid & Company would like to thank:

- Diane Bolin for her untiring efforts during the editing process of the book. Without her, we could never have kept the book organized.

- Mike Ellerbe for his contribution to the early part of the book and for free (semi-free) technical support in the wee hours of the morning.

- Kent Drummond for his work on the latter part of the book.

- Bill Gladstone and Dianne King for their work in bringing together the concept.

- The team at SYBEX, especially David Kolodney, the series editor, and Guy Hart-Davis, our editor.

- The combination SYBEX and Novell technical review team (John McCann of SYBEX and William Harding of Novell), who thoroughly put us through the wringer. Their careful scrutiny of the manuscript added tremendous value to the final product.

Tony Croes would like to thank:

- Guy "*Malleus Maleficarum*" Hart-Davis for infinite patience.

- William Harding for helping us keep a handle on new developments and for putting up with a great many last-minute questions.

- Rose Kearsley of Novell Press for consistently delivering the twenty-four–hour miracle.

- Cheryl Currid for accurately associating book production with the birthing process.

- Josh Penrod for agreeing in a moment of weakness—Bail! Bail!

Josh Penrod would like to thank:

- Tony Croes, for getting me into a lot of sleepless nights, bad fast food, some of the most frustrating months of my life, and the joys of pre-release and alpha software. It was worth it, wasn't it, Tony?

- The cheerful voice on the other end of the telephone, which usually said "Mike's tech support. Do you have your credit card ready?" Thanks, Mike.

CONTENTS AT A *Glance*

TABLE OF Contents

*I*ntroduction

Novell's Guide to NetWare 3.12 Networks is an easily read and understood escort through the challenge of installing and managing Novell NetWare 3.12. This book provides you with more than just a dry list of commands and procedures—it delivers a detailed explanation of why you should do something, as well as how to do it.

This book will take you through a wide range of topics from very basic discussions on general network theory all the way to advanced management subjects such as expanding the network and optimizing network performance. Overall, this book will provide you with an understanding of how to plan and install a new NetWare 3.12 network or upgrade an older version of NetWare, as well as give you the knowledge to configure and manage it effectively.

Who This Book Is For

This book contains information useful to a wide variety of readers. These include the ordinary network user, who might like to learn more about networking as one of the more productive business tools, all the way up to network administrators and installers, who need to know how to make the network more effective for the users. If you don't have much experience with networks, read the first four chapters closely to gain some background information about networking. If you have networking experience, you may want to skim these chapters in order to get to the later parts which deal with NetWare 3.12 in specifics.

How This Book Is Organized

This book is organized into five parts and four appendices:

Part I (Chapters 1 to 3) explains many networking basics including: What a network is, types of networks, networking theories and concepts, and the different components and technologies that allow network communication.

Part II (Chapters 4 to 7) covers considerations for the planning and implementation of your NetWare 3.12 network and provides you with details for the physical installation of network workstations, cabling, servers, and other network resources. Chapter 6 discusses the actual NetWare 3.12 software installation procedure. Chapter 7 explains the various client installations for workstations.

Part III (Chapters 8 to 11) deals with the generation of the user environment, including creating user accounts and user groups, developing a useful directory structure, customized login scripts, menus and drive mappings. Later chapters discuss network security strategies and implementation, as well as establishing network printer services.

Part IV (Chapters 12 to 17) covers network administration topics including network administrator skills and discussions of utilities available for users. Turn here for information on multi-server environments, software administration, disaster prevention and recovery, network backups, archiving of old data, maintenance of network disk space, and monitoring network use and security.

Part V (Chapters 18 to 20) covers advanced topics including optimizing the network through organization, monitoring network performance, and troubleshooting hardware and software problems. This section also discusses network communications and enterprise networking.

Appendices A to D give an in-depth look at the command-line and menu utilities for both the workstation and file server console (Appendix A) as well as discussions of the procedures for upgrading your server to NetWare 3.12 (Appendix B). Appendix C gives instructions for configuring and using the Net-Ware 3.12 Windows Client with an emphasis on the special VLM features and the NetWare Tools for Windows. Appendix D provides a dictionary of NetWare terms and key concepts.

PART I

Networks and Networking

▶ ·

Networks
and
Networking

Fast Track

There are seven basic steps to building a local area network   14

▸ Select the hardware and physical layout of the network
   (the topology)

▸ Design the layout and location of servers and workstations

▸ Install the network cabling and interface cards

▸ Configure the server hardware and peripherals (printers, etc.)

▸ Load and configure the server operating system and applications

▸ Create the user environment and implement security

▸ Set up ongoing LAN administration

NOTE
Mainframes are large-scale (usually proprietary) computers designed to serve hundreds of users. Mainframes are typically large, centrally located machines. Minicomputers are scaled-down versions of mainframes designed to be more economic and to handle fewer users.

In the last ten years, no single factor has changed corporate computing as much as the arrival of network computing. The explosive proliferation of low-cost, high-powered personal computers and peripherals, and of extremely versatile software, has driven the move to highly integrated local area networks. Support from manufacturers and developers who have been quick to adapt the enormous amounts of PC software and hardware into specialized "network-ready" products has caused many information systems professionals to reconsider the costs of minicomputer and mainframe solutions, especially when their computing needs might be met equally well by linking personal computers into a local area network (LAN).

In this chapter, we'll introduce some of the advances that have made local area networks consisting of personal computers more than just an inexpensive alternative to mainframes and minicomputers. We will describe some of the different types of networks and the benefits of using a LAN. Finally, we will walk you through an overview of the process of designing and building a local area network.

What Is a Network?

A network is a collection of computers and peripherals linked together so that they can share applications, data, and resources such as printers, modems, or CD-ROMs. While the initial concept may not appear earth-shattering, the implications of these abilities are actually quite extensive.

Types of Networks

Although there have been numerous schemes to allow a number of users swift access to the same information, there are only three basic types of networks:

- ▶ hierarchical central computer

▸ peer-to-peer networks

▸ server-client networks

In the following sections, we will describe the structure of each.

HIERARCHICAL COMPUTER SYSTEMS

Early computing environments were based on large-scale centralized computers. In this type of network, all users shared the same central computer, memory, disk space, and peripherals. There are several drawbacks to this type of system.

As Figure 1.1 shows, a hierarchical network is typically a single central computer to which multiple users are connected via terminals (often called "dumb" terminals because of their lack of local processing power). As such, all users to share a common Central Processing Unit (CPU), typically through a mechanism known as *timesharing*. In timesharing, the amount of work done by the CPU for a given time period is divided among the users of the system. As more users (and tasks) are added, the performance of the system begins to decline. From the individual user's point of view, the system slows down.

Mainframe and minicomputer vendors typically provided "development tools" with their systems rather than ready-to-run applications. This required users to write new programs or refine existing programs rather than buy new programs. Such writing and refining is expensive and time-consuming; this led to "kitchen-sink" programming strategies being applied to hierarchical networks. *Everything* that might be needed was included in the design of a program's screens, menus, and reports.

For example, a manager who needed access to information about the company's inventory might request a report from the information service department and receive as an answer a two-foot–high stack of printed material. Most managers will not willingly delve into an enormous stack of paper to find an answer that should fit on a single page. Worse, information contained in a printed report is most likely to be out of date by the time it gets used.

▶ · ◀

FIGURE 1.1

A hierarchical network

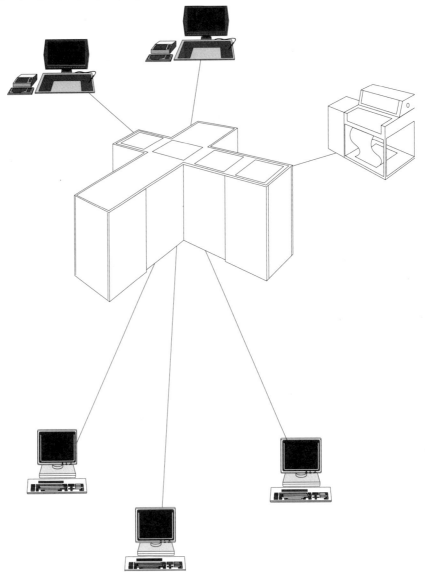

The Need for Distributed Access to Information

At the same time, personal computer users were discovering that their software packages would allow them to design and perform customized queries to obtain precisely the information they needed at the time. As these personal computer users became more and more sophisticated, software developers adapted many of the applications formerly handled by the mainframe for desktop personal computers. People do not want data—they want information. The fastest way to obtain information was to put the data on desktop computers, and that is just what the users did.

As more and more users began working on desktop computers, what was formerly a great continent of information became many isolated islands of data, each with its own government. Gaining access to processed information on another user's computer proved nearly as impossible as getting information from the mainframe. The idea of connecting these separate computers together into a "network" so that they could *share* data arose directly from these problems.

NOTE
A workstation is a computer—for example, a desktop PC—through which users can access the network.

The Need for Centralized Data Storage

Mainframe managers argue—rightly—that having all information stored at a central location is important in avoiding data loss. Data stored in several locations is in danger of being updated in only one location, which can result in inadequate or incorrect data in others. This often happens in "sneaker-net" environments, where users transfer data by carrying diskettes from one computer to another.

But end users want information to be distributed to their desktops, where they can get up-to-date information and more individualized responses. Unfortunately, the early information systems made it difficult for the mainframe manager and the end user to see eye to eye. Since then, software developers have resolved this conflict between central computing (for data security) and local desktop computing (for functionality) by providing in multiuser and networkable software packages the abilities previously found only in stand-alone applications.

NOTE
Peer-to-peer networks give network users access to resources (such as drives, printers, and modems) attached to other workstations.

NOTE
Dedicated network servers are committed to providing resources to the network and therefore cannot be used as workstations. Usually, workstations attached to a dedicated server can't share local resources either.

PEER-TO-PEER NETWORKS

Today the performance of desktop personal computers equipped with proper software rivals that of early mainframes and minicomputers. Enabling these computers to communicate with each other multiplies their usefulness.

One type of network that allows personal computers linked together to share their resources is called a *peer-to-peer network*. The most immediate benefit of this arrangement is that a single peripheral, such as a printer connected to a workstation, can be used by other network users. Another benefit is that one machine on such a network may be chosen to store a particular word processor, spreadsheet, or database for all other users on the network. This allows data to be centralized for better security, yet accessible to other network users. Although peer-to-peer networks multiply the usefulness of the computers connected to them, they also multiply support problems.

Limits of Peer-to-Peer Networks

Peer-to-peer networks are ideally suited to small organizations that already have an investment in personal computers but do not wish to dedicate one as a network server. However, peer-to-peer networks have a few drawbacks of their own. In a peer-to-peer network, the processing power of a workstation is divided between running a user's application and serving the network. As such, they typically cannot offer the performance a dedicated server would. Similarly, peer-to-peer networks can support fewer users than dedicated network servers. 20–30 users is a practical upper limit for most peer-to-peer networks.

Figure 1.2 shows a simple peer-to-peer network.

SERVER-CLIENT NETWORK

A third type of network is the *server-client* model, of which NetWare 3.12 is an example. Figure 1.3 shows a server-client network. In the server-client model, certain machines and devices on the network are dedicated to providing services to the network. The most important of these machines, the *file server*, is the computer around which the network is built.

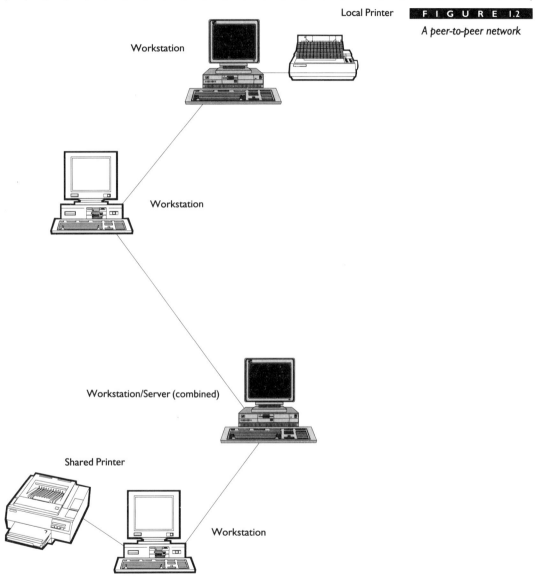

Local Printer

Workstation

Workstation

Workstation/Server (combined)

Shared Printer

Workstation

FIGURE 1.2

A peer-to-peer network

▶ . . . . ◀

A server-client model

network

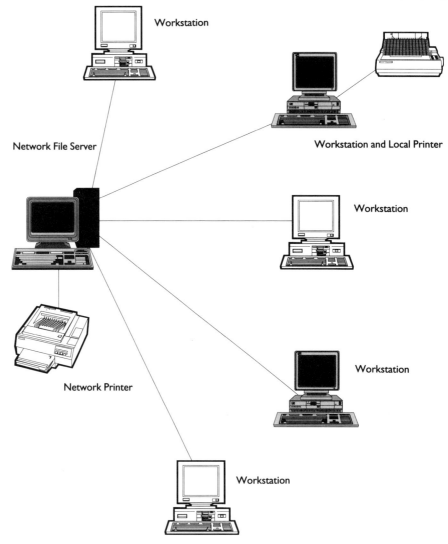

Workstation

Workstation and Local Printer

Network File Server

Workstation

Network Printer

Workstation

Workstation

The file server runs the network operating system and provides the link between the users and the disks that are used for data and application storage.

Aside from a file server, other common types of servers such as fax, printer, modem, e-mail, and database servers may be part of the network. By dedicating computers or specially designed peripherals to these tasks, performance is increased over that of a peer-to-peer network. In addition to the increased speed, the server-client network provides even further centralized data storage, helping ensure data security and reducing the amount of routine maintenance like backing up and archiving or software setup, installation, and administration that must be performed. (See Chapters 15, 16, and 17 for detailed information about server administration and maintenance.)

NOTE
Network servers are not always personal computers—they can include special peripherals such as network modems, fax servers, and print servers.

Benefits of Networks

There are many ways to justify a LAN, whether it be hierarchical, peer-to-peer, or server-client. Often, the installation is initially justified as a means of sharing peripherals. A single large hard drive, for example, can be used to support an entire workgroup. Expensive output devices, such as plotters and laser printers, can be shared, as can other specialty devices, such as fax boards, high-speed modems, and color printers.

But as the network grows and becomes integrated into the organization, device sharing usually becomes less important in comparison to the other advantages of networking. In particular, server-client and peer-to-peer link people as well as computers. LANs provide an effective tool for communicating through the use of electronic mail and other workgroup software. Messages can be sent instantaneously throughout the network, work plans can be updated as changes occur, and meetings can be scheduled without placing half a dozen phone calls.

Networking can also help reshape the way a company conducts certain business activities. Using workgroup software reduces the need for face-to-face meetings and other time-consuming methods of distributing information. At the same time, networking allows increased interaction among workers from their workstations. Networking can also enhance the effectiveness of communication, as people tend to put more thought into written communications than into informal conversation.

Because LANs provide direct access to workgroup information from each desktop, they also increase productivity. Everyone has access to the data and, by using the tools available on the network, can manipulate it and share the results with others. Users can improve efficiency by adding to the network any process that depends on input from many members of the organization. LANs reduce, or in some cases eliminate, the need for one person to finish a particular task before others can begin theirs.

An important side benefit of LANs is that software and data are much easier to maintain and protect than in a stand-alone desktop environment. Critical data can be backed up daily, or even hourly, if necessary. Similarly, when software needs to be upgraded, the job can be done at a single computer rather than at every personal computer running the program.

Building a Local Area Network

TIP
The First Rule of Networking: "The network will always outgrow your initial expectations." Plan accordingly.

Careful planning is essential to the successful implementation of a local area network. Even so, building a local area network is not difficult. The primary networking rule is "The network will always outgrow your initial expectations." Networks are modular. If you provide a solid base on which the network can be built, additional network needs can be added fairly simply.

There are seven basic steps to building a network:

1 · Select the hardware and physical layout of the network (*topology*).

2 · Design the layout and location of servers and workstations.

3 · Install (or have installed) the network cabling and interface cards.

4 · Configure the server hardware and peripherals (printers, etc.).

5 · Load and configure the server operating system and applications.

6 · Create the user environment and implement security.

7 · Set up ongoing LAN administration.

Once you've selected a topology (discussed in Chapter 3), specify the location of the server and workstations. We recommend that you have a reliable contractor come in and install the network cabling for you. The more organized you are at the outset, the more pleased you will be with the services provided by a third party, and the easier it will be for them to work with you.

You will also have to select the types of computers that will be used as workstations (discussed in Chapter 2). But before you do so, consider the types of software you wish to run, as this will influence the types of workstations you choose. Large databases and graphical user interfaces (GUIs) are memory-hungry applications that generally require more powerful workstations.

After the hardware has been installed and set up, it is time to configure the server and load the network operating system. Once the server is set up and running, it will be important to provide a directory structure that is logical and intuitive. The directory structure is a road map to the data and applications stored on the network; putting a little extra effort into designing it at the front end will greatly simplify future maintenance and upgrades.

The last two steps in the process will make the system easier for your users to use and easier for you to maintain. Prepare a common user interface for your users. This can be done by giving the log-in process the same look and feel for all users and providing your users with a menu or GUI to help them access the network applications. This will also assist you in establishing a security scheme to protect data on the network.

By the time you have done all of this, the network is basically ready for use. All that remains is to establish a sound set of procedures for supporting and maintaining the network.

The rest of this book is dedicated to helping you through these seven steps.

CHAPTER 2

Networks Components and How They Work

Fast Track

- Resources (printers, etc.) may be physically attached to the server

- Resources may be attached to other computers on the network and shared through the use of special software

- They may be independent of the file server and the workstations

- Bridges, which connect LANs that use similar methods of communication and network topologies

- Routers, which connect LANs that use different network topologies and addressing schemes.

- Internal routers, which reside in the file server and translate communications between segments of the same LAN that use different network topologies

- External routers, that may be either dedicated or non-dedicated computers that perform the translation function, or gateways, that are used to connect to systems that are different in their basic architecture. For example, a gateway would be used to allow a PC network access to a minicomputer or mainframe.

NetWare 3.12 continues Novell's flexibility in allowing you to configure your network to meet the needs of your organization. In most cases, the hardware and software that make up your network will be from many different manufacturers and vendors. Despite these differences, NetWare 3.12 is designed to allow products from many vendors to be integrated. In effect, Novell NetWare is the "glue" that binds many diverse products into a single entity which we call a network.

Like previous NetWare networks, NetWare 3.12 follows the server-client model. As we discussed in Chapter 1, this type of network has servers that are computers dedicated solely to providing a service to the network and clients that are workstations using these services.

A network may be as simple as a single server plus workstations; or as complex as an internetwork connecting multiple servers and hundreds of workstations together through bridges and gateways. Similarly, a network might take advantage only of central data storage and sharing printers; or it might provide enhanced services including access to reference materials on a CD-ROM, dial-in/dial-out modem access, electronic fax, or direct access to minicomputers and mainframes.

This chapter introduces you to some of the many options to consider as you design your network. While selecting the hardware, software, and network topology is not going to put you in a straitjacket, the tremendous variety of products supported by Novell makes this a job that will require your full attention. We'll begin by introducing you to file servers and workstations.

We'll discuss the software that allows a stand-alone computer to become a node on the LAN. We'll give you a basic introduction to the *topology* of a network—its physical layout. Finally, we'll introduce some of the different methods used to connect NetWare networks to other networks and computer systems.

NOTE
A *node* is a computer or peripheral capable of initiating and maintaining its own connection to the LAN.

Servers and Workstations

You'll remember from Chapter 1 that a network is a collection of computers and peripherals linked together so that users can share applications, data, resources, and peripherals. Although the network comprises many components, computers make up the bulk of the hardware on the network. All of these computers fall into two basic categories:

Servers
: A server is any device providing a service to the network. There can be many different types of servers providing anything from file storage on network disks, to printer, database, fax, and e-mail services. In many cases, servers are just souped-up PCs running special software (and sometimes hardware). They may also be products specifically manufactured to provide a service to a network—for example, network modems and fax servers.

Workstations
: A workstation is a computer used by a user to access the network. Workstations are generally just PCs running their own operating system (e.g., DOS or OS/2) along with additional communications software called a *shell* or *requester*. The shell or requester is simply a program that allows your users to access the network.

The file server is vital to the NetWare network. This is where the NetWare operating system runs and where the flow of data through the network is managed. A file server is a computer that provides central data storage, a communications link, and access to the applications to be shared across the network. File servers are sometimes used to perform other services as well. For example, a file server running additional software called

NetWare Loadable Modules (NLMs) can be used as a database server, a router, a bridge, or a printer server (we'll explain more about these shortly).

THE FILE SERVER

Given the file server's importance, and the fact that it is expected to serve many users, you will want to purchase a computer with enough performance to meet your needs. So, just how much is enough performance?

In general, you'd be wiser to spend money on high-speed network cards, high-speed disks and disk controllers, and ample memory than on a "killer CPU" for the server. Once you have invested in these other components as the foundation for your network, purchase the most powerful machine that fits into your budget. Under NetWare 3.12, we suggest using Table 2.1 as a rule-of-thumb guide for selecting your server. Table 2.1 represents a "minimum but adequate" approach to selecting a file server. When in doubt, buy a more powerful network server than you expect you'll need, or seek the help of a consultant or a knowledgeable vendor for recommendations.

More often than not, as a network becomes more and more useful, it will be expected to take on more tasks and more people than were initially planned for. Don't overlook the crucial rule of networking that states: *A network will always outgrow your initial expectations.* Don't be shy with your server. Starting with a solid foundation makes it easier to contend with future growth.

WORKSTATIONS

The only thing that differentiates a stand-alone computer from a networked workstation (a PC linked in as a network node) is the fact that a workstation has some extras: a network interface controller (NIC), network communications software, and a physical connection to the network. Under NetWare, the services accessed by the workstations are actually located on the network. The combination of network hardware and software gives an otherwise stand-alone computer access to disks, printers, modems, and other network peripherals as if they were directly attached to it.

NOTE
The file server on a Novell NetWare network *does not* do the calculation and processing for all computers on a network. The network's cumulative processing power is based on the processing power of the workstations attached to it and the speed of their information access from the server.

TABLE 2.1

*"Rule-of-thumb" guide for
selecting a Server*

SERVER TASKS

DOS-BASED APPLICATIONS ONLY

NUMBER OF WORK-STATIONS	NO DATABASE WORK	DATABASE WORK DONE AT WORKSTATION	DATABASE WORK DONE AT SERVER
0–25	ISA-based 386 SX	ISA-based 386 DX	ISA-based 486 DX
25–50	ISA-based 386 DX	ISA-based 486 SX	EISA or Micro Channel 486 DX
50–100	ISA-based 486 SX	ISA-based 486 DX	EISA or Micro Channel 486 DX
100–150	ISA-based 486 DX	EISA or Micro Channel 486 DX	EISA or Micro Channel 486 DX
150+	ISA-based 486 DX	EISA or Micro Channel 486 DX	Specialized Server

GUI- AND DOS-BASED APPLICATIONS

NUMBER OF WORK-STATIONS	NO DATABASE WORK	DATABASE WORK DONE AT WORKSTATION	DATABASE WORK DONE AT SERVER
0–25	ISA-based 386 DX	ISA-based 486 DX	ISA-based 486 DX
25–50	ISA-based 486 SX	EISA or Micro Channel 486 DX	EISA or Micro Channel 486 DX
50–100	ISA-based 486 DX	EISA or Micro Channel 486 DX	EISA or Micro Channel 486 DX
100–150	EISA or Micro Channel 486 DX	EISA or Micro Channel 486 DX	Scalar Architecture/ Specialized Server
150+	EISA or Micro Channel 486 DX	Scalar Architecture/ Specialized Server	Dedicated Database Server

NOTE
Physical network connections may not appear physical at all—for example, some network adapters support radio, microwave, and even satellite communications between the workstation and the network.

NOTE
The dot-pitch is the density at which dots or *pixels* can be displayed on a given monitor.

In a server-client network, almost all of the processing power for running applications resides at the workstation (database servers are a notable exception). The workstation *is* the network from the point of view of your users. Therefore, the more powerful the machines you can put in front of them, the happier they are likely to be with the network's performance. This, of course, also depends on the applications and the interface they will be using.

Although NetWare 3.12 will allow your existing computers (even old ones like the venerable PC-XT) to run applications on the network, when purchasing new systems it is wise to purchase fairly powerful PCs. In general, if your users are going to run only DOS applications, we recommend a 386 SX or more powerful PC that supports cache memory (cache memory is high-speed memory the CPU uses to reduce the number of times it must retrieve an instruction from "normal" memory). If these users are going to run very large spreadsheets or database applications, more memory than the standard 1 MB required for DOS and more powerful computers would be appropriate.

Similarly, if your users are going to run a graphical user interface (Microsoft Windows or OS/2, for example), we recommend that you purchase at least a 486 SX computer with at least 4 and preferably 8 MB of random access memory (RAM) and a high-quality video display.

In the PC environment, we recommend selecting a Video Graphics Array (VGA) or Super Video Graphics Array (SVGA) card and monitor combination; but be careful—they're not all alike. Even though a given monitor may support the frequencies needed to display higher resolutions such as 800 × 600, 1024 × 768, or 1280 × 1024, the quality of the display is determined by the monitor's *dot-pitch*.

In both the PC and Macintosh environments, try to select a monitor and card combination that supports higher *vertical refresh rates*. Typical vertical refresh rates are around 60 Hz—sixty times per second. In some instances, refresh rates of around 60 Hz exhibit *flicker*—the screen appears to flash or jitter during refresh. Flicker can cause eye discomfort after extended periods in front of a monitor; you may experience headaches and loss of focus, especially when viewing a monitor in your peripheral vision.

High-quality cards and monitors support more ergonomic refresh rates of 70 Hz or better. The higher the refresh rate the better, and the less chance the monitor will exhibit flicker.

WORKSTATION COMMUNICATIONS SOFTWARE

Before a computer can be used as a workstation, two additional pieces of communications software are needed to manage the network interface controller. One is a *packet driver* and the other a *network shell* or *network requester*.

A packet driver and shell allow workstations of different types on the same network to communicate with each other and share available resources. For example, a packet driver and shell enable a UNIX-based workstation to understand data generated by a Macintosh. The same is true of PC-AT–based computers and other types of workstations.

The packet driver is the program that causes the network interface controller to "talk to" the other devices on the network. The network shell allows the user to request access to network resources. The shell directs a user's commands to the proper resources, whether they are local or network devices.

The network user, in most cases, is completely unconcerned with which packet driver and shell are used to connect them to the network. To the user, the network simply appears as an additional drive, printer, etc., as if it were attached to their own workstation. For the network administrator, which packet driver and shell to use is determined by the network protocol (TCP/IP, IPX, AppleTalk, etc.), the operating system running at the workstation, and the applications the user needs access to.

NOTE
The vertical refresh rate determines the number of times per second that the image is redrawn.

How Programs Are Accessed through the Network

Figure 2.1 shows the layout of a simple network showing the file server and workstations. On this network, there are two workstations and a

FIGURE 2.1

A simple network

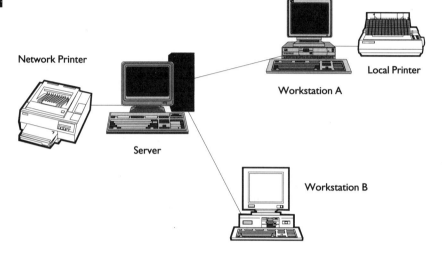

Network Printer

Local Printer

Workstation A

Server

Workstation B

printer attached to the file server. Both shared applications and data are stored on the file server's disks rather than at the individual workstations.

If a user at workstation A wants to run an application like WordPerfect, he or she simply changes to the correct drive and starts the program. The network shell determines whether the drive being accessed is a local or network drive, and directs the request to the proper location. An application located on a network drive is loaded into the workstation's memory just as it would be if it were located on a local drive. The user is then using the local memory and CPU of his or her workstation to run the application.

If the WordPerfect directory on the server is a shared directory, the user at workstation B can also run the program and access documents stored on the network. If both users attempt to use the same document, the first user to access the file will be the only one able to edit it. NetWare 3.12 manages access to files stored on the server through a file-locking mechanism. A file might be viewed or copied (depending on the type of lock a particular application uses), but not edited or deleted by other users.

Network Topology

The topology of a network is the network's physical layout. This is what defines the path that information must take to move from one place to another on the network. There are three basic network topologies:

- star

- bus or linear

- ring

In a star topology, all of the workstations and servers are connected to a centrally located device called a *concentrator* or *hub* (depending on the type of network being used). With a concentrator, all network segments are active at the same time and access to the network is based on a contention scheme (explained in Chapter 3). With a hub, only one sender and receiver are allowed to use the network at a time. This terminology has become a bit vaguer as networking technologies have begun to overlap. As such, you may often hear the terms *hub* and *concentrator* used interchangeably. In either case, in a star topology, a single segment of the network leads to each workstation or server, as shown in Figure 2.2. If you are using "intelligent" hubs, this arrangement has the added advantage of isolating network segments from one another in the event of a failure on one node.

In a bus or linear network topology, all workstations and servers are connected to a single cable called the *bus* (or sometimes the *backbone*). Networks of this type are built of "segments" of cable which lead from one workstation or server to the next. Linking computers together this way is called "daisy chaining." At the ends of the cable a device called a *terminator* is installed to complete the network circuit. Figure 2.3 shows a bus network.

In a ring topology, all workstations and servers are chained together in much the same way as they are in a bus network. The exception is that the cables at the ends of the network are connected together rather than terminated. As shown in Figure 2.4, the resulting network forms a physical "ring."

▶ · ◀

F I G U R E 2.2

A star topology

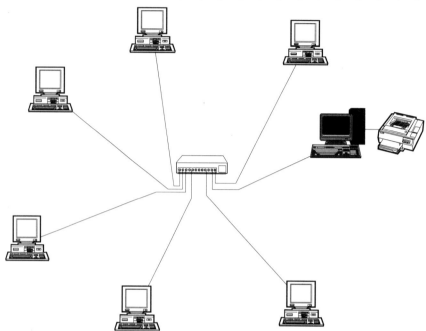

▶ · ◀

F I G U R E 2.3

A bus topology

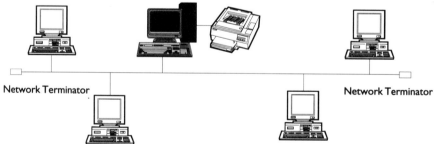

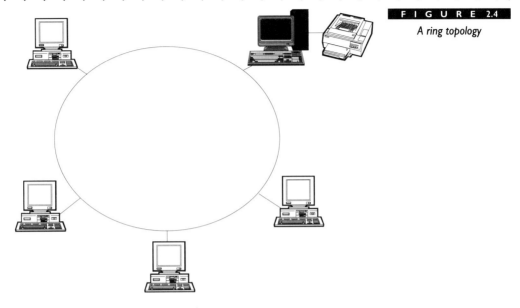

FIGURE 2.4

A ring topology

Although smaller networks might be based completely on one of these topologies, larger networks are often combinations of them.

Shared Resources

One of the great advantages of networks is the fact that resources attached to servers on the network can be shared among the network workstations. Instead of having to duplicate hardware and software at every workstation, these items can be purchased once and used by many users. On a NetWare network, resources can be shared in several different ways:

- ▸ They can be physically attached to a file server.
- ▸ They can be attached to other computers on the network and shared via special software.

▶ They can be completely independent of workstations and the file server.

If you have a small network, you can connect resources like high-quality printers and plotters directly to the file server. This is often convenient when the file server is located close enough that printers attached to it are still physically accessible to network users. In addition, most file servers will have unused parallel and serial ports that can be used for printing and plotting.

As networks grow, and there is the need for more resources and resources of different types, computers can be dedicated to sharing them. For security and other reasons we'll discuss in Chapter 4, it is probably not desirable to have the file server in the company copy room. On the other hand, this might be an ideal place to have printers and plotters. When resources are shared using dedicated computers and other devices as servers, they can be located wherever they are needed.

When resources are too expensive to purchase for every workstation on the network, sharing a single set of these resources over the network offers economies of scale. For example, all of your network users may need to get to an online database system accessed via a modem. Although many users will use the resources, they might use them only part of the time. This leaves phone lines unused most of the time and requires an initial investment in modems for all users. A dedicated phone line and modem connected to the network with modem-sharing software could be used much more efficiently.

Communicating with Other Systems

In many instances, there is a need to communicate with other networks or computer systems. NetWare provides software tools to turn servers and dedicated PCs into communications tools for connecting individual networks into internetworks of many LANs. In addition to these services, many specialized products are available from Novell and third parties for connecting NetWare-based networks to mainframes, minicomputers, and UNIX-based servers and networks, and other dissimilar systems.

BRIDGES AND ROUTERS

Often *bridges* and *routers* are used to connect isolated LANs together so that information can be shared across more than one LAN even when these LANs use completely different networking topologies and addressing schemes. In some cases, bridges can also be used to control the amount of traffic appearing on particular network segments. A bridge is typically used to connect networks of different protocols, while a router is usually used to connect networks that use similar communication methods.

Under NetWare 3.12, computers with network interface controllers can run software that turns them into "intelligent" routers. In addition to restricting unauthorized traffic between two segments, these routers are capable of performing many of the same functions as bridges. NetWare routers are capable of converting packets which originate on one topology with a particular addressing scheme to a completely different topology and addressing scheme. There are two types of NetWare routers, *internal* and *external*.

Internal Router

Whenever there is more than one network interface controller in a server, an *internal router* is formed. Internal routers are controlled by the server software. The server will automatically translate (when necessary) the traffic occurring on one segment of the network to the other segments attached to its other NICs. If a server has both an Ethernet segment and a Token Ring segment attached to it, a message sent by a user on one segment will be routed to the recipient on the other segment by the internal router. Internal routers are often used to connect several servers to a central network backbone. A single server can theoretically connect up to eighteen separate network segments together, though in reality the total number of network boards that you can install is determined by the available server resources (like I/O ports, memory space, and interrupts).

NOTE
See Chapter 20 for more detailed information about products for connecting NetWare-based networks to mainframes, minicomputers, and UNIX-based servers and networks.

External Router

An *external router* under NetWare is a computer that is running a router program. External routers may be either dedicated or non-dedicated computers that run Real or Protected modes. External routers run a special program called BRIDGE.EXE. Using this program, dedicated routers can also be used to run Value Added Processes (VAPs) such as print servers. In general, external routers offer better performance than internal routers and dedicated routers are more stable than non-dedicated ones.

GATEWAYS

Gateways are similar to external routers in that they are usually dedicated PCs running special software which is capable of transferring data between different topologies and cabling systems; but gateways are used when connecting to dissimilar systems that require special software translation as well. In general, a gateway is used when connecting beyond the LAN environment to systems of different architectures. Gateways are often used to allow networked PCs access to a minicomputer or mainframe. Some gateways can allow up to 256 users to simultaneously access a resource like a mainframe.

Summary

In this chapter, we introduced the components that make up a Local Area Network and gave a basic idea of how they operate. The computing environment already in place will most likely affect your decisions about which components to include with your network. If you are looking for more detailed information about connectivity with other types of systems, please refer to Chapter 20. *Options for Expanding Network Communications.* In Chapter 3, we'll introduce more of the technologies that can make up a LAN.

Network
Options

37   ***There are two basic methods used to control network access***

▸ CSMA/CD-based systems, in which several computers may transmit at the same time and must "listen" to the network to detect errors. If a collision occurs, the computer will keep sending the message until it is received intact.

▸ Token Passing schemes, in which the sending computer waits for a "token" to be passed around before transmitting the message. This allows the message to be sent without the risk of being corrupted by a message sent from another computer.

38   ***There are several popular network systems***

Ethernet is the most widely used because of its low implementation cost, lack of need for centralized control, and its ability to operate on several different types of cabling:

▸ Thick Ethernet

▸ Thin Ethernet

▸ Ethernet over twisted pair

▸ Ethernet over fiber optics

Token ring uses the Token Passing scheme of network control.
ARCnet also uses Token Passing, but can operate on more types of cabling.
FDDI is implemented on fiber-optic cabling and can operate at higher speeds than copper-based cabling.
CDDI is fairly new and, using the same scheme as FDDI but over twisted pair wire, promises to become useful for cabling to desktops from LANs that have FDDI as their backbone.

Local area networks typically use one of four types of network cable   *43*

▸ Coaxial, or "coax," which has better resistance to interference and better signal properties than other cabling

▸ Unshielded twisted pair, which is commonly used as telephone cable and therefore already installed in most buildings. However, this cabling is more susceptible to noise and cannot support the long distances that other cabling can

▸ Shielded twisted pair, which offers better noise protection and can carry signals for longer distances than unshielded twisted pair

▸ Fiber-optic cable, which offers the best noise protection and speed, and is capable of covering long distances, but can be very expensive

NOTE
If your network topology has already been chosen or determined by pre-installed wiring, skimming this chapter will introduce you to alternative wiring and media access schemes. Chapter 4 continues with instructions for planning your NetWare installation.

Novell NetWare is by far the most popular network operating system in use today, largely because of its ability to run on a wide variety of networking topologies and platforms. NetWare was the first to support, and still supports, more vendors, topologies, and protocols than any other network operating system.

NetWare won't limit you to purchasing proprietary hardware from a single vendor, nor will it force you to use a particular wiring scheme because it's the only one supported. The chances are good that NetWare can support any wiring scheme you already have installed; but if you're starting from scratch, you'll have many options to choose from.

Network topologies and data-passing schemes are a great source of ongoing debate. Today, more than ever, new technologies extend the limits of what was formerly thought state-of-the-art. Someone is always willing to push their favorite as the new king of the hill. The beauty of NetWare is that it allows your network to be as diverse as you need.

In this chapter, we introduce data-passing schemes, media-access systems, and network cabling. While we don't want to provide a highly technical discussion of networking systems, we will give enough of an introduction to let you avoid the winner-by-most-advertising approach to selecting your network system. We want you to see why one networking method may be better suited to your needs than another. This chapter will help you select the networking method or methods that will work best for you.

Network Data-Passing Schemes

Long before there were local area networks based on computers, communications engineers were working on ways to let communications devices use the same transmission medium (wire, microwave link, satellite, etc). Two of these schemes (called Medium Access Control Protocols) evolved over time as refinements of the earliest network access methods to become the ones predominantly used today.

In a LAN environment, a method is needed for controlling who gets to "talk" and when. There are basically two methods for controlling network access in use on most LANs today: *contention* and *token passing*.

CONTENTION

In a contention-based system, any computer may attempt to communicate at any time. There is no centralized control making sure computers take turns sharing the wire. If two computers try to send at the same time, the result is a corrupted message called a *collision*.

For this system to work, the sending computers must listen to the line to see if an acknowledgment is sent from the receiving computer indicating that the message was received. If no acknowledgment is received, the computer waits a random amount of time and then resends the packet.

The most common contention-based scheme in use today is called Carrier Sense Multiple Access with Collision Detection (CSMA/CD). This method of controlling network access is sometimes called "listening while talking." CSMA/CD is an improvement over earlier carrier-sense access methods because it listens for the actual collision rather than an acknowledgment of the received packet. The result is better use of the network because the sender does not have to wait the time it takes for the signal to reach its destination and return (its *propagation delay*). Ethernet uses CSMA/CD.

TOKEN PASSING

Token-passing schemes follow a much more orderly set of rules than the free-for-all that contention schemes are based on. In token passing, a data-packet representing a *free token* is passed around the network from station to station. Each station has an equal chance to take the token and hold it while it is sending data. A station wishing to transmit waits until it receives a free token and then issues a *busy token* immediately followed by the data it wishes to transmit. When a station finishes sending data or exceeds a preset limit (for example, time or amount of data transmitted), it reissues the free token to be passed on to the next station.

Since a high degree of control is required at the network station, token-passing controllers usually have some built-in "intelligence." There is also the possibility that the station holding the token will go down. To contend with this, there is a provision that will eventually issue a free token.

PERFORMANCE CONSIDERATIONS

There has been a long-standing debate about which data-passing scheme provides the best performance. Most LAN environments operate in *baseband*. Baseband means that network data is a sequence of discrete digital pulses or a *data packet* rather than an analog waveform (such as a television signal). The performance considerations for token-passing and contention schemes become more of a matter of preference, compatibility, and cost rather than rules.

As you add more users to a contention-based network (such as Ethernet), the network will slow down at a rate that can be predicted using statistical methods. It is theoretically possible to overload a contention-based network to the point of saturation, in which case no stations can send or receive. By contrast, the rate at which the performance of a token-passing network degrades is very predictable and network operation is not likely to be interrupted because of an increase in the number of stations.

Most comparisons made between Ethernet and Token Ring/ARCnet are based on the assumption that the network is completely loaded and that all stations are transmitting at their maximum rate—which seldom happens in real life. While each station added to a token-passing network adds a measurable time delay to the network, this is not always the case in an Ethernet network. As a rule of thumb, Ethernet networks are also less expensive to implement than Token Ring.

Media-Access Systems

Although there are many other options available, we have limited our discussion to the three most popular network systems. Ethernet and Token

Ring are based on standards established by the Institute of Electrical and Electronics Engineers (IEEE), while ARCnet is still maintained more by consensual agreement of the manufacturers than by formal standards. The FDDI and CDDI are maintained by the American National Standards Institute (ANSI) as standards, but the ANSI X3T9.5 committee is already considering the next generation called FDDI-2. Similarly, the CDDI is standardized; but the encoding scheme selected (MLT-3) does not meet FCC class B requirements and may still undergo changes.

ETHERNET

The CSMA/CD network access protocol was originally developed by Xerox as part of its "Ethernet" network. Today the network standard they developed is still known as Ethernet and is further defined by the Institute for Electrical and Electronics Engineers as IEEE 802.3. Ethernet is the most widely used networking protocol in use today, mainly because of the low cost of implementing an Ethernet network and the lack of need for centralized control.

Although Ethernet is very popular on *wide area networks* because of its ability to bridge and segment local networks into a much larger network, it can also link computers of many different types together. Most manufacturers support some form of Ethernet interface, regardless of the operating systems they support (UNIX, VMS, OS/2, the Macintosh OS, etc). Ethernet can run on coax, twisted-pair, and fiber-optic cabling, but the following forms are the most popular (cabling is covered in more detail in the *Cabling Options* section below):

- ▶ 10base5 or Thick Ethernet

- ▶ 10base2 or Thin Ethernet

- ▶ 10baseT or Ethernet over Twisted Pair

- ▶ 10baseF or Ethernet over Fiber Optic

10base5—Thick Ethernet

10base5, commonly called "Thick Ethernet," is based on heavy coaxial cable that has very good shielding and the capability of carrying a 10-Mbps signal for long distances (up to 500 meters). New stations, repeaters and bridges are added via a *vampire tap* that pierces the outer shell of the cable to get to the signal conductors. The tap (also called a *transceiver*) and the device being attached both have a connector called an *Attachment Unit Interface* (AUI). A 15-pin cable that cannot extend beyond 50 feet is used to connect the Ethernet device to the network tap. This form of Ethernet is often used as the backbone that connects several LANs together.

10base2—Thin Ethernet

10base2, commonly called "Thin Ethernet" or "Thinnet" and often nick-named "Cheapernet," is also based on coaxial cable. Thin Ethernet segments run at 10 Mbps and may be up to 300 meters in length, though 185m is typical. If repeaters (devices that carry the network signal to other segments) are used, the segments are restricted to 185 meters, but up to three of these 185-meter segments can be joined into the same network.

10baseT—Ethernet over Twisted Pair

10baseT is Ethernet running on Unshielded Twisted Pair. While most Ethernet networks are based on the linear bus, networks using this cabling scheme are based on the star topology. One segment of the network leads from each station to a centrally located concentrator. Twisted Pair Ethernet operates at 10 Mbps and individual segments may be up to 100 meters in length.

10baseF—Ethernet over Fiber Optic

10baseF is Ethernet running on a fiber-optic cabling system. Although the original specifications for Ethernet (IEEE 802.3) allowed for different types of media running from 1 Mbps to 10 Mbps, currently there are versions of 10baseF that run at up to 100 Mbps (though these are not yet standardized).

As with Thick Ethernet, this type of cabling scheme is best used as the backbone that connects multiple Ethernet LANs together. This allows you to use a high-speed backbone for all network traffic and less expensive cabling options where the increased speed is not needed. At present, it is still too expensive to run fiber optic to every desktop unless the application demands it.

Regardless of the cabling scheme you choose, today's Ethernet networks are rated at 10 million data bits per second or 10 megabits per second (Mbps). At the time of writing, some manufacturers were starting to announce new Ethernet technologies that would be capable of 100 Mbps over copper wire, putting them in the speed range of fiber-based systems. What remains to be seen is whether or not these new technologies will be incorporated into the IEEE standard.

TOKEN RING

Originally proposed in 1969 (the Newhall ring), Token Ring is the oldest of the token-passing topologies. Token Ring was popularized by Apollo, Prime Computer, and IBM in the early 1970s and is the only token-passing standard to be accepted by the IEEE 802 committee. As such, the Token Ring standard is known today as IEEE 802.5.

The two common types of Token Ring operate at 4 Mbps and 16 Mbps over a variety of cabling schemes including either Shielded or Unshielded Twisted Pair and Fiber Optics. Although the two schemes for supporting Token Ring at different speeds may often use the same type of cabling, both cannot run on the same network segment. If you need to support segments of both types, you can bridge them together. In addition, segments operating on Unshielded Twisted Pair support a maximum of 96 devices while segments on Shielded Twisted Pair can support up to 255 devices.

Although the name Token Ring implies a traditional ring topology, the physical layout of a Token Ring network appears to be a star because the segments leading to the previous station and the next station are contained in the same cable. These individual segments are connected into a ring at a device called a Multistation Access Unit (MAU). You can visualize the way the network operates by thinking of a network token traveling from the sending station to the MAU, and then on to the next station, and so on for all remaining network stations. Once the token reaches the last station, it will repeat the cycle.

Since Token Ring is the preferred standard for IBM products, networks that need to provide access to IBM mainframe hosts are well suited to Token Ring. Its benefits are its speed (16-Mbps version) and excellent stability. The major drawback to Token Ring is the high cost of wiring and intelligent network interfaces.

ARCNET

ARCnet (Attached Resource Computer Network), originally developed by Datapoint Corporation, is very popular because it is extremely flexible, inexpensive, and very dependable. ARCnet's flexibility lies in its ability to run on any cable type, in either a bus or star configuration.

Like Token Ring, ARCnet is a token-passing protocol. The major difference is in transmission speeds. Although both may not be run on the same system, ARCnet networks may be either 2.5-Mbps or 20-Mbps configurations, and you can run 2.5 Mbps and 20 Mbps on the same wire.

Today the ARCnet standard is maintained and closely monitored by manufacturers and vendors of ARCnet products rather than by a controlling committee. Even so, you may be reasonably certain that products from different vendors have been built to be compatible and will work in the same system.

ARCnet network segments may be a generous 2000 feet in length. ARCnet's extended coverage, stability, and flexibility explain its continuing strong position in the LAN market, even though most ARCnet LANs are the 2.5-Mbps version.

FDDI AND CDDI

The Fiber Distributed Data Interface (FDDI), one of the first High-Speed Local Networks (HSLNs), is implemented on fiber-optic cabling because it has a much greater capacity for throughput and speed than most copper-based networking schemes. The FDDI is based on a bidirectional token-passing scheme very similar to Token Ring, but FDDI runs at 100 Mbps rather than at 4 or 16 Mbps.

The major drawback in implementing FDDI networks is the cost of investing in a fiber-based system including cable plant, interface cards, and concentrators. Even so, if you foresee the need for higher bandwidth or coverage of long distances (fiber-optic segments can run up to 2 km), look to fiber now rather than as a replacement to an existing system. Optical fiber–based systems have the potential to go into the gigabits-per-second (Gbps) range in the not-so-distant future.

In June 1992, the American National Standards Institute approved a standard for the Copper Distributed Data Interface (CDDI). This is an implementation of the same scheme used in ANSI FDDI networks that works over copper wire. Though extremely new, this standard holds great promise for implementing LANs that support 100 Mbps over Shielded Twisted Pair and Unshielded Twisted Pair networks.

For Unshielded Twisted Pair networks, the cabling must be data grade UTP (Category 5 or Level 4), which has become widely available only recently. (See Table 3.2, Common Types of Unshielded Twisted Pair, in the next section for more information.). As CDDI LAN segments will be limited to 100 meters in length, networks-based on FDDI/CDDI will most likely use fiber backbones for long distances and network backbones with copper cable runs to the desktops.

Cabling Options

Cabling problems are probably the most frustrating source of network trouble. Although cabling problems are simple to solve at first, if left unchecked, they will become a source of severe distress in the long run. Network cabling problems can be intermittent, can affect performance, and can even shut down your LAN completely. When considering your options for network cabling, include a budget for third-party contractors, or at least the costs of proper maintenance and test equipment in your estimates.

Properly installed and tested cabling will most likely be one of the last things to worry about if your LAN has trouble. If you have confidence in your network cabling, tracking down occasional problems will be much simpler.

Local area networks typically use the following four types of network cable:

▸ Coaxial, commonly called "coax"

▸ Unshielded Twisted Pair

▸ Twisted Pair

▸ Optical fiber

The type of cabling you choose might be based on what you already have installed or on your expectations for future growth. Although most network systems will run on different types of cable, keep in mind that this does not mean that different systems can use cable with the same specifications. For example, ARCnet and Ethernet can both run on coax cabling, but ARCnet uses RG-62, 93-ohm–impedance cable while Ethernet uses RG-58, 50-ohm–impedance cable. These two cabling systems are not compatible. Cabling systems based on fiber optics will exhibit similar problems. On the other hand, most schemes that use Unshielded Twisted Pair will run on any Unshielded Twisted Pair—even though there are different cable grades. (When using newer technologies like Fast Ethernet or CDDI, you may find cable grade becomes an issue.).

Table 3.1 lists how the different cable types are commonly used.

COAXIAL CABLE

Coaxial cable is built out of a center conductor surrounded by an insulating material and a woven mesh outer conductor; it's called coaxial because the inner and outer conductors share a central axis. Coaxial cable has better resistance to interference and better signal properties than most other types

NETWORKING SCHEMES					
TYPES OF CABLING	**ETHERNET**	**ARCnet**	**TOKEN RING**	**FDDI**	**CDDI**
Coaxial	●	●			
Shielded Twisted Pair	●	●	●		●
Unshielded Twisted Pair	●	●	●		●
Fiber Optic	●	●	●	●	

of cabling. Coax's relative immunity to noise makes it an inexpensive alternative to fiber optic when you need long segments or segments passing through noisy environments.

If you are working in a building that has a large number of IBM 3270 terminals, chances are good that you have a lot of coax cable already run through the building. In this case, using a topology that supports the cabling already installed (ARCnet for example) would make a lot of sense and save on installation and testing costs.

Coax cable is often used in Linear Bus (Ethernet) networks as well. Instead of having to run every network segment back to a central hub or concentrator, segments are simply connected from one station to the next. This is a good way to wire networks working within a limited budget as the wiring is fairly inexpensive and you don't need concentrators or hubs. The drawback is that a problem with a single station or connection on the network is likely to affect every node on the network.

UNSHIELDED TWISTED-PAIR CABLE

Unshielded Twisted Pair (UTP) cable is quickly becoming one of the most popular cabling types, partly because UTP is commonly used as telephone cable and many buildings have an excess capacity already built in. Many network protocols run on UTP and use the star topology. Since telephone wiring is commonly run to a communications closet where telephone equipment is installed, this is also an ideal place to locate the concentrators and hubs for the network.

Consider two things before deciding to use UTP:

▶ First, high-quality UTP comprises at least two conductors twisted together to give at least six twists per inch. This arrangement provides the proper impedance (electrical resistance) to help reduce the effects of electromagnetic interference from fluorescent lights, telephone lines, and other sources. Even so, UTP (especially lower-quality UTP) is more susceptible to noise than other forms of cabling.

▶ Second, UTP is typically run through metal pipes called *conduits* to a communications closet. As such, it may follow a completely different path than you might expect. A run that appears to be fairly short might easily be 1000 feet. As UTP networking schemes usually support shorter distances than other schemes, this could become a problem.

NOTE
In LANs, attenuation is a decrease in signal intensity due to cable imperfections, faulty or poor-quality connectors, LAN length, or interference from other signal sources such as power or telephone lines.

If you plan on using existing UTP for your network, have a qualified communications technician test your cabling system. Make sure they test the cable for noise and attenuation as well as telling you the measured length of each cable segment.

Table 3.2 shows common types of Unshielded Twisted Pair cable.

SHIELDED TWISTED-PAIR CABLE

Although a Shielded Twisted Pair (STP) cable visually resembles a coaxial cable, it actually contains one or more sets of cable pairs molded into an insulating material. Outside this insulating material, there is often a braided shielding conductor. Given this construction, and the fact that the individual conductors are usually of heavier gauge than those used in UTP, STP cables offer better noise protection and are capable of carrying signals for longer distances.

TABLE 3.2
Common Types of Un-shielded Twisted Pair

CATEGORY/ TYPE	CON-STRUCTION	ATTENUATION (max) in db/1000 ft	IMPEDANCE (ohms ± 15 ohms)	CAPACITANCE (pf/ft max)	APPLI-CATION
3	24 AWG solid copper with Plenum PVC insulation	7.8 @ 1 MHz 30 @ 10 MHz 40 @ 16 MHz	100	20	LANs to 16 Mbps
4	24 AWG solid copper with Teflon FEP insulation	6.5 @ 1 MHz 22 @ 10 MHz 31 @ 20 MHz	100	14	LANs to 20 Mbps and extended-distance LANs to 16 Mbps
5	24 AWG solid copper with Teflon FEP insulation	6.3 @ 1 MHz 20 @ 10 MHz 28 @ 20 MHz 67 @ 100 MHz	100	14	LANs to 100 Mbps and extended-distance LANs

Tabular data on standards courtesy of Comm/Scope Inc., Claremont, NC.

Type 1 STP cable, the most common cabling system used in IBM Token Ring networks, consists of two shielded pairs of wiring, with one dedicated to transmitting, and one to receiving. In new installations, IBM type 2 cable is often preferable. Type 2 cable has four unshielded pairs of wire for voice communications in addition to the shielded transmit and receive pairs. As the manufacturing process is more stringent for STP (the number of twists per inch and the shielding are closely monitored) it is more expensive than Unshielded Twisted Pair. In some environments, Type 9 cable is often specified. Type 9 is similar to Type 1 except that the inner conductors are 26-AWG (American Wire Gauge) solid copper wire rather than the 22-AWG wire used in Types 1 and 2.

FIBER-OPTIC CABLE

A fiber-optic cable (also known as a "light pipe") is composed of a glass or plastic inner cable surrounded by an outer layer of the same material with slightly different light-bending characteristics. These cores are bonded together and enclosed in a protective teflon or plastic coating.

Some fiber-based networks operate in the *broadband* range, where the characteristics of the optical fibers are best used. The drawback of this type of network is that network interface controllers and concentrators are basically broadcast telecommunications equipment that is usually more expensive than baseband equipment like FDDI or FOIRL (Fiber Optic Inter-Repeater Link).

Though baseband systems are less expensive than broadband systems, they're still substantially more expensive than copper wiring.

Even so, if you need immunity to electromagnetic interference, very high speed, and coverage of distances up to 100 km (for LAN-to-LAN links), fiber-optic–based systems are the obvious choice.

If you are intending to install a fiber-based system, don't do it alone unless you are very experienced with splicing and pulling fiber-based cabling systems. The equipment to do the job properly and test the system thoroughly is highly expensive and requires extensive training. The contractors who specialize in installing fiber-optic cable are a good place to start, but don't overlook your local phone company. They often have a large installed base of fiber and the equipment and trained personnel to do the job. In either case, seek multiple bids for this type of work.

Summary

In this chapter, we introduced you to network data-passing schemes and media-access protocols. While providing a comprehensive reference on these subjects is far beyond the scope of this book, we've given you enough information to help you to make an intelligent decision. We also covered the most popular cabling options and described the different networking schemes available with each. In Chapter 4, we'll discuss site preparation and cable placement.

PART II

Installing and Configuring Your NetWare Network

Planning for NetWare Installation

Fast Track

56   **Novell NetWare is**
An operating system that allows communications and data sharing between computers. It handles requests for the file server's files from multiple network users and regulates the sharing of data among them.

57   **NetWare has two primary functions**

▶ It directs communication from a user to the appropriate location on the network (e.g., another workstation, printer, modem).

▶ It provides a shared location for storing data and applications that can be accessed by all users on the network.

57   **There are several versions of NetWare that accommodate a variety of networks:**

▶ NetWare Lite is a simple peer-to-peer operating system that is best suited for workgroups that are very small and have limited growth potential. It does not require a dedicated file server.

▶ NetWare 2.2 requires a dedicated 80286-based file server and is more suited to organizations that do not expect to run data intensive applications.

▶ NetWare 3.12 is a modular 32-bit operating system. The base system is a "kernel" to which modules and drivers are added to create a customized network.

▶ NetWare 4.0 is similar to NetWare 3.12, but it provides directory services that allow a user's preferences and privileges to be transferred to all the file servers on the network. This is especially important in organizations that have multiple file severs.

You need to consider several questions before installing a
NetWare-based network

- ▶ How many users will need to access the network?

- ▶ Who will be working together?

- ▶ What types of applications will be used?

- ▶ How are you going to use the network?

- ▶ How will the network be cabled?

- ▶ How is printing going to be handled?

- ▶ Who will maintain the network?

NOTE
Remember the Five
Ps: **Proper Planning**
Prevents Poor
Performance.

When planning for your NetWare LAN, pay close attention to the Five P's: Proper planning prevents poor performance.

Planning is the most important step in any network installation. Proper planning can prevent problems, help reduce maintenance, and simplify expanding the network. You might be able to get a poorly planned network up and running today, but the minute something changed, major time--consuming changes could be in store.

For example, in one case we know, the LAN architecture was so well planned from the start that some provisions were not put into effect until three years after installation. The designers quickly standardized file server names, user names, placement of bridges and routers, and even the way file directories and subdirectories were set up and applications installed. When network expansion was required, they accommodated it by simply incorporating the changes with minimum fuss and frustration. This particular installation has survived numerous changes in software (including new versions of NetWare), hardware (new servers), and radical increases in size.

In this chapter, we will outline planning steps for getting your NetWare LAN up and running. We will define NetWare, its versions, and look at what you need to consider before purchasing the materials for your LAN. Then we'll present a list of questions to help you start planning for your NetWare environment. Finally, we'll give you some planning advice that will help you answer each of the questions and begin to tailor your own NetWare LAN.

What Is NetWare?

NetWare is an operating system that allows communications between computers. Much like a stand-alone operating system, such as DOS, NetWare handles requests for files stored on the server's hard disk. The difference is that NetWare is designed to regulate these requests from multiple users across the network and to share needed data among them. But NetWare goes a few steps beyond a DOS or DOS-like operating environment.

NetWare has two primary functions:

- To act as a switchboard operator. The file server (one of the computers on the LAN) receives communications from one user and directs the responses back to the user. This enables users to communicate with one another. In the simplest case, this is accomplished by sending messages from one workstation to another. In other settings, users can access resources such as printers or modems that are physically located on another workstation.

- To provide a shared location for storing data and applications. In this capacity, NetWare provides a location for the storage of files that can be accessed by any user on the network. Data files can be shared by users, and application management can be improved in a networked environment. For example, if all the applications are placed in one location (the file server), you save the time needed to install them on individual hard disks *and* the hard disk space; it also makes software configuration easier. Further, when it is necessary to upgrade software, the administrator has only to work with one location instead of moving from workstation to workstation.

CHOOSING THE RIGHT VERSION OF NETWARE

Novell provides versions of NetWare able to accommodate a variety of organizations, from the two-person home office all the way up to the multinational corporation using hundreds of file servers and thousands of users spread all over the globe. Basically, NetWare is available in four versions:

NetWare Lite

NetWare 2.2

NetWare 3.12

NetWare 4.0

In this book, we cover the details of installing NetWare 3.12; however, we suggest that you carefully assess your organization's needs and choose the version of NetWare that is right for your specific environment.

The two main factors in deciding which is right for you are number of users and network complexity. Table 4.1 provides a breakdown, using these two criteria, for each version of NetWare.

For a closer look at the differences among the various NetWare versions, let's examine the distinguishing features of each.

What Is NetWare Lite?

NetWare Lite, Novell's simple peer-to-peer operating system, is best suited for a very small workgroup with only limited growth potential. It does not require a dedicated PC set up as a file server, and does not easily integrate with wide-area equipment, such as bridges and routers.

NetWare Lite is ideal for small-company or home-office use if you have two or more computers between which you need to share or transfer data. It is sold on a per-PC (or node) basis with a retail price of $99 for each participating PC.

What Is NetWare 2.2?

NetWare 2.2 (formerly called Advanced NetWare) is the next step up—moving toward a more complex operating system. NetWare 2.2 is a 16-bit operating system with advanced security features and sophisticated file- and disk-sharing capabilities. It requires at least one computer (a 286 or higher) set up as a file server.

NOTE
NetWare Lite is Novell's simple peer-to-peer operating system.

NOTE
NetWare 2.2 is a 16-bit operating system with sophisticated file- and disk-sharing capabilities.

T A B L E 4.1

Different NetWare Versions and Their Recommended Uses

VERSION OF NETWARE	RECOMMENDED NUMBER OF USERS	NETWORK COMPLEXITY
NetWare Lite	1–6	Very simple
NetWare v2.2	2–100	Simple
NetWare v3.12	2–1000	Simple to complex
NetWare v4.0	50–1000	Very complex

NetWare 2.2 offers much of the power to handle the needs of a 5–100 person network. A small business or a department within a large company can benefit from the advanced file-sharing and security features of NetWare 2.2.

NetWare 2.2 requires that the operating system be specially prepared for its hardware environment. For the most part, it must be configured, linked, and generated each time a change is made. Some enhancements to the basic operating system, such as databases or advanced communications services are available through special programs calls *VAPs* (*Value Added Processes*) that can be linked into the core of NetWare 2.2.

NetWare 2.2 is suitable for organizations that have very limited budgets for hardware, and that do not expect to run large data-intensive applications. Some of its limitations, especially when it comes to disk space, might become too confining to LAN users. (The maximum size of any volume on a NetWare 2.2 server is 255 MB. Many databases will outgrow this limitation.)

What Is NetWare 3.12?

NetWare 3.12 is a robust 32-bit operating system built from independent modules. It differs from both NetWare Lite and NetWare 2.2 in that its base system (or kernel) contains a minimum set of functions to which others are added. The kernel is the foundation to which modules and drivers are added to build a customized operating system. If your LAN requires any customization (and most do), you can add the modules needed to support your particular network activities. For NetWare 3.12, these modules are called NLMs (see Chapter 6). NLMs can support disk drives, network cards, databases, communications utilities, tape backup systems, or other network devices.

For example, a large corporation may require special disk controllers and hard drives in order to provide the disk space needed to support hundreds of users on a single server. All the special hardware are additional features that must be added to the operating system, and each one uses vital server memory and processing time. On the other hand, a small corporation may only need a common disk controller and a small hard drive. For this network, you would only need to add a few additional features to the operating

NOTE
NetWare 3.12's independent modules add extra capabilities to the basic system.

system, and require less system memory and processing time. Therefore a small company that didn't need as many added modules would not need the same caliber file server as the major corporation. You can save money without losing performance. The design of NetWare 3.12 gives you the power to get the most out of your file server by allowing you to choose only the services you actually need.

NetWare 3.12 is capable of considerably more activity than NetWare 2.2. Table 4.2 compares capacity differences between the two versions.

NOTE
NetWare 4.0 intro-
duced NetWare
Name Services, global
directory services that
can handle all the ser-
vers and users in a
large organization.

What Is NetWare 4.0?

NetWare 4.0 builds on the strengths of NetWare 3.12, making it a viable environment for large organizations with many file servers. This new version provides Directory Services that allow all the resources on the entire network to be directly available to all users.

In both NetWare 2.2 and 3.12, users log in to a file server. The file server maintains information about the user, his or her password, certain preferences (such as printers), and the security granted. If the user wants to change to another server, the other server must also have information about the

---

T A B L E 4.2

Comparing Capacity of NetWare 2.2 and NetWare 3.12

COMPARISON AREA	NETWARE 2.2	NETWARE 3.12
Maximum Server RAM	16 MB	4 GB
Maximum server disk space	2 GB	32 TB
Drives per server	32	2,048
Drives per volume	n/a	32
Volumes per server	32	64
File Size	255 MB	4 GB
Number of open files per server	1,000	100,000
Number of directory entries (per volume)	32,000	2,097,152
Users	5, 10, 50, 100	5, 10, 20, 50, 100, 250, 1000

user. In a large organization, with many servers, it is difficult to keep all the servers up-to-date with information about all the users.

With directory services available in NetWare 4.0, a user only needs to log in to the network, and the connections and paths needed to access all resources will be handled by the directory services. This is a boon to organizations with many servers.

But these additional services do not come without a price: Installing organization-wide NetWare 4.0 directory services is more complex and involved than installing either NetWare 2.2 or NetWare 3.12. In large organizations or organizations with multiple sites, the convenience and saving in maintenance in the long run far outweigh the extra effort in setup and configuration.

What Do I Need to Plan for?

Before installing a Novell NetWare–based network, ask yourself the questions below. Each question is important because it will provide you with a path toward an effective network. Keep in mind that you may not be able to answer all the questions right now, as many networks change in shape and complexity as they grow.

1 · How many users will need access to the network?

2 · Who will be working together?

3 · What types of applications will be used?

4 · How are you going to use the network?

5 · How will the network be cabled?

6 · How is printing going to be handled?

7 · Who will maintain the network?

We will discuss these questions in order. The answers are covered only briefly here and will be discussed in greater detail later in this book.

You'll notice that the question "How is the network going to be expanded?" is not on the list. That's because this question needs to be applied to each of the other seven.

1. How Many Users Will Need Access to the Network?

Estimating the total number (and location) of users who might eventually become a part of the network will give you a feel for the scope of the network that you are planning.

For example, if your network is originally set up to handle 28 people in the accounting department on the 5th floor, you're likely to purchase a single server and locate it close to the department users. But if the people in the accounting department have to interact with the marketing group on the 8th floor—and the 18 people in the marketing department also want a LAN—then you'll be better off trying to accommodate both groups at once. Perhaps they could even share a single file server; and you might find it convenient to locate the server centrally in a protected room.

As a rule of thumb, the more users who access the network, the more complex the environment will become. By knowing the number of users and the way the network will be used, you will have a few clues about server location and the user version of NetWare 3.12 you should buy.

Novell ships NetWare 3.12 in 5-, 10-, 20-, 50-, 100- and 250-user version licenses. Selecting the correct number of users will prevent you from having to upgrade immediately after setting up the network, or having a hundred extra user licenses that you will never use.

2. Who Will Be Working Together?

Knowing who will be working with whom is important in the overall installation of NetWare. This information is needed to assign users to file servers, set up workgroups, workgroup managers, user account managers, security, menu design, application needs, printer setup, and communication needs.

Are the users all physically located in the same building? Is there a requirement for remote access? Knowing who needs to share data and resources also plays a part in whether or not you need remote access (dialing in via modem or leased lines) or if certain users need an independent server.

At this point, it is very helpful to decide on naming conventions. Names on a network are like addresses for homes and businesses: If you do not have a unique name, information will get lost, as the system will not know where to send the data. But the names have to make sense or the users won't be able to remember them.

In general, consider expansion and simplicity when selecting your naming conventions. Objects (such as printers or queues) and users are named to simplify identification for network users, not for the server, so make your names meaningful.

Consider these questions:

▸ Will two different users get the same USERNAME?

▸ Are your server names informative?

▸ Will you be using groups to logically organize different organizational units like Accounting, Engineering, and Sales?

▸ Do you need different security levels within groups like Sales_Managers and Sales_Staff?

▸ Do names of print queues and printers need to indicate printer types and locations?

For more information on selecting user names and assigning group names, see Chapter 8. For information about naming printers and print queues, go into Chapter 11.

TIP
In NetWare, names help users identify network services and other users, so make your naming conventions informative.

3. What Types of Applications Will Be Used?

Don't overlook this vital consideration for installing a network. Your answers can provide solutions as to what types of workstations you need to purchase (running Windows-based applications requires more powerful

PCs and more disk space than simple DOS applications). If you are planning to use a lot of database applications, you may want to add a separate database server to your network or load the database-server software to your existing server as an NLM.

The types of applications that are to be used will also help you determine the qualifications your system administrator needs: The more complex the applications, the more specialized your administrator has to be. For example, hiring an administrator who doesn't understand Windows is not going to work well if you want to run Windows on all the workstations.

4. How Are You Going to Use the Network?

At first, this question may seem pointless, but actually it needs to be one of the first questions that you try to answer. Asking this question should generate further questions, such as:

- ▸ Will the network be a local area network or a wide area network?

- ▸ Do we need to plan for remote access?

- ▸ Do we need extensive security or just a little?

- ▸ Will our existing hardware meet our needs or do we need to purchase new and better computers?

The list goes on. Answering these questions will also serve as a guideline for purchasing the hardware and software that is best suited to your environment.

5. How Is the Network Going to Be Cabled?

Cabling is an aspect of network planning you cannot ignore. Since cables carry all the communication from workstations to the file server, it isn't simply a matter of laying a cable from point A to point B. Faulty cable can prevent the workstation from communicating with the server, or even corrupt the data being transmitted to the server.

Now use the information from Chapter 3 to decide what kind of network topology to use. The cable type you decide to use will affect the network from the time it is installed until it is either removed or recabled (not an inexpensive task). You also must decide who is going to do the cabling. Since cabling can be both time consuming and frustrating, you may need to delegate it to a qualified contractor (especially if you are planning to use fiber-optic cabling).

If you are planning to do your own cabling, or if you are hiring a contractor to do it for you, read the section on cabling in Chapter 5 for a better understanding of the basics of installing cable, as well as some do's and don'ts for cabling your network.

6. How Is Printing Going to Be Handled?

Sharing printers is one of the most-used features of a network, as the money saved by needing fewer printers can be used to buy higher-quality printers that all users can access.

Deciding how printing is to be handled will also help determine where to locate your printers. Shared printers need to be placed in an open and easily accessed location—for example, the copier room—rather than in lockable offices.

NetWare allows you to connect a shared printer to the file server, a workstation, a dedicated print server, or directly to the network cabling. Each of these has advantages and disadvantages.

Connecting a printer to a file server will add work to the server. If your server performance is already poor, adding a print server will reduce it even further. On the other hand, since the server is available at all times, a printer connected to the server will also be available at all times.

Placing a shared printer on a user's workstation reduces the work load for the server while allowing the printer to be used by all. The downside is that the program for managing printing requests will reduce the memory available to that workstation. Further, while the printer is printing, the workstation performance will be affected as the station is having to work on two tasks instead of just one.

TIP
**Place shared printers
in an open and easily
accessed location.**

Using a dedicated print server provides a printer that is always available, will not affect the users' performance, and will not increase the load on the server. The drawback is that it requires a computer with the sole function of managing print requests, and is therefore not available as a workstation.

If you don't have additional stations to dedicate to serving printers, or if space is limited, consider using a third-party print server. Many are available from companies like Castel, Intel, Hewlett-Packard, Compaq, QMS, Rose Electronics, and others who manufacture either printers that attach directly to the network or devices that can turn one or more stand-alone printers into network printers.

7. Who Will Maintain the Network?

Even though you haven't yet started on the installation, you need to consider how the system is going to be maintained. Who will be responsible for the network? What will that job entail? Will you use a small team of LAN administrators in the computer department or will duties be spread among users in each business unit?

We can offer you arguments to defend either a centralized or a decentralized LAN support organization. The right decision will depend on who has the time and training to adequately maintain the LAN.

We suggest, however, that you carefully consider the job duties of a LAN administrator, then choose a candidate early in the installation of the network.

NOTE
Chapter 12 discusses the responsibilities of the network administrator.

Summary

In this chapter, we addressed some of the basic planning questions you should consider before attempting a network installation. First we defined what NetWare is and what it does. Then we looked at the features and functions in the various versions of NetWare (not just version 3.12). We also looked at key planning areas spanning workgroup considerations, cabling, printing, applications, and even network administration. We'll revisit each of these topics in more detail as we proceed through our NetWare installation.

In the next chapter, we'll take a more focused look at actually setting up the hardware (servers, workstations, cables, etc.) for the network.

CHAPTER 5

Preparing
the Hardware

Fast Track

73   ***Consider the following when deciding where to locate the file server***

▸ **Security.** The file server needs to be located where it is not likely to be disturbed by persons other than the LAN administrator.

▸ **Power.** The file server needs to be protected from power fluctuations that can cause system lockups or board failures and can corrupt data.

▸ **Heat.** Heat can cause integrated circuits or boards to malfunction.

▸ **Dust.** Large amounts of dust can cause damage to the components of the server and increase the risk of electrical short.

78   ***Before installing NetWare, conduct an inventory of equipment to***

▸ Reveal what hardware needs to be purchased or modified.

▸ Make sure you have copies of the CONFIG.SYS and AUTOEXEC.BAT files for each system.

▸ Provide an inventory of printers and other shared devices and document how these devices should be configured.

81   ***Check the requirements of the systems to be connected to the network***

The file server needs to have sufficient:

▸ Disk space to accommodate all users and the applications that will be run on the network.

▸ Memory—at least 4 MB of RAM. (Additional RAM requirements are determined by disk capacity.)

The workstations will require:

- ▶ Network interface cards configured with the correct base input/output address, base memory address, and interrupt settings for each system.

- ▶ Memory to load network shells and run their applications.

When cabling the workstations, it is important to be aware of where the cable should be run. An ideal path will be: *87*

- ▶ Accessible; this will aid in troubleshooting and maintenance of cables.

- ▶ Free of obstructions, such as light fixtures in the ceiling or other forms of cabling, (such as power and telephone).

- ▶ Within the distance limitations of the cabling being used.

Cabling Do's *88*

- ▶ Pull more cable than is needed in anticipation of unexpected obstructions in the path and future growth.

- ▶ Use good quality cabling and connectors.

- ▶ Document the cable layout so that the LAN administrator will be able to locate a faulty cable and plan for changes in the network.

Cabling Don'ts *89*

- ▶ Build long LAN segments out of short, prebuilt cables.

- ▶ Run network cabling through the same conduits as power and telephone lines.

Installing a network isn't usually a weekend task. The old adage that patience is a virtue is just as true in networking as elsewhere. Take the time necessary to plan all the steps involved in properly installing a network. Considering how the installation might interrupt the normal activities of your organization is a good place to start—as is letting others in your organization know what's happening each step of the way.

In this chapter, we will actually start laying out the network. First, we'll explain how to find a good location for the file server that protects it from accidental damage.

Next, we will turn our attention to the file server itself. We'll discuss sizing (for disk space and memory). Then we'll set up systems to inventory workstation hardware and configure it to work with the network. We'll also set up the printers so that all the users on the LAN can use them.

Finally, we'll connect all the components. We'll do this by connecting each workstation to the network cabling and testing all the hardware so that we know it works. Preparing the hardware before installation speeds up installation.

Preparing the File Server Location

The file server is the heart of a NetWare 3.12 network—if the file server doesn't work, neither does the network. In most configurations, all the shared data, resources, and applications are dependent on the server, so it is important to select a proper location for it. You need to protect the server from accidents, heat, dust, and power problems.

NetWare file servers do not need the extensive environmental controls that mainframe computers require—you don't need to locate a file server in a 60-degree room with air cleaners and an independent power system. But do take some cues about site location and conditions from mainframe data centers.

Unfortunately, in the early days of LANs, many servers were placed in closets so that the network cabling would not be an eyesore to the rest of the office. The problem with closets is that they are generally not set up for the power needs of file servers, are rarely dust free, and generally have little or no air conditioning.

SERVER LOCATION OPTIONS

The file server will perform better, more reliably, and longer if you are careful about selecting its location. Consider these four points:

- ▸ security

- ▸ power

- ▸ heat

- ▸ dust

Physical Security

Frequently, the greatest risk to a file server is an *oops*-type accidental shutdown. For example, late one night, a coworker or the cleaning staff walks by the LAN administrator's office, notices that one of the PCs is left on, and decides to turn it off as directed by company policy for all work-stations. Oops, that was actually the file server. The next morning, the net-work will be down until the LAN administrator comes into work, discovers the problem, and brings up the system.

Even if *this* doesn't happen in your office, many other accidents can occur if you don't locate the file server in a suitable place. Unsuspecting users might not recognize it as a server and try to reboot it to use a word-process-ing application; the nightly cleaning crew could run over the power cord with a vacuum cleaner and unplug it; or someone could turn it off to save on the power bill.

Generally, the best location is a clean room where you can set up the serv-er and still have enough room to perform routine maintenance—for ex-ample, an unused office, with good ventilation and a lockable door.

WARNING
Beware of oops-type
risks to your file
server.

Power

All computers need an adequate and clean source of power. Unfortunately, plugging into the closest outlet will not necessarily provide you with access to good power. A recent survey of Novell resellers revealed that while 97% were using some form of power protection—usually an uninterruptible power supply (UPS) that stays on for a time if the power goes out—90% were *still* experiencing power-related problems.

Many office buildings are susceptible to power surges, drops, and spikes. If severe enough, these irregularities can harm sensitive electronic equipment. Power fluctuations can cause unexplained system lockups, board failures, and lost or corrupted data. If the power conditions are bad enough, your computers can reboot without warning. This is especially alarming since file servers generally keep many files open. If the server loses power at just the wrong time, say during a file write, it is possible to corrupt the file and it will not be able to easily restore it.

Since we recommend that you keep your file server up and running 24 hours a day, we also recommend that you protect it from poor power conditions.

Checking the supply of power isn't always straightforward. The unreliable way to check office power is to watch the overhead lights. If they dim during the day, it is a good indication that the building power is not going to be good enough for your server.

A more reliable test is to have an electrician check the electrical power output on the circuit you want to use for the server. Using a power-monitor device, the electrician can tell whether the circuit is overloaded or subject to spikes. Generally, it is best to monitor the power over several days—both day and night—to determine if fluctuations occur. This information can help you decide what type of power-conditioning equipment you need to clean up the electricity to your server.

If you want to be able to test the power yourself, or test it periodically, there are several manufacturers of electrical power monitors. You plug the monitor into the circuit you want to test (use the outlet your server will use), and an alarm will sound if there is any type of power fluctuation. The higher-quality monitors will allow you to print a report of all fluctuations on a tape like the ones used in adding machines.

There are several ways to protect your server from power fluctuations. You can have installed a *dedicated outlet* connected to a special circuit that, unlike the others in your office, is connected directly to the main building power and is not shared by other outlets. A dedicated circuit is protected from power drops that typically occur when a circuit is overloaded. For example, if you plug your server into the same circuit as the three copiers in the workroom, it will likely lose power when the copiers are being used at the same time. Plugging the server into a dedicated circuit prevents competition for power from other devices.

A second way to protect the server is to install an uninterruptible power supply (UPS) with power-conditioning features. A UPS is a battery backup device that also provides protection against major power spikes. The UPS works by maintaining a battery that will provide a constant supply of power even if the building power is completely shut off. A quality UPS will switch from commercial to its own battery power within a few microseconds when the commercial power drops below a certain threshold. In this case, the battery prevents the server from shutting down until the power returns to normal levels. If there's a major power failure, the UPS will use its battery to provide power to the server. Typically, the server is able to continue running for about 15–20 minutes—time enough to shut down the server properly.

NetWare 3.12 lets you monitor the UPS. This allows the server and the UPS to communicate with each other by linking the two with a serial cable and UPS monitoring card. The server is then configured for monitoring so that the UPS can indicate when a power failure has occurred. When power is lost to the UPS, a signal is passed to the server, which then executes the commands necessary for shutting down the file server without the administrator being present. This ability of the file server to shut itself down ensures that the server will be properly shut down even if the power failure occurs in the middle of the night.

Some experienced network managers also like to protect at least one workstation with a UPS. They install one UPS on each file server and one on a special workstation. If a power loss occurs, the LAN administrator can still operate the LAN for a short time to make sure that all open files are closed

NOTE
A dedicated outlet can protect your server from power drops.

NOTE
An uninterruptible power supply (UPS) provides protection against major power spikes.

NOTE
NetWare 3.12 lets you monitor the Uninterruptible Power Supply.

and the server is properly shut down before power is lost completely.

While most UPSs only provide the battery backup and surge protection, more advanced systems also offer line filters. The line filters help clean up the power signal as it is transmitted from the building power to the server. You need filters in buildings that have a lot of added noise to the power signal. The noise can be electromagnetic or radio frequency interference from the building's lighting and/or additional cabling near the power cable as it runs through the walls and ceilings. In most buildings, interference is not a major problem, but if you experience power problems that are not related to voltage drops or surges, you may benefit from a UPS that also includes filtering.

Heat

Heat is one of the silent killers of a network and can cause many problems for your hardware. Overheated disk drives can seize up and stop spinning, damaging the magnetic drive media. An overheated processor chip can cause processing errors or shut down the system completely. Memory chips also may overheat, causing parity errors. But the most common casualty to heat are the bearings in the cooling fan, which will cause the fan to stop, letting the other components overheat.

Placing the server in a closet can result in a heat buildup in the room, causing the server to overheat. Make sure you locate your server in a well-ventilated room that does not get too hot. You'll usually want a room with several vents, but you can use a closet if it has direct access to the air-conditioning system.

Most office buildings switch off the air conditioning on the weekends. This is a high-risk time for heat buildup. To reduce the amount of heat buildup, turn off the room's lights and all the video monitors. This will reduce the heat load in the room and allow the server to operate at a cooler temperature.

The main defense against heat is an insulated, ventilated, and relatively cool room.

WARNING!
Lack of ventilation can cause your server to overheat. Give your server plenty of ventilation.

NOTE
Make sure your server doesn't overheat on weekends, when most office buildings switch off the air conditioning.

By planning the server's location far enough in advance of the actual installation, you will have time to modify the server room without having to worry about damage to the server.

Dust

Dust can be another silent system killer. While dust problems are most common in industrial sites or where construction work is being carried out, dust will become a problem in almost any office over time. No matter how clean the building or room is, dust will accumulate unless extraordinary measures are taken to reduce it.

Dust tends to cause problems for the system gradually. First, dust can clog cooling fans, causing them to stop or even fail. Once a cooling fan stops, the rest of the computer will begin to overheat (and possibly fail as well).

Dust can also damage floppy disks and disk drives. If you are booting your file server from a floppy drive, dust becomes more important as you have to protect your server boot disk. Since dust can coat the diskette, it will find its way to the read/write heads in the floppy drive (and possibly destroy the drive's ability to read or write). Finally, large amounts of dust can also cause electrical shorts in a computer.

Fortunately, all of these problems occur only where there is a large amount of dust; usually you can catch it before too much builds up. You should be able to find a (relatively) dust-free room—look for a room where there is no construction and no major traffic. If dust *is* a major problem in your building, try getting the server access to an air filter such as the one used for the building's air conditioning.

Just because the server is up and running does not mean that it is free from potential problems. Check the inside of the file server periodically. Make sure the cooling fan is still working, check the fan housing for dust buildup on the blades, check the disk drives, and watch for dust building up on any of the chips on the computer's system board. By checking the server, you will be able to catch potential problems before they shut down your server.

**WARNING!
Check the inside
of your server
periodically for dust
build-up and other
problems. Just
because it's up and
running doesn't mean
it's free from
problems.**

Preparing Your Hardware to Run NetWare

Before you open the NetWare box and actually start installing the network software, ensure that your hardware is ready.

Conduct as complete a hardware inventory as possible so that you know what you already have, what you need to purchase, and what you need to modify. With this list of all the computers and their configurations, the administrator will find it easier to troubleshoot the network.

This is also the time to clean the workstations and carry out some preventive maintenance. Check each computer when you perform the inventory. Diagnostic software such as CheckIt or QAPlus/fe can give you thorough details about the computer and its components and offer diagnostic capabilities to discover and correct any existing problems. Bear in mind that the more problems you solve at this stage, the easier it will be later.

The table shown in Figure 5.1 lists what you'll need to know.

Add a copy of the CONFIG.SYS and AUTOEXEC.BAT files to the inventory to give details on a particular system's environment. Label all inventories with the computer's location, and write down the name of the primary user or users.

You can use one of a growing number of utility programs that perform your inventory for you and keep it available on line. Novell markets the NetWare Management System for OS/2 or Windows, which can manage your entire network. Software publishers such as Saber Software, Magee Enterprises, Intel, and Brightwork all produce packages for maintaining workstation information.

Next, perform an inventory of any printers or other shared devices that you want to use on the network. Write down what types of printers you have and how they need to be configured.

The table shown in Figure 5.2 lists the information needed for each printer you plan to use on the network.

FIGURE 5.1
*Sample Workstation
Inventory Sheet*

WORKSTATION INVENTORY SHEET

System Location	**A**dditional Drives: List type and number
Primary User Name	**M**onitor Type (VGA, Mono,...)
Processor Type	**N**etwork Card Configuration Node address
Amount of RAM installed	
BIOS Manufacturer	**M**odem Manufacturer BAUD Rate COM Port
Hard Drive Drive Type Controller Type Drive Capacity	
	Mouse
Floppy Drives Drive A: Drive B:	**S**ound Card Manufacturer Configuration
	Other

FIGURE 5.2

Sample Printer Inventory
Sheet

PRINTER INVENTORY SHEET

Printer Location	**B**AUD Rate
Printer Name	**D**ata Bits
Manufacturer	**S**top Bits
Model Number	**P**arity
Printer Type	**U**se X-on/X-off
Emulation Mode Additional Supported Modes	**S**ystem Connected to
Connection Port Parallel Serial	**P**ort Connected to

Collecting printer information will give you a ready resource and a guide to help you configure software for network users. For example, many software manufacturers require that you load a printer driver specific to each type of printer.

If a user wants to change the network printer that they are accessing, it will be easy for you to reconfigure their software if you know what type of printer they'll be using. If the application you are using will not accept the brand of printer you purchased, you will want to know what other types (brand and model number) of printers yours will emulate.

CHECKING COMPUTER REQUIREMENTS

Installing network computers is slightly different from installing a stand-alone computer. You'll need to add a network interface card to each computer. You'll also need to set up some workstations for attaching printers and other devices that can be shared across the network.

The File Server

The two most important computer requirements that you need to meet are available disk space and system memory (RAM) for your file server. Since the server is frequently the central point for storing data and applications, make sure it has enough disk space to handle the load. Typically, the more users you have, the more disk space you need.

Disk Space Requirements   As a rule of thumb, allow 10 MB of disk space for each DOS-based user to store data files, and 15 MB to 30 MB for each Windows- (or graphics-based) user. Database users, who often work with large files extracted from mainframe computers, will also require extra disk space.

Aside from calculating data-file disk-space needs, you also need to add up the space required by each of your applications. Some applications only require a small amount of space, but others require upwards of 15 MB to

20 MB each. Windows-based applications, for example, often use a tremendous amount of disk space. Consult the manuals shipped with your applications to find out the space they require.

Next, add in the disk requirements for the operating system. You'll need about 25 MB for NetWare 3.12. (See Chapter 16 for more information on administrator software.)

Server Memory Requirements   According to specifications, NetWare 3.12 requires a minimum of 4 MB of RAM to run the operating system, but this isn't necessarily the amount of memory you need for your server. File-server memory is affected by many factors: disk space, NLMs loaded, types of applications, number of users, and so on. The more extra features and people you have, the more server memory you'll need.

To accurately calculate the amount of memory required by NetWare, calculate the memory needed to maintain the disk space, and add 2 MB for the operating system.

The equation used by Novell (which can be found in the NetWare Installation manual) is

Volume size (in MB) $\times$ 0.023 + 2 MB (for the OS) = required memory

If your calculation comes to less than 4 MB, you will need to have 4 MB. Note that this is to calculate the *minimum* requirement: If you want better performance, add more memory.

In addition to the memory required to manage your disk space, the server also uses memory to load modules and handle network utilities, applications (like NLM-based databases) and communications. Remember that additional modules require server memory.

Consider also how many users your server will have to handle—the more users, the greater the amount of network traffic. If your server lacks enough memory to store incoming requests during the busy times, some data requests could get lost because the server is too busy handling others.

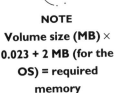

NOTE
Volume size (MB) $\times$
0.023 + 2 MB (for the
OS) = required
memory

Workstation Suggestions

Although installation requirements will change depending on what network interface card you are using, generally you need to configure each card with a base input/output address and a base memory address and set up the IRQ.

Base Input/Output Address	Interface cards you add to your PC will need a Base Input/Output address (Base I/O), a hexadecimal number the PC uses to uniquely identify each board in the system. Common values for Base I/O are the hex values 200h–360h. Each base address in the system needs to be unique.
Base Memory Address	Some types of cards use part of the PC's main memory for communication with the CPU. Cards use this type of memory (often called shared memory) to increase speed. Some other common types of cards in addition to NICs use shared memory: VGA controllers are often located at A000h or C000h, Monochrome cards use B000h, and some SCSI and disk controllers use a region around B200h. If you are using a Remote Boot ROM (special read-only memory containing executable programs that start the workstation's operating system, load the NetWare shell, and gain access to the network) rather than a floppy or hard disk to boot your workstation, you will need an additional memory area in this same region. Common shared memory addresses are A000h–E000h in varying increments.

Interrupt Request (IRQ)	Often NICs will also use an interrupt to tell the CPU that they have data ready and waiting. These cards will need to be assigned an interrupt value. As with Base I/O and Shared Memory addresses, an IRQ must be unique for each board (unless you are using a token ring or other adapter that supports shared interrupts). Some common IRQ values that are open in many PCs are IRQ2, IRQ3, IRQ5, IRQ9, IRQ10, and IRQ11. Most of the others are used by COM ports, printer ports, disk controllers, and other devices. We suggest, where possible, you set up the IRQ on your NIC to IRQ5, IRQ10, or IRQ11. These addresses are frequently not used by other adapter cards or PC ports. Some NICs will set these parameters through software rather than jumper settings.

First, your workstation will require a little tuning to set it up properly for LAN access. All PCs that access the LAN need to have network interface cards. The type of card (Token Ring, ARCnet, or Ethernet, for example) has to be the same as the one for the leg of the network that they will be connecting to.

Second, do all of your PCs have enough memory to run the applications you've planned for them? For example, if you are moving into a Windows environment, your computers will need at least 4 MB of RAM (preferably 8 MB) to run Windows 3.1 effectively.

On top of the memory needed to run the actual application, take into account the memory needed to access the network. Novell requires that you

NOTE
For Windows, your computers will need at least 4 MB of RAM.

load into memory several programs that allow your computer to communicate with the network. Typically these require approximately 64 KB of memory from the base 640 KB of memory allocated to DOS.

A user loading a lot of Terminate and Stay Resident programs (TSRs) may not have enough memory to load and run their programs. In this situation, consider using a memory-management program. Such programs allow you to use memory beyond 640 KB, and free up more memory for network shells and applications.

PREPARING NETWORK COMPUTERS

Use the list of devices commonly found in most personal computers in Table 5.1 to find the proper setting for your network cards.

HARDWARE DEVICE	IRQ	BASE I/O ADDRESS	BASE MEMORY ADDRESS*
COM 1	4	3F8–3FF	
COM 2	3	2F8–2FF	
LPT 1	7	378–37F.3BC–3BE	
LPT 2	5	278–27F	
Floppy disk controller	6	320–32F.3F0–3F7	
Hard disk controller	14	1F0–1F8	A000–E000
Mouse	2	230–23F	
Modem	3,4	3F8,2F8,3E8,2E8	
Network interface card	2–11	200–360	C000DFFF
Sound card	7,2,5,10	220–237,240–257	
Video		3B4–3BF,3C0–3CF 102	A000–CFFF

T A B L E 5.1

Typical Settings for PC Devices

The base memory address amount varies by device and monufacturer—this list is a range of addresses where shated memory typically resides.

NOTE
For the file server, note all the above settings for *every* card in the server. You have to tell NetWare which cards you have installed in the server and which settings each one is using.

NOTE
Though RS-232C is considered a standard, serial printers usually require more configuration than parallel printers. See your printer documentation for special cable requirements and information about baud rate, parity-bit and stop-bit settings.

Once you know which settings you can use for your network card, you can set the configuration. For Industry Standard Architecture (ISA) computers, you'll usually do this by setting a series of jumpers or switches. In this case, you set the jumpers on the card before you install it in the computer.

For Extended Industry Standard Architecture (EISA) and Micro Channel Architecture, you configure the card after inserting it in the system. On bootup, the system will notify the user that a new card has been added and a setup program will need to be run to configure the card (this is a *software configuration*).

Certain ISA network cards, such as Intel's EtherExpress 16 and SMC's EtherCard Plus 16, also use a software configuration. In this case, you install the card and run a software utility provided by the manufacturer to set its configuration. Once set, the configuration information is stored in flash memory or EEPROM (these chips remember even when power is removed).

Whichever method your card requires, read the manufacturer's documentation to answer any installation questions you have. You can also use manuals to configure a memory manager if a particular workstation needs one.

When you've installed the network interface card, connect it to a network cable and test it. Most network interface cards come with a diagnostic utility for testing both the card and the cable.

Finally, install the network software. See Chapter 7 for detailed instructions for generating the proper NetWare shells for your network.

PREPARING NETWORK PRINTERS

Preparing network printers is also important. Each printer that you are planning to use on the network will need to be configured and attached to the appropriate computer (server, workstation, or print server).

Be sure to place the printer where it will be once the network is up and running to check that the location is practical. Otherwise, you might find that you need a 35-foot cable to attach a new printer to the file server. Parallel cable normally should not exceed 25 feet, so you may have to reconfigure the printer and add a print server or a special printing box such as

Intel's Netport, which lets you set up a printer almost anywhere on the network (not just close to a file server).

Document each printer location documented (especially if serial), the station it is attached to, and which port it is using. You'll need all this information when you are setting up the printing services.

Cabling the Workstations

Cabling is the foundation of any network. In 99% of all local area networks, without cabling there can be no network (some wireless networks use radio waves to connect to the workstations).

Fortunately, you usually only need do large-scale cabling when the network is first installed. If you've never cabled a network before, consider contacting a professional cabling company or consultant who can help you plan a good cabling scheme and can properly install and test the cables.

If you are installing the cable yourself, read the following section for important considerations for setting up an effective cable system. In this section, we cover some of the basics for cabling the workstations in order to assist in your cabling or help you evaluate the company you have hired to do the cabling.

WHERE TO RUN THE CABLE

First, decide where to place the cables. Most office buildings have removable ceilings that will allow you to hide the cabling overhead. Use the following guidelines in choosing the path through the ceiling:

- ► Choose a path that is easily accessible. This will make the initial installation easier and it will also aid in troubleshooting and repairing cables down the line.

- ► Avoid placing the cable directly on light fixtures, air ducts, electrical cabling, or phone cabling. Light fixtures and other types of electrical devices can cause interference. All electrical systems radiate an electromagnetic field; if your network cable is too close, the field can interfere with communication between the workstation and the server.

If your topology permits, try running the main length of the cable segment down corridors or hallways. Corridors are accessible at all times, don't usually have employees working in them, and provide a central location for finding faulty cables.

The choice of cable placement is also important because it can add or reduce the length of the cable. Each type of cabling has distance limitations for each segment. Therefore, you may have a perfect place for running the cables, but it may require running the cables beyond the specified lengths to reach out-of-the-way workstations.

If this is the case, run a direct line to the workstation outside of the central cable run to stay within the segment-length restrictions and thus avoid ongoing communication problems. It is good policy, however, to try to keep stray cables to a minimum.

Generally, cabling will continue to function for most of the life of the network, and the increased maintenance time for tracking down the few cables that are not located in the central trunk will not be significant.

CABLING DO'S AND DON'TS

As you've seen, you have many choices of cabling for your network. Unfortunately, there are even more choices for installing the cable. This section will highlight some of the major do's and don'ts of cabling.

One of the golden rules to cabling is "Pull more cable than you need!" This means two things. First, and most important, pull extra length when running the cabling to ensure that you will be able to reach from the server to the workstation. Many an installation has failed to consider the air-conditioning duct that added three feet to the necessary cable length and discovered the problem only when the cable wouldn't reach all the way down the wall to the proper wall plate!

NOTE
Interference can dramatically affect the performance of your network. The more interference you have, the more excess "noise" you have on the network cable.

TIP
"Pull more cable than you need!"

There are three solutions to the cable that is too short. The first and least preferable is to mount the wall plate in the middle of the wall (about four feet above the floor). This solution not only looks bad as a finished product, but setting the end on a cable that high up is not an easy task.

The second option is to add a piece of patch cable to increase the length. This is better than the first option, but each connector adds an impedance and induces noise in the line that reduces the total distance the segment can reach. Additional connectors also add points of failure for the cable, so having additional connectors on a network segment increases the likelihood that the segment will fail.

The third, and preferred, solution is to repull the cable with a segment that is long enough to reach. This solution is often viewed as a complete waste of time and money, but it will result in a more stable cabling system (and will save a great deal more money in the long run).

Avoid using prebuilt cables. Some less-reputable cabling companies use prebuilt cables to reduce the time needed to perform the installation. Typically these cables are cut in 20-foot segments, and to make a 100 foot server-to-workstation connection would require five separate cables connected using barrel connectors, which are susceptible to failures (as are the connectors for each cable). This type of installation can greatly reduce the functional lengths for each segment, and can cause a great deal of trouble in the long run.

TIP
Avoid using prebuilt cables when you must use several to gain the desired length.

For example, in one installation, a network using thin Ethernet (*"cheapernet"*) consisted of 20-foot segments chained together with barrel connectors. This scheme worked well for about nine months, then each leg that measured over 400 feet would only function properly if there were fewer than eight workstations on it. This led to entire cable segments failing, and as a result the company had to recable most of the existing network.

The second translation for our golden rule is to plan for growth by pulling extra cable segments. Extra segments allow you to quickly replace a bad cable by switching the existing cable with a spare pulled early in the installation. Further, it is much less costly to pull two cables (one for the workstation and one extra) while installing the network than to pull a new cable to

NOTE
Using good-quality equipment is important in all aspects of your network, but cabling tends to be the place where most of the corner cutting occurs. Inexpensive cabling can function quite well for a small network with limited segments and short segment lengths. But even in a small network, you will have more performance problems with cheap cabling, and in many cases your network cabling will wear-out in a short time.

replace a faulty segment. These extra segments also allow you to expand the number of workstations without having to run new cable every time you add a new workstation. Carefully planning the use of extra segments can go far to ease network cabling maintenance and expansion.

Another important "Do" for cabling is to use good quality cabling and connectors.

One cabling company we have worked with discovered (with the help of several card manufacturers) that cheap twisted-pair cable, especially if poorly run, may cause your network card to "burn up" after only a year to year and a half's worth of service. The increased impedance generated by the low-quality cable caused the cards to overheat by constantly overdriving them, and this eventually reached a point where the cards could no longer function.

Once you've got the cable in place and the network cards installed in the workstations, it's time to test the hardware. Some NIC manufacturers provide utilities to test the network hardware. If any workstations fail, check the cabling, the network cards' configuration, and whether the card functions at all. Testing the hardware and making sure it's all working will help you catch problems early and make troubleshooting the network easier.

DOCUMENTING THE CABLE LAYOUT

The final step in any cable installation is to document where you've run each cable. By drawing the cable system out on a building blueprint, the administrator will be able to easily locate a faulty cable. Map each segment as it runs from the server to the workstation and mark both ends of the cable. Once you have a map of each segment, be sure to update the map every time you make any change in the layout so that you stay current on the layout and can identify any segments that may be having problems due to excessive length. This map will also help you plan any major changes to the network layout as well as network expansion.

Even so, don't stop your documentation at just a simple map of the cables. Include the location of all hubs, concentrators, and repeaters, as well as any patches added to cable segments. The locations of the hubs and repeaters will help a new administrator locate all the cabling hardware (including the repeater that is now buried in the back of the storage closet that no one's been into for three years). The maps will make passing the job of administrator on to a successor much easier.

In addition to maps, note in the documentation the type of cable used for the segments as well as any other hardware used (such as the make and model of the repeaters). Consider writing down the dates that any changes were made and the names of the technicians who performed the work. This will allow you to assess the age of each section of the cabling and will provide you with the name of the people who worked on it (this is especially important if you have different companies handling different sections of your cabling).

A well-documented cabling system will assist you in maintaining the existing network, planning for changes in layout, and increasing the scope of the network. Further, it can provide you with a complete history of the cabling system, which can be most helpful in troubleshooting cabling problems.

Summary

In this chapter we covered the important planning setups for your NetWare 3.12 installation. We prepared the hardware for its role in the network. The file server, workstations, and printers have been documented, configured, cabled, and set in their proper places. We explained why the server's location is especially important to protect it from damage, both accidental and hardware related. We finished up by looking at the cabling needed to connect all the elements together. In the next chapter, we will begin the actual NetWare 3.12 installation. It's finally time to open up the NetWare box and install the network operating system.

Installing
NetWare 3.12

Fast Track

NetWare Loadable Modules (NLMs)   *100*

are programs designed to add additional capabilities to the core NetWare
operating system. They may be:

- loaded as they are needed

- loaded into memory at all times

Partitions   *102*

are sections of the hard disk drive that are set aside for the storage of a
particular type of information. For example, when using the NetWare
operating system, a disk drive may have a DOS partition and a NetWare
partition.

NetWare may be started from: *104*

- a floppy disk drive

- a DOS partition on the hard disk

INSTALL.NLM is used to: *114*

- Create NetWare partitions

- Create NetWare volumes

- Copy the system and public files

- Create or edit AUTOEXEC.NCF and STARTUP.NCF files

TIP
Don't panic! NetWare 3.12 is extremely simple to install.

There's nothing like a huge stack of manuals to strike fear into the heart of would-be network managers! Because Novell NetWare is a complex network operating system with a tremendous number of features and capabilities, NetWare manuals must cover all of them—and the sight of the manuals is most imposing.

NetWare 3.12 is extremely simple to install. There are usually several ways to accomplish tasks in NetWare, and most installations will only use a fraction of them. For example, there is a complete volume on setting up network printing with more configurations than most networks will ever use. The chances are good that you will never need some of the documentation Novell provides with NetWare.

In this chapter, we'll lead you through installing NetWare and configuring a file server. We'll cover the way Novell network software is organized and the different ways you can install it. We'll introduce you to several concepts about how information is stored on a server's hard disk, how the server program and files are organized and where they are kept, and how to configure your server for automatic startup.

If you're upgrading from NetWare 2.1x or 2.2, please see Appendix B, *Upgrading to NetWare 3.12*. If you've installed NetWare 2.1x or 2.2 before, the concepts for installing NetWare 3.12 will be completely different, although pleasantly easier. If you're installing NetWare 3.12 on a new system, you are in the right place.

The Structure of NetWare

Novell NetWare 3.12 is a modern operating system built using a modular structure.

The core of the NetWare 3.12 operating system is a single ready-to-run program. When you need different components of the software (drivers, Network Loadable Modules, and other programs), you can load or unload them *while the server is running*. You don't have to perform any lengthy linking process before installing the server.

This design makes NetWare 3.12 simple to install, easy to maintain, and very flexible from the network installer/administrator's point-of-view. Installing NetWare 3.12 requires only six simple steps.

1 · Installing and documenting the configuration settings for hardware added to the server.

2 · Powering up the server under DOS and ensuring that it works properly as a stand-alone computer.

3 · Deciding where to store the components of the server software and using DOS to copy them there.

4 · Starting the server software and loading appropriate modules to allow access to the disks, network cards, etc.

5 · Loading the system and public files from the Novell disks.

6 · Customizing and saving the server's startup procedures.

SERVER FILES

The core of the NetWare operating system is the executable server program called SERVER.EXE located on the Program-1 disk included in the NetWare package. This is the operating system foundation to which other programs and modules are added (it may also be referred to as the operating system *kernel*).

To complete the server software, several different types of software modules are added. The programs which form the interface between the server software and the disk and network interface controllers, for example, are called *drivers*. Drivers are programs that enable NetWare to access the available hardware. Programs designed to perform a function such as monitoring the Uninterruptible Power Supply (UPS) or automatically backing up the server are called *NetWare Loadable Modules* (NLMs). NLMs are programs intended to extend the capabilities of the server software. In fact, drivers are a special type of NLM.

When SERVER.EXE is first run, it has virtually no knowledge of the different components that are installed in a system. To make NetWare aware

NOTE
With NetWare 3.12, you can load or unload different components of the software as you need them, even while the server is running.

of the installed hardware, you have to load drivers for the individual components. The two most common types of drivers are *disk drivers* and *LAN drivers*.

Disks and Disk Drivers

Before NetWare can access any of the hard disks installed in your system, it needs a disk driver for the disk controller (or controllers) you are using. PCs use many different types of drivers and controllers; below we list some of the more common types.

MFM   Modified Frequency Modulation drives. Used most often in early PC-XT and PC-AT class computers, MFM drives are rarely used in a file server because of limited capacities and speed.

RLL   Run Length Limited drives. Although used most often in early PC-XT class computers, RLL drives may also be found in PC-AT class computers. These drives are very similar to MFM drives, but they use an encoding scheme which allows the disk to hold more data. As with MFM drives, RLL drives are rarely used in a file server because of limited capacities and speed.

ESDI   Enhanced Small Device Interface. Early file servers most often used ESDI drives. These drives have extended capacities and are capable of greater throughput than either MFM or RLL drives.

IDE   Integrated Drive Electronics. These drives are gaining popularity as file-server drives. IDE drives are usually less expensive than other drive types and offer reasonable capacities and good performance.

SCSI   Small Computer Systems Interface. This is probably the most popular type of drive used in file servers. If you use a SCSI controller in your file server, you can attach other SCSI devices such as tape drives and CD-ROM players as well as disks to your system. SCSI is actually a specification for an interface which can support up to eight high-speed and high-capacity devices (of which one is the controller) chained to it.

In most cases, if you are using an MFM, RLL, ESDI, or IDE drive controller in your server, the disk driver will be ISADISK.DSK, located on the System-2 disk. This driver is for common controllers which work in Industry Standard Architecture (ISA) and some Extended Industry Standard Architecture (EISA) based computers. If you are using a SCSI controller designed to emulate a standard PC-AT disk controller, this driver may still work.

More often than not, though, when using a SCSI or other more specialized disk controller (a bus-mastering or drive-array controller, for example), the manufacturer will supply a driver with the controller. Check the documentation from the manufacturer to see if there is a specialized driver. If the manufacturer has supplied a special driver for NetWare 3.12, you are likely to get improved performance by using their driver rather than a generic one, even if both will work. Table 6.1 lists several other common types of disk drivers included with NetWare.

You can usually identify disk drivers by their filenames. Under NetWare 3.12, disk drivers typically follow a convention of using the same extension (.DSK), as in *ISADISK.DSK*.

Very few manufacturers have built special controllers that support more than one drive type. In order to use drives of different types in the same server and increase the number of drives which can be supported, NetWare allows you to install more than one disk controller in a file server. These different controllers may be of different types, so a driver for each board will need to be loaded.

NOTE
In most cases, a single controller can only handle drives of a single type—for example, an **MFM** drive cannot be connected to a controller designed to work with **SCSI** disks.

T A B L E 6.1

Disk Drivers Included with

NetWare

DISK DRIVER	INDUSTRY STANDARD ARCHITECTURE	EXTENDED INDUSTRY STANDARD ARCHITECTURE	MICRO CHANNEL ARCHITECTURE
DCB [1]	●	●	
ISADISK	●	●	
PS2ESDI			●
PS2MFM			●
IBMSCSI [2]			●

[1] **Requires Novell's Disk Coprocessor Board (DCB)**

[2] **Requires IBM's Optional SCSI Adapter**

LAN Drivers

Before NetWare can access the network, you must load a LAN driver for the network interface controller you are using. If you have more than one interface installed, you'll most likely need to load a driver for each additional card. Before you can successfully install the LAN drivers, you'll need to know what type of controllers you've installed and the configuration settings for each controller.

Network interface drivers under NetWare usually end with the extension (*.LAN*). NetWare provides support for a number of network interface controllers with the operating system. Table 6.2 lists some of the common LAN drivers included with NetWare.

NetWare Loadable Modules

NetWare Loadable Modules (commonly known as NLMs) are programs designed to add capabilities to the core NetWare operating system. Some of these programs are loaded only when needed, while others are intended to be run all the time. The functions provided by these modules can vary greatly.

For example, the installation program Novell provides with NetWare is an NLM that is only loaded when installing the server's files or when modifying a server's automatic startup files. This type of NLM might be

NETWORK BOARD	DRIVER	CABLING SYSTEM
16/4 Adapter	TOKEN.LAN	Token Ring
16/4 Adapter/A	TOKEN.LAN	Token Ring
EtherLink II	3C503.LAN	Ethernet
EtherLink Plus	3C505.LAN	Ethernet
EtherLink/MC	3C523.LAN	Ethernet
NE/2	NE2.LAN	Ethernet
NE/2-32	NE232.LAN	Ethernet
NE1000	NE1000.LAN	Ethernet
NE2000	NE2000.LAN	Ethernet
NE3200	NE3200.LAN	Ethernet
PCN	PCN2.LAN	IBM PC Network
PCN2	PCN2.LAN	IBM PC Network
PCN2/A	PCN2.LAN	IBM PC Network
PCN/A	PCN2.LAN	IBM PC Network
PC Adapter II	TOKEN.LAN	Token Ring
PC Adapter/A	TOKEN.LAN	Token Ring
RX-Net	TRXNET.LAN	ARCnet
RX-Net II	TRXNET.LAN	ARCnet ·
RX-Net/2	TRXNET.LAN	ARCnet

T A B L E 6.2

LAN Drivers Included with NetWare

categorized as a utility rather than a software enhancement. Other utility NLMs provided with NetWare include Monitor, Volume Repair, and Remote Console (see *File Server Commands* in Appendix A for a complete listing). An NLM for print service or network backup, by contrast, might always be loaded at startup and be continuously present during normal operation. This also is often the case with database servers such as NetWare's Structured Query Language (SQL) and Btrieve database products.

SYSTEM AND PUBLIC FILES

The bulk of the files and programs contained on the NetWare disks are utilities, printer definitions, and other programs stored in the SYSTEM and PUBLIC directories on the file server. During installation, you will be prompted to install many of the disks in the Novell package for the relevant files to be copied automatically to the file server. For a listing of the utility programs and a description of their functions, please see *File Server Commands* and *Workstation Commands* in Appendix A.

Parts III and IV of this book are dedicated to illustrating the use of the programs and utilities as tools for network administrators and users.

Preparing to Install NetWare

If you can, test the server hardware as a stand-alone DOS computer before attempting to install NetWare. Once you've installed all of the hardware in the server and documented the configuration values for the components, you're ready to power up the computer and start DOS from a floppy drive.

NetWare can be configured to start from a floppy drive or a hard disk. Depending on how your server will be configured, you may want to go ahead and prepare the server's hard disk and install DOS onto a section of the hard disk called a *DOS partition*. (See the section titled *DOS Partitions* below.) If you intend to store only the server program, drivers, and NLMs on the DOS partition of your disk, a partition of 3–5 MB should be sufficient.

WHAT IS A PARTITION?

Before NetWare (or any other operating system) can do anything with the disk drives in your system, they must be prepared and set up to store data. A *partition* is a portion of a hard-disk drive set aside for storage of a particular type of information. A hard disk may have several partitions, each used to separate one section of the hard drive from another. You can also use partitions to allow more than one operating system to reside on the same disk.

Most different operating systems store information on the hard disk in proprietary ways. Without special programs, for example, UNIX can't read a partition set aside for DOS. Similarly, DOS cannot directly read files stored on a NetWare partition. When using the NetWare operating system, we are mainly concerned with DOS partitions and NetWare partitions.

DOS Partitions

Partitions created by DOS are the most common type of partition used on Intel-based PCs with hard disks. DOS partitions are created when DOS is first installed and cannot usually be changed without destroying data on the hard disk.

When you install newer versions of DOS, the SETUP program will perform most of the tasks involved in partitioning the hard disk for you. If you want to use your hard disk with NetWare and DOS, you will need to prevent the DOS FDISK program from automatically assigning the entire drive to DOS, but you should allow FDISK to activate the DOS partition. (The active partition of the first hard disk in a computer is usually the one the computer boots from.) See your DOS manual for details on SETUP and FDISK.

NetWare Partitions

NetWare partitions are where NetWare stores 98% of the file server's files (some of the drivers and loadable modules may be stored on DOS disks). When you install NetWare, the installation program will copy the operating system, drivers, Network Loadable Modules (NLMs), and network utilities to a NetWare partition on a server drive. Once these files are on the NetWare partition, they can only be accessed from a workstation logged into the server or (in the case of NLMs) loaded from the server's console.

For this reason, it makes sense to store some of the file server's utilities on a DOS partition or on a DOS floppy disk. In particular, you'd be wise to keep on the DOS partition the utilities (such as VREPAIR) that assist in

NOTE
Most other operating systems take care not to disturb information stored on DOS partitions. However, if you are using a data compression driver or similar program on your DOS disk, back-up the DOS information before attempting the installation procedure.

recovering data after a server crash caused by a power failure or other problem. If you lose access to the NetWare partitions on your server from a server crash and the NetWare partition is the only place your utilities are kept, you'll have to return to using the installation floppy disks to recover your files.

The NetWare server program (SERVER.EXE) must be started from either a floppy or a DOS bootable partition of the hard drive. Starting NetWare from a floppy drive is usually slower than from the hard disk, but offers three advantages:

▸ You can use the entire hard disk for NetWare.

▸ If the server's hard disk fails, you will still be able to get to the repair utilities, configuration programs, and drivers without relying on your master disks.

▸ You can maintain better security because no one can start the server without the bootable floppy disk.

The disadvantage of storing these files on a floppy disk is the possibility that if the server is often shut down and restarted, the physical floppy media can wear out. If you intend to start NetWare from a floppy, save yourself future headaches by making more than one copy of your server's startup disk.

Installing the Server Software

WARNING
Before you start,
make a backup copy
of the NetWare disks!

As we just said, you can start NetWare from either a floppy-disk drive or from a DOS partition on the hard disk. If your computer boots normally under DOS and you're going to use the entire hard disk for NetWare, go to the next section, *Starting NetWare from a Floppy Drive*. If you are going to start NetWare from a DOS partition on your hard disk, proceed with the section titled *Starting NetWare from a DOS Partition*.

STARTING NETWARE FROM A FLOPPY DRIVE

To start NetWare from a floppy disk, you'll need one high-density floppy diskette formatted to boot DOS and enough space to hold the SERVER.EXE file, your NLMs, and driver files (in many cases the single bootable floppy is enough). Since the executable SERVER.EXE takes up almost 1 MB of disk space, you must use high-density drives. You don't *have* to partition the hard disk with DOS in order to install NetWare, but doing so won't harm you either. NetWare can create partitions without DOS and will allow you to create or delete partitions during installation.

Copy the contents of the disk *NETWARE 3.12 OPERATING SYSTEM-1* (called *SYSTEM-1* from here on) to the formatted diskette. If you don't have a second floppy drive or a place to temporarily store the NetWare files (such as a hard disk), use the DOS DISKCOPY command. When the copy is complete, retransfer the system files with the DOS SYS command and copy the command interpreter COMMAND.COM to the root directory (A:\, for example) in order to make the disk bootable. See your DOS manual for details on using these commands.

STARTING NETWARE FROM A DOS PARTITION

NetWare version 3.12 has a slightly different installation procedure than previous versions of NetWare.

Installing NetWare 3.12 with INSTALL

You can use the INSTALL.BAT (INSTALL.BAT will run the executable NWNSTLL.EXE) program on the NetWare INSTALL disk to create a DOS partition and begin the installation procedure; but Novell assumes that you will be doing this from the A: drive. (Make sure you have the proper disk media if you intend to use INSTALL). The INSTALL disk is a bootable DOS disk that can assist you in creating a DOS partition, automatically copy the first three server disks to the DOS partition, start the SERVER program and enter the NetWare installation utility INSTALL.NLM.

To use INSTALL, either reboot the computer and run the program INSTALL.BAT found on the NetWare INSTALL disk or place the INSTALL

WARNING
NetWare versions prior to 3.12 do not use an INSTALL disk when installing Net-Ware.

WARNING
If you use INSTALL, your server must boot from a DOS partition.

disk in drive A: and reboot the computer. The system will enter the main menu of the NetWare Installation Utility (see Figure 6.1).

From the main menu, select *Install new NetWare v3.12* to get to the Disk Partition Options menu. From this menu, you can choose to keep the currently defined partitions on your disk drive (if they exist) or allow NetWare to erase the existing partitions and create new ones.

If you allow INSTALL to erase the currently defined partitions, all information contained on them will be lost. Make sure that you have an adequate backup before selecting this option. The install utility will give you an opportunity to exit if you have incorrectly selected this option. If you use INSTALL to create the DOS partition, you will be prompted to enter the partition size in MB (NetWare will suggest a default value of 5MB). Enter a partition size and press ↵. The installation program will create the partition, reboot the computer, and attempt to format the new partition with DOS. (Should the format procedure fail, you will need to manually format the partition.)

If INSTALL finds an existing formatted partition on the disk, it will go directly to the Enter Server Name prompt. Enter a name for your server.

WARNING!
If you allow INSTALL to erase the currently defined partitions, all information contained on them will be lost. Make a backup first.

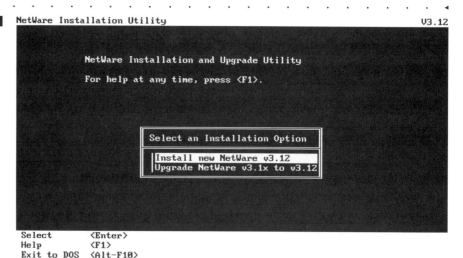

FIGURE 6.1

The NetWare installation utility

(You can change this server name later, but if you wish to set the permanent name now, see the suggestions for naming your server under the section *Firing Up NetWare.*) After you've selected the server name, you will be prompted for an Internal IPX number (see Figure 6.2). This number is a unique number used to identify the server. You may either enter a unique server number of your choice or accept the default provided by the INSTALL program.

From here the INSTALL program will request the SYSTEM-1 and SYSTEM-2 disks so that the appropriate files may be copied onto the DOS partition. By default, the INSTALL program will put these files in the directory C:\SERVER.312, but you may select any directory you wish (see Figure 6.3).

When the files have been copied, INSTALL will ask you if you want to modify the AUTOEXEC.BAT file. If you want the server to start up each time the system is rebooted, select yes. After you make your selection, INSTALL will give you the message *Invoking Server* as the server program SERVER.EXE is being started. At this point, you should proceed to the section *Firing Up NetWare.*

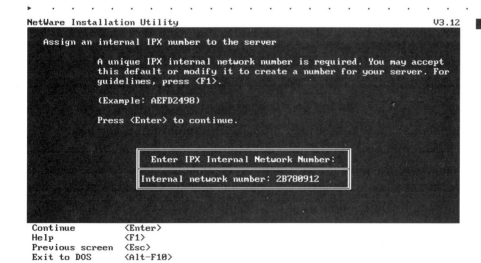

FIGURE 6.2

Selecting the Server's Internal IPX number

```
NetWare Installation Utility                                    V3.12

    Assign an internal IPX number to the server

          A unique IPX internal network number is required. You may accept
          this default or modify it to create a number for your server. For
          guidelines, press <F1>.

          (Example: AEFD2498)

          Press <Enter> to continue.


              ┌─────────────────────────────────────────┐
              │   Enter IPX Internal Network Number:     │
              ├─────────────────────────────────────────┤
              │ Internal network number: 2B780912        │
              └─────────────────────────────────────────┘


Continue          <Enter>
Help              <F1>
Previous screen   <Esc>
Exit to DOS       <Alt-F10>
```

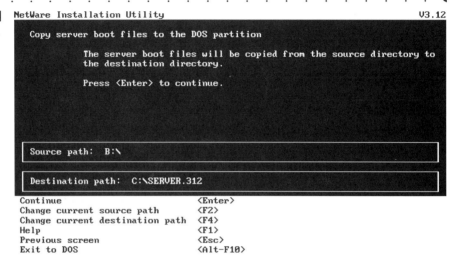

FIGURE 6.3

Selecting the DOS paths for
installation

Installing NetWare 3.12 Manually

To start NetWare from a DOS partition, first install DOS on the disk drive (DOS gets a little cranky if it doesn't get the first partition). Follow the installation procedure for your version of DOS. As mentioned before, during installation the FDISK program may try to automatically allocate all of the hard disk to DOS. Since you want to use part of the disk for NetWare, you need to manually select the size of the DOS partition. If you are only installing DOS to facilitate starting NetWare and storing its drivers and utilities, a 3–5 MB DOS partition should be sufficient. Make sure the DOS partition is marked as the active partition, or your server will not boot automatically. You can tell when the partition table has the wrong partition marked active or no partition marked active because the computer will respond with a message like this:

> missing operating system...
> Please insert a bootable disk into drive a:

Once your server can successfully boot up under DOS, copy the contents of the System-1 diskette to the DOS partition (this is usually the drive C:\

if you only have one DOS partition). To speed up installation, it is also helpful to copy the System-2 disk to the DOS partition.

Firing Up NetWare

Once you've copied the server software to the appropriate boot-up drive, the next step in installation is to fire up the server software. At the file-server console, reboot the machine and start the server software by running SERVER from the DOS prompt (if you're using INSTALL.EXE for NetWare 3.12, this has been done for you).

For example, if starting from the floppy drive, insert the bootable DOS floppy containing the copy of the System-1 disk into drive A: and type:

> A:\> SERVER↵

You should see the message *Loading* … while the server is starting up. This may take a minute or two from a floppy. Once the server has been loaded, you should be greeted with a message similar to the following:

> Novell NetWare System Console 3.12 (250 user) 12/21/92
> Processor speed: 346
> (Type SPEED at the command prompt for an explanation of the speed rating)

> File server name:

At this point, you're ready to give the file server a name. You'll be able to change the file server's name later, so don't worry about the software making permanent changes. Select your permanent file server name carefully. This might not seem important in a small office with only one server, but bear in mind that *the network will always outgrow your initial expectations* and plan ahead.

We recommend that you use a server name that is easy to type and remember and one that is not locked into a particular group or department. Often, servers initially bought for one department will end up serving

TIP
When selecting a name for your file server, choose something easy to type and to remember, and make sure it isn't tied to one group or department.

several. For example, it would not make sense for the server used by sales, accounting, and technical support to be named ACCOUNTING. Unless you plan for expansion, you can end up with server names that are meaningless or confusing to your users.

The reason for a server name which is easy to type and remember is that often server names are included in paths and drive mappings. It will quickly become uncomfortable to have to type **Systems_Engineering_File_Server _One** each time you want to remap a network drive.

NetWare must have at least two characters in the server name and will allow up to 47. The naming conventions otherwise are similar to those for a DOS filename: You can use alphanumeric characters, hyphens, and underscores, but not spaces, commas, or other punctuation.

For our installation example, we have named our file server CICERO. Some installations choose to merely number their file servers (e.g., FS1, FS2, etc.) but this scheme does not lend itself well to remembering which server is which. Examples of other *generic* file server names are: TOLSTOY, DICKENS, SIGMA, SUMMA, MAGNA, KIRK, SPOCK, MCKOY, ZEUS, APOLLO, JUPITER, NEPTUNE, MICKEY, MINNIE, DONALD (no snickering, Disney is big business), and so on.

NETWORK NUMBERING

After you've given your file server a name, you will have to assign it an internal network number. NetWare uses a network-numbering and node-numbering scheme to determine how to route information on the network. Network numbers and node numbers are akin to postal ZIP codes and addresses. Network numbers identify network segments; node numbers identify particular workstations and computers on the network. We're concerned with two types of network numbers: *internal* and *external* network numbers.

External Network Number or Physical Networks

A physical network number is a way of addressing a particular LAN segment. Each NIC in a server or router will be assigned a network number when its driver is loaded. If there are three file servers on a LAN segment, the common wire which connects them together is a physical network and must be assigned a unique number. This is the number that will be assigned when the LAN drivers for all three boards are loaded. See Figure 6.4 for an illustration of a physical network.

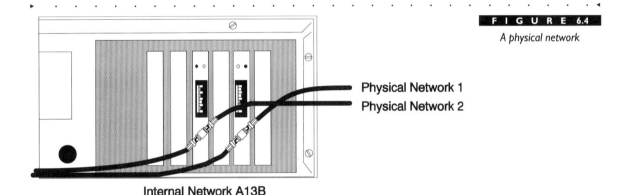

FIGURE 6.4

A physical network

Internal Network Number

An internal network number is a special kind of logical network inside of a server or router. If more than one interface card is installed in a server or router, you might visualize the internal network as the PC's internal bus with each of the boards being nodes on this logical network. Each internal network number on your LAN must also be unique. See Figure 6.5 for a representation of internal networks as they relate to physical networks.

Our test network has two LAN segments and our new file server is connected to the second segment. As such, three network numbers have already been assigned (two for the network segments and one for the internal network in the other file server). We chose an arbitrary but unique value of 10 for our file server. In larger networks it is advisable to develop a scheme for network numbering (perhaps by floor or by department), as multiple organizations or departments are likely to have their own servers and network administrators.

FIGURE 6.5

Internal and external
network numbers

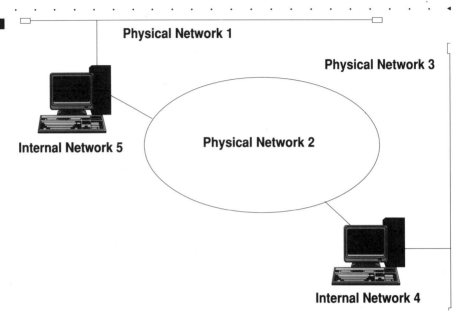

LOADABLE MODULES AND DRIVERS

Once you've named your file server and assigned a unique internal network number, you are officially running NetWare on your new server (you just can't talk to anyone yet). You will have to load the disk driver, LAN driver and installation NLM before the server will be able to complete the installation and charge off to the races.

LOADING DISK DRIVERS

NetWare's installation program will need to access the disks in your file server in order to create NetWare partitions and copy the files contained in the NetWare package. Before it can do this, you will have to load a driver for the disk controller. In most cases this driver is ISADISK.DSK and is located on the System-2 disk (or on the DOS partition if you copied System-2 there). The process for loading the driver is quite simple.

From the colon (:) prompt at the file server, type

: load [path] driver.dsk↵

For example, to load ISADISK.DSK from the System-2 disk in drive a:\,
type : **load a:\ISADISK**⏎. NetWare will respond with a message similar
to this:

> Loading module ISADISK.DSK
> NetWare v3.12   ISA Device Driver
> Version 3.1   December 17, 1992
> Copyright 1992   Novell, Inc.   All rights reserved.

In our test server, we were using one of the special controllers mentioned
earlier—an IDE drive-array controller for a Compaq System Pro. As with
most special drive controllers, this one uses a customized driver whose installation procedure differs slightly from ISADISK.DSK:

> : load a:\compaq\CPQDA386 slot=1⏎

LOADING NETWORK DRIVERS

At this point we could continue with the installation NLM, but if we load
a driver for a network interface controller and bind a protocol to it,
INSTALL.NLM will automatically place the necessary commands to load
the drivers in the server's auto-start files.

Loading the Driver

The process for loading a LAN driver is similar to that of a disk driver.
For example, to load a driver for a Novell (Eagle/Anthem) NE2000 card, we
typed:

> : load a:\NE2000⏎

NetWare responded by asking for the Base I/O address (port) of the card
in hex and then asked for the interrupt value. If installation is successful,
NetWare will sometimes respond with a message saying that the driver has
been loaded; this varies with the driver.

Binding a Protocol

You've only one step to go before the server can communicate over the network—binding a protocol to the interface controller. If you are running Novell's IPX/SPX protocol, you would bind this protocol to the board serving a particular physical network. In our example network, the command is:

```
: bind IPX to NE2000 net=10
```

The parameter *net=10* indicated to our driver that this card would be connected to physical network address 10. There are similar commands for binding other protocols such as TCP/IP and AppleTalk.

RUNNING INSTALL.NLM

Once the disks and network interface controllers are up and running, we are ready to let INSTALL.NLM take over. This file is located on the System-2 disk or on your DOS partition if you copied System-2 there. Load INSTALL with the following command:

```
: load [path] INSTALL↵
```

When INSTALL has loaded, you will be greeted by the screen appearing in Figure 6.6. This is the Installation Options menu of INSTALL.

We use the INSTALL program to perform several necessary operations:

- ▶ format the disk (if not previously formatted)
- ▶ create NetWare partitions
- ▶ create NetWare Volumes
- ▶ copy the System and Public files
- ▶ create the server's auto-start files.

We use INSTALL to format and partition the disk drives and create at least one *Volume* for the file server. Under NetWare, a Volume is a NetWare

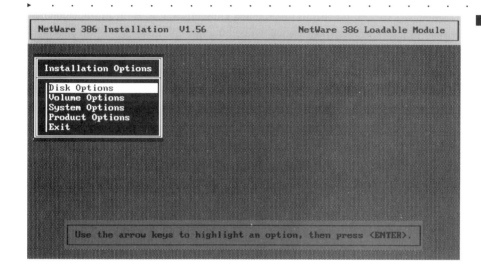

FIGURE 6.6
The opening screen of
INSTALL.NLM

partition, a portion of a partition, or a set of partitions that have been bound together into a single logical unit. To the network user, this logical unit will appear as a single drive.

The first thing to do to the disk is check to see if it has been formatted. If the disk has had another operating system installed on it, it has been formatted at least once. On new disks, you will need to check the documentation to see if the disk has been formatted at the factory (DO NOT format NetWare ready disks, SCSI disks, or IDE disks). In most modern disks, formatting is unnecessary.

If you need to format your disk, use the Disk Options menu. Select Disk Options and the Available Disk Options menu will appear. You can use the first option in this menu, Format (optional), to format disks.

Creating NetWare Partitions

Whether or not your disk had been previously formatted, or if you have newly formatted it with NetWare, you will need to use the Partition Tables option of the Available Disk Options menu to create at least one NetWare partition. Selecting the Partition Tables option will bring up the Available

WARNING!
If you delete a partition (DOS, NetWare, or other), the information that is stored there will be permanently erased. Be careful when using this option.

Disk Drives menu. If you do not see any disks listed, you probably have not correctly loaded your disk driver. Highlight one of the disks with your cursor keys and press ↵ to get the Partition Options menu, which appears in Figure 6.7.

In most cases, you won't need to modify your Hot Fix Redirection Area. Hot Fix Redirection is a method NetWare uses to relocate data that has been written to a questionable section of the disk. If you modify the Hot Fix parameters, be sure not to assign too small a value. Similarly, if you lengthen the Hot Fix Area to cope with problems you are already having with a particular disk, you are asking for trouble. It is generally best to accept the default values assigned by INSTALL.NLM.

Use the option Create NetWare Partition to assign free space on the drive to NetWare. NetWare will, by default, assign 98% of the free space as a data area and 2% for Hot Fix Redirection.

You can move to the field labeled Partition Size and change the value to create a partition of a different size. Once you have set the parameters for your partition, you can save it by pressing Esc.

FIGURE 6.7

The Partition Options menu

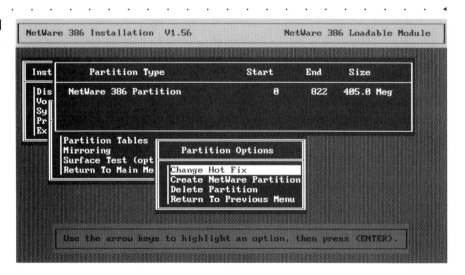

If there is no free space available on the disk, NetWare will indicate this with an error message. You can use the Delete Partition option to delete both NetWare and non-NetWare partitions to open disk space for your new partition.

Mirroring and Duplexing NetWare Disks

If you have more than one disk in your server, you can have NetWare automatically duplicate the data from a partition on one disk onto a partition on another for improved fault tolerance. If both disks are connected to the same controller, this is called disk *mirroring*. If both disks are connected to separate controllers, it is called disk *duplexing*.

To mirror or duplex a partition, select Mirroring from the Available Disk Options menu. Highlight one of the partitions appearing in the Partition Mirroring Status window and press ↵. The Mirrored NetWare Partitions window will appear and the entry you selected will have been inserted as a primary Mirrored partition. To link it with a secondary partition, press Ins and select one of the available partitions.

Creating NetWare Volumes

NetWare arranges partitions (single or multiple) into logical groups called *volumes*. All access to NetWare disks is through a volume name as a drive letter mapped to a particular volume. Volumes are created with INSTALL.

From the Installation Options menu, select Volume Options and a window containing the current volumes will appear. For a new file server, the window should be empty. In order to add a new volume, press Ins and a Volume Information window will appear. The first volume under NetWare must use the name (SYS:). After selecting this option, you should see the Volume Information menu which appears in Figure 6.8.

Under the Volume Information menu, you can change the segments included in a volume, change the volume name, change the volume's block size, and mount or dismount a volume. If you're using programs with very large database files on a particular volume, using a larger block size will

FIGURE 6.8

*The Volume Information
menu*

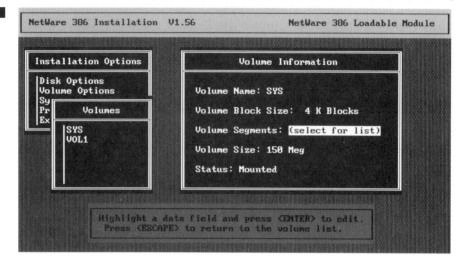

```
NetWare 386 Installation   V1.56              NetWare 386 Loadable Module
```

```
┌─ Installation Options ─┐     ┌──────── Volume Information ────────┐
│ Disk Options           │     │                                    │
│ Volume Options         │     │  Volume Name: SYS                  │
│ Sy ┌─── Volumes ───┐   │     │                                    │
│ Pr │               │   │     │  Volume Block Size:  4 K Blocks    │
│ Ex │ SYS           │   │     │                                    │
│    │ VOL1          │   │     │  Volume Segments: (select for list)│
│    │               │   │     │                                    │
│    │               │   │     │  Volume Size: 150 Meg              │
│    │               │   │     │                                    │
│    │               │   │     │  Status: Mounted                   │
└────┴───────────────┘   │     └────────────────────────────────────┘
```

```
┌──────────────────────────────────────────────┐
│ Highlight a data field and press <ENTER> to edit. │
│ Press <ESCAPE> to return to the volume list.      │
└──────────────────────────────────────────────┘
```

conserve server memory. By contrast, if you store many small files on a volume, a larger block size will waste disk space. In most cases, the default block size is adequate.

After you have chosen your volume configuration, all that remains is to mount the volume: Press ↵ at the Status prompt and select Mount Volume. If you wish to create more than one volume, follow the procedures outlined in this section. You may also mount or dismount volumes from this menu or from the server console (see Appendix A for more information).

Copying the System and Public Files

Once you have created and mounted the SYS: Volume, you can use INSTALL to copy the System and Public files to the file server. From the Installation Options menu, select System Options to bring up the Available System Options menu. The first item in the list allows you to copy these files to the server. Select this option, and NetWare will prompt you to install disks from the Novell distribution as in Figure 6.9. As you put in disks, INSTALL will copy the necessary files to their appropriate locations.

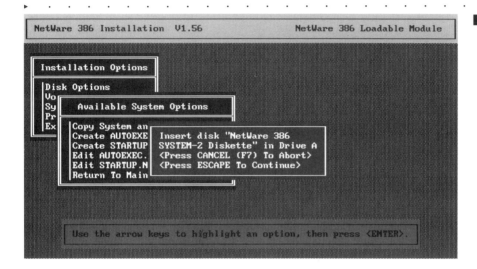

FIGURE 6.9

Copying the System and
Public files

Using INSTALL to create AUTOEXEC.NCF

At this point, all of the files necessary to start your system as a file server have been copied to either a floppy or DOS partition on the hard disk or to the SYS: Volume on the NetWare partition. Currently though, if you take the server down and bring it back up, you will have to manually load the disk drivers, LAN drivers, and NLMs necessary to start your server in addition to remembering all of the proper configuration values.

You can create two startup files to automate the process. The first file, AUTOEXEC.NCF, performs all tasks that you would manually perform at the server console, other than loading the disk driver. The file STARTUP.NCF located on your DOS partition or floppy drive will be used to load the disk driver. The reason for having separate files is to allow NLMs and drivers to be loaded from the NetWare partition as well as from the DOS partition or floppy disk. Once the disk driver has been loaded manually or by STARTUP.NCF and the Volumes have been mounted, NLMs and drivers are available from floppy disks, DOS partitions, and NetWare partitions.

You can use the Create AUTOEXEC.NCF option from the Available System Options menu to automatically include all of the steps you've done by

F I G U R E 6.10

An example
AUTOEXEC.NCF file

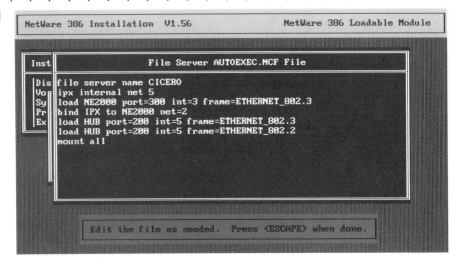

hand so far (except for loading the disk driver or INSTALL.NLM). After you select the Create option, your current settings will appear in a window, as shown in Figure 6.10.

If you don't wish to load anything further, press Esc to save this file. You can edit this file at any time with any standard ASCII text editor or with INSTALL.NLM.

Similarly, you can create the server's STARTUP.NCF file by selecting that option from the Available System Options menu. Figure 6.11 shows a sample STARTUP.NCF file (for our test server). You can save this file by pressing Esc.

Summary

In this chapter we took NetWare from the box and turned it into a file-server operating system. We structured the NetWare, made preparation for installation of NetWare, installed the server software, and fired up the Net-Ware. Now we are ready to begin customization so we can access NetWare services.

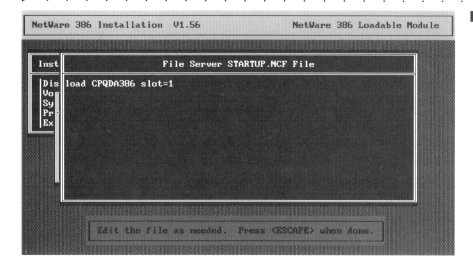

Creating Network
Access Programs

NetWare Core Protocol (NCP)   135

is a set of rules that the workstations follow when requesting that the
server alter a network connection, manipulate file servers, modify or create print queue entries, and so on.

A Terminate-and-Stay-Resident (TSR) program   136

is a program that stays in memory after it has been executed and the user
has been returned to DOS.

There are two ways in which extended memory is commonly con-   137
figured in PCs:

- extended memory

- expanded memory

Several utilities allow network drivers to be loaded into upper   137
memory:

- EMSNETx.EXE

- XMSNETx.EXE

To simplify the login process for your users,   147

create a batch file that loads the network-access programs whenever it is
called.

Connecting a new workstation to your NetWare server requires only a few steps. You need to install a network card (unless yours is built in), attach the station to the network, and configure special software (called client software) that allows the station to establish a connection with the server.

NetWare 3.12 is shipped with two different sets of client software for workstations running DOS: the DOS ODI Workstation Services and the NetWare Client for DOS and Windows.

▸ **ODI Workstation Services** is a set of programs that implement Novell's Open Data-Link Interface (ODI) to support more than one NIC per workstation and more than one protocol on a single NIC.

▸ **NetWare Client for DOS and Windows** also uses ODI technology, but replaces the network shell with a set of programs called Virtual Loadable Modules (VLMs).

In this chapter, we'll introduce you to both types of client software and the installation process for each. We'll lead you through configuring the client software to match the NIC you've installed in the workstation. We'll discuss loading the software and logging into a file server. Finally, we'll cover some basic troubleshooting methods in case you run into trouble.

Deciding Which Client to Use

Both the ODI Workstation Services and the NetWare Client for DOS and Windows are based on the same underlying technology. The Open Data-Link Interface (ODI) adds a number of capabilities that were not present in previous generations of NetWare client software. ODI allows a single network board to support more than one protocol and allows a single computer to support more than one network interface card. With this capability, a single workstation can connect to many dissimilar hosts on the same network or even connect to several physical networks.

In the NetWare Client for DOS and Windows, programs called *Virtual Loadable Modules* (*VLMs*) replace the network shells (NETX.EXE, EMSNETX.EXE, XMSNETX.EXE, BNETX.EXE) used with the ODI Workstation Services. These VLMs (collectively called a *requester*) add these capabilities to the client software:

- ▶ Packet Burst speed increases are automatic

- ▶ Large Internet Packets (LIP) improve speed on Internetworks

- ▶ the NCP Packet Signature improves security

- ▶ NetWare can support connections to multiple operating systems

- ▶ network workstations can be centrally backed up

- ▶ you can support Task-Switching environments

You must also use VLMs to access any NetWare 4.0 servers on your internetwork. In general, unless you have a compelling reason not to, you should use the NetWare Client for DOS and Windows. See Appendix C, *Configuring and Using the NetWare Windows Client,* for more information about the special features of VLMs and instructions for using the NetWare Tools for Windows.

Installing the NetWare Client for DOS and Windows

Installing the NetWare Client for DOS and Windows (called VLMs from here on) is really quite painless. Novell has automated the process with an installation procedure and a comprehensive set of drivers. You will need these four disks supplied by Novell:

(WSDOS_1) NetWare Workstation for DOS

(WSWIN_1) NetWare Workstation for Windows

(WSDRV_1) NetWare Workstation Drivers

(WSDRV_2) NetWare Workstation Drivers

The WSDRV_1 and WSDRV_2 disks contain drivers for a wide variety of network cards, but if the driver for your NIC is not included, or if you need an updated driver, you'll need to obtain a driver disk from the vendor as well. The ODI drivers for network cards are known as Multiple Layer Interface Drivers (MLID). These are hardware-specific drivers designed for a particular network board. The NetWare Workstation Drivers disks contain MLIDs for the cards listed in Table 7.1.

Once you've gathered the necessary disks, you're ready to install the client. Put the WSDOS_1 disk in a drive on the workstation, change to that drive, and type

INSTALL ↵

The opening menu shown in Figure 7.1 should appear.

If you will be installing the Windows client, the process is the same. The INSTALL utility on the DOS Client disk installs both the DOS and Windows clients. The DOS client must be installed regardless.

There are five steps listed in the main menu of the Install utility. In step one, you need to specify a directory where the client software will be installed or accept the default (C:\NWCLIENT).

TABLE 7.1		
NIC Support included with NetWare 3.12		
NETWORK		**DRIVER**
Novell/Excelan EXOS 205T Ethernet		EXOS.COM
Novell/Excelan EXOS 215 Ethernet		
Intel EtherExpress ISA Family		EXP16ODI.COM
Intel EtherExpress MCA Family		
Intel593		INTEL593.COM

NETWORK	DRIVER
Intel596	INTEL596.COM
Novell/Excelan LANZENET Ethernet	LANZENET.COM
Novell/Eagle NE1000	NE1000.COM
Ansel M1500	NE1500T.COM
Novell Ethernet NE1500T	
Novell/Eagle NE/2	NE2.COM
Novell/Eagle NE2-32	NE2_32.COM
Novell/Eagle NE2000	NE2000.COM
Wearnes 2107C	
Zenith Data Systems NE2000 Module	
Ansel M2100	NE2100.COM
EXOS 105	
Novell Ethernet NE2100	
Wearnes 2110T	
EXOS 235T	NE3200.COM
INTEL EtherExpress32	
Novell Ethernet NE3200	
Novell NTR2000 Token-Ring Adapter	NTR2000.COM
PCN II/A and PCN Baseband/A Driver	PCN2.COM
PCN II and PCN Baseband Driver	PCN2L.COM
IBM Token-Ring Network 16/4 Adapter/A	TOKEN.COM
IBM Token-Ring Network Adapter II & 16/4 Adapter	
IBM Token-Ring Network Adapter/A	
Novell RX-Net & RX-Net II	TRXNET.COM
Novell RX-Net/2	

```
NetWare Client Install  v1.02                    Friday  June 11, 1993  1:45 am


STEP 1. Type client directory name for Client Installation.
        C:\NWCLIENT

STEP 2. Client installation requires "LASTDRIVE=Z" in the
        CONFIG.SYS file and "CALL STARTNET.BAT" added to
        AUTOEXEC.BAT.  Install will make backup copies.
        Allow changes?  (Y/N):  No

STEP 3. Do you wish to install support for Windows? (Y/N):  No
        Windows Subdirectory:

STEP 4. Press <Enter> to install the driver for your network
        board.  You may then use arrow keys to find the
        board name.
        Press <Enter> to see list

STEP 5. Press <Enter> to install.


Esc-exit  Enter-select  ↑↓-move  Alt F10-exit
```

In step two, you specify whether or not you want to allow the Install utility to modify your CONFIG.SYS or AUTOEXEC.BAT files. We recommend that you allow Install to make the changes. It will automatically make backups of the original files and give them the extension .BNW.

In step three, you choose whether or not you wish to install the Windows client. In order to do so, you must have already installed Windows on the workstation's hard disk. On the second line of step three, you should specify the path to your Windows directory. Once you've filled in the relevant fields, your screen should look similar to Figure 7.2.

As with the CONFIG.SYS and AUTOEXEC.BAT files, originals of any Windows files that the Install utility modifies will be saved with the extension .BNW.

In step four, you choose the proper MLID for the network card you are using. To see a list of supported boards, press ⏎. A screen will prompt you for the location of the driver disks, as shown in Figure 7.3. If you are using a driver from your vendor or a third party, you need to indicate the full path to the driver files. The Install utility will look for files ending in .DOS or .INS as possible drivers. If you are using a driver from the NetWare Workstation Drivers disks, put WSDRV_1 in a workstation drive, select the

```
NetWare Client Install  v1.02              Wednesday  June 8, 1994  1:46 pm

  STEP 1. Type client directory name for Client Installation.
          C:\NWCLIENT

  STEP 2. Client installation requires "LASTDRIVE=Z" in the
          CONFIG.SYS file and "CALL STARTNET.BAT" added to
          AUTOEXEC.BAT.  Install will make backup copies.
          Allow changes?  (Y/N):  Yes

  STEP 3. Do you wish to install support for Windows? (Y/N):  Yes
          Windows Subdirectory:  C:\WINDOWS

  STEP 4. Press <Enter> to install the driver for your network
          board.  You may then use arrow keys to find the
          board name.
          Press <Enter> to see list

  STEP 5. Press <Enter> to install.

Esc-exit  Enter-select  ↑↓-move  Alt F10-exit
```

F I G U R E 7.2

INSTALL configured to install both DOS and Windows clients

```
NetWare Client Install  v1.02              Wednesday  June 8, 1994  1:47 pm

  STEP 1.     ┌─────────────  Network Board  ─────────────┐
              │ ▲ IBM Token-Ring Network Adapter/A         │
  STEP 2.     │   Intel EtherExpress ISA Family            │
              │   Intel EtherExpress MCA Family            │
              │   INTEL EtherExpress32                     │
              │   Intel593                                 │
              │   Intel596                                 │
  STEP 3.     │   Novell Ethernet NE1500T                  │
              │   Novell Ethernet NE2100                   │
              │ ▼ Novell Ethernet NE3200                   │
  STEP 4.     └───────────────────────────────────────────┘
          board.  You may then use arrow keys to find the
          board name.
          Press <Enter> to see list

  STEP 5. Press <Enter> to install.

Esc-exit  Enter-select  ↑↓-move  Alt F10-exit
```

F I G U R E 7.3

Selecting the location of your MLID drivers

appropriate drive letter and press ↲. A list of supported drivers will appear.

Select the appropriate board from the list and press ↲. A window will appear with the default settings for the network board you selected. If you modified the default settings when you installed the card, make the appropriate changes here. For instance, the base address for the card we used in our example is 320H. After pressing ↲, we were presented with a list of available base address settings for the card along with notes about our particular card (see Figure 7.4).

We needed to change our default frame type as well. In Figure 7.5, we added *Ethernet_802.3* to the default frame type, Ethernet 802.2.

There may be additional options for your particular network card. When you have set the configuration options correctly, continue the installation by pressing Esc. You will be returned to the main menu. Make sure the settings listed for steps one through four are correct and press ↲ on step five to complete the installation. When the Install utility requires new disks, you will be prompted to swap them. Once the Install utility has finished copying files and making changes to configuration settings, the screen in Figure 7.6 will appear indicating that you are through.

FIGURE 7.4

Selecting an I/O address through the Client Install

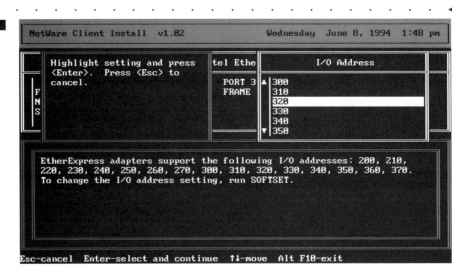

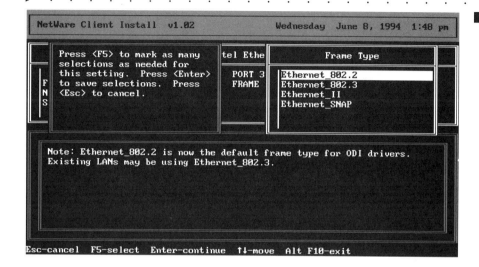

Adding or changing to a new frame type

```
NetWare Client Install   v1.02              Wednesday  June 8, 1994  1:48 pm

    Press <F5> to mark as many   tel Ethe         Frame Type
    selections as needed for
    this setting.  Press <Enter>  PORT 3   Ethernet_802.2
    to save selections.  Press    FRAME    Ethernet_802.3
 F  <Esc> to cancel.                       Ethernet_II
 N                                         Ethernet_SNAP
 S

    Note: Ethernet_802.2 is now the default frame type for ODI drivers.
    Existing LANs may be using Ethernet_802.3.

Esc-cancel   F5-select   Enter-continue   ↑↓-move   Alt F10-exit
```

The NetWare Client Install after a successful installation

```
NetWare Client Install   v1.02              Wednesday  June 8, 1994  1:53 pm

The Install Utility is finished.  Before rebooting your workstation do the
following:

1. Edit your AUTOEXEC.BAT and CONFIG.SYS files to remove any previous
NetWare workstation files.  The previous contents of these files have been
saved with .BNW extentions.

2. Reboot your workstation by pressing <Ctrl><Alt><Delete>.

Note: The Install Utility created or modified the NET.CFG and STARTNET.BAT
files in the client directory, and the WIN.INI, SYSTEM.INI, and PROGMAN.INI
files in the windows directory.  The previous contents of these files have
been saved with .BNW extentions.

Press <Enter> to exit install.
```

Testing the NetWare DOS and Windows Client

During the installation process, the NetWare Client Install utility will add commands to your AUTOEXEC.BAT that start the NetWare Client during bootup. (The line CALL C:\NWCLIENT\STARTNET is added to the AUTOEXEC.BAT file.) STARTNET.BAT is a batch file located in the NWCLIENT directory that contains all of the commands necessary to load the client software.

All of the settings for your client software are controlled by a configuration file called NET.CFG. NET.CFG is an ASCII file created during he client installation. Any time you need to change the configuration settings for your client software, you can edit this file and make appropriate changes. In *Configuring the Client Software with NET.CFG* later in this chapter, we cover the settings that are available in NET.CFG.

To test your current configuration, simply reboot your computer. If there are obvious errors during the loading process and your client software does not load properly, refer to *Diagnosing Problems with Client Software.* Otherwise, you are ready to proceed to *Logging Into the File Server.*

Setting Up DOS ODI Workstation Services

The DOS ODI Workstation Services have no installation utility. Installing ODI is a matter of creating a directory on the target disk and copying the appropriate programs to it. You can copy the client software to a floppy drive as easily as to a hard disk.

Most of the programs you need are stored on the DOS ODI Workstation Services diskette. You'll need the NetWare Link Support Layer (LSL.COM), the Internet Packet Exchange driver (IPXODI.COM), a driver for your network card (an MLID), and one of the NetWare shells. If you are using one of the network cards listed in Table 7.1, the MLID for your card is located on either the WSDRV_1 or WSDRV_2 disks and uses the name indicated. If you are using a network card that is not listed, you'll need a disk from the vendor that contains NetWare ODI driver support.

NETWARE SHELLS

Under NetWare, a *shell* is the program that controls the actions of your PC when logged into the network. The shell loads between the operating system and the application programs you will be running. The purpose of the shell is to intercept and direct requests to the proper location, whether it is a network or local device.

An *interrupt* is a mechanism used in the PC to halt execution of a program to take care of some other process that needs attention. Your PC uses several software interrupts during normal operation. The NetWare shell is a memory-resident program that interprets calls made to the DOS INT21, INT24, and INT17 service routines and directs the request to a service handler (a short program in memory). If the request is to a network device, it is translated into a NetWare Core Protocol (NCP) request. NCP is a set of rules that the workstations follow when requesting that the server alter a network connection, manipulate server files, modify or create print queue entries, and so on.

Older shells supplied with NetWare were specific to the version of the operating system running on the workstation. The *x* in the shell name (NETx.COM, EMSNETx.COM, or XMSNETx.COM) indicates the operating system's major version number. To load the shell NETx.COM under MS-DOS version 3.20, for example, you would look for the file called NET3.COM. The newer shells from Novell and those supplied with other versions of DOS (DR-DOS from Novell, for example) are non–version specific and can be identified by the presence of an *x* in place of the version number in the file name.

Just for the record, if you have computers running DOS version 5.0 and do not have NETx.COM for some reason, you must copy the file called NET5.COM from the DOS diskettes. If you have computers running DR-DOS, you can locate the file NETX.COM on the DR-DOS ViewMAX disk. If you have access to CompuServe, you can always download the latest shells from NETWIRE (Novell's Technical and Customer Support Forum). Simply type **GO NETWIRE** from any CompuServe prompt.

TSR'S AND COMPUTER MEMORY

The NetWare client software is made up of Terminate-and-Stay-Resident (TSR) programs. A TSR, as its name implies, is a program that stays in memory after it has been executed and you have been returned to DOS. As TSR programs take part of the PC's memory, some people prefer to load them into *upper* or *high* memory in order to have the maximum amount of RAM available for applications. Upper memory is memory located beyond the first 1 MB of memory in your computer. Some programs written to operate in *Protected Mode* can access memory above the 1-MB boundary. Conversely, your computer's first megabyte of memory is divided into two sections of 640 KB and 384 KB respectively. Programs not designed to run in Protected Mode (*Real Mode* applications) can only use the 640 KB section of memory called *lower* memory. The 384 KB of memory in between is used both by DOS and by hardware installed in the computer.

DECIDING WHERE TO LOAD THE NETWORK SHELL

If you will be using mostly Real Mode applications, it may make sense to load the network access programs into upper memory. Novell (and DR-DOS from Novell) provide additional network shell programs that load into upper memory. Determining which shell to use is based on preference and the type of memory in the workstation. There are two ways that memory above the first 1 MB is commonly configured in PCs:

Extended Memory
The extra memory in your computer may be used as Extended memory (called XMS) with a driver that conforms to v2.0 of the Extended Memory Specification. (Microsoft's HIMEM.SYS, Quarterdeck's QEMM.SYS, and DR-DOS's EMM386.SYS are examples of this.) This is the memory that Protected Mode applications are able to use.

Expanded Memory
The Expanded Memory Specification was written by Lotus, Intel and Microsoft and is hence known as either EMS or LIM memory. As with XMS, applications have to be specially written to take advantage of Expanded memory. NetWare shells have been written to work with v4.0 of this specification.

The NetWare shell that loads into Expanded (LIM/EMS) memory is called EMSNETx.EXE. The NetWare shell that loads into Extended memory (XMS) is called XMSNETx.EXE. As with NETx.EXE, the *x* refers to the DOS version being used on the workstation. Newer releases of the network shell are not DOS–version specific. You can identify these by the *x* that replaces the version number that was present in older shells.

In addition to running these special shells, if you are using DR-DOS from Novell, you can use the DR-DOS HILOAD command to load the network drivers into upper memory. There are several other utilities available as third-party programs that will also allow you to load your network drivers into upper memory (Above Disc and NetRoom are two examples).

If there are NetWare 3.11 servers on your network running PBURST.NLM to implement packet burst, you can use the BNETX.EXE shell to take advantage of the speed improvements, but there is a slight penalty in memory usage.

NOTE
VLMs automatically implement packet burst and take best advantage of available workstation memory.

Testing the Network Access Programs

For testing, we want to load each individual element of the client software manually while watching for error reports on the workstation monitor. For DOS ODI Workstation Services, the programs are loaded in this order:

LSL

DRIVER.COM (for example, NE2000.COM or EXP16ODI.COM)

IPXODI

NETX (or EMSNETX or XMSNETX)

All of the settings for your client software are controlled by an ASCII file called NET.CFG. If you are not using default configuration settings with your network board, you need to edit this file and make appropriate changes. Under the section titled Configuring the Client Software with NET.CFG later in this chapter, we cover the settings that are available in NET.CFG.

To load the Link Support Layer (LSL), type **LSL** ↵ at the command prompt. Loading LSL should pose no problems. If it does, see *Eliminate the Variables* under *Diagnosing Problems with Client Software* below. When working properly, your computer should respond with a message similar to the following after loading LSL.

```
C:\NWCLIENT>lsl

NetWare Link Support Layer v2.01 (921105)
(C) Copyright 1990, 1992 Novell, Inc. All Rights Reserved.

Max Boards 4, Max Stacks 4
```

The next item to load is the driver for your particular network card. In this example, we are using an Intel EtherExpress 16, so the driver name is EXP16ODI.COM:

```
C:\NWCLIENT>exp16odi
```

```
Intel EtherExpress(tm) 16 Ethernet MLID v2.28 (930115)
(C) Copyright 1992 Intel Corporation All Rights Reserved

EtherExpress 16 Adapter configured as follows:

Int 10, Port 300, Node Address 00AA002A3F6A L
Using RJ-45 connector
Max Frame 1514 bytes, Line Speed 10 Mbps
Board 1, Frame ETHERNET_802.3, LSB Mode
```

Load the packet driver by typing IPXODI ⏎ from the command prompt. If the driver is properly configured and successfully locates the NIC, you should see a message similar to the following:

```
C:\NWCLIENT>ipxodi

NetWare IPX/SPX Protocol v2.10 (930122)
(C) Copyright 1990-1993 Novell, Inc. All Rights Reserved.

Bound to logical board 1 (EXP16ODI) : Protocol ID 0
```

Depending on whether or not you want to load the shell into upper memory, you will load NETx.EXE, EMSNETx.EXE, or XMSNETx.EXE. For example, to load the Real Mode shell for MS-DOS version 5 from the NETWARE directory on drive C:, the command would be:

```
C:\NETWARE\NET5.COM ⏎
```

If successful, the computer will display a message indicating that the driver and shell have been loaded. Although the MLID will load if it finds your NIC, this does not imply that you have a valid network connection. By watching the response from the network *shell* however, you can usually determine if you are communicating on the network. When your network connection is good and your NIC is functioning, the shell will respond with a message indicating that you have attached to a server:

```
NetWare V3.10—Workstation Shell for PC DOS V5.x (910307)
(C) Copyright 1990 Novell, Inc. All Rights Reserved.
```

Attached to server CICERO
Sunday, July 8, 1994 8:32:50 pm

If you don't receive a positive response from the shell, see *Diagnosing Problems with Client Software* later in this chapter.

NOTE
The file NET.CFG is the ODI equivalent of SHELL.CFG and may include any SHELL.CFG commands as well as specific commands for the ODI programs.

TIP
NET.CFG files are moving targets to some extent. Be sure to check your latest Novell documentation or the documentation supplied with your NIC for more NET.CFG options.

Configuring the Client Software with NET.CFG

The ODI-based client programs for DOS use a configuration file called NET.CFG similar to the SHELL.CFG used with the earlier DOS Workstation Services (WSGEN).

The NET.CFG parameters allow you to modify the software configuration's settings for a NIC. Normally, when you use the ODI workstation programs, you shouldn't need to modify the default settings. If you do (because of a conflict with other workstation hardware or software for example), any of the NIC settings can be modified by changes to NET.CFG.

Each section of NET.CFG begins with main section headings under which different parameter values are set. The headings should be placed in the file left-justified. The parameters under each heading should be indented with a tab or spaces. See Table 7.2 for a list of possible parameters.

For example, if you are installing a Novell NE2000 that has jumpers set for a base I/O (port) address of 360H, and an interrupt of 5, you could use the following NET.CFG to set the software.

```
LINK DRIVER NE2000
    ;changing the interrupt
    INT 5
    ;changing the port address
    PORT 360
```

Notice that you can place comments in the file if they are preceded by a semicolon. If you want to increase the number of communication buffers

TABLE 7.2

Parameter Options for the NET.CFG file

OPTION	EXPLANATION
LINK SUPPORT	
BUFFERS *number [size]*	Sets current number of communications buffers and the buffer size.
	The product of *number* and *size* must be at or under 59 KB. Default *number* is 0. Default *size* is 1130.
MEMPOOL *number [k]*	Configures the number and size of the memory pool buffers that the LSL will maintain. This parameter is used by some protocols.
	The parameter *number* is the number of bytes to maintain. If the optional parameter *k* is included, *number* specifies KB.
PROTOCOL *protocol_name*	
BIND *name*	This parameter specifies the name of the NIC to which the protocol specified by PROTOCOL should be bound.
SESSIONS *number*	Configures the number of sessions that the protocol stack will be responsible for at one time.
LINK DRIVER *drivername*	
DMA *[#1	#2] channel*	Configures the DMA channel used by a NIC. If the NIC uses two channels, the parameter *#2* must be used.
	For example: LINK DRIVER *name* **DMA 3** **DMA #2 5**
INT *[#1	#2] irq*	Specifies the interrupt the NIC will use. If more than one interrupt will be used, the *#2* parameter must be used.
MEM *[#1	#2] base addr*	Specifies the base address of the shared memory address for a NIC. Some cards install memory into the region D0000 H. If this particular card uses D0000 and D4000H then the *#2* parameter must be used.
	For example: LINK DRIVER *name* **MEM D0000** **MEM #2 D4000**
PORT *[#1	#2] base addr*	Specifies the base I/O address port for a NIC.
	For example: LINK DRIVER NE2000 **PORT 360**

OPTION	EXPLANATION
	If the NIC uses two ranges, the parameter #2 must be used.
NODE ADDRESS *addr*	This parameter can be used to override a hard-coded node address set for the card at the factory. The parameter *addr* should be specified in HEX.
SLOT *number*	Specifies which board the driver should use. The driver settings will be used to configure the board in slot *number*.
FRAME *type*	Specifies a frame type to be supported by the NIC.
PROTOCOL *name id type*	Attaches new protocols to existing LAN drivers. Using this option, the NE2000 for example could support both Ethernet_802.3 and Ethernet_802.2. Replace *name* with the name of the new protocol (IPX for example). Replace *id* with the protocols assigned HEX id. Replace *type* with the new frame type used with the protocol.
SAPS *number*	Specifies the number of Service Access Points to be supported. The maximum value depends on the network interface controller. Used with the LANSUP driver.
LINK STATIONS *number*	Specifies the number of link stations needed. The maximum number depends on the network interface controller. Used with the LANSUP driver.
ALTERNATE	Specifies an adapter other than the primary adapter for the LANSUP, Token, and PCN2 drivers.
MAX FRAME SIZE *number*	This parameter specifies the maximum amount of data a Token Ring adapter can put on the wire. The default value is *number* =4216 unless you have at least 8 KB of shared memory available on the board, then the default becomes *number* = 2168.

for this card, you can add a parameter under the Link Support heading. For example:

```
LINK DRIVER NE2000
    ;changing the interrupt
    INT 5
    ;changing the port address
    PORT 360
LINK SUPPORT
    ;changing communication buffers to 60
    BUFFERS 60
```

You will need to check the documentation for the card to find out which parameters are available for your particular network card. For drivers supplied by Novell, you can look in the *Installation Supplements* guide or the *ODI Shell for DOS* guide for more information.

The NET.CFG file is also a superset of the SHELL.CFG file. As long as the SHELL.CFG commands are placed in the file left justified and before the headers understood by NET.CFG, any of the SHELL.CFG commands may still be used. If you are reconfiguring software to upgrade from IPX (WSGEN) to ODI Workstation Services or the NetWare Client for DOS and Windows and already have a SHELL.CFG file, you may leave it alone and create a separate NET.CFG file. The options in both files will take effect.

You can also place the SHELL.CFG commands at the beginning of your NET.CFG file. For instance, in the following example, the first four lines in this NET.CFG file are remnants of a former SHELL.CFG file.

```
LOCAL PRINTERS=0
LONG MACHINE TYPE=IBM_PC
PREFERRED SERVER=CICERO
SHOW DOTS=ON

Link Driver EXP16ODI
    PORT 300
    FRAME Ethernet_802.3

NetWare DOS Requester
    FIRST NETWORK DRIVE = F
```

SUPPORTING MULTIPLE VERSIONS OF DOS

If the computers on your network are from several different manufacturers and run different DOS versions, you should add a line to the NET.CFG file to specify a LONG MACHINE TYPE. In Chapter 8, we'll use this variable to determine where the workstation can locate its particular version of DOS when logged into the file server.

For now, choose a naming convention for this variable that will help you group computers of the same manufacturer and operating system together. For example, name all PC clones and IBM compatibles that run Microsoft OEM versions of DOS **IBM_PC**; or, if you have Compaq computers that run a version of DOS from Compaq, name these computers **COMPAQ**. Continue using a scheme like this for any unique versions of a particular operating system on all of your workstations. The name you choose should be six or fewer characters in length.

NOTE
The variable LONG MACHINE TYPE is a SHELL.CFG parameter, so it must be entered left-justified and at the top of a NET.CFG file.

DETERMINING THE FIRST NETWORK DRIVE

The first available network drive is controlled by a line in your CONFIG.SYS file if you are using NetWare Shells or by a line under the NetWare DOS Requester section of the NET.CFG file if you are using VLMs. In the CONFIG.SYS file, the line reads similar to the following:

LASTDRIVE=E:

If you don't have a CONFIG.SYS file on your boot drive or if you cannot locate a similar line in it, either create a new file or add the appropriate line (refer to you DOS manual for instructions). This line tells DOS to reserve drives A: through the indicated letter for DOS's local use. Novell assigns the first network drive to the next available drive letter.

If you are using the NetWare Client for DOS and Windows, include the line **FIRST NETWORK DRIVE** = *DRIVELETTER* in the NET.CFG file under the heading for the NetWare DOS Requester. For instance, the following example would set the first network drive to F.

NetWare DOS Requester
    FIRST NETWORK DRIVE = F

If you have users on your network with many local drives or logical partitions on their drives, it may be a good idea to assign a letter further into the alphabet so that all users can use the same *system login script*. (This file sets up the portion of the network environment that is uniform for all users. See Chapter 9 for details.) If you don't do this, different stations will have different assignments for the first available network drive.

Logging Into the File Server

To log into the network, you must first change to the first available network drive. From here, you can find a list of available servers with the command SLIST ↵:

Known NetWare File Servers   Network Node Address Status

CICERO   [5][1]Default
TOLSTOY   [565656][1]Attached

Total of 2 file servers found

The server listed as default is the file server that you will log into with LOGIN if you don't specify another server. You can view the syntax for the login command by typing LOGIN /HELP ↵ at the command prompt. LOGIN should respond with a message similar to the following:

F:\LOGIN>LOGIN /HELP
Usage: Login [/Options] [Server/] [Username] [Script-
Parameters]
Options : Clear screen
     No attach
     Script <path spec>

F:\LOGIN>

In most cases, you will just type LOGIN followed by your username if a "PREFERRED SERVER" line is included in your NET.CFG file. Optionally,

NOTE

If you are logging into a new server, there will only be two valid usernames: **GUEST** and **SUPERVISOR**. By default, neither will have a password assigned.

you can specify a particular server by typing LOGIN followed by a server name, a forward slash, and your username. After you have pressed ↵, LOGIN will prompt you for your password (if one has been set) and then log you into the network. If you are logging into a new server and have not yet set up new login scripts, your login will most likely look similar to the following example:

```
F:\LOGIN>login cicero/supervisor
Enter your password:
Good afternoon, SUPERVISOR.

Drive A: maps to a local disk.
Drive B: maps to a local disk.
Drive C: maps to a local disk.
Drive D: maps to a local disk.
Drive E: maps to a local disk.
Drive F: = CICERO\SYS: \SYSTEM

SEARCH1: = Z:. [CICERO\SYS: \PUBLIC]
SEARCH2: = Y:. [CICERO\SYS: \]
SEARCH3: = C:\
SEARCH4: = C:\DOS
SEARCH5: = C:\UTIL
SEARCH6: = C:\WIN
SEARCH7: = C:\SCAN

F:\SYSTEM>
```

If you don't specify a username on the command line, LOGIN will prompt you for your username and password.

Automatically Loading from the Hard Disk

Once you have established that your newly configured client software is functioning properly, you can simplify the login process for your users by creating a batch file (a small DOS program) to do the work for them. Depending on whether your users will log out often or will remain logged into the network anytime they are using their PC, you may want to have this batch file called from the AUTOEXEC.BAT file on the workstation.

For example, on our Ethernet LAN, the files LSL.COM, *DRIVER.COM* (for example NE2000.COM), IPXODI.COM, NETx.EXE, and NET.CFG are needed to log into the server. We have placed these files into a subdirectory called NETWARE on the workstations boot disk (A:\ or C:\). Using a standard DOS text editor to create an ASCII file, we created the following batch file to automate the login process:

```
@echo off
cls
c:
cd \netware
lsl
ne2000
ipxodi
netx
if errorlevel 1 goto neterror
echo.
f:
cls
echo Logging into CICERO ...
login CICERO/
goto endbat
:neterror
echo.
echo Error connecting to network!
echo Try again or contact your network administrator.
echo.
:endbat
```

When this batch file tries to load the driver, the driver will return what is known as an *errorlevel* to the operating system. The batch file will change its course of execution if an error occurs.

This file first changes to the boot drive, moves to the proper directory, loads the client software and places the user onto the login drive of the server. If you are using DOS versions previous to version 3.x, leave out the @ that appears before the call to turn echo off. This merely prevents DOS from displaying *echo off* during the execution of the batch file. The call *echo.* tells the batch file to echo a blank line. Batch files are far more capable than we hope to introduce here. If you have other uses for batch files, there are several books available on batch file programming.

If you want to automatically execute this program whenever the workstation is rebooted, you can accomplish this by calling the batch file from your AUTOEXEC.BAT file. Using a standard DOS text editor, include a single line in the batch file that reads **CALL FILENAME.BAT**. Using our example:

```
@echo off
prompt $p$g
path=c:\;c:\dos;c:\bat;c:\util;
rem Load Virus Scanning Software
cd \scan
vshield
cd \
rem Load Workstation Clients
CALL \NETWARE\NET.BAT
```

Be careful to use the DOS CALL command to run the batch file. Instructions that follow the execution of a batch file without the CALL command may have no effect. Once a batch file has changed directions to another batch file, the remaining instructions in the original batch file may be ignored.

Diagnosing Problems with Client Software

If you were unable to correctly load elements of the client software, or if after loading you were unable to connect to the server, there are several things you can check. The sections that follow outline a general troubleshooting method.

ELIMINATE THE VARIABLES

All of the programs that make up the client software are TSR programs. If you have trouble loading some of them, there is a possibility for conflict with other TSR programs or with a memory manager. Try starting again with a "clean" PC—copy your present AUTOEXEC.BAT and CONFIG.SYS files to a safe location and remove any suspect programs or drivers from the test versions. Some programs to try removing are mouse drivers, virus-detection programs, TSRs, and Extended or Expanded memory drivers. Examples of a bare-bones AUTOEXEC.BAT and CONFIG.SYS files are listed below.

AUTOEXEC.BAT:

```
@ECHO OFF
PROMPT $P$G
PATH=C:\;C:\DOS;C:\UTIL\;C:\BAT
```

CONFIG.SYS:

```
SHELL=C:\COMMAND.COM /E:512 /P
FILES=50
BUFFERS=30
```

TEST ALTERNATE CONFIGURATIONS

If you are unable to load the driver designed for your NIC, it may just be improperly configured. Check to make sure that the network card is configured for the same settings as those indicated in the NET.CFG file. If the configurations match, you may have a conflict with other devices in the computer. Try selecting a different configuration and making the appropriate changes to NET.CFG.

If you have tested several configurations and none have worked, try using another network card.

Different drivers for NICs will respond in different ways. Most, however, will give some indication of their configuration settings. When loading the

TIP
Some NIC manufacturers supply utility programs for automatically selecting the best configuration for your computer. In general, these utilities work well.

MLID driver for your NIC, make sure the reported settings also match those set in the NET.CFG file. (You should load the driver in the same directory as NET.CFG.) The example below shows the result of loading a NIC driver with incorrect settings:

> Intel EtherExpress(tm) 16 Ethernet MLID v2.28 (930115)
> (C) Copyright 1992 Intel Corporation All Rights Reserved
>
> EtherExpress 16 Adapter configured as follows:
>
> Int 3, Port 320
> Using BNC connector
> Max Frame 1514 bytes, Line Speed 10 Mbps
> Board 2, Frame ETHERNET_802.3, LSB Mode
>
>
> EtherExpress(tm) 16 board not found.
> The following is a list of probable causes:
>
>> 1) I/O conflict with another adapter
>> 2) EtherExpress 16 not installed
>> 3) NET.CFG I/O address differs from the EtherExpress 16
>> board's I/O address.
> EXP16ODH-DOS-6: The adapter did not initialize. EXP16ODH
> did not load.

CHECK THE PROTOCOL SETTINGS AND THE NETWORK CABLING

If all elements of the client software appear to load properly, but you are still unable to connect to the server, you may have a defective card or a network cabling problem. If possible, isolate the network to a server and the computer being tested and use only a single cable between them. If the shell does not report that you are attached to a server, the chances are good that you have either a network cabling problem or you are using an incorrect frame type. (Remember, if you are using Ethernet, the default NetWare frame type in version 3.12 is Ethernet 802.2 where it was Ethernet 802.3 in previous versions.)

If you have tested several configurations and none have worked, try looking for a diagnostic utility supplied by the vendor or using another network card. In most cases, the technical support provided by the vendor is very good. Do not hesitate to contact them when you feel you've exhausted your options.

Summary

In this chapter, we covered the steps needed to install and configure the software that turns a stand-alone computer into a network workstation. We described some of the differences between the network shell and VLMs. We covered some concerns about workstation memory and the programs used to get around problems with running out of lower memory. We described locating and logging into a file server. Finally, we outlined some generalized troubleshooting procedures for workstations. In Chapters 8 and 9, we will continue with procedures to be performed to get a new server set up for your users.

PART III

Creating the
User Environment

CHAPTER 8

Laying the Foundation for the Network

Fast Track

There are three ways to create users and groups in NetWare   *171*

SYSCON is useful for creating small numbers of users and groups. USER-DEF is useful for creating users through templates that automatically assign home directories and security settings. MAKEUSER is useful for creating large numbers of users.

Username Guidelines   *172*

▸ Usernames may contain up to 47 alphanumeric characters, and must be unique.

▸ Usernames are more easily remembered if personalized, but use a common scheme.

You can assign Account Restrictions to users to   *173*

Disable account, set an account expiration date, set the maximum number of concurrent connections, allow a user to change his/her password, require a password, force periodic password changes, and require unique passwords.

Network drives and drive mappings   *207*

▸ Drive mappings simplify access to network drives

▸ The NetWare MAP command is used to assign drive letters to network paths and search directories.

▸ The first available network drive is controlled either by settings in the NET.CFG file (if using the VLM requester) or the DOS LASTDRIVE variable (if using NETX shells).

▸ Search directories serve the same purpose as the DOS PATH. These locations are automatically searched when the execution of an application or utility is requested.

Installing NetWare and maintaining a Novell network is vastly different from setting up a personal computer for your own or someone else's use. In a single-user environment, people are used to putting applications and files where they want—in a pleasantly organized or (in many cases) a pleasantly disorganized fashion. On a network, idiosyncrasy can lead to confusion, disarray, chaos and a whole list of other nasty words.

Make efficiency and organization your key goals when designing your NetWare network. Many of your users may never have worked in a computing environment where data files and applications belong in specific locations or where access to resources depends directly on the privilege levels granted to the users. As a network often becomes the backbone of a company's information infrastructure, time spent here is time wisely spent.

This chapter will help you lay the foundation for a well-organized network. We'll cover directory structures and how NetWare deals with them. We'll discuss creating directories and building a logical directory structure. We'll go through setting up users, and, where appropriate, arranging these users into groups. Finally, we'll cover some things to know when setting up the users' environment, such as how to set up drive mappings and search paths.

Using Directories and Subdirectories

Most personal computers use a *directory structure* for logically arranging applications and data. If you are familiar with the directory structure used on DOS computers, you are already familiar with the type of structure used on most personal computers and workstations. This particular method of logically arranging applications and files is called a *tree* or *hierarchical* directory structure. An example tree structure appears in Figure 8.1. The highest organizational level in the structure forms the root and the directories and subdirectories and files form the trunk, branches, and leaves.

The analogy most often used to understand a tree directory structure is a file cabinet containing multiple drawers, dividers in each of the drawers, folders within these dividers, and documents. The cabinet itself is like the

```
Directory PATH listing for Volume SYSTEM
Volume Serial Number is 1753-15E1
C:.
    ├───ADAPTEC
    │       └───AFDISK
    ├───DOS
    ├───FAX
    │   ├───CAL
    │   │   ├───BIN
    │   │   ├───LIB
    │   │   ├───QUEUE
    │   │   └───TEMP
    │   ├───QUEUE
    │   └───SAVEDFAX
    ├───NETWARE
    ├───PROWIN
    │   ├───ASPECT
    │   │      └───DEMO
    │   └───DNLOAD
    │          └───ARCHIVE
    ├───UTIL
    └───WIN
           └───SYSTEM

C:\>
```

FIGURE 8.1

A tree directory structure

computer or file server; the cabinet drawers are equivalent to logical drives on the computers' disks; the folders in each of the drawers are like the directories in our file system; and finally, the directories contain the applications and data files stored on our disks just as folders in the file drawers contain documents.

In slightly more technical terms, the basic elements of a tree directory structure are a root directory, first-level directories created off the root, and subdirectories below these. As more directories are needed for a logical grouping and separation of files, subdirectories can be created further down the tree. Applications and data may be stored at any level in the directory structure. The idea is to logically arrange applications and data so that they are easy to find, use, and archive.

NOTE
DOS allows up to 32 levels of subdirectories; NetWare's default is 25.

USING NETWARE DIRECTORIES

NetWare uses a directory structure very similar to that used on DOS-based systems, but it allows you to specify additional information that single-user DOS computers don't need. Namely, the NetWare directory structure includes file server names and volume names. Under NetWare, the *path* that leads to a particular file includes server name, volume name, and directory path. (Think of a path as the address of the file to be found.)

For example, the full path to a word-processing file stored on a DOS-based system might be:

D:\DATA\WP51\LETTERS\EASAMS.003

On a NetWare file server, this same path (though it can use any drive letter) should work as well as it does on the DOS computer. Under DOS, it is only necessary to consider files located on drives physically attached to the workstation. Under NetWare, a file can be stored on a workstation's local drive or on a file server.

Just like a drive letter in DOS, the volume name in the NetWare path must be followed by a colon. For example, if you were logged into our example file servers, CICERO and TOLSTOY, and needed to copy a file stored on TOLSTOY to the directory you are presently in on CICERO, you'd need to include both the server name and volume name for the complete path to the file on TOLSTOY:

COPY TOLSTOY\VOL1:\DATA\WP51\LETTERS\EASAMS.003

As you can see, these pathnames are sometimes rather long. NetWare provides a way to simplify access to files on multiple servers through *drive mapping*. On network drives, drive mapping allows us to assign a server, volume, and path to a particular drive letter, so that whenever we use that drive letter, the path is already included. (See *Using Drive Maps* later in this chapter for details of drive mapping.)

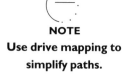

NOTE
**Use drive mapping to
simplify paths.**

USING SYSTEM DIRECTORIES

When you install NetWare, a standard set of system directories are created containing the NetWare utilities, NLMs, drivers, printer definitions, help files, and other files copied from the NetWare disks. The directory tree created by NetWare during installation should be similar to that shown in Figure 8.2.

When you log into a new server as the user SUPERVISOR, NetWare has a default script that places you in the system directory of the server's SYS:

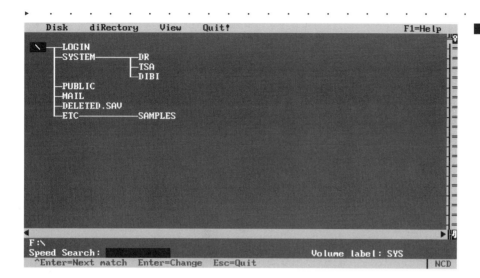

FIGURE 8.2

*The default NetWare
directory structure*

volume (usually F:\SYSTEM\). This is the directory where the NetWare system files are stored. By default, only the SUPERVISOR has privileges to use this directory. To see what is stored in the other directories, you can use the change-directory command (CD) to move from one directory to another. For example, to change to the public directory, type:

F:\SYSTEM\> CD \PUBLIC ↵

This will place you in the server's public directory. This directory is where almost all the NetWare utilities are stored. The conventions for moving from one directory to the next are similar for both DOS and NetWare:

CD \   takes you to the root directory of the current drive.

CD \DIRNAME   takes you from any current position on the drive to a directory called DIRNAME, if it exists.

CD DIRNAME   takes you to a subdirectory called DIRNAME, if it exists.

CD ..   takes you to the parent of the current
                                 directory.

NetWare has included a couple of enhancements to the change-directory command to make it more flexible than it is under DOS alone. First, you can move among volumes and even servers. If we are currently positioned in the public directory on CICERO and wish to change to a directory called UTILS on the server TOLSTOY, we can do this with the following command:

CD TOLSTOY\SYS:UTILS

This very powerful feature allows you to use a single drive letter to indicate paths on more than one file server. (In fact, this change-directory command actually *remaps* the current drive to another file server and directory.) From this point on, or until another server and volume are indicated, all change-directory commands performed on this drive will be to locations on TOLSTOY.

Second, NetWare 3.12 includes change-directory commands using multiple periods. Under DOS, the period (.), which appears in a directory listing, indicates the current directory. As such, the command CD . appears to have no effect, even though it actually resets your position to the current directory. (You just end up where you started.) Similarly, the dual period (..) in the directory listing indicates the *parent* of the current directory. (A parent is the directory that is located right before the current directory on the path.) Using the command CD .. will put you into the parent of the current directory. Under NetWare, you may indicate that you wish to move more than one directory up the directory tree with the command CD ... "Move to the parent of the parent of the current directory." For example, if you are in the archive subdirectory in the following directory structure:

G:\UTILS\ZIP\FILES\ARCHIVE

the command CD .... will put you into the UTILS directory on drive G: (G:\UTILS).

NOTE
You must first be attached (or logged in) to the servers with which you want to use DOS commands like CD

Directory Operations and Commands

Now that you have an idea of how you can maneuver around the network directory structure, let's get to the methods for creating one of your own. Under NetWare, you can perform most of the directory operations that you can under DOS:

- CREATE

- REMOVE

- COPY

To these basic abilities, NetWare has added command-line and menu utilities that give you the ability to rename directories and move or delete entire directory structures including the files they contain. (See Chapter 14 for instructions on FILER and Appendix B for the workstation command line utilities.)

CREATING DIRECTORIES

Creating directories is as simple as maneuvering around in them. To create a directory under NetWare, you can use NetWare utilities like FILER, or almost any utility that will create a directory under DOS. For simplicity, we'll use the DOS make-directory (MKDIR, or in short form MD) command from the command line in our examples. Using make directory is very much like using the change-directory command:

MD [PATH]DIRNAME↵

Under NetWare, the same rules apply for specifying a path as those in the change-directory command. To create a subdirectory from the current directory, simply type the make-directory command followed by a space and the subdirectory name. To create directories in other locations, specify the full path to the new directory—and of course make sure that the path exists! (You cannot create a subdirectory on a path with MD if its parent has

WARNING
You cannot create a new directory with MKDIR if its parent directory has not been created first. Directories must be created one at a time.

not been created first—you cannot create more than one directory at a time.) To create a directory called ARCHIVE under the root of TOLSTOY's SYS: volume, whatever directory you are currently in, you could use the following command:

MD TOLSTOY\SYS:\ARCHIVE ↵

You can accomplish the same thing equally well by using NetWare's FILER utility (see Chapter 14).

NOTE
This example assumes that you're logged in as the SUPERVISOR or have privileges to create directories on TOLSTOY's SYS: volume. See Chapter 10, *Establishing Network Security* for clarification.

REMOVING DIRECTORIES

The remove-directory command under NetWare (RMDIR or RD) follows exactly the same syntax as the make-directory command:

RD [PATH]DIRNAME ↵

However, before you can remove a directory with RD, two conditions must be met:

▶ The directory cannot contain any files or other subdirectories

▶ No other users can be using the directory.

TIP
Remember to remove hidden and systemfiles—these may not appear when the directory is viewed.

Most utilities that will remove a directory or directory structure under DOS will remove directories under NetWare as well. Some of these (including Novell's FILER utility, XTree NET from XTree, and QDOS 3 from Gazelle Systems) will remove an entire directory structure and the included files at the same time. In any case, if one of the directories is in use by another user, the command will result in an error.

Remember that a directory may be in use if a user has a drive letter mapped to it or if a user has opened a file in that directory.

COPYING AND RENAMING DIRECTORIES

Because the DOS copy command will only copy the files contained in a directory and not the directory itself, you use the DOS XCOPY or the NetWare NCOPY command to copy both directories and files. The format of these commands is similar to the DOS COPY command. Both require a source and a destination and can optionally use command line switches to change the way they operate. The NCOPY command, included with NetWare, understands complete NetWare paths including server names, volume names, and the directory conventions for other operating systems (such as Macintosh, OS/2, or UNIX). As with most NetWare utilities, following the command with a /h or /? will cause it to list its options:

```
F:\PUBLIC>ncopy /h

Usage: NCOPY [path] [[TO] path] [option]Options
  /s   copy subdirectories.
  /s/e   copy subdirectories, including empty directories.
  /f   copy sparse files.
  /i   inform when non-DOS file information will be lost.
  /c   copy only DOS information.
  /a   copy files with archive bit set.
  /m   copy files with archive bit set, clear the bit.
  /v   verify with a read after every write.
  /h (/?)   display this usage message.

F:\PUBLIC>
```

Using these options, you can copy an entire directory tree and the files it contains or a portion of the tree to another location with a single command. During the copy, all the new directories will automatically be created on the destination drive. For example, if we want to copy the UTIL directory and all subdirectories from the file server TOLSTOY to a new directory called TOOLS on the file server CICERO, we can use the following command:

```
NCOPY TOLSTOY\SYS:UTIL CICERO\VOL1:TOOLS /S /E /V
```

The options appended to the end modify the actions of NCOPY: /S forces NCOPY to include subdirectories located below the UTIL directory; /E forces NCOPY to copy empty subdirectories as well as those that contain files; and /V verifies the copies by comparing the copy to the original.

On the other hand, at times you might only want to rename a directory rather than copy it and its files to a new location. You can rename a directory through FILER or with the NetWare RENDIR command using the following syntax:

NOTE
RENDIR will work on your local drives just as effectively as it does on the NetWare volumes.

RENDIR OLDNAME NEWNAME↵

If we wanted the directories on both TOLSTOY and CICERO to match, we could rename the UTIL directory on TOLSTOY:

RENDIR TOLSTOY\SYS:UTIL TOLSTOY\SYS:TOOLS↵

Developing a Directory Structure

Now that you're armed with tools for manipulating directory structures under NetWare, you're ready to customize one that will meet your more specific needs. As stated before, the purpose of the directory structure is to allow applications and data to be logically arranged on the network volumes. This is where you begin laying the foundation for the administrator and the network users. It will help to design a directory structure on paper for each volume on your servers before implementing the overall system. Consider the following questions when designing your directory structure:

- What is the structure of the company or organization?

- What kind of applications will be run from this file server?

- How many users can be concurrently logged into this file server?

- How do I arrange applications and data to assist in implementing security?

If a company's organizational structure lends itself to division by departments, with each department having its own server and applications, many servers will have similar directory structures. Since each server serves the needs of a particular department and its applications, NetWare utilities, word processors, and spreadsheets are likely to be found on each server. Some programs, like an accounting package, CAD software, or an Inventory package, might be located only on the server for a particular department. Each server is likely to have its own administration and maintenance autonomously of the other network servers.

On the other hand, if all the users in the company need access to the same applications, it may make more sense to dedicate servers to providing a particular set of services to everyone. Some applications, like word processors, spreadsheets, and e-mail, for example, require less intensive data I/O than a database system. If all your users will need access to these resources, it makes sense to dedicate a server to serving the database users and another (or others) to serving other less intensive applications. Some utilities and applications will, by default, be duplicated across all the network file servers (DOS programs, NetWare utilities, etc. ...). Before deciding to separate applications by server, make sure that both the server and applications can handle a sufficient number of simultaneous users.

Network applications often limit the number of simultaneous users in much the same way as NetWare does. But other applications only allow a certain number of registered users and will not permit other users to use them. Regardless of the scheme used, each application will have its own method of *authenticating* (adding) new users. Often, it's as simple as purchasing licenses called *user packs* for the additional users.

In NetWare, you can check the File Server Information window of SYS-CON.EXE or the Version Information window of FCONSOLE.EXE to see how many users your NetWare version supports (see Appendix A for more information on these utilities).

As you can see, there is no clear-cut way to design a directory structure or to separate applications across network servers. Since a network provides both a method for storing information and a method for sharing it, look for places where the network can improve work flow by sharing information throughout the organization.

Once you have settled on a method for working in a multiserver environment, or if your network will only have a single server, select an organizational scheme for creating a directory structure that most closely matches your needs and implement it. In doing so, however, some very basic tenets will assist you with maintenance and upgrade tasks:

► If you use name spaces such as Macintosh or OS/2, separate these areas onto separate volumes. If possible, add the name space when you create the volume. (See Appendix A for more information on name spaces.)

► Create main directories like PROGRAMS, UTILS, and DATA. Under these, keep the application and data files separated into different subdirectories. Be careful not to load an application and fail to specify where to store the data files. If you do this, data files often end up in the same directory as the executable program files, making upgrades and reorganization difficult. You can avoid such problems by removing file create and file erase rights (see Chapter 10) for executable program directories and specifying dedicated data directories.

► Create subdirectories for all users called HOME, USER, or something similar, and give each user a private directory under this as their home directory. Under this directory, you can allow users to create subdirectories to arrange their own personal files in one location rather than scattered across the network. (Creating a home directory can be done automatically when creating users. See *Creating Users and Groups* below.)

► Create public or temporary data directories where shared information can be copied, shared, and stored. (If security is implemented as discussed in Chapter 10, you won't be able to copy a spreadsheet file directly into another user's home directory. You can use a public data directory as a convenient means of sharing files.)

▸ By default, NetWare will not allow a directory structure to be more than 25 levels deep. A soundly organized directory structure will (in most cases) not require more than this. (Even so, this parameter can be modified by adding the line **SET MAXIMUM SUBDIRECTORY TREE DEPTH** = *xx* to the server's STARTUP.NCF file, where *xx* indicates the new depth up to a maximum of 100 levels.)

▸ The SYS: volume will have a lot of traffic in temporary files such as print queues and e-mail. In some cases, e-mail data can be redirected to another volume, but it will help to locate applications that write to disk often or that need temporary swap files on other volumes.

NOTE
NetWare automatically creates a directory for each new user under the **SYS:MAIL** directory, where a user's personal login script is stored. (Scripts are discussed in Chapter 9.)

Once again, the primary networking rule applies—a network will always outgrow your initial expectations, so plan accordingly.

VIEWING THE DIRECTORY STRUCTURE

Novell has included a command in NetWare called LISTDIR to help you list the directory structure and display attributes, owners, creation dates, etc., as they relate to individual directories. By using the /SUB or /ALL options of this command, we can get an idea of the underlying directory structure. With these options, LISTDIR shows all directories and subdirectories from the specified directory down. Each subdirectory level is indented two spaces from its parent directory.

If you are only interested in seeing the structure, there are many utilities which display directory structures in a graphic format (e.g., Xtree, QDOS, and Norton Change Directory). Most people are visually oriented and can understand a directory structure more easily if it is displayed graphically. The DOS command TREE will show the current directory and subdirectories in a visual format similar to the one appearing in Figure 8.3.

If you use the MS-DOS shell program DOSSHELL, the Microsoft Windows File Manager, or the ViewMAX program in DR-DOS, the directories will be shown in a similar manner.

FIGURE 8.3

*A graphically represented
directory structure from the
TREE command*

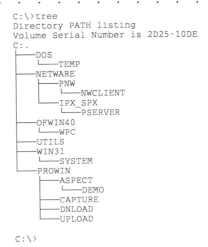

```
C:\>tree
Directory PATH listing
Volume Serial Number is 2D25-10DE
C:.
    ├───DOS
    │   └───TEMP
    ├───NETWARE
    │   ├───PNW
    │   │   └───NWCLIENT
    │   └───IPX_SPX
    │       └───PSERVER
    ├───OFWIN40
    │   └───WPC
    ├───UTILS
    ├───WIN31
    │   └───SYSTEM
    └───PROWIN
        ├───ASPECT
        │   └───DEMO
        ├───CAPTURE
        ├───DNLOAD
        └───UPLOAD

C:\>
```

Creating Users and Groups

NetWare creates two users by default during the installation process. One is a GUEST and the other is the SUPERVISOR. Before other users can log into the network, they will have to be created and assigned a user name, access privileges, and optionally a password.

If your company or organization already has a structure that is divided into separate groups or departments, you might use the same organization on your network servers. Users can be organized into groups that have common characteristics. For example, in a manufacturing company, you might have groups for ADMINISTRATION, MANUFACTURING, MATERIALS, PURCHASING, ACCOUNTING, ENGINEERING, and TECH_SUPPORT. Using groups makes it easier to send messages and e-mail to groups of users, or to control the login process for the needs of a particular group, than it would be for individual persons. For example, it is much easier to have a message about upcoming server maintenance displayed to the entire ACCOUNTING group during login than it would be to send the message to all the members individually.

DEFINING NETWORK USERS

There are three basic ways to define network users—with SYSCON, USERDEF, and MAKEUSER. Which one you use usually depends on how often your network users change and how large your organization is. SYSCON is a *public* utility (available for everyone's use and stored in the PUBLIC directory of the SYS: volume) and is the file server System Configuration utility. SYSCON has many more uses than simply creating users; these are covered under *Security* in Chapter 10 and in the *User Utilities* section of Chapter 15. In this chapter, we'll use SYSCON to create network users as this is the quickest way to assign user names and passwords to a small number of new users.

USERDEF is useful for creating single or small groups of users. With SYSCON, you can specify default values that affect all new users. Although you can go back and change any of these settings on a per-user basis, the USERDEF program makes it easier to create a user or users who require different defaults than those provided in SYSCON. With USERDEF, you can create *templates* that assign certain home directories and default security settings to all users created through that template.

MAKEUSER is a user-management utility capable of creating home directories, specifying security settings, and assigning groups for large numbers of users. The MAKEUSER utility is an *interpreter,* a program that accepts its commands from a script file and uses these commands to define new users and groups. You can create different script files to control how MAKEUSER creates and removes entire groups of users. In an environment where groups are temporarily assigned to work on a project together, or in an academic environment where classes are formed and dispersed at the end of the semester or seminar, MAKEUSER is an ideal utility.

Creating, Changing, and Deleting Users with SYSCON

Perhaps the simplest way to create a new user on your system is to use the System Configuration (SYSCON) utility. SYSCON is located in the PUBLIC directory of your server's SYS: volume. Unless the server's environment has been changed, all users have access to this directory and the

NOTE
User names may
contain up to
47 characters.

utilities stored there. To create a new user for the first time, you must log into the file server as SUPERVISOR. Run SYSCON by typing SYSCON↵ at the command prompt. You will be greeted by the opening menu which appears in Figure 8.4.

Selecting the User Information option at the bottom of the menu will bring up the current list of user names. On a new server, this list should only contain two users—GUEST and SUPERVISOR. To add a new user, press Ins, type the user name into the window that pops up, and press ↵.

Stick to a common scheme for user names. In a small office, using either first or last names might be perfectly acceptable. In larger installations, however, you are likely to have user-name conflicts using a simple scheme. Consider combining items likely to be unique for each user. For example, you could assign a combination of a user's initials and the last four digits of their social security number (e.g., TMC4651, RAP2908, J1C3482) or just assign completely unique user names outright. (Users find personalized names easiest to remember.)

FIGURE 8.4

The opening menu of
SYSCON

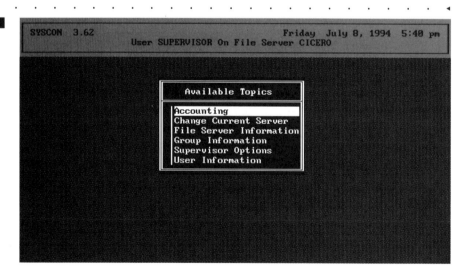

By default, NetWare will attempt to create a home directory for each new user in the root of the SYS: volume. On our file server, we have created a home directory on VOL1: (our server has two volumes SYS: and VOL1:) under which all our users' personal directories are stored. As we discussed in the section on *Creating Directories* earlier in this chapter, you might want to override NetWare's default and group your users together under a HOME or USER subdirectory. When prompted, you can modify the path and specify a new home directory for your user. From this point on, when SYS-CON creates new users, it will use the new path as the default for creating home directories. If the directory path you specify does not exist, SYSCON will prompt you to determine whether or not you want it to be created for you. Your new user will be added to your list of users.

If you highlight the new user and press ↵, the User Information screen will appear as it does in Figure 8.5.

From the User Information screen, you can change nearly every aspect of your user's personal identification or configuration.

If you have installed accounting on your system, the first option in the list allows you to specify the user's account balance. If you want to adjust an account balance, select this item and specify the upper and lower limits of the user's balance. Optionally, you can specify that the user have un-limited credit. If accounting is not installed, the first option is for setting the user's account restrictions. Selecting this option will bring up the Account Restrictions menu shown in Figure 8.6.

The settings in this menu determine the account restrictions for the user other than those imposed by security (see Chapter 10) and accounting if installed:

Account Disabled	Allows you (as the SUPERVISOR) to enable or disable this user's ability to log into the file server.
Account Has Expiration Date	Allows you to specify whether or not the user's account will expire and its expiration date.

TIP
Select a common scheme for user names. Personalize them to make them easy to remember.

NOTE
You can rename a user by highlighting their user name in the list and pressing F3, but this doesn't auto-matically modify their home directory name or login script.

FIGURE 8.5

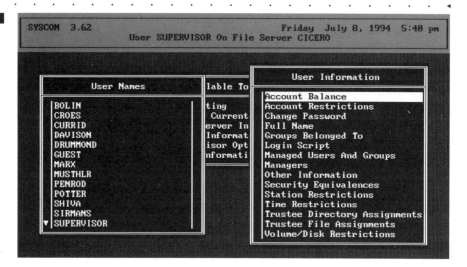

*The User Information
screen in SYSCON*

FIGURE 8.6

*Account restrictions for user
CROES*

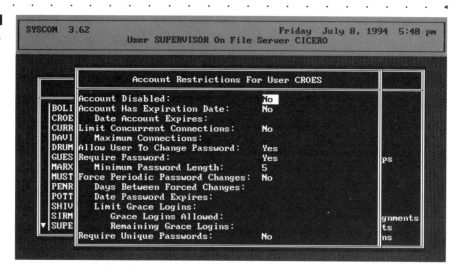

Limit Concurrent Connections	Allows you to specify the maximum number of times a user can concurrently login into the server. If this is set to Yes, the number indicated in the Maximum Connections field is the maximum number of concurrent login sessions a user can have.
Allow User To Change Password	If this is set to Yes, the user can change their password.
Require Password	If this is set to Yes, the user must have a password. If the password is left unassigned, the user will be able to log into the network under a *grace login* for the number of grace logins allowed. At each login, the user will be requested to specify a password. If the user does not specify a password within the number of grace logins allowed, the account will be locked.
Force Periodic Password Changes	If this is set to Yes, this option forces the user to change their password when the indicated number of days have elapsed. The Days Between Forced Changes option specifies the number of days between password changes. When set, this will determine the date the password expires. This expiration date can be overridden by typing a new date in the Date Password Expires field. The last two options specify the number of grace logins the user has once their password has expired.

Require Unique
Passwords

If this is set to Yes, the user will have to supply a new password that does not match one of the last eight passwords used.

Once you have set up the user restrictions, press Esc to return to the User Information menu.

The next option allows the SUPERVISOR or a user with SUPERVISOR equivalency to specify a user's password. As explained in the chapter on network security, passwords are stored in an encrypted form. There is no way for even the network SUPERVISOR to discover a user's password. This mechanism allows the SUPERVISOR to set a new user's password or override the password a user has assigned.

The Full Name option allows you to specify the user's full name. The user's full name can be used as a variable in login scripts and batch files. Additionally, another user can view information about a user from within SYS-CON. If the user's full name is set, it will be displayed.

The Groups Belonged To option allows the SUPERVISOR, an equivalent, or a workgroup manager to add or remove a user from groups. It also allows other users to view groups belonged to. In the case of the workgroup manager, only groups that the manager is in charge of can be affected. Groups are covered in a section below.

NOTE
Chapter 9 explains login scripts and script variables.

The user's login script generally controls the user's environment. You can use this option to create a user's login script, copy a login script from another user, or merely edit an existing login script. If the user does not have a login script assigned, a window will appear when this option is selected requesting the name of a user from whom to copy an existing login script. The default is the current user. If the current user is selected and does not already have a login script, a blank login-script–editing screen will appear. If the user already has a login script, an editing screen similar to Figure 8.7 will appear.

You can use the Other Information option to find out the last time a user has logged into the network, whether the user is a console operator, the disk space currently in use by the user, and the user's USER ID (number NetWare

▶ · ◀

```
SYSCON  3.62                          Friday  July 8, 1994  5:41 pm
                     User SUPERVISOR On File Server CICERO


                        Login Script For User CROES

MAP DISPLAY OFF
MAP INS S5:=CICERO\SYS:UTIL\EPSILON
MAP INS S6:=CICERO\SYS:TNA
EXIT <REDIR>
```

F I G U R E 8.7
*The login-script–editing
screen for a user who
already has a login script*

uses to keep track of a user). Don't put too much faith in the disk space in use option giving you an accurate picture of the disk space actually used by a user. Some DOS utilities, including DOS's XCOPY command, change the ownership of directories and files they copy to the user who copied them. Since SYSCON uses ownership to determine the amount of disk space in use by a particular user, this amount can be incorrect. If your users use FILER or NCOPY to move around large amounts of information, the ownership information will be intact.

The option at the bottom of the list, Volume/Disk Restrictions, can be used to specify a maximum amount of space a user can use on a particular volume. Selecting this option will bring up the list of volumes defined for the current server. After you select a particular volume, a menu will appear which allows you to specify restrictions for the current user. You can set space restrictions for the current user by typing **Yes** at the Limit Volume Space field. The Volume Space Limit field specifies the maximum number of 4-KB blocks the user may have on the current volume. By enabling space restrictions and setting this option to zero, you can effectively prevent the user from writing to the volume. The last prompt displays the current amount of space occupied on the volume by the user. As with the disk usage

WARNING
The disk space in use
option may be incor-
rect.

information displayed under Other Information, this number is determined by the ownership of files and directories and therefore subject to the same limitations.

The remaining options are useful in implementing network security. As such, they are merely mentioned here and covered more thoroughly in Chapter 10.

Managed Users and Groups	Specifies the users and groups that this user is a workgroup or user account manager for. (See *Defining Network Groups* later in this chapter.)
Managers	Specifies the people or groups who manage the current user.
Security Equivalences	Specifies users and groups with whom the current user has been set equivalent. The user gains the rights of any user or group listed here, but only up to the first 32 listed.
Station Restrictions	This is a list of stations that the user has been restricted to. If a list of stations has been specified, the user can log into the network only at one of the workstations listed. If the list is empty, the user is unrestricted.
Time Restrictions	This is a list of times the user is allowed to log in to the network. By default, a user may log in at any time. If this option is modified, the user will only be able to log in during the specified times and will be logged out if logged in when the time expires.

Trustee Directory Assignments	This is a list of directories and rights that the user has been granted for the directories listed.
Trustee File Assignments	Like directory assignments, this is a list of files and rights the user has been granted regarding these files.

Once you have specified the settings under the User Information menu, your user has been created and fully defined. Changing a user's options merely requires that you go back into SYSCON, access the User Information menu for the specified user, and modify the settings.

Setting Up Defaults for New Users with SYSCON

As you may have noticed after going through the previous section, it can be quite tedious to go through the complete procedure of defining and creating each user with SYSCON. To make your work a little simpler, you can specify defaults for most of the options in the User Information menu once within SYSCON and they will affect all users created from that point on. To set these defaults, log in as the SUPERVISOR and run SYSCON. From the main menu, select Supervisor Options. From this menu, you can specify the defaults for new users using the first two options—Default Account Balance/Restrictions and Default Time Restrictions. Selecting the account balance and restrictions option will bring up the menu shown in Figure 8.8.

From this menu, you can set defaults for the following:

Account Has Expiration Date	Specifies whether or not a user's account will expire and if so, the date on which the account will expire.

FIGURE 8.8

The Default Account
Balance/Restrictions menu

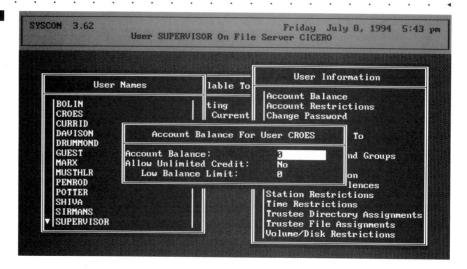

Limit Concurrent Connections		Specifies whether or not the user may have concurrent logins and the maximum number of times the user may be concurrently logged in.
Create Home Directory for User		Specifies whether or not a home directory should be created for each user.
Require Password		Specifies whether or not all users will be required to have a password and the minimum password length.
Force Periodic Password Changes		Specifies whether or not all users will be required to change their passwords, the length of time a password is valid, and the number a grace logins a user is allowed with an expired password.
Require Unique Passwords		Specifies whether or not a user may reuse one of his/her last eight passwords.

Account	These options are only valid if
Balance and	NetWare's accounting features have
Allow	been installed. If so, these options
Unlimited Credit	specify whether or not the user will
	have an account balance and if so, the
	user's upper and lower limits.

The Default Time Restrictions menu option allows you to specify the times users will be allowed to log into the network exactly as you might under the User Information menu of SYSCON. Once set, the options under these two menus will affect all new users created through SYSCON.

Defining Network Groups

A group is a collection of users who have something in common. As we've already described, it is sometimes useful to group people by departments so that it is easier to address an entire department at once. In addition, groups are useful for granting directory permissions and allowing access to different applications or data files. We might, for example, create a group called WINDOWS to allow members of the group to access the directories where the shared copy of Windows is stored. Using groups this way makes it very simple to give and remove permissions to use particular applications on the network: Any rights that belong to a group are automatically translated to the group members as well. The methods for selecting and setting directory permissions and rights are covered in Chapter 10, *Establishing Network Security,* and Chapter 16, *Techniques for Administering Software.*

Creating, Changing, and Deleting Groups with SYSCON

Creating groups is very similar to creating users with SYSCON. To create a network group, start SYSCON from the command prompt and select Group Information from the main menu. A list of currently defined groups will appear. To add a new group to the list, press Ins and type in the new group's name, then press ↵. The new group will be added to the list.

NOTE
Newly-created users automatically become members of the group EVERYONE. You can add users to other groups through SYSCON; a user can belong to up to 32 groups.

To modify the attributes and security or select members for a group, highlight the group and press ⏎. The Group Information menu shown in Figure 8.9 will appear.

From this menu you can use the Full Name option to specify a descriptive name for the group to help identify it. The Member List option will display a list of current group members. Network users and other groups may be group members. To add new users to the current group, press Ins while in the member list. A list of current non-members will appear. You may select them one at a time or many at a time by using the mark (F5) key. Once selected, press ⏎ to add the new users to the group. The Other Information option will display the GROUP ID number and whether or not group members are permitted to operate the system console.

The two items at the bottom of this menu are for implementing group rights and security. The Trustee Directory Assignments option allows you to give a group different permissions for particular directories while the Trustee File Assignments gives group members' permissions for particular files.

FIGURE 8.9

The Group Information menu

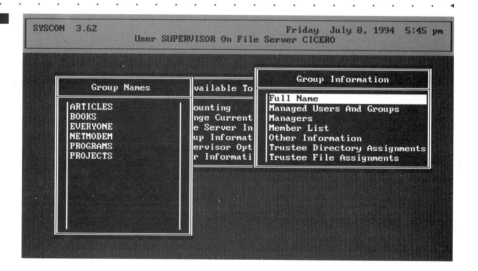

To see a list of current directories where the group has defined rights, press ↵ while highlighting the Trustee Directory Assignments option. To add to this list, press Ins. SYSCON will open a window requesting the new directory path. If you do not know the path, press Ins again to traverse the NetWare volumes and directories to specify the path. When you have reached the appropriate directory, press Esc and the current directory path will be indicated in the original window. Press ↵ to save it.

To assign new rights for a directory, highlight the directory in the list and press ↵. A list of currently defined rights will appear. You can add to the list by pressing Ins. If you wish to delete a directory from the list or rights from a directory, simply display the directory listing or the rights listing, highlight the entry, and press Del. SYSCON will prompt you before deleting the entry.

To see a list of current files with rights assigned, highlight the Trustee File Assignments option and press ↵. You can add to the list, add rights, and remove entries or rights exactly as you can trustee directory assignments.

There are two options in the Group Information menu that allow us to set up and view user account managers and the users or groups they manage. A *user account manager* is a person or group that has the rights and permissions necessary to manage the accounts of users in a particular group. These include the ability to change account balances (if system accounting has been installed), change user restrictions, change passwords, change security equivalences, and turn other users into user account managers.

Anyone listed under the Managers listing for a group is (at least) a user account manager for the group. User account managers assist the system SUPERVISOR by offloading many of the day-to-day tasks that need to be performed for the group (for example, resetting a user password).

Workgroup managers have the abilities of user account managers and the ability to create new users and groups. Workgroup managers are most useful when a network becomes too large for one or even a few SUPERVISOR equivalents to manage and when you don't want to spread SUPERVISOR equivalencies too far. The workgroup manager has basically the same rights as a SUPERVISOR for the group he or she controls: In addition to being able to manipulate users, a workgroup manager can create, manage, and delete print queues.

In most cases, managers are assigned to groups as user account managers and upgraded when the additional capabilities of the workgroup manager are needed. To make a user or group a workgroup manager, go into SYS-CON, access the Supervisor Options menu, and select Workgroup Managers. A list of current workgroup managers will appear. To add a new manager, press Ins to display a list of non-managers. Highlight the appropriate user or group and press ↵. The selected user or group now has workgroup manager capabilities for the groups they manage as user account managers.

Creating Users with USERDEF

The USERDEF utility is somewhat like SYSCON in the way it sets up a default configuration for users and then creates them. With USERDEF, though, there can be more than one set of defaults designed and stored in a template. USERDEF is first used to create these templates and then new users are created based on the settings in a particular template. Before you run USERDEF to create new users, there are some housekeeping functions to perform:

- ► If you will be using the system accounting features, you will need to enable them from within SYSCON before running USERDEF.

- ► USERDEF uses printer definitions that are already specified for the user SUPERVISOR. If you will be using print job configurations (see Chapter 11), you will need to use PRINTDEF and PRINTCON to create and define them for the SUPERVISOR before running USERDEF.

- ► Although USERDEF can add new users to existing groups, it cannot create new groups for you. If you need to add users to new groups, use SYSCON to create the groups before running USERDEF (see the section on creating groups in this chapter).

▶ Create the parent directory to the user's home directories. USER-DEF will (by default) create a home directory for each user. The parent directory where these personal directories will be stored must be created before running USERDEF.

Creating or Modifying Templates   You can start USERDEF by typing USERDEF ↵ on the command line. USERDEF should respond with the opening screen shown in Figure 8.10.

From this menu, you can use the Edit/View Templates option to create new templates for different user configurations. Highlight this option and press ↵ to see a list of currently defined templates.

On a new system, the only template will be the DEFAULT template. Press Ins to create a new template. You will be prompted to enter the template name. For our examples we created a template called GENUSER. After typing the template name and pressing ↵, you will be presented with the template menu, which has options for viewing the login script and viewing the current parameters. Press ↵ to view the login script. The default login script created by USERDEF appears in Figure 8.11.

TIP
If you don't want to have a home directory, you can back up and delete the home directory entry.

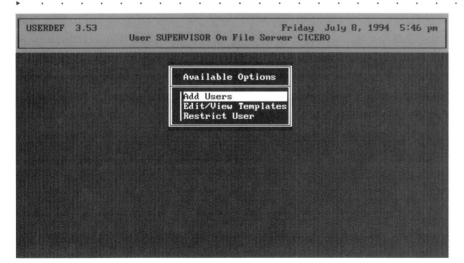

F I G U R E 8.10

The Available Options menu in USERDEF

FIGURE 8.11

The default login script
created by USERDEF

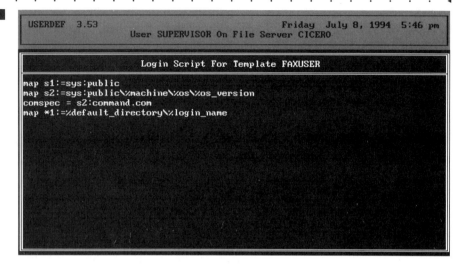

```
USERDEF  3.53                                  Friday  July 8, 1994  5:46 pm
                       User SUPERVISOR On File Server CICERO

                        Login Script For Template FAXUSER

map s1:=sys:public
map s2:=sys:public\%machine\%os\%os_version
comspec = s2:command.com
map *1:=%default_directory\%login_name
```

NOTE
See Chapter 9 for
details on login scripts.

If you understand login scripts and want to make changes to this default login script (login scripts are covered in Chapter 9), you can directly edit the script from this screen. When you are through making changes, press Esc and you will be prompted to keep or lose your changes.

The View Parameters option allows you to set up most of the same parameters you set up under the default account restrictions menu of SYS-CON. The parameters menu appears in Figure 8.12.

From this menu, you can set up the user's default home directory, print job configurations the user will use, groups the user belongs to, the user's security restrictions, and the user's accounting parameters. The first option sets the parent directory for the user's home directory. Below this, USER-DEF will create a subdirectory using up to eight characters of the user's login name. You don't need to specify the server name in this path. USER-DEF creates new users on the server displayed on the status line at the top of the screen.

The second and third options are where you can specify any printer configurations the user will use and the groups the user will belong to. To assign groups, for example, press ↵ on the prompt (See List) to get a list of current groups. To add groups, press Ins to display a list of currently defined

```
┌──────────────────────────────────────────────────────────────┐
│ USERDEF  3.53                       Friday  July 8, 1994  5:46 pm │
│              User SUPERVISOR On File Server CICERO             │
├──────────────────────────────────────────────────────────────┤
│                                                                │
│        ┌────────────────────────────────────────────────┐    │
│        │        Parameters for Template GENUSER          │    │
│        │                                                  │    │
│        │ Default Directory:  VOL1:HOME                    │    │
│        │ Copy PrintCon From: (see list)                   │    │
│        │ Groups Belonged To: (see list)                   │    │
│        │ Account Balance:              1000               │    │
│        │ Limit Account Balance:        No                 │    │
│        │      Low Limit:                                  │    │
│        │ Limit Concurrent Connections: No                 │    │
│        │      Maximum Connections:                        │    │
│        │                                                  │    │
│        │ Require Password:             Yes                │    │
│        │      Minimum Password Length: 5                  │    │
│        │ Force Periodic Password Changes: Yes             │    │
│        │      Days Between Forced Changes: 40             │    │
│        │ Require Unique Passwords:     Yes                │    │
│        └────────────────────────────────────────────────┘    │
│                                                                │
└──────────────────────────────────────────────────────────────┘
```

FIGURE 8.12

*The parameters set for the
template GENUSER*

groups, then highlight the group to add and press ↵ or F5 (if you want to add more than one). By highlighting multiple groups and pressing F5, you can specify that more than one group be added at once. If you accidentally add a group, or if you just want to remove a group, highlight the group in the Groups Belonged To: list and press Del. You will be prompted before the group is removed. When you are through, press Esc to return to the parameters menu.

If you have installed accounting, you can specify whether or not to limit users created through this template and if so, you may specify the upper and lower limits of their account balance. The remaining options are useful in setting up system security (discussed in Chapter 10). If you wish to specify the number of times that a user may be concurrently logged in to the server, you can specify a limit at the Maximum Connections prompt and enable this feature. The remaining elements modify the user's password requirements in the same fashion as the options under SYSCON. When you are through modifying these parameters, press Esc to save changes. The new template GENUSER should appear in the template list. Press Esc to return to the main menu.

Inserting the Names of New Users   Once you have created the template, you are ready to create new users. Select Add Users from the Available Options menu. A menu of the currently defined templates will appear. You can create more than one user at a time, but all new users will be created according to the parameters in the template you select. Select your template and a list of currently defined users will appear as in Figure 8.13.

To add a new user, press Ins and type the new user's name. Notice that the new user's name appears in the list with the flag (new) to the right of the user name. Continue pressing Ins and typing user names until you have added all users who need to conform to this template. You can use Del to remove any users you don't want created, but this command only affects undefined users—those with the (new) flag beside them. You cannot use USERDEF to delete users who have already been created. When you are through defining new user names, you can press the Esc key to have USERDEF create them.

USERDEF will automatically assign a temporary password for all the users it creates. The temporary password matches the user's login name. If any of your user's names are shorter than the minimum password length (as set in SYSCON), USERDEF will repeat the user name as many times as it takes to meet or exceed the minimum length. For example, if the minimum

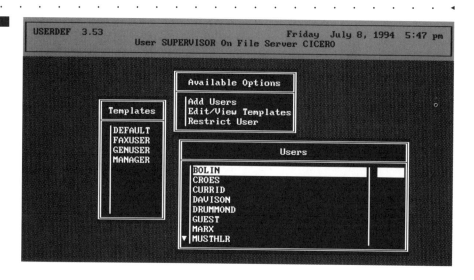

FIGURE 8.13

The current user list in USERDEF

password length is five and you create a user named TURK, USERDEF will prompt you to accept the password TURKTURK for this user or to specify an alternative.

On our file server, we are not using printer configurations. As such, after creating new users, USERDEF returns a message saying that it could not find any PRINTCON data files for the user SUPERVISOR. If you encounter this message and are not using printer definitions, this is not an error and can be disregarded. If you are using printer definitions, however, make sure that these have been assigned to the user SUPERVISOR before you run USERDEF.

The last screen you see should show the results of the operations USER-DEF has just attempted. Your screen should appear similar to Figure 8.14.

Using USERDEF to Assign Disk Space Limitations   The final function that USERDEF can perform is limiting the amount of disk space a user has access to. For example, to prevent your two new users (SIRMANS and TURK) from saving files onto the server's SYS: volume, you can use Restrict User to set their space allocation for this volume to zero. To do this for the

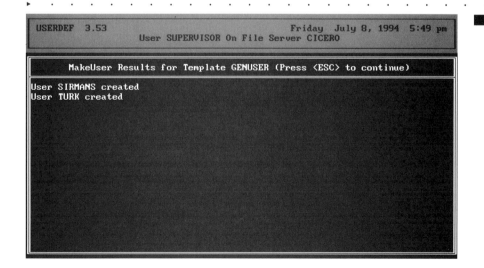

user SIRMANS, use Restrict User to select SIRMANS and the SYS: volume as in Figure 8.15

The screen which appears is the limitation information for this particular user on the volume you selected. For new users, there will be no restrictions set. Your screen should look similar to Figure 8.16.

Enable this option by typing **Yes** in the Limit Space field and specify the maximum amount of space available to the user in the Available field. If you want to completely restrict a user from writing to a volume, set the space available to 0 KB.

Creating Users with **MAKEUSER**

MAKEUSER is the utility that is best suited to creating large groups of new users. It is also more flexible than USERDEF or SYSCON. With MAKEUSER, scripts called *USR files* (because of their filename extensions) are interpreted by the MAKEUSER program to determine which new users should be created and the parameters that should be assigned to them. MAKEUSER can be run either from the command line or as a menu utility.

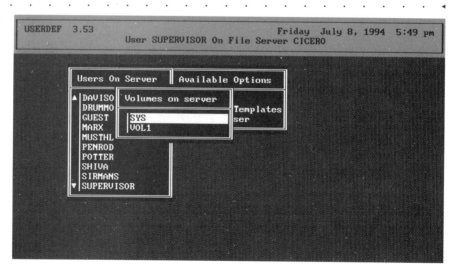

▶ . . . . ◀

```
USERDEF  3.53                          Friday  July 8, 1994  5:50 pm
                    User SUPERVISOR On File Server CICERO


        ┌ Users On Server ┐┌ Available Options ┐
        │     User Disk Space Limitation Information      │
        │                                                 │
        │  User:   SIRMANS                                │
        │                                                 │
        │  Volume: SYS                                    │
        │                                                 │
        │  Limit Space:      No                           │
        │                                                 │
        │  Available:            Kbytes                   │
        │                                                 │
        │  In Use:           0 Kbytes                     │
        │                                                 │
        └─────────────────────────────────────────────────┘
```

FIGURE 8.16

*The User Disk Space
Limitation Information menu*

If you choose not to use MAKEUSER from the command line, it will function as a menu utility as well. To start MAKEUSER as a menu utility, simply type MAKEUSER ↵ from the command line. MAKEUSER should respond with the screen that appears in FIGURE 8.17.

From the main menu, you can use the option Create USR file to create your first USR script. Selecting this option should bring up the editing screen for the USR file.

Control statements called *keywords* are inserted in the file to determine the actions performed by MAKEUSER. The order of the keywords is very important. Some keywords modify the actions of others, while some actually cause actions to be performed. See Table 8.1 for a list of the MAKEUSER keywords and their functions.

Using these keywords, you can create simple to complex scripts which will best create and organize the users you have on your network.

NOTE
**MAKEUSER scripts
are simple ASCII files
and may be created
with any ASCII text
editor.**

FIGURE 8.17

The opening menu of MAKEUSER

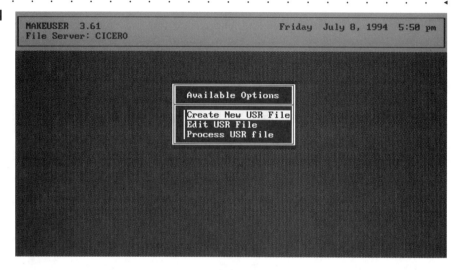

```
MAKEUSER  3.61                          Friday  July 8, 1994  5:50 pm
File Server: CICERO



                              Available Options

                         Create New USR File
                         Edit USR File
                         Process USR file
```

TABLE 8.1

Keywords available for use with MAKEUSER.

KEYWORD	EXPLANATION AND EXAMPLES
#ACCOUNT_EXPIRATION *month day, year*	#ACCOUNT_EXPIRATION specifies that the accounts for all users created after the occurrence of this keyword in the USR file will expire on *month day, year*. For example, to create users with accounts that automatically expire on December 31, 1995, place the following commands in the USR file: #ACCOUNT EXPIRATION December 31, 1995 #create PENROD^ #create KAPOOR^
#ACCOUNTING *balance, lowlimit*	#ACCOUNTING is used in conjunction with NetWare's Accounting features to set the user's starting balance and lower limit. Once users reach their lower limit, they will not be allowed to log in. You may allow users to run a negative balance by specifying a negative balance for *lowlimit*.

KEYWORD	EXPLANATION AND EXAMPLES
	For example, to create users whose accounts have balance restrictions, use the following sequence of commands: #accounting 1500, -200 #create BOLIN^ #create ELLERBE^ #accounting 1000, 0 #create DAVISON^ Each of the users in the above examples will have the account balance set by the occurrence of the keyword #ACCOUNTING located before they are created.
#CLEAR or #RESET	MAKEUSER can create more than one set of users from the same USR file, even if each set has completely different requirements. #CLEAR and #RESET nullify all keywords that occur in the file before them. They will not remove users who have already been created in the USR file, but after one of these keywords is used, you will start over with a completely different set of settings. For example, to create two sets of users who belong to different groups, one of which is using accounting functions, use the #RESET keyword: #groups MARKETING #accounting 1000, -100 #create PENROD^ #create SIRMANS^ #reset #groups ENGINEERING #create DEBONT^

TABLE 8.1

Keywords available for use
with MAKEUSER

(continued)

KEYWORD	EXPLANATION AND EXAMPLES
#CONNECTIONS *number*	Use the #CONNECTIONS keyword to specify the maximum number of simultaneous connections a user may have. For example, to restrict all new users to a maximum of 1 simultaneous connection, place the following command in the USR file: #connections 1
#CREATE *username* [option list]	#CREATE creates users and specifies other information about them. You must include a user name, but the additional parameters are optional. #CREATE offers these options:
where [option list] is one or more of:	**fullname** Set the user's full name.
[;fullname] [;password] [;group] [;directory (rights)]	**password** Assign the user's password. **group** Sets a list of groups the user will belong to (separate the groups with commas). **directory** [rights] Assigns rights to the indicated directories. The rights may be any of the NetWare directory rights (S,R,W,C,E,M, F,A) except the Supervisory (S) right. If you do not specify the rights only (,R, , , , ,F,) will be granted. To grant all rights include the keyword ALL after the directory name. If you want to assign rights to more than one directory, separate each directory/rights assignment with a comma. Each option of #CREATE must be preceded by a semicolon (;) and a plus (+) must be appended to the end of the first line if an entry wraps onto a new line.

TABLE 8.1
*Keywords available for use
with MAKEUSER
(continued)*

KEYWORD	EXPLANATION AND EXAMPLES

	For example, to create a user with a full name, password, and trustee directory assignments in the UTILS directory, we can use the following USR entry:
	
	   #create PENROD;Joshua A.
	      Penrod;thinkfast;;SYS:UTILS ALL
	
	Notice that the password has been followed by two semicolons to indicate that we are not assigning any groups.

#DELETE user1; user2, . . .	#DELETE is used to remove previously created users. You can delete more than one user with a single call to #DELETE, and you can remove information that is pertinent only to the indicated users.
	
	For example, by including the keywords HOME_DIRECTORY and PURGE_USER_DIRECTORY before the keyword #DELETE in the USR file, the home directory will be removed with the users:
	
	   #reset
	   #home_directory VOL1:HOME
	   #purge_user_directory
	   #delete STUART, STEPHENS, LEE

#GROUPS group1; group2; . . .	#GROUPS can be used before the keyword #CREATE to specify the groups new users will belong to. You may indicate more than one group, but these groups must already exist and be separated by semicolons in the list. MAKEUSER will not create new groups.

KEYWORD	EXPLANATION AND EXAMPLES
	For example, to include a new user in the groups accounting, inventory, and database, include the following sequence before creating them:
	#groups ACCOUNTING;INVENTORY;DATABASE
#HOME_DIRECTORY path	#HOME_DIRECTORY specifies the parent directory under which new users' personal directories will be created and the parent directory from which deleted users personal directories will be removed. If you are specifying this parameter before create, the parent directory must already exist as MAKEUSER will not create it for you.
	For example, to create a home directory under VOL1:HOME for a new user and remove the home directory for another, specify the #HOME_DIRECTORY keyword before the calls to #CREATE and #DELETE:
	#home_directory VOL1:HOME #create POTTER;lonestar;; SYS:PROGRAMS ALL #purge_user_directory #delete PENROD, CROES, ELLERBE
#LOGIN_SCRIPT path	#LOGIN_SCRIPT specifies the path and file name for the script file which will be copied as the user's personal login script.
	For example, to assign the script file default.scr in the SYS:PUBLIC directory to all new users, use the following command:
	#login_script SYS:PUBLIC\DEFAULT.SCR #create CURRID^ #create DAVISON^

KEYWORD	EXPLANATION AND EXAMPLES
#MAX_DISK_SPACE *vol,* *#blocks*	This keyword specifies the maximum number of 4 KB blocks a user can write to a particular volume. By default, a user may fill a disk completely as they have unlimited access to disk space. For this option to take effect, volume limitations will have to be enabled with DSPACE For example, to limit a user to 32 MB (32768 KB) of space on VOL1: and 4 MB (4096 KB) on VOL2:, use the following command before create: #max_disk_space VOL1, 8192; VOL2, 1024
#NO_HOME_DIRECTORY	#NO_HOME_DIRECTORY specifies that a personal home directory not be created for each user.
#PASSWORD_LENGTH *length*	#PASSWORD_LENGTH specifies the minimum length for the user's passwords. The value must be between 1 and 127 characters. Before setting the minimum password length, the keyword #PASSWORD_REQUIRED will need to be included in the USR file. For example, to set the minimum password length to 4 for new users, include the following command in the USR file: #password_length 4 Note that if you use this option, you'll need to enter a password for all #CREATE entries.
#PASSWORD_PERIOD *days*	#PASSWORD_PERIOD specifies the number of days a password is valid. After *days* days, the password will expire and allow the user a grace period of 6 logins. If this keyword is not used, the password will not be set to expire.

T A B L E 8.1

Keywords available for use
with MAKEUSER
(continued)

KEYWORD	EXPLANATION AND EXAMPLES
	For example, to force a new group of users to change their passwords once a month include the following command in the USR file: #password_period 30 #create CARLIN^ #create LIN^ Note that the user's password will expire at first login when this option is used.
#PASSWORD_REQUIRED	#PASSWORD_REQUIRED specifies that a user will have to have a password. If it is not used, the option of whether or not to use a password is left to the user. If this keyword is used and a password for new users is not specified, the new user will be given a grace period of six logins to specify a password before locking their account. For example, to omit the option of having a password and require that new users assign a password, put the following in the USR file: #password_required #create REYES;bigjohn^ #create BURNS^ As user BURNS was not assigned password in this example, he would be required to specify a password during one of his first six logins.
#PURGE_USER_ DIRECTORY	Use #PURGE_USER_DIRECTORY to purge a user's home directory and any subdirectories he or she has created when deleting the user from the system. To be in effect, this call must be placed in the USR file before the keyword #DELETE.

KEYWORD	EXPLANATION AND EXAMPLES
#REM OR REM	#REM is the specifier that allows comments to be placed into a USR script file. MAKEUSER ignores anything after a #REM keyword on a line.
#RESTRICTED_TIME *day, start, end*	#RESTRICTED_TIME can be used to restrict the times a user is allowed to log into the network. If the keyword is not used, the user can initially log in at any time. The keyword must be followed by the day, start time, and end time (separated by commas) that the user is restricted from accessing the network. For multiple days and times, the argument may be a list of days and times separated by semicolons: For example, to restrict the new user BROOKS from accessing the network on Monday & Tuesday, in the evenings, include the following in the USR file: #restricted_time mon,5:00 pm, 8:00 am;tue,5:00 pm,8:00 am #create BROOKS^ To restrict the user WILDER from accessing the network everyday during normal business hours, include the *everyday* modifier: #restricted_time everyday,8:00 am, 5:00 pm #create WILDER^
#STATIONS *network1,station1,station2;* *network2,station1,station2*	Use #STATIONS if you want to restrict your user to using a single workstation or group of workstations. If this keyword is not used, the user will be able to log in at any workstation. The complete address for a workstation includes *both a network address and a node address.*

TABLE 8.1

Keywords available for use
with MAKEUSER
(continued)

TABLE 8.1

Keywords available for use
with MAKEUSER

(continued)

KEYWORD	EXPLANATION AND EXAMPLES
	When the user is to be allowed on more than one station per network, each station should be added to the list following the network number and station numbers should be separated by semicolons. If stations on more than one network are allowed, separate the new network lists from the previous ones with semicolons. If you want to allow all stations on a network access, replace the station numbers with the keyword ALL.
	For example, to restrict the users DAVIS and SCHIPPA to the same set of three stations on two networks, use the following lines in your USR file: #rem Restrictions for network 003421, station FE and #rem network 100284, stations 05 and B3. #stations 003421, FE;1A;100284,05;B3 #create DAVIS^ #create SCHIPPA^
#UNIQUE_PASSWORD	#UNIQUE_PASSWORD prevents your users from using the same passwords over and over. This keyword causes NetWare to keep a history of the last eight passwords used by a user and prevents the user from reusing one of these.

Once the script has been created, you can use MAKEUSER to "compile" the script and check for syntax errors and other problems. If none are found, the new users will be created and the results of the script reported. Otherwise an error will be reported and no users will be created until the script is debugged.

Using Drive Maps

Simply put, the MAP command allows you to treat network drives as if they were local drives and network paths as if they were local paths. Without MAP, when you specify the location of a file or application on a network drive, you are forced to specify the entire path including server name, volume name, and subdirectories leading up to it.

MAP enables you to assign a network path, including the specification of the server, volume, and optionally a subdirectory path, to a single drive letter. Once a network drive has been mapped to a particular drive letter, we can treat it exactly as we would a local drive. If you don't use MAP, it would be impossible for many non-network–aware applications and utilities to access network drives—not to mention that it would make specifying the location of files and applications extremely tedious.

NetWare understands three types of drive maps:

Local drive maps	These are the drives that are physically attached to a workstation (e.g., floppy drives, hard drives, CD-ROM players). NetWare assumes that drives A:– LASTDRIVE are reserved by DOS as local drives. NetWare sets the first available network drive as the first drive letter after that specified in the DOS LASTDRIVE variable. If this variable has not been set in the CONFIG.SYS file, it will have a default value determined by the DOS version you use.

Network drive maps
Network drive maps are network drives attached to the workstation through a drive letter. Once assigned, it is possible to change to a network drive simply by typing the drive letter followed by a colon and pressing ↵.

Search drive maps
Search drive maps are NetWare's equivalent to the PATH in DOS. This is a set of directories searched by NetWare when you wish to run an application or utility that it not in the current directory. If the requested program is not located in one of the paths indicated by the search drives, the attempt will result in an error (usually the DOS *Bad command or filename* error).

Each of the different types of drive mapping uses one drive letter per map assignment. As there are only 26 drive letters available, there are only 26 drive letters to be divided among the different types of drive mappings. NetWare handles them using the model which appears in Figure 8.18.

▶ · ◀

F I G U R E 8.18

Drive letter assignments
under NetWare

```
F:\PUBLIC>map

Drive  A:    maps to a local disk.
Drive  B:    maps to a local disk.
Drive  C:    maps to a local disk.
Drive  D:    maps to a local disk.
Drive  E:    maps to a local disk.
Drive  F: = CICERO\SYS:  \PUBLIC
       -----
SEARCH1:  = Z:. [CICERO\SYS:  \PUBLIC]
SEARCH2:  = Y:. [CICERO\SYS:  \]
SEARCH3:  = C:\WIN31
SEARCH4:  = C:\
SEARCH5:  = C:\DOS
SEARCH6:  = C:\UTILS

F:\PUBLIC>
```

DOS defines the first floppy drive in a system to be drive A:, the second floppy as drive B:, the first hard disk in a system as drive C:, and so on. Each of the DOS partitions (see Chapter 6) on a PC's hard disk is assigned a logical drive letter.

These local drives typically start at the beginning of the alphabet and occupy the drive letters A: through the drive set with the DOS LASTDRIVE variable. Beyond this point, the drive letters in the remainder of the alphabet are available for mapping network drives, up to the point that they encounter search drive mappings. Search drive mappings are assigned from the end of the alphabet and progress toward the beginning. There is a limit of 16 search drive mappings in NetWare. This means that it is possible to use drives Z:–K: in search drive maps if one of these letters is not used as a network drive. The range of search drives will increase to accommodate network drive mappings and still support up to 16 search drives. If a drive letter is not used as a local drive letter or as a search drive map, it may be used to map network drives.

USING LOCAL DRIVE MAPS

The number of drives that are reserved by DOS as local drives can be controlled by a statement in the CONFIG.SYS file for a workstation. By including a LASTDRIVE=[DRIVE LETTER] statement in the CONFIG.SYS file, you reserve the drives A: through [DRIVE LETTER] as local drives. For example, if a workstation CONFIG.SYS file contains the line

    LASTDRIVE=G

the first available network drive will be drive H:. If there is no CONFIG.SYS file, or if it does not include a LASTDRIVE specification, NetWare will use the default LASTDRIVE for your version of DOS.

USING NETWORK DRIVE MAPS

By default the first available network drive is mapped to the login directory of the SYS: volume when the workstation software is loaded. Once

NOTE
**You can only map
drives after logging in.**

mapped, you can change to this drive just as you would a local drive. Assuming drive F: is the first available network drive, you can go directly to F:\LOGIN after loading the network shell by typing **F:**↵ at the command prompt. Once you're logged into the network, NetWare takes over to map network drives. To see the current map, type **MAP**↵ when logged into the network. The default drive mappings for NetWare appear in Figure 8.19.

▶ . . . . ◀

The NetWare Default

Drive Mappings

```
Drive  A:    maps to a local disk.
Drive  B:    maps to a local disk.
Drive  C:    maps to a local disk.
Drive  D:    maps to a local disk.
Drive  E:    maps to a local disk.
Drive  F: = CICERO\SYS:  \
       -----
SEARCH1:  = Z:.  [CICERO\SYS:   \PUBLIC]
SEARCH2:  = Y:.  [CICERO\SYS:   \]
```

To map additional drive letters to network drives, you use MAP like this:

MAP [DRIVE LETTER]:=[SERVER]\[VOLUME]:[PATH]

The directory path following the volume is optional. For example, if we had another volume defined on the server CICERO called VOL1:, we could map this volume into drive G: with the following command:

MAP G:=CICERO\VOL1:↵

To map G: to CICERO in the PUBLIC\TEMP directory of the SYS: volume, the command becomes:

MAP G:=CICERO\SYS:PUBLIC\TEMP↵

Changing drive mappings is a matter of specifying the path a drive should map to. If you were to change to drive G: and use the change-directory command to move to the PUBLIC directory on the SYS: volume, you would find that this alters the drive map just as it would on a local

drive. You could accomplish exactly the same thing with the following command:

    MAP G:=CICERO\SYS:PUBLIC↵

In addition to specifying alternate directories on the same volume, you can specify different volumes and even different servers. For example, the command

    MAP G:=TOLSTOY\VOL1:HOME↵

would map drive G: to a different server, volume, and path. If you were not attached to TOLSTOY when you performed the map, your user name on TOLSTOY, and a password (if you had one) would be requested before the MAP assignment could be completed.

NOTE
To MAP a drive letter to a server volume, you must have privileges to either a directory or at least to a file on that volume.

USING SEARCH DRIVE MAPS

Under DOS, you can set a variable named *PATH* that tells the operating system which directories to search when the user requests a file execution. DOS begins at the beginning of the list of directory paths and searches every directory in the list until it finds the requested file; if it doesn't find the file, DOS returns an error message.

Under NetWare, search maps serve exactly the same purpose. NetWare's default login script sets up a search path to the PUBLIC directory on the SYS: volume. Without this search drive, you would have to change to the PUBLIC directory in order to run any utilities stored there. With the search drive, you can run these utilities from any location. If you install an application or set of utilities that you need to be able to run from any location on the network, you can set up a search path to the desired directory. Setting search drive mappings is very similar to setting network drive mappings. The commands

    MAP INS S1:=CICERO\SYS:PUBLIC ↵
    MAP INS S2:=CICERO\SYS:\PUBLIC\MS-DOS\IBM_PC\V5.00 ↵

map the first two search drives (by convention drives Z: and Y:) to the public directory of CICERO's SYS: volume and to the shared copy of MS-DOS 5.0. To map the next search drive to the UTIL directory on VOL1: of TOLSTOY, you could use the following command:

MAP INS S3:=TOLSTOY\VOL1:UTIL⏎

You can continue this process to map up to sixteen search paths. If you do not know what the next available search drive is, you can substitute S16 to automatically select the next available drive:

MAP INS S16:=TOLSTOY\SYS:EMAIL⏎

Network drive mappings use part of the file server's memory out of the Alloc (short-term) Memory Pool, which in turn pulls memory as necessary from the File Cache Buffers into the Permanent Memory Pool. Once memory has been allocated from the File Cache Buffers to the Permanent Memory Pool, it cannot be recovered without shutting down the file server. Since File Cache Buffers are used to implement performance features in NetWare (like file caching, directory hashing, and directory caching), it is best to use as few search drive mappings as possible. Similarly, there is a limited number of drive letters available for use as local, network, and search drives. The more search drives used, the fewer drive letters are available to map as network drives.

Summary

In this chapter, we've covered a lot of ground about laying a foundation for your network. We discussed NetWare directory structures, setting up new users, setting up new groups, adding users to groups, and setting up the users' environments through drive mappings and search paths. In Chapter 9, we'll continue the process of building your network by showing you how to automate setting up your users' environments with login scripts and batch files.

Creating the
User Interface

Fast Track

As the system administrator, you have a tremendous amount of control over the look and feel of your network. Your users will see the network as the interface you present them, so try to provide a stable consistent interface for all of them. NetWare's login script commands, login script variables, and menu utilities assist you in setting up this interface.

Login scripts are used to perform routine tasks such as:

▶ mapping drives and search paths

▶ setting up environment and system variables

▶ providing a common user interface during the login process

▶ providing your users with any timely information that might affect their use of the network

In particular, you can use the system login script (a server-wide script executed for all users) to provide a consistent environment for everyone. If your users will not be using a graphical user interface (GUI) like Microsoft Windows, consider using the Novell or third-party menu utilities to provide a convenient way for your users to access the applications and resources they need. You can configure generic menus that apply to any user who needs them.

In this chapter, we'll describe the different login scripts used by NetWare and the purposes of each. Then we'll follow with a description of the syntax for login script commands and an explanation of script variables and how to use them. When we discuss the creation of login scripts, we'll describe how to distribute the tasks to be performed into the appropriate script. We'll describe the use of DOS batch files to dynamically modify the settings and drive mappings assigned at login time. Finally, we will cover the Novell menu system command structure and present a strategy for developing network menus.

Types of Login Scripts

When a user logs in to the network, at least one and typically more than one login script is executed. If you are on a new server that does not have customized scripts, a script called the *default login script* is run. This script is a very basic script that is *hard-coded* into the utility LOGIN.EXE. The default login script automatically maps the first available network drive to the SYS: volume of the current server, maps the first search path to the public directory, and maps the second search path to the SYS: volume. You can create two different types of scripts that will override the default login script:

- System login script
- User login script

THE SYSTEM LOGIN SCRIPT

The system login script is the first script run when a user logs into the network. Usually, this script contains commands to perform generalized drive mappings and other setups that might be necessary to maintain consistency for all users within an organization. The system login script can and should be used to set up a common environment for all network users. For example, this script might link all users into a shared e-mail system, display a system-wide message reminding users about upcoming scheduled maintenance and set up initial drive mappings and search drives common to all users.

USER LOGIN SCRIPTS

A user login script is a script that personalizes the user's environment after the previous scripts have set up at least the bare minimum needed to maintain a consistent environment. This script might set up a user's personal e-mail name, map a search path to a favorite utilities directory or start a personal menuing system.

Login Script Commands and Variables

Login scripts are ASCII text files that contain valid login script commands and variables. The program LOGIN.EXE interprets these instructions and takes the appropriate action. For the sake of simplicity and ease of maintenance, there are a few conventions that apply to login scripts:

▶ For greater readability, keep individual lines within a login script under 78 characters long (they can be up to 150 characters long).

▶ There can only be one login script command per line and each command in a login script should end with a carriage return. Commands that wrap onto additional lines but do not contain a carriage return are still considered a single command.

▶ Commands may be written in either uppercase or lowercase, but variable names should be typed in uppercase.

The commands that appear in Table 9.1 may be used in either system or user login scripts.

Many of the commands in Table 9.1 base their actions on values stored in login script or DOS variables. Variables allow you to write general purpose user login scripts that can be copied from one user to another without extensive modification. Even so, the more you put into the system login

TABLE 9.1 *Login Script Commands*	COMMAND	EXPLANATION AND EXAMPLES
	# program arguments	# causes external program execution. If possible, the command that follows the pound sign in the login script will be executed from the command line.
		For example, to clear the screen and run a user's menu system, include the # command and command line instructions in the user's personal login script:
		# cls # menu croes

TABLE 9.1

Login Script Commands

(continued)

COMMAND	EXPLANATION AND EXAMPLES
ATTACH *server/username; password*	ATTACH is used to automatically connect a user to more than one server during the login process. If the username and password parameters are not specified, the user will be prompted during the login process. If the server name is not specified, the program will attach to the current server (as reported by SLIST) and request a username and password.
	For example, if your users log into CICERO as their home server, but need access to a database on the server TOLSTOY, you can use attach to automatically log them into both servers when they log in to CICERO:
	``map display off`` ``attach TOLSTOY``
	If you work in a multiserver environment where users must attach to more than a couple of servers, you can simplify the login process by using NetWare's password synchronization features. If a user has the same username and password on the server he/she is attaching to, he/she will be attached without having to specify a username and password.
BREAK *on/off*	BREAK is used to specify the action to be taken if the user presses Ctrl-Break during the login process. If set to ON, the user can interrupt script execution by pressing Ctrl-Break. If set to OFF, the login script will prevent the user from exiting before the script has finished executing.
	Note that this command applies to login scripts only (see also DOS BREAK).
	For example, to prevent the user from exiting the script before the menuing system has been run, include the following commands in the login script:

	``BREAK OFF``
	``#cls``
	``# menu secure``

COMMAND	EXPLANATION AND EXAMPLES
COMSPEC [*path*]*filename*	COMSPEC specifies where the command processor (usually COMMAND.COM) can be found on network drives. Some programs remove the DOS command interpreter during execution to gain access to more memory. When these programs terminate, the DOS command processor must be reloaded.
	Although any valid path to the command processor will work, typically this variable will be set to search path number two (S2):
	MAP S2:=SYS:PUBLIC\%MACHINE\%OS\ %OS_VERSION COMSPEC=S2:COMMAND.COM
	where S2 is mapped to the directory that contains the particular version of the operating system running on the workstation.
DISPLAY [*path*]*filename* or FDISPLAY [*path*]*filename*	DISPLAY and FDISPLAY are used to display text files or other messages to users as they log in. Using these commands with conditionals, you can display a message-of-the-day or weekly reminders.
	DISPLAY is used when the file to be displayed contains only ASCII text. FDISPLAY (or Filtered DISPLAY) can be used when the file contains characters other than straight ASCII. FDISPLAY will remove all nondisplayable characters and tabs. If the specified path and file cannot be found, neither command will display an error message.
	For example, to display the message of the day to all members of the group ADMIN each time they log in before 10:00 am, use the following commands:
	IF MEMBER OF ADMIN AND HOUR24 <"10" THEN BEGIN DISPLAY SYS:PUBLIC\ MESSAGES\MOTD.TXT END

COMMAND	EXPLANATION AND EXAMPLES
DOS BREAK *on/off*	The DOS BREAK command is used to enable or disable the DOS BREAK facility. When DOS BREAK is set to *on* and the user presses the Ctrl-break key combination, the program will terminate the next time it makes an OS request. If DOS BREAK is set to *off*, this key sequence will have no effect.
DOS SET *variable* = *setvalue*	DOS SET can be used to assign DOS variables from within a login script. Once set, these variables can be used by batch files and other programs. For example, to set the DOS variable UNAME to the user's login name, use the following command in the login script: DOS SET UNAME="%LOGIN_NAME" Note: When using DOS SET to specify directory paths, you must use two backslashes wherever you need to specify a subdirectory. For example, to set the DOS variable INCLUDE to the include directory for Microsoft C, use the following command: DOS SET INCLUDE="R:\\ BIN\\C600\\INCLUDE"
DOS VERIFY *on/off*	DOS VERIFY determines whether or not files copied with the DOS copy command are automatically verified after the copy. The default is *off*. To set DOS verify to *on*, use the following command: DOS VERIFY ON
DRIVE [*driveletter:* or **drivenumber:*]	DRIVE sets the user's default drive under NetWare. Normally, the default drive is set to the first available network drive. Using the DRIVE command, you can override this value. For example, to set the user's default drive to H:, use the following command: DRIVE H:

COMMAND	EXPLANATION AND EXAMPLES
	Or, to set the default drive to drive number four, use the following command:
	DRIVE *4:
EXIT	EXIT can be used to cause immediate exiting from a login script. When used with an argument, it can exit the script and begin executing another program (like a menu program).
	Note: For the EXIT command to work with a computer that does not have the machine name IBM_PC, you must include the command PCCOMPATIBLE in the login script before the call to EXIT.
	For example, to exit the login script and start a user's menu program use the following command in the login script:
	EXIT "menu"
	Note: If you do not have *user* login scripts defined, the default user login script *will be* executed. This is sometimes undesirable as the default login script runs after the system login script and may override some of its settings. You can prevent the default login script from running by including an EXIT command in the system login script (this will also prevent user login scripts from running). If you don't want to execute another program, don't specify any arguments to EXIT. For example, use the command:
	EXIT
FIRE PHASERS N TIMES	FIRE PHASERS can be used to get the user's attention by causing sounds to be generated from the workstation's speaker.
	For example, to generate the phaser noise five times, use the following command in the login script:
	FIRE PHASERS 5 TIMES

COMMAND	EXPLANATION AND EXAMPLES
INCLUDE [*path*]*filename*	INCLUDE can be used to chain login scripts together. These *subscripts* are simply ASCII files that contain valid script commands. You may nest as many included script files as memory will allow. For example, to include a special script for all members of the group ACCT, include the following commands in the login script: IF MEMBER OF ACCT THEN BEGIN INCLUDE SYS:UTIL\SCRIPTS\ACCT.SCR END When you include an EXIT command in an included script, the subscript will execute and return to the parent (which will finish executing) before the EXIT instructions will be performed.
MACHINE="*name*"	MACHINE is used to reset the long machine type or set it if it was not set in the SHELL.CFG or NET.CFG. This command may be necessary when running NETBIOS programs. Machine names may be up to eight characters in length. Longer names will default to IBM_PC. For example, to set the long machine type to COMPAQ, use the following command: MACHINE="COMPAQ"
MAP [*options*] [*drive1*:=[*path1*]]; [*drive2*:=[*path2*]]where [*options*] = REM, DEL, INS, ROOT, DISPLAY [ON,OFF], ERRORS [ON/OFF]	MAP is probably the most-used command in script files. MAP performs several different functions controlled by *options*. The most prevalent of these operations is linking one of the 26 available drive letters to network volumes and search drives. Example of mapping a network volume to a drive letter: MAP H:=CICERO\VOL1:PROGRAMS

COMMAND	EXPLANATION AND EXAMPLES
	Example of mapping search drives:
	MAP S2:=SYS:PUBLIC\%MACHINE\ %OS_VERSION MAP S3:=SYS:UTILS
	To insert a new search path in front of S3 and move S3 to S4 in the previous example:
	MAP INSERT S3:=VOL1:PROGRAMS
	To remove drive mappings:
	MAP DEL S3 MAP DEL H:
PAUSE	PAUSE can be used to temporarily halt script execution and wait for the user to press a key.
	For example, to display a system message and give the user time to read it before going on, use:
	#CLS WRITE WRITE TO ALL USERS: WRITE WRITE The system will be down on THURSDAY from WRITE 10:00 am - 3:00 pm for hardware upgrades WRITE FIRE PHASERS 2 TIMES PAUSE

COMMAND	EXPLANATION AND EXAMPLES
PCCOMPATIBLE	PCCOMPATIBLE is used to tell the script interpreter that the workstation running the login script is compatible with the IBM PC and is running MS-DOS. If you want to use the EXIT command with computers whose machine name is not set to IBM_PC, you will need to use this command.
REMARK or REM	REM tells the script interpreter to ignore anything that follows on the same line. This command is used to include comments in scripts: REM This script executes for all members of the group ACCT IF MEMBER OF ACCT THEN BEGIN MAP ... END
SHIFT *n*	SHIFT is useful for system administrators who require a great deal of flexibility in their login scripts and who are doing batch-file programming in DOS. SHIFT allows you to shift the command line arguments of the LOGIN.EXE program *n* places to the right. Negative values will shift the command line arguments to the left. The first command line argument (%0) is the program name, the second (%1) becomes the next argument, and so on. By default, DOS will only accept ten command line parameters (%0-%9). By using the shift command, we can increase the maximum number of allowable arguments. Each successively shifted argument becomes available as %9. For example, to get access to the eleventh and twelfth argument in the following command line: F:\LOGIN> LOGIN CROES DOE RAY ME FA SO LA TEE DOE SEE SPOT RUN

COMMAND	EXPLANATION AND EXAMPLES
	Use the following commands:
	IF "%1" = "CROES" THEN …
	IF "%2" = " DOE" THEN …
	.
	.
	.
	IF " %9" = " DOE" THEN …
	REM and now we use shift to get to argument 11
	SHIFT 2
	IF " %9"=" SPOT" THEN …
	REM now we use shift to get to argument 12
	SHIFT 1
	IF " %9"=" RUN" THEN …
WRITE *"message"*	WRITE is used to send messages to the workstation's screen. Each message appears on a separate line unless the message ends in a semicolon. Lines ending in a semicolon are concatenated together onto the same line.
	For example, to say hello (appropriately for the time of day) to a user who is logging into the network, use the following commands in the login script:
	WRITE "Good %GREETING_TIME %FULL_NAME"
	WRITE "It is currently %HOUR:%MINUTE on %DAY_OF_WEEK"

TABLE 9.1
Login Script Commands
(continued)

COMMAND	EXPLANATION AND EXAMPLES
	You may also include compound strings and super characters in strings to be interpreted by WRITE: Super Characters: \r print a carriage return \n print a new line \" print the quote character \7 sound the system bell Compound Strings (these occur outside of quoted strings): ; concatenate previous and following strings * multiply two numbers / divide two numbers % modulo (remainder results of division) + add two numbers - subtract two numbers >>n shift right by n (truncate last n characters) <<n shift left by n (truncate first n characters)
IF...THEN...ELSE	The IF...THEN...ELSE command is the only control structure implemented in login scripts. This structure will perform conditional commands based on any of the available DOS or script variables (see Appendix A of the NetWare Installation Manual for a complete listing).

T A B L E 9.1	
Login Script Commands *(continued)*	

COMMAND	EXPLANATION AND EXAMPLES
	The IF…THEN…ELSE structure understands AND, OR, and NOR logical operations and the following relations:
	EQUAL may be represented as IS, =, ==, and EQUALS
	NOT EQUAL may be represented as IS NOT, !=, <>, DOES NOT EQUAL, and NOT EQUAL TO
	Other conditionals may be written out in all caps or in symbols:
	IS GREATER THAN is the same as (>)
	IS LESS THAN is the same as (<)
	IS GREATER THAN OR EQUAL TO is the same as (>=)
	IS LESS THAN OR EQUAL TO is the same as (<=)
	For example, the following two script segments perform the same functions:

```
IF LOGIN_NAME == "SUPERVISOR" THEN
    MAP H: =CICERO/SYS:SYSTEM
    MAP INSERT S5:=CICERO/SYS:SYSTEM
ELSE
    MAP H: =CICERO/VOL1:HOME/
    %LOGIN_NAME
ENDIF
```

```
IF LOGIN_NAME IS EQUAL TO
"SUPERVISOR" THEN BEGIN
    MAP H: =CICERO/SYS:SYSTEM
    MAP INS S5:=CICERO/SYS:SYSTEM
ELSE
    MAP H: =CICERO/VOL1:HOME/
    %LOGIN_NAME
ENDIF
```

script, the less of a maintenance headache you create for yourself. The list below shows the variables NetWare makes available during login scripts. For examples, see *Putting the Pieces Together* below.

VARIABLE	FUNCTION
<dos_variable>	Uses the DOS environment variable *dos_variable* as a string.
ACCESS_SERVER	Returns TRUE if the Access Server is allowing multiple NetWare AnyWhere sessions and FALSE otherwise.
AM_PM	Returns AM during the morning, PM during the day and evening.
DAY	Returns the current day of the month (01–31).
DAY_OF_WEEK	Returns the text for the day of the week (Monday, Tuesday, …)
ERROR_LEVEL	Returns the current DOS error level. The value will be nonzero if an error has occurred.
FILE_SERVER	Returns the name of the current file server.
FULL_NAME	Returns the user's full name as specified in SYSCON.
GREETING_TIME	Returns *morning*, *afternoon*, or *evening* depending on the time of day.
HOUR	Returns the time of day in twelve-hour format (1–12).
HOUR24	Returns the time of day in twenty-four hour format (00–23, with midnight = 00).

VARIABLE	FUNCTION
LOGIN_NAME	Returns the user's login name.
MACHINE	Returns the value set in the SHELL.CFG or NET.CFG files for Long Machine Type or the value set by the script . Otherwise it returns FALSE.
MEMBER OF "group"	Returns TRUE if the user is a member of group.
MINUTE	Returns the current minute (00–59).
MONTH	Returns the current month number (01–12).
MONTH_NAME	Returns the current month (January, February, ….).
NDAY_OF_WEEK	Returns the number for the day of the week (1–7, with Sunday = 1).
NETWORK_ ADDRESS	Returns the network address of the current network segment (XXXX XXXX h).
OS	Returns the workstations operating system (MS-DOS, etc.).
OS_VERSION	Returns the version of the operating system running on the workstation (vX.XX).
P_STATION	Returns the node address for the workstation (XXXX XXXX XXXX h).
SECOND	Returns the current second (00–59).
SHELL_TYPE	Returns the workstation's shell version.

VARIABLE	FUNCTION
SHORT_YEAR	Returns the current year in short format (93, 94, …).
SMACHINE	Returns the short machine name (IBMPC, etc.).
STATION	Returns the current connection number.
USER_ID	Returns the USER ID for the current user.
YEAR	Returns the current year (1993, 1994, etc.).

Creating System Login Scripts

The system login script is stored in a file in the PUBLIC directory of the SYS: volume called NET$LOG.DAT. The standard procedure for editing or creating this file is to access it from the Supervisor Options menu of SYS-CON; but any ASCII text editor can be used to edit it as well.

To create or edit a system login script, run SYSCON and select the Supervisor Options menu. One of the options listed will be System Login Script. Highlight this option and press ↵ to bring up the editing screen. If there is no system login script, this screen will be empty; otherwise the current system login script will be displayed.

SETTING UP DRIVE MAPS

As you may recall from Chapter 8, it would be somewhat cumbersome to have to map all your network drives and search paths manually after each login. Setting up drive mappings and search drives is an ideal procedure to put into the system or user login scripts.

TIP
SYSCON flags the NET$LOG.DAT file read-only, so you must remove this attribute before editing it—and reset it afterwards, if you are using a text editor instead of SYSCON.

The search paths and drive mappings that are common to all users are placed in the system login script. By convention, NetWare specifies that the first two search drives be mapped to SYS:PUBLIC and to the location of the OS files for the workstation. Setting up the first drive mapping (S1) is simple:

MAP S1:=SYS:PUBLIC

If you've specified the parameter long machine type in the NET.CFG file, you're already halfway there. If not, we'll show you how to set the variable for long machine type from the user's personal login script and use this to map S2. For now, we'll assume that you have specified the parameter in the configuration files and cover the other method under *Creating a User Login Script*.

Specifying S2 in the System Login Script

Each DOS workstation on the network will want access to a shared copy of its operating system files stored on the network. As we discussed in Chapter 8, only one copy of each unique OS version need be stored on the network for a given machine type. For our example, let's assume your network comprises the following PCs:

COMPAQ DESKPRO running MS-DOS V4.01

COMPAQ DESKPRO running COMPAQ DOS V5.00

HP VECTRA running MS-DOS V5.00

IBM PS/2 Model 50 running MS-DOS V5.00

PC Clone running MS-DOS V3.30

IBM PC-AT running MS-DOS V3.20

ACER 1100 running ACER DOS V4.00

The best and easiest way to fix this problem is to standardize DOS versions. But for the sake of this example, you will need six different versions of the DOS operating system stored on your network server to support these computers. In addition to the different OS versions, you will need to support three machine types. True, there are in fact five different computer manufacturers listed, but there are only three unique operating system suppliers in the list.

You need to identify unique versions of the OS—not necessarily unique hardware manufacturers—so that you can minimize the number of copies of the operating system that have to be stored. We have two COMPAQ DOS versions, two MS-DOS versions, and an ACER DOS version uniquely defined in our list of computers. The resulting directory tree needed to store these files would look something like Figure 9.1.

Given the directory structure appearing in Figure 9.1, there are three login script variables that can help determine where to specify the S2 drive mapping:

MACHINE	Identifies the computer's manufacturer and is set in either the SHELL.CFG/NET.CFG files or in the user's personal login script with the command MACHINE.
OS	Identifies the operating system and is reported directly by the operating system itself.
OS_VERSION	Identifies the version of the OS running on the workstation. It is reported directly by the operating system as well.

These variables must be preceded by the percent sign (%) when used in login scripts. For example, to map the second search path for one of the workstations in our list, we could use the following command:

```
MAP S2:=SYS:PUBLIC\%MACHINE\%OS\%OS_VERSION
```

F I G U R E 9.1

The PUBLIC directory with

DOS directories

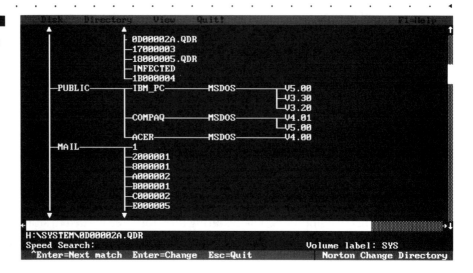

Once this search path has been mapped, we can set the COMSPEC parameter equal to search path two.

The COMSPEC script command specifies the location of the DOS command interpreter. Some applications will remove the DOS command interpreter from memory during execution to get access to the memory it occupies. When these applications terminate, the command interpreter must be reloaded. If COMSPEC has not been set, you will probably receive the following error message just before your PC locks up:

> cannot load COMMAND.COM
> System Halted

COMSPEC uses the S2 mapping as follows:

> COMSPEC=S2:COMMAND.COM

Specifying Other Search Paths

If you use applications on the network that need to be called from a search path, map a search drive to the directory where they are stored. NetWare ranks the search paths in increasing order from drive Z: backwards through the alphabet (e.g., Z:= S1:, Y:=S2, and so on). Because NetWare searches the search paths in this order, you should map the applications and utilities used most often among the leading search drives. For example, to map the next available search drive to the utilities directory on the file server, include the following command in the system login script if the next available search drive is known:

MAP S3:=SYS:UTIL

If the next available search drive is *not* known, use this instead:

MAP S16:=SYS:UTIL

Once done, any of the executable files located in the utilities directory will be available.

Search Drives and the PATH Variable

Before you login to the network, your workstation probably has a system variable called PATH that defines the directories searched by DOS to find an executable file that has been requested. The PATH is normally replaced by search drive mappings when you log in into the network file server. For example, suppose that the workstation has the following PATH before logging into the network:

PATH=C:\;C:\DOS;C:\CD-ROM;C:\UTILS;C:\W51

After the three search drives discussed in the previous section have been mapped, the PATH at the workstation would become:

PATH=Z:;Y:;X:;C:\UTILS;C:\W51

The first three items in the PATH have been replaced by the network search drive mappings.

If some of the search paths specified in the workstation's PATH variable are critical to the workstation's operation, you'll need to specify search drive mappings with the INSERT option. For example, if the CD-ROM player will stop functioning if the path to its files is removed, you'll need to prevent the path from being overwritten by using the INSERT modifier after the call to MAP and before the specification of the path:

```
MAP INSERT S1:=SYS:PUBLIC
MAP INSERT S2:=SYS:PUBLIC\%MACHINE\%OS\
%OS_VERSION
MAP INSERT S3:=SYS:UTIL
```

Calling MAP this way will result in the following path for the workstation after login:

```
PATH=Z:;Y:;X:;C:\;C:\DOS;C:\CD-ROM;C:\UTILS;C:\W51
```

As you can see, the three search drives have been placed in front of the DOS path that was already present.

Using the INSERT option to place the network search drive mappings ahead of the normal PATH is usually a good default for the entire network, but it's not without its limitations. The DOS PATH is an environment variable that can only hold a finite amount of information. If the defined path extends beyond this length, it will be truncated. By the same token, only 16 search drive mappings may be specified in NetWare and each of them requires a portion of the file server's memory. The bottom line is to map search paths only to those directories necessary. (You can use batch files to dynamically map search drives and network drive mappings to get around these limitations—see *Writing Batch Files with Dynamic Drive Mapping* later in this chapter.)

Mapping Network Volumes

Mapping network volumes in the system or user login scripts is simply a matter of including exactly the same commands described in Chapter 8 in the script file. In general, there should be at least one drive letter mapped to each volume on your file server to which users need access. For example, if your file server has two volumes defined as SYS: and VOL1:, map a drive letter to each volume so you can access the drive without specifying its full path each time. To do this, include the following commands in the system login script:

```
MAP F:=SYS:
MAP G:=VOL1:
```

In addition to the drive maps for each volume, it is useful to map additional drives to be used for dynamic drive mapping from within batch files and menus. This way, at least two drive letters are left as constants that point to the file server volumes. You can map the other drive letters to application directories, data directories, or even other servers as needed.

Mapping a Home Directory

A home directory is home base to network users. This is the directory under which the users may create files and make subdirectories, and is usually where they will launch applications and utilities. In addition to the drive maps for each volume and the free drive maps (for dynamic mapping), it is a good idea to map a separate drive to the user's home directory during login. This gives the users a place to go where their files are stored and which does not change unless they specifically remap the drive to another location.

To map a user's home directory and make the drive mapping the default drive when the user logs in, use the following commands in the system login script:

```
MAP H:=VOL1:HOME\%LOGIN_NAME
DRIVE H:
```

When users log in to the network, they will automatically be placed in their home directory.

DEFINING OTHER ENVIRONMENTAL PARAMETERS

Most *network-aware* applications will use a user name scheme to set up default directories, menu structures, color palettes, and the like. In many cases, these applications will allow you to specify the user name from the command line when the program is started. Instead of having your users memorize a (typically unique) user name for each network application they use, you can specify DOS variables in the login script that will set their respective user names. To do this, use the DOS SET command to assign the appropriate variable names.

For example, the character-based version of WordPerfect 5.1 for Networks uses a three-character user name to identify a network user. Based on this name, WP.EXE will change its menu setup, default directories, default printers, and other parameters unique to a particular user. The user name may be specified on the command line or interactively through menus. To automatically perform this operation for the user, you set a DOS variable to the user's WordPerfect user name in the login script and place the variable on the command line in the user's menu:

```
DOS SET WPUSER=T1C
DRIVE=H:
EXIT "MENU USERS"
```

When the menu calls up WordPerfect, the variable WPUSER can be placed on the command line to automatically log the user into the program. For example, the command line for WordPerfect would be:

```
WP /U=%WPUSER%.
```

NOTE
DOS variables use a percent sign both before and after the variable name.

SETTING NETWORK PRINTING PARAMETERS

When printing to network printers, there are typically two ways to route the print jobs to a network print queue. If you are using network-aware applications or NetWare utilities to print, the application will print directly to a print queue by specifying the queue name. Non–network-aware applications assume that they are printing to local printers attached to LPT ports on the workstation. For these types of applications to print on the network, the CAPTURE utility is used to *redirect* the output intended for a local port to one of the network's print queues. The commands that set up print capturing can be included in the system or user login scripts.

For example, to capture a workstation's local LPT ports 1 and 2 to a network laser printer queue and a wide-carriage dot-matrix printer queue automatically during login, include the following commands in a login script:

```
#CAPTURE /L=1 /Q=LASER /NB /NFF /NT /TI=5
#CAPTURE /L=2 /Q=WIDEPRINT /NB /NFF /NT /TI=5
```

Notice that you can include any of the normal CAPTURE parameters as well. (See *Establishing Network Printer Services* in Chapter 11 and Appendix A, *NetWare 3.12 Utilities Summary,* for more information.)

DISPLAYING A WELCOME MESSAGE

Part of creating a consistent user interface is displaying the same type of information to the users each time they log in. Consider creating a "welcome screen" that users see every time they log in. When the login process is consistent, the network users become able to inform you when something has changed or there is a network problem. (They might not be happy when they do, but they may discover the problem before you do.)

By using some of the parameters NetWare makes available to login scripts, you can make the login message informative as well as consistent. For example, the following script segment displays the login message for our test file server CICERO.

```
WRITE " "
WRITE "  Good ";GREETING_TIME;
WRITE ", "; FULL_NAME;". "
WRITE " You are logged on station: ";STATION; " using " ;
WRITE OS; " "; OS_VERSION
WRITE " Current time and date: "; HOUR;":";
MINUTE;":";SECOND;
WRITE " - "; DAY_OF_WEEK; " "; MONTH_NAME;" ";DAY;
    ", ";YEAR
WRITE " "

#WHOAMI
```

As you can see, this example greets the user, gives the date and time, and specifies the user name used to log into each server if the user is attached to more than one.

PUTTING THE PIECES TOGETHER

Up to now, we've been looking at individual tasks that you can put into a login script. Here, we've listed them all together in our example system login script. In this example, we attach another file server, map network drives and search paths, map a home directory, capture a local printer port, set the COMSPEC variable (for the location of the command interpreter), and display an informative greeting.

```
ATTACH TOLSTOY

MAP DISPLAY OFF
MAP F:=CICERO/SYS:
MAP G:=CICERO/VOL1:
MAP I:=TOLSTOY/SYS:
MAP V:=TOLSTOY/SYS:PROGRAMS
MAP INSERT S1:=CICERO/SYS:PUBLIC
MAP INSERT
S2:=CICERO/SYS:DOS\%MACHINE\%OS\%OS_VERSION
MAP INSERT S3:=CICERO/SYS:UTIL
MAP INSERT S4:=TOLSTOY/SYS:UTIL

IF LOGIN_NAME == "SUPERVISOR" THEN
    MAP H: =CICERO/SYS:SYSTEM
    MAP INSERT S5:=CICERO/SYS:SYSTEM
ELSE
    MAP H: =CICERO/VOL1:HOME/%LOGIN_NAME
ENDIF

#CAPTURE /TI=10 /I=3 /S=TOLSTOY /Q=HP_LASER_III NB NFF

COMSPEC = S2:COMMAND.COM

WRITE " "
WRITE " Good ";GREETING_TIME;
```

```
WRITE ", "; FULL_NAME;". "
WRITE " You are logged on station: ";STATION; " using " ;
WRITE OS; " "; OS_VERSION
WRITE " Current time and date: "; HOUR;":";
MINUTE;":";SECOND;
WRITE " - "; DAY_OF_WEEK; " "; MONTH_NAME;" ";DAY;
    ", ";YEAR
WRITE " "

#WHOAMI

DRIVE H:
```

If your users will not be using user login scripts, place the EXIT command at the end of the system login script to prevent the default login script from executing. If some users, but not others, will be using user login scripts, place the EXIT command in the scripts of users who would not have a user login script otherwise.

TESTING THE SYSTEM LOGIN SCRIPT

To ensure that you are only running the system login script during testing, include the EXIT command with no arguments as the last line in your system login script. If you don't do this, the default login script will be executed and may overwrite some of the settings from the system login script.

Log in as the SUPERVISOR and watch the login procedure for anything that looks unexpected. When the script has finished executing, check that the login script has placed you in the proper directory. You can use the MAP command without any arguments to verify that the drive mappings have been properly set and use the CAPTURE /SH command to see if the printer setup has been performed. After you have verified the system login script as the SUPERVISOR, try logging in as another user who does not have supervisor privileges. You may find that this will affect the way the login script acts.

It may take a few attempts to get everything right. Once you have a working system login script, *make a backup copy!* The file is stored in the PUBLIC directory of the SYS: volume in a file called NET$LOG.DAT.

TIP
Test your system login script first as **SUPERVISOR** and then as a user without supervisor privileges.

Creating a User Login Script

Creating user login scripts is very similar to creating the system login script. In some cases, user login scripts will be unnecessary. If you need to create them, you can do so from the User Information menu of SYSCON. Run SYSCON, select a particular user, and select Login Script from the User Information menu to edit the user's login script. If the user already has a login script, the editing screen will appear. If the user does not have a login script, a window will prompt you for the name of a user to copy an existing script from. This is a handy way of copying login scripts from one user to another.

The types of things to put in the user login scripts are commands that relate only to particular users or parameters that you want to control on an individual basis. If you must specify the parameter MACHINE in the user login script, include the command MACHINE=*manufacturer*, where *manufacturer* is the code you have chosen to identify the directory where unique versions of the operating system for these computers are stored. Once you've specified this parameter, add the command to map the second search path in the login script:

MAP S2:=SYS:PUBLIC\%MACHINE\%OS\%OS_VERSION

Once you've finished editing the user login script, press Esc to save it. User login scripts are stored in the user's mail directory (identified by the user's USER ID) in the SYS:MAIL directory. The file will be called LOGIN without any extension. To find out a user's USER ID, use SYSCON to view Additional Information for a particular user. The USER ID for the selected user will appear there.

Writing Batch Files with Dynamic Drive Mapping

As indicated in Chapter 8, each search drive mapping takes away one of the 26 available drive letters. To alleviate the problem of not having enough drives for search and network drive mappings to the most frequently used applications, you can use batch files to dynamically map drive letters as they are needed. The batch files may be kept in the users' home directory or in SYS:PUBLIC so that all may have access to them.

For example, let's assume that a user in accounting needs to use two applications: an accounts receivable system and Lotus 1-2-3. Further, let's assume that the 1-2-3 spreadsheets are stored in a data directory called WPS and that the accounting package is completely unsophisticated and requires that its data files be saved in the root directory of the data drive. (This is a very bad procedure on network drives. Once a user has access to the root of a volume, they have access to all subdirectories as well.) To minimize the number of drive letters that must be mapped, we'll dynamically map the drives before each application is loaded.

To do this for Lotus, we would map one drive to the directory where the Lotus executables are stored and another to the data directory:

```
@echo off
MAP K:=VOL1:PROGRAMS\LOTUS
MAP L:=VOL1:DATA\WPS
K:
123
H:
```

Using this example, both the executable program and data drives are mapped and the application is run. While the user is working, he or she should know to always save data files to drive L:. When the user exits the application, he or she will be placed in the proper home directory.

When running the accounting application, we would use the MAP ROOT command to trick the application into thinking it is accessing the

WARNING
If a user has access rights to the root directory of a network volume, they have the same rights in any subdirectory on the volume, unless specifically prevented. See *Using the Inherited Rights Mask* in Chapter 10 for more information.

root of the data drive. To map the drives for the Accounts Receivable package, we would use the following batch file.

```
@echo off
MAP K:=VOL1:ACCT\AR
MAP ROOT L:=VOL1:ACCT\DATA
K:
AR
H:
```

Since we have used the MAP ROOT command, the AR application won't know that it isn't writing to the root directory of the data drive. Using these types of batch files, it is possible to reuse the same set of drives (at times more than two may be needed) to run different network applications.

To deal with the accounting application, we'll use the NetWare MAP ROOT command to specify that a particular directory on a network volume emulate the root directory of a DOS drive.

Creating Menu Programs in NetWare 3.12

NetWare 3.12 includes a different menu-creation utility than that included in previous versions of NetWare. The NetWare 3.12 NMENU utility is actually a trimmed-down version of the Saber Menu System for DOS, created by Saber Software Corporation.

Using NMENU, you can create your own menu programs for your users. If you are upgrading an existing NetWare network to NetWare 3.12, and you already have menu programs that you created using the earlier MENU utility, you can use NMENU to convert those older menus. The following sections explain how to create new menu programs and how to update old ones.

NOTE
If you're using Net-Ware 3.11, see the next section, *Using the NetWare 3.11 Menu Utility*, for instructions on building a menu.

CREATING NEW MENU PROGRAMS

To create a menu program in NetWare 3.12, you first use a text editor to create a text file containing the commands you want the menu program to execute. Then you use the MENUMAKE utility, which takes the text file and "compiles" it into a program file. To execute the menu program file, use the NMENU utility.

The commands you can use in the text file to create your menu program are described below:

COMMAND	EFFECT
MENU	Identifies the heading of a menu or submenu.
ITEM	Indicates an option that will be displayed in the menu.
EXEC	Executes the commands necessary to complete an ITEM option when the user selects it.
SHOW	Displays a submenu.
LOAD	Displays a submenu from a different menu program.
GETR	Requests input from the user that is required for a menu item to be executed.
GETO	Requests input from the user that is optional.
GETP	Requests input from the user and assigns a variable to that input so that it can be reused.

To create this menu, first create two directories to hold the program and the temporary files that the menu program will generate. The temporary directories can be on the network or on the user's hard disk. Then use a text editor to create the following file. The text file has to be named with the extension .SRC or it cannot be compiled by the MENUMAKE utility. In this case, we'll name the file MANAGERS.SRC.

```
MENU 1, Select a Task
  ITEM ^SSpreadsheet
    SHOW 2
  ITEM ^WWord Processing
    EXEC WP
  ITEM ^MMail
    GETR Enter your email name: { } 8,, { }
    EXEC EMAIL
  ITEM ^EExit to DOS
    EXEC DOS
  ITEM ^LLogout
    EXEC LOGOUT

MENU 2, Choose a Spreadsheet File
  ITEM ^BBudget
    EXEC COUNT BUDGET
  ITEM ^IInventory
    EXEC COUNT INV
```

Notice that the sections of the file pertaining to each menu or submenu are separated from each other by a space, and the commands for each item within a menu are indented. Each ITEM command, which indicates an option on a menu, is followed by the EXEC command that executes that option.

In this menu, we want users to be able to select an item from the menu by typing the first letter of the option. To accomplish this, add a carat (^) and the letter that should be typed to the beginning of the ITEM command.

Under the Mail ITEM, the following GETR command appears:

GETR Enter your email name: { } 8,, { }

This command asks the user for his or her email user name before the option executes the command to load the email application. The syntax for the GETR command is as follows:

GETR *text {prepend} length, default, {append}*

In this example, the *text* is the statement "Enter your email name:". The *prepend* value is any value that should be automatically supplied to the beginning of the user's input. In this case, no value is needed, so type a blank space inside the brackets. The *length* indicates the maximum number of characters that a user's input can be. In our example, a user's email name can be up to eight characters long, so the supervisor entered the number 8. The next field in the commands lets you enter a default value that the user can select. However, for this menu there is no default user name, so we enter no value here. The two commas, however, are necessary; they show that there is no default value. Finally, the last field, *append* lets you enter any value that should be added to the end of the user's input. Again, in this example there is no value needed, so the brackets contain only a space.

After we finish creating the text file and save it as MANAGERS.SRC, it's time to compile the file. Instructions for compiling the menu file and adding commands to the login script to automate the menu program are explained later in this chapter. For more information about the creating and using menu programs with NMENU in NetWare 3.12, refer to the *NetWare 3.12 Utilities Reference* manual.

CONVERTING OLD MENU PROGRAMS

If you have a menu program that you created using earlier versions of NetWare's MENU utility, you can convert that menu program into an NMENU program. The older menu files have the .MNU extension, such as CLERKS.MNU.

To convert a menu file, complete the following steps.

1 • Create two directories to hold the program and the temporary files that the menu program will generate. The temporary directories can be on the network or on the user's hard disk. If you already have menu directories for your existing menu programs, you can use those directories.

2 · Use the MENUCNVT utility and specify the name of the menu file you wish to convert. The utility will create a new file with the .SRC file name extension, and will leave the old .MNU file unchanged. For example, to convert the CLERKS.MNU file, type

MENUCNVT CLERKS

3 · Edit the new .SRC file if necessary. For more information about the commands and format for creating .SRC files, see the previous section.

When you have finished converting the old menu file, you are ready to compile it and set up users' access to the new program in the login script, as explained in the next section.

COMPILING A MENU FILE

To compile the MANAGERS.SRC file, use the MENUMAKE utility, and type the following command:

MENUMAKE MANAGERS

It is not necessary to type the .SRC extension in the command. The MENUMAKE utility compiles the file and creates a data file called MANAGERS.DAT. This is the file that will execute when a user runs NMENU.

To allow users to access this new menu program, you must set up drive mappings in the user or system login script to the program and temporary directories. However, if you created the directories under SYS:PUBLIC, you do not need to add these drive mappings to the login scripts, because a drive is already mapped to SYS:PUBLIC.

Next, add DOS SET commands to the user or system login script that provide information about the location of the temporary subdirectories and about the workstation's ID number. For example, if the temporary directory is called MENUTEMP, and you created it in SYS:PUBLIC, you would add the following commands to the user or system login script:

```
SET S_FILEDIR="Z:\PUBLIC\MENUTEMP\"
SET S_FILE="%STATION"
```

Finally, if you want users to enter the menu program automatically after their login scripts have finished executing, add the command to execute the new menu program to the end of the login script. For example, to make a user enter the MANAGERS menu automatically, add the following line to the login script:

```
EXIT "NMENU MANAGERS"
```

Using the NetWare 3.11 Menu Utility

As mentioned in the previous section, NetWare 3.11 shipped with a different menu utility than NetWare 3.12. If you're using NetWare 3.11, read this section for a description of how to use the MENU utility.

NETWARE MENU BASICS

Using Menu is fairly simple. Novell provides you with a sample menu called MAIN.MNU in the SYS:SYSTEM directory. An easy way to see how MENU works is to give MAIN.MNU a spin. The syntax for the command to start a menu is MENU [PATH]*FILENAME*, where *FILENAME* is the name of a menu script file.

To see the main menu provided with NetWare, change to the PUBLIC directory on the SYS: volume and type **MENU MAIN** to display the Main Menu.

Each of the items appearing in this particular menu is preceded by a number. You can either press a number to move immediately to a menu item, or use your cursor keys to maneuver. The currently selected menu item is highlighted. To execute a menu item, select it and press ↵.

For example, to run the System Configuration utility, select item 4 and press ↵. Your screen will temporarily go blank as you enter SYSCON. Press Esc to exit SYSCON and return to the menu. NetWare menus follow conventions similar to the NetWare menu utilities like SYSCON. Namely, if you press Esc, you will be asked if you want to exit the menu.

CREATING NETWARE MENUS

You can create a menu script file using any text editor that can save to an ASCII format. You can set up menus to use any valid DOS or NetWare command. The menus you set up using NetWare will look and function just like regular NetWare menus that you see when running NetWare utilities, but you can also control the placement of the menu windows on the screen and the color scheme. The best way to go about learning how to create NetWare menus is to just jump right in and create a few, so let's do that now.

Menu Script File Components

Three basic things make up the menu script file—the menu (and/or submenu) title; option names; and commands.

The first thing you need to create a menu file script is a menu title, which is the first line of our example and has this format:

> %Menu_Title,Number_of_Rows,
> Number_of_Columns,Palette_Number

The percent sign tells NetWare that it is a menu title, and the numbers designate the position and color scheme for this menu. NetWare uses a grid-like system of 24 rows and 80 columns to place the menu on the screen. The first number in the menu title of our example indicates the number of rows down from the top of the screen. The second number is the number of columns from the left side of the screen. Finally, the third number designates the *color palette* or the color scheme. The default setting for all three numbers is zero.

Here is an example menu file we created called GENUSER.MNU.

```
%General User Menu,10,35,0
Network Utilities
    %NetWare
Applications
    %Applications
General Utilities
    %Utilities Menu
```

```
%Applications,12,40,0
Spreadsheets
        %Spreadsheets
Word Processors
        %Word Processors

%NetWare,12,40,0
1 - Print Console
        pconsole
2 - File Handline
        filer
3 - Show Users
        userlist
        pause
4 - Send a Message
        echo off
        send @1"Message (Use Quotes)" @2"To"

%Word Processors,14,45,0
1 - WordPerfect 5.1
        f:\programs\wp51\wp
2 - Microsoft Word
        f:\programs\ms_word\word
3 - WordStar
        f:\programs\wordstar\ws

%Spreadsheets,14,45,0
1 - Lotus 123
        f:\programs\lotus\123
2 - Quattro Pro
        f:\programs\quattro\qp

%Utilities Menu,12,40,0
2 - Memory Available
        mem
        pause
1 - DOS v5.0 Editor
        echo off
        edit @"Enter [path] filename to be edited"
3 - Copy All Files
```

```
copy @1"From [Path Only]"\*.* @2"To [Path Only]"\*.*
dir @2
pause
```

If we were to run this menu (by typing **MENU GENUSER.MNU**), we would have a basic menu entitled General User Menu located ten rows down from the top and thirty-five columns over from the left, and using color palette zero to designate the color scheme.

As you can see in our example menu script file, NetWare recognizes the unindented lines as menu options or choices. NetWare also will automatically alphabetize the options for you. If you don't want them in alphabetical order, place numbers or letters in front of the option names to specify the order. You can also have an option name or description up to 70 characters long. NetWare will automatically adjust the menu borders and placement to accommodate a large option name.

The final item that you must have for a menu script file is a command section. Every option name that you place in your menu must have a corresponding command section, or you will receive an error message. The command section can contain any valid DOS or NetWare commands, or it can contain a call to a submenu that you define. Commands and submenu calls are set off from menu titles and option names by indenting at least one space. Let's take a second to talk about submenus first, since our main menu has only submenu calls.

Submenus

Like commands, submenu calls must be indented by at least one space; but submenu calls must also be preceded by a percent sign (%). The percent sign and the submenu title can be the only things that appear on submenu lines. You can't have any DOS or NetWare commands preceding or following submenu lines.

After placing a call to a submenu as one of the items in your main menu, you define the submenu in the same fashion later on in the script file. The same rules for specifying actions apply. You can call a submenu from a submenu, as we have done from the Applications submenu.

In the General User Menu, we call a submenu called Applications, which contains options for two types of programs, spreadsheets and word processors. The Applications submenu in turn calls its own submenus, Spreadsheets and Word Processors, which contain the executable commands needed to start the applications. In this way, you can group applications or tasks that perform similar functions. Your submenu structure can be as deep as you want it to be, but consider your users and keep it as simple as possible.

Commands

The command can act just like a DOS batch file to perform tasks that require more than one command, and it can use DOS variables. Applications, NetWare utilities, DOS commands, and DOS batch files can be executed from the command section.

For instance, in our Word Processors and Spreadsheets submenu, we start applications by calling the appropriate executable or the batch file. Also, in our NetWare and Utilities Menu submenus, we use combinations of NetWare and DOS commands to perform simple tasks.

You can even prompt the user for information necessary to complete the task. For example, in our NetWare submenu, one of the options is to send a message to another user using NetWare's SEND command. The SEND command requires two sets of input, the message and the user it is to be sent to. You accomplish this by using a special variable designated with the @ sign. The @ sign tells NetWare to request input from the user and replace the variable with the input. Since in our case we need two sets of input, we will need to number our variables @1 and @2. You can also send a short message to the user with each prompt by following the input variable (no space between the variable and the message) with a message in quotation marks. For example, our Send a Message option will first prompt the user to enter a message in quotes and then prompt for the username before sending the message.

Because of the way MENU handles memory allocation and program execution, you should not load memory-resident programs from within MENU, nor should you recursively call menu (e.g., don't call other menu scripts from within a menu).

WARNING
Do not use commands that load Terminate and Stay Resident programs in the menu utility, and do not call other NetWare menus from within the MENU utility.

MENU takes up about 100 KB of memory. If you recursively call MENU, approximately 100 KB more of memory will be allocated and used. To make matters worse, when you exit a recursively called menu, you will find yourself back in the operating system, without all allocated memory being released. You could have one and possibly several more copies of MENU running on your machine that you couldn't terminate.

Menu Placement

As we mentioned earlier, you can control the placement of the menu on the screen through the first two numbers in the menu title. MENU uses a twenty-four–row by eighty-column (24 × 80) grid to determine where on the screen a menu is placed. The first number designates rows down from the top of the screen; the second, columns from the left side of the screen. The only exception to this rule is the default setting of zero, which tells MENU to center the menu. For instance, if you set your row and column coordinates to ten and zero respectively, the menu would be placed ten rows down from the top and equidistant from the left and right sides of the screen.

Don't place your menus close to or right on top of one another. Instead, try placing your menus so that each submenu is near the menu that called it while still leaving enough room to indicate that the current menu is a submenu. This way, users will be able to see where they are in the menu structure.

NOTE
The default setting of zero centers the menu.

TIP
Lay your menus out so that users can see where they are in the menu structure.

Creating and Modifying Menu Color Palettes

If you want to change the color scheme of a palette or want to create a new one, you can use NetWare's COLORPAL utility (for "color palette"), normally located in the SYS:PUBLIC directory. Simply type **colorpal** and you will see a list of all the defined palettes that are available to you. NetWare provides five predefined palettes numbered from zero (0) to four (4) for use with the menus that NetWare utilities call.

To define a new palette, press Ins and COLORPAL will create a new palette using the next free sequential number. For the first new palette you create, the new color palette will be named Color Palette 5. If you deleted

Color Palette 4 for some reason, COLORPAL would automatically renumber Color Palette 5 to become Color Palette 4.

Once you've created the new palette, change the colors from the defaults. Highlight the palette you wish to change in the Defined Palettes list and press ↵. COLORPAL will show you a list of five color attributes that you can control and an example menu that will show you how the changes will look as you make them. The attributes that you can control are Background Normal, Background Reverse, Foreground Intense, Foreground Normal, and Foreground Reverse. When you select an attribute to be modified, COLORPAL will provide you with a list of colors available for that attribute with the current setting highlighted.

Choose the new color that you want, and COLORPAL will show you how it will look on the sample menu. Use Esc to back out of COLORPAL when you have selected your new color scheme.

WARNING
Don't forget to save the changes as you exit COLORPAL.

USING NETWARE MENUS EFFECTIVELY

There are several ways in which using NetWare's MENU utility can help you. One of the most useful is to provide the novice network user with a way to start network applications and utilities, thus freeing you from having to constantly answer questions on the intricacies of DOS and NetWare.

Deciding on Menu Contents

When deciding on menu contents, first divide your users into groups with similar needs (e.g., using the same applications). You want to make your menus useful to as many users as possible so that you will not have to make so many menus. A menu for each user is probably a little unrealistic, especially if you are dealing with a large network and several hundred users. Remember also that if there are any changes to the network, you might be required to modify the menus so that your users will still be able to use them.

What should you put in your menus? The obvious answer is to use menus to start applications. You can also use them to change to the correct data directories that you want users to save to. Menus can also select different printers with the CAPTURE command, start CONSOLE to check on the progress of a print job, start FILER to manage their directories and files, or another other useful function that you think they would need.

Security

You can restrict users' access to the DOS command line by "trapping" them in an appropriate menu. In this way, you can have selective control over the applications and utilities the user can get to and you can prevent access to the DOS command line.

To restrict users' access to DOS, first carefully plan your menu system (taking note that some applications will allow a user to exit to a DOS shell) and place the commands to start the menu —**#menu genuser.mnu** and EXIT "**logout**"—in the user's login script.

The user will be able to do whatever the menu allows him or her to do. If they should leave the menu for any reason, control is returned to the login script, which completes the remaining commands. The next command, LOGOUT, terminates the user's session, preventing them from getting to a DOS prompt while logged into the network.

Naming Conventions

Follow NetWare's naming convention of having .*MNU* as the file extension for menu script files you create so you can easily identify menu script files and so you don't need to include the extension when using the MENU command to start the menu.

WARNING
Do not rely on trapping users in a menu as a mainstay of security—applications with shells may still let users reach DOS. But trapping can help prevent accidents by restricting a user's access.

Summary

In this chapter, we've discussed how to create a consistent user interface for your users. We covered login scripts, script variable, and the placement of script tasks into the appropriate script. We discussed using batch files for dynamic drive mapping, and we took a look at the Novell menu systems for NetWare 3.12 and NetWare 3.11 and how to use them.

Establishing
Network Security

Fast Track

- ▶ Effective user trustee rights for a directory are determined by direct user and group assignments. If the rights are inherited, then the IRM determines which rights are extended to the directory.

The third layer of NetWare security is the ability to set file and directory attributes or conditions and limitations that take precedence over a user's trustee rights.   **276**

- ▶ You can set the thirteen file attributes by using either the FLAG command or the FILER utility.

- ▶ You can set the five directory attributes by using either the FLAGDIR command or the FILER utility.

The fourth and last layer of security is prohibiting access to the file server, both physically and through NetWare: **281**

- ▶ Lock the file server in a secure place, disable the file server's keyboard to prevent unauthorized access to the file server console.

- ▶ Remove DOS from the file server's memory with the REMOVE DOS console command to prevent the loading of any NLMs not in SYS:SYSTEM.

- ▶ Use the password option from the MONITOR utility is a way to lock the file server console using NetWare.

- ▶ Choose carefully file server console operators (if any) so that there is little chance of an accidental file server shutdown or session disconnection through FCONSOLE.

One of the ideas behind networking technology is to allow users access to any piece of information they may need from anywhere on the network. Businesses use this concept to increase productivity by allowing groups (such as departments) to share resources such as data, applications, and devices. Ideally, users would have immediate access to any resource needed. Unfortunately, some types of data cannot be shared, and some devices should not be accessible to all.

Just as your home might need a security system that keeps intruders out of the house, teenagers out of your bank account, and toddlers out of the medicine cabinet, your network will need a security system to stop the wrong people accessing its resources. You may want to restrict access to the network to members of your company only, limit use of a printer to a certain group, or keep certain files for your eyes only. NetWare 3.12's flexible security system allows you to do this.

NetWare security is designed to offer a high level of protection for data and shared devices such as network servers. At the same time, it allows the administrator as much, or as little, security as they need. As mentioned before, the security structure is divided into four levels:

SECURITY LEVEL	LEVEL OF ACCESS
Username/Password	Initial (Login)
Rights	Directory/File Access
Attribute	Conditional Directory/File Access
File Server	File Server Console

The second and third levels build on the first, a very general means of limiting access, to give more specific means of restricting user activities. The fourth level prevents unauthorized access to the server console. Console commands are very powerful and when misused can cause great amounts of damage.

Depending on how each level is set up, as in to what depth, you can develop a security system as open or closed as you want. If you use only minimal security, your network will be much like a public library—nearly all the data and services will be available to anyone. On the other hand, you can create such a secure system that your LAN is more like a bank, with data so securely locked away that even the managers do not have access to all the data or services.

Developing a Network Security Strategy

Before you start establishing a security structure, you need to first have a strategy. First, decide just how much security your network needs. A small network may not need the extensive security that a large network needs. The general rule is "the greater the number of users and points of access, the greater the security needs." As with any rule, there are exceptions: Some small networks require a great deal of security.

In any case, *all* networks need at least minimal security. Every network will be threatened in some manner. In most cases, the greatest threat will be accidental data destruction. Possibly more data has been destroyed by users deleting files from the wrong directory than by any other means. Applications are most often damaged by users trying to modify their personal configuration but ending up modifying the application's default settings. Data files can be lost if a user mistakenly downs the server. An additional threat may be computer viruses.

Finally, all networks have the risk of being accessed by former employees, competitors, or "crackers" (malevolent hackers), all of whom can pose a significant risk to the data stored on the network. A thorough security scheme can greatly reduce the risk of a security breach. In view of the potential threats to any network, we recommend that all LANs implement a strong security structure to protect data, reduce maintenance time, and provide peace of mind.

Whatever level of security you establish, the easiest way to set up and maintain your structure is by using SYSCON and FILER, two menu utilities. SYSCON is the system (user and group) configuration utility for NetWare, and FILER helps manage directories and files. In this chapter, we focus primarily on SYSCON as it is the most useful tool in setting up your security structure.

Figure 10.1 shows the opening screen for SYSCON.

To build an effective security structure, you must have a good foundation to build on. The foundation for a NetWare security system is designed to limit access to defined users only. By creating a user (as discussed in Chapter 8), you allow that person access to the network, or at least a particular server. Once a user has access to a server, the next layer in the security structure is access to the files and directories on that server. By default, new users will have very limited access to information on the file server. The combination of access levels will provide you with the security structure you want to establish.

F I G U R E 10.1

The opening screen for
SYSCON

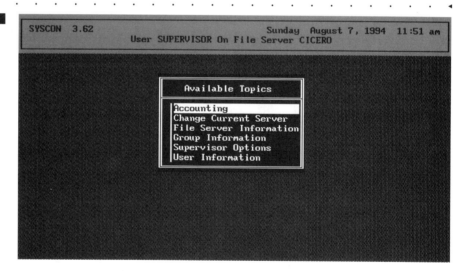

```
SYSCON   3.62                           Sunday  August 7, 1994   11:51 am
                      User SUPERVISOR On File Server CICERO



                         ┌─────────────────────────┐
                         │    Available Topics      │
                         ├─────────────────────────┤
                         │ Accounting               │
                         │ Change Current Server    │
                         │ File Server Information  │
                         │ Group Information        │
                         │ Supervisor Options       │
                         │ User Information         │
                         └─────────────────────────┘
```

Preventing Unauthorized User Access

The first, and most general, level of NetWare security is the User Name/Password level. As we saw in the list of security levels (above), this level allows initial access to the network. Here is where your security structure indicates who can log in to the network as well as when and where. Unfortunately, as this is the most general level, the only security question posed is "can this user access the network?" and the answer is either Yes or No.

This level relies on the user-naming scheme you developed in Chapter 8. As discussed there, to gain access to a NetWare file server, you have to have at least a valid user name and password (unless no password has been assigned).

This level of security is automatically built into NetWare. But because the user name alone cannot limit access (since any other user can get a listing of all valid user names), you need one more requirement for accessing the network—a password known only to the individual user.

IMPLEMENTING PASSWORD PROTECTION

NetWare uses encrypted passwords to verify that the user logging in is actually the one assigned to that user name. Passwords are encrypted so that there is no way to see what the passwords are. Further, by keeping their passwords secret, users can nearly guarantee that no one else can access their user account.

As with any security device (like the keys to your car), you will need to be careful how you store and use your password. One of the first rules for maintaining an effective password is "do not give anyone else your password." This rule covers several of the password *don'ts* listed below.

WARNING
If you enter a user name that does not appear on the list of users, NetWare will not notify you that it is not a valid user name but ask for a password. Regardless of what you enter for a password, you'll be denied access because the user name is invalid.

PASSWORD DO'S	PASSWORD DON'TS
Use words or phrases that you will be able to remember	Use words or phrases that are too complex to be remembered
Use at least five characters	Use fewer than five characters (short passwords can be cracked more easily by programs that go through the possible variations)
Change your password every few months	Write your password down

As the system administrator, you are able to force some of the "rules" from this list onto your users. By selecting Account Restrictions under User Information, you can both force the user to use a password, *and* set the minimum length of the password. Further, you can require that the password be changed every *x* number of days (90 days is the recommended MAXIMUM time frame), and when changed, it will have to be one that hasn't been used before. (The Require Unique Password should be set to YES.)

The list above covers some of the basic rules for maintaining password protection, but it is not complete. There are several pitfalls to avoid when setting up a password scheme for your users. One of the most important is to tell your users not to use the following selections for their passwords:

- ▸ Names of family members
- ▸ Names of pets
- ▸ Telephone numbers
- ▸ Birthdays
- ▸ The same character (such as 11111)

Why not? Well, these are the most commonly–used passwords, so someone attempting to gain access to your server might well try some or all the above in their effort to find out a password.

IMPLEMENTING INTRUDER DETECTION AND LOCKOUT

NetWare's Intruder Detection (ID) can monitor an account when a login attempt has failed. Once the server records an unsuccessful login attempt, it saves a record of the date, time, and station address of the last (and only the last) attempt. Since the network has to associate the invalid login attempt with a particular user, this information is only available when a valid user name is entered, but not the correct password.

How NetWare handles this information depends on whether or not you have activated the Intruder Lockout. Intruder Lockout (IL) tells the server to allow a certain number of invalid login attempts before locking the account. Once the account is locked, the server will not accept any attempts to log in with that particular user name until either the lockout period expires, or the system administrator removes the lockout. Using this feature helps protect the integrity of your network passwords by only allowing a few attempts to find the right one. Once the number of attempts is reached, the account is locked.

The number of allowed attempts is configured when setting both of the ID and IL options. These options are set globally, and are available under the Supervisor Options of SYSCON, as seen in Figure 10.2.

We recommend that you set the number of login attempts to three. This will allow a user to mistype a password a few times (usually it only requires two attempts to get it right) before the account is locked. We also recommend the use of three days for the amount of time for the account to remain locked.

Why use Intruder Lockout? Well, in almost every case, if someone is trying to gain illegal access to your network, you will want to know. If the account is locked while the user is trying to log in, they will receive a message that the account has been locked. At this point they either have to wait for the lockout period to end or call the system administrator to release the

FIGURE 10.2

Intruder Detection and

Intruder Lockout settings

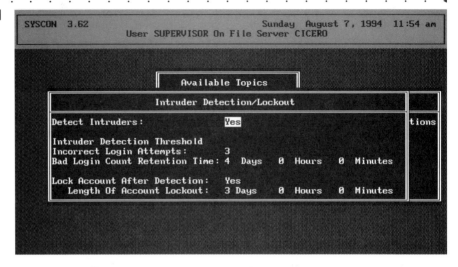

lock. Once they call, you can find out how the account became locked. If the user did not cause the lockout, it is reasonable to assume that someone was attempting to gain unauthorized access by using that account.

Why three days? The wait period of three days is needed if the unauthorized attempts were made on a Friday, the lockout will last until Monday, long enough for the user to get back to work and discover the lockout. You can set the wait period to be longer—we've known people set it for 30 days—but three should be the minimum.

Unfortunately, if a real intruder locks the account, and the real user tries to log in, the Supervisor can't tell the difference between an intruder attempt and a valid user mistyping.

LIMITING CONCURRENT SESSIONS

Another way to limit user access is to allow each user to be able to access the network from only one station at a time. By limiting the number of concurrent sessions to one, a user can only have one network session at a time: While they are logged into the network from, say, their desk, they will not be able to log in from any other workstation. If more than one session is attempted, the user will receive a message that they are attempting too many simultaneous logins. We recommend a global setting of one concurrent session for all users.

You can limit concurrent sessions globally by using the default settings under the Supervisor Options, or you can make the setting independently for each user through the Account Restrictions option. To set the restriction for an individual user, enter SYSCON and select User Information. Then highlight the user to be affected and select Account Restrictions (see Figure 10.3).

Even if this restriction is made on a global basis, you can still make exceptions on a case-by-case basis. Before making any exceptions, consider them carefully. Convenience should not be the sole factor in deciding to offer multiple sessions (especially for network administrators).

The Limit Concurrent Sessions setting is important because it can provide protection in two ways. First, it effectively locks out "crackers" during working hours. Typically, all the users will be logged in during the week, accessing the LAN and using needed resources. While a logged user is in and using their account, the network will not allow anyone else to access the same account. This is an easy way to eliminate unauthorized access during

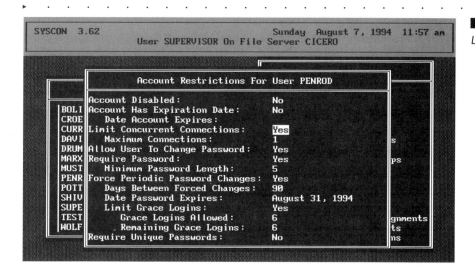

Limiting Concurrent Sessions

office hours, although it is not a perfect solution because your users may not always be logged in.

Second, limiting concurrent sessions protects users from themselves. Users often share their workstations with other users. For example, there's a meeting, and you need to show everyone a file located in your personal directory. To access the file, you log into the nearest workstation to access the appropriate data, and once the meeting resumes, you forget to log out. After the meeting, you return to your desk only to discover you are unable to access the network because you are already logged in. The system has just reminded you to log out of the other session.

What's more, any time you're logged into the network, that workstation has all the rights and privileges you have. If you are not actively using that particular workstation, then anyone can access your data (either departmental or personal data), and use your privileges. This is extremely important for system administrators as they will constantly log into different users' workstations when providing technical support. System administrators must handle many problems at once; it's easy to forget, as you jump from one fire to the next, to log out of every session you started.

NOTE
Restricting access time is very effective for limiting the number of hours contract personnel are eligible to work each day. If additional hours are needed, you can modify the settings, thus guaranteeing that your approval is given for any overtime hours.

RESTRICTING LAN ACCESS TIMES

Restricting access time allows you to set when a user can access the network. If your employees are supposed to be working only from nine to five, you can tell the system to allow them to log in only after nine. In addition, if the users are not logged out by five, the system will send them a five-minute warning that their access time is almost over, followed by a one-minute warning. At six minutes past five, if they are still logged in, the server will forcibly log them out.

You can set time restrictions for each user by selecting User Information, the user you want to restrict, and then choosing the Restrict Access Time option. Figure 10.4 illustrates setting time restrictions with SYSCON.

A star in each row and column indicates a day and time segment (in 30-minute intervals) when access is allowed. To remove blocks of time, you can use F5 and the cursors to highlight a block of hours. Then by hitting

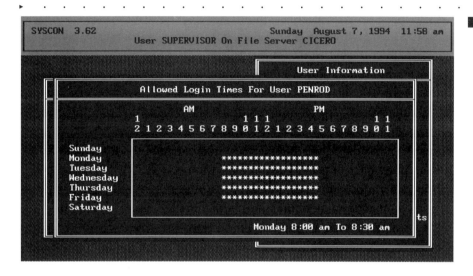

FIGURE 10.4

*Setting time restrictions
with SYSCON*

Del, you will remove access for the days and times you blocked out. Similarly, if you wish to add blocks, you can use F5 and the cursors to highlight blocks of time without asterisks. Press ↵ to add the asterisks that signify allowable access time.

SETTING STATION RESTRICTIONS

Have you ever had a wandering user, one unable to work on his or her own workstation? Typically, a user assigned an older and slower workstation will gravitate to another office to use a newer and faster workstation. One effective way to keep such users in their seats is to limit the user account so that they can only log in from their own workstation. On the other hand, if you don't want to limit this type of user to only one workstation, you can also set the station restriction to prevent them from logging into that one more desirable workstation.

Setting the station restrictions requires several steps. This setting, like most of the others we discussed, is available under the User Information option. But before you attempt to set the station restrictions, you have to know the Network and Node address for the station in question. The best way to obtain this information is to log into the workstation and

WARNING
**If you are using a
separate user ac-
count to perform
backups, be sure to
place the tightest
limitations on allow-
able login times and
workstation accesses
(only workstations
where backups can be
performed), since this
account is a
SUPERVISOR
security equivalent ac-
count and could pos-
sibly be used to
illegally access the
system.**

type **USERLIST /A** at the DOS prompt to display the list of logged-in users with their appropriate address information (see Figure 10.5). The station accessing the userlist will appear with a star next to the user name.

Once you have the network and node address, enter SYSCON and select the user you want. Next select Station Restriction and you will see a list of restrictions that have been set. To add a new restriction, simply press Ins and enter the network and node address, as illustrated in Figure 10.6. Once you've entered the information, the new restriction will appear on the list and the user will now be restricted to (or from) that particular station.

▶ · ◀

FIGURE 10.5

A listing of user connection information

```
G:\BOOK\NW386\SCREENS>userlist /a

User Information for Server CICERO
Connection  User Name       Network      Node Address   Login Time
---------------------------------------------------------------------------
     1      NETPORT       [     1] [  AA0010D04F]  5-02-1993   3:43 am
     3      BOLIN         [     1] [  AA00174EA5]  5-03-1993  10:19 am
     4    * SUPERVISOR    [     1] [  AA002A87FE]  5-03-1993  11:49 am
     5      DAVISON       [     1] [   C008FD24]   5-03-1993   7:58 am
     6      MUSTHLR       [     1] [   C013FD24]   5-03-1993   8:27 am
     8      CROES         [     1] [  AA002A3F6A]  5-03-1993  11:42 am

G:\BOOK\NW386\SCREENS>
```

▶ · ◀

FIGURE 10.6

Setting station restrictions

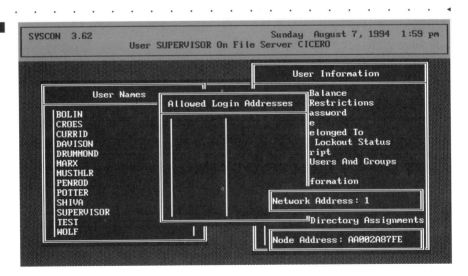

Adding Trustee Security

Once a user has gained access to the network, he or she needs access to directories and files to run applications and manipulate data. When first installed, by default Novell only grants access to all users in the PUBLIC and LOGIN directories. For users or groups to access any other directories and files, the system administrator has to assign them rights. The eight different rights that you can assign are listed with a brief explanation below.

	TRUSTEE RIGHT	RIGHT DESCRIPTION
S	Supervisory	Grants full rights to the directory, all files, and the entire subdirectory structure
R	Read	Open and Reads a closed file
W	Write	Open and Writes to a closed file
C	Create	Create a new file or directory
E	Erase	Delete a file or directory
M	Modify	Rename a file or directory
F	File Scan	Read the directory listing for a directory or specific file
A	Access Control	Grant rights to the file or directory to other users on the network

Implementing Directory and File Access Rights

The second level of security (also known as Rights) is the most flexible. By granting rights to a user or group, you are allowing access to that directory or file. In NetWare 3.12, you can assign specific rights to a particular user or group. The ability to grant individual rights to either a user or a group of users is where the flexibility is gained. For example, if you have just purchased a special package for the Accounting department and you do not want Sales or Manufacturing to be able to access it, grant rights only to Accounting, and Sales and Manufacturing won't even be able to *find* the application (much less access the data). As the example illustrates, your security structure can restrict or allow access on a case-by-case basis.

Be careful with the Access Control right (A), as this allows the user to grant rights to other users, whether or not the user with Access Control has the rights they are assigning. For example, if you have the following rights R, F, and A in a directory, you could grant someone else the following rights R, W, C, E, M, F, and A. With Access control, you can grant any right, except supervisory (S), to any user.

The rights you assign are important as they determine what kind of actions the user (or group) can take in that directory. If you don't grant enough rights, your users will not be able to work effectively on the network; if you grant too many, you may have maintenance problems as users delete, corrupt, or modify files they shouldn't. So take great care when deciding what rights you will grant.

Next, consider what rights you have to assign. This depends on what types of operations you need to perform. For example, applications require that all users have at least the ability to read the files (R) and the ability to scan the directory for existing files (F). If R and F are not granted to a user, they will not be able to access that application.

Some applications will require additional rights, which should be listed in the software documentation.

Be careful not to grant too many rights to applications. The fewer rights you have to grant, the more control you will have over the application. The greater your control, the fewer maintenance problems you will have, as most application problems are the result of changes in setup. If you give your users too many rights to an application, they can modify the default settings that affect all users.

WARNING
The Access Control right (A) allows the user to grant rights to other users, whether or not the user with Access Control has those rights.

NOTE
NetWare security prevents users from performing any action they don't have the right to perform. A user with F right in a directory can scan files but not read, delete, or rename them. All the rights are distinct and separate.

In the user's home directory, you will want to grant the user the ability to perform almost any action:

- ▸ Read

- ▸ Write

- ▸ Create

- ▸ Erase

- ▸ Modify

- ▸ File scan

WARNING
Grant the supervisory right only to supervisors!

We don't recommend granting supervisory (S) or access control (A) because users should not modify any portion of the security structure.

We strongly recommend that you allow only users with supervisor equivalency to have supervisory rights for directories. This right allows full functions in the directory in which it is assigned; this extends into the ENTIRE subdirectory structure from that point downward. Having the supervisory right is the same as having all the other rights combined. The main problems for the administrator are that the user with this right can grant or remove rights freely, or they can modify or delete any file they choose. Further, since the supervisory right cannot be blocked at a lower level, it is too powerful to grant to users.

You may want to grant the same rights to a common data directory. As all the users will need to be able to manipulate the data in the shared directory, they will need the same rights. You can do this easily by creating a unique group that these users can be a member of and assigning the group trustee rights.

Once the question of which rights to assign has been answered, the next question is how to best assign those rights. There are three possible answers to this question, and we examine each answer in the following sections.

NOTE
Once you assign a trustee right to a directory, that right will be available in any subdirectory under the assigned directory. In effect, the subdirectories *inherit* the rights assigned to the parent directory. This inheritance *cascades* throughout the subdirectory structure, unless modified by the Inherited Rights Mask (IRM) that will be discussed later in this chapter.

GRANTING TRUSTEE RIGHTS FOR DIRECTORIES OR FILES TO INDIVIDUALS

Granting trustee rights to an individual user is usually accomplished through SYSCON. Under the User Options menu, you can select a user and assign the trustee rights by selecting the Trustee Directory Assignments (or Trustee File Assignments, since the operations are similar) option. You will get a list of directories the associated rights already assigned to that specific user (see Figure 10.7). You will not see the list of rights granted for that user as a member of a group. You will need to view the group or groups they belong to in order to view their rights granted through group membership.

To add a trustee right, use the cursor keys to highlight the specific directory and press ↵. SYSCON will then display a list of the assigned rights. To add additional rights, press Ins, and a list of the available rights will be displayed. Using F5 to tag the rights you want to add, and pressing ↵, add the appointed rights to the directory assignment. To close the rights list menu, press Esc and you will return to the list of directories and their associated trustee assignments.

To add a new directory assignment from the list of directory assignments, press Ins. This action will open a window for entering the directory path

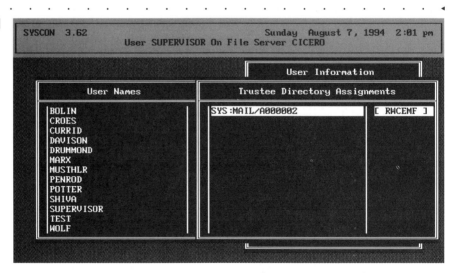

FIGURE 10.7

Assigning trustee rights with SYSCON

(see Figure 10.8). If you do not know the path or you don't want to type it in, you can again press Ins to get a window showing the current server.

At this point, use the ↵ key to make selections. By selecting the server, you will get a list of volumes, then a list of directories. Make your selections until the path is shown in the top window shown in Figure 10.8. When the path is complete, press Esc to close the directory-selection window, and finally press ↵ to return to the directory assignment list. The default rights assigned whenever you make trustee assignments are R and F. To add additional rights, follow the steps listed above.

You can also assign directory trustee assignments at the DOS prompt, and not using SYSCON. To grant rights for a directory, use the GRANT command. The syntax for this command is:

GRANT rights FOR [path] TO [USER|GROUP_NAME][options]

(See Appendix A, *NetWare 3.12 Utilities Summary,* for more information about GRANT.)

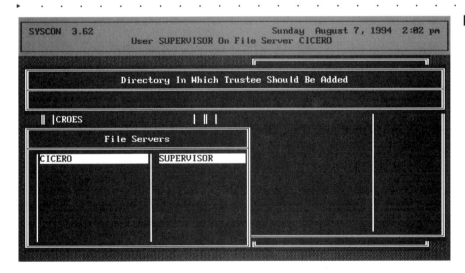

FIGURE 10.8

*Selecting the Trustee
Directory Assignment path*

A sample command would be:

GRANT R W F FOR G:\DEPT\ACCOUNT TO JOSH

This sample would give user JOSH Read, Write, and File scan to the directory \DEPT\ACCOUNT.

Although it may appear to be easier to assign rights with the GRANT command, you have to be careful when adding rights. Every time you use the grant command for a user, you have to list all the rights you want them to have. If you only list the right you want to add, the assignment will change to only allow the added right. For example, if in the previous example, you wanted to add the create right to JOSH and you type:

GRANT C FOR G:\DEPT\ACCOUNT TO JOSH

JOSH's trustee assignment to that directory would only be C, because you did not list *all* the rights you wanted him to have.

As you can see, setting up rights for users is not simple, and, if you had to add the same rights to every user, it would quickly become very tedious. To solve this potential problem, NetWare allows you to place users into groups.

GRANTING TRUSTEE RIGHTS TO GROUPS

Granting trustee rights to a group is almost exactly the same as granting them to a user. The only difference is that instead of using the User Information option, you will use the Group Information option. Under the Group Information option you will see the selection for Trustee Directory Assignments (see Figure 10.9) and Trustee File Assignments.

Selecting the Trustee Directory Assignments/Trustee File Assignments option will give you the list of current trustee directory and file assignments, and from this point on, the procedure is exactly the same as for individual users. The GRANT command is also identical, simply replace USER_NAME with GROUP_NAME.

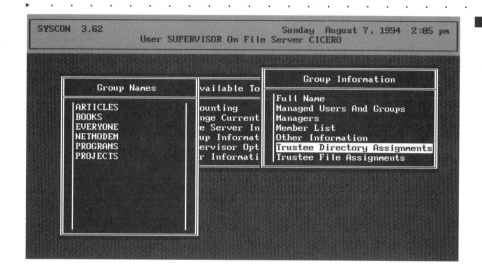

FIGURE 10.9

Assigning group trustee rights

The main advantage of assigning rights to groups is that you only have to enter the assignment once and it is then shared with all the group members. Further, making group trustee assignments also makes it easier to move a user from one group to the next. To add or remove trustee assignments for a user, simply add them to or remove them from the appropriate group We recommend that you use group assignments for all trustee rights except for specific requirements (such as home directories). Group assignments are especially good for applications.

One important note is all the user trustee assignments and group assignments are added together to define the total rights for each user in a given directory—you cannot give a group member fewer rights than the group. For example, if your group ACCOUNTING has full rights (RWCEMF) to the ACCT directory, but you want the manager of Sales to be able to access data in the ACCT directory without being able to modify it (R and F only), you cannot make him or her a member of ACCOUNTING as he or she would have the same rights as the rest of the ACCOUNTING group (RWCEMF).

TIP
If you have a user *and* group with the same name, prefix the name with "user" or "group".

GRANTING RIGHTS THROUGH SECURITY EQUIVALENCES

You can also assign rights by making a user exactly equivalent to another user or group. You can do so by assigning the same directory assignments and group memberships from one user to another, but it's easier to use the Security Equivalence option. Select the Security Equivalence option, and you will see a list of all the groups the user belongs to, as well as all users with whom the user is equivalent. All the groups are listed because by being a member of a group, you automatically are assigned all the trustee rights of that group. To make one user the same as another, in terms of trustee rights, you can make one the security equivalent of the other. To add an equivalence, press Ins to get a list of available users and groups, highlight the appropriate user, and press ↵.

For example, if an employee with the user name of TOM needed to access all the data and services of another user, FRED, you could add FRED to TOM's list of Security Equivalencies. Now TOM will maintain his own security setup, but will also have the rights and privileges of FRED.

The most common use for this selection is to create Supervisor Equivalents. Your network administrator needs to be able to access all the file and data areas on your network. The best way to allow full access to your network is to make the user the Security Equivalent of the SUPERVISOR.

Because no file or data areas are off limits to a SUPERVISOR Security Equivalent, we recommend not using this type of user for the day-to-day activities of your system administrators. System administrators are not above making mistakes when working on the network. Therefore, by using a basic user configuration for your system administrators when they are not performing network administrative duties, you will protect the network from mistakes they might make.

If you do set up your administrators as SUPERVISOR Security Equivalents, create a test user account set up like any other user to allow testing anytime the administrator modifies the security structure. Too often an administrator will install an application and test it as a SUPERVISOR Security Equivalent, but when the users try to run the application, they have problems. In this case, most of the problems are the result of not having

NOTE
Each user can have up to 32 different security equivalences.

NOTE
A SUPERVISOR Security Equivalent has all the rights and abilities of the user SUPERVISOR. Therefore, be very careful in assigning this level of equivalency as no file or data areas are off limits to this user.

enough trustee assignments. It didn't affect the administrator, so his or her first thought is to work on the application's configuration—which can waste a great deal of time if it is the security structure that's causing the errors.

Finally, when you have a user that was initially set up using a security equivalence, do not forget to assign the rights that user may need if they lose their equivalency. For example, if you are a SUPERVISOR Security Equivalent (and have been from the time the account was created), it is likely that you were not granted any rights to the network because it was unnecessary. Unfortunately, when you revoke the SUPERVISOR Security Equivalent rights, you then lose nearly all rights to the network (in some cases, you would not even be able to access your home directory). Therefore, be sure to set up all users in your security structure before adding any security equivalences.

REVOKING TRUSTEE RIGHTS

There will come a time when you will have to revoke a user's trustee rights. Revoking rights within SYSCON is nearly identical to adding rights. The main differences are that you highlight the desired assignment, and either delete the entire assignment by pressing Del (if you want to revoke all rights to that directory), or press ↵ to get the list of assigned rights. With the list of rights opened, use F5 to tag the ones to be revoked, and press Del.

You can also delete rights from the DOS prompt by using the REVOKE command. REVOKE is opposite of GRANT, and is used to delete trustee rights from a specific user. The syntax for REVOKE is as follows:

> REVOKE rights* FOR [path] FROM [USER|GROUP_NAME]
> [options]

(For more information on REVOKE, see Appendix A, *NetWare 3.12 Utilities Summary*.)

You need to have two points in mind when revoking trustee rights. The first is to consider if in deleting these rights, will you be limiting the user's ability to work. If your intent is to simply tighten up security, you will want to have the user test any changes that have been made. If you are attempting to revoke all access to a given directory, then testing the results is unnecessary. The second point is to be sure that the rights you are revoking from a user are not duplicated by one of the groups he or she belongs to or Security Equivalents (and vice versa). If you do not revoke the rights at both levels, you will not have completely revoked the trustee assignments.

Modifying Directory Security

Earlier in this chapter we mentioned inheriting rights and the Inherited Rights Mask. When you assign a trustee right to a directory, that right is inherited by the entire subdirectory structure that lies below the directory where the assignment was made (until a new specific trustee assignment is made). Therefore, if you need to have a set of rights for a directory structure that is several layers deep, you only need to assign the rights to the top of the directory structure, and not for every subdirectory.

NetWare allows you to restrict a right's ability to be inherited, so that you can modify rights as they are inherited from one directory to the next without having to resort to a new specific trustee assignment. By blocking the inheritance, you are able to reduce the rights for a directory further down the structure. This is called the Inherited Rights Mask (IRM) as it masks certain rights out of those being inherited.

USING THE INHERITED RIGHTS MASK

The Inherited Rights Mask (IRM) is assigned to every directory on the server. By default, the IRM allows all rights to be inherited. To change the IRM, you can use either the command line utility ALLOW to allow rights to be inherited or the FILER menu utility. In FILER, you can select the Current Directory Information option to display several pieces of information for that directory (see Figure 10.10).

FIGURE 10.10
*Current Directory
Information window for
FILER*

```
NetWare File Maintenance  V3.60           Friday  July 8, 1994  2:16 pm
                   CICERO\VOL1:BOOK\NW386\SCREENS

          ┌─────────────────────────────────────────────┐
          │        Directory Information for SCREENS      │
          │                                               │
          │  Owner: CROES                                 │
          │                                               │
          │  Creation Date:  November 1, 1992             │
          │                                               │
          │  Creation Time:  10:50 pm                     │
          │                                               │
          │  Directory Attributes: (see list)            │
          │                                               │
          │  Current Effective Rights: [SRWCEMFA]        │
          │                                               │
          │  Inherited Rights Mask: [SRWCEMFA]           │
          │                                               │
          │                                               │
          │  Trustees: (see list)                        │
          │                                               │
          └─────────────────────────────────────────────┘
```

To modify the IRM, simply select the Inherited Rights Mask option, and it will show you a list of the rights that can be inherited by this directory. To add rights to the IRM, press Ins and select the needed rights. To delete rights, simply highlight the right to be removed and press Del.

If you are using the IRM to prevent rights from being inherited, keep these two important points in mind. First, the IRM can block any right from being inherited except for the Supervisory right. As stated before, this right cannot be blocked once it is assigned. Second, if you block a right at one level, it cannot subsequently be inherited at lower levels. The IRM is only able to mask the rights that are inherited by the directory. The IRM can not add rights, it can only block their inheritance.

The IRM adds power to directory and file trustee assignments. Unfortunately, it is often confusing for administrators. Therefore, we recommend that you sparingly use the IRM. Instead, try relying on a carefully planned directory structure: Set the directory structure so that if you grant rights at one level, it is all right for them to be inherited.

NOTE
**The IRM is effective
only in a directory
where the user has
not been assigned
specific trustee rights.
Trustee rights are
considered explicit
rights assignments,
and take precedence
over any IRM
restrictions.**

DETERMINING EFFECTIVE RIGHTS

Effective rights are defined as the rights you are able to use in a given directory. There are several variables that factor into producing the effective trustee rights. The two most prominent are the trustee assignments, and the IRM. If you are using the IRM, here is where confusion may occur.

To calculate the effective rights for a directory, you have to add the trustee assignments for the user and any assignments that have been granted to any groups. The combination of these rights is the effective rights ONLY if the user (or group) was explicitly given the trustee assignment for this directory. If a trustee assignment was not given for the directory, then the rights are inherited. Therefore, the IRM for this directory will then remove any rights that are not allowed, and this will provide the effective rights. You can check the users' rights to be sure they are correct by logging in as the user in question, moving to the proper directory, and typing

rights↵

Adding File and Directory Attributes

The third layer of Novell security is the ability to set file and directory attributes. As Table 10.1 stated, this level is the conditional file and directory access. The reason this is called the conditional access is that by adding attributes, we are adding limits to the rights that have been assigned as trustee assignments to the individual users or to an entire group of users.

There is a difference, however: File and directory attributes affect the file and directory that they are assigned to and inhibit actions by all users, not just certain users. They are meant for all users or groups since the attributes are assigned directly to the directories and files and not to the user and group definitions as trustee rights are. For instance, if the users GEORGE, FRANK, and GLORIA as well as the entire group WORDPROC have Erase rights in the directory CICERO/VOL1:\PUB_DATA\WPFILES, but the Delete Inhibit attribute has been applied to this directory, none of those users would be able to delete the directory or the files it contains.

SETTING FILE ATTRIBUTES

The following table shows the thirteen file attributes and what they do:

	FILE ATTRIBUTE	DESCRIPTION
A	Archive Needed	Identifies files modified after last backup
CI	Copy Inhibit	Prevents Macintosh users from copying a file
DI	Delete Inhibit	Prevents users from deleting a file
X	Execute Only	Prevents .EXE and .COM files from being copied or backed up.
H	Hidden	Hides files from the DOS DIR scan and prevents them from being deleted or copied.
P	Purge	Purges a file as soon as it is deleted
Ra	Read Audit	Not currently used by NetWare 3.12; holdover from NetWare 2.x
Ro/Rw	Read Only/Read Write	Indicates whether a file can be modified or not; all files are marked "Rw" when created.
RI	Rename Inhibit	Prevents a file from being renamed

	FILE ATTRIBUTE	DESCRIPTION
S	Shareable	Allows several users to access a file at the same time
Sy	System	Hides files from the DOS DIR scan and prevents them from being deleted or copied.
T	Transactional	Activates the Transactional Tracking System (TTS). Prevents data corruption by ensuring that all changes are made to files being modified or none are.
Wa	Write Audit	Not currently used by NetWare 3.12; holdover from NetWare 2.x

There are two ways in which you can set or change file attributes. The first way is with the FLAG command. The syntax for the FLAG command is as follows:

FLAG path attributes

(leave off attributes to just view current settings).

For example, if you wanted to add the Copy Inhibit, Delete Inhibit, and Rename Inhibit attributes while removing Hidden and Purge from the file TEST.DOC in the directory G:\DEPT\ACCOUNT, you would type:

FLAG G:\DEPT\ACCOUNT\TEST.DOC +CI DI RI -H P

The other way to set and change file attributes is to use the FILER utility. Move to the directory containing the file whose attributes you wish to

NOTE
**The constants – and +
can be used to desig-
nate the addition or
subtraction of file at-
tributes. Additionally,
the additions must be
grouped together
as well as the
subtractions.**

modify and type:

FILER↵

From the main menu, select Directory Contents and choose the file to which you wish to add or subtract attributes and press ↵ (our example will again be G:\DEPT\ACCOUNT\TEST.DOC). You will then need to select View/Set File Information from the File Options menu to get the File Information for TEST.DOC. This screen has all sorts of useful information including the first field which contains a listing of TEST.DOC's attributes. Press ↵ to get a list of Current File Attributes. If you wish to add an attribute, simply press Ins and select the attribute from the Other File Attributes list that is provided (see Figure 10.11). Conversely, if you wish to delete one of TEST.DOC's attributes, simply highlight the attribute, press Del, and confirm the deletion.

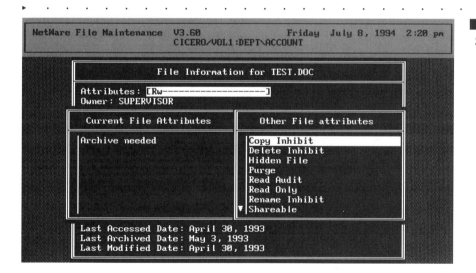

FIGURE 10.11

Setting file attributes using the FILER utility

SETTING DIRECTORY ATTRIBUTES

The following table shows the five directory attributes and what they do:

	FILE ATTRIBUTE	DESCRIPTION
DI	Delete Inhibit	Prevents users from deleting a file
H	Hidden	Hides files from the DOS DIR scan and prevents them from being deleted or copied.
P	Purge	Purges a file as soon as it is deleted
RI	Rename Inhibit	Prevents a file from being renamed
Sy	System	Hides files from the DOS DIR scan and prevents them from being deleted or copied.

There are two ways in which you can set or change directory attributes. The first way is with the FLAGDIR command. The syntax for the FLAGDIR command is as follows:

FLAGDIR path attributes

(leave off attributes to just view current settings)

For example, if we wanted to "hide" the directory G:\DEPT\ACCOUNT, we would type:

FLAGDIR G:\DEPT\ACCOUNT H

The other way to set and change directory attributes is to use the FILER utility. Move to the desired directory and type

FILER↵

(Our example will again be G:\DEPT\ACCOUNT). From the main menu, select Current Directory Information for a screen detailing all sorts of useful information about the current directory including the fourth field which contains a listing of the directory attributes. Press ↵ on the Directory Attributes field to get a list of Current Directory Attributes. If you wish to add an attribute, simply press Ins and select the attribute from the Other Directory Attributes list that is provided (see Figure 10.12). Conversely, if you wish to delete an attribute, simply highlight the attribute, press Del, and confirm the deletion.

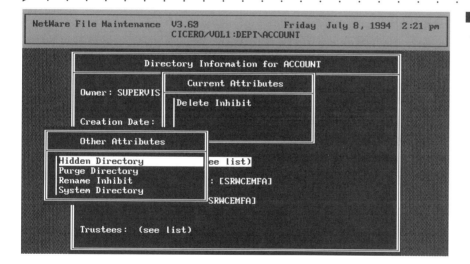

FIGURE 10.12

Setting directory attributes using the FILER utility

Adding File Server Console Security

The last level of NetWare security, as discussed at the beginning of this chapter, is that of file-server security. If not protected, the file-server console is the one location that someone (user or non-user) can affect the server. Unfortunately, if someone gains access to the file server, nothing can prevent them from shutting off the power and downing the server. But, Net-Ware does offer some protection for the server. At one level, the protection is placed at the physical console; the second is to limit the access by users for the options offered under FCONSOLE.

SECURING ACCESS AT THE CONSOLE

The easiest way to protect the file server is to lock the actual server console in a secure room. By securing the server console, you can limit which modules can be loaded, or you can lock the server's keyboard.

NetWare offers two ways to protect the server itself. First, you can remove DOS from the server's memory by entering the command REMOVE DOS at the server's console prompt. Removing DOS keeps the server from being able to access a DOS disk (or diskette).

As a result of removing DOS from the server's memory, the only NLMs that can be loaded are the NLMs stored in the server's SYS:SYSTEM directory, since the load command will no longer recognize a DOS path. Only users with access to the SYS:SYSTEM directory can load an NLM. This can help prevent unauthorized users from using the server's floppy drives or RCONSOLE (which is also located in the SYS:SYSTEM directory) to load unwanted NLMs.

The second way to protect the server is to use the password option from the MONITOR screen. When the password option is selected, the server will prompt you to enter a password to unlock the server console keyboard (see Figure 10.13).

Once the password is entered, all keyboard entries at the server are shut off until either the password you just entered or the password for the user SUPERVISOR is typed in.

Without one of the proper passwords, nothing can be entered at the server console keyboard, not even the DOWN command.

Securing the console with the password is preferable to removing DOS because you do not have to down the server if it becomes necessary to access a file on a DOS disk. It also prevents anyone from being able to type the DOWN command. Another advantage is that the password option also

NOTE
Removing DOS from the server's memory will increase the server's available memory pool as it no longer needs to maintain a memory range for DOS.

NOTE
The only SUPERVISOR password that will work is that of the user SUPERVISOR, not of a supervisor equivalent.

▶ . . . . ◀

```
┌─────────────────────────────────────────────────────────────────────────┐
│ NetWare v3.11 (250 user) - 2/20/91          NetWare 386 Loadable Module   │
├─────────────────────────────────────────────────────────────────────────┤
│                                                                           │
│                    Information For Server CICERO                          │
│                                                                           │
│     File Server Up Time:   39 Days 14 Hours 32 Minutes  9 Seconds         │
│     Utilization:              1       Packet Receive Buffers:      10      │
│     Original Cache Buffers: 3,714     Directory Cache Buffers:    161      │
│     Total Cache Buffers:    2,537     Service Processes:            3      │
│     Dirty Cache Buffers:        0     Connections In Use:           7      │
│     Current Disk Requests:      0     Open Files:                  58      │
│                                                                           │
│              ┌──────────────────────────────────────┐                     │
│                                                                           │
│        ┌──────────────────────────────────────────────────┐               │
│        │  Enter a password to use when unlocking the file server console. │
│        │                                                  │               │
│        │                                                  │               │
│        │      ┌──────────────────────────────────┐        │               │
│        │      │ Password:                        │        │               │
│        │      └──────────────────────────────────┘        │               │
│        └──────────────────────────────────────────────────┘               │
│              └──────────────────────────────────────┘                     │
└─────────────────────────────────────────────────────────────────────────┘
```

Setting the password for the server console

prevents the use of RCONSOLE to gain access to the console from a workstation. The user will still need to know the correct passwords to use the console remotely.

ESTABLISHING CONSOLE OPERATORS

The second area for securing the file server is to limit access to the functions and capabilities of FCONSOLE. FCONSOLE is a menu utility (see Figure 10.14) that allows a supervisor or console operator to make limited changes in the file server.

Although most of the options only allow minor changes (such as modifying the server's date and time), or broadcasting a message to all users, FCONSOLE has some powerful features. Under Server Status is the option for disabling logins, using which a user can prevent all new logins. Even more important, FCONSOLE can down the file server. Since FCONSOLE can be run on any workstation, take care when assigning console operators to prevent accidental downing of the server. The option for creating a console operator is located in SYSCON under the Supervisor Options selection.

From the Supervisor Options list, select the File Server Console Operators and press ↵ to receive a list of console operators. To add operators, press Ins to choose from a list of available users and groups. Highlight and press F5 over each user or group of users you wish to be operators and then press ⏎ to add them to the list of file server operators (see Figure 10.15). If you wish to delete operators, simply mark the

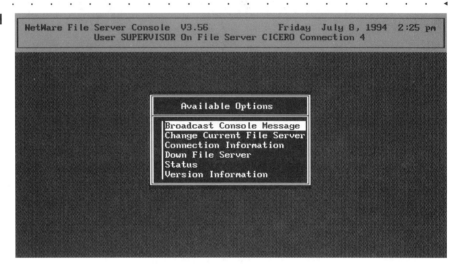

F I G U R E 10.14

FCONSOLE main menu

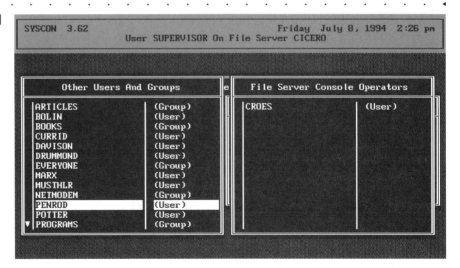

F I G U R E 10.15

Assigning file server console operators

operators to be removed with your arrow keys and F5, press Del, and confirm the deletion.

Because of the more powerful features of FCONSOLE such as downing the file server and being able to disconnect sessions, we recommend that you do not create any console operators. Instead, let SUPERVISOR or a supervisor equivalent (both are automatically console operators) be the only ones with access to the features to prevent the accidental downing of the file server or the disconnection of an important session.

Summary

As you can tell, it is extremely important to minimize the chances of data and applications being corrupted through ignorance, accidents, or malice. In this chapter, we have discussed the four levels of security that NetWare 3.12 provides to counter this problem: initial login protection, user account trustee rights, file and directory attributes, and file server security measures. With this powerful and flexible combination of limitations, you should be able to create a functional work environment for your network users that minimizes the chances of user-induced errors to both data and applications.

CHAPTER II

Establishing Network Printing Services

Fast Track

290   ***There are two types of printing on the network:***

▸ **Local printing:** A workstation prints to a printer directly attached to it. Local printing is independent of the network.

▸ **Network printing:** Print jobs are first placed in a network queue to wait until a printer serviced by the network is ready to print them.

291   ***There are four components of network printing:***

▸ A **printer driver** is software that translates application commands into printer commands.

▸ A **print queue** is a special directory located on a file server where print jobs are placed to wait for an available printer. A print queue is assigned users, operators, and servers.

▸ A **print server** is a combination of software and hardware (file server, dedicated workstation, external router, or third party device) which monitors its assigned print queues for print jobs to send to network printers. Print servers are also assigned users and operators.

▸ A **printer** can either be local (directly attached to the print server) or remote (attached to a workstation on the network) to a print server that controls it.

297   ***There are nine possible steps to setting up your printing services:***

▸ Organize and set up your printers.

▸ Create login accounts for dedicated print servers.

▸ Create and configure your print queues.

▸ Create and configure your print servers.

▸ Define your printers.

- ▸ Assign queue servers to queues.
- ▸ Set up queues, print servers, and printers on other file servers.
- ▸ Start print server operations using various PSERVER programs.
- ▸ Use RPRINTER.EXE to establish remote network printers.

CAPTURE and ENDCAP   334

are commands used to help print from applications that are not "network aware" and cannot see network queues.

NPRINT   336

allows you to print from the command line any DOS text files or any file that has been formatted by a DOS application for a specific printer.

PRINTDEF   336

allows you to give a printer a logical name and associate it with a predefined set of instructions on how the printer is supposed to print the print job.

PRINTCON   336

uses the forms and modes defined with PRINTDEF and creates a group of instructions that determines how a print job will print out.

Network printing is often one of the least understood and yet more versatile functions performed by NetWare. Just think how expensive it would be to outfit each workstation with its own printer, or how inconvenient it would be to have to wait in line to use a particular workstation just because you needed to print some data using the laser printer attached to it. Just as files can be shared on a network, so can printers.

In this chapter, we will discuss the difference between local and network printing, the components of NetWare's network printing, and what the components do. We will also step through establishing network printing services. After we have set up basic NetWare printing services, we will examine printing from applications, command-line printing, and give a quick overview of the differences in Macintosh printing from a NetWare environment.

Local Printing

When you're working with a local printer (illustrated in Figure 11.1), you're usually printing from an application and have already designated a

F I G U R E 11.1

A local printer

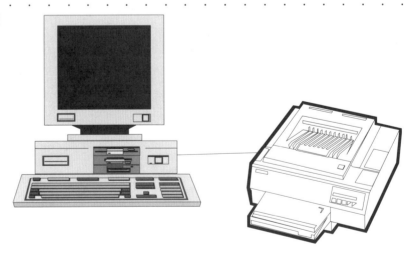

printer driver and the port the printer is plugged into. The application sends the print job to the correct printer port and uses the printer driver software to control the printer.

Network Printing

A print queue is a special directory at the file server. network printer works much the same way except for a few extra steps in the print job's journey to the printer. The application's output is still converted using a printer driver, but instead of traveling straight to the printer through a printer or communication port, the print job travels across the network to a *queue*, a special directory on the file server, to wait its turn to be printed.

A *print server* monitors the queue and sends the print job to the correct printer when the printer is available to print it. The print server generally sends print jobs to the printer on a first-come-first-served basis. In this manner, you can have many different users able to use the same printer, avoiding the need to have a printer at each workstation or waiting to use a particular workstation because of the printer attached to it.

NOTE
A print queue is a special directory on the file server.

Components

NetWare 3.12 uses four components to print a job for you:

- ▸ a printer driver
- ▸ a print queue
- ▸ a print server
- ▸ a printer

NOTE
Not all applications
need or use a printer
driver.

PRINTER DRIVERS

Most of the hundreds of printers available respond only to their own special *printer control codes*. A printer driver takes your file and converts the text to the language that the printer understands.

For instance, if you are using a Hewlett-Packard LaserJet III, you will need to insert special commands such as page format or fonting instructions that tell the HP LaserJet III exactly how to print the file so it appears as you want it to. These printer drivers are usually provided with the application that you are printing from and will do all the work of translating your file to code the printer will understand.

Some applications don't have the printer drivers necessary to tell the printer how to format your print jobs, in which case you have to use the printer–control codes provided with your printer documentation to specify page layouts and font changes. NetWare provides a way to standardize and customize this process using the PRINTDEF and PRINTCON utilities (discussed later in this chapter).

TIP
Even though a print
queue is a directory,
you don't need to
assign users trustee
rights to them.

PRINT QUEUES

A print queue is basically a directory created when you use PCONSOLE to make the queue, and it is usually located under the SYS:SYSTEM directory. Print jobs sent to a specific printer are stored in that printer's print queue as files until the printer is ready to print it.

The first step in starting network printing services is to create print queues using PCONSOLE. When a queue is created, PCONSOLE automatically assigns the user SUPERVISOR as the *print queue operator* and the user group EVERYONE as the *queue users*. At any time, you can change the default queue operator and user assignments by using PCONSOLE.

Print Queue Operator

The print queue operator is a user who can, among other things, delete jobs from the queue and modify the queue status (for example, telling the print queue to not accept any more print jobs). Queue operators can also change the order that print jobs are printed from the standard first-come-first-served basis by assigning a particular print job a higher priority to print it before other print jobs with a lower priority. Be careful whom you assign this privilege to—it can easily be abused.

Queue Users

Queue users are network users allowed to send print jobs to the queue. Since the default group of users is EVERYONE, this will initially allow any member of that group to use the queue.

Queue Servers

The queue servers are the print servers allowed to monitor and remove print jobs for printing. A queue can have up to 25 queue servers (print servers) servicing it.

PRINT SERVERS

Print servers take print jobs out of the queues that they service and send them to the appropriate network printer to be printed. In NetWare 3.12, a print server is a combination of software and hardware not unlike a file server, which makes it possible to allocate print jobs to sixteen different printers from as many as eight different file servers. The following list shows you the possible locations for a print server on your network and the associated software needed to create the print server in each case.

HARDWARE	SOFTWARE
File server	PSERVER.NLM
Dedicated workstation	PSERVER.EXE
External network router	PSERVER.VAP
Third-party print server	Supplied by the vendor

Although only one print server can be physically located on any one machine, there can be more than one print server on a network.

A File Server as a Print Server

Your file server can serve a dual role as both a file server and a print server. If you have a small network with few machines, this may be your best bet. You probably need all of your computers as workstations and won't be able to dedicate one to doing nothing but monitoring your print queues. Since your file server is serving this dual role, your network performance may decline. You use the NLM (NetWare Loadable Module) PSERVER to start print server operations on your file server.

Of the possible candidates for print servers, we recommend *not* using a file server as your print server—if possible—for these four reasons:

1 · If you have a large network, your file server will be responsible for two duties, and your network performance may suffer because of it.

2 · You may want to isolate your file server from your users so that they can't accidentally disturb it.

3 · You can locate your printers anywhere you want to, because they won't need to be attached to the file server.

4 · Depending on your network size and number of file servers, you may need to have multiple network cards in your servers. You'll then probably have a limited number of *interrupt requests* (IRQs) available. When you install hardware such as network cards and I/O cards (for more printer ports), you must assign that new piece of hardware a unique IRQ. It would be best to save the IRQs for the network and have your print server elsewhere.

A Dedicated Workstation as a Print Server

There are many reasons to dedicate a workstation as a print server. If you have a large network, you can improve your performance by setting up dedicated print servers. If you have more than 16 printers, you would have to have a second print server besides the one running on your file server. You could modularize your printing services by having a dedicated print server service the queues from several file servers or having groups of printers controlled by their own print server. The versatility of NetWare printing services allows you to set up your routes from user to printer to best suit your situation.

An External Network Router as a Print Server

If you have an external network router or bridge (discussed in Chapter 2), you might want to have it serve as a print server as well. Since the workstation has already been delegated to routing communications from one part of your LAN to another, why not have the external router also perform as a print server and avoid taking another workstation out of service?

An external router uses a special program called a *VAP* (*value-added process*), which is actually a program from NetWare 2.2. PSERVER.VAP runs "on top" of ROUTER.EXE (the utility run on the workstation to create the external router) in much the same way that WordPerfect runs "on top" of DOS.

However, like a file server, the external router will also be serving double duty, and performance of both the routing and the printer services run by the external router might fall off. Also, since external routers connect two or more LANs, the external router itself may not be accessible for maintenance or to retrieve printouts from the printers attached to it.

Third-Party Print Servers

Many companies, such as Intel and Castelle, make their own print servers designed and programmed to take the place of a workstation running NetWare print-server software. In fact, some more advanced (and expensive) printers actually have hardware built in that allows them to become their own print server. These print servers come with their own utilities that allow them to operate with NetWare. Unlike a NetWare server, the third-party print servers service only the printers to which they are physically attached.

Print Server Users

Like a queue, a print server also has users; the default is the group EVERYONE. The print server users only have the power to monitor the status of the print server. You don't need to be a print server user for the print server to print your print jobs. You need to be a queue user to get the print jobs into the queue. The print server will process your print jobs whether you are a print server user or not.

Print Server Operator

When the print server is defined using PCONSOLE, the print server operator is always initially set up to be the user SUPERVISOR. There can be several users with operator status, but all must be assigned by the SUPERVISOR (or SUPERVISOR Security Equivalent) by using PCONSOLE. A print server operator has the power to:

- ▸ Attach the print server to other file servers.
- ▸ Determine who should be notified if the printer needs service.
- ▸ Issue commands to the printer.
- ▸ Change forms for the printer.
- ▸ Change the queues serviced by a printer.
- ▸ Change queue priority.
- ▸ Down the print server.

A print server operator cannot, however, assign print server users or other print server operators. Only the user SUPERVISOR or SUPERVISOR Security Equivalent can assign those by using PCONSOLE. Like queue operator privileges, print server operator privileges should be guarded so that ordinary users can't circumvent the established printing hierarchy.

PRINTERS

Network printers, as illustrated in Figure 11.2, can be attached *local* to the print server, or *remote* to a workstation. Generally, a maximum of five printers can be physically attached to the machine serving as the print server through the three parallel printer ports of *LPT1*, *LPT2*, and *LPT3* and the two serial ports of *COM1* and *COM2*.

A remote printer is a printer attached to a workstation running a *terminate and stay resident* (TSR) program called RPRINTER.EXE that allows the print server to "see" the printer attached to the workstation. The workstation the remote printer is on will not be able to print directly to the printer, but will have to go through the network to the correct queue. This arrangement's response time is slower than when the printer is attached directly to your print server, so if you can spare the workstations to act as print servers, it will speed up printing if your printers are local to their respective print servers rather than remote.

Setting Up Network Printing Services

To set up your network printing services, you will need to:

- ▸ Organize and set up your printers.

- ▸ Create login accounts for dedicated print servers.

- ▸ Create and configure your print queues.

- ▸ Create and configure your print servers.

- ▸ Define your printers.

- ▸ Assign queues to servers.

- ▸ Set up queues, print servers, and printers on any other file servers if necessary.

▸ Bring up your print servers with PSERVER.NLM (if you are using a file server as a print server) or PSERVER.EXE (if you are using a dedicated workstation as a print server).

▸ Use RPRINTER to establish your remote printers.

FIGURE 11.2

*A print server with local
and remote printers*

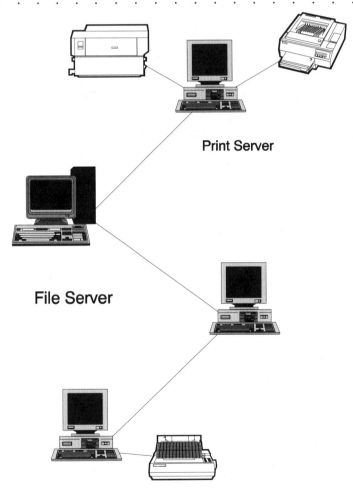

Print Server

File Server

Workstation with Remote Printer

ORGANIZE AND SET UP YOUR PRINTERS

First, consider who will be using your printers, how much they will be using them, and how many printers there will be. If you don't have enough printers, and different groups have to share printers, select a central location so everyone has access to them.

If you have enough printers for certain groups to have their own, concentrate them among the primary users. For instance, Sales may need the capabilities of a good PostScript laser printer for their dog-and-pony shows, while Accounting may need a wide-carriage dot-matrix printer for those really big and important spreadsheets. If you have enough printers, try to organize them in this fashion so that printers will not be overloaded and users will not have to wait for print jobs or walk a long way to retrieve their output.

Next, consider how many print servers you will need to set up and where to place them. A print server can service up to 16 printers, of which five can be local and the other 11 must be remote. Remember, however, that remote network printers are slower than local network printers. Therefore, it is advisable to make all printers local and not remote.

For most computers, up to five printers can be attached directly to the three parallel ports (LPT1, LPT2, and LPT3) and two serial ports (COM1 and COM2). Some machines allow you to have two extra serial ports known as *COM3* and *COM4*. These ports are of dubious value, however, because while they have unique hardware addresses, COM1 and COM3 share the same *IRQ* setting or *Interrupt Request* value. Likewise, COM2 and COM4 share the same interrupt. Some programs check both the hardware address and the interrupt so that they can differentiate between the ports of COM1 and COM3 and the ports of COM2 and COM4. Most programs, however, do not check the hardware address but use just the interrupt value to identify computer hardware and ports. Novell NetWare's PSERVER and RPRINTER use interrupt values only, so you would get an interrupt conflict if you tried to configure and use COM3 or COM4.

Configuring your printers and matching printers to print servers may be a problem. Many printers provide both a serial and a parallel interface. In most cases, your printer may have only a serial or a parallel interface port

WARNING
COM3 and COM4 are of dubious value because of IRQ conflicts with COM1 and COM2.

rather than both, although printers with this problem often have alternate port options that you can purchase and add on. You can also solve this problem by modifying the number of print servers or the placement of the printers.

If you have three serial printers, then you are going to have a problem because a print server can have only two serial ports. You can either set up another print server for the extra printer, or set up the printer as a remote network printer on an unused serial port on a nearby workstation.

Most newer computers include only two serial ports and one parallel port. If you need more printer ports, you can install I/O cards that can be configured to the ports that you need. Contact your vendor for the correct I/O cards and installation instructions.

When you are installing new cards such as an I/O or a network card, be careful that the interrupt you set for that card does not conflict with any other interrupt set on the machine in which you are installing the card. Record which interrupt is associated with each port and which printer is attached to which port. Check the documentation that came with the computer you are going to use as a print server for the interrupts you did not install. You will need this information later when you define your printers. Keep for each printer a separate log that includes its port, interrupt, and location.

WARNING
When installing I/O or network cards, make sure the interrupt you set does not conflict with an interrupt already set on the machine.

Finally, set the hardware communication parameters for each of the serial printers you are planning to use as network printers and plug them into the print server or the remote workstation. It is not necessary to record the hardware communication parameters for parallel printers. Consult the individual serial printer's documentation to find out and adjust the appropriate settings for *Baud Rate*, *Data Bits*, *Stop Bits*, *Parity*, and *XON/XOFF Protocol*. You will also need to record these parameters for each serial printer for when you define your printers for the print server.

CREATE LOGIN ACCOUNTS FOR DEDICATED PRINT SERVERS (OPTIONAL)

If you are going to use a dedicated workstation for a print server, you can activate your print server by running PSERVER.EXE from either a hard disk or boot disk at the workstation, or you can create a login account for the print server so that you can run PSERVER.EXE from the network. If you are going to run PSERVER from the network, restrict what this account has access to because it could be used as a "back door" around your normal security measures. For this reason, it would be better if you ran PSERVER from a local drive and did not have to log in to the network.

CREATE AND CONFIGURE YOUR PRINT QUEUES

Now you can define to the network the way print services should be organized. First, create queues for the print jobs:

1 · Pick a primary file server.

2 · Log in as the user SUPERVISOR.

3 · Run PCONSOLE by typing **PCONSOLE↵**.

4 · Select Print Queue Information.

5 · Press Ins.

6 · Type in the name of the queue you wish to create and press ↵.

7 · Select the new queue name and press ↵.

8 · Assign queue operators and users.

You must first pick a *primary* file server on which the print server object will be defined in the most detail.

▸ If you have only one file server, the choice for your primary file server should be easy.

▸ If you have a file server also be a print server, that file server will be the primary file server.

▸ If you have a print server running on a dedicated workstation, an external router, or a third-party print server, and that print server will be servicing queues on more than one file server, you can

choose any file server it will be servicing queues on as the
primary file server.

Choosing a primary file server for each print server is for your own convenience and will help you avoid confusion when you are defining your
print servers later on. The reason for this is that you will need to create and
define that print server as a *bindery object* (any physical or logical entity on
a file server that has been given a name) on *each* file server with print
queues the particular print server will be servicing. The primary file server
will have the print server bindery object that has the complete printer
definitions that the print server has attached to it either locally or remotely.

To complete the printer definitions, log in to the primary file server as
SUPERVISOR or SUPERVISOR equivalent and run PCONSOLE. You will
see a screen similar to the one shown in Figure 11.3. For this example, we
will be creating print services on a file server named CICERO.

From PCONSOLE's main menu, select Print Queue Information. You
will be given a list of print queues; it should be empty since none have been
created yet. Press Ins to add a new queue to the list. You will be prompted

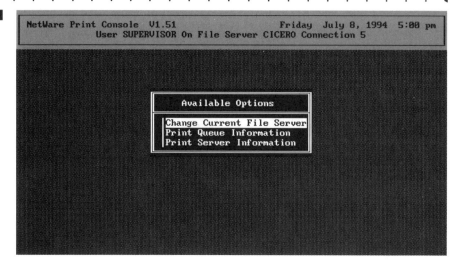

FIGURE 11.3

The main menu of
PCONSOLE

for the name of the new queue as in Figure 11.4. Type the new name and press ↵. Our example will use the name ENG_HP_LASER_III.

To keep things simple, we suggest you create one queue for each printer and name that queue in such a way so that you know which printer it matches. The name can be 47 characters long and can't contain spaces (if you enter a space, PCONSOLE puts in an underscore). Some good ideas for queue names might be some form of the printer type, make, or location so that users know where their jobs will be printed. Our example name, ENG_HP_LASER_III, indicates the queue for a Hewlett-Packard LaserJet III that the engineering department will use.

If you have several identical printers in the same place, consider making one queue feed all printers so that several printers handle the print load passing through the queue instead of one printer trying to service a back-logged queue while another printer stands idle because no jobs are in its queue. The printers need to be identical so that print jobs will be compatible with the printer's control codes no matter which printer is available for the job.

TIP
Print queue names can be up to 47 characters long, but we recommend keeping them shorter.

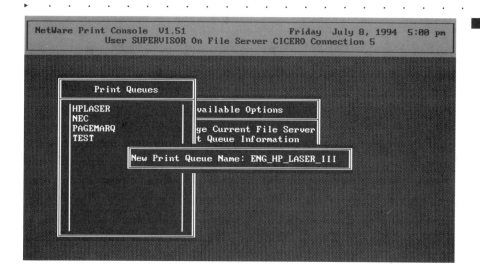

NetWare Print Console V1.51   Friday July 8, 1994 5:00 pm
                 User SUPERVISOR On File Server CICERO Connection 5

Print Queues

HPLASER   vailable Options
NEC
PAGEMARQ   ge Current File Server
TEST   t Queue Information

New Print Queue Name: ENG_HP_LASER_III

F I G U R E   11.4
Creating a print queue

Don't have one queue service identical printers in different places. A good printing system will have print jobs printed as close as possible to those who sent them to be printed. Although the print server can tell the user which printer it printed their job on, it would not improve your office popularity if users had to dash from printer to printer to retrieve their print jobs.

Assigning Print Queue Operators

The queue you just created should now appear on the Print Queues list. Highlight this new print queue and press ↵ to display the Print Queue Information menu (see Figure 11.5).

At this point, you will need to assign queue operators if the default operator of SUPERVISOR is not sufficient for your purposes. Remember that a queue operator can manipulate print jobs within the queue, so assign these rights as sparingly as possible. Operators who grow tired of waiting for some large and slow but important jobs to print before their own could easily change the print order to print their jobs, or even delete the other

FIGURE 11.5

The Print Queue

Information menu

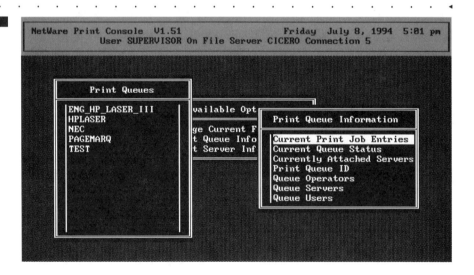

print jobs—which you as system administrator would certainly hear about!

We're not trying to make you paranoid, just make you think about your position as system administrator. Often, you may want to delegate some authority. If you have a large network, you can't be everywhere at once. If a print-out is needed quickly, an operator for a particular queue might need to simply move the print job in question to the front of the queue. The true test of any well-administered LAN is how efficiently and trouble free it runs when you, the system administrator, are not there.

Here's how to assign queue operators if you need to:

1 · Select Queue Operators from the Print Queue Information menu.

2 · Press Ins.

3 · Select from the listed users and press F5 (this will allow you to mark as many users as you like).

4 · Press ↵ to add all the marked users.

Use your keyboard arrows to highlight Queue Operators and press ↵. You will be shown a list of current operators for the queue you have selected. Since the user SUPERVISOR is the default queue operator, it should be the only one listed. Press Ins to show a list of available accounts that you can choose to be queue operators much like Figure 11.6.

Remember that this queue is located only on the server on which you created it. If you have more than one file server, any person you wish to have operator privileges must also have a user account there, or you will not be able to designate them as operators. Select a user from the list by highlighting the user and press ↵. The user you select should now appear on the list of queue operators along with SUPERVISOR. To add another user, simply press Ins to get the list of available users back, mark as many users as you need with the F5 key, and press ↵ to add them.

To remove a user from the list of queue operators, simply select the user you wish to remove, press Del, and confirm the deletion. The user will be removed from the list. When you are finished, press Esc to return to the Print Queue Information menu.

FIGURE 11.6

Selecting queue operators

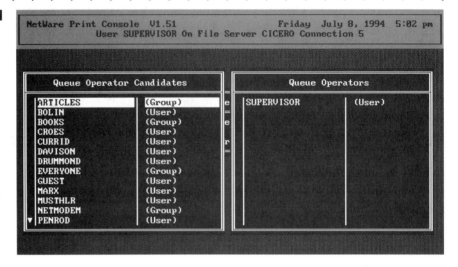

```
NetWare Print Console  V1.51                    Friday  July 8, 1994  5:02 pm
                   User SUPERVISOR On File Server CICERO Connection 5


    ┌─── Queue Operator Candidates ───┐        ┌───── Queue Operators ──────┐
    │ ARTICLES              (Group)   │e       │ SUPERVISOR          (User)  │
    │ BOLIN                 (User)    │═       │                             │
    │ BOOKS                 (Group)   │e       │                             │
    │ CROES                 (User)    │        │                             │
    │ CURRID                (User)    │r       │                             │
    │ DAVISON               (User)    │═       │                             │
    │ DRUMMOND              (User)    │        │                             │
    │ EVERYONE              (Group)   │        │                             │
    │ GUEST                 (User)    │        │                             │
    │ MARX                  (User)    │        │                             │
    │ MUSTHLR               (User)    │        │                             │
    │ NETMODEM              (Group)   │        │                             │
    │▼ PENROD               (User)    │        │                             │
    └─────────────────────────────────┘        └─────────────────────────────┘
```

Assigning Print Queue Users

By default, when you create a queue, the group EVERYONE is assigned as a queue user. To avoid conflicts between users, try to narrow the users of a queue to those who will need to use the printer servicing the queue.

Here's how to restrict the users of a queue:

1 · Select Queue Users from the Print Queue Information menu.

2 · Select EVERYONE and press Del.

3 · Confirm deletion by selecting Yes and pressing ↵.

4 · Press Ins.

5 · Select a user or a group and press F5 (this will allow you to mark multiple users).

6 · Press ↵ to add the marked users.

Adding and deleting queue users works in the same way as adding and deleting queue operators. Use your keyboard arrows to highlight Queue Users from the Print Queue Information menu. You will see a list of

Queue Users that should have the group EVERYONE as its only entry. Since we want to restrict the use of this queue, we are going to delete the group EVERYONE from the list. Make sure that EVERYONE is highlighted and press Del. You will be prompted to confirm the deletion, so highlight Yes and press ↵ as we did in Figure 11.7.

The list should now be empty and ready for you to make a list of only the users and groups that you want to be able to send print jobs to the queue you just created. Press Ins to show a list of users and groups. You can build your list from any combination of users and groups to allow only those who need to use the queue to be able to. Select your first choice and press F5. This will allow you to mark more than one user for addition. Press ↵ and your selections will be added to the list. Repeat this process until you have the list that you want. Press Esc to return to the Print Queue Information menu.

At this point, you would normally move on to designate a queue server. This process works exactly the same as assigning queue operators and users that we just discussed. But first we must define a print server to choose before we can designate the print server that will monitor the print queue

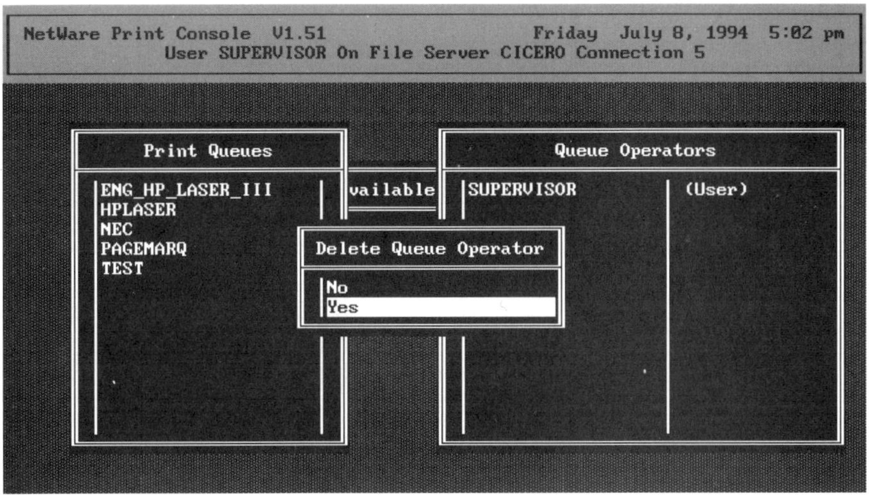

FIGURE 11.7

Deleting a user or group

```
NetWare Print Console  V1.51              Friday  July 8, 1994  5:02 pm
                 User SUPERVISOR On File Server CICERO Connection 5

        Print Queues                        Queue Operators

  ENG_HP_LASER_III    |vailable|  SUPERVISOR            (User)
  HPLASER
  NEC                  Delete Queue Operator
  PAGEMARQ
  TEST                 No
                       Yes
```

ENG_HP_LASER_III. Press Esc till you return to the Available Options screen of PCONSOLE.

CREATING AND CONFIGURING YOUR PRINT SERVERS

Now we are ready to create and configure the print servers on our network. Here's how to create a new print server:

1 · Select Print Server Information.

2 · Press Ins.

3 · Type the name of the new print server and press ↵.

After creating the print server, perform the following steps to define it.

1 · Select the print server you just created and press ↵.

2 · Set the password.

3 · Assign configuration options.

4 · Assign print server operators.

5 · Assign print server users.

When we last left off, we were logged into the file server CICERO, which is going to be the primary file server for this print server. We had just created and defined a print queue called ENG_HP_LASER_III using PCONSOLE and should still be at the Available Options menu. Creating a print server bindery object is very much like creating a print queue.

1 · Select the Print Server Information option and press ↵. You will be given a list of available print servers; it should be empty because we have not yet created any.

2 · Press Ins and you will be prompted, as we are in Figure 11.8, to type in the name of the new print server.

3 · Type in a name and press ↵.

FIGURE II.8

*Print Server Information
menu*

```
NetWare Print Console  V1.51              Monday  April 5, 1993  5:08 pm
             User SUPERVISOR On File Server CICERO Connection 5


          ┌───────────────────────┐
          │    Print Servers      │
          ├───────────────┬───────┤
          │CURRIDCO       │vailable Options
          │NETPORT        │
          │NETPORT-P1     │ge Current File Server
          │NETPORT-P2     │t Queue Information
          │      ┌──────────────────────────────────────┐
          │      │New Print Server Name: 2ND_FLOOR_PRINTER│
          │      └──────────────────────────────────────┘
          │               │
          │               │
          │               │
          └───────────────┴
```

Your new print server should now appear on the list of available print servers.

Like print queues, print servers should have names that are descriptive of which printers they send jobs to, which groups of users they service, or something unique to differentiate a print server that services the Sales' dot matrix printers from a print server that handles all of Shipping's printers. Names can be up to 47 characters long but can't contain spaces (PCONSOLE will substitute underscores for blanks automatically). Try to keep the names short (so that they are easy to remember and to type) while making them descriptive. For our example, we will name our print server 2ND_FLOOR_PRINTERS after the location of the printers it sends print jobs to.

TIP
**Give print servers
names describing the
printers and the users
they service. The
names can contain 47
characters but no
spaces.**

Using Passwords, Full Names, and IDs

Highlight the print server you just created and press ↵ to display a screen titled Print Server Information. The first option, Change Password, may or may not be very useful, since if the password option is enabled, it only prevents the print server from being started without it. If you should have a power failure or some other reason the print server would go down, it could not be restarted if you or someone else who knew the password was not available. Further, the print server does not have normal user access to the file server, so it may be more trouble to have a password for your print server than it is worth.

If you decide to set a password, select Change Password and press ↵. You will be prompted to type the new password and then to retype it to confirm. You can remove a password by following the same procedure, but when you are prompted to type and retype the new password, press ↵ only instead of typing a new password and pressing ↵.

To add a more descriptive name to the name you chose when the print server object was created, select Full Name and press ↵. Type in the full name at the prompt provided and press ↵. This feature is for your convenience only and is not necessary to the definition process.

Selecting the Print Server ID will show you the print server's unique bindery object number that NetWare assigns it and the server that the number is located on.

Assigning Print Server Operators

The next option, Print Server Operators, allows you to assign operator privileges to other users if you think that the default user SUPERVISOR will not be sufficient.

Remember that a print server operator can manipulate the priority of the queues the print server has control of, so assign these privileges with care. An unthinking print server operator could change your carefully thought-out priority for queues, or worse yet, reassign the queues a print server services. Changing priority could print important jobs after less necessary ones; moving queues to the wrong print server will direct users' print jobs to the wrong printer. Make sure that the people you assign these privileges understand the consequences of changes and when to seek your assistance.

All is not lost if operators make changes. Print server operator changes are all *dynamic*—they are not permanent changes. Only the user SUPERVISOR or SUPERVISOR Security Equivalent can make permanent changes.

Simply down the print server and then restart it to reset the print server to the original setup.

Here's how to set up other print server operators:

1 · Select Print Server Operators from the Print Server Information menu.

2 · Press Ins.

3 · Select from the listed users and press F5.

4 · Press ⏎ to add the marked users.

Assigning print server operators is identical to assigning print queue operators. Use your keyboard arrows to highlight Print Server Operators and press ⏎. You will be shown a list of operators for the print server you have just created. Since the user SUPERVISOR is the default print server operator, it should be the only one listed. Press Ins to show a list of available users and groups. Select from the list by highlighting the user or group and pressing F5. Press ⏎, and your selections should appear on the list of print server operators along with SUPERVISOR.

To remove a user or group from the list of print server operators, simply select the user or group you wish to remove, press Del, and confirm the deletion. The user or group will be removed from the list. When you finish adjusting your list, press Esc to return to the Print Server Information menu.

Assigning Print Server Users

When you create a print server, the print server users are automatically assigned to be the users who are part of the group EVERYONE. All a print server user is allowed to do is check on the status of the print server. A print server user can run PCONSOLE and will receive a menu similar to Figure 11.9 by selecting Print Server Information and the relevant print server name.

As you can see, the print server user has fewer options than the print server operator or the SUPERVISOR; note that Change Password and Print Server

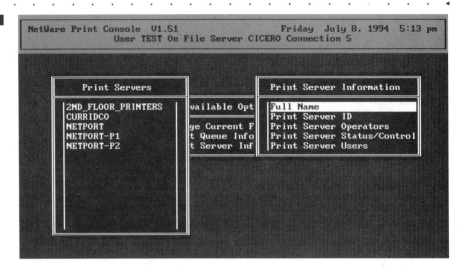

Configuration are not available. Figure 11.10 illustrates further options under Print Server Status/Control.

All of these options available to print server users shown in Figures 11.9 and 11.10 are informational only: Print server users may not change any information, only view it, so there is really no need to restrict this privilege because information cannot be changed accidentally. Also, you do not have to be a print server user to print out through the printers serviced by the print servers—you only need be a print *queue* user. The print server will retrieve jobs from a queue and send them to the correct printer regardless of whether you are a print server user or not.

If you still feel the need to restrict the users who can view the print server status information, here is how to do so:

1 · Select Print Server Users from the Print Server Information menu.

2 · Select EVERYONE and press Del.

3 · Confirm deletion by selecting Yes and pressing ↵.

4 · Press Ins.

▶ ·◀

```
NetWare Print Console  V1.51              Friday  July 8, 1994  5:14 pm
              User TEST On File Server CICERO Connection 5
```

```
       Print Servers
    ┌──────────────────────┐   vailable O   ┌─────────────────────────────┐
    │ 2ND_FLOOR_PRINTERS   │                 │ Print Server Status and Control│
    │ CURRIDCO             │                 │ ┌───────────────────────────┐
    │ NETPORT              │   ge Current    │ │File Servers Being Serviced│
    │ NETPORT-P1           │   t Queue In    │ │Notify List for Printer    │
    │ NETPORT-P2           │   t Server I    │ │Printer Status             │
    │                      │                 │ │Queues Serviced by Printer │
    │                      │                 │ │Server Info                │
    └──────────────────────┘                 └─────────────────────────────┘
```

5 · Select a user or group and press F5 to mark it.

6 · Press ↵ to add the marked users.

Adding and deleting print server users works in the same way as adding and deleting print queue users. Use your keyboard arrows to highlight Print Server Users from the Print Server Information menu. You will see a list of Print Server Users that should have the group EVERYONE as its only entry. Since we want to restrict who can view information about this particular print server, we are going to delete the group EVERYONE from the list. Make sure that EVERYONE is highlighted and press Del. You will be prompted to confirm the deletion, so highlight Yes and press ↵, as illustrated in Figure 11.11.

The list should now be empty and ready for you to make a list of the users and groups to have access to information about this print server. Press Ins to show a list of users and groups. You can build your list from any combination of users and groups to allow only those who you feel need this information. Select your first choice and press F5 to mark your selection, then select further choices. Press Enter to add your marked choices.

· · · · ·

FIGURE 11.11

*Deleting a print server user
or group*

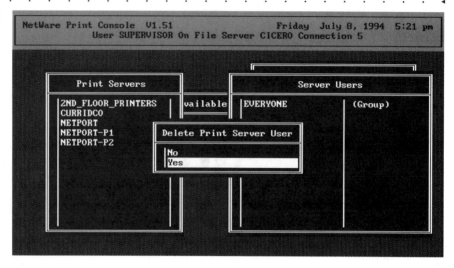

DEFINE YOUR PRINTERS

We have covered just about everything on the Print Server Information menu except for the Print Server Configuration option. To configure a print server, we need to do four things:

▶ List the file servers the print server will be servicing queues from.

▶ Configure the printers the print server will be sending print jobs to.

▶ Create a list of users to be notified when a printer needs maintenance.

▶ Assign queues to specific printers.

To begin, select Print Server Configuration and press ↵. You will be given a screen similar to Figure 11.12.

▶ • ◀

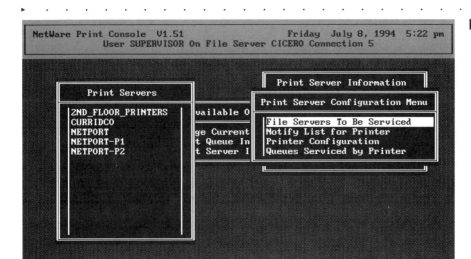

Print Server Configuration
menu

Assigning File Servers

From the Print Server Configuration menu, select File Servers To Be Serviced, and press ↵. You will see a list with the name of the file server into which you are currently logged in as SUPERVISOR. This is the default file server and can't be deleted from the list although other file servers can be added or deleted. If you have other servers that this print server will service, now is a good time to add to the list (up to eight) of file servers on which this particular print server will service queues.

Press Ins to show a list of available file servers. Highlight the desired file server and press ↵ to add it to the list of file servers being serviced by this print server.

To delete a file server, use your keyboard arrows to select the name of the server from the File Servers To Be Serviced list, press Del, and confirm the deletion.

To return to the Print Server Configuration menu, press Esc.

Configuring Printers

Next, we need to configure the printers to which the print server will be sending print jobs. Like queues, these printers will have to have unique names so that there is no confusion about which printer is which. We suggest that you give printers the same name or a form of the name of the queues that they receive their print jobs from. A printer's name can be up to 47 characters long. Add the name to your information log that you are keeping on all printers.

After you have settled on appropriate names for the printers this print server will serve, select Printer Configuration from the Print Server Configuration Menu and press ↵. You will be shown a list entitled Configured Printers (see Figure 11.13). This list is numbered 0–15 in the right column for the 16 possible printers this print server can control. The left column is for your unique printer names and will contain Not Installed until you configure that slot with a printer.

Highlight printer number 0 and press ↵ to display the Printer 0 Configuration form (see Figure 11.14). The default name will be Printer 0 and will be highlighted. The type will be Defined Elsewhere. All the other

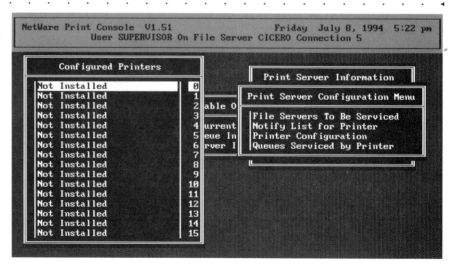

fields will be empty. Type in the name you have chosen for the printer and press ↵. Our example printer name will be HP_LASER_III. This makes our example printer name HP_LASER_III, the print queue name ENG_HP_LASER_III, and our print server name 2ND_FLOOR_PRINTERS. If your network is big or has many queues, printers, and print servers, you may have to be more creative with naming than we have been.

After you have named printer 0, highlight Type: Defined Elsewhere (located just under the name field) and press ↵. You will see a list of 16 printer types (see Figure 11.15). The first seven types are for local printers attached to the parallel ports of LPT1, LPT2, or LPT3 and the serial ports of COM1, COM2, COM3, or COM4 of the machine serving as your print server. Our example printer, HP_LASER_III, is locally attached to our print server of 2ND_FLOOR_PRINTERS through LPT1, so we need to highlight Parallel, LPT1 and press ↵.

If you're trying to configure a remote network printer, choose one of the remote port options. For example, if you have a printer attached to a network workstation through COM2, select Remote Serial, COM2 as your printer type. If you are going to set up a remote printer but do not know

F I G U R E   11.14

Printer 0 Configuration form

```
NetWare Print Console  V1.51              Friday  July 8, 1994  5:22 pm
          User SUPERVISOR On File Server CICERO Connection 5

        Co             Printer 0 configuration              ion
  Not In Name: Printer 0                                   on Menu
  Not In Type: Defined elsewhere
  Not In
  Not In Use interrupts:                                   iced
  Not In IRQ:
  Not In
  Not In Buffer size in K:                                 ter
  Not In
  Not In Starting form:
  Not In Queue service mode:
  Not In
  Not In Baud rate:
  Not In Data bits:
  Not In Stop bits:
  Not In Parity:
  Not In Use X-On/X-Off:
```

FIGURE 11.15

16 printer types

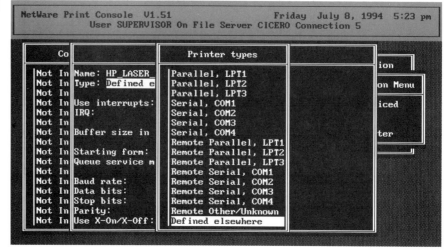

which port it will be attached to, choose the Remote Other/Unknown option. This option allows you to define the printer slot now without knowing the configuration details for the remote printer, and RPRINTER will pass along the information necessary to the print server later when RPRINTER is run.

The final printer type, Defined Elsewhere, is used for printers already configured on the primary file server for which you are setting up services on additional file servers that the primary file server's print server will be handling queues on (do not use this if you are presently configuring the printer on your primary file server—see *Setting Up Queues, Print Servers, and Printers on other File Servers* below for more explanation). If you choose either Remote Other/Unknown or Defined Elsewhere, you are finished with this printer's configuration; press Esc and confirm saving the changes.

After you have chosen a printer type, PCONSOLE will send you back to the Printer 0 Configuration screen, and the Use Interrupts field will be highlighted, containing Yes, the default answer. Using interrupts is generally faster, so accept the default by pressing ↵. If you do not know the interrupt setting for the port that the printer is attached to, press N↵ in the Use Interrupts field to disable the use of interrupts for this printer and move you down to the Buffer Size in K field. Disabling the use of interrupts is called *polled* printing.

If you answer Yes to using interrupts, PCONSOLE will automatically move you to the next field, IRQ, and will also try to anticipate the IRQ setting you will need according to which type of printer you designated. For instance, if you chose either a local or a remote LPT1 or the Remote Other/Unknown setting, the default value for the IRQ will be 7, while the default value for any of the other LPT ports will be 5. Similarly, COM1's default setting, either local or remote, will be 4, and the other COM ports will be 3. Check this default value against the IRQ setting you recorded for the port that the printer is attached to: If it doesn't match, change the default value to the IRQ setting you recorded.

PCONSOLE will only accept the numbers from 3 to 7 as correct IRQ settings. If the port where the printer is attached has an IRQ setting outside this range, you will have to reset the port's IRQ setting to conform or use *polled printing*. Press ↵ to move from the IRQ field to the Buffer size in K field.

The *buffer size* is the amount of RAM memory the print server sets aside for a buffer for your printer. As the print server begins processing the print job, it places the information ready for the printer in this buffer. The information is passed on to the printer as the printer is ready for it until the print job is complete. This saves time in printing because the printer can start printing the information that is ready instead of waiting for the whole job to be completely processed. The default buffer size is 3 KB, but you can designate any number of KB from 1 to 20. You may find that your printing performance improves when you increase the buffer size from 5 KB to 10 KB. Each printer normally requires about 10 KB of RAM, and if you increase the size of your buffers and have many printers attached to a print server, you will eat up your RAM quickly. Remember that a print server is a service provided to the network and can be run on a machine that is also providing other services such as a file server or a bridge, so you might need to be careful about how you allocate RAM. Type in the size of the buffer you wish and press ↵.

The Starting Form field will appear. This field is mainly used in conjunction with the PRINTDEF utility (which we'll explain in a minute). A *form* is a type of paper that a printer uses and is defined using PRINTDEF. For example, green-bar continuous-feed paper might be defined as 5, while legal size white paper might be 3. You can have up to 256 different forms with the designated code numbers 0–255. When the print server receives a print job, it will not process that print job until the proper form or paper is loaded on the requested printer. Accept the default of 0 for now by pressing ↵ until you decide whether or not you will define any forms using PRINTDEF.

The next field that needs your attention is Queue Service Mode, which tells the printer how it should handle form change requests. There are four ways that the printer can react:

Change Forms As Needed	The printer will stop and wait for the forms to be changed whenever it receives a form change request.
Minimize Form Changes Across Queues	All the jobs that use the currently loaded form will be printed from any queue the printer prints from. Queue priority is disregarded in this instance. After all those jobs have printed, the printer will then request a form change.
Minimize Form Changes Within Queues	All the jobs in the highest priority queue will be printed first with form changes requested as they occur from jobs in that queue before any jobs are serviced in another queue.
Service Only Currently Mounted Form	The printer will not request a form change at all, and any print jobs that require a change will not be printed.

The default will be Change Forms As Needed. To select one of the other options, press ↵ to get a list of service modes. Select the mode you wish and press ↵ to return to the Printer 0 configuration form.

If you are configuring a parallel printer, then you are through with this configuration. Press Esc and select Yes to save the changes for this printer configuration. You will now see the list of printers with your newly defined printer in slot 0. Press Esc to return to the Print Server Configuration menu. You are now ready to configure any other printers that this print server will be sending print jobs. Record the names that you gave them and which printer slot they were configured in.

If you are configuring a serial printer, you will need to specify to PCON-SOLE your serial printer's *Baud Rate*, *Data Bits*, *Stop Bits*, *Parity*, and whether or not to use the *XON/XOFF Protocol,* as in Figure 11.16. The default assignments are baud rate of 9600, 8 data bits, 1 stop bit, no parity, and not to use the XON/XOFF protocol. Check the records that you have been keeping for this printer and see if you need to make any changes to the defaults so they match the configuration of your serial printer. Press Esc and select Yes to save the changes for this printer configuration.

You will now see the list of printers with your newly defined printer in slot 0. Press Esc to return to the Print Server Configuration menu. You are now ready to configure any other printers for this print server. Remember

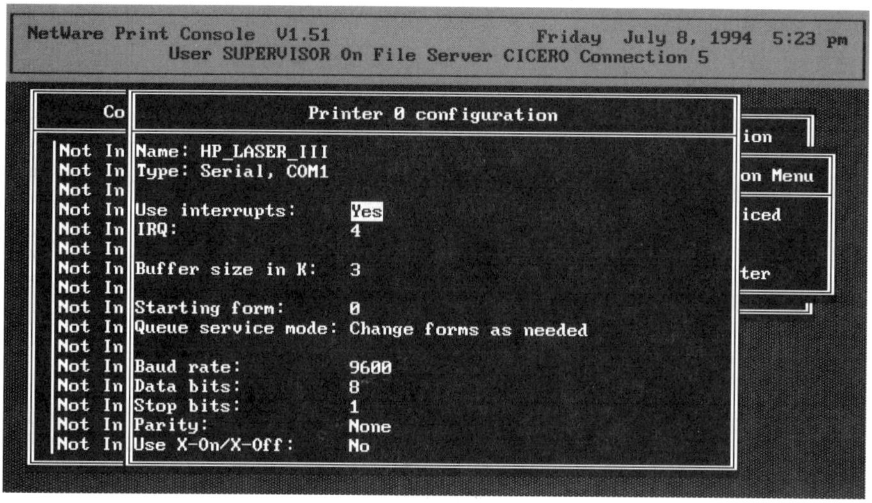

FIGURE 11.16

Sample serial printer configuration

to record the names that you give them and which printer slot they were configured in.

Creating a Notify List

A *notify list* for a printer is a list of users and groups to be sent a message when a printer needs human assistance such as a form change. Graphics programs, however, may interfere with the message sent to warn of a printer problem. If a user is running Microsoft Windows, a windows utility called NWPOPUP (usually installed when Windows is installed—see the Windows *User Guide*) must be running for the message to reach that user. Macintosh users will not receive a message at all.

To build your notify list, select Notify List for Printer from the Print Server Configuration menu, and you will be given a list of the printers defined for this print server. Select the printer name you wish to create the notify list for and press ↵. You will receive an empty list like Figure 11.17.

As with other list of users and user groups, press Ins to show a list of users and user groups available to choose from. There is also a special user listed in

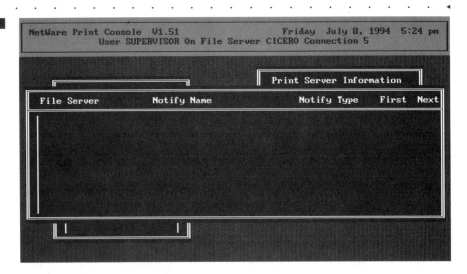

parentheses called *Job Owner*, and it is not listed as a user or group but as *Unknown Type*. By adding the user JOB OWNER, whoever sent the print job that needs human intervention will be notified along with the others who would normally be notified. Adding all of your print server operators and yourself as well as others sprinkled throughout your departments whom you consider capable of servicing the printer would be a good idea so that the chances of a problem cropping up with no one around to solve it will be small.

To add to the list, select the user or group to add and press ↵ to display a screen where you can specify the notification intervals. The default provides a notification after the first 30 seconds followed by another every 60 seconds. You can change the default to any number of seconds from 1 to 3600. Press Esc when you are finished and confirm the changes. Press Ins to show the available choices list again and repeat the process until you have built the list that you wish. When you finish building your list, press Esc till you return to the Print Server Configuration menu screen.

Assigning Queues to Printers

Next, assign which printers will receive print jobs from which queues. Select the Queues Serviced by Printer option from the Print Server Configuration menu. You will receive the list of printers defined for this print server. Select the one you want and press ↵. You should now see an empty list like Figure 11.18.

Press Ins to show a list of available queues. You can assign many queues to one printer or more than one printer to a single queue, depending on your organizational needs. Highlight the queue that you wish to send print jobs to this printer and press ↵. You will now be asked to assign a priority level to this queue. The default is 1—the highest priority—but you can choose a priority as low as 10.

If you have only one queue per printer, there's no need to change the priority from 1. If you have more than one queue sending jobs to this printer, such as a queue for management users and one for Sales personnel, you may want to set the management queue with a priority higher than the

FIGURE II.18

Assigning queues to printers

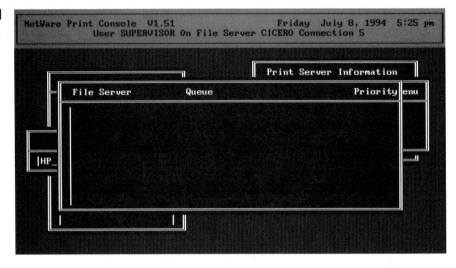

FIGURE II.18

Assigning queues to printers

queue for Sales. Once again, that depends upon how you want to minimize problems.

Enter the priority for this queue and press ↵ to add the queue to the list. Repeat this procedure to add any more queues that you want this printer to receive print jobs from. When you are finished, press Esc till you return to the Available Options screen or PCONSOLE's main menu.

ASSIGNING QUEUE SERVERS TO QUEUES

The final step in creating and configuring your print services will be assigning the queue servers. We've told NetWare which queues send jobs to which printers, but we have yet to specify which print servers service which queues. You'll remember that we couldn't do this when we created and defined our print queues because we hadn't yet created and defined our print servers.

Here's how to assign queue servers:

1 · Select Print Queue Information and press ↵.

2 · Select a print queue and press ↵.

3 · Select Queue Servers and press ↵.

4 · Press Ins.

5 · Select desired print server name and press ↵.

6 · Repeat if you want more than one print server servicing a queue.

From the Available Options menu, choose Print Queue Information and press ↵. You should see the list of print queues that you defined earlier. Select the print queue that you wish to assign a print server and press ↵. Our example list will only have the queue ENG_HP_LASER_III in it. You will see the now-familiar Print Queue Information menu. Select the Queue Servers option and press ↵. As with other lists we have built, the list of queue servers will be empty when we first view it. Press Ins for a list of available print servers. Our example list will only have one entry, the print server 2ND_FLOOR_PRINTERS. Select the print server that you wish to service this particular print queue and press ↵. The print server you chose will appear on the list as a queue server.

You can have more than one print server servicing a single queue. For example, if you have two dedicated print servers servicing twenty IBM 4019 laser printers in a large marketing department, you could have everyone in marketing direct their print jobs to one queue and the two print servers could both be removing print jobs from that queue and sending them to the laser printers. More than likely, you will just be assigning only one print server to monitor one queue. When you finish assigning print servers to this queue, press Esc twice to select another queue to assign print servers or three times to return to the Available Options menu.

SETTING UP QUEUES, PRINT SERVERS, AND PRINTERS ON OTHER FILE SERVERS

If you plan to have a print server service queues on file servers other than the primary server we just defined, you will need to create and define that same print server on *all* the file servers on which it will be servicing queues.

Use the exact same procedure discussed previously except:

I · On the printer configuration form, specify the type as Defined Elsewhere.

2 · Create new queues for the print server to service on the secondary servers.

You should still be logged into your primary server as the SUPERVISOR. From the Available Options menu, select Change Current File Server and press ↵ to display a list of the file servers you are currently logged into and under which user accounts you are logged in. In our example, we are only logged into the file server CICERO as the user SUPERVISOR. We will need to log in to a new file server called TOLSTOY to set up our print services there if we wish to use the print server 2ND_FLOOR_PRINTERS to service the queues. You will need to log in as the SUPERVISOR or SUPERVISOR Equivalent on that file server as well, because you can't make queues or print server definitions, or make permanent changes with PCONSOLE, unless you have supervisory privileges.

Select from the list of available file servers the name of the file server for which you wish to set up a queue that your print server will service and press ↵. You will be prompted for a user name to log in as. Type in **supervisor** or user equivalent and press ↵. Enter the correct password. Two things should happen now. First, the file server you were changing to, in our case the file server TOLSTOY, should now appear on the list of file servers that you are logged into. Second, the message on top of the Available Options menu should change from User SUPERVISOR On File Server CICERO Connection "Connection Number" to User SUPERVISOR On File Server TOLSTOY Connection "Connection Number".

You are now ready to create queues on this file server. Let's assume that this file server belongs to Accounting. The queue we wish to create will send print jobs to the Hewlett-Packard LaserJet III that we set up earlier for the print server 2ND_FLOOR_PRINTERS on the file server CICERO. We will call our new queue on the file server TOLSTOY, ACCT_HP_LASER_III. Set up this queue as we discussed earlier for the queue ENG_HP_LASER_III on the primary file server CICERO and assign operators and users as you wish.

After you have created and defined ACCT_HP_LASER_III, you will need to create and define the print server 2ND_FLOOR_PRINTERS on the file server TOLSTOY. You will use the same process as when defining 2ND_FLOOR_PRINTERS on CICERO. Obviously, you need to use the exact same name. You also need to define the printers in the same slot as well as give them the same names that they had before. For instance, we defined the printer HP_LASER_III in the configuration slot 0 for the print server 2ND_FLOOR_PRINTERS on the file server CICERO. We should then define that same printer as the printer HP_LASER_III in the configuration slot 0 for the print server 2ND_FLOOR_PRINTERS on the file server TOLSTOY.

One more item about printers: All you have to define about them this time is to give them the same name that they had previously and declare the type as Defined Elsewhere instead of having to specify a port. All the printer information has already been defined once and other than the name does not need to be defined again. Complete the print server configuration by assigning file servers to be serviced, creating a notify list, assigning queues to printers, declaring operator and user privileges, and assigning queue servers.

We are now ready to start our print services. Our example printing service has two queues called ENG_HP_LASER_III and ACCT_HP_LASER_III for two different groups of employees, namely Engineering and Accounting. These two queues both print to a common printer called HP_LASER_III. The same print server, 2ND_FLOOR_PRINTERS, monitors both queues even though they exist physically on different file servers, and removes print jobs from them as the printer HP_LASER_III finishes with a previous print job and is ready for another.

INITIATING YOUR PRINT SERVICES

With all of your print services created and defined, start the print server. Recall that you can have four different types of machines running the print server services, and each requires different software to start the print server. We will not discuss third-party print server installation, because that documentation will come with your third-party print server and varies from vendor to vendor.

When you as SUPERVISOR make changes to the print server or print queue configuration, such as creating a queue for that print server, configuring a printer, or moving a queue from one print servers control to another, you will need to down and then restart the print servers involved in order for them to recognize the changes.

Using a File Server as a Print Server

If you are going to use a file server for a print server, you will be using the PSERVER.NLM utility located in the SYS:SYSTEM directory. To start this type of print server, type at the command line of the file server's console

LOAD PSERVER *print_server*↵

where *print_server* is the name of the print server you are trying to start.

For instance, we would run our example print server called 2ND_FLOOR_PRINTERS on the file server CICERO by typing

LOAD PSERVER 2ND_FLOOR_PRINTERS↵

A screen similar to Figure 11.19 will appear, listing the status of each available printer the print server has configured in its configuration slots. Printers 0 through 7 will be shown on the first screen; printers 8 through 15 can be monitored from a second screen. Use the space bar to toggle between the screens. You can also press Alt-Esc to exit the PSERVER screen entirely.

On the PSERVER screen, you may see some of the following messages for a printer.

Not installed   No printer has been configured for this position.

Not connected

This is a remote printer that has been configured, but has not been connected using RPRINTER.EXE.

Waiting for job

The printer is ready to print.

Out of paper

The printer is out of paper or there is some problem with the printer such as the printer connection being broken.

If you wish to halt all print server activities, you can simply unload the print server module with the command:

UNLOAD PSERVER *print_server*

where *print_server* is the name of the print server you're trying to stop.

Using a Dedicated Workstation as a Print Server

If you are using a dedicated workstation as a print server, use PSER-VER.EXE to start your print server. There are several things you must do

```
                Novell NetWare Print Server V1.21
                Server 2ND_FLOOR_PRINTERS Running

0: HP_LASER_III              4: Not installed
   Waiting for job


1: Not installed             5: Not installed


2: Not installed             6: Not installed


3: Not installed             7: Not installed
```

F I G U R E   II.19

Print Server screen

first, however. You must have access to the following files either from a floppy disk, a local hard drive, or your network file server:

PSERVER.EXE

IBM$RUN.OVL

SYS$ERR.DAT

SYS$HELP.DAT

SYS$MSG.DAT

You must also increase the SPX connections in your NET.CFG file for the dedicated workstation by adding the line:

SPX connections 60

You do not have to be logged into the network, but you do need to have the workstation DOS Requester loaded. At the dedicated workstation's DOS prompt, type:

PSERVER *file_server print_server*⏎

where *file_server* is your primary file server and *print_server* is the print server you intend to start.

You will see the same screens and messages as with a file server doubling up as a print server (see Figure 11.19). If you wish to down this print server, you can use PCONSOLE:

1 · Log in to the primary file server as either SUPERVISOR or a print server operator.

2 · From the Available Options menu, select Print Server Information.

3 · From the Print Server Information menu, choose Print Server Status/Control.

4 · From the Print Server Status/Control menu, select Server Info.

5 · On the Print Server Info/Status screen, press ↵.

6 · Select either Down or Going Down After Current Jobs.

Using an External Router as a Print Server

If you are going to use an external router as a print server, use a *VAP* (*value-added process*) from NetWare versions 2.15c or above. You will need to have this program, PSERVER.VAP, located in the same directory as ROUTER.EXE (the utility run on the workstation to create the external router). When you run ROUTER.EXE to start your bridge, you will be prompted:

> Value Added Processes have been defined. Do you wish to load them?

Answer **Y** and press ↵.

To halt this print server for any reason, simply type **PSERVER STOP** and press ↵. This will accomplish the same thing as downing a dedicated workstation print server using the PCONSOLE utility. To restart your router/print server, type **PSERVER START** and press ↵.

Connecting Remote Network Printers

Next, connect any remote network printers to a print server using RPRINTER.EXE. RPRINTER is a *terminate and stay resident* (*TSR*) program—it is loaded into a workstation's memory and runs in the background until it is stopped or the workstation is rebooted. You do not have to be logged into the network, but you do have to have the NetWare workstation DOS Requester loaded. When PSERVER.EXE is run, it establishes its own session with the file server through NetWare Core Protocol (NCP) requests. If you had been logged in to run PSERVER.EXE, your connection will be broken while PSERVER.EXE establishes its own.

To make a remote network printer, you will need to add the line SPX connections 50 to the workstation's NET.CFG file, and you will need access to these seven files from a floppy disk, a local hard drive, or a network file server:

RPRINTER.EXE

RPRINT$$.EXE

RPRINTER.HLP

IBM$RUN.OVL

SYS$ERR.DAT

SYS$HELP.DAT

SYS$MSG.DAT

RPRINTER can be used as either a command-line utility by including the necessary options, or you will be prompted for them by menus. Here is the format for using RPRINTER as a command-line program:

RPRINTER *print_server printer_number -r -s*

where:

print_server is the name of the print server that this printer is defined under

printer_number is the configuration slot that this printer is defined in

-r is an option that disconnects the designated remote printer from the specified print server (do not use this option if you are using an extended or expanded memory shell: reboot the machine instead to disconnect the printer)

-s is an option that displays the status of the remote printer named

Here are three examples:

RPRINTER 2ND_FLOOR_PRINTERS 0	Connect the workstation's printer (defined in printer configuration slot 0) to the print server.
RPRINTER 2ND_FLOOR_PRINTERS 0 -r	Disconnect the workstation's printer (defined in printer configuration slot 0) from the print server.
RPRINTER 2ND_FLOOR_PRINTERS 0 -s	Display the workstation's printer (defined in printer configuration slot 0) status.

Whether you use RPRINTER as a command line program or a menu program, you will be prompted to fill in information about the printer if you declared the type to be Remote/Other Unknown. You will need to tell RPRINTER what port the printer is on, whether the printer is serial or parallel, what the IRQ value for the port is, and so on.

MACINTOSH PRINT SERVICES

To support Macintosh printing services on your network, you first need to have NetWare for Macintosh installed. NetWare for Macintosh is a set of NLMs and other programs that allow your NetWare file server to support an AppleTalk leg of your network. The print services are handled by ATPS.NLM (AppleTalk Print Services).

ATPS allows Macintosh clients to still print directly to Macintosh network printers, or you can "hide" the printers from the Mac clients and force them to use an ATPS queue. Using the queue allows you to ensure that important jobs can be given high priority and then printed faster than lower-priority jobs. ATPS.NLM even allows non-Macintosh clients such as DOS, OS/2, and UNIX, to print to an ATPS queue provided the jobs are formatted correctly.

Printing Using Applications and NetWare Utilities

One large problem associated with printing from your applications to network printers is that most DOS applications are still not *network-aware:* You can't send your print jobs directly to the print queue that services the network printer you wish to use. There are a few notable exceptions such as WordPerfect (which allows you to designate a network print queue with its printer selection menu), but most DOS applications will send your print jobs to a designated printer port such as LPT1 or COM1.

USING CAPTURE AND ENDCAP WITH DOS APPLICATIONS

We can redirect application printing to the correct printer queue by using the command line utility CAPTURE. You can redirect your print jobs to up to three different print queues in this manner, depending upon which parallel printer ports your application uses. The CAPTURE command uses this format:

CAPTURE *options*

where *options* are the different qualifiers that can be set—see Appendix A, *NetWare 3.12 Utilities Summary*.

We will be focusing on only two of these options, *local* and *queue*, to redirect application output to the proper queues. The syntax for the local option is L=*n*, where *n* is 1, 2, or 3, corresponding to your workstation's parallel printer ports of LPT1, LPT2, or LPT3. You do not necessarily need to have three parallel ports in your workstation because this is a logical connection. Any printing directed at a nonexistent parallel port can be redirected by the CAPTURE command. The syntax for the queue option is Q=*queuename*, where *queuename* is the name of the queue you wish your print jobs to go to.

Suppose you wish to print a letter from a word processor on a laser printer serviced by the queue LASER, a sales report from an accounting package on a wide-carriage dot-matrix printer serviced by the queue DOT_MATRIX, and a graph from a spreadsheet on a plotter serviced by the queue PLOTTER. We could redirect all these print jobs using the following commands:

```
CAPTURE L=1 Q=LASER
CAPTURE L=2 Q=DOT_MATRIX
CAPTURE L=3 Q=PLOTTER
```

WARNING
You cannot "capture"
COM port activity,
only LPT ports.

All we would have to do now is to have our applications send their output to the correct LPT port for them to be redirected to the correct queues. If we wanted to print with the laser printer, we would simply send our print jobs to LPT1. For jobs that needed to go to the dot matrix printer, we would direct them to LPT2, and plotter jobs now would be sent to LPT3.

These are not permanent commands, so every time the workstation is reset, the CAPTURE commands will be lost. You can prevent this by adding them to the user's login script using SYSCON.

If you no longer want to print to a network printer but instead to a local printer, use the ENDCAP or END CAPture command. This command resets the printer port captures that you have set up. The syntax for this command is:

ENDCAP *options*

where *options* are the different qualifiers that can be set—see Appendix A, *NetWare 3.12 Utilities Summary.*

We can cancel all the printer port captures with the option *all*, or selectively cancel the redirections using *local*. Here are examples of using ENDCAP:

ENDCAP ALL	Cancels all the previous CAPTURE commands. All subsequent application output will not be redirected to network print queues.
ENDCAP L=1	Cancels the CAPTURE command for LPT1 only. You can now print to a local printer through LPT1.

PRINTING FROM THE COMMAND LINE

NetWare can also allow you to print from the command line any DOS text files or a file that has already been formatted by a DOS application for a specific printer. The command-line utility to use is NPRINT (Network PRINT); its command format is:

NPRINT *path options*

where *path* is the directory path leading to and including the file name you wish to print, and *options* are listed and explained in detail in Appendix B, *Workstation Commands*. Here's an example:

NPRINT F:\PUB_DATA\WPFILES\README.TXT Q=LASER

This example sends the file F:\PUB_DATA\WPFILES\README.TXT, to a queue called LASER (Q=LASER).

Using PRINTDEF and PRINTCON

Sometimes you may need to use NPRINT, CAPTURE, or PRINTCON to print from outside of your network applications. If an application does not properly reset a printer when it is through printing or can't send the necessary printer codes easily to a printer, you may want to use the PRINTCON and PRINTDEF utilities to customize or standardize some print job configurations.

The PRINTDEF or PRINTer DEFinition utility allows you to give a print device a logical name and associate it with a predefined set of instructions on how the printer will execute the print job. In a sense, you're creating your own customized printer drivers. PRINTDEF allows you to define functions for that print device with escape codes found in the device's documentation. You can then use these functions to define modes or how you want the job to be printed, such as printed in condensed print. You can save these functions and modes in a special file called a PDF file (after the .PDF file-name extension). NetWare also has 34 predefined PDF files for many common printers. You can also define a form that can be any sort of paper type that you can get into a print device, from legal and letter size to checks and continuous feed paper.

The PRINTCON or PRINT job CONfiguration utility takes the forms and modes from PRINTDEF, as well as other options, and creates a group of instructions that determines how a print job will print out.

Summary

At this point you can see how powerful and versatile NetWare's printing services are, enabling you to avoid the confusion that can plague network printing. With some planning, nearly any combination of printers, print servers and print queues can be assembled to provide an efficient and smooth-running printing environment.

PART IV

Administering
the Network

What Is
a Network
Administrator?

Fast Track

The Network Administrator is also concerned with managing   *366*
day-to-day operations of the network, including:

► Establishing procedural documentation for network monitoring,
   planning, and usage

► Providing user support

► Developing user training

► Managing the network configuration

► Experimenting with new technologies

Time estimates for network administration tasks   *375*

Time estimates for network administration tasks vary with each LAN
depending upon such factors as user consulting, product installations,
and documentation required.

The Network Administrator, also known as a *System Administrator* or *LAN Administrator,* is the person responsible for maintaining and operating a local area network and providing support for network users.

As a Network Administrator, you help ensure that the investment made in your organization's local area network is used effectively. You will do more than maintain and troubleshoot. You must also help users and keep management informed about ways to improve productivity and to enhance the network for better performance.

This chapter describes the technical and administrative responsibilities a Network Administrator may have and the skills required to accomplish NetWare system administration tasks. Below we list the primary responsibilities and the associated tasks.

1 · Maintaining and Operating the Network

  ‣ Organizing Directories, Files, and Disks

  ‣ Setting Up Users and Access Control

  ‣ Managing Files

  ‣ Allocating Disk Space

  ‣ Backing Up the Network

  ‣ Performance Monitoring

  ‣ Troubleshooting

  ‣ Network Security

  ‣ Risk Management for Networks

  ‣ Disaster Recovery

2 · Enhancing the Network

  ‣ Assessing Software and Hardware Products

  ‣ Optimizing Network Performance

  ‣ Expanding the Network

  ‣ Internetworking

3 · Administering Network Operations

- ‣ Documentation
- ‣ Managing User Support
- ‣ Developing User Training
- ‣ Configuration Management
- ‣ Keeping Up with Technology

Network Administrator Skills

A Network Administrator's human-relations skills are very important to the success of the business. You must understand what your organization's goals are so you can make the network function to achieve these goals. Keep in touch with the business operations departments in the company so you know what is going on. Let each department manager know how the network integrates their data and processes, and that you can help them improve the productivity of their staff. You may have to spend time in meetings with the various departments to ensure you hear about their problems and participate in the solutions.

A Network Administrator should be well organized, think logically, and be able to develop procedures for routine tasks. By maintaining a close working relationship with each of the business departments, you can discover possible work flow bottlenecks, and duplicated or wasted efforts.

The Network Administrator should also be able to deal effectively with people, to communicate effectively one-on-one with users to answer their questions and resolve problems, to give presentations in front of groups, and to prepare written documentation including technical reports, procedures, instructions, training materials, plans, configuration baseline and change documents, and ad hoc studies.

Novell provides a host of NetWare-related courses, including those dealing with teaching technical subjects. Ask to attend *Train the Trainer* course so you can assist novice users by conducting in-house courses yourself or you can arrange for a vendor to do the training. By explaining how to use the network and teaching the users how to use their applications, you can save hours responding to unnecessary phone calls and repeatedly answering hundreds of routine questions. Many users' questions are nontechnical and concern their applications—"I can't log in," "the printer isn't working," or "why won't my spreadsheet sort properly?"

Although you need some fundamental technical training, you can support the organization best with a broad knowledge of the ways the network can improve users' productivity. Of course, you will have to deal with crises from time to time. You may need to have an outside support group help you with hardware failures, but you should be able to do basic troubleshooting to identify the causes of failures.

A Novell Network Administrator should have the following technical skills:

- ▸ A good working knowledge of DOS, and probably Windows, Macintosh, and OS/2

- ▸ A good working knowledge of Novell System Administration NetWare functions and commands

- ▸ An understanding of NetWare security rights

- ▸ An understanding of network hardware and software components

- ▸ The ability to create a workable directory structure, construct login scripts, create new users and directories and provide a working environment for users

- ▸ The ability to load applications, perform system backups, and define and control print queues

- ▸ The ability to create and maintain a database of network component and workstation configuration information.

If you are an aspiring Network Administrator, you will need to receive some training to carry out the maintenance and operations of your LAN.

The subjects required include:

- Hardware and software basics
- Directory structure
- Mapping
- Security
- Command line and menu utilities
- Supervisor utilities
- Console utilities
- Printing
- Login scripts
- Menu creation
- Loading application software
- Backup and restore

With the above knowledge and skills, you are prepared for developing procedures to conduct routine network maintenance and operations tasks.

Maintaining and Operating the Network

As an organization's Network Administrator, you should not have to spend all your time maintaining the local area network. If you can, establish a daily and weekly routine.

Routine daily tasks involve

- adding users
- cleaning up the file server hard disk drive

- installing software upgrades

- making backups

- restoring damaged or lost files

- monitoring traffic

- collecting accounting data

- generating reports for management

Some routine weekly tasks might include:

- monitoring and evaluating network performance

- managing and documenting the network configuration

- exploring and appraising new hardware and software technology

Use diagnostics frequently to help you spot potential problems so you can take corrective action. Your goal is to make the LAN as easy to use as possible and to reduce the time required to conduct these routine operations. The scope of your network administrator knowledge is more important than knowledge of every network component, but you should arm yourself with as much technical knowledge as possible to handle crises and become effective in training and talking with users. The following sections describe the routine technical tasks a Network Administrator should perform.

ORGANIZING DIRECTORIES, FILES, AND DISKS

A server's disk is organized into a hierarchy of directories and files much like a company organizes its departments. A typical hierarchy of a NetWare directory might include the items shown in Figure 12.1.

After establishing a directory hierarchy, you need to assign system and user drive mappings in the login scripts.

NetWare's SESSION menu allows you to control your current file server, default drive, network drive mappings, and search drive mappings. You also

FIGURE 12.1

Typical file server directory hierarchy

can send messages to users. Some of the options include:

- ▶ Change current file server—log in to another server

- ▶ Log out of a file server

- ▶ Display drive information

- ▶ Add, delete, or modify a drive mapping

- ▶ View, add, or modify search drive mappings

- ▶ Select the default drive

- ▶ View the user list and display user information

- ▶ Send a message to a user or a group

SETTING UP USERS AND ACCESS CONTROL

Use SYSCON for configuring the LAN and setting up users. Typically, you will set up system defaults which will apply to most users and use these defaults to add new users or delete those who no longer require LAN access. In your function as Network Administrator, you have access to a number of activities that require supervisor status. Here are some examples:

- ▶ Create or delete users.

- ▶ Assign or change a user's password.

- ▶ Assign, view, or delete a user's security equivalence.

- ▶ Assign, view, modify, or delete a user's trustee rights.

- ▶ Assign, view, or modify a user's full name.

- ▶ View, create, or modify user login scripts.

- ▶ List, create, rename, or delete server groups.

- ▶ Assign users to or delete users from a group.

- ▶ Limit disk space for a particular user

- ▶ View disk resource limitations

- ▶ Restrict Login to chosen workstations

- ▶ Specify default account balances and restrictions.

As we discussed in earlier chapters, adding several new users one at a time is slow work; it is better to organize them into groups according to the applications and peripherals they use and create them *en masse* using either the USERDEF or MAKEUSER utilities that we discussed in Chapter 8. For example, the technical publications department might need access to the word processing, graphics, and desktop-publishing applications, as well as a laser or color printer. An accounting group would need to access accounting applications and spreadsheet software and probably need a high speed printer for printing income and expense forms. By defining the directories, subdirectories, and applications software that each group should access, you can then easily add or delete users from the groups as necessary. Assign default access rights to each group. When necessary, generate exceptions for those users with special requirements.

MANAGING FILES

NetWare's FILER utility allows you to control the volume, directory, sub-directory, and file information on a file server. Major FILER activities include:

- ▸ View current directory, subdirectory, and volume information
- ▸ List and view files
- ▸ Change file attributes, creation dates, modification dates and times, archive dates and times, owners, sizes, and directory paths.
- ▸ Display general defaults
- ▸ Specify file deletion, copy, and overwrite information
- ▸ Add or delete file search attributes per session
- ▸ Set file to execute-only
- ▸ Index large files

Additions, deletions or changes to the directories, subdirectories, ownership, trustees, and adding, deleting, copying, or renaming files requires your supervisory rights.

ALLOCATING DISK SPACE

There are many ways to allocate network disk space to create working environments for your network users. Here are some suggestions for developing your own disk space–allocation philosophy.

First, group your network applications together. You could place your network copies of applications such as word processors, spreadsheets, and databases in a separate subdirectory for each under a directory named PROGRAMS. For instance, you could place your network copy of Word-Perfect 6.0 in a subdirectory of PROGRAMS called WP60. You could do the same for your utility programs and call the directory UTILS. Control tightly which users have access to these directories and their subtrees, and how many rights these users have. You can't go too far wrong by being as stingy as possible with access rights to these program files. If a mistake is made with these files, the consequences will affect every user who needs to use an application or utility that has been accidentally corrupted, changed, or erased.

In addition to your PROGRAMS and UTILS directories located off the root, create a directory structure that contains only the public data files generated by the network applications. You could call the main directory PUB_DATA and have subdirectories for each application's data files. Only the users with access to a particular application should have access to its public data files.

Your users will also need a directory in which to keep private files. The base of this structure could be a directory named HOME or USER, which could also be located off the root. Beneath this directory should be a sub-directory that bears the user's login name and is the beginning of the user's private network domain. Here they can create their own directory structure to store their personal data and applications. You can also have a common directory called TEMP to which all users can have access, so that they can use it to swap data. This directory would be cleaned out periodically to stop it from growing too large.

Now that you have a basic design for organizing your applications and data files, you can actually allocate disk space (so that no user hogs the available disk space). Use SYSCON to restrict users to a specified amount (in KB) of the available disk space on a particular network volume. The ownership attribute assigned to each file created and stored on the network tells NetWare which user a file belongs to. NetWare keeps track of the kilobytes of files owned by each user and prevents a user from putting files on the network that exceed their limit. This should help you limit users' disk space and force them to police their own files. If they need more space, they will have to rid themselves of unnecessary files or convince you that they should have more space.

NOTE
Use SYSCON to restrict the amount of disk space on the network that users can use.

BACKING UP THE NETWORK

To ensure that your users do not lose data stored on the network, backups should be performed at least weekly and preferably daily for critical data. NetWare provides two utilities for backing up valuable information. Use NBACKUP to back up the network from a workstation, and SBACKUP (an NLM loaded on the file server) to back up the network from the file server.

One of your more difficult tasks will be to track the accumulation of files on the server, which can fill up very quickly. As we mentioned earlier, managing and controlling the disk space users take up can be a difficult and persistent activity. Some users believe they can back up their complete hard disk to the file server. Others prefer to use their workstation storage. It's best to set limits on disk space for each user and inform the users what these limits are. You might also provide an archive directory where users can add files they don't need, but want to retain. By using a daily or weekly archiving schedule, these files can be archived on tape, WORM drives, or Bernoulli disks, and removed from the server. You can also use third-party backup utilities, which offer the convenience of backing up the system from a workstation to a tape drive. This helps to minimize the possibility of crashing the file server while performing the backup function.

You can save yourself many hours of backup time by configuring the hierarchy of directories and subdirectories so that all the data you need to back up periodically is in one or two directories. If you have more than one hard disk on your server, you may want to dedicate one drive for data that must be backed up daily or weekly and the other for applications software and data files that change infrequently. Often, however, you may configure two drives as a single volume, so using a third-party backup utility is recommended to eliminate the server down time required for large disks.

One backup strategy is to backup only those files that have changed on a daily basis and do a complete backup weekly. Retain at least two or three copies of each type (daily and weekly) of backup. For example, after you make the third backup, then for the next backup you can use the first tape drive or set of floppy disks. Labeling is important so that when you have to restore files, you can identify the backup with the correct version of the files. The backups should be moved to an off-site location in a fireproof safe or in a bank's safe deposit box for safe keeping.

Although most Network Administrators use tape backup systems, new types of backup systems are appearing on the market and include continuous backup systems that maintain backups every time data is changed so no data is ever at risk. Unattended backup systems can perform backups at specified times. Whatever system you chose, pick one compatible with NetWare and that will backup the server's disk completely. Some vendors offer helical scan digital tape drives that back up 2.2 gigabytes; digital audio tapes often hold 1.1 to 1.4 gigabytes.

PERFORMANCE MONITORING

Network performance monitoring can help you identify potential bottlenecks and problems before they occur. You may want to invest in diagnostic hardware (such as a managed network hub) and software (such as Blue Lance's LT AUDITOR program) to monitor resource use. With such devices, you can monitor and observe the frequency of file server disk accesses, total traffic volume, user response times, and how the peripherals on the network are being used. For example, if 70% to 80% of the users are sending their documents to a single LAN printer, you may want to add another printer or relocate an existing one to make it more accessible for users to pick up their print jobs.

You can work with users to arrange to have their larger documents printed before 8:00 a.m., during the lunch hour, or after 5:00 p.m. The same approach can be used with database users who attempt large database queries and sorts. In any event, you as Network Administrator have the capability to see the symptoms of degraded performance. Listen to users' complaints to determine whether there is a network problem you need to investigate and whether the network is keeping up with the users' demands.

Software monitors are the most common type of performance measurement tool and the easiest for Network Administrators to use. NetWare 3.12 provides the MONITOR utility, which helps you determine how efficiently

NOTE
MONITOR lets you view current information, but does not record it.

your network is operating (as explained in Appendix A). You can use MONITOR to view information about the following:

- Percentages of utilization and overall activity
- Status of cache memory
- Connections and their status
- Disk drives
- Mounted volumes
- LAN drivers
- Loaded modules, including the amount of memory they are using
- File lock status
- Memory usage

Some software monitors run on a separate workstation, not the file server, and can continuously track traffic levels, error rates, and numbers and names of active workstations. Reports can be generated with the collected information that allow you to do trend analysis and sampling to uncover potential problems. Recent tools such as NetWare Services Manager v1.5 for OS/2 and NodeVision by Fresh Technology use Windows 3.x to produce performance and diagnostic reports on file servers and network clients. These products track levels of activity and generate reports on how resources are used. Frye Computer Systems, Inc., markets a DOS-based management utility for NetWare 2.2 and 3.12. It includes graphical and reporting functions and provides for disaster recovery support, enhanced troubleshooting and diagnostics. It also features weekly maintenance reports and performance-tuning information. Protocol analyzers can provide more advanced information such as network utilization statistics and traffic simulations. As the level of sophistication increases, so does the cost of the diagnostic tool.

TROUBLESHOOTING LANS

LANs usually malfunction because something in the system was changed. Use one of the many utility programs developed by third-party vendors such as Blue Lance's LT STAT or LAN Support Group's BINDVIEW NCS to document changes to the NetWare bindery for your LAN so that when problems occur, you can investigate the most recent changes first. Network Administrators become experienced with the common problems that occur with their networks, because they work at solving them daily. Moreover, NetWare automatically sends you the following alert warnings:

- ▸ Volume is getting full

- ▸ Volume is full

- ▸ No more connections slots available

- ▸ Available memory for allocation is low

- ▸ All available memory of allocation to additional file server resources is gone

- ▸ Volume was dismounted due to a failure

- ▸ Bindery was opened or closed

- ▸ Login was remotely disabled or enabled

- ▸ File server time was remotely changed

- ▸ Transaction Tracking System (TTS) was enabled or disabled or another TTS event occurred

The abovementioned alerts are placed in one of three error log files depending on whether they pertain to the system (SYS$LOG.ERR), a volume (VOL$LOG.ERR), or the Transaction Tracking System (TTS$LOG.ERR). SYS$LOG.ERR is located in the SYS:SYSTEM directory and can be viewed either using any text editor or though SYSCON. TTS$LOG.ERR is always located in the root directory of the SYS volume and can be viewed with any text editor. Finally, there is an error log file for each volume that is always named VOL$LOG.ERR and is always located in the root directory of each volume.

VOL$LOG.ERR can be viewed with any text editor. Review these files daily to help identify problems early.

Trying to fix major equipment or system failures can be time consuming and stressful. In most cases, you'll want to have an outside support service you can call for help. It's best to make these arrangements at the time the network is installed. The *Novell System Administration Manual* provides a Troubleshooting Guide that covers common problems with the file server and hard disk, communications, workstations, and applications. For component hardware failures, you can use the diagnostic utilities mentioned above to help research the problem.

Troubleshooting is a problem-solving process, and as a Network Administrator, you will need to understand the operation of each of the LAN components to detect the source of possible problems. Once you isolate the problem as hardware, software, or procedural, you can narrow down the possibilities and attempt to simulate the problem at a single workstation. In addition to the troubleshooting documentation provided by the equipment and software vendors, excellent technical notes are available on Novell's bulletin board system called NetWire, which is available through CompuServe. Often you will find that a problem with the same symptoms as yours has been identified and solved. Consequently, arrange to access the bulletin board periodically to identify potential problems. This research effort is particularly important when you are installing a software upgrade, e.g., upgrading from Windows 3.0 to Windows 3.1.

Many problems are identified by users. They may not be able to access their files or print to a network printer. Often, users forget their passwords and call to get help logging into the network. By creating an effective user interface as a Network Administrator, you can teach users how to select passwords they can remember.

NETWORK SECURITY

The security of a network or any of its components consists of three elements:

> **integrity**—ensuring that transmitted data is received intact

availability—the network services are performed within an acceptable time frame

confidentiality—preserving the privacy of an organization's information.

As the Network Administrator, you are responsible for network integrity and availability. Confidentiality is the responsibility of all, but should be backed up by strict control of rights to files and directories.

Network data integrity is ensured when data transmitted over the network is protected during transmission from modification by accident, error, or willful alteration. Data is of little use if it is not correctly received. The use of established protocols, network error detection, correction components, consistent periodic file backup, and archiving usually provides the necessary data integrity except in cases of accidental or deliberate introduction of virus software.

Computer viruses continue to multiply, according to a recent article in the *New York Times*, which reported the results of a survey of 606 large North American companies and government agencies with 300 or more personal computers. From January through September of 1992, nine percent of the companies and agencies experienced a computer virus that affected a quarter of their PCs. Although the number of viruses and their level of sophistication is increasing, many organizations do not have any protection from computer viruses.

Virus detection and eradication software will offer good protection against such intrusion. Ensure that each workstation and file server on your network has virus-scanning software so that a virus can be detected at bootup time, not after it has a chance to modify network or workstation files. Several products are available, including Fifth Generation's Untouchable for Networks and Symantec's Norton AntiVirus (NAV) Software. Both of these products provide virus detection and eradication features that can be used on Novell NetWare networks.

Because your users rely on the availability of the network for access to computing resources, network availability is vital to the success of the organization's operations. Protective measures against network abuse include user authentication and network monitoring. The network file servers and intra- and internetwork connecting components such as cable termination blocks, gateways, routers, and bridges should be physically protected by locking them in a terminal room, closet, or office, and limiting access only to the Network Administrator or maintenance personnel. Some installations include tamper-proof seals to enable intrusion detection.

Logical access controls include mechanisms such as passwords that permit only authorized users access to a LAN component. It is also important to have system records so that security problems may be traced and resolved. Furthermore, the only way to ensure that a server's security controls remain in place is to practice good configuration management. This requires that you take the following precautions:

- ▶ Load the file servers only from authorized distribution software.
- ▶ Make only authorized changes to the server configuration.
- ▶ Maintain a copy of the current LAN configuration data sheets.
- ▶ Periodically review device configurations.
- ▶ Maintain at least one backup copy of server software.
- ▶ Test software thoroughly on a backup server if possible before introducing it to your network, to prevent incompatibilities that could crash your system.

The NetWare security system is structured after a mainframe security environment. As discussed in Chapter 10, information is protected by four types of security at four levels of access:

SECURITY LEVEL	LEVEL OF ACCESS
Username/Password	Initial (Login)
Rights	Directory/File Access

SECURITY LEVEL	LEVEL OF ACCESS
Attribute	Conditional Directory/File Access
File Server	File Server Console

One way to prevent unauthorized access through the system console is to use the SECURE CONSOLE command from the server console command line: Type **secure console** at the command line to implement the following NetWare security measures:

- ▸ Prevent loadable modules from being loaded from any directory other than SYS:SYSTEM.

- ▸ Prevent entry into the OS debugger.

- ▸ Prevent anyone other than a console operator from changing the date and time.

- ▸ Remove DOS from the server to prevent access to floppy drives.

As your network grows, take precautions by keeping track of what access permission you assign to a group. For example, you may initially assign a group of accountants access to the accounts receivable applications. A new employee is hired and after you've given her the same rights, she asks to have access to the budget application. If you give the whole group rights to the budget, you may also give them access to confidential or proprietary files they shouldn't see. Consequently, you may want to create a new group and assign the new employee to that group or assign rights specifically to that user.

RISK MANAGEMENT FOR LANS

LAN risk management is an ongoing process which defines, analyzes, and controls the risks of operating the LAN's information resources. Two documents comprise the risk management process for a LAN: a Risk

Analysis Report and a Disaster Recovery Plan. Risk analysis for LANs begins by identifying the following:

- Computing assets in the LAN

- Potential threats to those assets

- Existing controls and residual vulnerabilities

- Impact or loss that could be incurred if residual vulnerabilities are exploited

A *risk analysis report* includes the above information and an inventory of the LAN hardware and critical applications software.

LAN DISASTER RECOVERY PLANNING

The criticality of the applications and data on the LAN determine the need for continuity of operations following a disaster. You, as Network Administrator, must determine where and how to perform backup operations. You must decide which hardware, telecommunications, software, and data are required to establish a minimum acceptable level of operating capability as well as the actions and schedules necessary to begin production level operations.

You must also determine how the LAN will be returned to full operating capability. As Network Administrator, your job will be to determine how to recover the LAN equipment, software, and data resources. Your input to the plan should identify the location of one or more replacement file servers.

As in the case of mainframe backups, store a backup of your current week's data files and copies of your applications in another building or fireproof safe. In areas where hurricanes or tornadoes are common, you will want to store backups in a commercial brick and steel building away from areas likely to be flooded or to receive wind damage.

You should continually remind users to backup their data files to prevent extensive lost time in recreating them should a mishap occur. Building electrical systems fail infrequently and lightning strikes do not often cut off the power, but when they do occur it is usually while a person is in the middle of creating a large document or updating a database.

As Network Administrator, you should prepare a plan for various disaster scenarios and include foreseeable disasters and their impact on the LAN, which in turn affects the business. The plan should identify the precautions needed to protect the equipment and data, and if it is destroyed, the steps necessary to mobilize a recovery work force to reestablish the LAN and critical business functions at another location. The recovery plan should identify priorities for reestablishing network services, applications, and the specific tasks for each member of the recovery staff. The most important parts of the plan are identifying a recovery location such as a remote branch office, retrieving off site backups, and obtaining temporary computer equipment. The plan should be updated at least annually, because of turnover of personnel and changing assignments, and the frequent changes to your network's configuration.

Enhancing the Network

New technology and demands from users challenge the Network Administrator to enhance the network by optimizing its operation, adding new functions to the LAN, and expanding the network to include more users and servers or connecting to other networks. The Network Administrator has four tasks that involve enhancing the network:

1 · assessing hardware and software products

2 · optimizing performance

3 · expanding the network

4 · internetworking and wide area networks

ASSESSING SOFTWARE AND HARDWARE PRODUCTS

Part of your job as a Network Administrator is to keep up with the trade magazines on new products and to evaluate both software and hardware that may improve the operation and performance of a network or provide new capabilities for users to make them more effective workers. Because of the hundreds of new products and product upgrades that are announced each year, you have to become very selective. Install neither product upgrades nor new products automatically without first evaluating their benefits and their ability to operate on your network. If there are no specific benefits such as functionality, performance improvement, or easier use, then you may want to wait for a later upgrade or another product.

You can obtain information about a product's features directly from vendors or dealers, and often the trade magazines provide assessments with comparable products. Once you've decided to try a product, prepare a test plan and test it thoroughly during off-hours or on a test network. Involve some of the users in the testing to determine if they run up against any bugs or anomalies. They can provide important feedback on the capabilities of the product for their work.

If you are evaluating a product to perform a critical function, e.g., a higher-capacity disk for your file server, keep your original disk operating and do testing in parallel until you've worked out all the problems with the new disk drive.

When you start receiving complaints about slow service, investigate the nature of the complaints, which users are noticing the delays, and when. Use your performance-monitoring tools, analyze the source of the bottlenecks and then decide on a solution. You may have to add more capacity, or redistribute the users to another server or fix a LAN malfunction. In either case, you may need to justify your proposal to management: If you do, you will need to summarize your performance data, identify the scope and impact of the problem on users, and propose one or more solutions with their costs. In some cases, building a model allows you to identify all known parameters affecting the system's performance, narrowing down the alternative solutions.

INCREASING PERFORMANCE

Today's Windows and OS/2 operating environments require faster and more powerful computers and file servers. The easiest way to accommodate these systems is to buy faster computers with larger memories and larger disk capacities. As you monitor declining performance, you may need to make management aware of the need to add higher-performance hardware and software.

As your network grows, current tape backup systems may become too slow to handle the additions of new users or file server disks may have reached their capacity. Users may find their disk space is limited or their workstation memory level can handle only two applications running under Windows.

You can do three things to ensure that your network's performance doesn't degrade below the users' needs:

- ▸ keep periodic records of the network's performance, problems, and upgrades

- ▸ keep your management informed about the impact of any persistent drop in performance

- ▸ prepare a plan and budget for upgrading your LAN

Depending on the organization, your management may wish to replace the users' older equipment and software over a long period, a year or more, but they may be willing to invest in higher-powered file servers, new cabling, and common user software in a single procurement. You will have to prepare to justify and recommend the investment and develop a plan for accomplishing the effort.

EXPANDING THE NETWORK

As Network Administrator, always look for ways the network can do new jobs: Follow the trade magazines, listen to users about their needs, talk to vendors, and participate in network users groups.

You can subscribe to Computer Select, a compact disk (CD) system, available through Computer Library Products (212-503-4400), that contains copies of articles published in 135 computer journals. It also lists descriptions of hardware and software products introduced over the past year through an interactive menu system. Each monthly version of the CD contains the past year's copies of the articles and product descriptions. You can configure to access Computer Select on the network, so users could access it from their offices. Users could then read the articles or print them out at their network printers.

As Network Administrator, attempt to learn about the work of your whole organization, whether it's a company, institution, or government agency. By attending management meetings and learning about the work in other departments of the organization, you become familiar with the organization's problems and successes. You also become aware of users' needs, and you may find ways for the network to provide solutions for these needs.

INTERNETWORKING AND WANS

Wide Area Networks (WANs) are networks that span large distances such as cities, states, countries or continents. Each WAN is a network that allows remote connections to far off locations, but operates at slower speeds than other technologies and has much greater delay between connections. WANs typically operate at 9.6 Kbps to 45 Mbps. At some time, your organization may require connection to a WAN, so you should become familiar with the requirements, benefits and limitations of WANs.

Internetworking is a new open system technology that accommodates multiple hardware technologies by providing physical connections and a new set of conventions. Internetworking is common at NASA's Johnson Space Center, where the buildings have been connected with fiber optic cable and each building may have one or several local area networks. NASA built an internetworking system that allows users to communicate among any of the LANs and with the host computers via routers and gateways on the internetworking system.

Some of your users may want to access the Internet, a worldwide network of colleges and universities, government research labs, and military installations in over a dozen countries. In 1990, the Internet included over 3,000 active networks and over 200,000 computers. Since the Internet uses TCP/IP protocol, you must provide a *gateway*, an interface, to access the Internet. Gateways, which are often called *internet protocol (IP) routers*, are special-purpose, dedicated computers that attach to two or more networks and route packets from one to the other. They interconnect two physical networks and make IP decisions. Gateways route packets to other gateways until they can be delivered to the final destination.

When you determine there is a need for internetworking, analyze the requirements and prepare a plan for developing a model or prototype, conducting tests on the prototype, validating the users' satisfaction, and implementing the internetworking capability.

Administering Network Operations

Administration deals with managing the daily operations of a LAN. It includes coordinating actions among people in the organization; and because the network is the system that integrates all the organization's activities, processes, and data, it is essential that the Network Administrator give these tasks a high priority.

Earlier, we said that it was important to proceduralize the maintenance and operations functions of the network. This means that time can be allocated to ongoing administrative tasks. These tasks include defining your responsibilities in the organization, preparing the necessary documentation, and integrating network operations with those of the business and service departments.

To ensure effective integration, an organization needs a coordinating mechanism for setting information system requirements, approving changes, and seeing that they are carried out. Some organizations use a steering committee made up of the business operations department managers. Others may employ a Chief Information Officer (CIO) who is responsible for managing the integration of the data processing support with the corporate business operations managers. The Network Administrator may take direction from the steering committee, the CIO, or a supervisor reporting to them, and implement their directives.

To effectively process changes to the network, an organization will need procedures for review and approval of all proposed changes before they are implemented. The authority should come from the CIO or steering committee and any proposed changes should be reviewed by the department managers who may be affected.

Throughout the technical discussion of the Network Administrator's responsibilities and tasks, we have referred to a number of planning documents. Writing plans for network performance improvements, increased user productivity, testing new hardware and software, and user training should be among your highest priorities. Sometimes Network Administrators are terrified of writing of any sort and the easiest way to start is by reviewing existing company policies, procedures, plans, training manuals, feasibility studies, and status reports.

Before you start any document, talk to your manager to make sure you understand what information is needed, who your readers will be, and what style, layout, and format should be used. Some companies hire technical writers to assist with the writing; if you need to develop this skill, take a course in technical writing to prepare yourself.

What are the documents you will need to administer your network?

The Network Administrator needs several types of documents. All are about equally important. The first group of documents cover network configuration and operations information:

- Network status reports and problem log

- Network and user workstation configuration baseline diagrams and specifications

- Configuration Change Requests

The second group of documents deals with daily maintenance of the network and includes procedures such as:

- modifying and adding users and groups
- installing applications
- backup and restoring the file server

The third group of documents cover plans for expansion, emergencies and training:

- Network expansion plan including internetworking
- Test plan for evaluating new products or product upgrades
- Network Security and Risk Management Plan
- Disaster Recovery Plan
- User training plans and course materials

Network record keeping and configuration management documentation is vital to maintaining a successful and operating network. When the network is initially installed, collect a set of configuration baseline documents which include: the descriptions of the network components, e.g., cable diagrams, workstations, file servers; complete lists of all hardware and software including the version numbers; lists of users and groups; and lists of directories and files. Change requests should be written to document upgrades and modifications to the network for hardware, software, and user information.

MANAGING USER SUPPORT

Begin keeping a journal or log of all important activities relating to the operation of the network. If possible, note all calls from users and a description of their complaint, idea, or problem and its resolution. Some organizations maintain help desks which have the responsibility for logging user problems. However, you may be the only person who can answer network-related questions and resolve users' network problems, so the calls will probably be forwarded to you for resolution. You can also get help by typing **help** or **help** and the name of a specific NetWare command or utility, for example:

    help fconsole

The most important part of the network is the user interface. Windows, OS/2 and Macintosh systems provide an easy-to-use interface, because when the user understands how to use one system, he can usually learn others very quickly. These systems use common types of screens with pull-down menus and can be manipulated using a mouse or a keyboard. Systems like these are easy to use and consequently users become more productive. You can encourage users to explore their applications, so they tend to feel comfortable trying new ways of handling their tasks.

DEVELOPING USER TRAINING

It's important that you participate in the process of developing user training programs. The more knowledgeable the users, the less time you'll spend supporting them. Beginning users should first receive training covering basic computer operations and networks. This should be followed by training covering the applications and procedures they use in their jobs and how the network supports their work. Although self-paced instruction is the most inexpensive, we have found that classroom instruction is the most effective. Users can return to their workstations and begin immediately to apply what they have learned and then take advanced courses to build on their knowledge.

CONFIGURATION MANAGEMENT

If you take over a Network Administrator's position with no configuration documentation, you will have to initiate a systematic inventory. You can run a network software utility produced by Cheyenne Software called Cheyenne Utilities to inventory the hardware and software on the workstations using the network. Figures 12.2, 12.3, and 12.4 illustrate the reports these utilities produce. Your purchasing agent and the accounting department can also provide you with copies of the purchase orders, packing slips, invoices, and warranty or support contract information about all workstation hardware and software procurements.

You will also want to make a diagram of your server's volume and directory structure and a list of the functions the network serves for your organization. Cable diagrams may be difficult to maintain unless the cable modifications must be approved by a Configuration Control Board. You may have to contact the cable support contractor or building maintenance supervisor to obtain cabling information.

KEEPING UP WITH TECHNOLOGY

The computer industry is filled with technically superior products that have never caught on because the market has not embraced them. The driving force for upgrading with new technology is the pressure of intense competition. However, be wary of vendors' promised delivery dates. As Network Administrator, you want to explore new technology; a good guideline is to find technologies that are scheduled to ship two years before you need them. Your job is to project the acquisition and upgrades needed in the next three years. Although there is no crystal ball, the trade magazines identify several technologies that can serve as the foundation for your evolving architecture. They include client/server, object-oriented programming, and mobile computing.

A few of the technologies and products we feel worth investigating are as follows: faster workstations like the 486-66 PCs from IBM, Dell, and Compaq, and Apple's Quadra. Redundant Arrays of Inexpensive Disks (RAID) technology is designed to increase data safety by duplicating disk information. Six levels of RAID technology have been developed thus far. RAID technology seeks to minimize the possibility of data loss caused by disk failures.

```
Jan 19, 1994  01:02PM                         USER REPORT
Cheyenne Utilities v 1.0                      Page     1
                    Cheyenne Utiltities

              ========| USER REPORT |========
                        -----------
Executed By: DBELL      NetWare Version:            3.12
File Server: JSCCSC1    Maximum Number of Volumes:    64
                        Maximum Number of Connections: 100
*****************************************************************
--------------------------------
Name : KDRUMMON
ID   : 8200002D
--------------------------------
        Group Membership
        ----------------
        DEPT150 (Department 150)
        EVERYONE
        LAN (Special Projects Group)
        RABBIT (Rabbit for DOS Users)
        XPERT

        Account Restrictions
        --------------------
        Account Disabled:              No
        Account Has Expiration Date:   No
           Date Account Expires:
        Limit Concurrent Connections:  Yes
        Allow User To Change Password: Yes
        Require Password:
           Minimum Password Length     5
        Force Periodic Password Changes: Yes
           Days Between Forced Changes: 30
           Date Password Expires:      01/25/94
           Limit Grace Logins:         Yes
              Grace Logins Allowed:    3
              Remaining Grace Logins   3
              Require Unique Passwords: Yes

        Intruder Lockout Status
        -----------------------
        Account Locked:                No
        Incorrect Logic Count:
        Account Reset Time:
        Time Until Reset:
        Last Intruder Address: 86760000:00001B0021E0:4003
        Station Login Restrictions
        --------------------------
           Station (s) Restricted To
           =========================
           No Station Restrictions
```

FIGURE 12.2

Example of Third-Party

User Report

FIGURE 12.3

Example of Third-Party
Vendor Disk Usage Report

```
=========| DISK USAGE REPORT |=========
          -----------
Executed By: DBELL        NetWare Version:                    3.12
File Server: JSCCSC1      Maximum Number of Volumes:            64
                          Maximum Number of Connections:       100
--------------------------
Volume Name:   SYS:
--------------------------
      Capacity:          Occupied Space:     Available Space:
================== ================== ==================
321,556,480 Bytes 259,653,632 Bytes        61,902,848 Bytes
     78,505 Blocks     63,392 Blocks            15,113 Blocks
                       11,132 Directories       21,540
Directories
                          81 Percent           19 Percent
                             Space        Space
Occupied
User Name       Dirs   Files   Occupied    Available
Percent
---------------- ----- ------- -------- ---------- -------
ABUFOX            1      3       28,672  61,902,848   0.1%
AHOLLAND          0      0            0  61,902,848   0.0%
AHOLLMAN          1      3       20,480  61,902,848   0.0%
BHESTER           8    201    1,753,088  61,902,848   3.3%
DBELL            43    641    6,688,768  61,902,848  12.6%
DISKBACKUP        3    112    7,200,768  61,902,848  13.6%
-
-
-
-
-
-
-
-

Jan 31, 1994 09:17AM                    DISK USAGE REPORT
Cheyenne Utilities v 1.0                         Page   2
```

OS/2 Version 2.1 has similar features to Windows 3.1. You may want to ask users to test its performance to determine whether it can improve their productivity. Microsoft's new Access database management system (DBMS) lets programmers build custom applications using a variant of Visual Basic

01/8/94 13:03   Machine Record for DBELL   Page 1

Administrative information:
         Primary login: DBELL
     Primary full name: DBELL
   Last hardware audit: 11/18/93 12:22
       Secondary login: Supervisor
   Secondary full name: Supervisor
            Department: 130
               Project: UWS Consultant /LAN Admin.
              Building: Space Center One Room: 5038
            Machine id: Adosea 386/25

Machine information: Drive information:
        Machine class: Clone PC/AT 386   # floppies: 2
           OS mfg/ver: MS-DOS 6.00   # hard drives: 2
             CPU type: Intel 80386SX-25   last drive: M
             FPU type: N/A   Total hard drive: 178,080KB
        BIOS signature: AMI   Available hard drive: 33,074KB
            BIOS date: 04/09/92   1st physical disk type: 35
             Bus type: ISA   2nd physical disk type: 0
        Battery state: Good

RAM (KB):   EMM:
Total Conventional: 640   LIM version: N/A
Avail Conventional: 539   Frame segment: 0000H
   Ext. BIOS memory: 0   Total page count: 0
     Total extended: 7,168   Available page count: 0
      Avail extended: 0
      Total expanded: 0
      Avail expanded: Video:
                                     Adapter: VGA
                                     Monitor: Analog
                                        Mode: 80x25 Text
Mouse:
         Type: None   Buffer Address: b800H
      Version: N/A   Adaptor Memory: 256 KB

Server:
        Name: JSCCSC1

Shell:
        Shell Version: 3.26a
             Protocol: ODI 3.10

LAN Card:
         Description: ET200 (T) Ethernet
       Configuration: IRQ 5, Port 0300
          Network id: 0040f620ca29

language. Access works with MS SQL Server, and it has hooks for Oracle, Rdb, and DB2.

In addition to Novell's bulletin board and technical reports, there are a number of LAN magazines that provide information about new hardware and software products. Some of these are:

LAN Magazine

LAN Times

Network Computing

PC Week

Corporate Computing

NetWare Technical Journal.

Some useful books include the following:

Building Local Area Networks with Novell's NetWare by Patrick Corrigan and Aisling Guy. M&T Books, 1989.

The Computerland Handbook for Local Area Network Administrators by Ben Melnick. Computerland Books, 1991.

Mastering NetWare by Michael L. Hader. Hayden Books, 1989.

Internet with TCP/IP, Volume I: "Principles and Protocols, and Architecture," and *Internet with TCP/IP*, Volume II: "Design, Implementation, and Internals" by Douglas E. Comer and David L. Stevens. Prentice Hall, Inc., 1991.

The Whole Internet User's Guide & Catalog by Ed Krol. O'Reilly & Associates, Inc., 1992.

Time Estimates for Administering a Network

The table below shows an example of some estimated maximum times required for each of the tasks discussed in this chapter. The times will vary depending on the amounts of user consulting, product installations, and documentation required.

NETWORK ADMINISTRATOR TASKS	ESTIMATED MAX TIME REQUIRED
1. Organizing Directories, Files, Disks	Daily 1–2 hours
2. Setting Up Users and Access Control	Daily 1 hour
3. Managing Files	Daily 1 hour
4. Allocating Disk Space	Daily 1 hour
5. Backing Up the Network	Daily 1–3 hours
6. Performance Monitoring	Weekly 1 hour total
7. Troubleshooting	Daily 1 hour
8. Risk Management for Networks (Documentation)	Annually 1 month
9. Disaster Recovery (Documentation)	Annually 1 month
10. Assessing Hardware and Software Products	Monthly
11. Increasing Performance	Monthly
12. Expanding the Network	Semiannually
13. Internetworking	Annually
14. Documentation	Integrated with Other Tasks

NETWORK ADMINISTRATOR TASKS	ESTIMATED MAX TIME REQUIRED
15. Managing User Support	Daily 2–3 Hours
16. Developing and Delivering User Training	Monthly 3–6 hours
17. Configuration Management	Weekly 2 hours
18. Keeping Up With Technology	Weekly 1–2 hours

Summary

This chapter discussed the technical and administrative functions of a Network Administrator. The responsibilities for managing a network require both technical and administrative skills. Your success as a Network Administrator will depend on your ability to work effectively with your manager and the network users. Your skill mix should include both technical and human relations abilities. You should emphasize participation in user training to reduce the time required to respond to users' problems with their network applications. Training one or more assistant network administrators will ensure continuity of operations and give you time to take a vacation. Preparing for disasters by performing risk analysis, daily backups of the file servers, and developing a plan for handling various disaster scenarios is critical to the survival of the organization.

CHAPTER 13

Techniques for Administering Users

Fast Track

380   ***NetWare allows two additional types of network managers:***
- User Account Managers
- Workgroup Managers

380   ***User Account Managers can***
change the rights and attributes of users in a particular group:
- change account balances
- set user restrictions like login times and account expiration
- change passwords
- set security equivalences
- turn other users into user account managers

User Account Managers are listed under the managers listing for a particular group.

381   ***User Account Managers cannot***
- create new users
- create groups
- create print queues

381   ***Workgroup managers***
have all the capabilities of a User Account Manager and can create new users, groups, and print queues.
Workgroup managers are set up under the Supervisor Options menu of SYSCON.

By now, you've probably discovered that managing a network can be a lot of work—especially if you are trying to manage a multiserver network with a large number of users. Fortunately, as the network grows, the support organization can grow along with it. NetWare has built-in capabilities that enable the supervisor to offload some of the work to other network users.

In this chapter, we'll discuss having user account managers and workgroup managers as tools for distributing the network management workload from the network supervisor to other network users. We'll cover the concept of the HOME server and its place in a multiserver environment. Finally, we'll describe some useful techniques for working in a multiserver environment, including the use of ATTACH and MAP to gain access to other servers.

Using User Account Managers and Workgroup Managers

When the network environment becomes too large for a single network administrator to handle, some of the tasks the supervisor would normally perform can be delegated to other users. This is often the case in a large company that has multiple servers and no centralized department in charge of managing the network. Under NetWare, you can define two additional types of network managers:

- ► user account managers

- ► workgroup managers

USER ACCOUNT MANAGERS

A *user account manager* is a person or group that has the rights and permissions necessary to manage the accounts of users in a particular group.

A user account manager can:

- ▸ change account balances (if system accounting has been installed)
- ▸ change the restrictions placed on users
- ▸ change passwords for users
- ▸ change security equivalences for users
- ▸ turn other users into user account managers

Two options in the Group Information menu of SYSCON allow you to set up and view user account managers and the users or groups they manage. Anyone listed under the Managers listing for a group is (at least) a user account manager for the group. User account managers assist the system supervisor by offloading many of the day-to-day tasks that need to be performed for the group, such as resetting a user password. User account managers cannot create new users or print queues.

WORKGROUP MANAGERS

A workgroup manager not only has the abilities of a user account manager but can create, rename, and delete users, groups, and print queues. Workgroup managers are most useful when a network becomes too large for one, or even a few SUPERVISOR equivalents to manage, and when you don't want to spread SUPERVISOR equivalencies too far. The workgroup manager has basically the same rights as a supervisor for the particular group he or she controls.

You create workgroup managers through the Supervisor Options menu of SYSCON. In most cases, managers are assigned to groups as user account managers and upgraded when the additional capabilities of the workgroup manager are needed.

To make a user or group a workgroup manager, access the Supervisor Options menu and select the last option in the list, Workgroup Managers, to display a list of current workgroup managers. To add a new manager, press Ins, and a list of non-managers will appear. Highlight the appropriate

NOTE
A SUPERVISOR equivalent is a user with the same rights as the user **SUPER-VISOR**. You can give a user these rights by adding **SUPERVISOR** to the list of Security Equivalences for the user in the User Information menu in **SYSCON**.

user or group and press ↵. The selected user or group now has workgroup manager capabilities. Which groups the new manager has control over is determined by the groups they manage as user account managers or that they create.

To see how workgroup and user account managers are useful, let's take a look at how the management of a particular department might be organized. We chose an accounting department as our example as these employees are likely to work with information that is sensitive and guarded from other network users.

Let's assume that the two most-used software packages in the accounting department are Lotus 1-2-3 and an accounting package called INMASS. Using normal rules for developing a directory structure (as discussed in Chapters 8 and 16) and network security (as discussed in Chapter 10), we would have developed a directory structure for accounting similar to that shown in Figure 13.1.

Notice that a main directory for the accounting department called ACCT has been created from the root of the volume. Since Lotus 1-2-3 is used by other network users, the executable programs have been installed in a

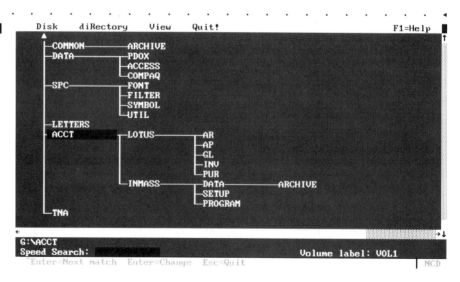

FIGURE 13.1

The subdirectory structure for the Accounting department

public "programs" directory elsewhere on the volume. However, the data files accessed by Accounting have been placed in a LOTUS subdirectory under the ACCT directory. Each of the different types of files for accounts receivable, accounts payable, general ledger, etc., has its own subdirectory.

A subdirectory for the INMASS programs has been created under ACCT as well. The accounting program is only used by the accounting department and managers with authorized access, so the program files have not been installed in a public programs directory. The data files for the program have been located in one subdirectory of INMASS and the executable programs in another.

To simplify managing the users who need access to these resources, we could create a group called ACCOUNTING and assign a workgroup manager to manage it. The SUPERVISOR would assign all rights for the ACCT subdirectory to this workgroup manager. Then the workgroup manager would be ready to start creating her own users and groups and granting access to the accounting applications and data.

The workgroup manager might create several groups to individually grant access to certain spreadsheet files as needed: one group called AC-COUNTS RECEIVABLE, one called ACCOUNTS PAYABLE, one for IN-VENTORY, and so on. Since the accounting software is likely to have built-in security, a single group called INMASS would be created. To each of these groups, the workgroup manager would assign appropriate rights for the subdirectories they need access to.

For example, to ACCOUNTS RECEIVABLE, the workgroup manager might grant SCAN, READ, MODIFY, and WRITE access to the directory VOL1:ACCT\LOTUS\AR. For INMASS, she might grant ALL RIGHTS to the directory VOL1:ACCT\INMASS\DATA and only SCAN and READ rights to VOL1:ACCT\INMASS\PROGRAM (so executable files are not accidentally erased). Once the groups have been created and the directory rights have been assigned, the workgroup manager is ready to add existing users the appropriate groups or create new users. As discussed before, members of a group have the rights and privileges assigned to the group.

If there were a special laser printer dedicated to the accounting department, the workgroup manager might also create a new print queue specifically for this printer and assign him- or herself as the print queue manager. Access to the printer could then be granted to the members of the group accounting and prevented for all other network users. A user account manager could perform most of these responsibilities with the exception of creating users, groups, and print queues.

The "Home" Server Concept

When you work in a multiserver environment, it does not make sense to have to log out of one server and into another each time you need the services of another file server. NetWare tools are capable of working with more that one server at a time. Just as users have a home directory on the file server, the server they log into using the LOGIN command is their *home* server.

The system login script for the home server is the first script that will be run to setup the user's environment. This is also the file server where the user's home directory and user login script will be stored. Any of the common files like utilities and OS files are likely to be accessed from search drives on the home server rather than from any other servers the user eventually attaches to. Using this server as a home base, the user can access the resources of other servers on the network by using NetWare utilities like ATTACH and MAP.

The home server ensures that the user's environment is set up appropriately to access the resources of that server. A user needing access to resources on another server must have a login name on the server and privileges to resources there (like directory rights, or print queue rights). But the ATTACH command will not execute a system or user login script for the server being attached. So the user must use some other method to MAP volumes on the other servers to network drive letters: Manually MAP them after attaching, use DOS batch files, or ATTACH to other servers and MAP appropriate drives in a login script on the home server.

WORKING IN A MULTISERVER ENVIRONMENT

The first step in accessing the resources of another file server is to ATTACH the required server. To see a list of available servers, use the SLIST utility. ATTACH may be used like LOGIN to attach a particular user name to a particular server. For example, to attach to the file server TOLSTOY, use the following command:

ATTACH TOLSTOY/SIRMANS

If the user SIRMANS has a password defined on the server TOLSTOY, he will have to type it before gaining access. Once a server is attached, volumes and services provided by the server become available to the user, if the user has the proper permissions to access them.

As we did in Chapter 9, we can use dynamic drive mapping to use the resources of attached network servers. For example, if we attach to the server TOLSTOY in order to use a Paradox database stored there, we can use a batch file to set up the network data drive and search drive using the MAP command. The only difference in a multiserver environment is that you must specify the full path to the mapped directories in the batch file. Since Paradox uses a configuration file to setup the default data directories, the network user name, and programming parameters, we'll map a search drive to the Paradox program directory and execute the program from the directory where the configuration files are stored:

```
@echo off
MAP S16:=TOLSTOY\SYS:PROGRAMS\PDOX4
MAP K:=CICERO\VOL1:HOME\SIRMANS
MAP L:=TOLSTOY\SYS:DATA\PDOX
K:
Paradox
H:
```

Even though the data files being accessed in this example are actually stored on a different file server, MAP has enabled us to set network drive maps that allow us to simultaneously access files on more than one server.

USING WINDOWS IN A MULTISERVER ENVIRONMENT

Drive letters become especially important if the users are working in Windows. Windows understands network drives but does not directly understand NetWare volumes. Therefore, access to network drives must be accomplished through drive mapping. If a user logs into a server other than their home server, there is no guarantee (and in fact it is quite unlikely) that the icons within Windows will correctly launch network applications. To solve the problem, attach to other servers during the login process and always map volumes on other servers to the same drive letter.

Another problem you might encounter in a multiserver environment under Windows occurs when users with different home servers use a sharable network application like a database. Shared network applications often use a "control" file to handle file and record locking and set up system-wide defaults for directory locations, print queues, and such.

If the network control file specifies default directory paths, you must ensure that users have the same drive letters mapped to the appropriate directory paths, regardless of which server is their home server. For example, if drive M: is mapped to the control file directory and drive N: to the data directory for users whose home server is CICERO, then drives M: and N: must be mapped to the same paths (on CICERO) for users whose home server is TOLSTOY. For more information about using Windows with NetWare, see Appendix C.

Summary

In this chapter, we've introduced the idea of user account managers and workgroup managers as tools for distributing the network management workload. We've explained that user account managers have some abilities to manage users and groups and that workgroup managers have the same abilities as a network supervisor for the groups and users they manage.

We've defined the concept of the "home" server as the home base for network users and the server that sets up the user's environment. Finally, we've described the use of NetWare utilities and batch files to enable you to simultaneously use the resources of more than one file server.

CHAPTER 14

Using the
NetWare 3.12
Utilities

392   *NetWare 3.12's menu utilities have many similar keyboard conventions that can help a user with an unfamiliar menu utility, such as:*

- ▶ Getting help with F1

- ▶ Exiting your current situation or action with Esc

- ▶ Selecting an item or close a data field and move on with ↵

- ▶ Displaying a list to select from with Ins

- ▶ Removing the highlighted item with Del

- ▶ Marking an item with F5

- ▶ Maneuvering around lists with ↑, ↓, Ctrl-↑, and Ctrl-↓

- ▶ Editing text fields with ← and →

- ▶ Canceling the current action with F7

- ▶ Going straight to the exit menu with Alt-F10

395   *SYSCON can allow some limited actions and provide the ordinary network user with valuable information such as:*

- ▶ Accounting charges and service rates, if the accounting functions are installed

- ▶ Change the current file server

- ▶ View group information

- ▶ View user information and personal login scripts

SESSION allows the network user to change   **408**
characteristics of their current session such as:

- ▸ Changing the current server
- ▸ Changing the default drive
- ▸ Displaying and changing drive mappings
- ▸ Displaying and changing search drive mappings
- ▸ Send messages to and view groups
- ▸ View user information and send messages to users

FILER provides the network user with file and directory management   **417**
and information such as:

- ▸ Displaying volume information
- ▸ Displaying directory information
- ▸ Change current directory
- ▸ Displaying file information and managing files
- ▸ Changing FILER options

NetWare 3.12 also provides the network user with several command-   **425**
line utilities that can perform useful tasks such as:

- ▸ Sending messages to other users or groups using SEND
- ▸ Allowing and blocking messages using CASTON and CASTOFF
- ▸ View current connection information about all sessions with USERLIST
- ▸ Changing passwords with SETPASS
- ▸ Displaying personal connection information with WHOAMI

NetWare 3.12 comes with a set of utilities to help you examine and manage your files and directories and to interact with other users on your network, whether you are the Network Administrator or an ordinary user. In this chapter, we'll look at some of these utilities and see how you can use them to increase productivity. We'll look first at some of the menu utilities, then at some utilities that you can call from the DOS command line. We'll only consider those aspects of these utilities that will be useful to you as a user, when you are not using supervisor privileges. The utilities most useful for administration are covered in Part Three of this book, and in other chapters in Part Four.

Some NetWare Menu Utilities

In this section, we'll go over some of the menu utilities that come with NetWare, and look at the features they offer the non-supervisory user. Some of the menu utilities are described elsewhere in this book (PCONSOLE, PRINTDEF, and PRINTCON in Chapter 11, and FCONSOLE in Appendix A) but they all use the same keyboard conventions as the utilities described in this chapter. Therefore, once you know the key sequences for one utility, you will find that they are all easy to use. With this in mind, let's look at some of the most useful key sequences.

KEY SEQUENCES FOR ALL MENU UTILITIES

This section describes some of the most useful key commands for the menu utilities. To see the other function key sequences, or to quickly refresh your memory on these while you are working in a utility, just press F1 twice while using any of the menu utilities. You will see a screen like the one in Figure 14.1, and you can use the PageUp and PageDown keys to move between the screens that list all the function keys for the utilities. Here we describe the ones you are most likely to use.

```
┌──────────────────────────────────────────────────────────────┐
│ SYSCON  3.75                       Tuesday  June 7, 1994  6:30 pm │
│            User SUPERVISOR on NetWare Server TOLSTOY             │
└──────────────────────────────────────────────────────────────┘
┌──────────────────────────────────────────────────────────────┐
│ The function key assignments on your machine are:               │
│                                                                  │
│ Esc            Esc            Escape                             │
│ Exit           Alt F10        Exit Program                      │
│ Cancel         F7             Cancel Changes                    │
│ Backspace      Backspace      Delete Left                       │
│ Ins            Ins            Insert                            │
│ Del            Del            Delete                            │
│ Modify         F3             Rename/Modify/Edit Item            │
│ Select         Enter          Accept                            │
│ Help           F1             Online Help                       │
│ Mark           F5             Toggle Mark                       │
│ Cycle          Tab            Cycle Screens                     │
│ Mode           F9             Change Modes                      │
│ Up             Up arrow       Move Up One                       │
│ Down           Down arrow     Move Down One                     │
│ Left           Left arrow     Move Left One Space               │
│ Right          Right arrow    Move Right One Space              │
│ Ctrl+PgUp      Ctrl PgUp      Beginning                         │
└──────────────────────────────────────────────────────────────┘
```

FIGURE 14.1

The Function Key Help

screen

Getting Help with F1

You can press F1 at any time in the NetWare menu utilities to display a windowful of text that describes the current screen, field, or menu item.

Escape

In the NetWare menu utilities, Esc always exits your current action. If you are working in a particular submenu and want to return to the previous one, press Esc. Similarly, if you are entering text in a text field and change your mind about altering the field, Esc gets you out of the entry and restores the old entry (except when you're entering a new password; see *User Information* later in this chapter). If you have changed a field on a menu or screen and the cursor is still on that field, when you press Esc your cursor will move to the next field. Press Esc again to exit that menu or screen. Remember that the Esc key is the only way out of some data-entry screens.

Enter (↵)

Pressing ↵ selects the menu item on which your cursor currently rests, or tells the utility that you have finished editing the current field.

Ins

Generally, when your cursor is on a field that accepts input from a list of options, pressing Ins will display a list from which you can make your selection. If you are editing a field that does not recognize Ins, pressing it will have no effect.

Deleting with Del

Pressing Del removes the current item from the list you are editing. NetWare utilities will always ask you to confirm any deletions before deleting the item, so you don't have to worry about pressing this by accident and destroying information. If you press Del while on a field that does not recognize it, nothing will happen.

Marking Items with F5

You can use F5 to select several items in a list. Press it to mark the current item, and press it again to unmark a marked item. Press ↵ when you have finished marking, and the utility will perform the current action on all the marked items. If you are working in a list where actions on multiple items are not possible, pressing F5 will have no effect.

Moving Around in Lists

↑ and ↓ move you up and down in lists. To move to the top or bottom of the current list, press Ctrl-↑ or Ctrl-↓.

Editing Text Fields

← moves your cursor one character to the left, unless you are already at the start of the field, and → moves the cursor one character to the right, unless you are at the end of the field. Backspace moves the cursor one character to the right, deleting the character that was there (up to the start of the field), and Del deletes the character your cursor is on, if any. ↵ concludes the editing, and Esc or F7 cancels it, leaving the field with its old value. Editing is always in insert mode instead of overstrike mode, which means that the characters you type in that field will get inserted to the left of your cursor, rather than on top of the character the cursor is resting on.

Canceling Actions

When you press F7, the utility will cancel the current action and return you to your previous menu or screen. It will first ask you to confirm the cancellation, so don't worry about pressing it by accident and losing all your changes.

Exiting a Utility

Press Alt-F10 from anywhere in a menu utility, and the utility will go straight to the Exit menu. This can be a time-saver if you are working several levels deep in a utility and don't want to press Esc for every level, as shown in Figure 14.2.

USING THE SYSTEM CONFIGURATION (SYSCON) UTILITY

SYSCON is the NetWare system configuration utility. The system administrator uses it for many system maintenance functions, including setting up accounts for new users, modifying settings for existing users, creating and managing groups of users and their access rights, and managing the system accounting. Most of these features are not available to other users, for the protection of both the users and the system. As a non-supervisory user, you will probably use SYSCON mostly for changing your password and editing your login script. You can access both tasks via the User Information menu item described below. You can also use SYSCON to

FIGURE 14.2

Quick exit with Alt-F10

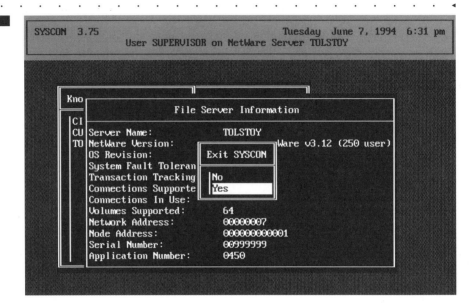

view information about the server and the network, and we'll cover those items as well.

Figure 14.3 shows the top menu of the SYSCON utility. With the access rights of a typical user, you will be able to view settings for the various subsections, but will not be able to change anything that will affect anyone's network configuration besides your own. With that rule in mind, let's look at each of the SYSCON menus.

Accounting

When you select this menu item, you will either see a message saying "Accounting is not installed on server" or the menu in Figure 14.4. If your system has NetWare Accounting running, you can use the functions from this menu to view the charges for various system services. On some systems, services heavily used at certain times of the day might cost you more to use at those times than others. You can find out the rates by using features in this menu, so that you can budget your account accordingly. Figure 14.4 shows the Accounting menu.

▶ . . . . ◀

F I G U R E 14.3

The SYSCON top menu

```
SYSCON  3.75                          Tuesday  June 7, 1994  6:31 pm
               User SUPERVISOR on NetWare Server TOLSTOY

                    ┌─────────────────────────┐
                    │    Available Topics     │
                    ├─────────────────────────┤
                    │ Accounting              │
                    │ Change Current Server   │
                    │ File Server Information │
                    │ Group Information       │
                    │ Supervisor Options      │
                    │ User Information        │
                    └─────────────────────────┘
```

▶ . . . . ◀

F I G U R E 14.4

The Accounting menu in
SYSCON

```
SYSCON  3.75                          Tuesday  June 7, 1994  6:32 pm
               User SUPERVISOR on NetWare Server TOLSTOY

                    ┌─────────────────────────┐
                    │    Available Topics     │
                    │                  ng     │
          ┌──────────────────────┐ urrent Server │
          │      Accounting      │ ver Information│
          ├──────────────────────┤ formation      │
          │ Accounting Servers   │ or Options     │
          │ Blocks Read Charge Rates│ ormation    │
          │ Blocks Written Charge Rates│
          │ Connect Time Charge Rates│
          │ Disk Storage Charge Rates│
          │ Service Requests Charge Rates│
          └──────────────────────┘
```

Use the first menu item, Accounting Servers, to select the server about which you want to view accounting information. Once you select a server, you can use any of the other five menu items to view charges for services on that server. In our example we will look at charges for connect time, as shown in Figure 14.5, but the accounting screens for the other menu items behave the same way.

Note that on the left side of the screen you have a list of rate codes with charges next to the codes. The values in the table at the right are the rate codes, each corresponding to a rate in the list at the left. In this example, you can see that it will be more expensive for you to log in during weekdays than in the evenings or on weekends. You can scroll through the times of day by using the arrow keys or the PageUp and PageDown keys.

Change Current Server

If your network has more than one server, you can move between them using this menu item. When you select it, you get a list of all the servers you

FIGURE 14.5

Connect Time Charge Rates
screen

SYSCON 3.75							Tuesday June 7, 1994 6:33 pm

User SUPERVISOR on NetWare Server TOLSTOY

		Sun	Mon	Tue	Wed	Thu	Fri	Sat
Connect Time Charge Rates	11:30am	1	2	2	2	2	2	1
	12:00pm	1	2	2	2	2	2	1
	12:30pm	1	2	2	2	2	2	1
Wednesday	1:00pm	1	2	2	2	2	2	1
5:00 pm To 5:29 pm	1:30pm	1	2	2	2	2	2	1
	2:00pm	1	2	2	2	2	2	1
Rate Charge Rate Charge	2:30pm	1	2	2	2	2	2	1
1 No Charge 11	3:00pm	1	2	2	2	2	2	1
2 2/1 12	3:30pm	1	2	2	2	2	2	1
3 13	4:00pm	1	2	2	2	2	2	1
4 14	4:30pm	1	2	2	2	2	2	1
5 15	5:00pm	1	2	2	2	2	2	1
6 16	5:30pm	1	1	1	2	1	1	1
7 17	6:00pm	1	1	1	2	1	1	1
8 18	6:30pm	1	1	1	2	1	1	1
9 19	7:00pm	1	1	1	2	1	1	1
10 20	7:30pm	1	1	1	1	1	1	1
(Charge is per minute)	8:00pm	1	1	1	1	1	1	1

are logged into. Use the arrow keys to move down to the server that you want as your new current server, and press ↵. The list vanishes, and your current server is now the one you just selected.

If the server you wish to access is not on the list of servers you are logged into, press Ins to bring up a list of available servers that you are not logged in to. Choose from this list, press ↵, and enter the password.

File Server Information

To get information about your current server, select this menu item. You will see a window like the one in Figure 14.6. Here you can see what version of NetWare you are running, how many connections your server supports, network and node addresses, and other information. In normal usage of your network, you will probably not need much of this information.

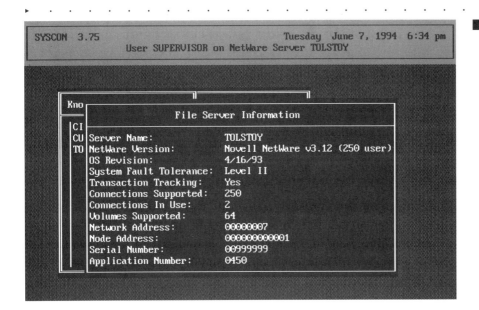

F I G U R E   14.6

File Server information

Group Information

With Group Information, you can view all the groups on your server and can also view information about the groups. When you select this menu item, you see a list of all the groups on your server. Use the arrow keys to move to the group about which you want more information, and press ↵. At this point, one of two things will happen. If you are not a member of the selected group, you will see a window with just two menu items, as in Figure 14.7. Otherwise you can view several different items about the group, as shown in Figure 14.8. Since the non-member information is also in the member-information menu, we'll look at the latter.

Full Name	Displays the full name of the group, if any. The administrator might choose a short and easy-to-type group name and put a longer name here that describes the purpose of the group more completely. This full name is optional, however, and if it is not present for the current group, you will see a message to that effect.
Managed Users and Groups	Lists the users and groups (if any) managed by this group
Managers	Lists the users authorized to manage this group. These users can create or remove users from the group and modify the user accounts, among other tasks. They have supervisor rights only within the group that they manage. See Chapters 10 and 13 for more information.
Member List	Lists all the members of the current group.

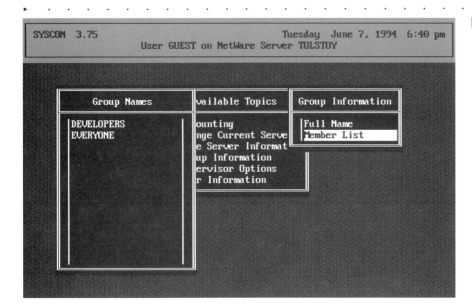

F I G U R E   14.7

*Group Information if you're
not a member of the group*

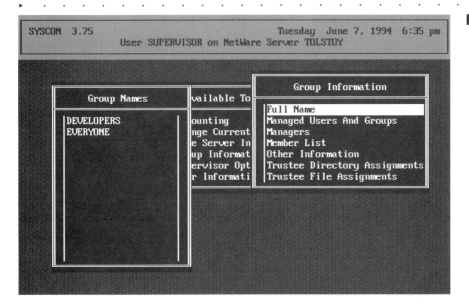

F I G U R E   14.8

*Group Information when
you are a member of the
group*

Other Information	Displays some miscellaneous parameters relating to the group. As a non-supervisor, you will only be able to view the group's ID number, which is the number (also called the *bindery number*) that NetWare uses to refer to the group. You'll probably never need to know this number.
Trustee Directory Assignments	Displays a two-column list: on the left are the directories to which members of this group have rights, and on the right the rights the members have within those directories, as shown in Figure 14.9. Their rights in a particular directory will trickle down into that directory's subdirectories, unless the subdirectories have rights blocked with the Inherited Rights Mask. See Chapter 10 for more information about these rights and masks.
Trustee File Assignments	Lets you view special access rights per file that apply to your group. The system administrator might have set these rights if the group needs access to particular files within a directory, but not to the whole directory, or conversely, if the group needs access to all the files in a directory except for a small number of special cases. If your group has any such files, this menu item will show you a list of them, in a two-column structure much like the one for Trustee Directory Assignments, above.

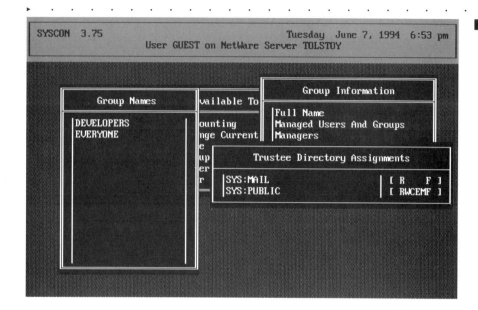

FIGURE 14.9

Viewing Trustee Directory
Assignments

Supervisor Options

Since you do not have Supervisor access rights, you will not be able to access any of the features in this menu. For information on administrative activities, including this menu, see Chapters 10, 12, and 13.

User Information

This menu is probably the most useful of all the SYSCON menus to non-supervisory users. With features in this section you can view and change information about your account and view some information about other users. When you select this item, you will see a list of users; use the arrow keys to move up and down within the list and ↵ to select which user to view. Now you will see one of two things: either a short list of items if the selected user is not yourself, as in Figure 14.10, or a longer list for information about your own account, as in Figure 14.11. Since the items in the short list also appear in the longer list, we'll go over all the items in the complete list.

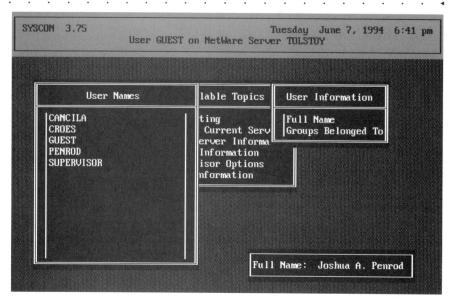

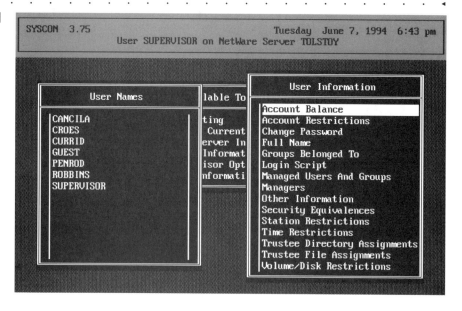

Account Balance	Only appears if your server has system accounting enabled. If it does, you can view your current account balance, whether your account allows credit, and the lower limit on your account.
Account Restrictions	Shows you several parameters about your account, and most of them are self-explanatory (you can press F1 for help screens). Limit Concurrent Connections tells whether you can log into the server from more than one station. This screen describes the details of what type of password protection your account has.
Change Password	You should change your password periodically, and you can use this menu item to do it. Change Password will prompt you to enter the current password (for security), then to enter the new password twice (to make sure you don't make a typo).
Full Name	Displays the full name of the currently selected user. This might either be the person's full name if the account belongs to one person, or a more informative description of the type of user if this is an account that several users share.
Groups Belonged To	Lists all the groups to which the currently selected user belongs.

Login Script	The system executes your login script every time you log into your account. Unless the Network Administrator provides otherwise, with this menu item, you can edit the script to perform whatever actions you wish. The types of things that typically go into login scripts are drive and search drive mappings, messages, and parameter settings unique to this user. Drive and search drive mappings, messages, parameter settings, etc., common to all network users should be defined in the System Login Script located under the Supervisor Options of SYSCON's main menu. Figure 14.12 shows the Login Script editor screen.
	When you are editing your login script, $\uparrow$, $\downarrow$, $\leftarrow$, and $\rightarrow$ move you around in the text, and Del and Ins work together, so that you can insert text with Ins that you previously deleted with Del. The lines of the script must be 150 characters or less, and must have only one command per line. The commands must be NetWare login script commands, as described in Chapter 9.
Managed Users and Groups	Displays a list of any users or groups you manage.
Managers	Displays a list of the users who manage your account, other than the SUPERVISOR.

Other Information	Shows the last time you logged in, whether you are a console operator, how much disk space you are using, and your user ID.
Security Equivalencies	Shows you which user you are equivalent to (if your network administrator has set up your account to have the same security rights and restrictions as another user's, rather than setting all the parameters individually for each user account).
Station Restrictions	Shows the address for the workstation to which you are restricted if your network administrator has restricted you to one particular workstation; otherwise you will get a message saying that your account is not restricted.
Time Restrictions	Displays a screen showing what times you will be able to log in (see Figure 14.13). The asterisks show times when you have access to the system, and the spaces indicate when you cannot be logged in. In Figure 14.13, the user can log in only during normal business hours on weekdays, on Saturday mornings, and late on Wednesday evenings.

Trustee Directory Assignments	Presents a screen divided into two columns, listing the directories on the left and the rights you have to each directory on the right. The Trustee Directory Assignments menu item for users works exactly the same as the one for groups (described above).
Trustee File Assignments	Lists files having special rights on the left side of the screen and their access rights on the right. The Trustee File Assignments for users works just like the one for groups (see *Group Information* above).
Volume/Disk Restrictions	Shows whether your system administrator has limited the amount of disk space you can use on a particular volume, how much space you can use altogether, and how much you are currently using.

USING THE SESSION MANAGEMENT (SESSION) UTILITY

SESSION is the utility you use to change characteristics of your current network session. The changes you make using this utility will last until you log out, so if you want to make them effective every time you are logged in, go into SYSCON and add the commands to your personal Login Script (in the User Information menu off the main menu).

Using SESSION, you can change your current server, change your current drive and your drive mappings, and view information about users and groups. Figure 14.14 shows the SESSION top menu. We'll look first at the server and drive functions, then at the user and group functions.

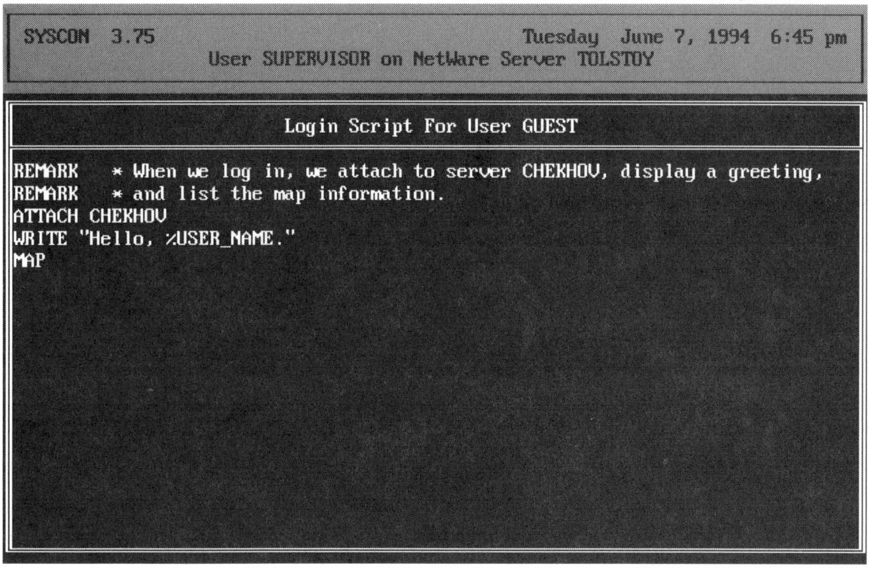

FIGURE 14.12

Editing a login script

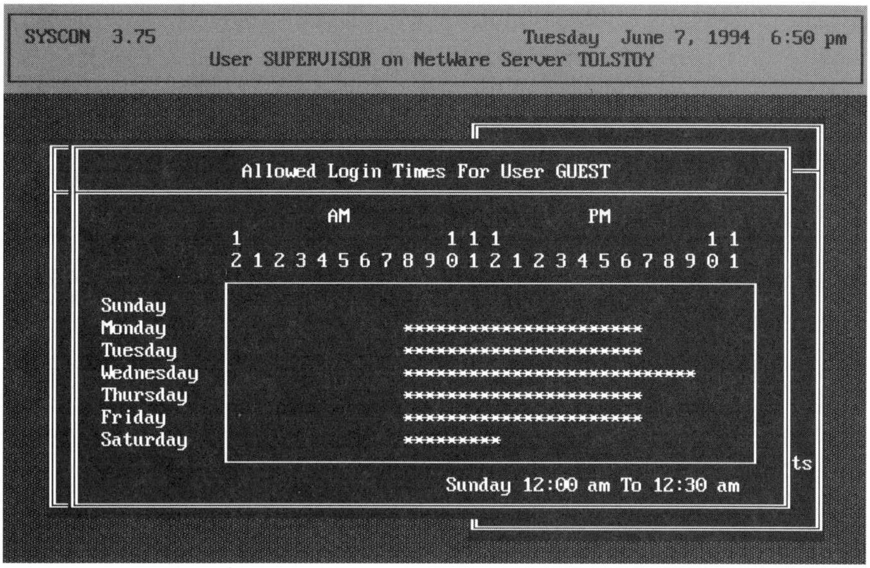

FIGURE 14.13

The Time Restrictions Screen

FIGURE 14.14

The SESSION top menu

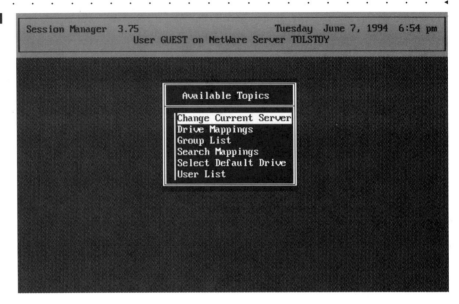

Changing Your Current Server

Select Change Current Server to display a list of servers on the network that you are logged into. If there is more than one server on the list, use the arrow keys to move to it, then press ↵ to select it, making that server your new current server. Now all the commands you execute will apply to that new current server.

To log out of a server, select Change Current Server again and use the arrow keys to move to the server from which you want to disconnect. Press Del, and the system will ask you to confirm logging out. If you select YES, you will be logged out of the server.

Changing Your Default Drive

Your default drive, also known as your *current drive*, is the focus of your activities. When you type the DOS command DIR, for instance, the directory information it displays will be for the current directory on your default drive.

You can change your default drive by selecting Select Default Drive on the SESSION menu. This displays a list of all your drive mappings and search drive mappings, as shown in Figure 14.15. The highlight bar will be on your current default drive. Use the arrow keys to move the highlight to the drive you want for your new default, then press ↵ to select it.

Note that Ins and Del do not work in this list. To add or delete drive mappings, see the next section.

Displaying and Changing Drive Mappings

Drive mappings give you a shorthand way of referring and moving to directories. This can be especially useful if you have directories on several different servers, or directories with long path names. For instance, if your data files are in the directory SYS:PUBLIC\DATA\MARCH, you would have to type the whole path name every time you wanted to refer to a file in that directory. With drive mappings, you can just map a drive letter to that directory—for example, S:. Now you can refer to files in the directory by typing

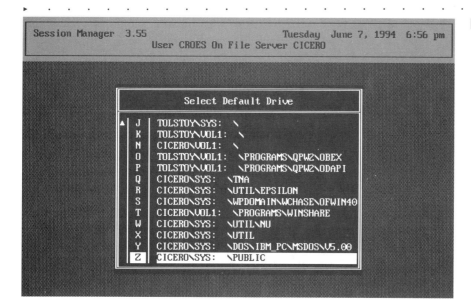

F I G U R E 14.15

Selecting a new default drive

s:file1, s:file2, etc., and you can move to the directory by typing s: instead of typing cd sys:public\data\march.

You can alter your drive mappings by selecting Drive Mappings on the SESSION menu. This displays a list of all your drive mappings (see Figure 14.16).

For completeness, your local drives are listed as well as your network drives, but you cannot change the mappings of any local drives.

To delete a drive mapping, highlight that drive with the arrow keys and press Del. The system will ask you to confirm before performing the deletion.

To add a new drive mapping, press Ins. You can do this no matter where you are in the list. A box will pop up listing the next available drive letter; you can press ↵ to accept it or backspace over it and type your own selection. You must use a letter, and you can't reuse a drive letter that is already mapped. If you want to reuse one, delete the old mapping first.

Once you have selected the drive letter, you will see another box pop up prompting you for a directory name. Enter the name of the directory that

```
Session Manager  3.55                        Tuesday  June 7, 1994  6:56 pm
                      User CROES On File Server CICERO


                         Current Drive Mappings

           A   (Local Drive)
           B   (Local Drive)
           C   (Local Drive)
           F   CICERO\SYS:   \DOS
           G   CICERO\VOL1:  \
           H   CICERO\VOL1:  \HOME\CROES
           J   TOLSTOY\SYS:  \
           K   TOLSTOY\VOL1: \
           N   CICERO\VOL1:  \
           O   TOLSTOY\VOL1: \PROGRAMS\QPW2\OBEX
           P   TOLSTOY\VOL1: \PROGRAMS\QPW2\ODAPI
           Q   CICERO\SYS:   \TNA
```

will be mapped to the drive letter, including the server and volume names if necessary. If you are unsure of the correct path, press Ins and choose from the lists of available servers, volumes, and directories to build the path you desire. Press Esc when you are satisfied. Figure 14.17 illustrates this process.

Displaying and Changing Search Drive Mappings

Search drives tell the system where to look for applications and other executable files. They are much like the directories in the DOS PATH environment variable. When you type in a file name, the operating system will look in each directory till it is found. The order used is defined by the PATH environment variable.

You can view, add, or remove search drives from your search list by selecting Search Mappings in SESSION. This displays a window like the one in Figure 14.18. Note that both your network search drives and your DOS PATH directories appear in this list.

```
Session Manager  3.55                      Tuesday   June 7, 1994  6:57 pm
                    User CROES On File Server CICERO

┌──────────────────────────────────────────────────────────────┐
│                       Select Directory                         │
├──────────────────────────────────────────────────────────────┤
│CHEKOV/SYS:USR\DATA                                             │
├──────────────────────────────────────────────────────────────┤
│  B  │ (Local Drive)                                            │
│  C  │ (Local Drive)                                            │
│  F  │ CICERO\SYS:  \DOS                                        │
│  G  │ CICERO\VOL1:  \                                          │
│  H  │ CICERO\VOL1:  \HOME\CROES                                │
│  J  │ TOLSTOY\SYS:  \                                          │
│  K  │ TOLSTOY\VOL1:  \                                         │
│  N  │ CICERO\VOL1:  \                                          │
│  O  │ TOLSTOY\VOL1:  \PROGRAMS\QPW2\OBEX                       │
│  P  │ TOLSTOY\VOL1:  \PROGRAMS\QPW2\ODAPI                      │
│  Q  │ CICERO\SYS:  \TNA                                        │
└──────────────────────────────────────────────────────────────┘
```

F I G U R E   14.17

Adding a new drive mapping

FIGURE 14.18

Using Search Mappings in
SESSION

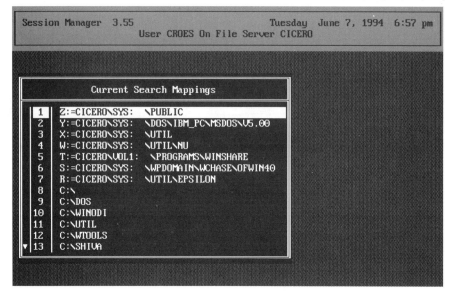

If you will be running programs out of a couple of directories, you can delete the extra search drive mappings one at a time by moving the arrow keys to highlight the extra search drive, then pressing Del. The system will ask you to confirm before it deletes the mapping. This will prevent the system looking in every directory for your programs for the current session. You can also delete several drives at once by moving the arrow keys to each one, pressing F5, and moving to the next one. When you have selected all the search drives you want to delete, press Del and the system will delete them all at once (after asking you, of course).

To add a new search drive to the list, press Ins. A box will pop up displaying the next available search drive number. Press ↵ to accept it or backspace over it and type your own selection. Note that the system refers to search drives by number instead of drive letter in this list; the number indicates the order in which they are searched. If you want to add a new drive before an existing one, type the number of that drive and the system will insert it there.

Once you have selected a search drive number, another box will pop up asking you for the directory to search. Enter the full path name, including the server and volume names if necessary, as shown in Figure 14.19. Again, press Ins if you are unsure of the correct path.

View and Send Messages to Groups

SESSION offers a quick, easy way to view all the groups on your current server and to send messages to them. First, select Group List from the SESSION top menu. You will see a window listing all the groups on your server. Use the arrow keys to move the highlight bar to the group to which you want to send a message, and press ↵ to select that group. The system will prompt you for the message, as shown in Figure 14.20.

To send a message to several groups, highlight each group in turn and press F5. When you've selected all the groups, press ↵, and the system will prompt you for the message.

FIGURE 14.19

Adding a new search drive

```
Session Manager  3.55                    Tuesday  June 7, 1994  7:01 pm
                     User CROES On File Server TOLSTOY


┌──────────────────────────────────────────────────────────────┐
│                      Select Directory                          │
├──────────────────────────────────────────────────────────────┤
│ D:\APPS\USERPROG                                               │
└──────────────────────────────────────────────────────────────┘
    ┌─────────────────────────────────────────────────────────┐
    │  2 │ Y:=CICERO\SYS:   \DOS\IBM_PC\MSDOS\V5.00             │
    │  3 │ X:=CICERO\SYS:   \UTIL                               │
    │  4 │ W:=CICERO\SYS:   \UTIL\NU                            │
    │  5 │ T:=CICERO\VOL1:  \PROGRAMS\WINSHARE                  │
    │  6 │ S:=CICERO\SYS:   \WPDOMAIN\WCHASE\OFWIN40            │
    │  7 │ R:=CICERO\SYS:   \UTIL\EPSILON                       │
    │  8 │ C:\                                                  │
    │  9 │ C:\DOS                                               │
    │ 10 │ C:\WINODI                                            │
    │ 11 │ C:\UTIL                                              │
    │ 12 │ C:\WTOOLS                                            │
    │▼13 │ C:\SHIVA                                             │
    └─────────────────────────────────────────────────────────┘
```

Sending a message to a

group

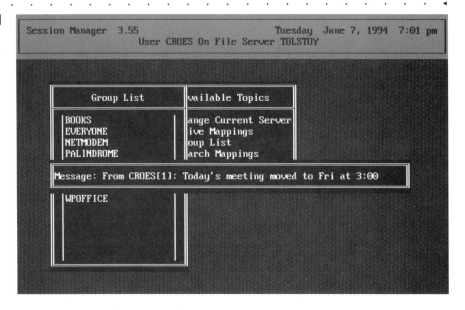

View User Information and Send Messages to Users

Just as SESSION lets you view all the groups on your server and send messages to them, it also lets you view and send messages to individual users.

Select User List from the SESSION main menu. SESSION checks to see which users are logged in, and displays them in a list. Use the arrow keys to move up and down in this list, and press ↵ to select a user to view. Now you get an Available Options menu with two items: Display User Information and Send Message. If you select Display User Information, you see a window like the one in Figure 14.21. This window displays the user's full name, the object type of the connection (in this case, the object type is always User, but in other contexts it could be a printer or other object), the time the user logged in, and the user's address and node ID.

If you want to send a message to the user, select Send Message from the Available Options menu. The system will present you with a prompt box; enter the message and press ↵ to send it.

FIGURE 14.21

User Information Window

```
Session Manager  3.55                    Tuesday  June 7, 1994  7:10 pm
                      User CROES On File Server TOLSTOY


    ┌─────────────────────────┬──────────┬──────────────────┐
    │ Current Users           │ Station  │ble Topics        │
    ├─────────────────────────┼──────────┼──────────────────┤
    │CANCILA                  │   001    │Current Server    │
    │CROES                    │   002    │appings           │
    │ROBBINS                  │          ├──────────────────┴─────────────────┐
    │                         │          │Full Name:      Margaret Robbins     │
    │                         │          │Object Type:    User                 │
    │                         │          │Login Time:     Tuesday  June 7, 1994  7:08 pm │
    │                         │          │Network Address: 00000001            │
    │                         │          │Network Node:   480b03709706         │
    │                         │          └─────────────────────────────────────┘
    │                         │
    └─────────────────────────┴
```

To send a message to several users, highlight each in turn and press F5. When you've selected all the users, press ↵, and the system will prompt you for the message.

USING THE FILE MAINTENANCE (FILER) UTILITY

FILER gives you a quick way to display information about directories and files, and to move around in network directories. It also has some options that you can use to change its behavior. Figure 14.22 shows the top FILER menu.

Note that FILER only works with network directories, so your current drive must be a network drive before you can use FILER.

Displaying Volume Information

Using FILER, you can view some basic statistics about your current volume. Select the Volume Information menu item from the FILER top menu, and you will see a window like the one in Figure 14.23.

▶ · ◀

F I G U R E 14.22

The top menu of the Filer
Utility

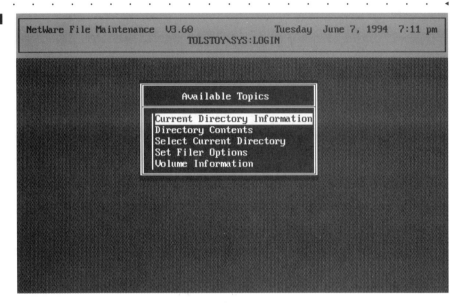

▶ · ◀

F I G U R E 14.23

The Volume Information
Window

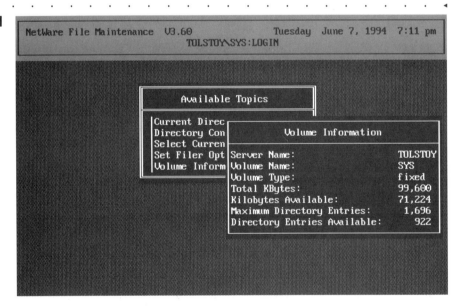

From this window, you can see the current server name, the name of the volume you are currently using and its type, and the volume's total capacity and amount of unused capacity, both in terms of kilobytes and directory entries.

Displaying Directory Information

To view information about your current directory, select Current Directory Information from the top FILER menu. The Directory Information window appears, showing the directory name relative to the current volume across the top of the window, and a list of other data items about the directory (see Figure 14.24). These include the owner of the directory, the date and time the directory was created, the directory attributes, your effective rights for this directory, and your inherited rights for this directory.

If you have rights to change the parameters of this directory, you will be able to use the arrow keys to move around in this screen and view the data about the directory. In particular, you can view the directory attributes, as shown in Figure 14.25.

NOTE
See Chapters 9 and 10 for more information about rights and attributes.

▶ · ◀

```
 NetWare File Maintenance   V3.60           Tuesday  June 7, 1994  7:12 pm
                            TOLSTOY\SYS:LOGIN

        ┌──────────────────────────────────────────────────┐
        │          Directory Information for LOGIN           │
        │ ┌────────────────────────────────────────────────┐│
        │ │ Owner: SUPERVISOR                               ││
        │ │                                                 ││
        │ │ Creation Date:  June 7, 1980                    ││
        │ │                                                 ││
        │ │ Creation Time:  12:00 am                        ││
        │ │                                                 ││
        │ │ Directory Attributes: (see list)                ││
        │ │                                                 ││
        │ │ Current Effective Rights: [SRWCEMFA]            ││
        │ │                                                 ││
        │ │ Inherited Rights Mask: [SRWCEMFA]               ││
        │ │                                                 ││
        │ │                                                 ││
        │ │ Trustees:  (see list)                           ││
        │ └────────────────────────────────────────────────┘│
        └──────────────────────────────────────────────────┘
```

FIGURE 14.24

The Directory Information window

FIGURE 14.25

Viewing a directory's
attributes

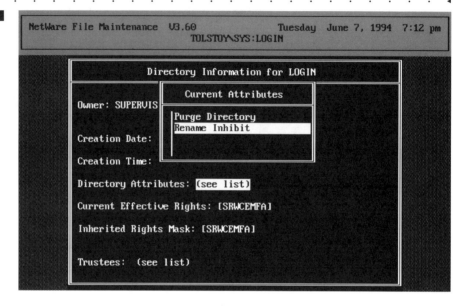

```
NetWare File Maintenance  V3.60              Tuesday  June 7, 1994  7:12 pm
                            TOLSTOY\SYS:LOGIN

          ┌─────────── Directory Information for LOGIN ───────────┐
          │                                                       │
          │                  ┌── Current Attributes ──┐           │
          │  Owner: SUPERVIS  │                        │          │
          │                   │ Purge Directory        │          │
          │                   │ Rename Inhibit          │          │
          │  Creation Date:   │                        │          │
          │                   └────────────────────────┘          │
          │  Creation Time:                                       │
          │                                                       │
          │  Directory Attributes: (see list)                     │
          │                                                       │
          │  Current Effective Rights: [SRWCEMFA]                 │
          │                                                       │
          │  Inherited Rights Mask: [SRWCEMFA]                    │
          │                                                       │
          │                                                       │
          │  Trustees:  (see list)                                │
          │                                                       │
          └───────────────────────────────────────────────────────┘
```

Change Current Directory

To change your current directory, select Select Current Directory from the top FILER menu. FILER will pop up the Current Directory Path prompt window showing the current directory name. You can add to the end of this name to move to a subdirectory, or backspace over it to erase it and enter a new directory name. It is easiest to press Ins and let FILER search the directories for you. FILER will display the Network Directories window, which contains a list of all the subdirectories of the current directory; you can select one by using the arrow keys and pressing ↵. Figure 14.26 illustrates the Current Directory Path and Network Directories Windows.

Note that, just as in DOS, the ".." directory refers to the parent of the current directory. If you select that directory, you get a new window showing the subdirectories off that directory. The directory name in the Current Directory Path window gets updated with each selection you make so that it reflects your choices. When the desired directory appears in this window, press Esc to exit the Network Directories list, then ↵ to make that directory your new current one.

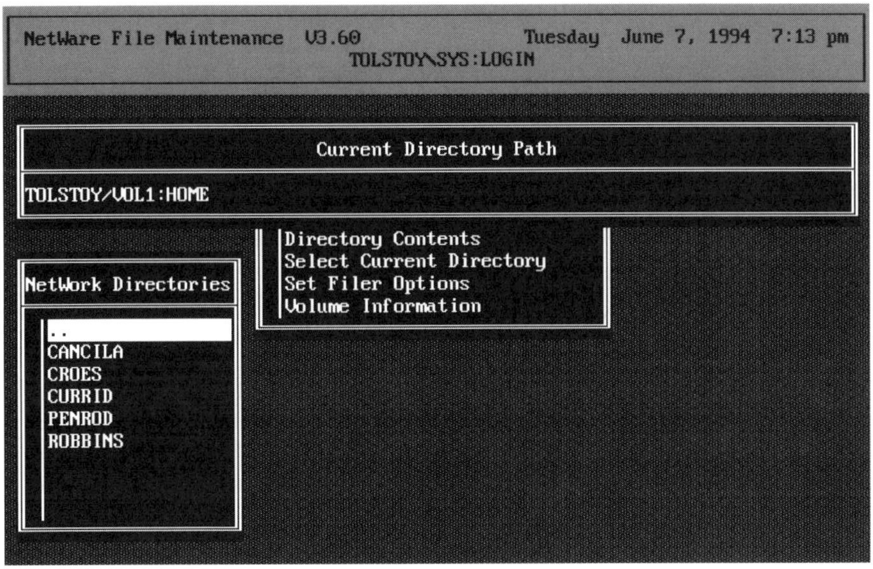

FIGURE 14.26

*The Current Directory Path
and Network Directories
windows*

To leave your current directory unchanged, press Esc at the Current Directory Path prompt.

Displaying File Information and Managing Files

Now that you have selected a directory, you may want to see what files are in the directory, and possibly copy, move and delete them. Select the Directory Contents menu item from the FILER main menu. When you do, the system displays a window listing the files and subdirectories in your current directory. You can use the arrow keys to move up and down in the list, and ↵ to select an item in the list.

Your available options depend on two things: Whether you have rights to change anything in this directory, and whether the selected item is a subdirectory or a file. If you do not have the appropriate rights to perform the action you have selected, the system will tell you so with a warning window. For this discussion, we will assume you do have the necessary rights to the directory.

NOTE
See Chapter 10 for a
more complete discus-
sion of file rights.

If you select a file, the system will display the menu shown in Figure 14.27. It offers you the options of copying, moving, or viewing the contents of the file, viewing information about the file (such as its attributes, owner, rights, and access dates), and displaying a list of users who have rights on the file and what rights they have.

You can press Ins while viewing this list, and the system will prompt you for the name of a new subdirectory. If you enter one, it will create a subdirectory by that name. You can also press Del; the system will ask you to confirm deleting the currently highlighted file, and will delete it if you answer Yes.

If you select a directory, you will see a menu like the one in Figure 14.28. Using this menu, you can perform the following actions on the directory:

Copy the Subdirectory's Files	Copies all the files in the subdirectory to another directory that you specify.
Copy the Subdirectory's Structure	Copies the entire tree of files and subdirectories under the current directory to another directory that you specify.
Make This Directory Your Current Directory	Does exactly the same thing as the Select Current Directory option off the main FILER menu.
Move the Subdirectory's Structure	Moves the entire tree of files and subdirectories, including the current directory, to another directory that you specify.
View and Set Directory Information	Displays the same window of information as the Current Directory Information option off the main FILER menu, but here you can modify the data.

▶ . . . . ◀

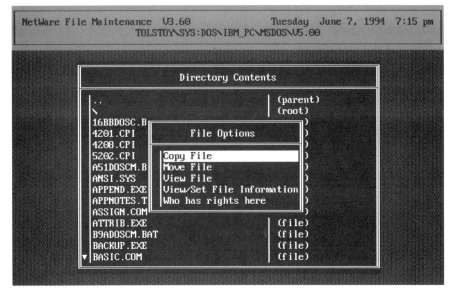

Tasks you can perform on files

Tasks you can perform on directories

View which users have which rights in the directory

Who Has Rights Here lists all the users who have any rights in the current directory, and displays which rights they have. Figure 14.29 shows an example.

As you can see, many of FILER's features are accessible in several different ways. This makes it easy for you to use the most convenient method for the task you are performing.

F I G U R E 14.29

The Who Has Rights Here option lists which users have which rights in the current directory.

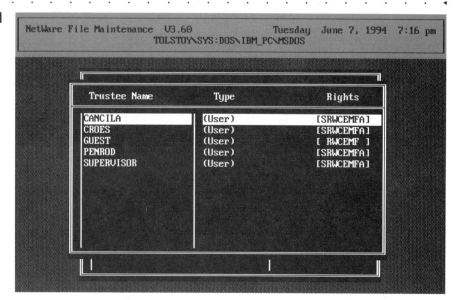

```
NetWare File Maintenance   V3.60              Tuesday  June 7, 1994  7:16 pm
                       TOLSTOY\SYS:DOS\IBM_PC\MSDOS
```

Trustee Name	Type	Rights
CANCILA	(User)	[SRWCEMFA]
CROES	(User)	[SRWCEMFA]
GUEST	(User)	[RWCEMF]
PENROD	(User)	[SRWCEMFA]
SUPERVISOR	(User)	[SRWCEMFA]

Changing FILER Options

You can change some aspects of FILER's behavior by selecting Set Filer Options from the main FILER menu. Many of these options are safety features. You can tell FILER to warn you before it overwrites a file or truncates a filename, for instance. You can also describe file search patterns here. If you never want to see files whose names end in .ERR, for example, you would put *.ERR in the Exclude Directory Patterns list. Press F1 for a detailed description of each of these settings. Figure 14.30 shows the Filer Settings window.

```
NetWare File Maintenance   V3.60              Tuesday  June 7, 1994   7:18 pm
                               TOLSTOY\SYS:

                               Filer Settings

          Confirm Deletions:   No
          Confirm File Copies:   No
          Confirm File Overwrites:   Yes

          Notify Extended Attributes/Long Name Lost:   No
          Preserve File Attributes:   Yes

          Exclude Directory Patterns:   (see list)
          Include Directory Patterns:   (see list)

          Exclude File Patterns   (see list)
          Include File Patterns:   (see list)

          File Search Attributes:   (see list)
          Directory Search Attributes: (see list)
```

F I G U R E 14.30
The Filer Settings window

Using Command-Line Utilities

Many of the things you can do with the menu utilities, you can also do with command-line utilities. Command-line utilities are single-function utilities that you can execute from the command line rather than going through a series of menus. Some command-line utilities do more than the corresponding menu commands. We'll look at just a few of the most useful ones here; see Appendix A for a complete list.

SENDING MESSAGES

The SEND command lets you send messages to other users. The messages must be brief, no more than 48 characters minus the length of your user name. The system will truncate longer messages. You can send your message to a particular user, a group of users, a workstation, or to users, groups, or workstations on different servers. Only those users or workstations currently logged in will see your message. Note that SEND only works on DOS or OS/2 workstations; users on Macintosh workstations, for instance, will not see your messages.

Sending Messages Using SEND

The SEND command has several forms, depending on your addressees. The general form is:

SEND "message" addressees

In every case, the message is the first part of the command, and must be entered within double quotation marks. The first example simply sends a message to a particular user:

SEND "Nancy, are you ready for lunch?" NCONNELL

The next example sends a message to a group:

SEND "Does anyone have a DOS 6.0 manual?" ENGINEERING

In this example, we send a message to selected users on different servers:

SEND "What time is the meeting?" SRV1/JONES, SRV3/FISHER

As a special case, you can also send messages to the system console:

SEND "Printer5 appears to be out of paper" CONSOLE

And finally, this example shows how to send a command to a user at a particular workstation (here, logical station 147), in case that user is logged in at several workstations. (You can find workstation numbers with the USERLIST command.):

SEND "Is anyone attending the seminar?" 147

Once your message has been sent, you will get a confirmation message on your screen.

For more detail on using this command, just type SEND at the DOS prompt, and you will get a message describing the syntax.

Blocking Messages

Sometimes you are performing a task that should not be interrupted by messages from other users. Some mainframe emulator programs, for instance, will behave unpredictably if a message appears on your screen during the emulator session. To prevent messages from other workstations from reaching your workstation, type:

CASTOFF

at the DOS prompt.

To prevent messages from other workstations *and* the console from reaching your workstation, type:

CASTOFF ALL

When you have finished your task and want to again receive messages, type:

CASTON

and messages will again arrive at your workstation.

LISTING USERS

The USERLIST command lets you view information about all the users logged on to your current server. To use it, just type USERLIST at the DOS prompt. It displays the connection number, the user name, and the time that user logged in. You will see an asterisk (*) next to your connection, as shown in Figure 14.31.

If you want to see information about a particular user, type that user's login name after the command:

USERLIST SMITH

You will see a display like the one in Figure 14.32. If the user SMITH is logged in several times, typing **USERLIST SMITH** will show you all of SMITH's connections and login times.

CHANGING A USER PASSWORD

You can change your password using SYSCON, as we discussed above, but if you don't want to go through all those menus, the SETPASS utility offers the quickest way to change your password. At the DOS prompt, type:

SETPASS

The system will first prompt you for your current password. (This is a confirmation step to prevent someone from changing your password while

---

FIGURE 14.31

Listing users with USERLIST

```
C:\>userlist

User Information for Server TOLSTOY
Connection   User Name        Login Time
----------   --------------   --------------------
        3    * ROBBINS        7-08-1994  5:45 pm

C:\>
```

FIGURE 14.32

*Displaying information
about a specific user*

```
C:\>userlist robbins

User Information for Server TOLSTOY
Connection   User Name        Login Time
----------   --------------   --------------------
        3    * ROBBINS        7-08-1994  5:45 pm

C:\>
```

you are away from your workstation.) Next, it will prompt you for the new password. You must enter the new password twice, and if the two entries don't match, the password will remain unchanged. This saves you from making a typo and changing the password to something unknown. If you mistype the password both times, this could still happen—in which case you should contact your network administrator.

DISPLAYING USER INFORMATION WITH WHOAMI

If you use several different login names or servers, it can be easy to forget which ones you are currently working on. The WHOAMI command lets you check easily, and also displays your login time and version information about NetWare on each server. To see this information, type **WHOAMI** at the DOS prompt. Figure 14.33 shows a sample WHOAMI display.

If you want information about only one server, type that server name after the command name (example: **WHOAMI SRVR1**).

WHOAMI offers several options to enable you to display detailed information. We describe some of these below. To use these options, type them after the WHOAMI command on the command line.

OPTION	MEANING	EFFECT
/S	Security	Display security equivalencies
/G	Groups	Show groups to which user belongs on each server
/R	Rights	Show effective rights on each server
/A	All	View all information

```
C:\>whoami
You are user ROBBINS attached to server TOLSTOY, connection 3.
Server TOLSTOY is running NetWare v3.12 (250 user).
Login time: Friday  July  8, 1994  5:45 pm

C:\>
```

FIGURE 14.33

Using the WHOAMI Command

To view your groups on all your current server connections, for example, you would type:

WHOAMI /g

Summary

Among the large number of utilities in NetWare, several are of particular interest to non-supervisory users. In this chapter, we discussed how to change passwords, configure login scripts, and view information about files, the server, the other users and groups, and one's own account. You can find descriptions of other commands in Appendix A, and information on supervisory tasks in Chapters 9, 10, 12, and 13.

Maintenance
Techniques

Fast Track

Regularly clean out your network's "common area"   **442**
(where users can exchange data) so that it does not grow too large. Be
sure to warn the network users first.

Monitoring for duplicate files   **443**
can save you space and also can help you discover problems such as a
bad drive-mapping or if users are keeping multiple file copies and why.

Other maintenance checks to perform in addition to disk-space   **445**
monitoring include:
- Checking the volume root directories for files that do not belong and determining how they got there
- Using the SECURITY utility to examine for possible lapses in security such as checking for: accounts without passwords, old passwords, weak passwords, supervisor rights, root directory rights, or global directory rights
- Monitoring network use to discover performance bottlenecks
- Preparing and implementing file server disaster prevention and recovery techniques:
- Safeguarding the file server's physical environment
- Providing hardware redundancy
- Performing routine backups of the file server
- Recovering from a file server crash

Your network should now be up and running smoothly, and your users happy. But don't sit back and rest yet, because you need to put some maintenance plans in place. With careful organization and some foresight, you can ensure that your network continues to run smoothly and that any problems that do occur have minimal impact. In this chapter, we will discuss some techniques to help you implement good maintenance habits, so that your problems will be few and will affect you and your users as little as possible.

Network administration is certainly a technical job, but it also requires plenty of interpersonal communication skills. If the network has a problem, users may be unable to do their work, and will likely become frustrated, angry, and worried. If some aspect of the network changes unexpectedly, users may very well have similar reactions. Handling all this is also part of your job, and the best way to ease it is to keep communications open at all times.

Before you change anything, let people know what will be changing and why. If a problem does occur, let the users know as quickly as you can what it is, or—if that's not possible—at least what happened and what is being done to correct it. This may be the hardest part of your job—it's tough to be calm and explain things to irritated people when you yourself may be frustrated and anxious. If your users know what's going on and feel involved, however, they are likely to be much more supportive of you and your efforts, which will make your job easier and more enjoyable.

Monitoring Disk Space

Keeping track of disk space on your network drives is one of the simplest of maintenance items. With careful tracking, you might find ways to use space more efficiently and free up hundreds of megabytes or save your users time and confusion.

WHY KEEP TRACK OF DISK SPACE?

Since your network drive is probably quite large, it may be tempting to just let users put their files on it as they wish. If you tried this, you might be amazed at how quickly the disk filled up. Without some structure to your file system, users could put files anywhere, keep many duplicates and unnecessary backups, and store files that they seldom use on the network. Suddenly your large hard drive is full, it's taking much longer than usual for users to access their files, and you have a big problem on your hands. By regularly checking disk space, you can ensure that performance does not suffer and that you are using disk space as efficiently as possible.

BASICS OF TRACKING DISK SPACE

Regular checking is the key to tracking disk space. When you first bring up your network, check your disk space once a week using the VOLINFO utility. VOLINFO shows you a window for every volume on your server, up to 32 volumes, and the amount of free space on each volume. Note the free space per volume each week and graph it. Eventually this graph will show you what 'normal' usage means for your network, and will enable you to spot unusual situations that might indicate problems. Figure 15.1 shows a sample VOLINFO screen.

After about six months, you can start checking disk space less often, perhaps dropping back to every two weeks or even once a month, depending on how heavily your network is used. If you do see a large change in disk usage, find out why it happened. It might indicate a problem—users might have a drive mapped incorrectly, for instance, and might be saving files to duplicate directories instead of their storage directory. On the other hand, an increase in disk usage could simply reflect an increase in network usage. As your network grows, your usage naturally will too, and you will at some point probably need to bring another disk or server on-line to support it.

FIGURE 15.1

The VOLINFO screen

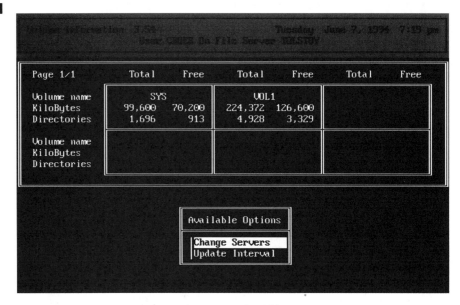

DISPLAYING SPECIFIC DISK-USAGE INFORMATION WITH NDIR

You will need several different views of your network files to get a clear picture of disk usage. The NDIR utility lists files and attributes of files, and has command-line options that let you specify which files and attributes you want to view. In this section, we'll look at several types of information that NDIR can provide.

NDIR is very similar to the DOS command DIR, but has many more options and capabilities, and shows much more information in its standard display format, as shown in Figure 15.2. Therefore, you might want to get in the habit of using NDIR all the time and not using DIR anymore. However, NDIR only works on network drives.

You will usually be using NDIR to look at a large number of files, probably more than will fit on your screen. NDIR automatically breaks the list up into chunks that will fit on your screen, and waits for you to press a key before showing the next screenful. To save a list to a file for reference,

```
TOLSTOY\SYS:

Files:                   Size      Last Updated        Flags              Owner
------------------    ----------   --------------    ----------------   ---------
BACKOUT      TTS        28,672     7-20-93  6:16p  [Rw-A-HSy----------]  SUPERVISO
DIRSTAMP     SYS       442,368     6-07-93  7:26a  [RwSA-HSy----------]  SUPERVISO
TTS$LOG      ERR         2,656     7-15-93  3:08p  [Rw---------------]   SUPERVISO
VOL$LOG      ERR         2,227     7-15-93  3:08p  [Rw---------------]   SUPERVISO

                     Inherited    Effective
Directories:          Rights       Rights        Owner       Created/Copied
------------------   ---------    ---------    ----------    --------------
CONF         HGW    [SRWCEMFA]   [SRWCEMFA]    CANCILA       7-09-93   2:13p
DOS                 [SRWCEMFA]   [SRWCEMFA]    CROES         6-07-94   7:16p
ETC                 [SRWCEMFA]   [SRWCEMFA]    TOLSTOY       6-07-93  10:07a
LOGIN               [SRWCEMFA]   [SRWCEMFA]    SUPERVISOR    0-00-00   0:00
MAIL                [SRWCEMFA]   [SRWCEMFA]    SUPERVISOR    0-00-00   0:00
NCDTREE             [SRWCEMFA]   [SRWCEMFA]    CROES         6-07-93   6:24p
PROGRAMS            [SRWCEMFA]   [SRWCEMFA]    CANCILA       7-02-93   2:51p
PUBLIC              [SRWCEMFA]   [SRWCEMFA]    SUPERVISOR    0-00-00   0:00
SYSTEM              [SRWCEMFA]   [SRWCEMFA]    SUPERVISOR    0-00-00   0:00
TNA                 [SRWCEMFA]   [SRWCEMFA]    SUPERVISOR    6-08-94   8:54a
UTIL                [SRWCEMFA]   [SRWCEMFA]    CROES         6-14-94   9:50a

Strike any key for next page or C for continuous display...
```

FIGURE 15.2

File Listing with the NDIR
command

or so that you can print it, use the DOS file-redirection capability as follows:

ndir > filelist.txt

Of course, you can use any filename you like; just make sure it's in a directory where you have Write and Create access.

In the examples below, we won't show file redirection, but if you use it, put the greater-than sign (>) and filename after all the options to NDIR.

NDIR has many options, of which we will discuss only a few here. See the Novell NetWare Utilities manual for information about the other options, or type **ndir /help** at the DOS prompt for a list.

Finding Files That Have Not Been Modified in a Long Time

To keep your disk tidy, you will probably want to keep track of which files are not being used so that the network disk space is only used by files to which your users need constant access. You can back up other files to tape, diskette, or some other media, then remove the files from the disk. You can use NDIR to find the oldest files.

To find out which files in the current directory have not been changed lately, use this command:

ndir /sort up

The options mean *SORT by the date of the last UPdate.* With this command, you will see a screen like the one in Figure 15.3.

Note that in Figure 15.3, the oldest files are listed first, so you can scan through the listing until you get to files whose modification dates are more recent. To see the newest files listed first, tell NDIR to reverse the sorting order, like this:

ndir /rev /sort up

Before you remove those old files, check with the users. Make sure they understand that the files will still be available, but that there is not room on the network to store files that no one is using. The users may not have used the files for some time, but will need them soon, in which case it would be best to remove other files. Users might have concerns about the accessibility

FIGURE 15.3

The NDIR Command

```
TOLSTOY\SYS:

Files:                 Size     Last Updated       Flags            Owner
---------------        ------   ------------       -----            -----
DIRSTAMP    SYS        442,368  6-07-93  7:26a  [RwSA-HSy----------] SUPERVISO
TTS$LOG     ERR          2,656  7-15-93  3:08p  [Rw----------------] SUPERVISO
VOL$LOG     ERR          2,227  7-15-93  3:08p  [Rw----------------] SUPERVISO
BACKOUT     TTS         28,672  7-20-93  6:16p  [Rw-A-HSy----------] SUPERVISO
FIG15_02    TIF        112,190  7-08-94  5:55p  [Rw-A--------------] ROBBINS

                       Inherited  Effective
Directories:           Rights     Rights      Owner      Created/Copied
------------           ---------  ---------   -----      --------------
CONF        HGW [SRWCEMFA] [SRWCEMFA]  CANCILA    7-09-93   2:13p
DOS             [SRWCEMFA] [SRWCEMFA]  CROES      6-07-94   7:16p
ETC             [SRWCEMFA] [SRWCEMFA]  TOLSTOY    6-07-93  10:07a
LOGIN           [SRWCEMFA] [SRWCEMFA]  SUPERVISOR 0-00-00   0:00
MAIL            [SRWCEMFA] [SRWCEMFA]  SUPERVISOR 0-00-00   0:00
NCDTREE         [SRWCEMFA] [SRWCEMFA]  CROES      6-07-93   6:24p
PROGRAMS        [SRWCEMFA] [SRWCEMFA]  CANCILA    7-02-93   2:51p
PUBLIC          [SRWCEMFA] [SRWCEMFA]  SUPERVISOR 0-00-00   0:00
SYSTEM          [SRWCEMFA] [SRWCEMFA]  SUPERVISOR 0-00-00   0:00
TNA             [SRWCEMFA] [SRWCEMFA]  SUPERVISOR 6-08-94   8:54a

Strike any key for next page or C for continuous display...
```

of files that are not immediately available. Users might also have some suggestions on other files that can be moved off-line. The main point is to keep them informed, and to keep yourself informed in the process.

Finding Files That Have Not Been Accessed in a Long Time

What about files that no one has even *accessed* in some time? The update dates of files change only when the files themselves change, so the update dates of application files and program files will not change when people use the programs. How, then, do you find out if anyone is using the applications?

Happily, NDIR lets you view the date a file was last accessed. This date is updated when anyone opens the file, which happens when someone views the contents of a data file or runs an application file. To list files in the order of earliest access to latest, use this command:

```
ndir /sort ac
```

Again, even if no one has accessed a file in some time, it is a good idea to warn your users before you remove it from the network, to give them time to find an alternative if they were still using it occasionally, or to give them a chance to talk you out of it.

Finding Files That Have Not Been Archived Since the Last Backup

When you run a backup, NetWare automatically sets the Archive Needed flag to 'no' for all files that it backs up. When a user subsequently modifies a file, NetWare sets that flag to 'yes.' If you do a 'modified only' type of backup (see Chapter 17), NetWare will only back up those files that have this flag set to 'yes.' You can see which files those will be for the current directory with the following command:

```
ndir /a
```

Determining When Files Were Created

To sort files by creation date, use NDIR like this:

ndir /sort cr

This will give you a list of files sorted from earliest creation to latest. Again, you can use the '/rev' option to reverse the order of the sorting.

Listing All Files on a Volume

Like the DOS (5.x or 6.x) command DIR, NDIR lets you list files in the current directory and files in its subdirectories as well. To see all the directories on the SYS: volume, for instance, use this command:

ndir sys: /do /sub

The DO option tells NDIR to list directories only. To see all the files on the volume, omit this option.

Finding All Files Belonging to a Particular User

To find all the files on the current volume that are owned by user ADAMS, for instance, type:

ndir /ow eq ADAMS

You can remember this command more easily if you read it as *NDIR all files with OWner EQual to ADAMS.*

TIP
Be sure to type the username correctly, as NDIR does not validate the username entered.

REVIEWING USERS' DISK SPACE WITH SYSCON

With SYSCON, you can limit the disk space allocated to a particular user, and can review how much space that user is currently using. Enter SYSCON by typing **syscon** ↵ at the DOS prompt. Follow these steps:

1 • From the SYSCON main menu, select User Information.

2 · You will see a list of all the users for the current server. Use the arrow keys to move the highlight bar to the user name you want to view, and press ↵.

3 · Select Volume/Disk Restrictions from the User Information menu.

SYSCON will display a window like the one in Figure 15.4. It shows whether the user's disk space is limited, and if so, what the limit is, and how much space the user's files are currently using.

You can change the amount of disk space that user can occupy, or whether the user's disk usage will be restricted, with this menu (see Chapter 14 for information on using the NetWare utilities).

▶ · ◀

F I G U R E   I5.4

Viewing user's disk space
with SYSCON

RECOVERING SPACE FROM DELETED USERS

To preserve your network's security and ease of use, you should delete users from the network when they leave your organization. Chapter 8 discusses how to do this. At this time, also perform these steps:

- ▶ Back up their files
- ▶ Remove their directories
- ▶ Run BINDFIX

Before you delete any files, be sure to archive them so other users can access them later if necessary. If users need files in the deleted user's directory, move those files to a central place before removing the directory.

BINDFIX checks and updates the *bindery*, the set of files NetWare uses to store information about users, groups, accounting, and other system tracking. BINDFIX will delete the mail directories and trustee rights of any users that have been deleted since the last time you ran BINDFIX, after asking you to confirm the deletions.

To run BINDFIX, be sure no one else is logged in to the network. You must be logged in as SUPERVISOR or with SUPERVISOR equivalence. Run it from the SYSTEM subdirectory, by typing **bindfix** ↵ at the DOS prompt. BINDFIX will display information about its status as it runs.

MONITORING COMMON FILE AREA SPACE

WARNING
Clear out common file area space occasionally. Warn users before doing so.

Many networks have a directory designated as a place where users can share files. Often that directory is called COMMON or TEMP, and is a subdirectory off the root of the SYS: volume. No matter where you keep it, you will need to sweep it out occasionally, or it will get too full for anyone to use. You can warn everyone before you clean it out, but this doesn't help those users who are traveling at the time. A better approach to maintaining this directory is to issue a policy about when it will be cleaned and make sure all users are aware of it (you could use a special message when they log in). Make sure they know that the directory should be used only for temporary storage, and let them know the cleaning schedule. Depending on usage, you might want to sweep the directory daily, weekly, or monthly.

The batch file below, called SWEEP.BAT, will perform this housekeeping operation on the server TOLSTOY when the user types SWEEP on the command line.

```
ECHO OFF
: Batch file to remove files from the COMMON directory.
: CAUTION! This program will delete ALL files in the COMMON
directory!
:
ECHO *** ERASING ALL FILES IN THE COMMON DIREC-
   TORY***
MAP N: = TOLSTOY/SYS:COMMON
N:
DEL *.* < H:Y.CMD
H:
ECHO *** SWEEPING COMPLETED ***
```

Note the use of the Y.CMD file. This is a file that you must create in your home directory which contains just the letter 'y' and a RETURN. By using this construct, you automatically tell DEL Yes when it asks you

```
n:\common\*.*: Are you sure? (Y/N)
```

This "Are you sure?" check is how DOS tells you that you are about to delete all the files in a directory, and it is an important safeguard. Omitting this check is what makes SWEEP.BAT so dangerous; be very careful when you run it!

Create both SWEEP.BAT and Y.CMD with a text editor, and store them in the home directory of your supervisor login account, so that no one else can access them and run them inadvertently.

MONITORING DUPLICATE FILES

In your quest for disk space, you will probably find that some files appear on the network in more than one place. This is a problem not only because they take up precious disk space, but multiple copies of files can confuse your users and may lead to mistakes that result in data getting lost. Solving the problem of duplicate files can be troublesome, however, because the duplicates may be different versions of a file with the same name, or they may be exact copies of each other. Further, it may take some sleuthing to find out why the duplicates are getting created. Following these guidelines should help.

First, get a utility that finds duplicate files. There are some that run on DOS systems and you can use them on your network drives as well. Many of them are limited, though, because they will not span NetWare volumes. You will have to run them on each volume separately. It's better, therefore, to find one specifically designed for NetWare; every little bit of time saved helps. A good utility that might be useful is SHOWDUPE.EXE, which you can download from *PC Magazine's* bulletin board, PCMagNet.

Once you have found duplicate files, decide which to delete. There are two types of duplicates: exact copies and different versions of files with the same name. If the files are exact copies, it shouldn't matter which one you delete; if they are versions, your task is more complicated. Are they direct steps from each other? Or is one file a seed for several versions, none of which contain each other's changes? Consult with the file's owners and any other users who access the file to determine which version to keep.

Now that you have only one copy of every file on your network, take a look at how the duplicates were created. We discuss several possible causes below.

Do Your Users Keep Several Copies of Files?

If they do, find out why this is necessary. Listen carefully to the explanation, because it will tell you something about changes you need to make to the way you administer your network. The users might not trust the network backups, or they might be trying to override a security system, or they might simply not realize that their practices can cause problems. Find out, and correct the problem as quickly as possible.

Do Some Users Have Some Drive-Mapping Errors?

If users have their drives mapped to incorrect directories, they could be inadvertently placing data files in directories where they do not belong. Check the owners on the duplicate files, and check those users' login scripts and workstation startup files (such as AUTOEXEC.BAT). Explain to users the importance of correct drive mappings, and perhaps prepare a tutorial on the topic to prevent these mistakes in the future.

Do Users Need Several Versions of Files Maintained?

In work that goes through many revisions, all of which are products that need to be preserved, it is important to be able to access old versions of the working files. Program source code files for developers are a good example of files of this type. Of the duplicate file troubles, this is the simplest to solve, because many good version-control systems are on the market. Try PolyMake Version Control System (commonly called PVCS), from PolyMake.

Performing Further Maintenance Checks

Keeping an eye on disk usage and making sure your network uses disk space efficiently is a big part of network maintenance, but you need to perform several other checks as well. You must make sure security is strong, keep the root directory or directories (if you have multiple volumes) clear of extraneous files, and monitor general network use. If the network does crash, you need to take fast action to get it running again. Let's look at these tasks in more detail.

CHECKING THE ROOT DIRECTORIES

Despite your care, sometimes files may get saved in the root directory or directories. You need to clean them up periodically. Keep track of what should be in the root directories in your log, and remove anything that does not belong there. Once a month should be often enough to perform this check, because your organized approach to all aspects of security should prevent anything from getting into the root directories that does not belong there. If you do have to remove files, find out first who owns them and how they were saved in the root, and close that gap in the system to prevent a recurrence.

PERFORMING SECURITY CHECKS WITH SECURITY

The amount of attention you pay to security issues will depend on how your network is used. A few organizations do not require security at all: Everyone works on everything and all data is available to everyone. In most organizations, some types of information must be shielded from at least some users. Payroll records, for instance, are generally not left open for public viewing. Proprietary information such as product designs needs to be protected as well, from intruders if not from the other people in the organization.

In Chapter 10, you learned how to set up your initial security system; here we describe a utility you can run to make sure your system stays secure and to find any potential gaps or trouble spots. The utility is called SECURITY, and you run it from the SYS:SYSTEM directory when you are logged in to your SUPERVISOR account. It will check for common security-system weaknesses and warn you about:

- accounts without passwords

- passwords that have not been changed in some time

- weak passwords

- accounts that have supervisor rights

- accounts that have rights in root directories

- accounts that have rights in global directories

To run SECURITY, change your current directory to the SYS:SYSTEM directory and type **security** ↵ at the DOS prompt. As it checks the system, SECURITY will issue status messages. When the checking is complete, it will display the results on your screen, or in a file if you redirect the output to one, which is recommended as SECURITY produces many screensful of data. The report lists first all the user accounts with potential security breaches, then groups, also with weak points listed for each. Important security points are described below.

Checking for Accounts without Passwords

Logging into the network through accounts that do not require passwords is one of the easiest ways for intruders to access your system. One important piece of information they could get is a list of all the user names on the system, which they could then use to access other accounts. To close this gap, use SYSCON to set the Require Password parameter for all accounts to YES. This item is available from the Account Restrictions screen of the User Information menu and Default Restrictions under Supervisor Options.

Checking for Old Passwords

If an account's password has not been changed within the last 60 days, SECURITY will tell you. To require users to change their passwords, use the SYSCON utility. Select User Information off the main menu, then select the user from the user list. The Account Restrictions menu item brings up the screen that lets you set password time restrictions. (You can also set password time restrictions with Default Restrictions under Supervisor Options.)

Checking for Weak Passwords

Someone determined to access your system without authorization will try certain common passwords first. These include passwords that match the user's name, names of the user's family members, and passwords that have to do with the user's hobbies or interests. Short passwords are also easier to crack than longer ones. Encourage your users to select passwords with these points in mind. SECURITY can't check for all these conditions, of course, but it will warn you about passwords that are short or that match the user's name.

Checking for Supervisor Rights

Occasionally you might want to grant SUPERVISOR equivalence to an account temporarily. SECURITY will warn you about accounts that have these rights. Minimize the number of such accounts; someone with supervisor rights can inadvertently wreak havoc on your network. (This includes you, the network administrator! Don't log in as SUPERVISOR unless absolutely necessary.)

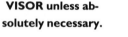

TIP
Don't log in as SUPER-
VISOR unless ab-
solutely necessary.

Checking for Root Directory Rights

A user with privileges at the root of a volume will have the same rights for the entire volume unless the rights are revoked at a lower subdirectory. Access Control rights are particularly powerful, since users with such rights in the root can grant themselves rights to the entire volume. Therefore SECURITY warns you of rights granted in root directories.

Checking for Global Directory Rights

No users should have rights in the SYSTEM directory, and they should have only Read and File Scan rights in PUBLIC and LOGIN. They should have Write and Create rights in the MAIL directory. SECURITY will warn you if any user has more rights than these in any of these global directories, because that gives them the ability to view or damage files that will affect other users.

MONITORING NETWORK USE

In a small to medium-sized network, you will probably not need information about cable use, transmission errors, and connection quality. If you have more than about 70 users, however, these statistics become more important, giving you a guideline for normal network performance. If performance later degrades, you can compare the statistics for normal operation to those for the slowed network, and this comparative data should help you determine where the bottleneck lies and what you can do to correct the problem.

Since so many different brands of equipment combine to form your network, NetWare itself cannot provide these figures. Ask your vendor to recommend some network monitoring equipment. When you evaluate it, look for systems that are easy to run and that provide concise, easy-to-use reporting mechanisms. You will need to run the checks at least monthly, so look for tools whose use you can automate.

RECOVERING FROM FILE SERVER FAILURES

Don't wait for disaster. As a network administrator, one of the best things you can do for yourself is to plan for catastrophe. Some day, some part of your network is going to fail. By planning for the failure, however, you can greatly reduce its impact.

Cables, network interface cards, and workstations can fail, but none of these is likely to affect the entire network as much as a failure of the server's hard drive controller, or the hard drive, or the server itself. If one of the drives stops working, a large percentage of your users will probably be affected. Let's go over the prevention steps you need to take now, including careful system setup and frequent backups, then we'll go over recommendations for when the unthinkable does happen.

TIP
Prepare for file server failures. Some day, some part of your network will fail.

Environmental Prevention Steps

In Chapter 5, we covered some considerations about the server's physical environment. Don't dismiss these points—they can be the difference between the health and demise of your server. Briefly:

- Place the server in a closed area, away from the normal traffic of the organization.

▶ Make sure the room is clean and free of dust, that it has adequate ventilation and air conditioning, and that it is running on an uninterruptible power supply (UPS).

Network administrators' horror stories include tales of servers placed next to the system printer, where the printer dust can clog fans and drives, or servers in crowded companies that are placed in users' offices, vulnerable to soda spills, bumps, and getting turned off. Particularly grim is the tale of the company that was forced to close its doors when the pipes in the server closet burst, ruining the server. All their product designs were lost.

We mention these considerations again, because you will need to review the server environment periodically for dangerous situations. You may have installed it carefully initially, but over time the environment may change. As the organization grows, people might store boxes in the server closet, or the efficiency of the air conditioner might decrease, or more equipment might get moved into the room. Don't let these factors place your server at risk.

Hardware Redundancy—Mirroring and Duplexing

NetWare allows you to mirror drives. *Mirrored drives* are two drives connected to the same disk controller. If you use mirrored drives, everything written to one drive is automatically also written to the other drive as well. This way, if one drive fails, you still have access to all the data, because you have an exact copy on the other drive.

Another form of hardware redundancy is *duplexed drives*. A network with duplexed drives has pairs of drives with duplicated data, much like mirrored drives, but each drive has its own hard drive controller. With mirrored drives, if the controller stops functioning, you probably won't lose data, but you won't be able to access it until you install a new controller. With duplexed drives, even if a controller fails, you still have the duplicate one, so your network users should experience no loss of network services.

Backups

Making sure that you have regular backups of the system is a major part of your job as network administrator. We'll cover this large topic in detail in Chapter 17, but since we're on the topic of maintenance and recovering from file server failures, let's look quickly at some key points about backups.

1 · Make backups as often as you can afford to lose data. This advice probably sounds absurd; of course you can't afford to lose any data. If that's really true, you should have your hard drives mirrored. But hard drives are expensive. Can you afford to have two? Evaluate the costs and benefits carefully. The main point here is that the length of time that elapses between backups matches the maximum amount of work that will be lost if your server fails. We know of companies that perform full backups once a month, and no backups in between; they stand to lose a month's worth of work if their server crashes. Other organizations back up nightly; they will lose at most a day's work if disaster strikes their server. For many companies, the risk of losing one day's work is acceptable when weighed against the cost of a spare hard drive.

2 · Store backups in off-site or fireproof storage. One of the things backups guard against is fire. If your building burns and your backups are stored in the same room as your file server, you have lost everything. Many companies store their backup media at another site for this reason, and your city may even have courier companies that will come to your site periodically, pick up your new backups, and bring you your obsolete backups so you can reuse the media. Ask your dealer for a recommendation.

3 · Test your backups. Even if you back up the server every twenty minutes, you will have gained nothing if you can't use the backups you have made. As part of your monthly maintenance, test the backups. These tests serve three purposes: they ensure that the backup media are reliable; they prove that your backups are storing the right data, every time; and they give you practice in restoring the file server from backups. You will be very glad of this practice if you do have a file server crash; with hordes of frustrated users breathing down your neck, the last thing you want to be doing is trying to figure out how and whether the restoration process works.

To thoroughly test your backups, you will need a computer configured as much as possible like your file server but not connected to the network. Restore the backup onto this system and check it against the main file server. Do all the applications function? Are the latest data file changes intact? You will probably need to enlist the help of your users to confirm the backups; you might want to work with management to select key users from each area to help you. Taking this precaution will not only ensure that the network data is safe, it is a great way to further gain the trust and cooperation of your users.

Getting the Server Running Again

Despite all your planning and care, your file server crashed. This is the most difficult and stressful aspect of your job, so try to remember: *Don't panic!* Even in a worst-case scenario, since you've been making careful backups, you would have no trouble restoring the system data. Depending on the frequency of your backups, you may lose some data, as we discussed above. With that in mind, let's go over the six steps to successful server recovery.

1 · **Calm the users.** This is critical. When the server crashes, everyone is affected. They will be concerned about their data and will wonder when they can get back to work. You will probably feel very stressed and anxious, and would prefer to jump right into troubleshooting without talking to anyone. If you take a few minutes to share with the rest of the organization the nature of the problem, to the extent that you know it, you go a long way toward calming people. Tell them what happened, what you are doing to correct it, and when you will issue an update (and make

sure you do issue updates as scheduled). Go ahead and tell them more than they need to know, even though they might not understand it. Information is always a balm in a crisis, and it's just possible that someone will even be able to offer some help.

2 · Find the problem. Now that your users are quieted down, move on to solving the problem. The problem may be obvious, but if it's not, remember the number one rule of troubleshooting: Assume the problem lies in the part of the system you know the least about. Once you notice your tendency towards this approach, you will have gone a long way towards forming an objective problem-solving strategy.

Now remember the number two rule: *Use a binary search to find the problem.* Divide the system into two parts. Which half is the problem in? Okay, you've just ruled out half of the potential problem areas. Now divide the remaining part into two parts, and repeat. Continue until you've isolated the problem. This approach is very useful when trying to track down cabling problems, but with creative application can be extended to any other problem solving situation as well.

NOTE
**Use a binary search to
find the problem.**

Some things to check? First, look for an obvious cause for the problem (e.g., natural disasters, loss of server power, or —worse—smoke). The second thing to check is the server itself. If any of your workstations can still see the server, the server is most likely still up. A quick way to find out if the server is running is to check the console.

If the server appears to be running and is accepting input from the console or remote console, check to see if all of the volumes are properly mounted. NetWare will indicate any errors with the volumes on the console and in the file server error logs (look for the file VOL$LOG.ERR in the root of each volume).

If nothing appears out of the ordinary on the file server, check with users on each leg of the network to identify a fault with a particular network segment. Any number of things, a failed bridge or router, a malfunctioning hub, a cable break, or faulty NIC in the server, can cause communications between the server and the workstations to fail.

If the file server has obviously locked up, try rebooting and watching the reboot process. Look for some indication of a hardware failure during the power-on self-test. If a disk channel or system memory has failed, the problem will often be indicated on the system monitor during reboot. If no obvious hardware problems exist, watch the server while restarting NetWare. Net-Ware will check NetWare volumes during boot up.

Every network is different, so unfortunately we can't offer much more advice on finding the problem in yours. But if you remember to keep an open mind and a systematic approach, the task will be much easier.

3 · **Repair or replace the faulty component.** Once you've found the problem, you need to get the failed part out of the network as quickly as possible, and get a replacement installed. Depending on which component failed and the quality of support that is available to you, this could take minutes or weeks. This is where a good maintenance contract comes in handy.

The problem may be simple; and NetWare provides a utility to fix such problems. If you have mirrored drives and you get a mir-roring error when you boot the server, you may have some corruption in the primary file allocation table. This can occur as the result of a power loss, and is one reason you might want to get an uninterruptible power supply (UPS). The NetWare utility to correct the damage is called VREPAIR, and you can run it on the damaged, dismounted volume while the other volumes are running normally unless the troubled volume is SYS:, in which case you would have to load VREPAIR from a floppy or from the bootable DOS partition since the volume must be dismounted for the repair to occur. Even so, back up all the server files before performing this or any other server-maintenance operation that may change the file allocation table.

The format of the VREPAIR command is

load n:vrepair

where n: is the drive letter mapped to the directory where you have stored the VREPAIR utility. You should keep it in the root directory of the boot partition of the server, so that you can access it even if all volumes fail to mount. See the NetWare System Administration guide for more information about VREPAIR.

4 · Restore the data. Now all that practice with backups pays off. You have a working server again, and all you have to do is restore the latest full backup onto it, then restore any incremental backups that you have made since then. Be careful to keep the incremental backups in order. Read Chapter 17 carefully for tips on backing up and restoring from backups.

5 · Test the system. Before you give everyone the all-clear sign, test out the server with the newly restored files. This test will be much like your backup-testing drill. Are all your applications accessible and functional for all users? Are the data files the latest versions? If you have users from each group who help you test your backups, enlist them now to test the restored server. Their experience will be invaluable in finding subtle problems.

It is probably not possible to test exhaustively for all restoration problems, but taking some time to test before letting everyone log back in can help you find problems at a time when they will be much easier to correct. If you wait until everyone is logged back on to the server before you look for gaps, someone could change something that might render correcting a problem impossible. Go slowly and cautiously; it will pay off.

6 · **Aftermath.** A server crash may be the most difficult thing you have to deal with in your job as network administrator. Once everything is back on-line, sit back and congratulate yourself for getting through it so well, and start looking ahead. The repercussions may echo throughout your organization for some time, especially if some data was lost. Think about what could have made the effects less severe, and what you need to change in your administrative habits to mitigate the effects of such crises in the future. Be patient with the network's users, who may be wary of storing their files on the network for some time to come. Do whatever you can to reassure them, perhaps including offering education about what strategies are in place in case of future network crises, and what they can do to make sure they are less vulnerable to loss.

Summary

A number of tasks go into keeping the network running smoothly and efficiently, and making sure your organization is getting the most out of its investment in network equipment. We discussed strategies for maximizing disk space, one of the most precious network resources, and we discussed other housekeeping tasks which, if performed regularly, will help assure that you have a productive, trouble-free network that people expect to have.

CHAPTER 16

Techniques for Administering Software

Fast Track

▶

Develop a logical file–naming scheme　　467
to prevent the creation of duplicate files.

▶

Load certain applications onto workstations instead of the file server　　467
to improve performance and to save on network disk space.

▶

Choose , test, and allow access to your software carefully,　　469
taking into account user needs, software reliability and ease of maintenance, and the need for a standard software to cut down on support
requirements.

▶

You can protect your network from computer virus infection by　　472
routinely scanning for viruses, training users to scan for viruses, controlling the installationof software, providing only diskless workstations,
routine scanning of the network for possible infections, write-protecting
application master diskettes, and using the EXECUTE-ONLY file attribute whenever possible.

▶

Do not violate　　475
your software licensing agreements. Read their details.

▶

Solicit feedback from network users　　475
to determine better ways to administer a network.

Applications are what make computers useful—without applications, your computers would just be expensive paperweights. At a minimum, your network will probably have accounting applications, spreadsheets, and word-processing applications. If you do software development, you will very likely have a compiler, a version-control system, and an application-building utility. If your organization does manufacturing design, you probably will have a computer-aided design (CAD) program.

All of these applications and their files must be accessible to the network users, so they will probably reside on your server. In addition, the users will need to get to their data files, whether designs, spreadsheets, desktop-publishing text, or software source files. Obviously, this is a lot of data for you to administer. Your job is to keep it all up to date and easily accessible. To do this successfully, you will need to be as organized as possible. Using the suggestions in this chapter will help.

Create a Meaningful Directory Structure

Before you load any software on your server, work out how the software will be used and by whom, so that you can decide where everything will go. Organize your directories so that it is easy to assign access rights. Recall that in NetWare, access rights are inherited by subdirectories unless you specify otherwise. Arrange files so that you don't have to exclude rights in subdirectories, and your job will be much easier.

Top directories should correspond to the largest organizational structures; subdirectories should represent categories within those structures. Study your organization and how users will use the network to decide what organization to use at the top level.

Some companies organize the server drives by department, with one major directory tree for Accounting, another for Marketing, and so on. Other companies organize on the basis of projects, so everyone in Engineering, Accounting, and Marketing working on a particular project has access to the same data files and applications. Many companies use a combination of these approaches. Furthermore, you will need to make some applications accessible to nearly everyone (the company word-processing application, for instance), so you will want a directory to which many or all users have access rights.

As you lay out your directory structure, keep this guideline in mind: *Avoid structures with pathnames more than four levels deep.* Long pathnames can cause several problems:

TIP
Avoid structures with pathnames more than four levels deep.

> ▸ If users have the pathnames in their DOS path statement, their DOS environment will fill up quickly. (If you are not familiar with DOS environment variables, the PATH statement, or the COMMAND.COM file, refer to the DOS manual.) You can overcome this problem with judicious use of drive mappings, so it becomes a quite manageable issue.

> ▸ Worse, some applications make assumptions about the lengths of pathnames, and if they encounter a pathname longer than their assumed maximum, they may fail, sometimes spectacularly.

> ▸ Long pathnames can slow down the performance of your network, because the operating system has to spend more time searching for and accessing files.

Keep Applications and Data Separate

On the basis of the directory structure you have outlined, you will load your application into its own directory on your server. Users will run the application by accessing files in that directory and storing their newly-created files into the directory you designate for data files. We strongly advise you to map their drives so that these data files do not get stored in the same directory as the application's files.

WHY KEEP DATA AND APPLICATIONS SEPARATE?

You need to keep data separate from applications for several reasons:

▶ ease of making backups

▶ ease of software upgrades

▶ protection from accidents

▶ easier to issue protective rights

▶ better network performance

Let's look at each of these points in more detail.

Ease of Making Backups

An application's files typically do not change unless you buy and install an upgrade to the application. Therefore you don't need to back them up as often as you back up other files on the server. Data files, for instance, may well change daily, so you need to back them up more often. If applications and data are in separate places, you can back up the data files as often as necessary, and the application files less often. This means that most of your backups are shorter than they might otherwise be, which means you don't have to change tapes as often during a backup and tapes don't wear out as quickly—all of which means your job is easier.

Ease of Software Upgrades

When you get a new version of the software, you will probably want to install it into the same directory as the old version. The files in the old version whose names match those of files in the new version will get overwritten. If you know that only application files reside in that directory, you can proceed with the update without concern. But if you have data files in the same directory, you will have to install a dummy copy of the new version in a separate directory and copy the files into the old directory by hand, comparing them to the old ones one by one, to be sure you are not overwriting any user data files. You probably have better things to do with your time.

Protection from Accidents

To save their data files, users will require Create, Write, and Erase rights to the directory in which the data files reside. If that directory is the same as the one in which the applications reside, it becomes possible for users to overwrite or delete the application files. Accidents of this type can render the application useless for other users.

A more subtle version of this type of accident is a user overwriting or erasing a configuration file that the application requires. This type of problem can be difficult to trace. If users have only File Scan and Read rights in the application directory, you can breathe easier.

Easier to Issue Protective Rights

Organize your directories so that everyone who has rights to a particular directory has rights to all the subdirectories below as well. By doing so, you will spare yourself the trouble of having to exclude rights on subdirectories and simplify maintenance. Issuing protective rights will be much easier if all your data files are in their own directories.

Better Network Performance

You can organize your data and applications to improve the performance of your network, by placing applications on one drive or server and data on another. That way, the operating system can access the application at the same time as it is accessing the data, which should speed up the network's response time.

HOW TO SEPARATE APPLICATIONS AND DATA

Now that you are convinced that you need to keep data away from applications, how do you do it? Use NetWare's MAP command to map a drive letter to a particular directory. For example, assume you have a word-processing program called WORDPROC.EXE stored on the main file server, FS1. The application directory is \DOCPROGS\WORDPROC, and you want to store data in \DOCS\REPORTS. Create a search drive mapping for the application directory, and a drive mapping for the data directory, like this:

```
MAP INS S3=FS1:\DOCPROGS\WORDPROC
MAP R:=FS1:\DOCS\REPORTS
```

With these mappings, your users can invoke the application with the command

```
wordproc r:newfile.txt
```

or

```
wordproc r:oldfile.txt
```

and the application will use the files in the specified directory.

You don't have to type in these drive mappings every time you log in. If you use them often, add them to the system login script or to the login scripts of the particular users who require them. See Chapter 9 for information on using SYSCON to edit user login scripts.

Some applications decide where to look for data by examining the value of DOS environment variables. If you're having trouble with data files getting created in directories other than where you've mapped them, check the application's documentation for its use of environment variables. If you need to use a particular environment variable setting, add it to the users' AUTOEXEC.BAT files or login scripts. (See your DOS manual if you are not familiar with AUTOEXEC.BAT.) Other applications (such as WordPerfect) have a setup file for each user in which the data file directory is set and other preferences are set automatically.

Put Each Application in Its Own Directory

You might find it tempting to put all applications in one master directory and give everyone access to it, rather than maintaining dozens of mappings and keeping track of who needs access to which applications. Resist this urge! Instead, create a directory for each application on your server, for these four reasons:

TIP
Create a directory for each application located on the network.

- ▸ ease of upgrades

- ▸ ease of backups

- ▸ simplified file searching

- ▸ reduced risk of file overwriting (*clobbering*)

In particular, the risk of *clobbering* is greatest. If all applications are stored in one directory (as is common under UNIX), you may find that your applications will operate incorrectly or completely fail to function.

EASE OF UPGRADES

If all the files for a given application are under one directory, it will be simple to install an upgrade to the application. Most installation procedures ask you into which directory to install the application, and if you know that there are no other files in that directory, you can let the application's automatic procedures perform the upgrade. Furthermore, if your applications are in their own directories, you can glance through the directories to determine which version of each application you have. This way you can easily tell whether you need to upgrade to a new version (we'll look at some other upgrade considerations later in this chapter).

EASE OF BACKUPS

If you need to back up some applications more often than others, it will be much easier to have them all in separate directories.

SIMPLIFIED FILE SEARCHING

Sometimes you need to know which files belong with which application. Obviously, you'll have a much easier task finding associations between files if your applications each have their own directories.

REDUCED RISK OF FILE OVERWRITING

Since application developers do not arrange unique file names, several applications might have files with the same name. SETUP.EXE is a common file name among DOS applications, for instance. If you install two such applications into the same directory, the second will overwrite (or *clobber*) the first, and you may have lost a critical portion of your first application.

APPLICATIONS THAT WRITE TO THE ROOT DIRECTORY

Some applications assume that they can create and change files in the root directory of the drive on which they're running—but since you have put them in a subdirectory on your network server, they cannot. If an application will not run except in the root directory, you can trick it into thinking it's in the root by using the ROOT option to the MAP command:

```
MAP ROOT P:=FS1\ODDPROG
```

Don't Alter the Application's Directory Structure

TIP
Don't alter the directory structure an application creates at the time of setup.

Many applications create directory structures of their own. These directories may contain several subdirectories and may descend several levels. This can look untidy at first glance, and you might be tempted to streamline the structure so that you need only provide a single drive mapping to all files in the application. Again, resist the temptation! Combining the directories will cause you far more problems than it will solve, particularly when you need to upgrade the software. If you change the directory structure of the application, you will have to make the same changes again to the upgraded version. If you use the application's own structure, on the other hand, the upgrade will proceed automatically.

Accessing files will be easier if you leave the application's structure in place, too. Many applications incorporate their directory structures throughout their file-access procedures, so you would have to find every place the application accesses a file and change the access path to the one you created. In a large application, this would be very time-consuming.

Create a Naming Scheme for Data Files

Duplicate files can be a serious network administration problem. Server drives can fill up quickly if your network does not have a structured mechanism for storing files in various stages of revision.

Some administrators solve the problem by requiring users to name their files with extensions that indicate the status of the files, and by creating different directories for the different stages of work. You might, for instance, call an intermediate version of a file DATA.INT, and store the final version in DATA.FIN.

It will also help to create a directory for working copies of files and one for completed files, especially if the files already have a particular extension name. Encourage all users to adhere to the naming convention. If files are named consistently, users will more easily find the ones they need, and you will more easily keep track of network activity.

TIP
Create a file-naming scheme that will produce unique but descriptive names.

Loading Your Applications on Workstations

In some cases, you might want to load applications not on the server, but on an individual user's workstation. This would be a particularly good idea for users working regularly without network connections or working on very large networks (networks with more than 200 users). If some users need applications that would make heavy use of the network and slow down other users' response times, consider loading these applications on the users' own workstations.

Applications that use temporary *swap files* to simulate memory or store temporary data are prime candidates for local storage. Database programs, graphics programs, and GUI-based interfaces like Windows often use swap files. Though the applications themselves can be loaded onto the network, the swap file location should definitely be on a local drive. Placing swap files on network drives puts a severe burden on the network.

Server disk space is also a consideration: If only one or two users will require the application, it might be appropriate to load their copies locally and reserve the server drive space for more widely-used applications. Most applications are priced by the number of users rather than the number of copies, so cost will probably not be a factor in deciding whether to load an application on the server or a workstation.

NOTE
Store temporary swap files on local drives. Putting swap files on network drives places a severe burden on the network.

Storing Your Data Files on Workstations

Users will often need to keep interim copies of their data as they work on them. Your naming scheme will prevent them from leaving multiple interim copies on the server drive. As long as only one person works on a file, you should have no problems. But when two or more people work on a file simultaneously and then copy it back to the server directory, the last file to be copied back to the server will overwrite the others, destroying any changes made by the other users.

If you have ever seen this happen, you know how frustrating it can be. If this situation seldom comes up in your organization, it might be sufficient to educate the users and encourage them to be careful when sharing files.

If your users often need to work on the same files at once, however, consider investing in a version-control system, which keeps track of all changes to files and prevents situations like the one in this example.

Choosing Software

Once you have identified the applications you need to purchase, how do you go about deciding between the candidates? For every application you can imagine, there are dozens of different software products on the market.

Study reviews in industry news magazines and the computer section of your newspaper. These reviews will often rate software packages on several different points, including ease of installation, speed, ease of use, and reliability. You will probably value some of these points more than others; cost will likely also be a consideration. Weigh all the benefits and disadvantages with respect to how you intend to use the system before you make your decision.

Don't rule out an application strictly on the basis of the size of the company that created it. Many useful and highly innovative programs are created by small companies.

Some people will advise you never to buy software that has a release number of 1.0. True, first releases of products are likely to be less robust and complete than later releases; but remember that new releases (no matter what number they use) almost always introduce new problems even while they fix old ones. Furthermore, some products are reliable and rich in features even in the first release. Rely on the experts to help you in this area, by reading product reviews and talking with experienced users.

If your network currently sports several different brands of the same type of application, you will probably want to try to standardize on one product for each application. You might have some people creating spreadsheets with Lotus 1-2-3 and others using Microsoft Excel, for instance. If everyone used the same spreadsheet program, you would spend less time supporting them, and everyone would be able to share spreadsheet files easily. Software upgrades would be easier, too.

Standardizing networked programs takes time, however. Many users are too busy to learn a new application, and will resist doing so if their current one is serving them adequately. If you do try to standardize applications, plan on a transition period of at least a few months, and be patient. Work with the users to overcome any problems that arise during the transition.

Keeping Track of Software

Keep an original document file for each software product that you buy. This file should contain the purchase receipts, a record of when and where you bought the software, the version number, and serial numbers for every copy you own. If you ever need support on the product, this information will probably be essential. For the same reason, be sure to register your software. Some companies will not support software for unregistered users (this policy gives them some protection against illegal copies). You can also keep vital information like version, serial number, etc., in a database of your software so that you can get to the information more easily.

Include in your file information about how you have configured the software:

▸ the directory in which you installed it

▸ the directory structure in which you keep the data

▸ the access rights for all directories

▸ any changes you made to the installation defaults

▸ descriptions of any user menus you created

If you have all these items well organized and easy to find, you will have a much easier task when it is time to upgrade the software.

Test the Software on an Off-Line System

This rule applies to any change you make to the network: *Test it before you add it to the network and give other users access.* Test new applications during periods of low network usage to make sure you don't interrupt the work of any of the network users. Many network administrators keep unusual hours, because they often need to work late at night or other times when few people are using the system.

Creating good, representative test scenarios can be tricky. Your goal is to simulate the users in your network environment as much as possible for your test, so that you can find any problems with the new software before your users do.

TIP
Test everything you
add to the network
during "off" hours.

Restrict Users, Including Yourself

An important part of administering the network software is maintaining proper access rights to the files. In general, restrict access rights as much as possible, to prevent accidental file overwrites or erasures, and to guard against malicious actions.

In application directories, you should only need to give users Read and File Scan rights. Most application files must be marked Shareable. Grant Read Only access if possible, giving Read Write rights only to those users who will need to change the files. You can use FILER to set these file attributes (see Chapters 10 and 14), or FLAG (see Chapter 10 and Appendix A).

Unfortunately, some applications require users to have Write, Create, and Erase access rights in their application directories, because they create temporary files in those directories. If the application fails to run and gives you file access errors, try adding these rights to its directory, or check the application's documentation for an alternative solution.

We have seen how important it is to restrict user rights as much as possible, but don't forget to restrict your own rights as well. With supervisor

TIP
Use your SUPER-
VISOR account only
when absolutely neces-
sary. Use a regular
user account most of
the time.

privileges you can delete or overwrite any file on the server, so mistakes can be disastrous. Create another user account for yourself with the access rights of a regular user, and use that account for most of your network functions. Use the SUPERVISOR account only when absolutely necessary.

Virus Protection

In early 1992, computer viruses began to receive worldwide attention. The virus named Michaelangelo was about to become active, and it was known to be extremely destructive. The network administrators in many companies spent days running virus-detection software on the PCs of every user in their companies, and on the network server drives as well. Suddenly magazines, newspapers, and casual conversations were full of discussions of viruses, how they work, what damage they can do, and how to protect against them. When the date of Michaelangelo's activation passed with very few people experiencing any problems, many people were tempted to dismiss viruses as a fabricated threat, or perhaps even a clever scam perpetrated by companies that create virus detection software.

Don't lapse into this complacency or cynicism. Viruses are a real danger to your data, and you must take precautions against them. Though the chances of infection may be low, the potential damage is enormous.

Like biological viruses, computer viruses spread by replicating themselves. Most viruses lodge themselves into application files and spread when someone executes them. So be very careful when you load new applications onto network drives, and train the network's users to be careful as well.

Here are some steps you can take to make your network less vulnerable to virus infection.

GET A VIRUS-SCANNING PACKAGE

Your first line of defense against viruses is a good virus-scanning program. This is one product you want to be sure to purchase from a large company or a company with a solid reputation for quality software and strong support. You might consider Symantec's Norton Anti-Virus or Central Point Anti-Virus and Anti-Virus Plus.

Before you buy, check the upgrade policy. New viruses arise constantly, so the more current your scanning software, the more likely it is to catch all the viruses that might infect your systems. Good virus-scanning software gets upgraded frequently to cope with these new strains. If possible, purchase a scanning product that gives you a discount on one or two upgrades, a feature that many products offer.

TRAIN USERS TO SCAN FOR VIRUSES

Educate your users on the nature and dangers of viruses and what they need to do to prevent infection. Instruct them to scan every diskette that they use to load or download data onto their workstations or onto the server. They—and you—should be especially wary of software that someone has downloaded off a computer bulletin board. Most reputable bulletin board operators run virus-scanning software regularly, but bulletin boards remain one of the main avenues of virus infection.

LOAD SOFTWARE ONLY THROUGH A CENTRAL POINT

Personal computers run a huge number of applications, and users will each have their favorites. They may bring in their own software to personalize their workstations, and, despite your warnings, be lax about scanning the disks before loading these applications. For these reasons, it is very difficult to control every application that gets loaded onto workstations or the server drives, especially in a large organization with many users. Nonetheless, you may want to issue a policy that all applications on the server get loaded by a central person or group. This person is responsible for scanning the software before loading it onto the server.

GIVE USERS DISKLESS WORKSTATIONS

If users do not have floppy drives on their workstations, they will not be able to load software onto workstations or onto the server drives. This is an extreme step for virus protection, but it might be a necessary one for other reasons, such as data security. If the workstation does not have a floppy drive, the user cannot copy data to a floppy and remove it from the premises.

SCAN THE ENTIRE NETWORK PERIODICALLY

No matter how well you control access to the server drives, you should run the virus-scan software on the server from time to time. Once a month should be sufficient for most networks. Be sure to run it at a period of low or no network activity. Refer to the documentation for the scanning software for more information about running scans on network servers.

WRITE-PROTECT MASTER DISKETTES

As soon as you remove new diskettes from the shrink wrap, before installing the software, back the new software up on work diskettes and put write-protection labels on both sets of diskettes. Write protection will prevent the common viral trick of the virus writing itself to a diskette. If you ever have to reload the software, be sure to do so using these protected master diskettes. Note that some applications write their serial numbers or other codes to one of the master diskettes during the installation process, for copy protection. If your installation fails due to the write protection, remove the label while installing and replace it afterward.

WARNING
Once set (through FILER), the Execute-Only attribute cannot be removed, so ensure you have a backup copy of the application first.

USE THE EXECUTE-ONLY FILE ATTRIBUTE

In many cases, you can set the Execute-Only file attribute on the application file. This way, the application file never changes, so the modifications that a virus would make never get written. Using this attribute can have unexpected results if you use it with an application not intended to support the execute-only attribute. Check the documentation that came with the application to see if it is compatible with this usage. More often than not, you will have to use trial and error to determine which application can be designated execute-only.

Legal Issues

Having applications on a network drive does not mean that you will now save money by sharing software among all the users on the network. Most software companies are very explicit about shared usage of their products, and are quite serious about their license agreements.

For most applications, you must still purchase one copy for each user, even if you store it in a single location on the server. Some products offer site licenses, which means that you pay according to how many users will be using the product at a single time.

You might wonder how they—or you—can enforce these licensing agreements. One way is the honor system. You know only three people use the accounting software, so you pay for three copies. When the number of users goes to four, you pay for another copy.

Another method of enforcing licensing is called *site locking*. Some applications have site locking built in. In this case, the application keeps track of how many people are currently using it, and when that count reaches the number of copies licensed, no one else can access the application until one of the copies becomes available.

Even if your applications do not have site locking built in, you can get the benefits by purchasing a site-locking program for your applications. SiteLock is one such product. Once the allowed number of users are accessing a tracked application, SiteLock prevents any other accesses until someone relinquishes their hold on the application. For this reason, site locking requires cooperation between users—they can't start up their spreadsheet application in the morning and leave it running unused all day, for instance. Some people might have to change some of their habits.

Talk with Users, and Listen to Them

The network's users are an invaluable resource in administering the network. Make a habit of talking casually to a wide variety of users, and listen carefully to what they say. They can tell you more about efficiency and needed features than any management meetings or industry magazines ever will. Watch users at work and notice which tasks are awkward and where inefficiencies occur. Discuss solutions with them; solicit feedback. Keep communications open with users at all times, and your job will be much more rewarding and even fun.

Summary

Ruthless organization is the key to an easy-to-maintain network. In this chapter, we've looked at a number of important points that will help you when you initially configure your network drives and as you add new applications and users. The larger your network gets, the more essential careful organization becomes. Time spent now on tidying will pay off hugely in the long run; a well-structured network file system is a thing to be proud of. In the next chapter, we'll discuss what you need to do to preserve your handiwork.

CHAPTER 17

Backing Up and Archiving the Network

Fast Track

The absolute bare minimum   **493**
is to perform at least a partial backup *every day.*

You can use NetWare's NBACKUP utility   **495**
for a workstation-based backup solution.

You can use NetWare's SBACKUP utility   **497**
for a server-based backup solution.

Early one morning, a very strange Austrian author awoke as a cockroach and wandered into a rapidly growing company's computer facility. Trying desperately to avoid the many wingtips descending his way, he slipped into the file server's case, and in a bright flash of light and a puff of magic smoke, he brought network services to its collective knees *and* ended a promising literary career. And there followed much lamentation and gnashing of teeth. "How will we process our documents?" wailed the desperate LAN users. It was indeed a dark day for network computing.

But wait! Hearing the whimpering and sobbing coming from various high rooftops and window ledges, a mild-mannered network administrator dashed into the nearest broom closet and emerged as *NETMAN!* "Don't worry, network citizens, I will save your data!" he boomed. "In fact, I already have. Unbeknownst to you, I have been routinely performing backups on our dear departed file server." And there was much rejoicing!

Sounds a bit hokey until you realize that backing up your network file server is the final authority in preventing and recovering from a catastrophic data loss.

Backing up your system is meant to protect your network from human error such as the inadvertent deletion of important files, devastating mechanical failures like the file server being knocked over by the cleaning crew or a lightning strike melting sundry important chips on the inside of your server, or just plain sabotage such as a computer virus. Let us assure you from brutal experience that these examples are not as unlikely or flippant as they sound. Furthermore, hardware such as a hard disk can simply wear out and fail. Whether or not your system folds due to user inexperience, equipment failures, or natural calamity, it is definitely too late to be implementing a backup system or wishing a better backup schedule had been followed. Always plan for the worst—that way, you'll never be taken completely by surprise.

In this chapter, we'll discuss the difference between backing up your system and archiving old data, things to consider when deciding upon an appropriate backup system, establishing sound backup procedures, and the NetWare backup utilities, NBACKUP and SBACKUP.

Backing Up vs. Archiving

Backing up your system and archiving important or old data are basically the same operation with slightly different intent. Backing up prevents the loss of data through mechanical failures or human errors by making a copy of your LAN and placing it on storage media such as tapes or optical disks. From this copy, you can restore the system and data files as they were at the time of the last backup. The only data lost would be the changes since the time of the last backup. While this loss would doubtless be inconvenient, it would be much preferable to losing everything. This is also why you should strive to have the most recent backup as possible.

Archiving is different only in the reason why you are duplicating and saving data. This data is archived to save it over time as well as to prevent its unexpected destruction. Archiving your old data is used in addition to making backups and is not intended to take the place of regular backups. For instance, your accounting department will definitely want to save financial records for several years in case of that odd IRS audit. Files that you need to keep but hardly ever use should be archived or copied on to tapes, floppy disks, or other storage media and saved in a safe place such as a safety deposit box or a fireproof safe. This will free up room on your file server that could be used more effectively.

Record what data is on your archived or backed up media and what procedure you used to save it. Since there is no telling how long this data may need to be kept, this will help whomever is going to try to restore the data in case you are not available or you have changed to a new backup system or procedure.

NOTE
Back up your system frequently so that you lose as little data as possible when things go wrong.

Backup System Considerations

Third-party vendors such as Tecmar, Mountain, Colorado Memory Systems, and Palindrome provide backup devices and software that you can use in your backup system. Some of these devices can also be used with

NetWare's backup utilities NBACKUP and SBACKUP. The difference in capabilities and storage media used for the vast array of backup devices available means there are quite a few things which you will need to consider when purchasing a backup system. Because of the importance of keeping your system backed up, don't skimp on equipment here. Other things to consider are:

▸ server-based versus workstation-based backups

▸ security

▸ how file problems will be handled

▸ available types of media for storing the backup

▸ "file-by-file" vs. "imaging" backups

▸ error detection and correction

▸ backup size and speed

▸ file structure that will help facilitate backups

SERVER-BASED VS. WORKSTATION-BASED BACKUPS

There are two basic types of backup software, *server-based* and *work-station-based*. Server-based backup software is simply an NLM and is run directly on the file server. The tape system, optical drive, etc., must also be attached directly to the server. Workstation-based backup software has the backup system hardware and software installed directly at a workstation.

Server-based backup systems have several advantages over workstation-based systems. For one thing, server-based backups are faster because the data transfer occurs across the file server's bus instead of across the network. The process is also more secure, since the entire operation is internal to the file server and can't be used to gain unauthorized entry to the file server as is possible with the workstation process.

A server-based system also has disadvantages compared with a work-station-based backup system. The performance of a server-based backup is generally faster, but this speed can be deceptive. If you have more than one

NOTE
Server-based backup systems are faster and more secure than workstation-based systems.

file server, then the network drives on the primary server will have the advantage of using just the server's bus to facilitate the transfer. The other network drives on other file servers, however, will not have this benefit since the data transfer in this case will have to occur across the network. The larger the transfer across the network becomes, the smaller the benefit. Also, running the backup NLM along with the NLMs you would normally be running could slow the file server's core processes and degrade your network performance.

Another weakness with the server-based method is that the backup system usually needs a Small Computer System Interface (SCSI) drive subsystem on the file server it will be attached to. While the actual installation of the SCSI devices is not that much of a problem, if the server drives are SCSI devices as well as the backup system, the coordination of drivers for the SCSI devices, network drives, the backup software, and NetWare is. Unfortunately, only certain revisions of SCSI drivers are actually compatible with each system in the server. To maintain performance and compatibility, you may find yourself installing more than one SCSI interface and using different drivers. This confusing tangle of drivers, if not in sync, could lead to a file server crash by the very system that is supposed to be a safety valve in case of a file server breakdown. On the other hand, if the backup process fails at a workstation, your file server is generally insulated from the failure. You will then be able to figure out what the problem is and try again.

When you are trying to restore from a file server crash, you run into another disadvantage to a server-based backup system when compared to a workstation-based approach. The crashed volumes must first be restored in both the server and workstation-based situations. The disadvantage occurs because of the fact that the server-based approach runs and stores its software directly on the file server's volumes. Some server-based backup systems also store their important control data files on the file server's volumes. If this software and control information is on the volume or volumes that crash, you will have to reinstall the software from the original diskettes and recreate the control files before you can even begin to restore your data. If your backup software is unable to handle open files during the backup process, you will not have a copy of the control files, and you will have to rebuild your entire catalog by reading all the data to be restored. Once the control data has been restored, then you can finally begin the process of restoring the lost data to the crashed volumes. This process could add hours to an already tense situation.

The workstation-based backup software, however, can be run directly from the workstation's hardware. Any control data the software needs to keep for administrative purposes can also be stored at the workstation. The workstation approach does not lose time reinstalling software or rebuilding pointers and indexes but can begin directly restoring lost data as soon as the volumes have been returned to working order. It is important to remember that you are able to perform backups during relative calm and tranquillity, while trying to execute a data restoration after a volume has gone down is at best a high-stress situation. In most cases you will not be losing great amounts of time with the workstation approach, when you consider how much extra time and inconvenience you could go through by using a server-based approach.

SECURITY

Security for a server-based backup system is not much of a problem as was discussed earlier. Your file server should be kept under lock and key at all times as well as having the console locked. If someone can get to your file server with ill intent through these precautions, there is not much they can do except for outright sabotage of your equipment.

In the case of a workstation-based backup system, you have one very large security problem that you will have to minimize to protect against data theft or destruction. To perform a complete backup, you need to be logged into the network as the user SUPERVISOR or a user account with supervisor privileges.

Leaving a workstation logged in with that kind of access to the network while the backup is being performed is not a bright idea. It is also not very productive for you to waste your time or somebody else's baby-sitting the workstation to make sure someone does not steal your backups or stop the backup and use the supervisor privileges for mischief.

One way to solve both problems is to limit access to the workstation that is performing the backup. You could keep the workstation in the same locked room as your file server.

Another way to improve security on a workstation-based backup system is to set up a specific user account designed for the sole purpose of performing the backup procedure. You could set up the user account BACKUP, for example, using the SYSCON utility. It must have supervisory privileges and mappings to where the backup software is located, but you can restrict its use so that BACKUP can only login at a certain workstation, with only one concurrent connection, and only during the times that will be used for regular backup sessions. You can further restrict the BACKUP user account by having the login script call all the necessary backup programs, perform the backup, and then log the BACKUP account out when the backup is complete. You could also include programs in the procedure that will disable the Ctrl-Break function and enable you to lock the keyboard with a password. Some machines also allow you to physically lock out the keyboard with a key.

Your workstation should now be reasonably secure from inquiring minds. What can you do, however, to prevent the theft of data by simply taking the backups? Some backup software can allow you to assign passwords to each tape or disk to prevent the unauthorized access to the data contained therein. Another thing you could do is store the backups somewhere off-site such as a safety deposit box or fireproof safe. This is good practice anyway to prevent a natural catastrophe such as a fire from destroying your file server as well as your backup library and archived files. You could recover from the loss of one or the other, but not both.

At the end of the day, you should be able to simply load up the backup system with a tape or disk large enough to hold the entire backup, log in as BACKUP, provide any information necessary to start the backup, lock the keyboard through either software or hardware, and leave, letting the backup system do its thing inside a secured room.

TIP
Set up a specific user account solely for performing backups.

FILE-HANDLING PROBLEMS

Since hardware continually outpaces software, make sure that the hardware and software you eventually choose can handle large files or an ever-increasing directory tree.

NetWare has many peculiarities to its file system that distinguish it from DOS. Like NetWare-specific data, Macintosh files on your server can pose a problem if your backup software can't properly handle them. Because of this, backup software designed to work with DOS may not copy files, attributes, and directory structures that DOS does not recognize. You need to determine if your prospective software will recognize NetWare's bindery data, directory rights, trustee assignments, and extended file attributes as well as how they handle the associated data forks and resource forks for Macintosh files.

Another important file-handling aspect is how your backup software will deal with open files. When files are backed up, there are usually modifications made to that file such as resetting the *archive-needed* attribute. This is why there is usually a problem with open files, since both the backup software and a user can't be using and therefore modifying the same file at the same time.

Some software requires that your file server be free of user login sessions, which guarantees that all the files will be closed, eliminating the issue of what the software will do about open files. This is not very efficient because it also guarantees that no work can be done while a backup is being performed. An important principle for planning your backup routine is to make it as easy and convenient as possible to encourage adherence to the schedule. Usually, backups should be performed after hours when the use of the file server is lowest. But what would happen if users were working late to finish an important project? You would either have to wait until they were finished to perform your backup or skip it entirely. Neither is a very inviting idea.

Backup applications handle the problem of open files in several ways. Many backup software packages will halt the backup procedure when they encounter an open file. The person performing the backup then can stop the backup completely, try to back up the file again, or skip that file entirely.

The application will usually keep track of all the files bypassed in this manner so that they can be backed up later when they are not open. Now, if you can't think of something more useful to do than watch filenames flashing across the screen for hours on end, you are a late-stage computerholic and should seek professional help immediately. All kidding aside, backups are at best a tedious thing to behold. Most software allows for unattended backups (thus the need for tighter security discussed earlier) so that no one will need to monitor the backup session. You can either set the software to skip over and record in an error log any open files encountered, or the software might have some sort of timing device whereby, if it doesn't receive an answer to a specific number of queries on what to do with an open file, it will continue with the backup after recording the unopenable file.

A few backup applications are able to access open files if the files have been assigned the NetWare attributes of *shareable* and *read only*. The *shareable* attribute means that more than one user can use that file at the same time, and the *read-only* attribute prevents a user from making any changes to the file. The user can only view a file when it is marked *read only*. When a file is in use by someone on the network, it becomes a *read-only* file to everyone else on the network, even though that attribute has not been assigned to that file. This is accomplished by placing a "lock" on the *modify* privilege where this file is concerned for everyone on the network *except* the user who accessed the file first. When the backup software runs across this *modify lock,* the program will be forced to halt and ask what to do because it can't modify the attribute for the file that it needs to, namely the *archive needed* attribute. When the file is actually specified to have the *read-only* attribute, there is no need for this *modify lock* to prevent changes from being made.

If the open file is also flagged *shareable*, the backup application can make its changes, back up the file and move on. If the file is open, and it is not *shareable* or marked *read only*, then the application will not be able to access the file and will have to halt and wait for instructions or enter the file in an error log and move on.

AVAILABLE TYPES OF MEDIA

Many choices of storage media are available, including floppies, removable hard drives, optical disks, and magnetic tape. Magnetic tape is probably the most popular because of its relatively large capacity and low cost. Keep in mind that you need to select a media large enough to contain a complete backup. With magnetic tapes and optical disks, you can use tape changers and disk "jukeboxes" that will change the disks or tapes for you when the backup has filled up a disk or tape.

Magnetic Tape Drives

Magnetic tape is the most popular form of backup media with three types of format in use today: Quarter-Inch Cartridge (QIC), 8mm Tape, and Digital Audio Tape (DAT). Quarter-Inch Cartridge tape drives record data in serial fashion on long serpentine tracks running the length of the tape. The drive will be constantly winding and rewinding the tape when it performs backups or restores. Earlier versions of this system suffered from performance problems but have lately come to rival 8mm and DAT for speed and accuracy.

8mm tape drives and DAT cartridges use *helical scan,* a method of storing data quite different from QIC. Rotating read and write heads magnetize the tapes in short diagonal tracks. DAT cartridges are smaller than 8mm tape cartridges. DAT tape changers are also available that enable you to back up very large file servers without having to "baby-sit" the process in order to change tapes.

Optical Drives

Optical drives make use of the same compact-disk technology found in your stereo system. In fact, if you looked at a music CD and a CD containing computer files, you would not be able to tell the difference. A laser heats the disk to its Curie point, and a magnetic field is then used to change the affected area to a 0 or a 1. Two types of optical disk technology are available for backups—Write Once Read Many (WORM) and rewriteable or erasable.

WORM technology lends itself to archiving of important files because of its ability to write to an optical disk. Remember, however, that once you have written to a WORM disk, it becomes permanent and can't be erased or written over like magnetic media. This could be useful in archiving important files since you can store those files on a WORM disk and you will not have to worry about them being written over by accident. But overall a WORM drive's inconvenience makes it a poor choice of media, especially as optical technology is much more expensive than magnetic media.

Optical technology's saving grace is erasable or rewriteable disks and multifunctional optical drives which could support both the new erasable disks and the older WORM disks. This newer technology allows you to erase and reuse optical disks just like magnetic disks. This makes optical disks as convenient as their magnetic counterparts, with the added bonus of an optical disk's durability—a shelf life of up to 100 years. Since it still costs much more than tapes, optical technology is not ideal for routine backups and archiving but would be most efficiently used on critical backups of important data.

Removable Hard Drives

Removable hard disks are excellent for backing up critical data that may need to be restored quickly, such as applications or your SYS:SYSTEM and SYS:PUBLIC directories containing your NetWare NLMs and executables. Removable hard disks have limited storage capacity but are much faster at accessing data than magnetic tape or optical media since they do not have to search for it in a sequential manner as do tapes and optical disks. If you suffer a file server crash, you will need to gain access to certain NLMs such as VREPAIR to restore your server to working order. Having the necessary software available on a removable hard drive may save you valuable time when you are trying to recover from a server crash.

Floppy Drives

With the leaps that technology has been taking, hard drives have become far too large for floppy disks to be realistic for regular backup procedures—

it would take 140 1.44-MB floppies to back up a file server with even a 200 MB hard drive, and with a 2-GB system, you'd be feeding floppies from now until doomsday. Floppies are best used by individual users to back up important files they do not want lost, erased, or corrupted by accident.

FILE-BY-FILE VS. IMAGING BACKUPS

Backup software comes in two major types, differentiated by how they back up data. The first type is *imaging*. With imaging backup software, the application skips the operating system entirely and makes an exact copy of the hard disk by transcribing the sectors one by one in order. Imaging is fast because it is simply copying data to the storage media and ignoring the operating system's structures—but it is very inflexible. Because the operating system structures are not taken into account, it is very difficult to restore a specific directory or even a specific file. This could be a serious inconvenience if you need to quickly restore a very important file from yesterday's backup. The file server also needs to be downed to perform this type of backup. Because of this inflexibility, imaging has not gained a wide following.

The second—and far more popular—type of backup software is *file-by-file*, which copies files instead of sectors. Since this procedure is concerned mainly with files, it permits you to specify which files to backup. You can designate a complete backup where all files are saved, or you can choose specific types of files. File-by-file backups can restore specific files and directories, whereas imaging backups cannot. Most file-by-file backup software will also allow you to restore files to a different directory than the directory that they were backed up from. Finally, the file-by-file approach permits the file server to be up and running while a backup is being performed. File-by-file's flexibility makes it probably the best choice for backup software.

ERROR DETECTION AND CORRECTION

As with just about everything associated with computers (hence the need for backups), something can always go wrong with the data transfer to the media you have chosen. Be sure that the software you choose has some form

NOTE
File-by-file backup software is more flexible than imaging backup software and is probably a better choice.

Warning
Choose backup software with error detection and correction.

of error detection and correction. Stay away from applications that do not have this feature or where it is only an option. Options are often not used and omitting error detection and correction could be deadly because of the possibility for errors being introduced into your backup data. Remember that your backup needs to be as correct as possible since it is a major lifeline designed to save you from catastrophic data loss.

Backup software addresses error detection and correction in two main ways; each has its advantages and disadvantages. These methods of error detection and correction are *read-after-write verification* and *redundant copies* of the data. The read-after-write method does exactly what the name implies: After a block of data is written to the media of choice, it is compared directly to the original block on the hard drive to make sure the copy is exact. If an error is detected, the block is rewritten to the storage media and the process of reading and comparing to the original is repeated until an exact copy is obtained. In this manner, *hard errors* (errors actually recorded on the storage media) are eliminated.

Where read-after-write runs into trouble is when data is being restored, as there is a chance for errors in interpretation. Dust or debris can be caught between the read/write drive head and the storage media and cause an error in reading the backup copy during the restore procedure. These kinds of errors are called *soft errors* because they are misreadings of the storage media rather than errors recorded on the storage media.

The other popular method of error detection and correction is the *redundant* method. When a block of data is backed up, a duplicate is also copied to a different location on the storage media. If an error is detected during the restore, the correct information can be rebuilt from the two copies of the data. The problem with the redundant method is that it takes much longer to back up since you are essentially backing up your file server twice.

BACKUP SPEED AND SIZE

When you are designing your backup system and procedures, keep in mind how long it will take to complete a full backup. The less time a backup takes, the less time there is for a power surge or blackout to ruin it. To back up two gigabytes, using a workstation and a tape drive running at a relatively fast 10 MB a minute, would take about three hours and 20 minutes and would probably only need one tape. This is not too bad, but a ten-gigabyte system would take about 16 hours and 40 minutes and would use several tapes (depending on the tape size and compression rate)—far less convenient. If we left this backup at 5:30 pm to run overnight, it would still be running the next morning at 10:00 am!

You could use a tape changer to change the tapes, but time is a little more difficult. You could structure your server so that you could easily perform a partial backup on only the data likely to be modified often such as placing data files in VOL1 and application files on the SYS volume. You could back-up VOL1 daily and then do a complete backup of both volumes on the weekends when your server would be seeing very little use. If you only have one volume, you could group the directories in a similar fashion with two main structures coming off the root, one for data files and the other for applications. Another way would be to have two tape backup systems and have them backing up different volumes at the same time.

Vendors such as Palindrome have come up with a more elegant way to solve this problem. The Network Archivist uses a backup system that keeps a database of files that it backs up, an aging of each file backed up, and the location of the file on the storage media. This backup software will in essence be doing a complete system backup the first couple of times that a backup is performed. Meanwhile, the database that the software creates and updates is keeping track of where every file is located on the storage media and is aging the files—recording whether or not each file has been modified since the last backup. After a certain amount of times backing up a file that has not been modified at all, the software tags it as rarely used and will not back it up again until it has been modified. You end up having a complete backup each time you run the procedure, but it gets faster and faster because time is not wasted recopying files where no modifications have been made.

Establishing Backup Procedures

Let's review what we have covered so far.

- You should have a workstation-based approach because the security risks are easily nullified and the time lost due to having the data travel across the network instead of the server's bus is negligible compared with running the risk of crashing your server with a server-based approach.

- You should also have a software package that will handle all the different types of files for any operating system on our network as well as have error detection and correction capabilities.

- Your software should also be able to adequately handle open files.

- You should have an accompanying tape system because of its large storage capacity and relatively low cost when compared to other media. The tape should be big enough for the entire network system to be stored on it, or if your network is too large for one tape, then a tape changer will do nicely.

- Finally, you should have your file server structured to facilitate your backup procedure.

Now we need to discuss what to do with this setup.

SIMPLE BACKUP SCHEMES

You might be tempted to do a full backup and then fall into the habit of once a week, once a month, or—worse yet—no set schedule at all. A lot of the things we have discussed so far help to make the backup process as painless as possible because it is very important that backups be done. How much trouble will it be if several days of data were lost because backups were not kept up to date? How about a week? A month? Your data is too important to be lost when the way to protect your network is so easy to perform.

Some form of backup, whether a full or partial, should be performed *every* day. Some simple schemes could include a full backup every day using a different tape for each day. Mark them by which day they were used for the backup. For instance, on Monday, you would use the "Monday" tape for your backup. This way you would have at any one time five working days of "history" so that if the file you need to restore was deleted accidentally two days ago, you could go to the tape made three days ago and restore it from that.

You could also make a complete backup every week and only a partial backup of the files that were modified on each of the other four days. Make sure in any case that you always have two complete backups before you begin reusing your complete backup tapes. For example, on Friday, you would make a complete backup of the system and call it FRIDAY1. On Monday through Thursday you would make a partial backup every day. Depending on the size of the network and how many files were altered in between backups, you might be able to store all four of those backup sessions on the same tape—although you might want to keep the sessions on separate tapes just to be paranoid. Remember, paranoid is good when we are talking about backups! On Friday, you would again make a complete backup except with a different tape from the last complete backup, and you could call it FRIDAY2. The following Monday you would perform a partial backup with the tape labeled MONDAY. The partial backup procedure is repeated as before for Tuesday, Wednesday, and Thursday. On Friday, we can now reuse the tape labeled FRIDAY1 because we have a more current backup on the tape FRIDAY2 as a safety net in case the backup does not go as planned. This scheme leaves you with two weeks of history at any one time.

"GRANDFATHER, FATHER, SON" SCHEME FOR BACKUPS

Now you should be getting the idea how to rotate tapes and how to devise a procedure that will ensure that you always have a way to restore your network with only the possibility of the loss of one day's data. The earlier simple schemes show you the rudiments of what is called the "Grandfather, Father, Son" method of backup scheduling and tape rotation.

You start this method out on a Friday with a complete backup that we will name GRANDFATHER1 and place it in your archives. On Monday through Thursday of the first week, you will be performing partial backups that we will call SON1, SON2, etc. On the Friday of week one, you will perform another complete backup, call it FATHER1, and place it in your archives. Week two will consist of your partial backups on Monday through Thursday, for which you will reuse the SON tapes. On Friday of week two, you will again make a complete backup, name it FATHER2, and archive it. Week three will follow the pattern that you should see by now. The partial backups performed daily on Monday through Thursday will reuse the tapes marked SON1–4 and the complete backup on Friday will be named FATHER3 and placed in storage with GRANDFATHER1, FATHER1, and FATHER2. You would then round out week four with partial backups on Monday through Thursday using SON1–4, but on Friday, the complete backup will be named GRANDFATHER2.

Month two will proceed just like month one did except that you can start reusing the Father tapes beginning with FATHER1. You should repeat this pattern until you have four GRANDFATHERs in your archives. That will mean that you will have four months' worth of history, and this should be long enough to have discovered any discrepancies. For month five you can start reusing the GRANDFATHER tapes beginning with GRANDFATHER1.

At any one time, this rotation scheme should let you look at what was on your server at the end of the last four months (the four GRANDFATHER tapes). You will also have a complete backup from the last four weeks (the three FATHER tapes and the most recent GRANDFATHER tape). Finally, you should also have partial backups for the last four days. With this setup, you will not ever lose more than one day's work if the server crashes, and you will be able to restore data from as far back as four months.

NBACKUP

NetWare has two backup utilities available for your use, NBACKUP and SBACKUP. NBACKUP is the workstation-based variety of backup software.

NBACKUP can be used by users to backup data from directories where they have *File Scan* and *Read* rights and restore information to directories where they have *Create, Erase, File Scan, Modify*, and *Write* rights. Only the user SUPERVISOR or users with supervisory privileges can use NBACKUP to backup a file server.

There are some other important limitations to NBACKUP. You must restore the data to the system type you backed it up from. In other words, if you back up data from a v2.x server and intended to restore it on a v3.1x server, it will not work. It would also be taboo to try to restore data backed up from a local drive to a network drive.

NBACKUP also will back up and restore only DOS and Macintosh files. You would have to use SBACKUP to back up or restore any other operating systems files such as OS/2. Macintosh file names are case sensitive, while DOS names are not. Also, DOS files can use "wild card" characters while Macintosh files can't. When you are designating Macintosh files or directories, you would use a colon (:) instead of a backslash (\) in the path. For example, say you have a directory called MACAPPS with a subdirectory called MACFILES located in VOL1. You would designate those Macintosh directories in the following manner:

VOL1::MACAPPS:MACFILES

NBACKUP can use a variety of DOS and non-DOS devices to back up to. These are the DOS devices that NBACKUP can use:

- workstation floppy drives

- workstation hard drives

- network drives on another server

- tape drives with a DOS driver

- optical multi and WORM drives with DOS drivers

NBACKUP can also use any non-DOS device that has a *Device Independent Backup Interface* (DIBI or DIBI-1) device driver. NetWare is bundled with a

DIBI device driver for Wangtek tape drives and will appear as a choice along with DOS Devices when you first run NBACKUP. If you do not have a DOS or DIBI device driver for your backup device, you will need to get one from either your vendor or from Novell's NetWire bulletin board on Compu-Serve. You will need to add the DIBI device driver to the SYS:PUBLIC directory and modify the data file, SYS:PUBLIC\DIBI$DRV.DAT. This process is described in more detail in Appendix B.

You will then need to log in as SUPERVISOR or equivalent, choose whether you are going to use a DOS or non-DOS device, select Backup Options, and choose a working directory. A working directory can be either a local drive, an unrelated server network drive, or the storage media you are going to back up to. The working directory will contain two files, a backup log called WBAK$LOG.xxx and an error log called WBAK$ERR.xxx. These logs will help you troubleshoot your backup session. You will then need to choose Backup File Server or Backup By Directory, set your backup options, press Esc to save them, and start the backup process right away or set the time and date when you want it to start.

The restore process works a little differently. Select Restore Options from the main menu and enter a working directory. From here you choose Restore Session, select the session you wish to restore, set your restore options, press Esc to save your options, and start the restore process.

SBACKUP

SBACKUP is a server-based backup package and bears the advantages and detriments of a server-based system. The backup device is attached directly to the file server and operates only with DIBI-2 device drivers. It is executed from the file server console, runs as an NLM, and has a similar procedure to NBACKUP. It is more versatile than NBACKUP in that it can backup not only DOS and Macintosh directories and files but also OS/2, HPFS, NFS, and FTAM files. NBACKUP and SBACKUP backup methods are not compatible, so don't try to mix backup data.

SBACKUP has two command-line options that you can set to control the number of buffers and the buffer size. The number of buffers is controlled with the "BUFFER=*x*" where *x* is the number of buffers in the range of 2 to 10 (4 is the default). The size of the buffers is determined by the option "SIZE=*xxx*" where *xxx* is the buffer size of 16, 32, 64 (default), 128, or 256 KB. The following is an example of loading SBACKUP on the console with six 128 KB buffers:

LOAD SBACKUP BUFFER=6 SIZE=128

NetWare 3.12 has added a new feature to SBACKUP that may make your life much easier. SBACKUP can now be used to back up workstations that have a program loaded called a Target Service Agent (TSA). A TSA does several things:

▸ passes the data request from SBACKUP to the target

▸ receives and processes commands from SBACKUP so that the target's operating system can handle the request for data

▸ receives the requested data from the target and returns it to SBACKUP in standard Storage Management Services (SMS) format.

You need to do four things to set up workstation backups:

1 · Load the device drivers for controllers or storage devices. (If the SCSI controller and its device driver are ASPI compatible, you can use TAPEDAI.DSK. Otherwise, consult your vendor, local Novell office, 1-800-NETWARE, or NetWire for a driver for your storage device.)

2 · Load TSA_DOS.NLM at the server.

3 · Load TSA_SMS.COM at the workstation (see accompanying table for option details).

4 · Load SBACKUP.NLM at the server console.

TSA_SMS.COM OPTIONS	SYNTAX	EXPLANATION
Help	/H	Displays all the options for TSA_SMS.COM.
Buffers	/B=*n*	TSA 1 K buffers (*n*=2 through 30, default is 1). Increasing the buffers increases your throughput but decreases the available RAM.
Drive	/D=*xxx*…	Indicates the DOS drives you wish to backup data from. Replace an *x* with a DOS drive letter you wish to access (ex. /D=CDE, where C:, D:, & E: will be accessed).
Name	/N=workstation_ name	Sets a workstation with a unique name up to ten characters long.
Password	/P=password	Sets a password for the station that anyone wishing to access through the TSA must know.

TSA_SMS.COM OPTIONS	SYNTAX	EXPLANATION
Trust	/T	Can be used instead of password to let anyone with supervisor equivalency to access the workstation through the TSA.
Server	/SE=server_name	Specifies the name of the server you want to back up the workstation.
Stack	/ST=n	Specifies the stack size as a decimal (512 through 4096, default is 2048).
Unload	/U	Unloads TSA_SMS.COM from the workstation's memory.

Summary

The ideal backup situation would be to perform at least a partial backup every day and a full backup once a week. This backup should be scheduled for after hours, when network activity is lowest. The backup would be safest and easiest if it were performed from a workstation. The workstation and backup user account need to be as secure as possible. The most storage for the least money would be a tape drive. The tape should be capable of holding a complete file server backup—if not, several tapes and a tape changer should do the trick. This will allow the person performing the backup to load up the storage media, set up the backup parameters, start the backup, and leave it running in a locked room overnight secure in the knowledge that a new backup will be there to greet him or her in the morning. That's the real secret—make it so easy that there is no excuse for not performing a routine backup.

You should also leave this chapter with a good healthy paranoia about protecting your data, because any number of unforeseen things can happen to it. Remember that your business in this day and age could be held hostage easily by any number of small catastrophes that snowball into a major crisis. If you are ready to weather that storm, those unforeseen circumstances will remain simply a minor nuisance.

PART V

Fine-Tuning the Network

CHAPTER 18

Monitoring System Performance and Troubleshooting

Fast Track

How would you feel if you paid for the aerodynamic styling, composite materials, and engineering work necessary to build an Indy car, but the initial test drive left you feeling like you had purchased a Model T? You can be sure that slow performance on a network will elicit similar reactions from those who commissioned it. Fortunately, Novell NetWare will really scream on an "Indy car" network, and even a "Model T" network will perform admirably with proper tuning and a matched set of components.

Unfortunately, the responsibility for network performance falls almost without fail on the shoulders of the network administrator (whether the administrator designed the network or not). By paying careful attention to performance indicators and providing the server with additional resources when they become necessary (remember, the network will always outgrow your initial expectations), you optimize the performance of your NetWare network.

In this chapter, we'll describe performance bottlenecks that affect network servers. We'll discuss monitoring network performance with the tools and resources commonly available through sources like CompuServe. Finally, we'll cover some basic methods of troubleshooting network hardware and software problems.

Potential Bottlenecks for Network Servers

TIP
Well-balanced networks will perform better than networks combining high-performance components with mediocre components.

Because a network environment is far more complex than a stand-alone PC, the operating system and server hardware must be capable of handling many tasks at the same time. Whenever the use of a computing resource must be divided among users, performance can drop. NetWare was designed for multitasking and multiuser processing and to make the best of resource sharing. Even so, a well-balanced network design will do more for network performance than a few high-performance components scattered here and there, especially if the remainder of the network's components have only mediocre performance. (You can't drive a Ferrari flat-out on a 55-mph freeway. Similarly, you'll hamstring a Herculean super-server if the maximum effective throughput of your cabling to the workstation is 150 Kb/second.) Without the proper balance, the performance potential of many of your network's higher-performance components is completely lost.

Bottlenecks are weak links in the system that adversely affect network performance. Bottlenecks can be caused by hardware and software limitations, hardware and software incompatibilities, poor-quality network connections, faulty network components, and so on. While faulty components and poor connections can easily be remedied, other bottlenecks are the result of the network's design. The following areas on your network may well limit performance if the capabilities of one system does not match the capabilities of the rest:

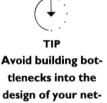

TIP
Avoid building bottlenecks into the design of your network!

- ► the sustained-throughput capacity of the server disks and disk controllers

- ► the type of NICs used in the server and workstations

- ► the server's bus architecture

- ► the bandwidth of the physical network media

- ► the number and types of bridges, routers, and repeaters used

- ► the amount of memory in a file server

- ► The processor in the file server

- ► the type of workstations used

You could compare server and network performance (roughly!) to the checkout at a grocery store: When only two of a store's 20 lanes are in use, the store has a great deal of *unused capacity*. If a few more checkout lanes were opened, the customers could be serviced much more quickly (*better performance*). Barring *non-deterministic* problems (technical difficulties like a checker getting clothing caught in the cash drawer or having a CSMA/CD network access scheme on a highly loaded network), twice the number of lanes would roughly double the performance. At some point, however, there are just too many people in the store and the service would be better if half of them had decided to shop across the street.

Information flow in a computing environment is really not all that different from this simplistic model (dyed-in-the-wool networkers and telecommunications experts will have a coronary hearing this, but for our purposes it's basically true). The more holes you can put in a bucket, the faster it will drain water.

THE SERVER'S BUS ARCHITECTURE

Can you get superior performance from advanced and proprietary bus architectures? Yes, but maybe not as much as the manufacturers claim. Yet while the Industry Standard Architecture (ISA) is not the best bus available for your network server, in many cases an ISA computer will be able to outperform other components on the LAN so that changing to a more advanced architecture is unwarranted. At its maximum of 8 MHz, the ISA bus has the capability to handle 5.33 MB/sec in data transfers across its bus. In practice, 2 MB/sec is a better figure. Unless the combined throughput of your server's disks, disk controllers and NICs can saturate this capacity, ISA will do. In such a case, an ISA bus computer will probably serve you well as a network server.

On the other hand, advanced architectures like the Extended Industry Standard Architecture (EISA) and Micro Channel Architecture have capabilities that extend far beyond those found in ISA. These advanced buses typically use a 32-bit data path for transferring data and are capable of true *bus* mastering modes (explained shortly). Theoretical limits for the EISA bus are approximately 32–33 MB/sec and Micro Channel Architecture has working speeds of 20–30 MB/sec with the theoretical capability of running in a "Streamlined Mode" at speeds of up to 160 MB. (Controllers capable of these speeds, however, are by no means run-of-the-mill.)

The prices of advanced-architecture PCs and workstations are dropping so drastically that soon it will make very little sense to buy anything other than a computer with an advanced bus. However, while the host computer costs are similar, the add-in cards for advanced architectures and the

NOTE
Advanced and proprietary bus architectures can give superior performance, but your network may not need them.

software to properly exploit them are more expensive. Fortunately, the chances are good that your current equipment can still be used in an advanced architecture. For example, ISA cards are still quite viable (though limited to the same performance levels as ISA) in an EISA bus computer. Even if you don't yet need the performance levels of the advanced bus, it makes sense to buy the computer with the advanced bus for future expansion if it only costs a little more.

Bus Mastering Controllers

Perhaps the most significant advantage that advanced architectures have over ISA is the capability to use bus mastering cards. During normal bus transfers, without bus mastering, the CPU must either *poll* the bus devices (the CPU checks every so often to see if there is data to be read or written) or operate with an interrupt mechanism (a board can interrupt the CPU when it has or needs data). In both cases, the intervention of the host CPU is necessary during the data transfer. In a bus mastering configuration, a bus mastering card can take control of the bus away from the CPU and perform data transfers on its own. The CPU is then free to perform other operations during the transfer, so long as they don't require use of the bus.

ISA computers can only employ a rudimentary form of bus mastering that allows a single card to interrupt the host and use Direct Memory Access (DMA) to directly access or write to data in memory. Advanced-architecture computers use a bus arbitration scheme to allow up to 6, 8, 10, or even 15 bus masters to be simultaneously present in the system. Since many of the tasks performed by the CPU are not related to bus transfers, the result is greatly improved system performance.

SERVER DISKS AND DISK CONTROLLERS

Although a network may have many different types of servers (including print, fax, database, image storage, and document retrieval), one of the primary services of the network is access to central data storage for application and data files. The speed at which a user can access a file on the network is directly related to the speed at which the server can retrieve the file from the server's disks and pass it through the network to the station. The data must pass through several interfaces—the disk, the disk controller, the server bus, the server NIC, the network media, and the workstation NIC. The server's disks and controllers can be the weakest link in this data path.

In most cases, the connection between the bus and the disks in a server is a *serial* connection—data are transferred from the disk to the disk controller in a sequence, one bit at a time. (ST-506 and, ESDI are serial interfaces designed specifically to connect to disk drives.) In some cases, however, a disk drive controller is really an interface between two different bus architectures: One is the host's expansion bus and the other is a bus to which disks and other devices are attached. The SCSI is a *peripheral* bus or a bus that can be used to connect both a host or *master device* and peripheral devices together.

Either type of interface, SCSI or peripheral, has the potential to adversely affect performance. For example, a SCSI bus is a multitasking, multi-threaded bus capable of transfers at 8 MB/sec and faster. Since the ISA bus in a PC can only realistically transfer 2 MB/sec, attaching a SCSI bus to the ISA bus introduces a bottleneck for the SCSI bus and drives attached to it.

Similarly, a single SCSI controller in an ISA computer can't really overload the bus on its own. Because of the differences in the way the two buses operate, ISA bus limitations, and software limitations, a SCSI controller can only force about 600 KB to 1.2 MB/sec through the ISA bus. Having more than one controller in the bus allows a greater amount of information to be passed and allows the potential bandwidth of the ISA bus to be met. In general, these problems are less apparent on an advanced bus architecture, but still, the more holes you can put in a bucket, the faster it will drain water.

The table below lists some common throughput capacities for disks typically used in server applications. But remember, even though a particular type of disk is capable of these capacities, the bus and disk controller in the server will in some cases not be able to exploit the full potential of the disks' speed.

DISK TYPE	TYPICAL PERFORMANCE	THEORETICAL MAXIMUM
IDE	4–8 Mbps or 500 KB/sec – 1.0 MB/sec	10–12 Mbps or 1.2–1.5 MB/sec
ESDI	15–17 Mbps or 1.8–2.1 MB/sec	24–33 Mbps (burst) or 3.0–4.1 MB/sec
SCSI	24–32 Mbps or 3.0–4.0 MB/sec	32 Mbps or 4.0 MB/sec
SCSI II (Fast/Wide)	24–80 Mbps or 3.0–10.0 MB/sec	80 Mbps or 10.0 MB/sec

NETWORK INTERFACE CONTROLLERS

The type of network controller you use can affect network performance more than many people realize. Although the theoretical limits of a 10baseT network are 10 Mbps, a given network interface controller will generally not be able to deliver this performance level—a NIC with an 8-bit host interface is most certainly slower than a NIC with a 16-bit interface. By the same token, bus mastering controllers may be faster than other types, but this should not be considered law. While some bus mastering network controllers are available, most network controllers use *memory-mapped* or *I/O-mapped* methods of communication with the host.

An I/O-mapped controller communicates with the PC bus through registers on the card. Each byte of information requires a bus transfer to the card. Memory-mapped controllers have the potential to give better performance than I/O mapped controllers. A memory-mapped controller has an on-board memory buffer *mapped* into the PCs *address space*. A memory-mapped card will still need a bus I/O location for control of the card, but for data transfer, the CPU may communicate with the card as if it were memory. In general, memory accesses are faster than I/O transfers.

NETWORK PROTOCOLS AND PHYSICAL MEDIA

Everyone seems to have their own favorite network protocol, topology, and media-access scheme. We covered some of the performance considerations for the most popular schemes in Chapter 3. Here we will point out how the network's physical media and protocols can affect performance. Regardless of which topology, protocol, and media access scheme you use, several stations operating simultaneously will very likely degrade network performance.

For example, though the theoretical bandwidth of most Ethernet set-ups is 10 Mbps, most workstations would have a difficult time (because of the overhead involved in protocols, the NICs performance, etc.) completely using the bandwidth of Ethernet. A single station might have a throughput of 300–600 KB/sec or 2.4–4.8 Mbps. However, several stations operating at the same time can effectively use the full 10 Mbps bandwidth. Once this happens, the bandwidth of the network is divided (not necessarily equally) among the network stations.

On the other hand, a Token Ring network only lets a single station transmit at a time. In doing so, the station may use as much of the cable bandwidth as it has the potential to (e.g., 4 or 16 Mbps). Even so, this is not likely to be the full bandwidth. During the transmission, other stations on the network must wait for their turn with the token.

The real bottleneck across the LAN occurs with the overhead involved with higher level protocols, the type of error detection and correction used, and the performance of the NIC. Third-party drivers that add peer-to-peer support for things like disk sharing, fax, etc., can often have a negative effect on network performance. The NetBIOS protocol, for example, is a connection-based protocol that has its own error-correction scheme, which adds a tremendous amount of overhead. By contrast, with IPX there is no added overhead needed to establish and maintain a network connection.

Under NetWare, NetBIOS is implemented as a high-level protocol that sits on top of IPX. The net effect is both IPX and NetBIOS each perform their own acknowledgments and/or session-management schemes. The added overhead to maintain the connection and perform requests and acknowledgments in NetBIOS can require anywhere from four to eight times the information transfer a normal IPX transmission would.

Similarly, although IPX is more efficient than NetBIOS, it is less efficient at working with large data requests (over 1500 bytes) than when working with small data requests.

Ordinarily, the NetWare Core Protocol (NCP) requires that every transmission between a station and the server be answered with an acknowledgment from the server. Over large networks, especially internets with many bridges and routers and Wide Area Networks, this can result in a severe performance bottleneck. Novell's Burst Mode protocol deals with this problem. This protocol has the capability to transmit several IPX packets (up to 64 KB in total length) in an adaptive, self-tuning, *sliding window* that requires an acknowledgment only after the last packet in the window has been transmitted. Performance gains from this technology can be anywhere between 10 percent and 300 percent, depending on the network. The highest performance gains take place when wide area links are present.

Under NetWare 3.x versions prior to 3.12, the Burst Mode protocol must be loaded in NLM form (PBURST.NLM). Once loaded, it becomes active when workstations running the proper shell (BNETX.COM) log into the network. The shell used for packet burst requires more of the workstation's memory than conventional shells. The amount of workstation memory is determined by parameters set in the NET.CFG file, capabilities of the network media, and an additional 4–5 KB for the shell. The NET.CFG needs to contain the line

PB BUFFERS = N

where N indicates the number buffers to allocate to activate packet burst. The value may range from one to ten; the default is two. If the burst mode shell is unable to set up a burst mode connection with a particular file server or if the PB BUFFERS parameter has not been set in NET.CFG, it will default to using standard NCP communication mode.

NetWare 3.12 has the Burst Mode protocol technology built into the OS. To use this enhanced protocol, enable it from within the NET.CFG file by adding the PB BUFFERS line. As with NetWare 3.1x, you must be running the proper NetWare shells to realize packet burst mode at the workstations (BNETX.COM for ODI workstation services or VLM.EXE for the NetWare DOS and Windows client).

HOW BRIDGES, ROUTERS, AND REPEATERS AFFECT NETWORK PERFORMANCE

In general, bridges, routers, and repeaters should affect network performance minimally when implemented properly. When misunderstood or used improperly, the layout of your LAN as well as the types of bridges, routers, and repeaters used can drastically affect performance—in particular the way NetWare routers are used.

Third-party routers are usually devices that attach to the network and are dedicated to performing a specific function. Some will function as repeaters: They merely pass information appearing on one segment to other attached segments. Others will function as routers: They determine the best route for a packet to get to its destination and repeat signals only on the appropriate segments. Finally, some will function as bridges: They connect and repeat information to dissimilar systems.

NetWare uses two types of routers: *Internal* and *external*. NetWare routers function as multiprotocol routers and bridges in some instances and simply as routers in others, depending on the types of LAN segments that are attached. External routers may run in protected or real mode and be either dedicated or non-dedicated. Internal routers are part of the NetWare OS. In general, dedicated external routers can offer 10–20 percent better performance than internal routers. Even more important than the type of router, however, is their placement.

Figure 18.1 shows a simple network that employs a performance-robbing method of using internal routers to connect several servers together.

If you will recall from Chapter 6, NetWare uses the concept of internal and external network numbers when describing network segments. Each NIC in a server is connected to an external network with its own network number, while the server's bus is an internal network with a network number. In our example, the external networks (LAN cables) and internal networks (server buses) are numbered from one to nine. For the workstation labeled STATION

TIP
Dedicated external routers can offer 10–20 percent better performance than internal routers.

▸ . . . . ◂

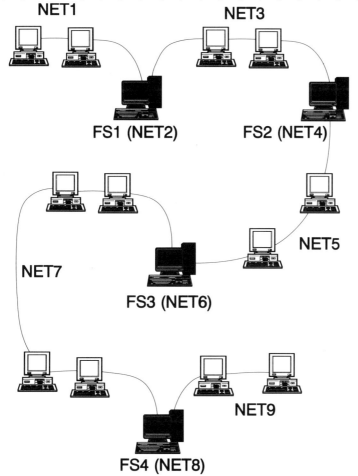

1 to communicate with the file server FS4, its packets must cross over several networks and internal routers. (Each packet will encounter six *hops* before finding the file server FS4: NET2, NET3, NET4, NET5, NET6, NET7. A hop occurs when packets must cross over one network to reach another.) Each of these hops across internal routers and external networks adds a time delay.

For improved performance, the network should have been set up like the one in Figure 18.2. This network uses a backbone (NET5) to

FIGURE 18.2

*A network connected via a
backbone*

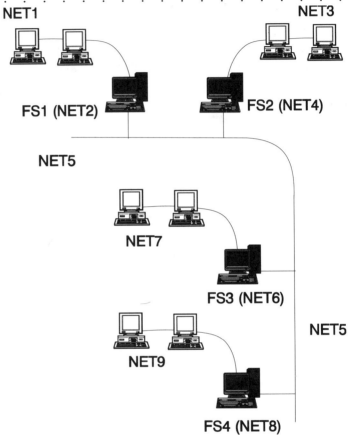

connectall the servers together.

While each server still has two NICs installed and the total number of network segments is still nine, the performance of the network using a backbone will be far superior to the previous example (possibly 40–80 percent better). On this network, STATION 1 will only have to cross NET2 and NET5 in order to reach the file server FS4—two hops as opposed to six as in the previous example. In fact, the total number of hops from any one station to a server will never be more than two in this configuration.

To get information about the networks known to a particular file server, use the command DISPLAY NETWORKS at the file server console. The

DISPLAY NETWORKS command will display the networks known to the router in the file server, the number of hops to each network, and the time delay for a packet to reach each network (in $\frac{1}{18}$ths of a second). This information is useful when you are trying to identify network bottlenecks. For more information on DISPLAY NETWORKS, see Appendix A, *NetWare 3.12 Utilities Summary,* or the NetWare System Administration guide.

SERVER MEMORY AND PERFORMANCE

Memory has faster access times than any other storage medium—period. When software is able to make effective use of memory, many of the shortcomings in the server and network hardware will probably not be apparent until the system is consistently loaded and usage is high. This is certainly true of the NetWare OS. Novell NetWare was designed to make very efficient use of server memory and employs several schemes to do so:

- ▸ Directory Caching

- ▸ Directory Hashing

- ▸ File Caching

- ▸ Elevator Seeking

- ▸ NetWare Memory Pools

Directory Caching

NetWare stores information about the ownership of files and directories in a Directory Entry Table (DET) on each network disk. A DET stores three types of entries: entries for files and directories, entries for file trustees, and entries for directory trustees. Each of these entries contains the following information as it applies: information about assigned trustee rights, file names and ownership, directory names and ownership, date and time of last update, and the address of the first block on the network disk if the entry is for a file.

NetWare caches the most recently accessed parts of the DET in server RAM. Since the DET must be searched each time a file or directory is accessed, accessing it from RAM is much quicker than reading it from the server's disks. NetWare 3.0 was the first version that did not cache the entire DET in server memory. (Previous versions stored the entire table.)

Directory Hashing

NetWare uses a File Allocation Table (FAT) to store information about files stored on network disks in much the same way DOS uses a FAT to store information about files on local disks. The FAT is like a road map to each data block that comprises an application or file. The entire FAT is stored in cache memory on the server to speed up access to files. Before a file can be accessed on a network disk, both the DET and the FAT must be searched.

Directory Hashing allows the server to more efficiently search the portions of the DET stored in server memory. Normally the DET is unsorted. Directory *Hashing* is the process of sorting the portions of the DET stored in server memory into alphabetical order. This allows the server to employ a more efficient search algorithm when looking for information about a particular file. Instead of searching the entire DET to find information about a file, the server searches only a few entries.

File Caching

File Caching allows the server to store entire files or parts of files in the server's memory. When files are accessed, the entire file is loaded into memory. Subsequent accesses to the file occur from server memory rather than from disk. If a file is not frequently used, it is eventually replaced by one that is. File caching has a profound impact on server performance. In some cases, files may be accessed up to 100 or more times faster than files that must be accessed from the server's disks.

Elevator Seeking

Although not directly a memory-related function, elevator seeking is employed by NetWare to improve performance when reading and writing disks. Disk access occurs according to priorities assigned by the addresses of the data locations on the disk. The queued addresses are read or written as the disk heads encounter the proper address—even if the requests are satisfied out of requested order. The result is a smooth in-and-out motion as the heads scan the disk rather than the random movement of non-prioritized disk access.

NetWare Memory Pools

Most of the NetWare's performance enhancing functions rely on server memory. When a server is first brought up, all available memory is allocated to File Cache Buffers. From this, all of the server's memory is reallocated to other *Memory Pools* as needed. As the demand increases for other types of resources, the number of file cache buffers decreases and the memory is reallocated to the task or process that requested it. The memory reallocated has many different purposes:

- ▸ When a NLM is loaded, memory from the cache buffer pool is assigned to the NLM. When the NLM is unloaded, the memory is returned to file cache buffer pool.

- ▸ When a volume is mounted, memory is allocated to store portions of the File Allocation Table (FAT) in server memory.

- ▸ The server allocates memory for the storage of portions of a drive's Directory Entry Table (DET).

- ▸ The server allocates memory for Directory Hashing.

- ▸ The server allocates memory for a special index called the Turbo FAT. (Turbo FAT performs a function for the FAT analogous to that of directory hashing for the Directory Entry Table. The Turbo FAT index allows NetWare to jump directly to the needed FAT entry rather than scanning all previous entries.

Since all server memory is initially allocated to File Cache Buffers, the memory needed by other memory pools must be allocated from this memory. NetWare uses the following other memory pools:

- ▶ Permanent Memory

- ▶ Semi-Permanent Memory

- ▶ Alloc Memory (short term memory)

- ▶ Cache Movable Memory

- ▶ Cache Non-Movable Memory

Permanent Memory   Permanent Memory is used by the server for long-term storage needs like directory cache buffers (for storing DETs), permanent table storage, and packet receive buffers (temporary storage for incoming network data packets). Permanent memory cannot be reallocated for use by NLMs or other processes and is never returned to the file cache buffer pool. The Permanent Memory pool is allocated according to need and grows dynamically during system usage. Memory from the Permanent Memory pool is used for the Alloc and Semi-Permanent memory pools.

SemiPermanent Memory   When a NLM is loaded that will require memory for long periods of time (such as file system or protocol support), memory is allocated from the Semi-Permanent memory pool.

Alloc Memory   Alloc Memory is short-term memory used by NLMs and other processes as well as for storage of other temporary services:

- ▶ connection information for users

- ▶ drive mapping information and search paths

- ▶ information about open or locked files

- ▶ information advertising services that are currently available from the server

- ▶ service requests, like file read/write requests

▸ messages that are waiting to be broadcast

▸ information about queue managers

▸ temporary table storage for NLMs

Cache Movable Memory   Cache Movable Memory is borrowed from the File Cache Buffer memory pool for storage of tables likely to grow dynamically. Directory Entry Tables, File Allocation Tables, and Directory Hashing Tables are likely candidates for Cache Movable memory. Cache Movable memory is considered moveable because it can be organized to prevent fragmentation of the main memory pool. (It becomes more difficult to find a section of contiguously open memory when portions of the File Cache Buffer are used by other memory pools. In these cases, Cache Movable Memory can be relocated to open a contiguous region of server memory.) Cache Moveable Memory is only allocated as needed and is returned to the File Cache Buffers when no longer needed.

Cache Non-Moveable Memory   Cache Non-Moveable Memory is used when NLMs need to allocate large memory buffers. Like Cache Moveable Memory, it is assigned and reallocated as needed, but it is not relocatable.

HOW THE SERVER MICROPROCESSOR AFFECTS SYSTEM PERFORMANCE

How the server processor affects network performance is directly related to the number of tasks the server must manage for the network. Accordingly, network file servers that must run a print server, database server, or router software in addition to maintaining the normal network management functions will depend heavily on the processing power of the network server.

One of the great misconceptions about NetWare file servers is that the processor in the server is shared by all network users when running their applications. When a server is merely running in a file server capacity, its processor is dedicated to handling network-management functions and access to the server's disks. In most cases, even a 386SX processor with a passable clock speed (16–20 MHz) can handle the needs of file access.

Marketing campaigns touting Scalar Architecture and multiprocessor Super Servers rarely mention that these specialized computers are intended for environments where the server is running a client/server database package (like Btrieve, NetWare SQL, Oracle, or Lotus Notes) or other processes where the server actually *does* process information at the server, or when the network server must support 200 or more simultaneous users. With a client/server package, the processing power of the server is divided among the network users accessing its resources.

In some cases, the processor in your file server will be capable of outrunning the cabling scheme being used on your network. On our test network, we have two file servers—a Compaq SystemPro 486DX/33 EISA (CICERO) and a clone 386SX/20 ISA bus computer (TOLSTOY). Because of the limitations of the cabling scheme, network hubs, and NICs we're using, the aggregate capacity of our network is a maximum throughput of approximately 7.3 Mbps, or about 0.9 MB/second. Consequently, during our performance testing, the clone server and the SystemPro turned in nearly identical marks. It should be noted, however, that the SystemPro was running half loaded (47 percent CPU utilization) while the clone was having to run nearly at full bore to keep up (93 percent CPU utilization). In this case, it is obvious that the processing capabilities of the SystemPro were being underused.

Monitoring Key System Performance Areas

To your users, the performance of the network will vary depending on the type of workstation they use, the type of network they are attached to, and the NIC in their system. The performance of the server and the LAN, however, should provide the same potential performance to each workstation on a given LAN segment. The next two sections tell you how to test and monitor the performance of LAN segments and the file server itself.

USING NOVELL'S PERFORM UTILITY

Novell's PERFORM utility is available on CompuServe in the NOVLIB forum (at this writing, PERFORM3 was the latest version and was located in Library 16—Public Domain/Text under the name PRFRM3.ZIP). PERFORM is useful for measuring the capacity of the network cabling scheme as well as the performance of the server's CPU and memory. PERFORM *is not* useful for measuring the capacities and throughput of network drives. PERFORM measures the amount of information that a workstation or workstations can transmit to the server in different size blocks. The server must respond to and acknowledge each transmission, making this utility useful for measuring the throughput between workstations and the server.

PERFORM will measure the performance of one station or many stations under the coordination of a master station. It stores the results in two files, one has the extension .TXT and the other .OUT. The .TXT file is ASCII text of the results displayed on screen as the test is performed. The .OUT file is a data file for the PLOTOUT utility, which will display a histogram of the aggregate performance of the network. Typing PERFORM3 at the command line with no arguments will cause it to display its options:

PERFORM3 version 1.61

The syntax is:

>PERFORM3 <graph name> <...configurable options...>

where options are:

```
<test time seconds to test (12 to 65535)>    default = 12
<start size (1 to 65535)>   default = 1
<stop size (start size to 65535)>    default = 4096
<step size (stop—start+1)/512 to (stop—start+1)> default =
(stop—start+1)/128
```

The defaults will cause PERFORM3 to step through record sizes of 1 to 4096 bytes every 12 seconds in steps of 128. The record size determines the

NOTE
Use PERFORM (available on CompuServe) to measure the capacity of network cabling and the performance of the server's CPU and memory.

amount of data sent from the workstation to the server. The test time determines the total time for a testing with a particular record size. The step size determines the next record size. For example, a step size of 128 will cause PERFORM3 to use a record size of 4064 (calculated from [4096 − 1 + 1]/128 = 32 bytes), which is 4096 − 32 bytes for the second 12-second test interval.

We performed tests on a five-station 10baseT network as an example. We started the tests using the following command-line options at the master station (the master station is a workstation chosen to start the testing for all stations at the same time):

PERFORM3 TEST1 12 2048 4096 256 ↵

After you press ↵, a menu appears while the program polls the network for other stations being tested. The test does not begin until you press ↵ again at the master station. The results of the test were written to the files TEST1.TXT and TEST1.OUT. The file TEST1.TXT contains information about the throughput for the station and the aggregate throughput for the network. If only one station is being tested, the values in these columns will match. The contents of our output file appear below:

```
4096 bytes. 390.63 KBps. 390.63 Aggregate KBps.
3840 bytes. 382.25 KBps. 382.25 Aggregate KBps.
3584 bytes. 372.65 KBps. 372.65 Aggregate KBps.
3328 bytes. 362.29 KBps. 362.29 Aggregate KBps.
3072 bytes. 383.33 KBps. 383.33 Aggregate KBps.
2816 bytes. 371.50 KBps. 371.50 Aggregate KBps.
2560 bytes. 358.24 KBps. 358.24 Aggregate KBps.
2304 bytes. 342.83 KBps. 342.83 Aggregate KBps.
2048 bytes. 369.21 KBps. 369.21 Aggregate KBps.
390.63 Maximum KBps. 370.33 Average KBps.
```

To test more than one workstation at a time, simply set up the parameters at the master station the same way as before and then type PERFORM3 with no arguments at each of the workstations to participate in the test. At the master station the *Stations in test:* should increment with each additional station. To begin the test for all stations, press ⏎ at the master station.

The following five figures illustrate how PERFORM can be used to measure network performance. Figure 18.3 shows the histogram result of a single workstation under test, Figure 18.4 the result of two workstations, Figure 18.5 the result of three, Figure 18.6 the result of four, and Figure 18.7 the result of five workstations.

Figure 18.3 indicates that the results of aggregate network throughput are the same as those for the single workstation being tested. So far, the bandwidth of the network has not been used completely. In Figure 18.4, two stations have come closer to using the full bandwidth, but both stations are still able to transfer information at an average rate of 360–370 KB/sec. In Figure 18.5, Figure 18.6, and Figure 18.7, the full bandwidth of the network has been reached. The aggregate throughput for the LAN is approximately 936 KB/sec or 7.5 Mbps. Each workstation is getting some

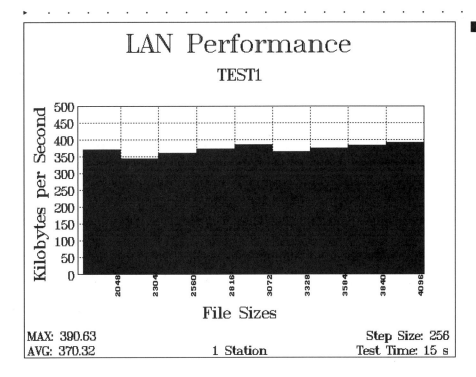

FIGURE 18.3
Results of PERFORM with one workstation

Results of PERFORM with
two workstations

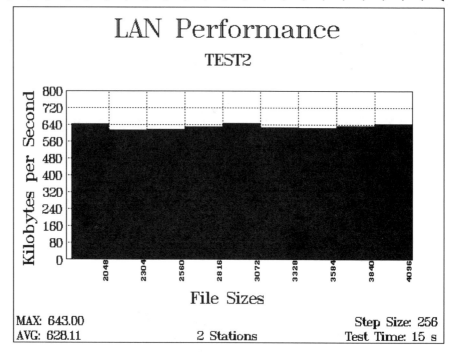

portion of the total bandwidth because each is transmitting at the same time. When three stations are active, they are getting an average 310 KB/sec. With four stations active, the average is around 255 KB/sec. With five stations active, from an individual workstation's point of view, the performance of the network has dropped to 215 KB/sec.

USING OTHER PERFORMANCE TESTS

PERFORM does not exercise the disks in the file server during its performance testing. If you want to test the capabilities of the server's disks as well as LAN performance, try the public-domain utility TESTNET.EXE, written by Scott Taylor, and available on CompuServe in the NOVLIB forum (look for the file TSTN22.ZIP in Library 15). TESTNET.EXE uses two forms of

FIGURE 18.5

Results of PERFORM with

three workstations

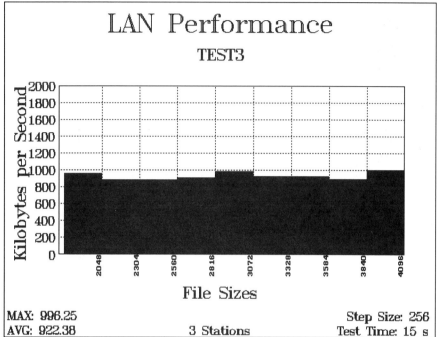

testing, one of which exercises the server's disks. Similarly, other commercially available utilities packages (such as Norton Utilities System Information) include the ability to test the performance of a LAN and server drives.

Troubleshooting

Troubleshooting network problems is a black art at best. Unfortunately, there are virtually no magic wands, miracle cures, or sorcerers' spells. When you experience trouble with your network, there is no single sure-fire method that will help you solve the problem. The best troubleshooting tools for a network administrator are a keen eye, good documentation of the network components and layout, common sense (the reasons for calling it *common* are quite elusive), and—most of all—patience.

FIGURE 18.6

Results of PERFORM with
four workstations

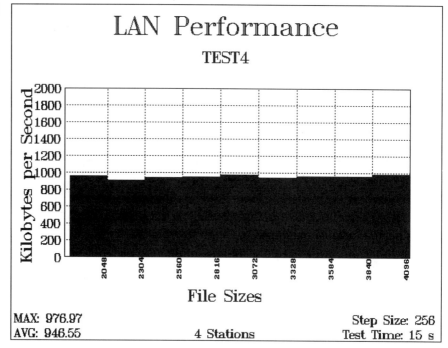

FIGURE 18.6

Results of PERFORM with four workstations

Usually, the easiest problems to solve are those tied to a particular event—for example, every time a user prints to print queue ALPHA, a segment of the network halts. Unfortunately, most network problems are *intermittent*—they only manifest themselves some of the time. To find the cause of such problems, you usually have to identify the event or series of events that cause the problem to occur. The most difficult problems to solve are those that are both intermittent and unpredictable. The problems that you cannot link to a particular event or simulate at will are the ones that will require the most patience.

TROUBLESHOOTING SOFTWARE PROBLEMS

Don't overlook the error message if there is one. Although many error messages are cryptic (or worse, undocumented), they can often assist you

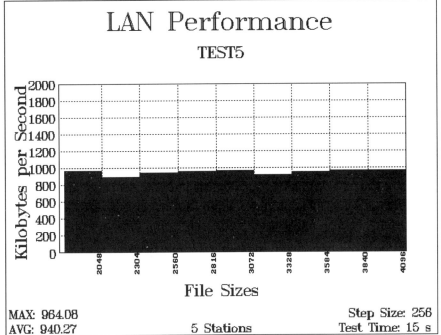

in finding software problems. Software problems are often caused by inadequate permissions or directory access rights in areas that you might not expect. Similarly, many software problems are caused by allowing multiple users to use non–network-aware applications on a network. These programs may not properly implement file or record locking.

Finding these kinds of problems is tedious but not all that difficult. You can often find problems caused by inadequate rights by testing the software both as a supervisor and as a user without supervisor privileges. In general, install software as the network supervisor so that directories and files created when an application is installed belong to the supervisor. Installing the software with supervisor privileges will also allow you to determine whether or not the software is functioning properly without having to worry about rights and privileges. It then is simple to grant privileges incrementally to users until they are able to run the software.

Pay careful attention to the software documentation. The software developer will often indicate the minimum rights necessary to run the software. Even so, test the software as a user other than a supervisor equivalent to make sure that it is functioning properly. To illustrate the point, consider the following incident.

We once discovered trouble with the editing section of network fax software. The software had the ability to allow a user to place textual information on received faxes. This worked flawlessly for the system supervisor, but not for other users. After checking the documentation thoroughly, we discovered that the user needed certain rights in the directory where faxes were stored and other rights (READ and SCAN only) in the directory where the executable software was stored. With the appropriate rights, the user was indeed able to edit the faxes, but could not save them. We used the Novell RIGHTS utility to verify that the correct permission levels were set in the proper directories and retested. If the user was granted the identical rights in the *data directory* as those listed for the supervisor (meaning all rights), the user was still unable to save modified faxes. The error message was *File Creation Error.*

To solve the problem, we used the NetWare MONITOR utility from the system console to see what activities were occurring when the supervisor and other users saved modified faxes. We selected Connection Information from the main menu of MONITOR to display the active network connections, then selected a user and pressed ↵ to display a list of files currently in use by the user. This list changes dynamically as the user uses the network. While watching the list, we had someone perform a save of a modified fax file. We discovered immediately that when saving a fax that had been modified, the software attempted to create temporary files in the executable program directory (the one which normally had only READ and SCAN rights). Granting the users the ability to create, modify, and erase files in that directory solved the problem. To prevent a user from accidentally erasing one of the executable files, we used FLAG to mark the executable files as share and read-only (SRO).

TROUBLESHOOTING HARDWARE PROBLEMS

Hardware problems are sometimes glaringly obvious and it is easy to determine that a component has failed and will most likely not operate again. (If the PC is smoking, it's probably broken.) Unfortunately, in most cases the problems do not jump out and wave white flags. Troubleshooting hardware problems can be extremely difficult when they occur without the complete failure of a component. Problems like this are *intermittent* (problems consistently present are *nonintermittent*).

Here is how to track down a nonintermittent problem:

► Check the obvious, even if you are sure things are in order. For example, make sure the power is on (yes, this can be embarrassing!), make sure that cables are connected properly, make sure the correct command and syntax are used when issuing commands, and so on.

► If the problem occurs on more than one station, try isolating entire systems. Remove systems from the network one-by-one and watch for differences and changes.

► Replace a suspect component with a spare or borrowed part. If you don't suspect any particular component of a system, replace the entire system with another (if possible) and see if the problem still exists.

► If changes to the server or stations don't have any effect, have the LAN cabling checked. (LAN cabling is often the cause of hardware problems, but since testing workstations and components is relatively easy, that is a good place to start.)

The best tools for tracking down intermittent problems are patience (your #1 tool), a network log book, assistance from your users, and your attention. If the problem seldom manifests itself, enlist your users' help in documenting it. Whenever the problem occurs, have your users write down what they were doing at the time, what steps they took to get there, and when they noticed the problem. If a system is reporting error messages, document these as well. Eventually a pattern may emerge that is completely different from what you might suspect.

In one case where we had an intermittent conflict between a NIC installed in the server and a parallel printer port, one leg of the LAN would go down for a few seconds or minutes at a time. On occasion, the server would halt with a Non-Maskable Interrupt (a hideous sort of error that gives highly cryptic error messages) message: *NMI—Memory Parity Error.* We tried everything from changing server memory, to suspecting non-network applications, to suspecting our word processor (the most often–used piece of software) of causing the problem.

Eventually, the secretary noticed that the LAN only locked up while one of the laser printers was active. A little checking revealed that both a NIC and the third parallel port were sharing an interrupt in the file server. Although a simple problem to fix, this took about ten days to locate and solve.

Summary

In this chapter, we have described how hardware and software can affect network performance. We have discussed optimizing the placement of bridges and routers and organizing the layout of a LAN. We have covered file server memory and its effect on performance. We have shown a simple methodology for using the Novell PERFORM utility and other utilities commonly available to assist in measuring LAN performance. Finally, we have introduced some basic tenets that will assist you in solving both hardware and software problems on your LAN. Now that you know how to measure the performance of a LAN, in Chapter 19, we will look into using the tools provided by NetWare for server optimization.

Configuring the Network for Maximum Efficiency

Fast Track

NetWare's MONITOR utility 543

is one of the most useful tools for helping a LAN administrator determine the current level of performance a file server is exhibiting.

▸ The System Module Information option will list the NLMs currently loaded in the system and the associated resources that must be allocated for their operation.

▸ The Resource Utilization option tracks the usage of file server resources like memory and server processes.

▸ Loading MONITOR with the /p option will provide the Processor Utilization feature which lists the available processes and can show the corresponding CPU utilization.

The SET console command and the file server's startup files 550

can also "tune" most of the server performance parameters available to the MONITOR utility.

Even though your network may be up and running smoothly, there is most likely still room for improvements in server performance. Networks often grow faster than they were intended to, and the capabilities of a network do not always grow at the same rate as its needs.

In this chapter, we will discuss a few areas where performance may be improved by configuring software and hardware. In particular, we pay attention to the server CPU, the configuration of disks and controllers to achieve the highest performance levels, we cover the tunable parameters of the NetWare operating system, and we discuss the use of NetWare tools to monitor system performance

Using the Right Size Hardware for the Server

File servers are commonly used for a lot more than just sharing files across a network. There are database packages, fax servers, print servers, CD-ROM software, backup systems, LAN management software, and many other applications that run as server modules.

Each additional software package that runs on the server itself takes away some of the server's processing capabilities. The more applications you run on your network server, the more processing power, memory, and disk capacity it will require. In Chapter 2, we briefly covered the idea of file servers and distributed processing on a network. Table 2.1 listed some common recommendations for file servers based on the types of applications that the file server will be expected to handle.

An ISA-based 80386 SX motherboard running at 25 MHz might be perfectly capable of handling the network management and file I/O on your network. However, installing a database system like NetWare SQL or Btrieve onto the same server might well slow it down to the point of being impractical. Meanwhile, the same environment running a 33-MHz 80386 DX might be completely acceptable. The table below lists some of the relevant differences in CPU architectures.

CPU TYPE	TYPICAL CLOCK SPEED	MEMORY BUS WIDTH	INTERNAL CACHE/FLOATING POINT UNIT
80386 SX	16–25 MHz	16 bits	N/A / N/A
80386 DX	16–40 MHz	32 bits	N/A / N/A
80486 SX	20–25 MHz	32 bits	8K / N/A
80486 DX	25–33 MHz	32 bits	16K/built in
80486 DX/2	50–66 MHz internally (25–33 MHz externally)	32 bits	16K/built in

If your file server must handle large amounts of raster data, document retrieval data, network fax traffic, database activity, or CAD activity, consider dividing the tasks to be performed among multiple servers rather than trying to build a single server capable of handling all of them. The principle is the same as we described in Chapter 18 when discussing disk controllers—the more processors you can allocate to perform server tasks, the more performance you can extract from your network.

NOTE
Raster data refers to graphics data represented in a pixel format—each data element (typically a byte) is used to represent a color and intensity for one pixel (dot) on the screen.

Setting Up Disks and Volumes for Performance

Getting the best performance out of the disk system in a network server sometimes requires more than just buying the fastest, largest drives and high-speed controllers available.

Improving the performance of drive and data storage systems requires the consideration of much more than raw data capacity and access times. The fastest hard drives in the world are worthless if they stop functioning because of a component failure. When assessing the performance of a data-storage system, consider reliability and fault tolerance on equal terms with the data-transfer capabilities of a system. NetWare has been providing several methods for enhancing data reliability directly in the OS for quite some time. In the following sections, we describe these as well as other available technologies.

DISK MIRRORING

Since its early versions, NetWare has been capable of implementing a data-protection scheme known as *disk mirroring*— attaching drive pairs to a network server and using one of the drives in the pair to store exactly the same information as the other. One of the drives is selected to be a primary drive and the other as the secondary drive which *mirrors* the information stored on the primary drive. While this scheme implements a form of data redundancy far superior to running single drives, the complete capacity of one of the disks is lost to maintaining data redundancy. Similarly, since the data must be written to two drives, there is added overhead in the write process. But writes are performed in the background, unless the system is overtaxed, and thus the effect on performance is negligible.

NOTE
Redundancy is having two exact copies of data.

DISK DUPLEXING

Disk duplexing, like disk mirroring, maintains a complete copy of the data stored on a disk. But disk duplexing requires that a separate controller be used for each disk in the mirrored pair. Because there are two channels to the data on the disks, read accesses can occur more quickly than they can in a mirrored system. Since the data stored on the drives is duplicated, it makes no difference whether the data is read from the primary or secondary drive. The ability to read from the first available drive is called a "split-seek." There is, however, no added benefit over mirroring for write accesses. In addition to the speed improvement and redundancy achieved through mirrored data, another measure of redundancy is added because a duplexed system can tolerate the failure of either a drive controller or a disk without the loss of data.

SPANNING DISKS

When using a multitasking bus like the SCSI or multiple controllers as the interface to your disks, you can increase data storage space and get additional performance by *spanning* more than one disk into a single volume. When more than one disk is available as a single volume, a write request can be handled by the first available drive as opposed to waiting for another transaction to finish. Similarly, if the Volume FAT indicates that the necessary file is stored on an idle drive, a read request can take place while another transaction is occurring. This is especially true if you use more than one controller as in disk duplexing. While the data redundancy capabilities of such a system are reduced to the level of a single drive (in fact the expected MTBF is reduced below that of a single drive), the performance of a spanned system can be double or triple the performance of a single drive system.

REDUNDANT ARRAYS OF INEXPENSIVE DISKS (RAID)

Redundant Arrays of Inexpensive Disks, a technology originally used in the mainframe and supercomputer environments, is becoming more and more predominant in the LAN environment. Originally conceived at the University of California (Berkeley) as a solution for mainframes and workstations to have better disk performance and fault tolerance, RAID has become a very viable technology for enhancing the performance and reliability of network data storage. Although a thorough description of each level is beyond the scope of this book, we have included the introduction to the technology and a basic description of the six RAID levels.

RAID Level 0

In level 0, the disk array is performance oriented rather than data redundancy oriented. Multiple disks are connected in parallel so that reads and writes may span several drives. The data is *striped* (spread and balanced) across the drives in the array. With RAID level 0, you must be very confident of the quality of the drives used in the array. The Mean Time Between Failure (MTBF) of one of the drives is divided by the number of drives in the array. For a three disk array with disks that have a 150,000 hour MTBF, the MTBF for the array becomes 50,000 hours. Disk spanning supported by NetWare implements RAID Level 0.

RAID Level 1

In level 1, the data on one drive is mirrored on another for data redundancy. RAID Level 1 is supported by NetWare through disk mirroring and disk duplexing. The drawback of the system is that half of the storage capacity of the array is lost to data protection and there is the possibility of a data write penalty imposed because the data must be written to two drives.

RAID Level 2

In level 2, the features of both Level 1 and Level 0 are incorporated. The data is striped across the drives, but instead of keeping a mirror image of each drive, an Error Correction Code (ECC) is spread across multiple disks and used to rebuild corrupted data. This type of array retains more of the data capacity of the drives in the array and is still fault tolerant.

RAID Level 3

In level 3, the drives in the array are synchronized to reduce latency (the time delay caused by head positioning) and data is written to the disks in parallel at the bit level. Level three uses a parity drive for data redundancy. This arrangement is most useful when large amounts of sequential data (like graphics and imaging information) are being accessed. The performance of level 3 is very good when data is likely to span several drives and small transactions are kept to a minimum. As such it is generally not well suited to the LAN environment.

RAID Level 4

Level 4 is similar to level 3 except that data is written in parallel at the sector level rather than at the bit level. This implementation permits simultaneous reads of data, but performance still suffers when writing data.

RAID Level 5

In level 5, both data and parity information is striped across the drives. The drives are unsynchronized and may act independently. This makes RAID 5 well suited to environments with a large number of transactions where the files are not likely to span drives (like a LAN). Since RAID level 5 can support concurrent reads and writes and makes efficient use of space for error correction information, it is the most viable in a LAN environment.

Hardware and Software RAID Solutions

RAID systems are available as completely software solutions (they use the file server CPU to calculate striping) or in hardware-based implementations. The software-based solutions often allow you to use off-the-shelf components or even make use of the drives and controllers you already have. The hardware-based systems are more expensive, but they usually have redundant power supplies, *hot-swap* capability, appear to the host as a single drive (usually a SCSI peripheral) and free up the CPU for other tasks. Hot-swapping is the ability to replace a disk without bringing the system down.

Whatever your performance or fault tolerance needs, there is likely a disk system supported by NetWare or a RAID array that will meet them. Just remember, a redundant drive system is not a replacement for a thorough backup procedure. Any system can fail—ultimately, backups are the final line of defense against data loss.

Using Monitor Information

NetWare's Monitor utility is one of the most useful utilities for helping a LAN administrator determine the current level of performance a file server is exhibiting. Monitor is a NetWare Loadable Module that is run at the file server console. MONITOR.NLM can display information about the current memory status for the server, current server connections, current server processes, file lock status, and resource utilization. Figure 19.1 shows the Monitor main screen.

The top window, Information for Server *Servername,* gives information at a glance about the current status of the server. In particular, the statistics for cache memory buffers and service processes is immediately available:

Original Cache Buffers	Shows the total number of cache buffers available for allocation when the server was first booted.
Total Cache Buffers	Shows the number of cache buffers that are currently in use for file caching. Memory that is required for other memory pools or cache buffers will be allocated from this area.

FIGURE 19.1

The main screen of

MONITOR.NLM

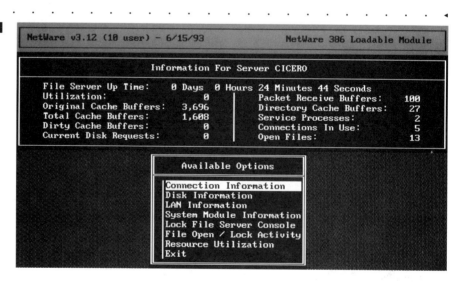

```
NetWare v3.12 (10 user) - 6/15/93          NetWare 386 Loadable Module

                    Information For Server CICERO

    File Server Up Time:    0 Days  0 Hours 24 Minutes 44 Seconds
    Utilization:              0         Packet Receive Buffers:   100
    Original Cache Buffers:  3,696      Directory Cache Buffers:   27
    Total Cache Buffers:     1,608      Service Processes:          2
    Dirty Cache Buffers:         0      Connections In Use:         5
    Current Disk Requests:       0      Open Files:                13


                       Available Options
                   Connection Information
                   Disk Information
                   LAN Information
                   System Module Information
                   Lock File Server Console
                   File Open / Lock Activity
                   Resource Utilization
                   Exit
```

Packet Receive Buffers	Shows the number of cache buffers allocated to temporarily queuing workstation requests. The tasks received here are serviced by Service Processes so the two parameters are related. The more Services Processes there are, the less likely it is that you will need to increase the number of Receive Buffers.
Directory Cache Buffers	Shows the number of buffers allocated to caching the Directory Entry Tables and File Allocation Tables. When this number reaches 100, the number of available buffers should be increased.
Service Processes	Shows the maximum number of processes dedicated to handling tasks from workstation requests. If this value reaches 20 and at least 20 percent of the Total Cache Buffers are free, you might consider increasing this number in increments of five.

SYSTEM MODULE INFORMATION

Each of the NetWare Loadable Modules presently in the system will appear in a list when this option is selected. Some of the modules should be recognizable as disk drivers, LAN drivers, and utilities you have loaded from the console or the AUTOEXEC.NCF file. Figure 19.2 shows a listing of system modules that might appear in Monitor.

Each NLM defines tags (names) to resources that must be allocated for its operation. To see a list of the resource tags for a given module, select the module from the list and press ↵. A screen similar to the one in Figure 19.3 will appear.

*The System Modules listing
in MONITOR*

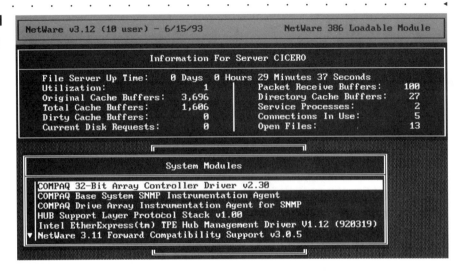

*The resource tags
associated with an NLM*

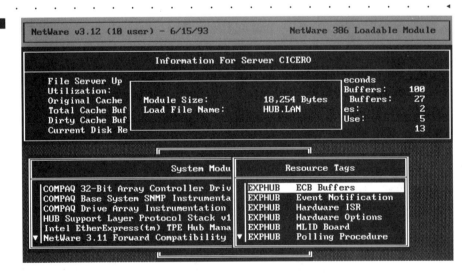

After identifying specific resource tags, you can press ↵ or use the Resource Utilization option from the main menu to get more information about the amount and types of resources the NLM is using.

RESOURCE UTILIZATION

NetWare tracks the usage of the file server resources like memory and file server processes. To see the server's memory usage statistics or see a list of the tracked resources, select Resource Utilization from the Available Options menu of Monitor. A screen similar to the one in Figure 19.4 will appear.

Check two parameters in particular—Alloc Memory Pool and Tracked Resources. Alloc Memory Pool can indicate a misbehaving NLM. If this number continually grows over a period of time, try to track down (using resource tags) the NLM using the additional memory. The Cache Buffers percentage should never go below 20 percent. If this ever happens, you are running short on file server memory and should add memory to the server.

The Tracked Resources window holds the name of the resource being used (see Figure 19.4). When looking at the resource tags assigned to a

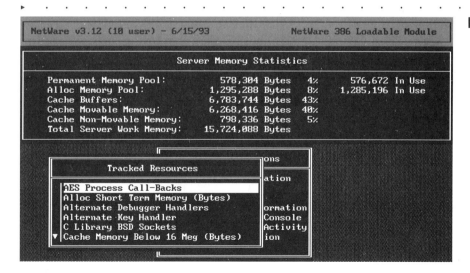

FIGURE 19.4

Server Memory Statistics

particular module, one of the items listed for each tag is the name of the resource being used. By selecting a particular resource, you can determine which modules are using it and the name of the tag the module has assigned to the resource. See the list of resource tags in Figure 19.5.

FIGURE 19.5

Listing of the resource tags

using a particular resource

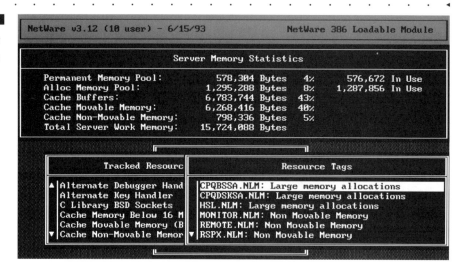

```
NetWare v3.12 (10 user) - 6/15/93              NetWare 386 Loadable Module

                          Server Memory Statistics
        Permanent Memory Pool:          578,304 Bytes    4%      576,672 In Use
        Alloc Memory Pool:            1,295,288 Bytes    8%    1,287,856 In Use
        Cache Buffers:               6,783,744 Bytes   43%
        Cache Movable Memory:        6,268,416 Bytes   40%
        Cache Non-Movable Memory:      798,336 Bytes    5%
        Total Server Work Memory:   15,724,088 Bytes


          Tracked Resourc              Resource Tags

        ▲ Alternate Debugger Hand     CPQBSSA.NLM: Large memory allocations
          Alternate Key Handler       CPQDSKSA.NLM: Large memory allocations
          C Library BSD Sockets       HSL.NLM: Large memory allocations
          Cache Memory Below 16 M     MONITOR.NLM: Non Movable Memory
          Cache Movable Memory (B     REMOTE.NLM: Non Movable Memory
        ▼ Cache Non-Movable Memor   ▼ RSPX.NLM: Non Movable Memory
```

PROCESSOR UTILIZATION

Monitor's Processor Utilization feature does not appear in the menu by default. To see the amount of CPU time a particular process or interrupt is using start Monitor with the (/P or -P) option. When Monitor loads, an option called Processor Utilization will appear in the list of Available Options. Select this item to bring up a list of the available processes and interrupts. You can view the utilization of a particular process one at a time, or use F5 to tag several before pressing ↵, as shown in Figure 19.6.

Figure 19.7 shows the window with a histogram that this option displays when giving information about CPU utilization. The Load parameter is the percentage of the overall CPU time a particular process is using. Press F1 to get detailed help for this option.

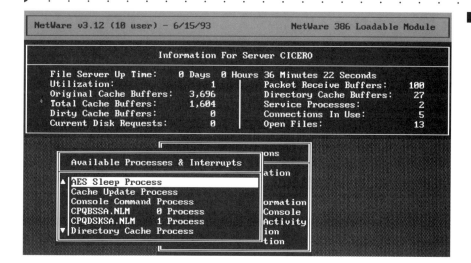

FIGURE 19.6

The Available Processes &

Interrupts menu

FIGURE 19.7

CPU utilization for a set of

processes

Using the Console Set Command and the STARTUP.NCF File

Most of the parameters just discussed are *tunable* either through the server's startup files or with the SET command at the console. The SET command can affect nine categories of file server performance: Communications, Memory, File Caching, Directory Caching, File System, Locks, Transaction Tracking, Disk, and Miscellaneous. Some of these different categories and the parameters within them are listed in the table below. (See Appendix A for a more complete listing.)

TABLE 19.0

SET command parameters

PARAMETER	DEFAULT VALUE	DESCRIPTION
COMMUNICATIONS		
Maximum Packet Receive Buffers	100	Determines the maximum number of receive buffers that can be allocated by the server OS. Busy servers often raise this value to 300 or even 500.
Minimum Packet Receive Buffers	10	Must be set in STARTUP.NCF. If the file server is slow when first starting, it may be because it has not yet allocated more receive buffers. Can be used to set the minimum available at startup.
MEMORY		
Maximum Alloc Short Term Memory	2 MB	Alloc short term memory is used for storing variables like user's drive mappings. The default value should be sufficient to support the mappings for 250 simultaneous users. If the operating system issues a warning about this memory area, it can be increased in increments of 1 MB up to a maximum of 16 MB.

PARAMETER	DEFAULT VALUE	DESCRIPTION
Auto Register Memory Above 16 Meg	ON	Must be set in the STARTUP.NCF file. Determines whether or not the OS should automatically register memory above 16 MB in an EISA bus computer. If you are using a Bus Mastering Controller or NIC that uses DMA, this parameter will most likely need to be set to OFF to prevent memory conflicts.
Cache Buffer Size		Must be set in the STARTUP.NCF file. An advanced parameter that should only be changed in very specific circumstances. If the block sizes on all Volumes in a server are greater than 4096, this parameter may be used to improve performance. Set it equal to the smallest block size used on the server Volumes. (Any Volume that has a smaller block size than the Cache Buffer Size will *not* be mounted.)
FILE CACHING		
Minimum File Cache Buffers		Sets the minimum number of allowable File Cache Buffers.
Directory Caching		
Maximum Directory Cache Buffers	500	Each Directory Cache Buffer takes memory away from the File Cache Buffers. This parameter can be used to control the number of Directory Cache Buffers allocated by the server. If directory searches become sluggish, you may need to increase this parameter.
Minimum Directory Cache Buffers		Sets the minimum allowable Directory Cache Buffers.

PARAMETER	DEFAULT VALUE	DESCRIPTION
MISCELLANEOUS		
Maximum Service Processes	20	An advanced parameter that should only be changed in very specific circumstances. File Service Processes (FSPs) are task handlers that take care of requests from workstations. Maximum Service Processes is usually self-tuning. Increasing the value will help only if there are 20 stations being simultaneously delayed by lack of buffers or processes.

Summary

In this chapter, we discussed the differences in different CPU types that may be used in the file server. We introduced a few areas where performance may be improved through the configuration of either software or hardware. We covered the tunable parameters of the NetWare operating system and discussed the use of NetWare tools to monitor system performance.

Options for
Expanding Network
Communications

Fast Track

- ▸ leased lines like T1 or T3 supporting multiple protocols
- ▸ satellite-based communications

Dial-up lines   563

are perhaps the simplest form of wide area communications to implement, requiring only a set of modems and a local or long-distance phone call.

Public Data Networks (PDNs)   564

are networks that can be accessed via a phone call or a direct connection. PDNs provide services to subscribing organizations.

Leased lines   566

provide higher-performance lines than dial-up lines and PDNs and are justifiable when your WAN needs to support heavy traffic or interactive services.

Communications satellites   568

are capable of providing several services for data communications, including emergency backup to land-based systems on an as-needed basis, typical data rates of around 19.2 Kbps for point-to-point communications, and potential for high-speed data channels.

Novell provides for connecting LAN-based workstations to   568
mainframe hosts

through a gateway by using software that allows the workstation to emulate IBM terminals and printers.

The installation of a network is often justified as a means of helping a small workgroup like a single department or a small office share information and improve productivity, regardless of the overall size of the organization. Many large organizations have multiple LANs that evolved as separate islands of information rather than as part of an organization-wide network. As growth in an organization-wide network is evolutionary, it is likely that these islands of information will eventually need to be connected. If this possibility was considered during the initial LAN design and was implemented from the beginning, the roots of an organization-wide LAN should be already available.

In this chapter, we'll introduce some of the options for expanding your NetWare LAN or connecting your LAN to networks of different types. As this area of LAN technology changes daily, this chapter is intended to be an overview of some of the available technologies rather than a detailed exploration. The best sources for information about what is currently available are your vendor, your communications company (e.g., your telephone company, long distance carrier, or network service), and the hardware manufacturers themselves.

Expanded LAN communications take many forms: access to a LAN from remote sites, single sites that have multiple LANs connected together, Metropolitan Area Networks (MANs) that are limited to a specific geographic region, and Wide Area Networks (WANs) that are not limited to a specific geographic region. The needs of each LAN will determine the best solution. In this chapter, we'll cover single-site connectivity and extended network communications, including some of the technologies used to implement MANs and WANs.

NOTE
Metropolitan Area Networks (MANs) are groups of interconnected LANs within a region of approximately 160 sq. km (or with a radius of 15–16 km). Wider networks are WANs.

Expanding Single-Site Communications

Expanding single-site communications is when you connect more than one LAN in the same building into a larger network or when you provide dial-in and dial-out services for your network. The ability to connect multiple servers and LAN segments into a larger LAN is built into NetWare.

LOCAL LAN-TO-LAN BRIDGING

Perhaps the simplest way to extend your LAN is to use the internal and external router capabilities provided with NetWare. An *internal router* is created whenever more than one NIC is added to a NetWare server. An *external router* is either a workstation with more than one network card that is running a router TSR or a dedicated computer with multiple network cards that is running NetWare router software.

In either case, a NetWare router can combine multiple file servers and network segments into the same network. In addition, NetWare routers translate between different protocols and topologies automatically. For example, you can run a Token Ring and an Ethernet LAN segment out of the same server simply by installing a network interface card for each. For an even larger system or for optimal performance, you can combine multiple LAN segments (e.g., multiple Ethernet, ARCnet, Token Ring, etc.) into the same logical network by connecting all of the network servers to a common backbone—all of the protocol translation and connectivity issues (like segmentation and reassembly) are handled transparently by NetWare.

MODEM SHARING

For implementing remote communications on a budget or when working with a small number of remote users, few solutions can beat Asynchronous modems. Additional telephone lines are usually inexpensive, as are modems and sharing software. There are several ways to use modems to implement remote communications: modem pooling, network-connected modems, and workstation-based modems. NetWare provides two methods of attaching a pool of modems to the network. The first method is the NetWare Asynchronous Communications Server (NACS); the second is the NetWare Access Server.

NOTE
Internal and external routers are discussed in **Chapter 2;** performance issues are discussed in **Chapter 19.**

NOTE
Since Token Ring and ARCnet use larger packet sizes than Ethernet, bridges and routers must disassemble packets going to and re-assemble packets coming from an Ethernet network. The process is called *segmentation and reassembly.*

NetWare Asynchronous Communications Server (NACS)

The NetWare Asynchronous Communications Server, an NLM for the NetWare 3.12 operating system, allows up to 32 users to share asynchronous serial ports attached to the server. The NLM may run either on a network file server or on a dedicated communications server using the NetWare Runtime version of the server software.

The NetWare NACS NLM supports general-purpose asynchronous communications devices that are directly attached to the server and may be used for modem pooling. Either native (COM1–COM4) ports can be used or intelligent multiport solutions from manufacturers like Digiboard, Hayes, Microdyne and Newport Systems Solutions can be used for increased capacity. The software comes in 2-, 8-, and 32-port versions.

Devices attached to these server-based ports are available to all network users subject to normal network security (through NetWare security). Accessing a network port is simply a matter of specifying the port's name. Resources attached to that port are placed at the disposal of the network user who made the request (for example, if the attached resource is a modem, the user can use modem communications software at the workstation to control the remote modem as if the modem were attached directly to the workstation). Examples of attached resources might be a serial connection to another host computer (like a minicomputer or UNIX host), an asynchronous modem, dial-up access to an X.25-based Public Data Network, or a serial device like a plotter.

The NetWare Access Server (NAS)

The NetWare Access Server can turn any compatible 80386- or 80486-class computer into 16 virtual-computer sessions. As with the NACS, each port controlled by the local computer session can be used to support either direct connection to a serial host, an asynchronous modem connection, or dial-up access to an X.25 or other Public Data Network. However, while both NACS and NAS supply general-purpose serial communications to LAN-based or remote users, the NACS must use a LAN-based workstation for the remote user's computational requirements. The NAS, on the other hand, uses advanced features of the 80386/80486 processors to support multiple users on a single computer. When a remote user needs to access LAN resources, he or she does not have to tie up a LAN workstation with a NAS as they would if using a NACS.

The NAS also provides general-purpose processing power to local users. A user at a local workstation can log into the Access Server and use one of the virtual PC sessions there to perform a task that otherwise might tie up the local user for long periods of time (for example, querying a database or transferring a file from a remote system). The LAN users would still be able to use their local workstations for other tasks.

Using Remote-Control Software

Remote Control Software is one of the simplest and most ingenious solutions to remote computing. This type of software establishes a *session* between a remote computer (or even a terminal) and a workstation located on the LAN. Once connected, control of the remote and local keyboards and displays is switched—meaning that the remote keyboard can control the LAN based workstation and the remote display shows the same information as the workstation display. (In most cases, the display and keyboard of the LAN workstation can be enabled or disabled for security purposes.)

The LAN-based workstation loads and executes applications as it normally would, but they can be under control of either the local or the remote user. The performance perceived by the remote user is as good as the capabilities of the LAN workstation—doing a database query should take no longer than it would locally, for example—although screen refreshes take longer. Another difference is that users on remote software must use a file transfer, rather than a DOS COPY, to move files between the remote and the LAN workstation. See Figure 20.1 for a graphical representation of the way information flows between the host and remote computers.

There are many packages available for remote control. Some of the more popular packages are Avalan Technology's Remotely Possible, Microcom's Carbon Copy, Norton-Lambert Close-Up and Close-Up LAN, Symantec's PC/Anywhere IV and PC/Anywhere IV LAN, and Triton Technologies'

Information flow with
remote control software

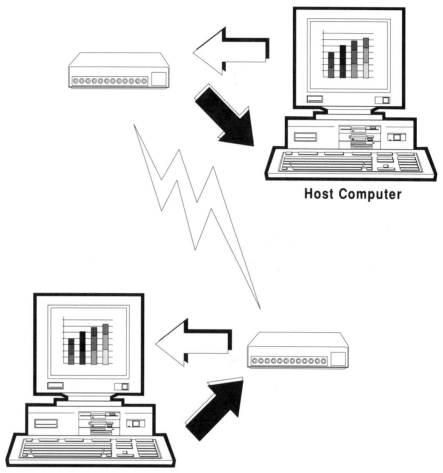

Host Computer

Remote Computer

CO/Session family of products. The single-user versions typically allow any single workstation with a modem to act as a remote or host workstation for another computer. The LAN versions of the software often provide additional capabilities for sharing across the LAN: the ability to control other computers on the LAN as well as remote computers, the implementation of a gateway for outgoing modem sharing, and the ability to direct incoming calls to a host on the LAN or at another remote site.

Using Router Software

An alternate solution to taking over a LAN-based workstation or having an Access Server would be to route IPX/SPX (or even other protocols) directly over an asynchronous router to the remote workstation. If IPX packets are directly routed to the remote station, it can log into the LAN just as if it were locally connected. A workstation does not have to be dedicated to providing computing power for the remote user.

The remote user can copy files to and from the network, access network-based data files (like word-processing documents or e-mail), or even run applications from the network under the control of their own CPU and memory. Since communications over asynchronous links are much slower than being locally attached, however, this type of arrangement is best used when only small amounts of data need to travel back and forth across the link (for example e-mail or small file transfers). Using large applications or accessing a database from the LAN would not be practical with an asynchronous router connection.

Two different approaches are often used to provide remote router capabilities to a LAN. The first is a software solution that works in conjunction with a LAN based workstation acting as a router; the second uses network-attached intelligent modems.

The software and workstation solutions generally support a greater number of simultaneous remote sessions because the workstations can be outfitted with intelligent multiport controllers and each port of the controller can be used to support a communications device. An example of this type of software is Intercomputer Communications Corporation's Remote LAN Node, a remote router capable of routing IPX/SPX, TCP/IP, NetBEUI, OSI, and other protocol types.

The network-attached–modem approach does not require that a workstation be dedicated as a router and generally has a very small footprint (the size of an external modem). See Figure 20.2.

Some of these LAN modems have a special port that allows another external modem to be attached to the LAN modem. This way one connection to the network can support two remote connections.

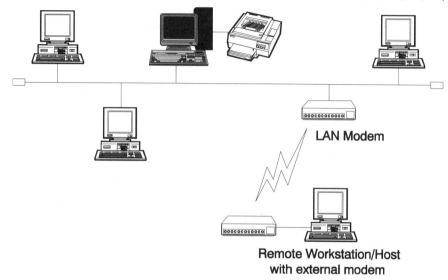

FIGURE 20.2

A network-attached modem connected to a remote station

LAN Modem

Remote Workstation/Host
with external modem

In addition to being used as remote routers, network-attached modems can also provide gateway services (like a NACS) for incoming and outgoing asynchronous communications. Examples of network-attached modems are Microtest's LANMODEM, Shiva's NetModem/E, and UDS/Motorola's LANFast DM20 and LANFast DM25.

Extended Area (MAN/WAN) Communications

Extended area communications extend beyond a single site and take the form of either Metropolitan Area Networks (MANs) or Wide Area Networks (WANs). A regional network within a radius of 15–16 km (or a circular region of approximately 160 sq. km) is usually considered a MAN, while networks that extend beyond this distance are considered WANs.

In many cases, MANs are built on the same cabling scheme that LANs use—for example, 10Base2 Ethernet backbones and Token Ring networks that cover more than one building, or even a campus. When high performance and distances are an issue, MANs will use higher-performance technologies like the Fiber Distributed Data Interface (FDDI) or Distributed Queue Dual Bus (DQDB). FDDI can cover distances of up to 100 km, with a maximum distance between nodes of 2.5 km.

The DQDB was recently approved by the IEEE 802.6 committee as the standard architecture for MANs. DQDB is designed to cover larger regions than FDDI, but is still fiber based and supports signaling at up to 100 Mbps. Future MANs will likely use FDDI technology to connect workgroups and buildings, and these FDDI networks will likely interconnect into wider areas via DQDB. Local-exchange carriers and long-distance companies are likely to begin offering DQDB as a subscriber service.

Networks built around wide-area communications use a variety of communications mechanisms: Asynchronous or Synchronous communications over dial-up lines, X.25 or Frame Relay over Public Data Networks, leased lines like T1 or T3 supporting multiple protocols, and satellite-based communications. However, when trying to understand wide-area communications, it is important to understand that there is a physical media (or set of media) over which you are communicating and a higher-level protocol (or even multiple protocols and levels) being used across the link.

What does that mean? Your connection to a remote LAN might occur over a dial-up line, over a public data network, over a leased line or satellite link, and in each case use the same protocol on one link as you might use on a completely different type of communications link. (For example, X.25 can be supported on a dial-up line, a leased line, a public data network, or a satellite.) Protocol does not necessarily dictate a particular physical medium.

USING DIAL-UP LINES

Dial-up lines are perhaps the simplest form of wide-area communications to implement. All that's required is a set of modems and a local or long-distance phone call. Dial-up lines over public and private networks are typically charged according to connect time and the distance covered by the call. When using a dial-up line, the physical medium across which the data is transferred is usually irrelevant from the user's standpoint. A voice-grade phone call made over fiber, copper, or microwave links should still perform like a voice-grade dial-up connection because you are using only the portion of the potential bandwidth necessary to support your call.

Dial-up connections usually support communications rates of 9.6–38.4 Kbps with the upper end only occurring under ideal conditions. However, when using high-speed modems supporting the V.32 signalling standard, and V.42/V.42bis standards for error correction and compression, effective throughputs of 57.6 Kbps are theoretically possible. Typical data transfer rates are between 9.6 and 19.2 Kbps.

There are several ways to implement dial-up communications for your LAN. Novell provides a software solution called the NetWare Asynchronous Remote Router, which supports LAN-to-LAN communications at speeds of up to 19.2 Kbps over voice-grade lines. The remote router can use an internal modem that emulates COM1 or COM2, external modems attached to server serial ports (COM1 or COM2 only), or a WNIM+ board for placing calls. When using the local serial ports, however, the maximum data rate is reduced to 2400 baud. A WNIM+ board has local memory and an on-board processor to offload communications tasks from the server CPU.

Alternately, network-attached modems like Microtest's LANMODEM, Shiva's NetModem/E, and UDS/Motorola's LANFast DM20 or LANFast DM25 modems can be used to route data between LANs over dial-up connections (see Figure 20.3).

These modems typically support the higher communications speeds (14.4 Kbps for V.32 bis) and data-compression/error-correction standards (like V.42/V.42bis) to make asynchronous routing more practical for transferring larger amounts of data or for remotely executing programs.

USING PUBLIC DATA NETWORKS

Public Data Networks (PDNs) are networks that can be accessed via a phone call or a direct connection. PDNs are public only in the sense that

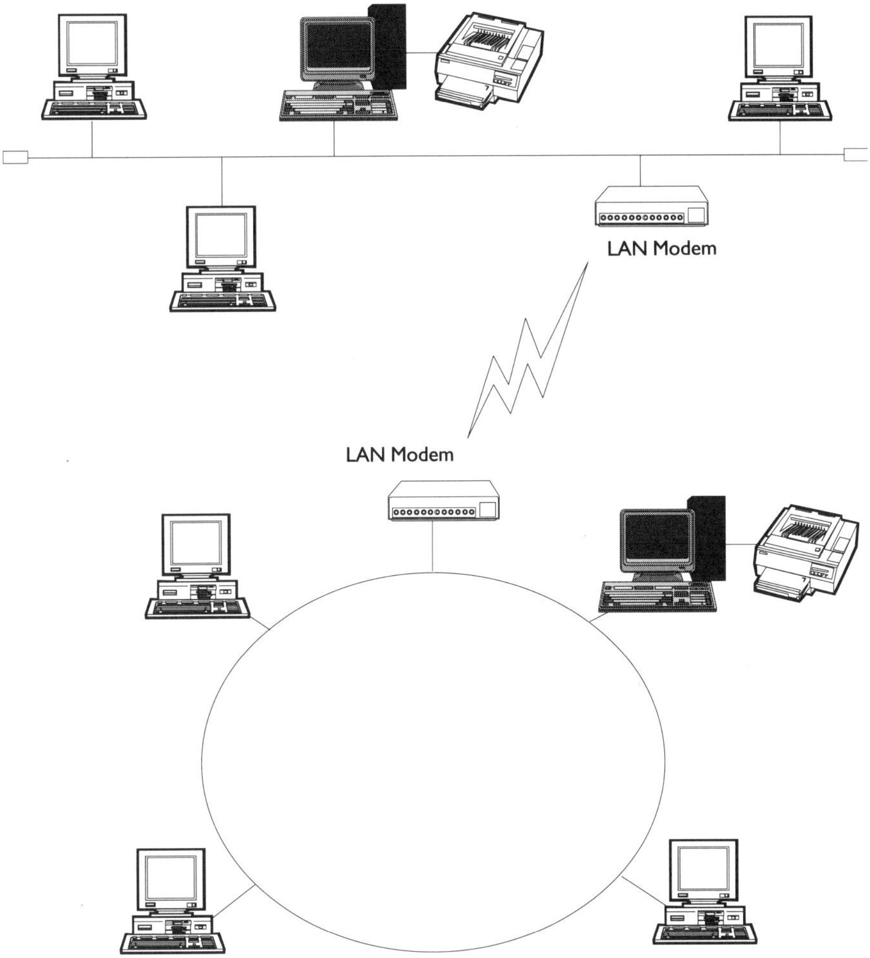

FIGURE 20.3
Using LAN based modems
for asynchronous routing

LAN Modem

LAN Modem

the phone system is public; they are networks set up to provide services to organizations that subscribe to the service.

Because PDNs are used by many organizations and are typically packet switched, they are usually more robust than fixed lines between networks. A packet-switched network does not require that a dedicated connection be established between the source and the destination. When using a packet-switch protocol (like X.25 or Frame Relay), the data stream to be transmitted is divided up into smaller data segments called *packets,* each of which has a destination address. As packets are received by network nodes, they are stored and forwarded from node-to-node until the final destination is reached. Even if there are hundreds of hosts on the network, you needn't be concerned with how the information gets to its destination. Similarly, because there can be many nodes on a Public Data Network, the same access point, communications link, and equipment can be used to reach many remote hosts.

Local connections to a PDN are sometimes made through dial-up lines, but direct digital access to the network is preferable. Digital access to a network requires a digital-capable phone line, a Data Service Unit (DSU), and a Channel Service Unit (CSU). A DSU is the interface between the Data Terminal Equipment (like a LAN bridge or NetWare router) and the CSU; the CSU is the interface between the DSU and the telephone line.

Digital access is preferable to dial-up access for two reasons: First, direct digital access can provide higher data rates than dial-up access, and second, high-speed modems are often more expensive than the DSU/CSUs needed for direct digital access. Since the connection between your network and the PDN is typically a local connection, PDNs are a very convenient way of connecting a single network to multiple remote networks. Some of the more popular packet-switch networks are CompuServe, Telenet, Accunet, and Sprintnet/Tymnet.

USING LEASED LINES

If your network requires access to a computer used for transaction processing or one centrally located for security reasons or mission-critical applications, you'll most likely need higher performance levels than dial-up lines or PDNs can provide. You can justify the higher-speed communications links when you need to support interactive services (like transaction-processing and on-line database systems) or when you have enough traffic to support ten or more 64-Kbps channels.

Leased lines come in different grades (for example, T1 or T3) and can provide communications links at speeds up to 45 Mbps. A T1 link is the most common and provides a communications link capable of 1.544 Mbps. (E1, the European equivalent of T1, can provide communications links at up to 2.048 Mbps.)

Since the measured throughput for most LAN workstations is between 400–750 Kbps, T1 or even fractional T1 is often more than adequate for LAN interconnections (fractional T1 is a means of dividing the bandwidth available from a T1 link into several smaller bandwidth links). In fact, fractional T1 is most often used for data communications needs; the remaining T1 bandwidth is used to carry digital voice signals (each digitized voice channel typically requires a communications link capable of 64 Kbps). Many companies offer excess T1 capacity as fractional T1 links to other organizations that use them for data traffic (typically at rates of 384, 512, and 768 Kbps).

For extremely high–performance communications needs, T3 can support communications links to 45 Mbps. T3 speeds would amount to overkill for LANs in most instances without the addition of voice or other data over the link (except maybe for mission-critical applications).

The cost for a particular link is relative to its performance; a T3 link can cost upwards of $100,000 per month. For more modest performance needs, Digital Data Service (DDS) is available from many phone companies and long distance carriers. DDS can support digital communications links at speeds of up to 56 Kbps.

With Novell's NetWare Link and appropriate communications hardware (like a DSU/CSU, Digital PBX, or T1 multiplexer), your NetWare LAN can directly route LAN data over digital communications media. The software comes in two versions, NetWare Link/64 and NetWare Link/T1. Each must be used in conjunction with a Novell Synchronous/+ adapter or a third-party adapter.

NetWare Link/64 is designed to handle communications rates between 9600 bps and 64 Kbps, while NetWare Link/T1 is designed to handle communications rates up to 2.084 Mbps. The adapter and software combination enable a NetWare server or dedicated router to directly connect to your data communications equipment. Different versions of the Synchronous/+ adapters support RS-232 (up to 19.2 Kbps), RS-422 or V.35 (to 2.048 Mbps), and

NOTE
T3 can support communications links to 45 Mbps for extremely high–performance communications.

V.35 (to 2.048 Mbps). The adapter used is determined by the interfaces available on your communications equipment.

USING SATELLITE COMMUNICATIONS

Communications satellites typically reside in a geosynchronous orbit 35,784 km above the surface of the earth—the distance at which their orbital velocity matches the rotation of the earth. *Geosynchronous* means that their position relative to the movement of the earth is fixed so that they continually cover the same geographic region.

Communications satellites are capable of providing several services for data communications, including emergency backup to land-based communications systems on an as-needed basis, typical data rates of around 19.2 Kbps for point-to-point communications, and the potential for high-speed data channels (for example, a single channel might provide a single data link in the 50 Mbps range or 16 links of 1.544 Mbps each—effectively at or greater than T3 and T1 speeds.)

Although the technology is extremely promising and readily available, satellite communication has proven more expensive than alternatives like PDNs and leased lines for the same performance levels. Satellites also have a characteristic transmission delay of about a quarter of a second, which makes them somewhat unsuitable for real-time and interactive applications. Even so, satellite communications are especially useful in areas where land-based communications systems are not readily available or where satellite communications' immunity to problems (like accident or natural disaster) that would incapacitate terrestrial systems is needed.

Expanding LAN-to-Host Communications

Novell also provides tools for connecting LAN-based workstations to mainframe hosts. Since the processing power in a mainframe resides at the host, typically terminals or printers are attached rather than workstations.

In an IBM environment, these terminals, printers, and other devices are connected to the mainframe through a cluster controller. A cluster controller can be either Channel Attached (directly connected to the mainframe) or Remote (connected via a communications link to a Front End Processor that is Channel Attached).

In NetWare, LAN workstations use a software package (the NetWare 3270 LAN Workstation for PC, Macintosh, or OS/2 environments) to emulate IBM terminals and printers. These workstations are connected through the network to a 3270 Gateway (a network PC running 3270 gateway software). The gateway can be connected directly to a Channel Attached or Remote Cluster Controller or it can be directly connected to a Front End Processor. A connection to the cluster controller can be made via a 3270 emulator card or Token Interface Connection (Token Ring). A connection to the Front End Processor can be made via a Synchronous Data Link Control (SDLC) card. Each of the different configurations supports a certain number of simultaneous connections to the mainframe: A 3270 emulator card supports up to five sessions, SDLC supports up to 128 sessions, and a Token Interface Connection supports up to 254 sessions.

Alternatively, NetWare for SAA is Novell's new strategy for connecting to mainframe hosts. NetWare for SAA is an NLM that can be run on a file server or dedicated gateway PC running NetWare Runtime to support up to 508 simultaneous terminal, printer, or application connections to an IBM host. NetWare for SAA supports communication over Token-Ring, SDLC, and QLLC/X.25 to mainframe Front End Processors or directly to IBM AS/400 hosts. On the LAN side, any network architecture supported by NetWare can be used. NetWare-based workstations can access applications on an AS/400 transparently through NetWare for SAA.

Summary

In this chapter, we've introduced some of the options for expanding your NetWare LAN to support remote and extended area communications. Expanded LAN communications can include anything from an internet of connected LANs, to access to a LAN from remote sites, to Metropolitan Area Networks and Wide Area Networks.

This chapter gave a brief overview rather than a detailed exploration of communications (there are volumes dedicated purely to this subject). Before deciding on a particular communications solution, seek the advice of people experienced in network communications. Some of the better sources of information about what is currently available are your vendor, your communications company, and the manufacturers of communications products.

NetWare 3.12
Utilities Summary

Introduction

This summary explains the different types of utilities included in Net-Ware 3.12 and gives general information about each type. It also includes a summary of each utility's function. Where it is helpful or meaningful, the explanation is followed by examples of how to use the utility and some of its options. NetWare utilities fall into two general categories: workstation and server console.

Workstation Utilities

Workstation utilities are executed from a workstation logged into the network. Workstation utilities include both command-line and menu utilities. Two types of online help are available from the workstation:

- ▶ At the command line, type HELP and then the utility name to get syntax information and instructions for using the utility.

- ▶ From within a menu utility, highlight the item you want specific help for and press F1.

Using the Workstation Utilities

The sections below summarize the NetWare 3.12 workstation utilities and give examples of how to use them.

ACONSOLE

This utility is a communication program that controls a modem attached to a workstation. It must be on any workstation that you use to establish an asynchronous remote console connection with a server. It works with other remote console programs and loadable modules, especially the RS232 NLM, which must be loaded on the server you want to connect to.

To bring up the menu and establish an asynchronous connection, type:

ACONSOLE

ALLOW

Use this command-line utility to set or change the Inherited Rights Mask (IRM) for a directory or file. You can also see the current IRM settings that apply to any directory or file.

When you assign a right or a set of rights to a file or directory, only the rights you specify are allowed; all other rights are blocked. If you do not assign specific rights to a file or directory, all rights are allowed by default (unless they were blocked at a directory level above the one you are in).

For example, if you created a directory in volume SYS: called INFO to store informational files that you wanted users to read, but not copy or modify in any way, you would type:

ALLOW SYS:INFO R FS

This would allow users to see a list of the files in the INFO directory, and to open and read the files. It would not allow the files to be modified or deleted.

This utility has a total of ten rights that can be assigned at the command line.

ATOTAL

If you have turned on the accounting function for a server, you can use this command-line utility to see a total of all the accounting charges for the server.

You can use the SYSCON menu utility to determine the services you want to charge for and set charge rates for those services.

To see the total of all accounting charges on a server, type the following at the command line:

ATOTAL

A screen is displayed showing totals for connection time (in minutes), service requests, blocks read and written, and disk storage per day (in blocks).

This utility has no command-line options.

ATTACH

Use this command-line utility to attach to servers other than the one you are logged into. Attaching to a server makes its file system and resources available to you without requiring you to log out of your current server.

ATTACH is different from LOGIN in two ways:

- ▸ No login script is run.

- ▸ You can be attached to more than one server at a time.

After attaching, you can map a drive to the server and access files on that server. This saves you the time and effort of logging out of your current server and logging in to another server to access its resources. Attaching also means that you have the file systems of both servers available to you.

For example, if you are logged in to server SERV1 and you need to read a file located on SERV2, you can attach to that server using the following command:

ATTACH SERV2

After answering the prompts for your username and password for SERV2, you are attached to the server.

This utility has no command-line options.

BINDFIX

Use this command-line utility to repair the server bindery. If you have problems deleting or modifying users, passwords, or rights, you might need to run BINDFIX. During the repair processes, you are notified of the items being checked, and you'll be prompted for changes you want to make to the bindery.

To run the utility, notify all users to log out of the server. Then change to the SYS:SYSTEM directory and type:

BINDFIX

The utility locks the bindery files and makes a copy of the files (named with an .OLD extension). After the bindery is rebuilt, it re-opens the bindery so the server can be accessed again. If you have problems with the repaired bindery, see BINDREST.

This utility has no command-line options.

BINDREST

If you have run BINDFIX and the bindery fix failed, use the BINDREST command-line utility to restore the copy of the bindery that existed before BINDFIX was run (named with an .OLD extension). BINDREST deletes the new bindery files and replaces them with the .OLD files, so the bindery is restored to its previous condition.

To restore the old copies of the bindery files, make sure users are all logged out of the server. Then change to the SYS:SYSTEM directory and type:

BINDREST

The three bindery files with the .OLD extension replace the existing bindery files.

This utility has no command-line options.

CAPTURE

This command-line utility allows you to redirect print jobs so you can sprint to a network print queue from within network-unaware applications. You can also redirect screen displays to a queue, and redirect data to a network file. Additional options let you set up a print job to use a specific form (by name), specify the number of copies you want to print, etc. You do not need to use CAPTURE if you use a NetWare-aware application that is set up to send print jobs to queues. If you prefer, you can set your print options in PRINTCON instead of using CAPTURE at the command line.

To send a print job to a print queue named "Sales" and use a form named "Charts," you would use the following command:

CAPTURE Q=Sales J=Charts

To create a file and send data to it, use the "Create" option. For example, if you wanted to redirect data to a file in your current directory and name it "Myfile," you would type the following command at the prompt:

CAPTURE CR=MYFILE

If you wanted to create the file in another directory, you would type the full path to the file instead of only typing the file name.

Other options are available that are not shown here. The CAPTURE utility has a total of 21 command-line options.

CASTOFF

Use this command-line utility to stop network messages from being displayed on your workstation. Since messages "freeze" the workstation screen and any processes being run by the workstation until they are manually removed (by pressing Ctrl and ↵ simultaneously), it is a good idea to use CASTOFF when you don't want to be interrupted or when you run a process unattended on a workstation.

To stop a workstation from getting messages from other workstations, type:

CASTOFF

This utility has one option. If you want to stop a workstation from getting server messages as well as messages from other workstations, use the ALL option. Type:

CASTOFF ALL

To enable the workstation to get messages again, see CASTON.

CASTON

If you used CASTOFF to stop your workstation from getting network messages, you can enable it to get messages again using the CASTON command-line utility. At the workstation prompt, type:

CASTON

If you get a message on your workstation screen, it will not be cleared until you press Ctrl-↵.

This utility has no command-line options.

CHKDIR

This command-line utility lets you view a volume or directory's disk space limit, the amount of space currently used, and the amount of space still available.

If you are at the volume or directory you want to check, you simply type the command at the workstation prompt:

CHKDIR

If you are not at the volume or directory you want to check, enter the path leading to and including the directory or volume. For example, if you are logged in to SERV1 in volume APPS and you want to check the PUBS directory on volume SYS:, you would type the following command at the prompt:

CHKDIR SYS:PUBS

If you have a drive mapped to the directory you want to check, you can enter the drive letter after the command.

This utility has no command-line options.

CHKVOL

Use this command-line utility to view the following information about a volume:

- Total disk space allowed for the volume

- Amount of space currently used

- Amount of space being used by deleted (but not purged) files

- Total remaining space available for the volume

- Amount of user disk space unused in the volume's directories

If you are in the volume you want to check, you simply type the command at the workstation prompt:

CHKVOL

If you are not in the volume you want to check, enter the path leading to the volume. For example, if you are logged in to SERV1 in volume APPS and you want to check volume SYS:, you would type the following command at the prompt:

CHKVOL SYS:

If you have a drive mapped to the volume you want to check, you can enter the drive letter after the command.

You must be logged in or attached to a server whose volume you want to check. If you are not logged in to the server where the volume resides, see ATTACH.

This utility has no command-line options.

COLORPAL

You can use this menu utility to set the screen colors for NetWare menu utilities and menus you create for users (using the NMENU utility). When you change the default color settings, the changes apply to all utilities on your network. You can set colors for the following items:

- Active window border

- Active window text

- ► Alert window text and border
- ► Background and inactive windows
- ► Error window text and border
- ► Help window border
- ► Help window text
- ► Key description
- ► Key name
- ► Quick help area
- ► Screen header
- ► Selection bar

To bring up the main menu, type:

COLORPAL

DOSGEN

Use this command-line utility to set up workstations so they can boot from a server instead of a boot diskette or local drive. DOSGEN creates a boot file on the server and copies the workstation's boot files to this server file. The file, NET_DOS.SYS, is located in the server's SYS:LOGIN directory. You must run DOSGEN to create boot files for each workstation that will boot from the server. If you create multiple workstation boot files on the server, DOSGEN gives each set of boot files a unique name. This utility has no command-line options.

DSPACE

Use this menu utility to manage a server's disk space. You can limit the amount of disk space that can be used by directories and users. You can also attach to other file servers from within this utility.

To bring up the main menu, type the following command at the workstation prompt:

DSPACE

ENDCAP

This command-line utility frees your workstation's local print port (if you used the CAPTURE command to capture the port and send data to a network printer or file). If you did not use the "Timeout" or "Autoendcap" options with your CAPTURE command, you must use ENDCAP before your data will be printed or sent to a file.

For example, if you had captured printer port 2 and you wanted to free the port, you would type:

ENDCAP LOCAL=2

If you wanted to end the capture of printer port 2 and discard any data that you had sent to the port, you would type:

ENDCAP LOCAL=2 CANCEL

Other options are available that are not shown here. This utility has a total of five command-line options.

FCONSOLE

This menu utility allows network supervisors to manage the file server from a workstation. If you have supervisor rights, you can:

► Log in to or out of file servers.

► Broadcast console messages to workstations that are logged in to the server you are managing.

► View information about user connections to the server.

► View or change server status.

▸ Bring down a file server.

Users also have access to the utility, but they cannot do the same tasks that a supervisor can. Users can:

▸ Log in to or out of file servers.

▸ See server connection information.

To bring up the main menu, type the following command:

FCONSOLE

FILER

Use this menu utility to manage the NetWare file system. Almost any task that is required for the file system can be done from FILER. Following is a list of the types of tasks you can do with FILER.

▸ View information about files, directories, and volumes.

▸ Modify or view attributes of files and directories. (Attributes determine what operations can be done with a file or directory.)

▸ Modify or view rights and trustee assignments for files and directories.

▸ Search for files and directories according to a search pattern.

▸ Copy or move files and directories to another location in the file system.

▸ Delete files and directories from the file system.

To bring up the main menu, type the following command:

FILER

FLAG

This command-line utility allows you to view or modify a file's attributes. The attributes determine what operations can be done with the file.

You can also use FLAG options to view detailed information about a file or to change a file's owner. If you want to set attributes from a menu utility (which is easier to do), use FILER.

To run FLAG on a file, you must either be at its location in the directory structure, or you must include the complete path with the FLAG command. For example, if you are at the command line and you want to see the attributes of a file named ACCOUNTS in the SYS:PUBLIC directory, you would type:

FLAG SYS:PUBLIC\ACCOUNTS

To add or remove attributes, use the plus (+) or minus (−) characters. For example, to flag the file in the previous example so it can be read, but not modified or deleted, type:

FLAG SYS:PUBLIC\ACCOUNTS +RO

If the "Accounts" file's attribute is set to Read Only and you want to change it to Read Write, type:

FLAG SYS:PUBLIC\ACCOUNTS -RO +RW

Other attributes are available that are not shown here. There are a total of 16 file attributes that you can set.

FLAGDIR

This command-line utility allows you to view or modify a directory or subdirectory's attributes. The attributes determine what operations can be done with the directory.

You can also use FLAGDIR options to view detailed information about a directory or subdirectory, or to change its owner. If you want to set attributes from a menu utility (which is easier to do), use FILER.

To run flag on a directory or subdirectory, you must either be at its location in the file system, or you must include the complete path with the FLAGDIR command. For example, if you are at the command line and you want to see the attributes of a subdirectory named MARKET in the SYS:PUBLIC directory, you would type:

FLAGDIR SYS:PUBLIC\MARKET

If you want to make sure that the MARKET directory is not erased, even by users who have the "Erase" right, type:

FLAGDIR SYS:PUBLIC\MARKET DI

If you want to make sure that MARKET is not renamed, even by users who have the "Rename" right, type:

FLAGDIR SYS:PUBLIC\MARKET RI

Other attributes are available that are not shown here. There are a total of seven directory attributes that you can set.

GRANT

Use this command-line utility to give users rights to use directories and files in your file system. When a user has rights to a directory or file, he or she is a trustee of that directory or file. You can also grant rights using the FILER menu utility.

For example, suppose your server name is SERV1 and you have created a HOME directory in volume SYS: for each user. To give user Alan all rights in his HOME directory, type:

GRANT ALL FOR SERV1/SYS:HOME/ALAN TO ALAN

If you are in the directory where you want to assign rights, you do not need to enter the full path to the directory. In the example above, you would move to the ALAN directory and type:

GRANT ALL TO ALAN

If you have a directory named ACCOUNTS that contains information that you want Alan to be able to read, but you do not want him to delete or modify any information, you would give him the "Read" trustee right. Type:

GRANT R TO USER ALAN

Other trustee rights are available that are not shown here. There are a total of ten trustee rights that you can assign to users.

LISTDIR

This option allows you to see information about subdirectories in the directory where you run the utility. You can see a list of all subdirectories and the creation date, Inherited Rights Mask, and your effective rights for each subdirectory.

If you are in the directory whose subdirectories you want to view, you need only type the command and the options you want. If you are not in the directory, you must enter the complete path (including the volume) to the directory.

For example, to see your effective rights to the subdirectories in directory MARKET, type:

LISTDIR MARKET /E

If you want to see all the available information for MARKET, type:

LISTDIR /A

You will see the creation dates, IRMs, and your effective rights for each of the subdirectories in directory MARKET.

Other options are available that are not shown here. This utility has a total of five command-line options.

LOGIN

This command-line utility allows you to log in to a NetWare server and run the login scripts available to you (System and User). For example, to log in to server "Serv1" as user Fred, type:

LOGIN SERV1/FRED

After you enter a valid password, you are logged in to "Serv1." You can only be logged in to one server at a time, for example, if you log in to another server, you will be logged out of Serv1. If you need resources from more than one server, see ATTACH.

LOGOUT

Use this utility to log out of a server (or all servers) that you are attached to.

For example, if you want to end your network session and log out of all servers, type:

LOGOUT

If you are attached to "Serv1," "Serv2," and "Serv3," and you want to log out of "Serv1" only, type:

LOGOUT SERV1

Your connections to other servers will not be affected. The LOGOUT utility has no additional command-line options.

MAKEUSER

Use this menu utility to automate the process of creating and deleting users and user accounts. If you create and delete user accounts on a regular basis, you can save time by using this utility. MAKEUSER lets you create, edit, or process a USR file, which is a script file made up of key words that you use to create or delete users and set up user accounts. The key words are executed (like commands in a batch file) when MAKEUSER processes the file.

MAP

This command-line utility allows you to view, create, or change network and search drive mappings. You can assign a total of 26 mappings, including network, search, and local drives.

- ▸ A local drive mapping points to a hardware device, such as a hard drive in a workstation.

- ▸ A network drive mapping points to a directory or file in the Net-Ware file system.

- ▸ A search drive also points to a directory or file. The difference is that the operating system automatically scans search drives for files when the files are not found in the current drive. This capability allows a user working in one directory to access application or data files located in a different directory. It is not necessary to move to the directory containing the needed file.

If you want to see a list of all your drive mappings, type:

MAP

If you are not sure what drive letters you have assigned and you do not want to overwrite any of your existing mappings, you can assign the next available drive letter to a new mapping. To assign the next available drive letter to the "Accounts" directory (located in SERV1/SYS:PUBLIC), type:

MAP N SERV1/SYS:PUBLIC/ACCOUNTS

To assign the drive letter "G" to the same directory instead of assigning it to the next available drive letter, type:

MAP G:=SERV1/SYS:PUBLIC/ACCOUNTS

To map your fourth search drive to the applications subdirectory in SYS:SYSTEM, type:

MAP S4:=SYS:SYSTEM/APPS

This map command assigns the search drive letter "W" (the fourth letter from the end of the alphabet) to the applications directory.

Other options are available that are not shown here. The MAP utility has a total of eight command-line options.

MIGRATE

Use this menu utility to upgrade a NetWare v2.x server to NetWare v3.x. (You do not need this utility to upgrade from one version of v3.x to another.) The utility lets you upgrade the server operating system and transfer your existing bindery objects, rights and trustee assignments.

To bring up the main menu and start the upgrade process, type:

    MIGRATE

NCOPY

This command-line utility allows you to copy files and directories from one location on the network to another and to specify how they are copied.

You can use NCOPY options to specify if you want extended attributes and name space information retained, whether to copy subdirectories of a directory, and other options.

For example, to copy the ACCOUNTS directory with its files and sub-directories from SYS:SYSTEM/ACCOUNTS to network drive G, type:

    NCOPY SYS:SYSTEM/ACCOUNTS TO G: /S

Typing *TO* in an NCOPY command is optional. To copy a file named SALES in the directory shown in the previous example to your local drive and rename the file SALES2, type:

    NCOPY SYS:SYSTEM/ACCOUNTS/SALES TO C: SALES2

If you are in the ACCOUNTS subdirectory when you copy the SALES file, you do not need to enter the complete path name. You only need to type the file name. For example,

NCOPY SALES TO C:

Other options are available that are not shown here. The NCOPY utility has a total of eight command-line options.

NDIR

This commandline utility provides a powerful search function to help you find and sort information about files and directories in your file system. The following types of options are available:

- display options
- format options
- sort options
- attribute options
- restriction options

These options are discussed below.

Display options

Display options allow you to view specific volume information, including volume space limitations. You can also display only directories, only files, or only subdirectories. For example, to see a list of directories on drive G:, type:

NDIR *.* /DO

There are nine display options available for NDIR.

Format Options

Format options allow you to view specific information about files and directories. You can display update, archive, access, and create dates, as well as name space and rights information. For example, to see a summary of the Inherited Rights Filter, effective rights, and attributes for all files in your current directory, type:

NDIR *.* /R

If you are not in the directory you want information about, you will need to enter the complete path to the files. There are five display options available for NDIR.

Sort Options

Sort options are used to view files and directories according to criteria you specify, such as owner name, size, creation date, and file size. For example, to sort files in your current directory by date last accessed, from earliest to latest, type:

NDIR *.* /SORT CR

There are seven sort options available for NDIR.

Attribute Options

Attribute options allow you to sort file and directory information by attribute assignment. You can search for all files flagged Read Only or Read Write, or you can search for all files that have been compressed or migrated. For example, to search for all files in the directory SYS:PUBLIC/AC-COUNTS that are marked Execute Only, type:

NDIR SYS:PUBLIC/ACCOUNTS/*.* /X

There are 14 attribute options, including status flags.

Restriction Options

Restriction options allow you to search for files within owner, size, or date restrictions that you set. You can also use "NOT" to view a list of all files except those within the specified limits. For example, if you want to view a list of all files except those created by user Ben in the current directory, type:

NDIR *.* /OW NOT EQ BEN

To view a list of all files created by Ben, you would enter the same command without "NOT."

There are six restriction options available for NDIR.

NETBIOS

Use this command-line utility to see if NETBIOS is loaded and what interrupts it is using. You can also unload NETBIOS with this command.

For example, if you want to see information, type:

NETBIOS I

To unload NETBIOS, type:

NETBIOS U

NMENU

This command-line utility executes menu utilities created for workstation users. To start up a menu, you can add the command to exit to a menu screen or to a user's login script. A menu can also be invoked from a workstation command line. For example, if you create a menu program called "Wordprocessing," a user would type the following command to bring up the Main menu:

NMENU WORDPROCESSING

If you want a menu to appear on a user's screen whenever he or she logs in, put the following command at the end of the user's login script:

EXIT "NMENU WORDPROCESSING"

NPRINT

You can use this command-line utility to print a file that has been formatted by an application for a specific printer. You can also use the utility and its options to set up and print an ASCII file. NPRINT options override default print queue and print job configuration settings.

If you have existing print job configuration settings that you want to use with NPRINT, you can specify that you want to use them for the job you are sending. For example, to print a sales report file and use a print job configuration named "Report," type:

NPRINT SYS:SALES/SALES.RPT J=REPORT

Other options are available that are not shown here. The NPRINT utility has a total of 16 command-line options.

NVER

Use this command-line utility to see workstation, server, OS/2 Requester, and driver version information. To see version information for these items on your network, simply type

NVER

This utility has only two options: Help and Continuous (which causes information on the screen to scroll without pausing).

PAUDIT

If you have turned on accounting for a server, all of the server events are entered into a file called NET$ACCT.DAT. PAUDIT lets you see the contents of this audit file. To see the file, type:

PAUDIT

This utility has only one option. If you do not want the utility to pause after each screen, type /C after the utility name. This will cause the information to scroll continuously.

PCONSOLE

Use this menu utility to set up and manage print queues and print servers on your network. Most printing setup and management tasks can be done from PCONSOLE. Here is a list of the types of tasks you can do with PCONSOLE.

- ▸ Create, delete, modify, and monitor print queues.
- ▸ Assign print queue operators and users.
- ▸ Manage print queue assignments to print servers.
- ▸ Define and manage print job configurations.
- ▸ Create, delete, modify, and monitor print servers.
- ▸ Configure printers and make print server assignments.

To bring up the main menu, type the following command at the workstation prompt:

PCONSOLE

PRINTCON

Use this menu utility to manage print job configurations on your network. You can create new configurations, and view or modify configurations that you have already set up. You can also specify default configurations to be used with print jobs sent using CAPTURE, NPRINT, or PCONSOLE.

To bring up the main menu, type the following command at the workstation prompt:

    PRINTCON

PRINTDEF

This menu utility allows you to create, view, or modify printer definitions. You can also use it to create and modify printer forms to use as defaults for CAPTURE, NPRINT, and PCONSOLE. If you have an existing printer definition that you want to use for another printer, you can import the definition to the new printer, saving you the time it would take to set up a definition for each printer.

To bring up the main menu, type the following command at the workstation prompt:

    PRINTDEF

PSC

Use this utility to control printers and print servers from the command line. You can also use it to view network printer information.

For example, to display the status of the printers on a print server named PSERV1, type:

    PSC PS=PSERV1 /STAT

To remove a printer named PRINT1 from a list of network printers, type:

    PSC P=PRINT1 /PRI

Other options are available that are not shown here. The PSC utility has a total of 13 command-line options.

PSERVER

If you installed print services on a workstation to create a dedicated print server, you can run this executable file to see information about printers assigned to the print server.

For example, if you create a print server named "Pserv1" and assign printers to it, you can see a print server screen showing information about all the assigned printers by typing:

PSERVER PSERV1

If you want to install a print server on a file server, see PSERVER in the Server Console Utilities section for information about the PSERVER.NLM.

PURGE

This command-line utility allows you to remove deleted files from your file system. Since deleted files are saved on a server's hard disk, you might want to purge the files to free disk space. PURGE removes deleted files from the path you specify. Using PURGE with the "All" option removes deleted files from subdirectories under a directory you specify.

For example, if you want to purge deleted files from the directory "Accounts" and all of its subdirectories, move to the directory and type

PURGE *.* /A

This utility has only two command-line options: All and Help.

RCONSOLE

This command-line utility allows you to manage NetWare servers from a workstation. RCONSOLE establishes a connection to the server you choose, turning the workstation or PC into a virtual server console. You can then manage the server as if you were at the console.

RCONSOLE will not work unless the NetWare Loadable Modules (NLMs) that enable remote sessions are loaded on the server. This utility has no command-line options.

REMOVE

This command-line utility allows you to remove all of a user or group's trustee assignments from a directory or file by removing the name from its trustee list. (If you want to use a menu utility to modify trustee rights, see SYSCON. Generally menu utilities are easier to use when modifying network security.)

For example, if user FRED moved from the Accounting department to a new job and you did not want him to have access to your department's directory, you would move to the ACCTG directory and type:

REMOVE FRED FROM ACCTG

If you are not in the directory where you want to change the trustee rights, you must enter the complete path to the directory. To remove FRED's rights in this case, you would type:

REMOVE FRED FROM SERV1/SYS:ACCTG

If you want to take a right away from a user, but you don't want the user removed from the trustee list, see REVOKE.

RENDIR

This command-line utility allows you to rename a directory. Be careful when renaming directories, because it could affect your drive mappings. If you have mapped drives to a directory whose name is changed, you will need to change mappings to the new name.

To change a directory named "SALES" to "NY_SALES," move to the directory and type:

RENDIR :/ NY_SALES

The colon and backslash characters represent your current drive.

There are no command-line options, with the exception of "Help" available for RENDIR.

REVOKE

This utility allows you to remove a specific right of a user or group without removing the user or group's name from the directory or file's trustee list. (If you want to remove the name from the trustee list entirely, see REMOVE.)

For example, if the group "Sales" has Read, Write and Erase rights to the directory SYS:SALES/APPS and you decide that you don't want them to delete any of the files in the subdirectory, you can revoke the Erase right by moving to that subdirectory and typing:

REVOKE E FROM SALES

If you are not at the subdirectory where you are revoking rights, you must enter the entire path to that location. To use the example above, you would type:

REVOKE E FOR SYS:SALES/APPS FROM SALES

If you prefer to modify rights using a menu interface, see SYSCON.

RIGHTS

You can use this command-line utility to see what rights you have in a file, directory, or volume. You will see your effective rights, which take into account trustee assignments, Inherited Rights Filter settings, and in some cases, rights you have inherited from directories above the one you are checking. In other words, you will see the sum of all of your rights.

For example, to see your rights to the directory ACCNTG move to the directory and type:

RIGHTS

If you are in a different location in the file system than the volume or directory that you want to check, enter the complete path to the volume or directory. For example, to see your rights to SYS:SALES/ACCNTG from another directory, type:

RIGHTS SYS:SALES/ACCNTG

RPRINTER

This executable utility allows you to use a printer attached to a workstation as a network printer. When RPRINTER is loaded, the printer can receive jobs from a print server.

To bring up the main menu and connect the printer to the network, type:

RPRINTER

This utility has two options. You can type -r after the command to remove the printer from the network, and you can type -s after the command to see the remote printer's status.

SALVAGE

This menu utility allows you to recover files that have been deleted. When you delete a directory, it is saved for a time in a directory called DELETED.SAV. When you delete a file, it is saved in the directory it was deleted from. In either case, you can use SALVAGE to view lists of deleted files and directories, making it easy to find the data you want to recover.

To bring up the main menu, type:

SALVAGE

SECURITY

Supervisors can use this command-line utility to check the security of their networks. SECURITY can alert you to potential problems by checking user accounts for:

▸ No password assigned.

▶ Passwords that are easy to guess (passwords match usernames, are less than five characters long, are not changed for an extended period of time, etc.).

▶ Supervisor security equivalence.

▶ Rights granted at the root directory of a volume.

▶ No login script (which would allow an intruder to create one).

▶ Excessive rights in the SYSTEM, PUBLIC, LOGIN, or MAIL directories in volume SYS:.

Security problems are displayed on the screen as they are discovered. If you want to stop the screen from scrolling, you can do so by pressing the Ctrl and S keys simultaneously. Any key will start the information scrolling again. You can also send the information to a file using the DOS redirector (>) command.

SEND

This command-line utility allows you to send messages to other users on the network.

For example, to send a message to members of the Sales group on your network, type:

SEND "Remember our meeting today at 2:00" TO SALES

All users in the group will receive the message, unless users have used the CASTOFF utility to accept no messages at their workstations.

This utility has no command-line options.

SESSION

This menu utility gives users an easy way to do normal network tasks without having to remember command-line utility syntaxes and options.

Use SESSION to:

- ▶ Attach to other file servers.

- ▶ Log out of a specific file server.

- ▶ Create, delete, and change your drive mappings.

- ▶ See a list of groups on a server.

- ▶ Send messages to a group or another user.

- ▶ Change to another server, or to another drive you have mapped.

SETPASS

Use this command-line utility to change your password. For example, to change your password, type:

SETPASS

You will be prompted to enter your current password first, then you will be asked to enter the new password. If you are attached to other servers and your password is the same on the servers, you can change those passwords as well.

If you need to change another user's password, you must enter the username. For example, to change user FRED's password, type:

SETPASS FRED

Of course, you must know Fred's current password before you will be allowed to change it.

This utility has no command-line options available.

SETTTS

Use this command-line utility to view and set the physical and logical record locks for the Transaction Tracking System (TTS), which protects database applications from corruption by backing out incomplete transactions in case of a hardware or software failure.

Valid TTS values are 0 to 254. The number you set determines how many record locks will be ignored before a transaction is tracked. For example, if you set the value at 1, TTS tracks every transaction. The settings are reset to zero whenever you log out or turn off your workstation.

For example, if you want to see your current TTS settings, type:

SETTTS

If you want to change your settings, just enter the new ones. For example, to set the logical and physical levels to 4, type:

SETTTS 4 4

There are no other options are available for this utility.

SLIST

Use this utility to see a list of all available file servers on the network. You also see each server's network number, node address, and status. To see the list, type:

SLIST

You can also specify if you only want to see information about a specific server. For example, if you want to see the network number and node address of SERV1, type

SLIST SERV1

SMODE

This command-line utility allows you to specify search instructions for executable files. Normally, the default works best for executable file search modes. However, if you have a specific data file that contains instructions, you can specify a different search mode for the executable file that needs those instructions.

To see a list of search mode settings for all executable files in a directory, move to the directory and type:

SMODE

If you want to see the search mode setting for a specific executable file, type the file name after the command. For example, to see the search mode setting for all of the executable files in the APPS directory in volume SYS:, type:

SMODE SYS:APPS

This command also shows you the search-mode settings for subdirectories in APPS.

SYSCON

Use this menu utility to manage the file servers on your network. Most supervisor tasks required to maintain network file servers, security, and users can be done with this utility. You can:

▸ Set up accounting and specify charge rates for services.

▸ View information about the type of NetWare running on a server.

▸ Create and manage groups (assign trustee rights, group members, etc.).

▸ Create workgroup managers and console operators.

▸ Create and manage users.

▸ Assign login time restrictions and user account restrictions.

▸ Create and manage system and user login scripts.

▸ Assign and manage file system rights.

To start the utility and bring up the main menu, type:

SYSCON

SYSTIME

This command-line utility allows you to set your workstation's date and time to match the date and time of a server.

For example, if you want to set your workstation's date and time with those on your default server, type:

SYSTIME

To set your workstation's date and time with a server named SERV1, type:

SYSTIME SERV1

These options are the only ones available for SYSTIME, with the exception of the Help option.

TLIST

This command-line utility allows you to see who has trustee rights to a directory, subdirectory, or file. You will see all users and groups who have rights, and a list of the trustee rights each user or group has been given.

For example, if you want to see who has rights to the "Accts" directory in volume SYS:, move to the directory and type:

TLIST

If you are not in the directory where you want to see the rights list, you must enter the complete path. In the example above, if you were not in the "Accts" directory, you would type:

TLIST SYS:ACCTS

USERDEF

This menu utility allows you to apply a template when you create users, giving them a default set of rights and properties on the server. You can apply the template provided, or you can create custom templates. The advantage of using this utility when you create users is that they are automatically set up with a simple user login script, a home directory, a password, and a print job configuration. You can also apply account and disk space restrictions if you want to.

To bring up the main menu, type:

USERDEF

USERLIST

Use this command-line utility to view information about the objects that are attached to the server. You can see:

► Users currently logged in to the file server

► Connection number, network address, and node address for each user

► Each user's login time

For example, to see user, connection number, and login time information for a server, type:

USERLIST

If you also want to see the network and node addresses of the users, type:

USERLIST /A

There are two other options. The /O option lets you see the type of object at each connection, and the /C option scrolls information continuously on the screen.

VERSION

Use this command-line utility to check the version of any NetWare Loadable Module (NLM) or utility on a server.

For example, to see the version of SYSCON that you are using, move to the directory where the file is stored and type:

VERSION SYSCON

If you are in a different location in the file system, you must type the complete path to the utility instead of entering only the utility name.

VOLINFO

Use this menu utility to see information about the volumes on a server. The information is updated regularly. You can see a list of all the volumes mounted on a server, and the storage capacity and number of directory entries allowed for each volume.

To bring up the main menu, type:

VOLINFO

WHOAMI

Use this utility to see connection information. You can see information such as groups you belong to, effective rights and security equivalences, etc.

For example, if you are logged in to a server named SERV1 and you want to see a list of groups you belong to, type:

WHOAMI SERV1 /G

To see all information available about your connection on this server, type:

WHOAMI SERV1 /ALL

Other options are available that are not shown here. This utility has a total of eight command-line options.

WSUPDATE

This command-line utility allows you to search for and update worksta-tion files in multiple directories or subdirectories. This utility is useful if you need to update files on many workstations, since you are not required to go to each station and manually update files.

For example, if you have a new NET3.COM file in your SYS:PUBLIC/WORK file and you want to search all workstation local drives and copy the new file over existing ones, type:

> WSUPDATE SYS:PUBLIC\WORK\NET3.COM /LOCAL /C

Sometimes workstation and executable files are flagged Read Only to protect them from being deleted or overwritten. You can still update the files using WSUPDATE.

For example, if the NET3.COM files in the previous example were marked Read Only, you would add another option to the command. The additional option is shown in the command below:

> WSUPDATE SYS:PUBLIC\WORK\NET3.COM /LOCAL /C /O

To search all mapped drives instead of only local drives, you would use the All option instead of the Local option.

Server Utilities

Server utilities are used to manage the network from the NetWare server console.

Server utility commands are entered at the console prompt, or you can execute them at a workstation if you have set up remote console software on your workstation and server. When you start a remote console session on your workstation, your keyboard and screen become the server console and monitor. You can do most server management tasks from a remote console, with the exception of file and directory copying. For security reasons, you can copy files to, but not from, a server.

Server utilities consist of console commands (command-line and menu utilities) and NetWare Loadable Modules (NLMs).

CONSOLE COMMANDS

Use these commands to perform tasks such as controlling how server resources are used by workstations, changing how server memory is allocated, and monitoring server performance and resource use.

NETWARE LOADABLE MODULES

NLMs link resources into the server operating system. For example, LAN and disk drivers are linked to the server operating system (OS) when they are loaded at the server console. You can also link in OS support for name spaces for Macintosh and OS/2 file systems. Some server management applications also link into the OS as loadable modules.

Using The Server Utilities

The sections below summarize the NetWare 3.12 server utilities and give examples of how to use them.

ABORT REMIRROR

If you have mirrored disks in your server, you must unmirror them if you make changes to a disk, such as changing the size of a disk partition. After making necessary changes, you can reset mirroring and synchronize the data on the changed partition by remirroring it with the secondary partition. If, for some reason, you decide to stop the remirroring process, you will use this command.

For example, if you are remirroring logical partition number three and you want to abort the process, type:

    ABORT REMIRROR 3

ADD NAME SPACE

In order to store non-DOS files on a volume, the volume must be set up to support the name space required for the files. You do this by loading the name space NLM on the server and then adding support for that name space to the volume where the files will be stored.

For example, if you want to store Macintosh files on volume SYS:, you would load the MAC name space (using the LOAD command) on to the server. After the name space is linked into the operating system, type the following command at the console prompt:

ADD NAME SPACE MAC TO SYS

If you want to see a list of the name spaces you have loaded on a server, type:

ADD NAME SPACE

BIND

When you install a network board in a server, the board or its driver must be bound to the protocol being used to send packets across the network. When you install NetWare or add boards or drivers using INSTALL.NLM, the system defaults to binding the IPX protocol.

Most of the time you will not need to enter the commands to LOAD drivers and BIND a protocol to them, since INSTALL adds the applicable commands and options to the server's startup file (AUTOEXEC.NCF) for you. However, you might want to use other protocols on the network. If so, you can edit the .NCF file and add the necessary commands so the drivers and protocol will be linked automatically whenever the server is booted.

For example, to bind a protocol at the command line and accept the server default settings (options), type the following command at the console prompt:

BIND IPX TO NE2000

If you do not want to accept the default settings, you can specify options in the BIND command. There are six driver parameters and one protocol parameter. Additional parameters might be specified in the documentation that came with your network board.

BROADCAST

This command allows you to send a message from the server console to workstations on the network. You can send messages to all users (workstations) who are logged in, or you can send a message to a specific user, group, or workstation connection number.

For example, if you want to bring down the server and you need to notify all users so they can close their files and log out, type:

```
BROADCAST "Server going down in 5 minutes. Please
log out."
```

If you want to send a message to a specific group, add the name of the group to the end of the command. For example, to notify the Sales group of a department meeting, type:

```
BROADCAST "Sales meeting in 20 minutes. See you there."
TO SALES
```

CDROM

This NLM allows you to use a CD-ROM disk as a read-only volume on your server. After this module is loaded, you can mount the volume represented by the CD-ROM disk and access the information stored there.

For example, to load volume INFO from the console, first make sure the CD-ROM module is loaded, and then type:

```
CD MOUNT INFO
```

For more information about how to load the module, see LOAD.

CLEAR STATION

If a workstation crashes while it is logged into a server, you can use this utility at the console command line to clear the workstation's connection to the server. Clearing the connection closes all open files on the workstation and erases workstation information stored on the server's internal tables.

To use this command at the console prompt, you need to know the workstation's connection number. If you do not know the number, it is easier to clear the connection using MONITOR, which gives you a list of connections to choose from.

For example, if a workstation is attached to the server as connection number 18, you clear it by typing:

CLEAR STATION 18

CLIB

This module is a C Interface Library. It provides other loadable modules with an interface to the operating system, so that each NLM does not need its own built-in library. CLIB is usually linked to the operating system at run time.

CLIB and STREAMS work together, so both must be linked to the operating system before dependent NLMs can be loaded.

Most NLMs that depend on CLIB and STREAMS will look for them at load time. If the CLIB and STREAMS are not found, the module will autoload them before it loads itself.

Since STREAMS and CLIB are required for many other modules to run, they have probably already been loaded on your server. If they have not, and you want to be sure they are loaded each time the server is booted, consider adding them to an .NCF startup file.

CLIB has no options or parameters available. To load it at the command line, type:

LOAD CLIB

If you need more information about loading modules, see LOAD.

CLS

Use this utility to clear information, messages, etc., from the server console screen. At the console prompt, type:

CLS

This command does the same thing as the OFF command.

CONFIG

Use this utility at the console prompt to see configuration information about the server. You can see the following information:

- ► Server name
- ► Server internal network number
- ► LAN drivers loaded
- ► Network board information such as node address, frame type, network number, and communication protocol

To see configuration information about the server, type:

    CONFIG

DISABLE LOGIN

Use this utility if you want to prevent users from logging in to a server. If you must make changes or repairs to the server that affect its setup files (requiring you to reboot the server to use the new settings), or if you want to back up server information or load an application, you will probably want to disable user logins until you are finished.

If users are already logged in to the server when you disable logins, they are not affected. If you want all users to log out, you will need to send a BROADCAST message to all logged in users and ask them to do so.

To disable logins to the server, simply type the command at the console prompt. This utility has no options available.

    DISABLE LOGIN

When you want to allow users to log in again, you must type the ENABLE LOGIN utility at the console.

DISABLE TTS

Use this command if you have used ENABLE TTS to enable transaction tracking on the server. In most cases, the server will disable TTS if it is necessary. For example, TTS will be disabled if the server runs out of memory or if the SYS volume gets full (the SYS volume is used as the back-out volume by TTS).

However, if you need to free up NetWare server memory that is being used by TTS, you can disable it yourself at the console prompt.

To disable TTS at the console, type the command at the console prompt. This utility has no options available.

DISABLE TTS

To enable TTS after you have disabled it, you will need to type ENABLE TTS at the console prompt. TTS is also re-enabled automatically if you reboot the server.

DISKSET

Use this utility when you install a disk subsystem or replace a hard disk on a server, before you bring up or reboot the server.

DISKSET adds identification and configuration information about the new hard disk or subsystem on the host bus adapter's EEPROM chip. It also formats external hard disks when you add them to your disk subsystem so they can communicate with the server through the adapter.

DISKSET

If you are not in the directory where DISKSET is stored, you will need to type the complete path to the file instead of only typing the utility name.

DISMOUNT

This utility allows you to unload a volume from the server. When you dismount a volume, it is cleared from server memory.

You might want to dismount a volume if you need to repair it (using VREPAIR), or if you want to change or upgrade a disk driver without bringing down the entire server. You can also free up server memory if the server is running slowly by dismounting volumes that are not used very often.

If you are using the INSTALL loadable module, you can select and unload the volume you want to dismount. If you are at the console prompt, you type the command and the name of the volume you want to dismount.

For example, if you were having problems with volume SYS: and you wanted to run VREPAIR to see if it would find and solve your problem, you would send a message to anyone who might be logged in and using the volume and ask them to log out. Then you would type:

DISMOUNT SYS

When you want to reload the volume and make it available again, use the MOUNT command at the console prompt.

DISPLAY NETWORKS

Use this utility if you have a server set up as a router and you want to see all the networks available to the router. You can also see the network number of the cabling system for each available network.

To see the available networks for your router, type this command at the router's console prompt:

DISPLAY NETWORKS

This utility has no options available.

DISPLAY SERVERS

Use this utility if you have a server set up as a router and you want to see all the servers available to the router. To see the available servers, type this command at the router's console prompt:

DISPLAY SERVERS

This utility has no options available.

DOWN

This utility allows you to bring down the server in a way that protects data integrity. When you use this command, it ensures that all cache buffers are written to disk and files are closed before services are terminated.

Before you bring down a server, you might also want to use the BROAD-CAST command from the console to notify users who are logged in, and to allow them to save their work, close open files, and log out. Of course, if you just bring down the server, the files will be closed and the users logged out, so nothing will be corrupted, but it is better to let users know beforehand so they can finish whatever they are working on.

To bring down a server, all you have to do is type the following command at the console prompt:

DOWN

When you are ready to bring the server back up again, you must type "SERVER" at the DOS prompt to execute the SERVER.EXE file.

EDIT

Use this NLM to create or edit text files on the server, such as the server .NCF files. You can edit files on either DOS or NetWare partitions. EDIT does have one limitation; you can only edit text files that are smaller than 8 KB. However, most server text files are smaller than this.

To use this module, you simply load it at the console prompt and then specify the name of the file you want to edit.

ENABLE LOGIN

Use this utility if you disabled logins for the server and you are ready to reenable them. You will only need to use this command if you are not rebooting the server after disabling logins, because logins are automatically enabled whenever the server is booted.

To enable logins, type the following command at the console prompt:

ENABLE LOGIN

To find out about disabling server logins, see DISABLE LOGIN.

ENABLE TTS

Use this utility if you disabled TTS on the server using DISABLE TTS, or if it was disabled automatically by the operating system because of lack of memory or volume disk space.

You will only need to use this utility if you are not rebooting the server after TTS is disabled, because TTS is automatically enabled whenever the server is booted.

When you are ready to re-enable TTS, type the following command at the console prompt:

ENABLE TTS

This utility has no options. To find out about disabling TTS on a server, see DISABLE TTS.

EXIT

This utility takes you back to DOS after you bring down a server. From there you can access DOS files if you want to. You also start NetWare on the server from this location, by typing SERVER.

If you removed DOS from the server earlier, to free up the space, EXIT will not take you to the DOS level; it reboots the server.

For example, if you bring down a server and you need to access utilities on the DOS partition, type the following command at the console prompt:

EXIT

This utility has no options available.

INSTALL

This NLM is one of the most often used modules for managing, maintaining, and updating NetWare servers. The NLM is structured like a menu utility, which makes it easy to use. You can do the following types of tasks with INSTALL:

- ▸ Create, delete, and manage disk partitions on the server, including DOS partitions

- ▸ Install NetWare (including the operating system and NetWare Directory Services)

- ▸ Load and unload disk and LAN drivers

- ▸ Create, delete, and manage NetWare volumes on the server's hard disk(s)

- ▸ Add, remove, mirror, unmirror, check, and repair hard disks

- ▸ Modify server startup and configuration files (.NCF files)

- ▸ Install additional products (besides NetWare) on the server

Before you can use INSTALL to do any of these tasks, make sure it is loaded on the server. Sometimes NLMs are unloaded by network supervisors if the server's response time is slow and memory or disk spaces need to be freed for other processes. If you need information about loading the module, see LOAD.

After INSTALL is loaded on the server, type the following command at the console prompt:

    INSTALL

INSTALL has only one option. If you want to load INSTALL without the help screens (and save 16 KB of memory), type:

    INSTALL NH

IPXS

This NLM must be loaded on your server before many other NLMs you might load. It supports the NetWare standard IPX protocol. Since other modules depend on this NLM, it should be loaded automatically whenever the server is booted.

To autoload the NLM, simply place the command to load it in a server startup (.NCF) file. If you need more information about using the load command for NLMs, see LOAD.

KEYB

This NLM allows you to use keyboard types on the server other than U.S. English. When you load KEYB, a list of valid keyboard types appears on the console screen. Five types are supported: English (U.S.), French, German, Italian, and Spanish.

For example, to load KEYB and use the German keyboard, type:

LOAD KEYB GERMAN

LIST DEVICES

This utility gives you a list of all devices, such as tape, disk, and optical disk or other storage device, attached to the server. From the console prompt, type:

LIST DEVICES

LOAD

This command is used with all loadable modules to link the modules to the NetWare operating system. To use a module, it must first be loaded. The following types of modules are loaded with this command:

▸ Disk drivers

▸ LAN drivers

- ▸ Name space modules

- ▸ NetWare Loadable Modules (NLMs)

You can use LOAD to load commands at the console prompt, or you can put load commands in one of the server start-up (.NCF) files for modules that you want loaded automatically whenever the server is booted.

For example, to load a LAN driver, you would place the following command in an .NCF file (since you'll need the driver to load whenever the server is booted):

LOAD NE2000

If you use LOAD with only the module name, the operating system assumes the module is in the default directory (where it was copied during installation). If a module is moved to a different directory, you must enter the complete directory path to the module.

MAGAZINE

Use this utility at the console prompt after being prompted to insert or remove a media magazine from the server. The server automatically prompts you to insert or remove a magazine when applicable, but you must enter an option to notify the server of your action. Four options are available. They are:

- ▸ Removed

- ▸ Not removed

- ▸ Inserted

- ▸ Not inserted

Type one of these options after the MAGAZINE command at the console prompt. For example, if you were prompted to insert a magazine, you would insert it and then type:

> MAGAZINE INSERTED

If you were prompted to insert a magazine and you decided not to insert it, you would type:

> MAGAZINE NOT INSERTED

MATHLIB

If your server has a math coprocessor chip, you need to load this NLM to link it to the operating system. (If it does not, you must load MATHLIBC.)

This module cannot run without the CLIB and STREAMS modules. Most modules that depend on STREAMS and CLIB will autoload them if the modules are not linked to the operating system when the NLM tries to load.

Since STREAMS, CLIB, and either MATHLIB or MATHLIBC are required for many other modules to run, they have probably already been loaded on your server. If they are not, and you want to be sure they are loaded each time the server is booted, consider adding them to an .NCF startup file.

To load MATHLIB, type the following command at the server console:

> LOAD MATHLIB

This module has no parameters or options available. If you need more information about loading modules, see LOAD.

MATHLIBC

If your server does not have a math coprocessor chip, you need to load this NLM. (If it does, you must load MATHLIB.)

This module also relies on the CLIB and STREAMS modules. Most modules that depend on STREAMS and CLIB will autoload them if the modules are not linked to the operating system when the NLM tries to load.

Since STREAMS, CLIB, and either MATHLIB or MATHLIBC are required for many other modules to run, they have probably already been loaded on your server. If they are not, and you want to be sure they are loaded each time the server is booted, consider adding them to an .NCF startup file.

To load MATHLIBC, type the following command at the server console:

LOAD MATHLIBC

This module has no parameters or options available. If you need more information about loading modules, see LOAD.

MEDIA

Use this utility at the console prompt after being prompted to insert or remove media from the server. The server automatically prompts you to insert or remove media when applicable, but you must enter a media option to notify the server of your action. Four options are available. They are:

- ► Removed

- ► Not removed

- ► Inserted

- ► Not inserted

Type one of the options after the MEDIA command at the console prompt. For example, if you were prompted to insert media, you would insert it and then type:

MEDIA INSERTED

If you were prompted to insert media and you decided not to insert it, you would type:

MEDIA NOT INSERTED

MEMORY

Use this command to see how much of the server's installed memory that the operating system can use. This command gives you information only. To see this information, type the following command at the console prompt:

MEMORY

MIRROR STATUS

Use this command to see a list of all the server's partitions. You will also see information about the mirrored status of each partition. This command gives you information only. To see this information, type the following command at the console prompt:

MIRROR STATUS

Mirrored partitions exist in one of five states: Not mirrored, fully synchronized (data is identical), out of synchronization (data is not identical), orphaned (integrity of data not guaranteed), or being remirrored.

MODULES

This utility allows you to see information about the loadable modules you have loaded on the server. You can see each module's short name, and descriptive string (long name). Where applicable (such as for LAN and disk drivers), you will also see version numbers of the loaded modules.

This module is for information only. It has no additional options or parameters. To see module information, type the following command at the console prompt:

MODULES

MONITOR

This loadable module is the one you will use most often to get information about your server. Current statistics, updated as the server runs, let you assess how efficiently the server is running and how heavily it is being used.

You can see information such as:

- How long the server has been running since it was last booted

- The percentage of time the server's processor is busy

- The number of blocks available, and the number of blocks of data that are waiting to be written to disk

- Number of disk requests waiting to be serviced

- Buffer information such as the number available for station requests and directory caching

- The number of connections to the server

- The number of files being accessed

- The information about server disks, LAN drivers, volumes, and attached media devices

This information can help you configure your server in a way that will best use its resources, and it can help you track usage, see potential problems, and reallocate resources to solve them before they affect the server.

Although you can not change these statistics directly, you can make adjustments to your server and view additional information about its usage, because MONITOR provides a menu interface that allows you to perform server maintenance tasks.

MONITOR also loads with a built-in screen saver, which protects your console and the MONITOR information from being accessed by unauthorized users. To load MONITOR, simply type the command at the console prompt, as shown below:

LOAD MONITOR

Once MONITOR is loaded, you can just type MONITOR when you want to bring up the screen.

MOUNT

Use this command to load a volume onto the server. Mounting volumes makes the file system data on the volume available to users.

You can mount volumes while the server is in use; there is no need to bring down the server to mount or dismount volumes. For example, if you are having problems with a volume, you might want to dismount it, run VREPAIR to check and fix the volume, and then remount it.

MOUNT has two options available. You can mount a specific volume or you can mount all volumes with a single command. For example, to mount a volume named VOL1, type:

MOUNT VOL1

If you want to mount all volumes, type

MOUNT ALL

NAME

This utility lets you see the name of the server. This is the name that is assigned during the server installation. All you have to do is type the command at the console prompt. For example,

NAME

The server name will appear. This utility has no additional parameters or options.

NLICLEAR

This loadable module allows the server to clear unauthenticated connections so they can be re-used. When the module is loaded, it checks the server periodically and automatically clears unauthenticated connections.

Unauthenticated connections are caused by incomplete logins, such as when a user logs in but does not complete the procedure by entering a password.

To load the module and begin checking for unauthenticated connections, type:

LOAD NLICLEAR

If you need additional help loading the module, see LOAD.

NMAGENT

This module is used with network hub and management programs. It passes network information from the server and LAN drivers to the management program. If you are using network management on your network, load this module on each server that you want to see on your program:

LOAD NMAGENT

This NLM has no additional parameters or options. If you need help loading the module, see LOAD.

NUT

This loadable module is the NLM utility user interface for NetWare v3.x loadable modules. It must be loaded on v3.x servers in order for most utilities to function.

You will probably not need to load the module at the command line, because the modules that depend on NUT will autoload it if they can not find it when they try to load. You can see if NUT is loaded by using the MODULES utility at the console prompt to get a list of the modules currently loaded on your server.

If you must load this NLM at the server console, type the following command at the prompt:

LOAD NUT

NWSNUT

This loadable module is the NLM utility user interface for NetWare 4.0–based modules. If you buy an NLM based on the v4.0 operating system, you need this module loaded on your server.

You will probably never need to load the module at the command line, because the modules that depend on NWSNUT will autoload it if they can not find it when they try to load. You can see if NWSNUT is loaded by using the MODULES utility at the console prompt to get a list of the modules currently loaded on your server.

If you must load this NLM at the console, type the following command at the prompt:

LOAD NWSNUT

OFF

Use this utility to clear information, messages, etc., from the server console screen. At the console prompt, type:

OFF

This command does the same thing as the CLS command.

PROTOCOL

This utility allows you to see a list of the protocols and frame types registered on your server. You can also use it if you need to register additional protocols, although this is not usually necessary because most protocols either register themselves or are automatically registered by the LAN driver they communicate with.

To see a list of protocols and frame types currently loaded on your server, type this command at the console prompt:

PROTOCOL

If you need to register a protocol (for a new, unusual media type, for example), type the command below, followed by the new protocol and its frame type.

PROTOCOL REGISTER

You will have to get the protocol and frame type information from the documentation that comes with the media or module you are adding to your server. To make sure the protocol is registered each time the server is booted, add the command to the server's AUTOEXEC.NCF file.

PSERVER

This loadable module links a print server to the server operating system. Loading this module is the final step in setting up printing for your network. Before you load it, you must use PCONSOLE to set up and configure the print server.

For example, after creating a print server named PSERV1, load this NLM by typing the following command at the console prompt:

LOAD PSERVER PSERV1

This NLM has no additional parameters or options. If you need help loading PSERVER, see LOAD.

REGISTER MEMORY

If you add memory to your server, you will need to register it so the server knows where it starts and ends. This helps avoid memory address conflicts.

To register the memory, you need to specify the starting address of the memory and its length (in hexadecimal numbers). For example, if you added 8 MB of memory to the server above its standard 16 MB, you would type the following command at the console prompt:

REGISTER MEMORY 1000000 800000

To make sure the memory is registered automatically whenever the server is booted, add the command to the server's AUTOEXEC.NCF file.

If you want to see how much memory the server is currently addressing, use the MEMORY command at the console prompt.

REMIRROR PARTITION

If your server stopped remirroring for some reason, or you aborted a remirroring procedure, use this command when you are ready to restart it.

You will not normally need to use this command, because the server automatically takes care of partition mirroring.

For example, if you had to abort a remirroring procedure for partition 3 and you wanted to restart the process, you would type the following command at the console prompt:

    REMIRROR PARTITION 3

REMOTE

This loadable module allows you to access the server console from a workstation or from a PC with a modem. The workstation utility RCONSOLE can establish a connection to any server running the REMOTE NLM and the RSPX NLM (the remote SPX protocol). When you have these modules linked to the server, you can manage the server as if you were at the console.

You can also set a password for REMOTE, so only users with the password can access the console. For example, to restrict access to the remote server console by adding the password "manage," type:

    LOAD REMOTE manage

Immediately after you load REMOTE, you must load RSPX. For more information, see LOAD and RSPX.

If you want the server to be available for remote access automatically each time it is booted, add these LOAD commands to the server's AUTOEXEC.NCF file. This NLM has no additional options or parameters.

REMOVE DOS

This command allows you to free the memory used by DOS on the server and return it to the NetWare operating system. You might want to remove DOS if your server's available memory is low and you want to alleviate the problem.

If you remove DOS, it is no longer resident on the server, so any modules loaded on the DOS drive are not available. When DOS is removed, the EXIT command, which normally takes you to the DOS level, will reboot the server.

To remove DOS from the server, type the following command at the console prompt:

REMOVE DOS

No additional parameters or options are available for this command.

RESET ROUTER

If the router table in your server becomes corrupted or is inaccurate because servers are down, you can use this command to reset it. When a server is down, packets are still sent to that server until the other servers on the network update their router tables, which removes the inoperative server from the table. In the meantime, packets sent to that server for routing are lost.

Router tables are automatically updated every two minutes, so if you can wait that long, the router will be reset for you. If you do not want to wait, however, you can use this command on each server that is still running to update the router tables.

To reset a router table for a server, type the following command at the console prompt:

RESET ROUTER

This command has no additional parameters or options.

ROUTE

This loadable module allows you to set up and control the routing of Net-Ware packets across an IBM bridge to a Token-Ring network.

ROUTE has nine options available. However, in most cases where you have a simple configuration, loading route with the default settings (no parameters) will work fine. The only exception is the board number parameter, which will have to be specified if you do not have the Token-Ring driver loaded first. For example, if you want to set up routing for a Token-Ring network on your NetWare LAN, and you know that the driver for the Token-Ring board will be the third one loaded by the system, type:

LOAD ROUTE BOARD=3

If you want routing to be enabled automatically whenever the server is booted, place this command in the AUTOEXEC.NCF file. If you need more information about loading modules, see LOAD.

RPL

The RPL (Remote Program Load) loadable module allows you to connect diskless workstations to your network by enabling them to boot from files on the server instead of requiring boot files on the workstation.

Before workstations can boot from a server, you must set up a directory on the server and copy boot files for each workstation to those files.

Once you have boot files set up, load this module on the server by typing the following command at the console prompt:

LOAD RPL

There are no additional parameters or options available for this module. If you need help loading the module, see LOAD.

RS232

This loadable module sets up an asynchronous communications port on the server so workstations can access the server console through a modem.

It works with the REMOTE module, so both must be loaded in order for a workstation to access the console through an asynchronous connection.

When you load RS232, you must specify the communications port number you will use and the baud rate of your modem. For example, after loading REMOTE (which must be loaded first), you can load RS232 and use communications port 2 with a 4800-baud modem by typing:

> LOAD RS232 2 4800

If you don't specify the parameters with the LOAD command, you will be prompted for each parameter the system needs. If you want the communications port to be set up automatically whenever the server is booted, put the command immediately after the LOAD REMOTE command in the AUTOEXEC.NCF file.

RSPX

This loadable module loads the SPX driver on the server so workstations cabled to the network can access the server console.

RSPX works with the REMOTE module, so both must be loaded in order for a workstation to access the console. For example, after loading REMOTE (which must be loaded first), you can load RSPX by typing:

> LOAD RSPX

No additional parameters or options are available for this module. If you need help loading modules, see LOAD.

SBACKUP

This loadable module allows you to back up data to and restore data from a storage device attached to a NetWare server. You can back up NetWare server data, such as user information, trustee assignments, and file system data. You can also back up DOS, Windows, and OS/2 workstations to the storage device.

SBACKUP works with TSAs (Target Service Agents), which must be loaded on the machine whose data is being backed up. The TSA interprets the data and communicates information about its characteristics to SBACKUP, so that data types (such as name spaces) that are not familiar to the server can be backed up accurately.

To bring up the SBACKUP main menu, type the following command at the console prompt:

LOAD SBACKUP

From the menu, you can choose F1 help to get more information about running the program.

SCAN FOR NEW DEVICES

Use this utility to look for devices that have been added to the server since it was last booted. When a server is booted, it scans for all devices attached to it and gathers information about each device. However, if you add a device after the server is booted, it may not be aware of it.

To have the server scan for devices added since the last time it was booted, type the following command at the console prompt:

SCAN FOR NEW DEVICES

This command has no additional parameters or options available.

SEARCH

This command lets you set search paths that tell the server where startup files and loadable modules are stored in the file system. It is similar to the MAP command used to map drives for workstations. The default search path for the server files is SYS:SYSTEM, so if you change the directory structure and move the loadable module and the .NCF file, you will need to create new search paths so the server can find them.

This command allows you to add new server search paths, delete existing paths, and view the current paths. For example, to see a list of the search paths you already have, type:

> SEARCH

If you loaded new NLMs on your system at the root of the SYS volume in a directory called NLMS, you would type:

> SEARCH ADD SYS:NLMS

SECURE CONSOLE

This utility allows you to use the console (if you are authorized), but it prevents security breaches. While it does not lock the console (which can be done in MONITOR), it allows NLMs to load only from volume SYS. This protects the server and the network from someone loading an NLM from a floppy diskette or from DOS and then using it to break the network security.

This utility also prevents anyone other than the console operator from changing the server date and time. Accounting and auditing features rely on date and time to determine exactly when certain procedures were done or when files or rights were changed.

If you use SECURE CONSOLE, you can only disable it by rebooting the server. To secure the console, type the following command at the prompt:

> SECURE CONSOLE

This command has no additional options or parameters available.

SEND

This command allows you to send a message from the server console to workstations on the network. You can send messages to specific users (workstations) who are logged in, or you can send a message to a workstation connection number.

For example, if you want to send a message to users, type the message and the usernames as follows:

> BROADCAST "Staff meeting in 20 minutes. See you there." TO Fred, Susan, Jeff

If you want to send a message to a group of users, or to all users who are logged in, use BROADCAST instead.

SERVER

This utility boots your server and starts NetWare. Whenever you bring down a server, you will type this command to start it up again.

When you run this utility, it executes the startup files (STARTUP.NCF and AUTOEXEC.NCF) and mounts volume SYS:. SERVER has options that allow you to circumvent the startup files and use replacements, and you can also change the block size of the cache buffer, but these changes are not recommended. The default files are the best way to bring up the server.

To bring up a server with NetWare, type the following command at the DOS prompt:

> SERVER

SET

This utility allows you to set operating system parameters from the command line. SET is an extensive utility with many parameters.

To help you understand the types of parameters you can set for a server, they are divided into 12 categories:

Communications parameters

These let you set values for packet receive buffers (server memory set aside to hold data packets) and packet size. You can set watchdog functions, which automatically terminate workstation connections to the server if no activity is detected.

Memory parameters

These let you control the Short Term Memory pool. You can set values for automatically registering memory above 16 MB, and set the cache buffer block size.

File-caching parameters

These let you manage file cache buffers in the server's memory. You can set minimum file cache buffers that the server will allow, and you can manage disk cache settings.

Directory-caching parameters

These let you manage how the directory entry table is stored in memory by setting directory cache buffers and limits.

File system parameters

These let you set warning thresholds for full volumes, set the maximum subdirectory depth for the file system, and manage how and when deleted files are purged from disk.

Locks parameters

These let you specify how many open files workstations can have and how many the server can handle.

Transaction tracking parameters

These let you set TTS flags for backout and abort (off and on), and set TTS backout file truncation and unwritten cache wait times.

Disk parameters

These let you set read after write verification and some Hot Fix parameters.

Miscellaneous parameters

These let you set alert messages and displays, specify the maximum number of service processes that can be created, and specify whether passwords can be encrypted or unencrypted.

Most operating system parameter defaults have been set so the server will perform efficiently and accurately. Make sure you do not change server settings unless you know how the change will affect your server.

If you want SET parameters to be implemented each time the server is booted, enter them in a server startup (.NCF) file.

SET TIME

Use this utility to modify the server's internal date and time.

The two parameters for this command control the time and the date. They are "month/day/year" and "hour:minute:second." Several formats are acceptable for each parameter. To reset the server time to 2:30 p.m., April 18, 1993, type:

> SET TIME 4/18/93 2:30:00 PM

SET TIME ZONE

This utility sets a time reference in CLIB. The time information is used by other NLMs that depend on CLIB. It does not change the server time.

You can set parameters for the time zone, hours from Greenwich Mean Time, and daylight savings (if you live in an area where this applies). You can see the current setting by entering the command with no parameters.

To change the time zone setting to Central Standard Time, enter the code for that zone and its hours from Greenwich Mean Time by typing:

> SET TIME ZONE CST6

SPEED

This utility allows you to see your processor's CPU speed setting. To get the most from your CPU, you should read the documentation that came with your computer to calculate and set the highest CPU setting allowed.

To see the CPU speed setting, type:

SPEED

This utility has no additional parameters or options available.

SPOOL

Use this command to set up default print queues for print jobs created with NPRINT and CAPTURE.

For example, if you create a print queue named "Queue1," you can set it up by typing:

SPOOL 0 TO QUEUE1

You can also use PRINTCON to set up defaults, which is somewhat easier than using this command at the console prompt.

SPXCONFG

This loadable module allows you to set configuration parameters for SPX. You can change SPX parameters such as watchdog timeouts, retry counts, and maximum concurrent SPX sessions.

To load the SPXCONFG module, type the command, as shown below, at the console prompt:

LOAD SPXCONFG

This module has a total of seven options available.

SPXS

Use this loadable module if you are using a STREAMS-based SPX protocol on your server. If you want this module loaded each time the server is booted, put the command to load it in a startup (.NCF) file.

To load the SPXS module on the server, type the following command at the console prompt or in a server .NCF file:

LOAD SPXS

If you need help loading the module, see LOAD.

STREAMS

This loadable module works with the CLIB module to provide a C interface library and STREAMS protocol services to other NLMs. Since they work together, both should be loaded on the server before the NLMs that are dependent on them are loaded.

These NLMs are usually linked to the operating system at run time. An NLM that depends on CLIB and STREAMS will look for them at load time. If the CLIB and STREAMS are not found, the module will autoload them before it loads itself.

Since STREAMS and CLIB are required for many other modules to run, they have probably already been loaded on your server. If they have not, and you want to be sure they are loaded each time the server is booted, consider adding them to a startup .NCF file. STREAMS must be loaded before CLIB.

To load STREAMS, enter the following command at the console prompt or in the .NCF file:

LOAD STREAMS

This NLM has an option available for changing the maximum message file size, but the default is usually sufficient. If you need more information about loading modules, see LOAD.

TIME

This utility displays the server's date and time.

To get this information, type the following command at the console prompt:

TIME

This utility has no additional parameters or options available.

TLI

This module provides the transport layer for network communications services. It is loaded with the modules it works with, such as STREAMS, CLIB, SPXS, or IPXS.

You can see what modules are loaded on your server by using the MODULES utility at the console. If this module is not loaded, you can load it at the console prompt, or you can place the command to load it in an .NCF file so it is loaded each time the server is booted.

To load TLI, type the following command at the console prompt, or in an .NCF file (after the commands to load STREAMS and CLIB):

LOAD TLI

No additional parameters or options are available for this module.

TRACK OFF

If you have the Router Tracking screen displayed, you can clear the console screen and turn it off with this utility. Just type the following command at the console:

TRACK OFF

TRACK ON

This utility displays the Router Tracking screen, which shows you incoming information (network data received by the server), outgoing information (data being broadcast to the network by the server), and responses by the server to "get nearest server" requests.

The screen is for routing information only, you cannot set any router parameters with this utility. To display the screen, type the following command at the console prompt:

TRACK ON

No additional parameters or options are available for this utility. To turn off the Router Tracking screen, see TRACK OFF.

UNBIND

If you want to remove a network board from your server or bind a different protocol to a board, you will first need to unbind the current protocol from the board's driver.

Specify the protocol and the name of the LAN driver you are unbinding so the operating system will know which protocol to unload. If you have several identical network boards, include enough information in the command to make it unique, such as its interrupt or port number.

For example, if you want to remove an NE2000 board from the server, unbind the protocol from its driver by typing the following command at the console prompt:

UNBIND IPX FROM NE2000

If you remove the network board permanently, you will need to remove the command to load and bind it from the AUTOEXEC.NCF file.

UNLOAD

This utility allows you to unload NLMs and other loadable modules from a server. Unloading the module removes its services from the server's operating system and returns the resources it was using.

If your server is running out of memory, you might want to use the MODULES command to see a list of the modules you are running and unload any that are not needed (such as old LAN and disk drivers, or a module you use occasionally, such as INSTALL).

For example, if you did not need the INSTALL module loaded all the time, you could unload it by typing the following command at the console prompt:

UNLOAD INSTALL

Anything that is loaded with the LOAD command can be unloaded using UNLOAD. Be careful about unloading modules such as CLIB, STREAMS, and drivers, since many other processes depend on them.

UPS

This loadable module allows you to link an uninterruptible power supply (UPS) system to your server. After installing the UPS hardware and connecting the power, load UPS.

You must specify several parameters when you load the module, to let the server operating system know what interface board and port number are being used. This information can be found in the documentation that comes with the UPS hardware. You can also specify how long the server will function on UPS power and how long the battery should recharge after it is used.

The easiest way to set up all of this information is to type the command to load the UPS and the driver, and then the system will prompt you for the additional information it needs. For example, type:

```
LOAD UPS TYPE=DCB
```

The system will prompt you for the information it needs to complete the linking process. To have UPS loaded whenever the server is booted, place the LOAD command and parameters in a startup (.NCF) file.

UPS STATUS

This utility allows you to view current information about your UPS system. You can also see the current network power status. This is helpful if the network is on battery power and you need to know how much power is left to keep it running.

To see UPS information, type the following command at the console prompt:

```
UPS STATUS
```

This utility has no additional parameters or options available.

UPS TIME

This utility allows you to change the discharge, recharge, and wait settings for the UPS. An older UPS will need the discharge and recharge settings adjusted, because it takes longer for it to recharge.

To change these settings for your power supply, enter all the settings at the command line, or simply type UPS TIME and you will be prompted for the changes you want to make.

For example, to increase the recharge time to 175 minutes from the command line, type the following command at the console prompt:

UPS TIME RECHARGE=175

You should also be aware that your current settings don't show on the screen at the time you make them. You have to use UPS STATUS to see the new settings.

VERSION

Use this utility to see the version of NetWare that is running on your server. At the console prompt, type:

VERSION

This utility has no additional parameters or options available.

VOLUMES

This utility allows you to list all the volumes currently mounted on the server. To see this list, type the following command at the console prompt:

VOLUMES

This utility has no additional parameters or options available.

VREPAIR

This loadable module finds volume problems and corrects them so the volume operates properly when it is remounted on the server. The server and its mounted volumes are not affected by VREPAIR; you do not need to bring down the server. All you have to do is dismount the volume before you run VREPAIR to fix it.

The following options are available for running VREPAIR:

▸ Specify if you want name space support removed from the volume during the repair process. If you added a name space to a volume and then started having problems, you might want to remove it to see if the name space is the cause of the problem.

▸ Choose what directory and file allocation table (FAT) information is written to the disk. You can have the entire table rewritten, or just the entries with errors.

▸ Choose whether to write changes to the disk immediately or save them in memory and write them later. If you have enough memory available on the server, writing them later helps VREPAIR run faster.

▸ Choose whether to purge deleted files from the disk while it is being repaired.

For example, if you were having problems with VOL1 on your server, you would first use DISMOUNT to unload it from the server, and then you would type:

LOAD VREPAIR VOL1

If you need more information about loading modules, see LOAD.

Upgrading to
NetWare 3.12

Introduction

Because NetWare 3.12 handles organizing, storing and accessing data as well as security differently from the format of 2.x, the data from a 2.x file server can't just be placed directly on a 3.12 server. Many modifications to all the files and directories need to be carried out first. This appendix covers the three main ways NetWare 3.12 transforms a 2.x server into a 3.12 server. Although the extensive reformatting required to transform a 2.x server to a 3.12 server is not necessary, the three techniques to be discussed can also be used to upgrade a server from versions 3.0, 3.1, and 3.11 of NetWare. The migration techniques can also be used to upgrade an IBM LAN server or PCLP to 3.12. However, we will concentrate mostly on upgrading from the NetWare 2.x environment.

NetWare 3.12 has three ways to upgrade a server:

▸ The **Across-the-Wire Migration Method** allows you to translate the 2.x data and bindery into the 3.12 format and send it from the old 2.x file server to the new 3.12 server using the network as the medium for the data transfer.

▸ The **Same-Server Migration Method** uses your current backup system to store the network data and application files and a working directory to store a translated copy of the bindery. The old 2.x server is then installed with the 3.12 software, and the data and bindery are restored to it.

▸ The **In-Place Upgrade Method** makes all the changes to the files, directories, and bindery right there on the network hard drive. The data is not moved to another location as with the other two methods, but is modified in place.

The following table lists the methods that can be used to upgrade a server, the version of NetWare the server is initially running, and the utilities used by each method.

UPGRADE METHOD	NETWARE VERSION	3.12 UTILITY
Across-the-Wire Migration	2.0a or better	MIGRATE.EXE
Same-Server Migration	2.0a or better	MIGRATE.EXE
In-Place Upgrade	Any version except 2.0, 2.0a and 3.0	2XUPGRDE.NLM (2.x)
		INSTALL.NLM (3.1 and 3.11)

Preparing a NetWare 2.x Server for Upgrade to NetWare 3.12

As in many other significant operations, overlooked details can be the kiss of death, and can turn a relatively easy and straightforward procedure into a confusing nightmare. Do the following to ensure that upgrading your NetWare 2.x server proceeds smoothly and as planned:

- ► Make working copies of the NetWare 3.12 diskettes

- ► Install NetWare 3.12 on a different server (Across-the-Wire Migration)

- ► Check the 2.x server naming conventions for long directory and filenames

- ► Check the 2.x server for System and Hidden directories

- ► Remove unnecessary files

- ► Check the 2.x server's maximum subdirectory depth

- ► Develop a plan for information migration (if combining two or more 2.x servers)

- Allow for Macintosh support if you have or will support them

- Prevent users from logging in during upgrade

- Rebuild the 2.x file server bindery with BINDFIX

- Make two complete backups of the 2.x server

- Create a working directory and copy the MIGRATION diskette to it (migration procedures)

To begin with, work from copies of the NetWare 3.12 diskettes to prevent any accidental corruption of the original diskettes. If you are using the Across-the-Wire Migration to upgrade your 2.x server, the method in which all the directories, files, and bindery information is changed to fit the 3.12 format and is sent to the new 3.12 server across the network, you need to install NetWare 3.12 on a new server using procedures discussed in Chapter 6. Your NetWare 2.x server allows for directory structures, security attributes, and naming conventions that conflict with NetWare 3.12; these must be addressed before you can begin upgrading. Also, you will need to perform some preparatory housecleaning on the 2.x server. If you have or intend to support Macintosh workstations, you will need to purchase special NetWare software to run on your new 3.12 server so that Macintosh files and folders can be supported on the new server. Users need to be logged out. You also need to make backups of the entire 2.x server system before the upgrade procedure begins. If you intend to use the migration methods, you will also need to choose a working directory and copy the MIGRATION diskette files to it.

CREATE WORKING COPIES

To prevent any accidental corruption of your original NetWare 3.12 diskettes, always work from working copies and store the original diskettes in a secure place. Label your high-density 3.5 floppies exactly as the original diskettes are and use the DOS DISKCOPY command to make exact copies of the original diskettes.

If you wish to make copies on high-density 5.25 floppies instead of the original 3.5 floppy format, the procedure will be a bit more complicated than using a simple DOS command. For each disk you will need to determine if it is a bootable disk or not. If the original is a bootable diskette, than the copy will need to be also. To make a bootable diskette, use the /s switch when you format the disk. You will then need to copy all of the files from the original diskette to the working copy using either the DOS COPY or XCOPY commands. Finally, make sure that you provide the working copy with the correct 11 character volume label. You can use the DOS LABEL command for that.

NAMING CONVENTIONS

NetWare 2.x allows you to use up to 14 characters in the names of files and directories, but NetWare 3.12 uses the DOS naming conventions of an eight-character name followed by a three-character extension. If you have used this feature of NetWare 2.x, you can either rename conflicting 2.x server directories and files so that their names conform to DOS practices, or you can allow the upgrade procedure to rename them by truncating the names to eight-character names with three-character extensions. If you allow the upgrade procedures to truncate directory and file names automatically, check that the truncated names won't conflict with each other.

If you had support set up for Macintosh clients, you will not need to change or modify files with Macintosh naming conventions since that support will be passed on through the upgrade procedure.

NOTE
NetWare 2.x allows 14-character names for directories and files; NetWare 3.12 uses DOS-style names of eight-characters with a three-character extension.

SYSTEM AND HIDDEN FLAGS

If you are upgrading from the later versions of NetWare 2.x beginning with 2.15, you may have problems with some of the security attributes of these versions. These NetWare versions allow you to designate any directory as System and/or Hidden, which effectively prevents these directories from being upgraded. If this is the case, you can do one of two things: Save the affected directories to diskettes or tapes and restore them to the new server after the upgrade; or remove the System and/or Hidden flags from the directories, upgrade your 2.x server to a 3.12 server, and then redesignate them as System and/or Hidden after the upgrade.

REMOVE UNNECESSARY FILES

Removing unnecessary files can save you disk space that you may need later. Temporary files such as .BAK and .LST files can be deleted from the source server or prevented from migrating if you are using the migration techniques. Value Added Processes (VAPs) are no longer used in NetWare 3.12. VAPs need to be replaced with NLMs that perform the same functions. The VAPs can be deleted since they are of no use after the upgrade.

The following NetWare 2.x files are not compatible with 3.12 and will be prevented from migrating to the new server. You will need to delete these files if they are outside the SYS:SYSTEM and SYS:PUBLIC directories or if you are using the In-Place upgrade method:

LARCHIVE.EXE

LRESTORE.EXE

MACBACK.EXE

NARCHIVE.EXE

NRESTORE.EXE

ENDSPOOL.EXE (2.0a)

Q.EXE (2.0a)

QUEUE.EXE (2.0a)

SPOOL.EXE (2.0a)

WARNING
NetWare 3.12 does
not by default allow
for more than 25
levels of
subdirectories.

SUBDIRECTORY DEPTH

A potential trouble spot between NetWare 2.x and 3.12 is that a 3.12 server does not by default allow for subdirectories with more than 25 levels. If your 2.x server has subdirectories with more than 25 levels and you do not wish to shorten your directory structure, you will need to modify your

3.12 server to accommodate the greater number of levels by modifying your 3.12 server's STARTUP.NCF file using the INSTALL utility. If you are going to use the Same-Server Migration to upgrade your 2.x server, you will have to wait to fix this problem until after you have used the migration utility to back up your 2.x server's bindery, and you have installed NetWare 3.12 on your old server.

1 · Log into the 3.12 server as SUPERVISOR and load INSTALL.

2 · Select System Options.

3 · Select Edit STARTUP.NCF File.

4 · Enter the pathway to your STARTUP.NCF File.

5 · Add the line:

SET MAXIMUM SUBDIRECTORY TREE DEPTH = n

6 · Save changes to STARTUP.NCF and exit INSTALL.

7 · Down and restart the 3.12 server.

Log into your 3.12 server console as the SUPERVISOR and type LOAD INSTALL. You should recognize the Installation Options menu from installing 3.12 on this server. From the Installation Options menu, select Systems Options and then Edit STARTUP.NCF File. Enter the correct pathway to your STARTUP.NCF file.

If you are normally going to boot your server from drive A:, press ↵ to accept A:\STARTUP.NCF as the correct path to your STARTUP.NCF file.

If you are normally going to boot from a DOS partition on the hard drive, then press HOME. Delete A and replace it with C. The pathway should now read C:\STARTUP.NCF. Press ↵ to continue.

Once inside the STARTUP.NCF, add the line

SET MAXIMUM SUBDIRECTORY TREE DEPTH = n

where *n* can be any number between 26 and 100 that corresponds to the depth of your subdirectories. Save the changes to your STARTUP.NCF file and exit the INSTALL module. Down the server so that when you reboot, the changes to the STARTUP.NCF file will take effect.

MERGING TWO OR MORE SERVERS

If you are planning to merge two or more existing 2.x servers into a single 3.12 server using the Across-the-Wire migration, you need to be aware of the following. You can control what data is migrated according to how you want your consolidated server to be set up. You can control the migration of the following items or combinations of items.

Data files	Migrates all data files and their DOS and NetWare attributes. Will not overwrite a file with the same name.
Trustee assignments	Migrates rights that are assigned to users and groups for directories and files to the corresponding 3.12 rights. With this selection, you must also choose **Users**, **Groups**, and **Data files** if the users and data files do not already exist on the destination server.
Users	Migrates users, user print-job configurations (PRINTCON.DAT), and user login scripts unless they already exist on the destination server.
User restrictions	Migrates user account restrictions, station restrictions, and time restrictions, but not volume restrictions. If this type of information is chosen, **Users** must also be migrated. If restrictions already exist on the destination server, the source server's user restrictions will not overwrite them.

Groups	Migrates group members and group trustee rights for directories and files. If the groups from the source server already exist on the destination server, the source and destination groups will be merged.
Default account restrictions	Migrates the default account restrictions. This option will overwrite any existing restrictions on the destination server.
Accounting information	Migrates the accounting charge method for network services charged to individual user accounts. The source server's information will be kept intact.
Print queues and print servers	Preserves your network printing services by transferring print queues and print servers and their corresponding setup information.

You will need to plan carefully the order in which you want to migrate your servers and what data you wish to restrict or not restrict. For instance, if you wanted to keep the default account restrictions from one particular server, you would allow it to migrate its default account restrictions to the new server and overwrite the ones already there. Any server that followed, you would prevent from migrating their default account restrictions.

PRESERVING MACINTOSH SUPPORT

If you have supported Macintosh workstations on your old 2.x server and/or intend to support them on your new NetWare 3.12 server, you will need to do several things. First you will need to add Macintosh support when you install the new 3.12 server by installing NetWare Services for Macintosh. This will allow for native-mode support for Macintosh workstations that log into your new 3.12 file server.

Then you need to add the line

LOAD MAC

to the STARTUP.NCF file (see Chapter 6 for instructions on modifying your STARTUP.NCF file) to load the Macintosh name space module. Next, you will need to type the console command:

ADD NAME SPACE MAC TO volume_name

where *volume_name* is the name of each volume where you are going to use Macintosh naming conventions.

This command only needs to be used once for each volume that will have to support Macintosh naming conventions. Adding a name space is normally permanent, but it can be erased using the VREPAIR.NLM utility and destroying all non-DOS data.

Check your System Administration Guide for more details on the ADD NAME SPACE console command. Carefully check the additional memory that adding a name space will require. If you do not have enough extra memory on your server to accommodate the name space overhead, the volume will not mount.

LOG USERS OUT OF THE 2.X SERVER

All user accounts, including accounts used by network devices such as print server, must be logged out during the upgrade. The only account that can be active during the upgrade is the SUPERVISOR account. In addition, all files, with the exception of bindery files, must be closed. To ensure this, you can use the SYSCON utility to clear all the login connections and then use the console command, DISABLE LOGIN, to prevent user login attempts until after the upgrade has been completed.

PERFORM BINDERY HOUSECLEANING

Use BINDFIX on the 2.x server to delete unnecessary mail directories for users who have been removed from the network. The BINDFIX utility will search each volume on your 2.x server for directory trustee rights that belong to users who no longer exist on the server. When orphaned rights are found, they will be removed. The resulting bindery written to the server's system directory should be relatively free of extraneous material.

MAKE TWO BACKUPS OF THE 2.X FILE SERVER

For safety, make two complete backups of the 2.x file server using the backup method that you normally use. With these backups, you can be sure that your data will not be lost if some unforeseen accident should occur such as a power failure. You can rebuild your old 2.x server repeatedly from your backup and try to upgrade as many times as it takes you to succeed.

CREATION OF A WORKING DIRECTORY

If you are going to use either of the migration methods to upgrade your 2.x server, you will need to create a working directory with which to work from. A working directory is a place where the migration procedures will store session files that contain error messages and session information from the data transfer procedure. During the Same-Server migration, the working directory will also store a translated copy of the bindery being migrated. A working directory *cannot* be on a removable device (e.g., a floppy disk)—it *can* be on a hard disk in the workstation the upgrade is performed from or a network drive from a file server that is neither the source server nor the target server.

Simply create a subdirectory of the root of the C drive called MIGRATE. This will give you the working directory that is the MIGRATION utility's default. You can, of course, use any directory you like for the working directory as long as it conforms to the two restrictions stated above. Also, if you are going to use the Same-Server migration, you need to choose a workstation with access to at least 5 MB of disk space for the working directory above and beyond the space the MIGRATION diskette files will require.

Copy the contents of the MIGRATION diskette to the working directory you have prepared with the DOS COPY command:

```
COPY A:\*.* C:\MIGRATE\*.*
```

How Data Is Migrated

The MIGRATE utility has certain rules by which it handles the data transfers required. Files from the source server with the same name as a file that exists on the target server will not be migrated. You will have to rename these files so that they will migrate. If you do not, an error will be logged in the migration report explaining why the file was not migrated. Another special case is the system login script, which will not be migrated at all. Directories with the same name will be merged and will contain a conglomeration of both sets of files. If this is not what you want, you will have to rename one of the two directories. Also, passwords are not migrated. You will have to reassign them, or let the migration process randomly generate them.

The Across-the-Wire Migration Method (2.x to 3.12)

The Across-the-Wire Migration Method does exactly what the name implies. The entire network environment consisting of all the data files, application files, and bindery information is copied from the old 2.x server, translated into the 3.12 format, and sent to the new 3.12 server using the network as the media for the transfer.

The Across-the-Wire migration is the most versatile of the three upgrade procedures. It allows you to upgrade your 2.x server to NetWare 3.12 without any risk of data loss. Since the original 2.x server is never altered by the procedure in any way, you will not be left at the mercy of an unforeseen circumstance that prevents the upgrade from completing or corrupting the data in route. If such a circumstance were to occur, you could simply repeat the procedure as many times as needed to obtain a successful upgrade. You can also merge several servers into one 3.12 server. Other pluses include the capability to limit the data that you wish to migrate and direct data to a specific volume or directory. The one big drawback, however, is the fact that you need a 3.12 server installed in addition to the 2.x server that you are planning to upgrade.

Planning for the Across-the-Wire Migration Method

You will need the following to upgrade your 2.x server using the Across-the-Wire Migration Method:

- ▸ two file servers, the current server running NetWare 2.x, and a computer with a 386 or better processor that NetWare 3.12 will run on

- ▸ a workstation with at least 640 KB of memory, a high-density drive, and access to 5 MB of free disk space on a local or unrelated network drive

- ▸ working copies of the NetWare 3.12 diskettes (not the originals)

- ▸ enough disk storage on the new 3.12 file server

Check to see that the data from the 2.x server (or servers if you are consolidating more than one 2.x server by migrating them to the new 3.12 server) will fit on the new 3.12 server. Bear in mind that NetWare 3.12 requires a little more file and directory overhead than NetWare 2.x does. Also, you will need to take into account the DOS partition size you will need if you plan to boot your 3.12 server from the hard drive instead of a floppy. Another potential troublespot could be the additional users and their related login scripts added to the SYS volume through the merging of 2.x servers to a consolidated 3.12 server. Novell suggests allowing at least 6 MB of additional disk space for the SYS volume for each 2.x server to be consolidated. If the 3.12 server does not have adequate room for the 2.x server's files, then you may have to transfer only certain volumes or directories until you can add more disk space.

BEGIN THE ACROSS-THE-WIRE MIGRATION UPGRADE

A good place to begin would be to add the new 3.12 server to your LAN by using the installation procedures described in Chapter 6, followed by the installation of the client software for a workstation for the new 3.12 server using instructions found in Chapter 7. Check through the *Preparing a NetWare 2.x Server for Upgrade to NetWare 3.12* section earlier in this appendix to see which of the preparations apply to your situation.

With your preparatory work done, you are ready to begin the migration of the 2.x server to the new 3.12 server using your LAN as the medium of the exchange. Log into your 3.12 server as SUPERVISOR using a workstation that has at least 640 KB of memory and a high-density drive. Make sure that the workstation is booted without any terminate-and-stay-resident programs (TSRs) loaded. From the DOS prompt, run the MIGRATE utility from the working directory.

The Select a Migration Option menu will appear, as shown in Figure B.1. You have the option of choosing between a Standard migration and a Custom migration. The Standard migration only allows you to pick the working directory and the servers involved. You will basically be transferring all the data from the 2.x server to the 3.12 server and will not be able to designate

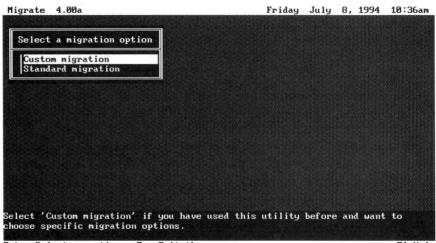

FIGURE B.1

The Migration Main Menu

a change of volume for the data as you would with the custom option.

The Custom migration option allows you to not only choose what data is transferred but also to designate which volume the data is to be sent to. We will choose the Custom migration option in our example since it will give us the most control over how our file server is transferred.

The next screen (see Figure B.2) will allow you to choose between the two types of migrations, Across-the-Wire and Same-Server. Select the Across-the-Wire option.

You will now be asked in the next two screens to select both the source LAN type and the destination LAN type (see Figure B.3 and Figure B.4). Choose the NetWare 2.x option for the source and the NetWare 3.x for the destination.

This will bring you to a screen similar to Figure B.5. This screen allows you to set options for the migration utility and both the source and destination servers.

For the migration utility, you are allowed to set the working directory and the action to be taken in the event of an error. The source server settings allow you to designate the server to be migrated; it will log you into that server if you are not already logged into it. Simply press Enter to bring up

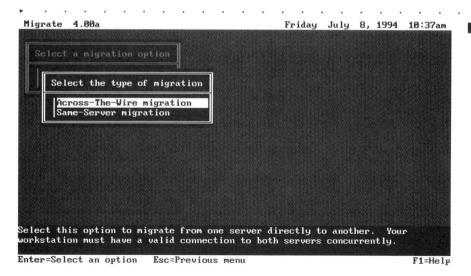

FIGURE B.2

Determining the Type of Migration

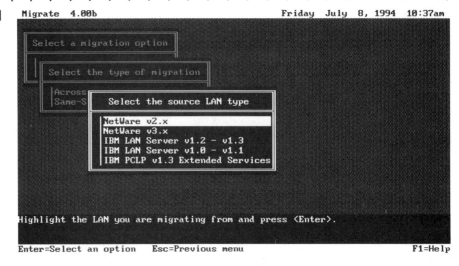

FIGURE B.3

Selecting the Source LAN Type

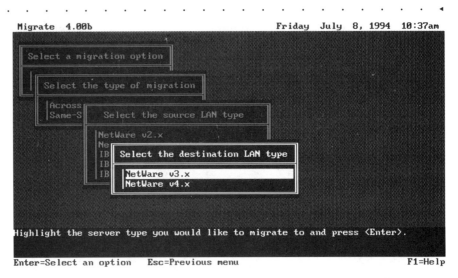

FIGURE B.4

Selecting the Destination LAN Type

a list of servers and the associated user names that you are logged into. If the server that you need to designate is not on the list, press Ins and choose from the list of Other NetWare Servers. You will need to supply the username SUPERVISOR and the correct password. The 2.x server that you need should now be available for you to select as the source server.

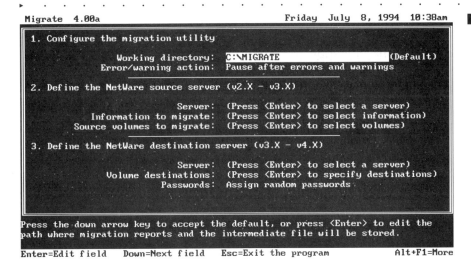

The Migration
Configuration screen

You can also set the migration to include all the information from the source file server with the All information option or a combination of the following information: Data files, Trustee assignments, Users, User restrictions, Groups, Default account restrictions, Print queues and print servers, and Accounting information (see the table in the *Preparing a NetWare 2.x Server for Upgrade to NetWare 3.12* section). These will be the options that you will rely heavily upon to shape a consolidated server.

You can even limit the information transferred to the new server to only the volumes that you select in the third source server option. For instance, if you did not wish to transfer the example server TOLSTOY's VOL1 volume, your would remove it from the list of source volumes to be migrated by highlighting it and pressing Del.

The final three options that you need to set for a custom Across-the-Wire migration have to do with the destination server. First, you are able to choose the destination server name similar to the way you chose the source file server name. Once again, if you are not logged in, the migration utility will allow you to log in at this time by pressing the Ins key and choosing from the available servers.

Next, you can designate which volume of the destination server you want the source server's information to be migrated to. For instance, you could tell the migration procedure to transfer the information from the TOLSTOY:SYS source volume to the CICERO:VOL1 destination volume.

Finally, you will need to decide how you wish passwords to be handled. Passwords are not upgraded along with other user information in the upgrade. You have several options for handling this. You can have MIGRATE assign no passwords to any account, and you can reassign them later or let the user set their own at their next login. If you are going to use this route, we suggest reassigning them so that this security function will still be in place. The users can always set their own later on. MIGRATE can also assign random passwords to each account. These passwords are stored in the file NEW.PWD in the SYS:SYSTEM directory and can only be accessed by the user SUPERVISOR.

Once you have selected your options for the Across-the-Wire migration, press F10 to bring up the Select a Migration Action menu (see Figure B.6). You have four options at this point. You can begin the migration, return to the configuration form to change a migration option, view a migration report, or exit the utility and return to DOS. Unless you wish to change a configuration option, you are ready to continue with the migration. Select Start Migration to begin the upgrade.

You will see the migration report being generated on the screen as is illustrated in Figure B.7. The report or log file name will be shown on the top of the screen as it is being generated. When the procedure is finished, press ↵ to return to the Select a Migration Action menu. Now it is time to view the migration report to check what was transferred and view any errors that might need attention. Use the View Migration Reports option to bring up a list of reports (depending on how many times this procedure has been run) stored in the working directory and select the one this upgrade session generated. If there are no errors that require that you repeat the upgrade, you are ready to proceed to the *Clean Up After an Upgrade from 2.x* section of this appendix.

```
Migrate  4.00a                         Friday  July  8, 1994  10:46am

1. Configure the migration utility

              Working directory:  C:\MIGRATE                    (Default)
           Error/warning action:  Pause after errors and warnings

2. Define the NetWare s┌────────────────────────────────┐
                       │   Select a migration action    │
                       ├────────────────────────────────┤
        Information    │ Start migration                │
      Source volumes   │ Return to configuration      d)│
                       │ View migration reports         │
3. Define the NetWare d│ Exit (return to DOS)         X)│
                       └────────────────────────────────┘
                 Server:  CICERO
     Volume destinations:  (Destinations specified)
              Passwords:  Assign no passwords


Select this option to start the migration.

Enter=Select an action    Esc=Return to configuration          F1=Help
```

FIGURE B.6

The Across-the-Wire
Migration Action menu

```
Migrate  4.00a                         Friday  July  8, 1994  10:46am
┌──────────────────────────────────────────────────────────────────┐
│              Migrating... (log file: MIG000.RPT)                   │
│      Trustee : CROES (user), [R    F  ]                            │
│      Trustee : EVERYONE (group), [R    F  ]                        │
│      Trustee : PENROD (user), [R    F  ]                           │
│      Trustee : SUPERVISOR (user), [R    F  ]                       │
│                                                                    │
│  SYS:PROGRAMS\QPW2\ODAPI                                           │
│      Trustee : CANCILA (user), [R    F  ]                          │
│      Trustee : CROES (user), [R    F  ]                            │
│      Trustee : EVERYONE (group), [R    F  ]                        │
│      Trustee : PENROD (user), [R    F  ]                           │
│      Trustee : SUPERVISOR (user), [R    F  ]                       │
│                                                                    │
│  SYS:PROGRAMS\QPW2\OBEXPOST                                        │
│      Trustee : CROES (user), [RWCEMF  ]                            │
│      Trustee : CANCILA (user), [RWCEMF  ]                          │
└──────────────────────────────────────────────────────────────────┘
The spacebar was pressed during the migration process.  Select an action.

Spacebar=Continue    Esc=Stop migrating                        F1=Help
```

FIGURE B.7

Migration Report
Generation

The Same-Server Migration Method (2.x to 3.12)

The Same-Server Migration Method uses the backup system that you have already been using all along. You do not even need any special NetWare drivers as with previous versions of NetWare 3.x. With the Same-Server migration, you simply back up your 2.x server using your normal backup procedure. Next you migrate the 2.x server's bindery information to a working directory, changing it to the 3.12 format during the process. Then you will create a 3.12 server on the machine that previously served as your 2.x server and restore the data files from your backup. Finally, you will need to migrate the upgraded bindery information from the working directory to the new 3.12 server to complete the upgrade process.

The Same-Server Migration Method is not quite as adaptable as the Across-the-Wire procedure, even though it requires only one server to perform. You can only designate what server information to migrate with this procedure. If you recall, the Across-the-Wire migration could also merge several file servers and redirect data files to different directories and volumes from where they were originally located. There is also the issue of losing data. With the Across-the-Wire method, you can always reperform the migration from the original 2.x server if the migration was not successful. With the Same-Server method, you will have to rely entirely on your backup system to rebuild the 2.x server if something serious goes wrong in the migration. If your backup system fails, you could sustain some permanent data loss. This is why we suggest that you make two complete backups of the 2.x server before beginning the migration procedure.

PLANNING FOR THE SAME-SERVER MIGRATION METHOD

To use the Same-Server Migration Method, you will need:

► the current server running NetWare 2.x with a 386 or better processor

▸ a workstation with at least 640 KB of memory, a high density drive, a backup device, and a hard drive if you only have one server on the network

▸ working copies of the NetWare 3.12 diskettes

Once again, it is important to check to see that the data from the 2.x server will fit on the new 3.12 server. Bear in mind that NetWare 3.12 requires a little more file and directory overhead than NetWare 2.x does. Also, you will need to take into account the DOS partition size you will need if you plan to boot your 3.12 server from the hard drive instead of a floppy. If the 3.12 server does not have adequate room for the 2.x server's files, then you may have to transfer only certain volumes or directories until you can add more disk space.

MIGRATING THE BINDERY TO THE WORKING DIRECTORY

Much of this section will sound similar to the *Across-the-Wire Migration Method* section with some notable exceptions.

First, check through the *Preparing a NetWare 2.x Server for Upgrade to NetWare 3.12* section earlier in this appendix to see which of the preparations apply to your situation. With the preparatory work out of the way, you are ready to begin the actual migration of the 2.x server to the new 3.12 server using your normal backup system as the main conduit for the exchange.

Log into your 2.x server as SUPERVISOR using a workstation that has at least 640 KB of memory. Make sure that the workstation is booted without any terminate-and-stay-resident programs (TSRs) loaded as they will only use up RAM that you might need during the migration. Make a complete backup of your 2.x file server from which to work with. You should now have three complete backups—one to use during the upgrade process, and two as a safety net.

Next, run the MIGRATE utility from the working directory you have created. The Select a Migration Option menu will appear. You do not have the option of choosing between a Standard migration and a Custom migration. The Standard migration is used for the Across-the-Wire method only and cannot be used in this case. Choose the Custom migration option.

The next screen you will see will allow you to choose between the two types of migrations, Across-the-Wire and Same-Server. Select the Same-Server option. You will now be asked in the next two screens to select the source LAN type and the destination LAN type. You will need to choose the NetWare 2.x option for the source and the NetWare 3.x for the destination. This screen allows you to set options for the migration utility and both the source and destination servers.

For the migration utility, you are allowed to set the working directory and the action to be taken in the event of an error. The source server settings allow you to designate which server is to be migrated, and it will log you into that server if you are not already. Simply press Enter to bring up a list of servers and the associated user names that you are logged into. If the server that you need to designate is not on the list, press Ins and choose from the list of Other NetWare Servers. You will need to supply the username SUPERVISOR and the correct password. The 2.x server that you want should now be available for you to select as the source server.

You can also set the migration to include all the information from the source file server with the All information option or a combination of the following information: Data files, Trustee assignments, Users, User restrictions, Groups, Default account restrictions, Print queues and print servers, and Accounting information (see the table in the *Preparing a NetWare 2.x Server for Upgrade to NetWare 3.12* section).

You can even limit the information transferred to the new server to only the volumes that you select in the third source server option by creating a list of volumes and/or directories to be migrated. This only will affect the bindery information. You will also have to prevent the data files that you wish to exclude from being restored from your backup.

The final three options that you need to set for a custom Same-Server migration have to do with the destination server and should be left alone for the moment. Press F10 to bring up the *Select a migration action* menu as seen in Figure B.8. This menu is slightly different from the one you saw in the Across-the-Wire section. You now have five actions possible, migrate the bindery to the working directory, migrate the bindery to the target server, return to the migration process configuration screen, view migration reports, and exit the migration utility. If there are no changes that you would like to make to the migration configuration, select the *Migrate to the working directory* option.

You should now see the migration report being generated on the screen. The report or log file name will be shown on the top of the screen as it is being generated. When the procedure is finished, press ↵ to return to the Select a migration action menu. Now it is time to view the migration report to check what was transferred and view any errors that might need some attention. Use the *View migration reports* option to bring up a list of reports (depending on how many times this procedure has been run) stored in the working directory and select the one this upgrade session generated. If there are no errors that require that you repeat the bindery migration to the working directory, you are now ready to move on.

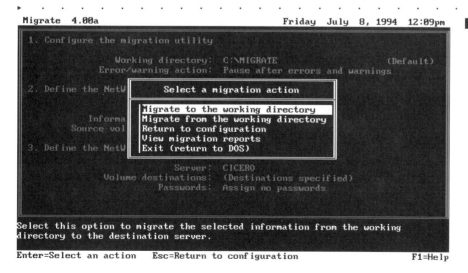

FIGURE B.8

The Same-Server Migration Action menu

MIGRATING THE BINDERY TO THE TARGET SERVER

At this time, you need to add the new 3.12 server to your LAN by using the installation procedures described in Chapter 6 followed by the installation of the 3.12 client software for the workstation you are working from using instructions found in Chapter 7. Check through the *Preparing a Net-Ware 2.x Server for Upgrade to NetWare 3.12* section earlier in this appendix to see if any of the preparations might apply at this time. Next, you will need to use your backup system to restore the data files to the new server. Remember to put them in the correct directories and volumes if you intend to redirect them when you migrate the bindery from the working directory.

Next, you will need to restart the migration utility you have copied in your working directory. You need to return to the configuration menu that you only partly filled out before you migrated the bindery to the working directory. Select the menu options in the following order:

- ▸ Custom migration

- ▸ Same-Server migration

- ▸ NetWare 2.x to select source LAN type

- ▸ NetWare 3.x to select destination LAN type

You should now be at the configuration screen. Do not change any of the settings you have previously set for the first migration—they need to remain as they are. Instead, use ↓ to reach part three where the destination server options are to be set. First, you are able to choose the destination server name similar to the way you chose the source file server name. Once again, if you are not logged in, the migration utility will allow you to log in at this time by pressing the Ins key and choosing from the available servers.

Next, you can designate which volumes and directories of the destination server you want the source server's information to be migrated to. For instance, you could tell the migration procedure to transfer the information from the TOLSTOY:VOL1 source volume (2.x server) to the TOLSTOY:SYS destination volume (3.12 server). Make sure, however, that when you restore the data files from your backup, you remember to redirect the files correctly.

Finally, you will need to decide how you wish passwords to be handled. Passwords are not upgraded along with other user information in the upgrade procedure. You have several options, though, for handling this situation. You can have MIGRATE assign no passwords to any account, and you can reassign them later or let the user set their own at their next login. If you are going to use this method, we suggest you reassign them so that this security function will still be in place. The users can always set their own passwords later on. MIGRATE can also assign random passwords to each account. These passwords are stored in the file NEW.PWD in the SYS:SYSTEM directory and can only be accessed by the user SUPERVISOR.

Once you have completed selecting your options for the migration to the destination server (see Figure B.9), press F10 to bring up the Select a migration action menu. Select *Migrate from the working directory* to transfer the bindery to the destination server. Again, you will see a migration report being generated on the screen. When the procedure is finished, press ↵ to return to the Select a migration action menu, and use the View migration reports to view the migration report. If there are no errors that require that

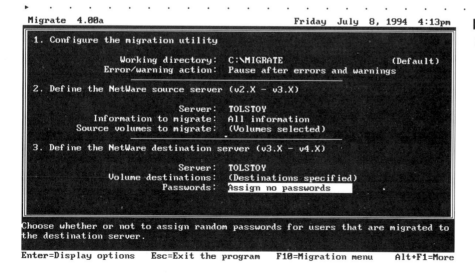

```
Migrate  4.00a                        Friday  July  8, 1994  4:13pm

1. Configure the migration utility

              Working directory:  C:\MIGRATE                    (Default)
           Error/warning action:  Pause after errors and warnings

2. Define the NetWare source server (v2.X - v3.X)

                         Server:  TOLSTOY
          Information to migrate:  All information
        Source volumes to migrate:  (Volumes selected)

3. Define the NetWare destination server (v3.X - v4.X)

                         Server:  TOLSTOY
            Volume destinations:  (Destinations specified)
                      Passwords:  Assign no passwords

Choose whether or not to assign random passwords for users that are migrated to
the destination server.

Enter=Display options    Esc=Exit the program    F10=Migration menu    Alt+F1=More
```

FIGURE B.9

Example configuration for a same-server migration

you repeat the upgrade, you are ready to proceed to the *Clean Up After an Upgrade from 2.x* section of this appendix.

In-Place Method

The In-Place upgrade is probably the easiest of the three upgrade procedures to plan for. All you need to perform this upgrade is a working copy of the 3.12 diskettes and your 2.x server. No other equipment is necessary because all the data files and bindery information is altered to fit the new 3.12 format without having to be moved to working directories or other servers. The flip side to this procedure is that if the procedure is interrupted before completion, you could have to rebuild your 2.x server from your system backups. Also, you have no control over what data and bindery information are transferred like you do with the other procedures. You will have to perform any data-file manipulations either before or after the upgrade. In addition, the In-Place upgrade will not work with NetWare 2.0, 2.0a, and 3.0.

TRANSFORMING THE 2.X SERVER WITH 2XUPGRDE.NLM

To begin with, make sure that you have taken all the preparatory steps discussed earlier that apply to you. The next thing you will need to do is bring up a 3.12 server so that you use 2XUPGRDE.NLM to convert the 2.x server. Down the 2.x server and reboot it with the working copy of the UPGRADE diskette. You will boot up in DR-DOS. Insert the working copy of the SYSTEM_1 diskette and run SERVER.EXE. After SERVER.EXE has loaded into memory, you will have a 3.12 server active, although there are quite a few more things to be done before it will be useful.

You now need to assign the server a name. Use the 2.x server's name so that changes to be made to mappings, login files, and batch files will not have to be made. You also need to assign an internal IPX number unique to this server. The internal IPX number must be a hexadecimal number of up to eight digits. As you can see, this part of the upgrade procedure is very similar to creating a new server, as discussed in Chapter 6. Use the information in Chapter 6 to load the correct disk driver and LAN driver so that you can access the server's disks and communicate with the network. You also need to load Macintosh name-space support at this time if you are going to support Macintosh workstations. The drivers for the hard disk(s) and network card(s) as well as MAC.NAM can be found on the working copy of the SYSTEM_2 diskette.

If you intend to create a DOS partition and have an IDE disk drive, do not use the IDE.DSK driver, but instead use the ISADISK.DSK driver with the /b and /l switches. Creating a DOS partition with FDISK will cause the IDE driver to obtain its head, sector, and cylinder parameters from the CMOS tables instead of from the disk drive. This problem will allow the NetWare and DOS partitions to overlap, resulting in data loss or corruption.

Running 2XUPGRDE.NLM in Batch Mode

The next big decision you are going to make is whether or not to run the In-Place upgrade method in batch or interactive mode. If you have performed an In-Place upgrade before and feel comfortable about what is happening, then the batch mode might be what you need. You simply load 2XUPGRDE.NLM with the appropriate parameter switches and confirm that you have a recent backup of the 2.x server. The In-Place upgrade will perform the four-step process (discussed in more detail with the interactive mode) that will rebuild your 2.x server disks into the 3.12 format without any further assistance from you. The table below shows you the parameters that you can set for the 2XUPGRDE's batch mode.

PARAMETER	EXPLANATION
/B	Runs the upgrade process in batch mode
/BATCH	Runs the upgrade process in batch mode
/BATCH2	Runs the upgrade process in batch mode, no pause for errors

PARAMETER	EXPLANATION
/BINDERY	Upgrades the 286 bindery only (skips to Phase 4)
/F	Skips the memory and disk resource check (Phase 1)
/FAST	Skips the memory and disk resource check (Phase 1)
/H	List of batch-mode parameter switches
/HELP	List of batch-mode parameter switches
/?	List of batch-mode parameter switches
/P0	Does not create a DOS partition on the SYS volume disk
/Px	Creates a DOS partition of x megabytes (0 to 32, with 5 as default) on the SYS volume disk
/R	Assigns random passwords
/R+	Assigns random passwords
/R-	User accounts will not have a password (default)

An example of 2XUPGRDE's usage in batch might be:

LOAD A:2XUPGRDE /B /R /F /P10 ↵

The above example of the In-Place upgrade would run in batch mode (/B), assign random passwords to the user accounts (/R), skip Phase 1 of the process, which is the memory and disk resource check, and create a 10 MB DOS partition. When the upgrade of your 2.x server disk(s) is completed, you will be shown the Final Status screen.

You are now through with the 2XUPGRDE utility, so press any key to return to the server-console command line. Type **MOUNT ALL** to confirm that all the volumes will mount and that there are no obvious errors. Down the server and type **EXIT** to return to DOS.

Running 2XUPGRDE.NLM in Interactive Mode

If you have not upgraded a 2.x server using the In-Place upgrade method, then we suggest that you use the interactive mode for 2XUPGRDE, so that you see what is happening and react accordingly if something unforeseen should come up. To begin the upgrade procedure, you will need to load 2XUPGRDE.NLM from the working copy of the UPGRADE diskette by typing:

LOAD A:2XUPGRDE ↵

You will receive a warning screen that basically asks if you have a complete, current backup of your 2.x server. If you do not or wish to end the utility for some reason, answer n and the utility will abort. If you are ready to proceed, answer y to the query and the utility will move on to the next item of business, determining the DOS partition size.

2XUPGRDE will need to know what size DOS partition you would like to have. It is much faster to boot the server from the hard drive than it is from a floppy. Also, you could keep various repair and maintenance utilities on the DOS partition, and they could be used even if the SYS volume is not mounted. For these reasons, we suggest that you go ahead and create a DOS partition. You can designate the partition to be any size from 1 to 32 MB. The default is 5 MB. If you do not want a DOS partition, answer 0.

2XUPGRDE is now ready to begin the four phase operation that will turn your 2.x disks to 3.12 disks. Phase 1 or the System Analysis Phase inventories each disk and each volume of your server. It also determines if your server has enough memory and free disk space for the upgrade process to work properly. Phase 1 is a nondestructive process. This means that the upgrade procedure can be interrupted for some reason without any adverse effects to the 2.x data because the 2.x data has not in any way been modified to this point. When Phase 1 is complete, you will be prompted to press any key to continue with the upgrade or press Esc to terminate the procedure.

Phase 2, or the Disk Analysis Phase, analyzes each server disk and builds an image of the new NetWare 3.12 disk. This image is stored in memory. This phase is also nondestructive, allowing the upgrade process to end without having to restore your server from the backup afterwards. Once again, when Phase 2 is complete, you will be prompted to press any key to continue with the upgrade or press Esc to terminate the procedure.

Phase 3, or the Disk Modification Phase, is your point of no return, so to speak. In this phase, 2XUPGRDE writes the new NetWare 3.12 file system to the disk. It also moves blocks of data that were in one volume in the 2.x server but may now be physically located in another volume due to the addition of a DOS partition among other things. This phase is a destructive phase because the 2.x server data is being modified and then overwritten to conform to the 3.12 format. Because of this, you are asked to confirm that you do, in fact, want this phase to begin. If, for some reason, the upgrade procedure were to be terminated after this phase has begun, you would have to restore the 2.x server from the backup and start the upgrade process from the beginning.

2XUPGRDE will proceed directly to Phase 4 or the Bindery Phase. At this point, the SYS volume will be mounted and any changes or modifications to the bindery will be made. Also, you will be asked whether you wish 2XUPGRDE to assign the user accounts random passwords or not, since a user account password cannot be updated. If you allow random passwords to be generated (by answering Y to the query), the new passwords will be located in a file accessible only by the SUPERVISOR named NEW.PWD in the SYS:SYSTEM. If you do not allow passwords to be generated (by answering N to the query), the user accounts will not have a password assigned to them. You will need to assign them passwords after the upgrade procedure is finished. When the bindery has been upgraded, the SYS volume will be dismounted, and you will be shown the Final Status screen.

You are now through with the 2XUPGRDE utility, so press any key to return to the server-console command line. Type **MOUNT ALL** to confirm that all the volumes will mount and that there are no obvious errors. Down the server and type **EXIT** to return to DOS.

PREPARING THE DOS PARTITION

If you had 2XUPGRDE create a DOS partition for you, then you need to prepare it for use. Use FDISK located on the UPGRADE diskette to create the DOS partition and designate it as the active partition. After the DOS partition has been created, you will need to use the FORMAT utility also located on the UPGRADE diskette to format the DOS partition by typing the following:

FORMAT C: /S /X

The /X is to tell DR-DOS that the drive is a hard drive; MS-DOS does not need this switch.

After you have formatted the DOS partition, insert the working copy of the INSTALL diskette and type, **INSTALL** to bring up the Select an Installation Option menu (see Figure B.10) and choose the Upgrade NetWare 3.11 option.

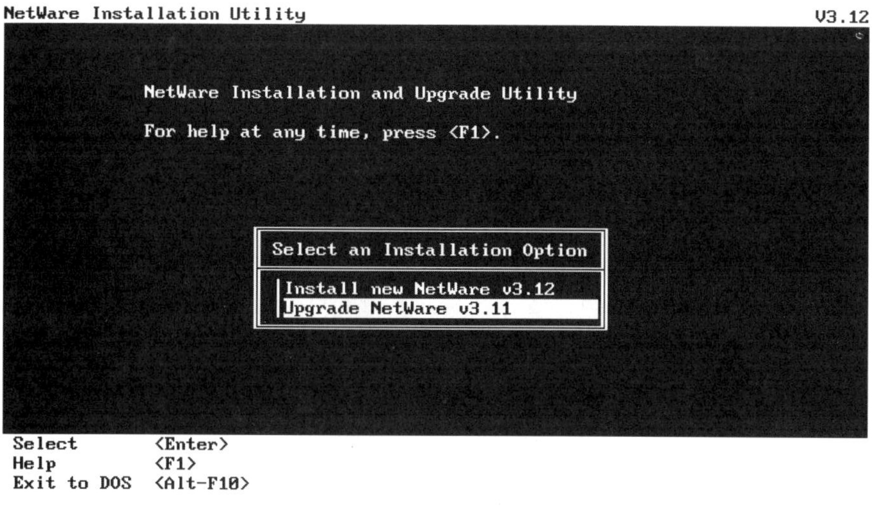

```
NetWare Installation Utility                                      V3.12

           NetWare Installation and Upgrade Utility

           For help at any time, press <F1>.




                    ┌─────────────────────────────────┐
                    │  Select an Installation Option   │
                    ├─────────────────────────────────┤
                    │ Install new NetWare v3.12        │
                    │ Upgrade NetWare v3.11            │
                    └─────────────────────────────────┘





Select        <Enter>
Help          <F1>
Exit to DOS   <Alt-F10>
```

FIGURE B.10

*Choosing an Installation
option*

You are going to be copying selected files to the DOS partition, including the files necessary for starting up the server.

The source of the files you are going to copy should be a floppy drive. If you need to change the source path, press F2 to move to that field, make your change, and press ↵ to continue. You will also need to set the destination path for the files to be copied. Press F4 to reach that field, add the destination path that you desire as is illustrated in Figure B.11, and press ↵ to continue. If you designate a path including directory names that do not exist on the DOS partition, you will be asked if you wish to create them. Press ↵ to begin copying the necessary files to the DOS partition after you have both the source and destination paths to your satisfaction. You will be asked for various working copy diskettes from time to time.

When the files are finished copying to the DOS partition, you will see a screen for setting up the Language Configuration as seen in Figure B.12. If you do not normally use a country code or code page in your DOS configuration, then accept the default settings and press F10 to continue.

Next, you have the choice of using DOS-compatible filenames or 3.11-equivalent filenames (see Figure B.13). We recommend that you use the DOS compatible names so that both DOS and the NetWare DOS Requester

▶ · ◀

FIGURE B.11

Selecting a destination directory

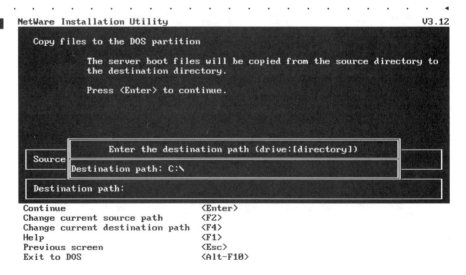

```
NetWare Installation Utility                                         V3.12

 Copy files to the DOS partition

         The server boot files will be copied from the source directory to
         the destination directory.

         Press <Enter> to continue.




            ┌──────────────────────────────────────────────────────────┐
            │         Enter the destination path (drive:[directory])    │
     ┌──────┤                                                           │──┐
     │Source│Destination path: C:\                                      │  │
     │      └──────────────────────────────────────────────────────────┘  │
     │ Destination path:                                                   │
     └─────────────────────────────────────────────────────────────────────┘
 Continue                              <Enter>
 Change current source path            <F2>
 Change current destination path       <F4>
 Help                                  <F1>
 Previous screen                       <Esc>
 Exit to DOS                           <Alt-F10>
```

```
NetWare Installation Utility                                      V3.12
```

These are your current DOS values for country code and code page. You may
accept these, or select new values. You may also choose a country specific
keyboard driver. Selecting new values will not change your DOS configuration,
but will only affect the server.

If you do not normally use a country code or code page in your DOS
configuration, choose country 1 and code page 437.

```
┌──────────────────────────────────────────┐
│           Language Configuration          │
│                                           │
│    Country Code:         1                │
│                                           │
│    Code Page:           437               │
│                                           │
│    Keyboard Mapping:    None              │
└──────────────────────────────────────────┘
```

```
Help              <F1>              Accept locale settings  <F10>
Previous screen  <Esc>              Change value            <Enter>
Exit to DOS      <Alt-F10>          Select field            <UP, DOWN>
```

```
NetWare Installation Utility                                      V3.12
```

This server may use either NetWare 3.11 or DOS equivalent filenames. NetWare
3.11 allows certain lower case characters in filenames. Neither DOS, nor the
NetWare DOS Requester (VLM), allow these characters in filenames. It is
recommended that you choose DOS filename compatibility. However, if you are
certain you need to use 3.11 equivalent filenames, you may do so, but you must
use a shell such as NETX, to access files whose names contain these
characters.

There are 25 lower case characters that are allowed in 3.11 equivalent
filenames, which DOS for the code page that you have chosen will not allow as
filename characters. Press <F9> to view a list of those characters.

```
┌──────────────────────────────────────────────┐
│   Select the format you desire and press <ENTER> │
│  ┌────────────────────────────────────────────┐ │
│  │ DOS Compatible Filenames (recommended)     │ │
│  │ 3.11 Equivalent Filenames                  │ │
│  └────────────────────────────────────────────┘ │
└──────────────────────────────────────────────┘
```

```
Help <F1>                              Previous screen <Esc>
```

can recognize the names. If you do not, then you will have to use a shell
such as NETX to access those files that are not compatible with DOS.

Finally, you are asked whether you wish to invoke an existing START-
UP.NCF file or not. If you answer Yes, a STARTUP.NCF file will be invoked
from the boot directory you copied files to. Choose No, since a STARTUP.NCF

file does not exist yet. The INSTALL.BAT program will then invoke the SERVER.EXE program. You are ready to complete the upgrade using the INSTALL.NLM.

COMPLETING THE IN-PLACE UPGRADE WITH INSTALL.NLM

Now, this is where those of you who created DOS partitions and those of you who didn't can get back on the same page. You have converted all your data to the 3.12 format. All that remains is to configure your server and copy the SYSTEM and PUBLIC files. Perform the following actions to complete the In-Place upgrade. See Chapter 6 for more details on how to set up a server.

1 · Run SERVER.EXE.

2 · Type in the old 2.x server name (this will be the new name for the 3.12 server).

3 · Assign an internal IPX number.

4 · Load the disk driver(s).

5 · Load the NIC driver(s).

6 · Bind IPX to the NIC driver(s).

7 · Mount all the volumes.

8 · Load Macintosh name-space support (optional).

9 · Load INSTALL utility from the SYSTEM_1 diskette.

10 · Create the STARTUP.NCF file and save it to the DOS partition.

11 · Create the AUTOEXEC.NCF.

12 · Copy the SYSTEM and PUBLIC files.

13 · Exit the INSTALL utility.

Clean Up After an Upgrade from 2.x

Now that your server has been upgraded, you need to do the following:

- ▸ Delete all of the 2.x operating system files and VAPs. They are no longer needed and the space could be used.

- ▸ Review and update in your login scripts, especially if you changed the server's name and/or redirected volumes and directories.

- ▸ Check the user accounts for restrictions and accounting charges to see if they are correct.

- ▸ Check directory and file attributes to see if they are in line with your security strategies.

- ▸ If passwords were generated randomly, distribute the new passwords to the users and have them change them as soon as possible. If passwords were not generated, assign them using SYS-CON, distribute them to the users, and have the users change their passwords as soon as possible.

- ▸ Install any new NetWare Loadable Modules to replace the functions that VAPs used to provide.

- ▸ Check to see if your applications are working correctly, especially if you changed the server's name and/or redirected volumes and directories. You may need to reinstall some.

- ▸ Restore any Hidden or System directories.

Upgrading from a 3.x Server

When upgrading from an earlier version of NetWare 386 (3.0, 3.1, or 3.11), you can use the same three techniques that we discussed earlier for the 2.x versions. The one big hurdle was the need to convert the data and bindery from the 2.x format to the 3.12 format. That is no longer a problem because the earlier versions of NetWare 386 use the same format for the data and bindery. Otherwise, the same advantages and disadvantages still apply. The migration methods will work in the same manner except you will choose the NetWare 3.x (3.00—3.11) option for source LAN type instead of the NetWare 2.x (2.1—2.2) option.

The In-Place method upgrade is a much simpler process when upgrading from a 3.1x server than upgrading from a 2.x server. First of all, the 2XUPGRDE utility is not needed since the data is already in the correct format and locations. If you are using Ethernet, load INSTALL and check your AUTOEXEC.NCF for a frame type inconsistency. NetWare 3.12's default frame type is 802.2, although you can use either 802.3 or 802.2. If you are using 802.2 anyway, then you will not have to worry about creating a new AUTOEXEC.NCF. If you are using 802.3, then be aware that if you attempt to create a new AUTOEXEC.NCF, NetWare 3.12 will try to use 802.2 unless you edit the new file and save the changes.

Next you need to down the server and type **EXIT** to return to the DOS prompt. If you are booting from a DOS partition, backup all the old boot files as a precaution. At this point, if you boot from a DOS partition, you are ready to proceed with the upgrade as it is described earlier in the Preparing the DOS Partition section except that you do not need to use the FDISK and FORMAT commands on the DOS partition. The upgrade for both those who boot their servers from a DOS partition and those who boot from a floppy is finished using the procedures described in the *Completing the In-Place Upgrade with INSTALL.NLM* section. The only exception is that when you are asked if you would like to invoke an existing STARTUP.NCF, you can answer Yes and skip steps 1 through 8, 10 and 11 and move directly to copying the new System and Public files using the INSTALL utility.

Upgrading from an IBM LAN Server v1.3 or PCLP v1.3

NetWare 3.12 also gives to you the capability to transform an IBM LAN Server v1.3 or PCLP v1.3 to the 3.12 format through the upgrade procedure. You can only use the Across-the-Wire and Same-Server methods to do this. Once again, the procedures are no different from the ones we discussed earlier. You simply must substitute either IBM LAN Server v1.0—v1.1, IBM LAN Server v1.2—v1.3, IBM PCLP v1.3 Extended Services for NetWare 2.x as the source LAN type.

Here is a list of important things to know when performing this type of upgrade:

- ► LAN Server components that are not migrated to the NetWare environment include: ALERTER, AT, AUTO LOG OFF, external resources, MACHINE ID, NETRUN, REPLICATOR, RIPL, and station restrictions.

- ► LAN Server rights are not inherited by subdirectories as is the case with 3.12. When the rights are migrated to 3.12, they will be inherited down the directory structure. The rights may need to be changed after the upgrade if this situation alters your security scheme.

- ► You need to add /API /NMS:2 /NVS:2 to the DOSLAN.INI file. Consult your LAN Server documentation for more information.

- ► You must be either the domain administrator or have administrative privileges in the domain.

- ► OS/2 extended attributes and long names are not migrated but may be truncated in order to conform to DOS naming conventions.

▶ For workstation setup, use Novell's ODINSUP or LANSUP protocol stack to allow for loading dual requesters on DOS clients in order to access both a LAN Server and a NetWare server resources.

▶ You must be logged into the domain server you want to migrate from before you run the migration utility.

▶ You can migrate only the following data categories to a 3.12 server: Access Control Profiles, All Information, Data Files, Groups, Print Queues, and/or Users.

▶ You will have to set up your print services from scratch after migrating to 3.12.

Summary

In this appendix, we have discussed the three methods available to convert a file server running NetWare 2.x or 3.x to a file server running 3.12, the Across-the-Wire, Same-Server, and In-Place upgrade methods. You can also upgrade an IBM LAN server or PCLP to a NetWare 3.12 server using the Across-the-Wire method.

▶ The Across-the-Wire Migration Method takes the old 2.x data, adds the new modified file and directory attributes, adjusts the bindery and sends it all across the network to the new 3.12 server.

▶ The Same-Server Migration Method does essentially the same thing except to just the bindery, which is then stored in a working directory on a workstation or unrelated network drive. The old server can then be upgraded to NetWare 3.12, followed by the restoration of the data from a backup and the modified bindery from the working directory.

▸ The In-Place Method is different from the other two in that the data and bindery do not have to be moved to another location but are instead modified in-place.

All three upgrade methods allow you to preserve the look and feel of your old server while converting the bindery and data into the new 3.12 format.

Configuring the NetWare Windows and DOS Clients

As we mentioned in Chapter 7, NetWare 3.12 ships with a new form of client workstation software called the NetWare Client for DOS and Windows. This software is based on Open Data-Link Interface technology for its first four layers, but has the added capabilities of the new DOS requester as the last. The DOS requester is a TSR program that loads and manages client software modules called *Virtual Loadable Modules* or *VLMs* that add additional capabilities to the requester. The analogy is similar to NLMs on a files server. These programs, together with the management program (VLM.EXE) and the various modules (VLMs), are known collectively as the *requester*. We have listed some of the additional capabilities VLMs provide below:

- improved speed through Packet Burst (Pburst) and Large Internet Packets (LIP)

- improved security with NCP Packet Signature

- support for NDIS Drivers and OS/2 Named Pipes

- backup of network workstations from a file server with SBACKUP

- additional support for Task-Switching environments in DOS and Windows

In this appendix, we'll briefly introduce you to these services and their capabilities. We'll describe the settings in the NET.CFG file that enable or disable the performance features and the backup service agent. Since a formal introduction to network interfaces like NDIS and Named Pipes is beyond the scope of this appendix, we'll introduce you to the features VLMs can support and refer you to the appropriate Novell documentation. Finally, we'll introduce you to the NetWare Windows Tools included with the NetWare Client for DOS and Windows.

Improved Speed through Packet Burst and Large Internet Packets

Both Packet Burst (Pburst) and Large Internet Packets (LIP) are designed to improve network performance. Though you will see performance gains on most networks, the most dramatic performance increases will occur across an internet with bridges and routers.

Packet Burst is a protocol that allows a client or server to send multi-packet messages across the network. A workstation will negotiate a packet-burst connection with a server and "burst" packets whenever there is a write request in excess of a single packet.

Large Internet Packets allow the size of individual packets to be increased in size. The default maximum packet size is 576 bytes. LIP allows bridges and routers to service blocks of data at up to 64 KB in size. The workstation and the server negotiate an appropriate packet size when establishing a connection.

To illustrate how this affects performance, consider that a read request for a 64 KB file without Packet Burst and LIP would require that the client and server exchange 128 separate request/response packets. Since every read request would require a subsequent response from the server without packet burst, there is a substantial amount of idle time on the network. With the performance enhancements in place, this exchange is reduced to a single read or write request. Over a wide area link, the speed increase can be dramatic.

By default, both Packet Burst and Large Internet Packets are enabled in the DOS Requester. To disable Packet Burst, reduce the amount of available buffers to zero in the NET.CFG file (set PB BUFFERS = 0). Similarly, you can disable Large Internet Packets by including the line LARGE INTERNET PACKETS = OFF in the NET.CFG file.

Improved Security with NCP Packet Signature

NCP Packet Signature is a security feature designed to protect clients from forged NetWare Core Protocol (NCP) requests. NCP Packet Signature requires that both the server and the client "sign" each packet transmitted across the network. The signature changes with each packet. If an attempt is made to forge a valid NCP packet, an alert message is sent to the file server console, the client, and to the file server error log.

The implementation of NCP Packet Signature requires that a security signature level be assigned for both the client and the server. On the client side, you enable security by setting the variable SIGNATURE LEVEL = {0, 1, 2, or 3} in the NET.CFG file. Since NCP Packet Signature can affect the performance of the network, it is set to level 1 in the NET.CFG file by default. The following list shows what each level signifies.

level 0	The client workstation does not sign packets
level 1	The client workstation will only sign packets if the server requests it (server signature level is 2 or greater).
level 2	If the server is capable of signing packets, the client will sign them as well (server signature level is 1 or greater).
level 3	The client signs and requires that the server sign packets. If the server does not sign packets, the login process will fail.

On the server side, there are corresponding signature levels (0, 1, 2, or 3). The following table shows the relationship between the packet levels at the client and the server.

	SERVER = LEVEL 0	SERVER = LEVEL 1	SERVER = LEVEL 2	SERVER = LEVEL 3
Workstation = Level 0	no signature	no signature	no signature	no login
Workstation = Level 1	no signature	no signature	signature enabled	signature enabled
Workstation = Level 2	no signature	signature enabled	signature enabled	signature enabled
Workstation = Level 3	no login	signature enabled	signature enabled	signature enabled

Support for Coexistence of ODI and NDIS Drivers

The two main network driver interfaces are the Network Driver Interface Specification (NDIS) and the Open Data-Link Interface (ODI). The NetWare Client for DOS and Windows can support both of these driver specifications simultaneously. This feature is called Open Data-Link Interface/Network Driver Interface Specification Support (ODINSUP) and allows you to load workstation software for different networks (e.g., LAN Manager, 3+Share, and NetWare). Once done, you can access files and applications on other networks as if they were on the same network. Enabling ODINSUP will depend on the type of NDIS network you are connecting to. For information on specific networks, refer to Novell's *NetWare Workstation for DOS and Windows Guide.*

Support for OS/2 Named Pipes

The NetWare Client for DOS supports connection to networks that support the Named Pipes protocol through the Named Pipes extender for DOS

(DOSNP). In order to use the Named Pipes extender, you must have an OS/2 Named Pipes server operating on your network. Once installed, DOSNP allows DOS to access the services of remote Named Pipes. For information on installing and using DOSNP, refer to Novell's *NetWare Workstation for DOS and Windows Guide*.

Supporting Workstation Backup with TSA Support

With VLMs, the server backup utility SBACKUP can backup both the server and client workstations (OS/2, DOS, Windows) that are running an appropriate Target Service Agent. TSA_SMS supports several levels of security and operates in the background on the station being backed up.

Using TSA_SMS is a matter of loading an agent on the client station and loading the storage device drivers and an agent at the server before running SBACKUP. For DOS-based workstations, the client agent is called TSA_SMS.COM and is located on the WSDOS_1 diskette.

Command line options for TSA_SMS specify a name for the workstation, a password, and a trust level for the backup procedure. The command line options of TSA_SMS appear in Table C.1.

T A B L E C.1	COMMAND-LINE OPTION	SYNTAX	DESCRIPTION
The Command-Line Options for TSA_SMS	Buffers	/B=n	Indicates the number of 1 K buffers allocated to TSA (n=2 through 30, default is 1). Increasing the buffers increases your throughput, but decreases the available workstation RAM.

COMMAND-LINE OPTION	SYNTAX	DESCRIPTION
Drive	/D=*xxx*	Indicates the DOS drives you wish to back up data from. Replace an *x* with a DOS drive letter you wish to access (ex. /D=CDE, where C:, D:, and E: will be accessed).
Help	/H	Displays all the options for TSA_SMS.COM
Name	/N=name of workstation	Gives the workstation a unique name. The name can be up to 10 characters long.
Password	/P=password	Sets a password for the station that anyone wishing to access through the TSA must know.
Remove	/R=server name, workstation name	Removes the workstation address from NDS. (Not applicable with 3.12 servers.)
Server	/SE=server name	Specifies the name of the server that will back up the workstation.
Stack	/ST=*n*	Specifies the stack size as a decimal (512 through 4096; the default is 2048). It is best not to change the default value.
Trust	/T	Can be used instead of password to let anyone with supervisor equivalency to access the workstation through the TSA.
Unload	/U	Unloads TSA_SMS.COM from the workstation's memory.

For example, the line below indicates that the server TOLSTOY should perform the backup, the user performing the backup must indicate the password RAPIER, the local drives C:, D:, and E: will be backed up, the number of buffers has been increased to 10, and the name of the workstation is GRENDEL:

```
TSA_SMS /SE=TOLSTOY /P=RAPIER /D=CDE /B=10
     /N=GRENDEL
```

Support for Task-Switching Environments in DOS and Windows

Some applications (like network fax service and modem-sharing software) directly request access to the IPX or SPX protocol. If you need to use these applications in a task-switching environment in DOS or in the Microsoft Windows environment, you can use the Novell Task Buffer Manager (TBMI2.COM) to support sessions with multiple applications. If the applications do not directly access IPX/SPX, or if you are only running one such application, you probably don't need TBMI2.

The Task Buffer Manager files are located on the WSWIN_1 disk. Before using them, you must unpack them to a directory on your hard disk or a network disk. There are two files required to support task switching under Windows (TBMI2.COM, TASKID.COM). For DOS task switching, only TBMI2.COM is needed. The syntax for unpacking them is as follows:

```
UNPACK source_drive:TBMI2.CO_
     dest_drive:TBMI2.COM
UNPACK source_drive:TASKID.CO_
     dest_drive:TASKID.COM
```

All that is required to use the Task Buffer Manager in DOS is to load TBMI2.COM before loading the task-switching software. For example, load TBMI2 before loading DOSSHELL for MS-DOS or TASKMAX for DR-DOS.

In Windows, each task running in a DOS shell window must be given a unique task ID. Before starting Windows, load TBMI2. After you have initiated a DOS shell and before you start the application, run TASKID to assign a unique task ID to the window. Run your application normally. After you have finished with the application and wish to close it, unload TASKID with the command TASKID /U before returning to Windows with the EXIT command.

Using the NetWare Windows Tools

If you installed the NetWare Client for Windows when you installed the NetWare Client for DOS, you will have a new group icon called NetWare Tools in the Windows Program Manager. After starting Windows, select this group and you should see an icon for User Tools. If you double-click on this icon, you will bring up a set of utilities called the NetWare Windows Tools. The opening screen for this utility appears in Figure C.1.

By default, the program opens on NetWare Drive Connections. If you look at the button bar below the title bar, there are several icons for the different utility functions. Currently, the Drive icon should be depressed. If you logged into the network before running Windows, this screen will also show your current drive mappings in the Drives: window and the available network resources in the Resources: window. If you did not login, these lists will be blank.

With the NetWare Tools for Windows, you can perform the following NetWare functions from within Windows:

- ► log into and out of network servers

- ► map network drives

- ► capture printer ports to network print queues

- ► send messages to other network users and groups

FIGURE C.1

The Opening Menu of the
NetWare Windows Tools

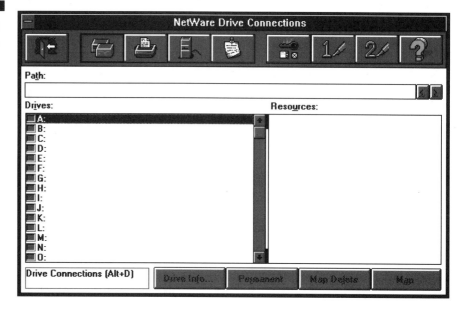

TIP
When you load your
requester in DOS, it
will attach to either
the first server to
respond or to the serv-
er indicated in
NET.CFG with
PREFERRED SERV-
ER. This server is indi-
cated in the Connec-
tions: list in NetWare
Tools with an asterisk
(*).

If you're not logged into a file server, you need to log in before you can perform any of these functions. To log in, select the server icon from the button bar. A list of available servers should appear in the Resources: window, the window title will change to NetWare Connections, and the button bar across the bottom of the window will display new options. See Figure C.2.

To log into a server, simply click on one of the servers in the resource list and press the login button on the lower button bar (or double-click on the server). A dialog box will appear requesting your username and password. You can also elect to log into the server as a guest by pressing the Guest radio button. See Figure C.3.

If your login attempt was successful, the server will appear in the Connections: list on the right hand side of the window.

Once you've successfully logged into a server, you can use the other utilities. To map network drives, click on the drive icon in the button bar. A screen similar to the one appearing in Figure C.4 should appear.

FIGURE C.2

The NetWare Connections Window

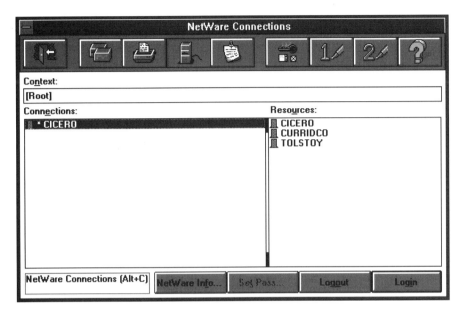

FIGURE C.3

The Login Dialog Box

In this example, we've logged into two servers called CICERO and TOLSTOY. The Resources: window displays a list of available network volumes. To map a drive letter, simply select the drive letter with the mouse, select a volume from the resource list, and press the Map button on the lower button bar. (You can also drag a network volume to a drive letter.) As

FIGURE C.4

NetWare Drive Connections

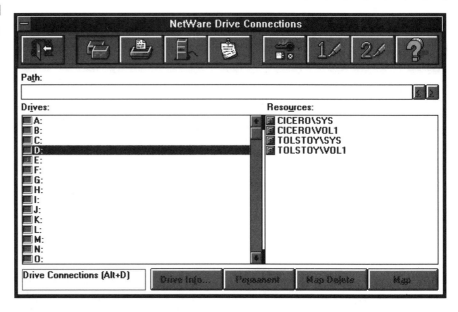

you can see in Figure C.5, the Drives: list changes as you map network drives.

Figure C.5 also shows the expanded resources list being used. If you double-click on a volume in the Resources: list, the directory tree will expand to show you the directories on the volume. The display will continue down the tree as you double-click on individual sub-directories. As you select directories further down the path, the Path: window will show your current position. If you press the Map button on the lower button bar, the current path will be mapped to the selected drive letter. See drive H: in Figure C.6 as an example.

At any time, you can get information about a drive by selecting the drive letter and pressing the Drive Info button on the lower button bar. The Permanent button places the currently highlighted drive map into the permanent map list. If you'll notice in Figure C.6, drives F:, G:, and H: display an icon to the left of the drive letter that indicated that these drives are permanently mapped. Any time you enter Windows, drives that are in the permanent map list are re-mapped automatically.

Mapped Drives in
NetWare Drive Connections

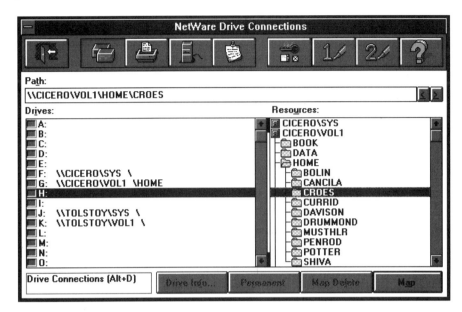

Mapping drives further
down the directory tree

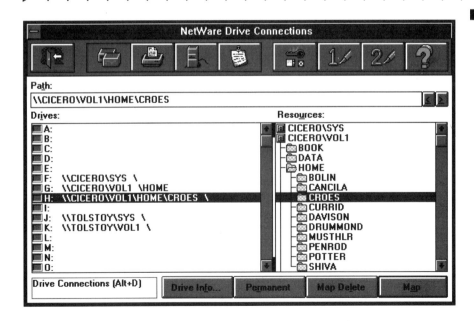

Capturing printer ports is as easy as mapping network drives. To capture a port, select the printer icon on the upper button bar. A window similar to Figure C.7 should appear.

The left hand Ports: list displays the current status of the ports while the Resources: list on the right displays a list of available network print queues. You can capture a port by selecting a port, selecting a queue, and pressing the Capture button on the lower button bar. You can also select and drag a print queue to the appropriate port. After capturing ports, your Ports: list should look similar to Figure C.8.

By default, ports captured with the NetWare Windows tools will print a banner with your username and a form feed command with every document. You can control the current port settings with the LPT Settings icon on the lower button bar. Pressing this button will bring up a window similar to the one that appears in Figure C.9.

In this window, you can set the printing options for a particular port. To remove the banner and the extra piece of paper at the end of the print job,

F I G U R E C.7

NetWare Printer
Connections

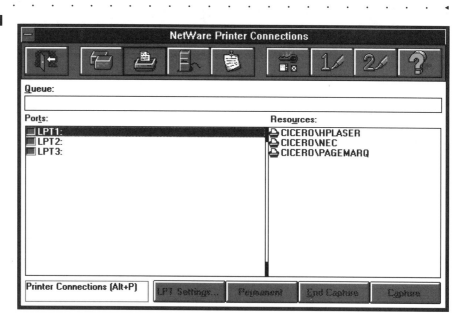

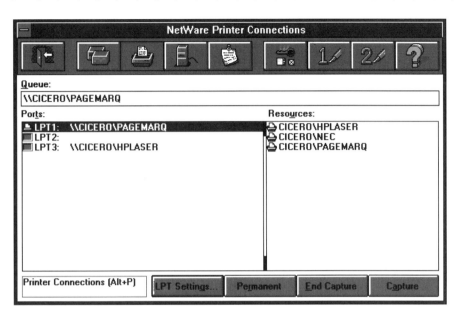

use the mouse to deselect the Form Feed and Enable Banner check boxes. Press OK when you are through making changes.

As with network drive mappings, you can make these connections and settings permanent by selecting the Permanent button from the lower button bar. Each time you run Windows, those ports marked with the printer icon next to the port name will be recaptured with the same settings automatically.

The note icon on the upper button bar is used to send messages to other users and groups. If you select this button, a window similar to Figure C.10 will appear.

The Connections: list will show the servers you are connected to. The Resources: list on the right shows a list of the users for the currently selected server in the Connections: list. To send a message, select a user from the Resources: list, type a message into the Message window, and press send. A dialog box like the one appearing in Figure C.11 will appear on the remote user's screen if they are using Windows. If they are using DOS, it will appear at the bottom of their screen.

F I G U R E   C.10

NetWare Send Messages window

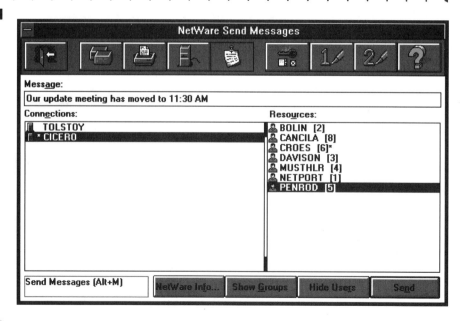

You can also send a message to a group of users. The Hide/Show Groups and Hide/Show Users buttons on the lower bar are toggles for displaying or hiding user and groups. Figure C.12 shows the list with both user and group icons present.

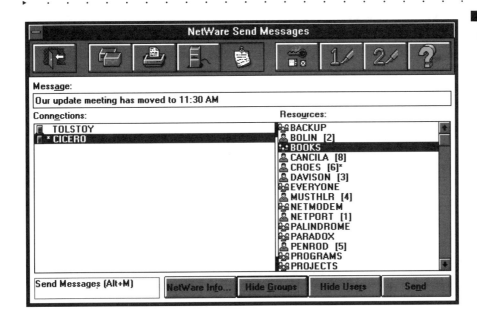

F I G U R E   C.11

A NetWare Broadcast
Message dialog box

F I G U R E   C.12

A Resources List of Users
and Groups

If you need additional information about a particular user or group, select the appropriate icon and press the NetWare Info button on the lower button bar. A dialog box will appear with information about the user or group.

The group of buttons on the right hand side of the button bar are used to customize the NetWare Windows Tools, define user buttons, and access the help system. The question mark button accesses help. The number 1 and 2 buttons are user definable.

To define a user defined button, press the button and a command line dialog box will appear. If you wanted to install the MS-DOS editor to button 1, for example, you would press the 1 button and type **EDIT.COM** in the command line box and press the OK button. From then on, when button 1 is pressed, the DOS editor would run in a DOS shell window.

The last button on the button bar is for setting the configuration of the NetWare Windows Tools. If you press this button, the NetWare Settings window in Figure C.13 will appear.

F I G U R E C.13

*The NetWare Settings
window*

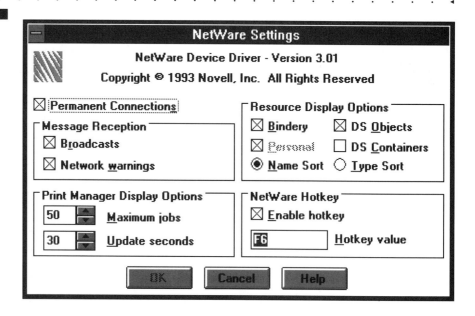

From this window, you can set the following options:

Permanent Connections	If marked, permanent drive maps and captured printer ports are possible. The default is marked.
Broadcasts	If marked, other users can send you broadcast messages. The default is marked.
Network Warnings	If marked, you will receive server network warning messages. The default is marked.
Maximum Jobs	Sets the maximum number of jobs the Windows Print Manager will display. The default is 50.
Update Seconds	Sets the number of seconds before the Windows Print Manager will update print queue status. The default is 30.
Resource Display Options	These boxes select which resources will be displayed in the Resource lists. If you have no NetWare 4.0 servers, the DS Objects and DS Containers boxes have no effect. The Personal box is for Personal NetWare. The radio buttons select if the list is sorted by name or object type.
NetWare Hotkey	The checkbox enables the hotkey when marked. By default, the hotkey is the F6 key. When selected, the F6 key will bring up the NetWare Windows Tools from anywhere within Windows.

Summary

In this appendix, we've briefly introduced you to the additional capabilities of the NetWare Client for DOS and Windows. We've described how to use the NET.CFG file to enable or disable VLM features and we've introduced you to the NetWare Windows Tools included with the NetWare Client for DOS and Windows.

Dictionary of
Key Concepts

A

ABEND (ABNORMAL END)

A message issued by the operating system when it detects a serious problem, such as a hardware or software failure. The abend stops the file server.

ACCESS CONTROL RIGHT

A file-system right that grants the right to change the trustee assignments and Inherited Rights Mask of a directory or file.

ACCOUNTING

The process of tracking resources used on a network. The network supervisor can charge for network services and resources by assigning account balances to users that they draw from as they use the services and resources.

The network supervisor can charge for blocks read, blocks written, connect time, disk storage, and service requests.

ACTIVE HUB

A device that amplifies transmission signals in network topologies. See *hub*.

ADD-ON BOARD

A circuit board that modifies or enhances a personal computer's capabilities. Examples:

- ▶ *Memory board*—increases the amount of RAM within a personal computer.

- ▶ *Network board*—installed in each network station to allow stations to communicate with each other and with the file server.

ADDRESS

A number that identifies a location in memory or disk storage, or that identifies the location of a device on the network.

APPLICATION

A software program that makes calls to the operating system and manipulates data files, allowing a user to perform a specific job (such as accounting or word processing).

- ▸ *Stand-alone application.* An application that runs from the hard disk or floppy disk in a self-contained, independent computer. Only one user can access the application.

- ▸ *Network application.* An application that runs on networked computers and can be shared by users. Network applications use network resources such as printers. Advanced network applications (such as electronic mail) allow communication among network users.

ARCHIVE

A transfer of files to long-term storage media, such as optical disks or magnetic tape.

ARCHIVE NEEDED ATTRIBUTE

A file attribute, set by NetWare, indicating that the file has been changed since the last time it was backed up.

ATTACH

To establish a connection between workstation and file server. The server assigns each station a connection number and attaches each station to its LOGIN directory. When you log in, your workstation is attached to the nearest file server.

ATTRIBUTES

The characteristics of a directory or file that tell NetWare what to do with the directory or file; also called *flags*. Attributes override rights and prevent tasks that effective rights would allow. For example, attributes can be used to prevent the following: deleting a file or a directory, copying a file, viewing a file or a directory, or writing to a file.

If users have the Modify right for a directory or a file, they can change the attributes and complete any task allowed with their effective rights.

AUTOEXEC.BAT

A batch file that executes automatically when DOS or OS/2 is booted on a computer.

A workstation's AUTOEXEC.BAT file, located on the bootable floppy or hard disk, can contain commands that load NetWare client files, load other files required by the hardware, set the DOS or OS/2 prompt, change the default drive to the first network drive, and log the user in.

A file server's AUTOEXEC.BAT file, located on the hard disk's DOS or OS/2 partition, can contain the command that loads the NetWare operating system (SERVER.EXE).

AUTOEXEC.NCF

A file server executable batch file, located on the NetWare partition of the server's hard disk, used to load modules and set the NetWare operating system configuration.

The AUTOEXEC.NCF file stores the server name and internal network number, loads the LAN drivers and settings for the network boards, and binds the protocols to the installed drivers.

AUTOMATIC ROLLBACK

A feature of TTS (Transaction Tracking System) that returns a database to its original state. When a network running under TTS fails during a transaction, the database is "rolled back" to its most recent complete state, preventing corruption from an incomplete transaction.

B

BACKING OUT

Abandoning an incomplete database transaction because of system failure.

NetWare's Transaction Tracking System (TTS) views a sequence of database changes as a single transaction that must be wholly completed or wholly "backed out" (no changes made at all). TTS stores all the information necessary to back out of a transaction and return the database to its previous state.

BACK UP

To copy a file, directory, or volume onto another storage device (such as a magnetic tape or an optical disk) so that the data can be retrieved if the original source is corrupted or destroyed.

BACKUP

A duplicate of data (file, directory, volume), copied to a storage device (a floppy diskette, cartridge tape, or optical disk). A backup can be retrieved and restored if the original is corrupted or destroyed.

The type of backup you perform and the storage media rotation method you use are dictated by

- The number of backup sessions you are willing to restore in the event of data loss.

- The number of duplicate copies of data you want and are willing to store.

- The desired age of the oldest data copy.

Perform backups when the fewest files are likely to be open. (Files in use at the time of the backup aren't backed up.)

BACKUP HOSTS AND TARGETS

A *backup host* is a file server that has a storage device and a storage device controller attached.

A *target* is a server that contains data you back up or restore data to. Any server, workstation, or service (such as NetWare Directory Services) on the network can be a target, as long as it contains Target Service Agent (TSA) files.

BASE I/O ADDRESS

The beginning address of an I/O port. The base I/O address allows the microprocessor to find the correct port for communicating with a particular device.

BASE MEMORY ADDRESS

A configuration option available on many network boards.

Network boards often use the base memory address as a buffer. When the network or device attached to the board sends information before the processor is ready, the information is placed in a buffer.

Since the address for each device is unique, the memory address of each buffer should also be unique. A common source for hardware conflicts within a machine is having two devices trying to use the same memory address for a buffer.

BAUD RATE

Under serial communication, the signal modulation rate, or the speed at which a signal changes.

BINDERY

A database that contains definitions for entities such as users, groups, and workgroups. The bindery allows the network supervisor to design an organized and secure operating environment based on the individual requirements of each of these network entities.

The bindery is composed of three components:

- *Objects* represent physical or logical entities, including users, user groups, workgroups, file servers, print servers, and any other entity that has been given a name.

- *Properties* are the characteristics of each bindery object. Passwords, account restrictions, account balances, internetwork addresses, lists of authorized clients, and group members are all bindery properties.

- *Property data sets* are the values assigned to an entity's bindery properties.

BINDING AND UNBINDING

The process of assigning a communication protocol to network boards and LAN drivers, or the process of removing it.

Each board must have at least one communication protocol bound to the LAN driver for that board. Without a communication protocol, the LAN driver can't process packets.

You can bind more than one protocol to the same LAN driver and board. You can also bind the same protocol stack to multiple LAN drivers on the server. You can also cable workstations with different protocols to the same cabling scheme.

BIOS (BASIC INPUT/OUTPUT SYSTEM)

A set of programs, usually in firmware, that enables each computer's central processing unit to communicate with printers, disks, keyboards, consoles, and other attached input and output devices.

BLOCK

A unit of stored data. In NetWare, the default block size is 4 KB, or 4,096 bytes, of data. For example, a 40-MB hard disk contains roughly 10,000 blocks of data-storage area.

BOOT FILES

Files, like AUTOEXEC.BAT and CONFIG.SYS, that start the operating system and its drivers, set environment variables, and load NetWare.

BOOT RECORD

Information that ROM-BIOS uses to determine which device to boot from.

ROM-BIOS loads a short program from the boot record to determine disk format and the location of system files and directories. Using this information, ROM-BIOS loads the system files (including two hidden files, IBMBIO.COM and IBMDOS.COM) and the command processor (COMMAND.COM).

BRIDGE

A device that retransmits packets from one segment of the network to another segment. A router, on the other hand, is a device that receives instructions for forwarding packets between topologies and determines the most efficient path.

BUFFER

An area in server or workstation memory set aside to temporarily hold data, such as packets received from the network.

C

CABLING SYSTEM

Part of a network's physical layout. See *topology*.

CACHE BUFFER

A block of file server memory (RAM) in which files are temporarily stored. Cache buffers greatly increase file server performance.

Cache buffers allow workstations to access data more quickly because reading from and writing to memory is much faster than reading from or writing to disk.

CACHE BUFFER POOL

The amount of memory available for use by the operating system after the SERVER.EXE file has been loaded into memory.

The operating system uses cache buffers in a variety of ways:

- ▶ The operating system loans cache buffers to loadable modules (such as LAN drivers, disk drivers, the INSTALL utility, etc.).

- ▶ The operating system allocates sufficient cache buffers to cache each volume's entire File Allocation Table (FAT) in memory.

- ▶ The operating system allocates enough cache buffers to cache parts of each volume's directory table.

- ▶ The operating system uses cache buffers as needed to cache parts of files that users want to access.

- ▶ The operating system allocates cache buffers to build a hash table for all directory names.

- ▶ The operating system allocates cache buffers to build Turbo FAT Indexes for all open files that are randomly accessed and have 64 or more regular FAT entries.

CHANNEL

The logical location of hard-disk controller hardware for the flow of data. For instance, a hard-disk controller in a PC is installed in a channel, or a DCB (disk coprocessor board) and its disk subsystems make up a disk channel.

Available channels normally include 0 through 4. Channel 0 is normally used by internal controllers and hard disks.

CHARACTER LENGTH

In serial communication, the number of bits used to form a character.

CLIENT

A workstation that uses NetWare software to gain access to the network. Under NetWare, client types include DOS, Macintosh, OS/2, UNIX, and Windows.

With the respective client software, users can perform networking tasks. These tasks include mapping drives, capturing printer ports, and sending messages.

CMOS RAM

(Complementary Metal-Oxide Semiconductor RAM) Random-access memory used for storing system configuration data (such as number of drives, types of drives, and amount of memory). CMOS RAM is battery powered to retain the date, time, and other information that requires power when the computer is turned off.

COM PORTS

Asynchronous serial ports on IBM PC–compatible computers.

COMMAND FORMAT

Instructions that show how to type a command at the keyboard; also called syntax. In NetWare manuals, a command format may include constants, variables, and symbols.

COMMUNICATION

The process of transferring data from one device to another in a computer system.

COMMUNICATION PROTOCOLS

Conventions or rules used by a program or operating system to communicate between two or more endpoints. Although many communication protocols are used, they all allow information to be packaged, sent from a source, and delivered to a destination system.

Workstation Protocols

NetWare workstations may use protocols such as IPX (Internetwork Packet eXchange), SPX (Sequenced Packet eXchange), TCP/IP, NetBIOS, OSI, and AppleTalk (for Macintosh).

Server Protocols

NetWare 3.12 has six layers of communication between an application and the hardware in the computer. These layers are based on the OSI model. The six communication layers are

- ▸ Application Layer

- ▸ Service Protocol Layer

- ▸ Communication Protocol Layer

- ▸ Link Support Layer

> ▸ Driver Layer

> ▸ Hardware Layer

In the server, communication protocols allow the Service Protocol Layer to communicate with the Link Support Layer. IPX, part of the operating system, is the default communication protocol.

You can use more than one protocol on the same cabling scheme because the Link Support Layer allows the LAN driver for a network board to service more than one protocol.

CONFIGURATION (HARDWARE)

The equipment used on a network (such as servers, workstations, printers, cables, network boards, and routers) and the way the equipment is connected—the network's physical layout. Hardware configuration includes:

> ▸ The specific hardware installed in or attached to the computer, such as disk subsystems, network boards, memory boards, and printer boards.

> ▸ The set of parameters selected for a board. For many boards, these settings are made with jumper and switch settings; for other boards, settings are made using configuration software.

CONFIGURATION OPTIONS

Settings on network boards that allow all boards in a system to be uniquely identified. Configuration options can include four settings:

> ▸ interrupt

> ▸ DMA

> ▸ base memory address

> ▸ base I/O address

The way jumpers or switches are set determines the configuration number for a board. Most network boards are factory set to a default option (0).

When more than one network board is installed in a workstation or file server, the configuration options for those boards must be unique so that conflicts do not occur.

CONNECTION NUMBER

A number assigned to any workstation that attaches to a file server; it may be a different number each time a station attaches.

The server's operating system uses connection numbers to control each station's communication with other stations.

CONNECTIVITY

The ability to link different pieces of hardware and software (Macintoshes, PCs, minicomputers, and mainframes) into a network to share resources (applications, printers, etc.).

CONSOLE

The monitor and keyboard at which you view and control server activity. At the console, you can enter commands to control printers and disk drives, send messages, set the file server clock, shut down the file server, and view file server information.

CONTROLLER ADDRESS

The number the operating system uses to locate the controller on a disk channel. The number is physically set (usually with jumpers) on a controller board.

CONTROLLER BOARD

A device that enables a computer to communicate with another device, such as a hard disk, network board, or tape drive. The controller board manages input/output and regulates the operation of its associated device.

COPY INHIBIT ATTRIBUTE
A file attribute (valid only on Macintosh workstations) that prevents users from copying the file.

CREATE RIGHT
A file-system right that grants the right to create new directories.

CYLINDER
A distinct, concentric storage area on a hard disk that roughly corresponds to a track on a floppy diskette. Generally, the more cylinders a hard disk has, the greater its storage capacity.

D

DATA FORK
The part of a Macintosh file that contains information (data) specified by the user. See *Macintosh files*.

DATA PROTECTION
A means of ensuring that data on the network is safe. NetWare protects data primarily by maintaining duplicate file directories and by redirecting data from bad blocks to reliable blocks on the file server's hard disk.

Protecting data location information
A hard disk's directory table and File Allocation Table (FAT) contain address information that tells the operating system where data can be stored or retrieved from. If the blocks containing these tables are damaged, some or all of the data may be irretrievable.

NetWare greatly reduces the possibility of losing this information by maintaining duplicate copies of the directory table and FAT on separate areas of the hard disk. If one of the blocks in the original tables is damaged, the operating system switches to the duplicate tables to get the location data it needs. The faulty sector is then listed in the disk's bad block table, and the data it contained is stored elsewhere on the disk.

Protecting data against surface defects

NetWare hard disks store data in *blocks*, specific data-storage locations on the disk's magnetic surface.

Due to the constant reading and writing of data to disk, some storage blocks lose their capacity to store data. NetWare prevents data from being written to unreliable blocks by employing two complementary features known as *read-after-write verification* and *Hot Fix,* as well as by storing duplicate copies of data on separate disks.

Read-after-write verification   When data is written to disk, the data is immediately read back from the disk and compared to the original data still in memory. If the data on the disk matches the data in memory, the write operation is considered successful, the data in memory is released, and the next disk I/O operation takes place.

If the data on the disk doesn't match the data in memory, the operating system determines (after making appropriate retries) that the disk storage block is defective. The Hot Fix feature redirects the original block of data (still in memory) to the Hot Fix redirection area, where the data can be stored correctly.

Hot Fix   A small portion of the disk's storage space is set aside as the Hot Fix redirection area. This area holds data blocks that are redirected there from faulty blocks on the disk.

Once the operating system records the address of the defective block in a section of the Hot Fix area reserved for that purpose, the server won't attempt to store data in the defective block.

Disk mirroring or duplexing   You can also protect your data with disk mirroring or duplexing. Mirroring stores the same data on separate disks on the same controller channel; duplexing stores the same data on separate disks on separate controller channels.

DATA SET

A group of data that can be manipulated by SBACKUP. Data sets can contain different items depending on which Target Service Agent (TSA) they are related to.

DCB (DISK COPROCESSOR BOARD)

An intelligent board that acts as an interface between the host microprocessor and the disk. The DCB relieves the host microprocessor of data storage and retrieval tasks, thus increasing the computer's performance time. A DCB and its disk subsystems make up a disk channel.

The NetWare operating system can handle up to four DCB channels. NetWare allows each DCB a maximum of eight SCSI (Small Computer System Interface) controllers, with each controller supporting up to two disk drives. External SCSI disk drive subsystems can be daisy-chained off the DCB port.

DEDICATED IPX DRIVERS

IPX.COM files created with WSGEN. These drivers work only with the IPX protocol. If you want to use other protocols, such as TCP/IP, you need to load ODI (Open Data-link Interface) drivers.

DEFAULT DRIVE

The drive a workstation is using. The drive prompt, such as A> or F>, identifies the default drive letter.

DEFAULT SERVER

The first server you log in to. The LOGIN command lets you change your default server.

DELETE INHIBIT ATTRIBUTE

A file-system attribute that prevents any user from erasing the directory or file.

DELIMITER

A symbol or character that signals the beginning or end of a command or of a parameter within a command.

In the command **NCOPY F:*.* G:**, for example, the blank space between F:*.* and G: is a delimiter that marks two distinct parameters.

Other delimiters used in NetWare include the comma (,), the period (.), the slash (/), the backslash (\), the hyphen (-), and the colon (:).

DEVICE DRIVER

An NLM that forms the interface between the NetWare operating system and devices such as hard disks or network boards. See *disk driver*; *LAN driver*.

DEVICE NUMBERING

A method of identifying a device, such as a hard disk, to allow the device to work on the network. Devices are identified by three numbers:

> **Physical address**. Set with jumpers on the boards, controllers, and hard disks. The physical address is determined by the driver, based upon those jumper settings.

> **Device code**. Determined by the physical address of the board, controller, and hard disk. In the device code #00101, the first two digits (00) are reserved for the disk type. The third digit (1) is the board number; the fourth (0), the controller number; and the

fifth (1), the disk number.

Logical number. Determined by the order in which the disk drivers are loaded and by the physical address of the controller and hard disk.

After device numbers are assigned, NetWare also assigns physical and logical partition numbers to the partitions created on the hard disks. Hot Fix messages use the physical partition number when recording which hard disks have blocks of data that need to be redirected.

All physical partitions are assigned logical partition numbers. These numbers are assigned to both the mirrored disks and the DOS and nonNetWare partitions. Mirroring messages use the logical partition number to record which hard disks are being remirrored or unmirrored.

DEVICE SHARING

The shared use of centrally located devices (such as printers, modems, and disk storage space) by users or software programs. By attaching a device to a network that several workstations are logged in to, you can use resources more efficiently.

DIRECTORY AND FILE RIGHTS

Rights that control what a trustee can do with a directory or file.

DIRECTORY CACHING

A method of decreasing the time it takes to determine a file's location on a disk.

The File Allocation Table and directory tables from the file server's volumes are written into the file server's memory. The area of memory used to hold the most-often–requested directory entries is called directory cache memory.

The file server can find a file's address (from directory cache memory) and the file data (in the file server's cache memory) much faster than if it had to retrieve the information from the hard disk. As the directory cache fills, the least-used directory entries are eliminated.

DIRECTORY ENTRY

Basic information for file server directories and files, such as the file or directory name, the owner, the date and time of the last update (for files), and the location of the first block of data on the network hard disk.

Directory entries are located in a directory table on a network hard disk and contain information about all files on the volume. The server uses directory entries to track file location, changes made to the file, and other related file properties.

DIRECTORY PATH

The full specification that includes server name, volume name, and name of each directory leading to the directory you need to access.

DIRECTORY RIGHTS

Rights that control what a trustee can do with a directory.

DIRECTORY STRUCTURE

The hierarchial system used to organize network files and directories on a file server's hard disk. Each file is given a file name and stored at a specific location in a hierarchical filing system so that files can be located quickly.

The file server is divided into one or more volumes, which are divided into directories, which contain files or subdirectories.

Volume The highest level in the NetWare directory structure. To a user, a volume appears much like a hard disk in a stand-alone system.

You can store directories at the volume level. Storing files at this level is possible but, for security reasons, isn't recommended.

Directory   A place within a volume where you can store files or other directories. Directories within directories are called subdirectories. A directory can contain any number of files and subdirectories.

Files   Individual records that can be created in or copied to any level of the directory structure (except, in practice, the volume level).

Directory path

A file or directory is located by its path, which states where the directory or file is on a volume. Under DOS and OS/2, directory names and file names contain one to eight characters, followed with an optional file-name extension.

Basic directory structure

When volume SYS: is created, it contains four predefined directories:

- *SYS:SYSTEM* contains NetWare operating system files as well as NLMs and NetWare utilities used for managing the network.

- *SYS:PUBLIC* allows general access to the network, and contains NetWare utilities and programs for network users.

- *SYS:LOGIN* contains programs necessary for users to log in.

- *SYS:MAIL* is used by mail programs compatible with NetWare. This directory also has an ID number subdirectory for each user that contains the user login script and print job configurations.

Types of directories

You can create directories for both executable files and data files, depending on what types of directories best fit the needs of your network.

Operating system directories   These store workstation operating system files. The number of DOS or other operating system directories you need depends on the number of different operating systems, versions, and workstation types on the network.

Application directories　Although applications can be accessed from local drives, installing them on the network provides convenient access.

Data directories　These are work directories for groups and users to keep work files in. You can also create a directory to transfer files between directories on the network.

Home or user-name directories　To provide personal workspace for users, you can create home or user-name directories. You can create a parent directory in volume SYS: called HOME or USERS. Or, you can create a separate HOME or USERS volume, then you can create a subdirectory for each user. The name of each subdirectory should be the user name.

Although data can be created and stored in a home or user directory, when data is stored in a user's directory, no other user (except network supervisors or managers assigned file rights) can access it. So, to allow users to share data, you can create work directories and make trustee assignments for groups or users who need access to these directories.

DIRECTORY TABLE

A table that contains basic information about files, directories, directory trustees, or other entities on the volume. The directory table occupies one or more directory blocks on the volume. Each block has 4K (4,096 bytes) of data. A directory entry is 32 bytes long, so each block can hold 128 directory entries.

Volume SYS: starts out with six blocks for its directory table. When a volume needs to add another block to its directory table, the server allocates another block.

The maximum directory blocks per volume is 65,536. Since each block can accommodate 32 entries, the maximum directory table entries per volume is 2,097,152.

In NetWare 3.12, a volume can span multiple drives, so each drive can have more than one directory table.

DISABLE

1 · To turn off; to render inactive. For example, the **DISABLE LOGIN** console command prevents workstations from logging in to the file server.

2 · To prevent certain interrupts from occurring in a processing unit (such as a network board) by setting a switch or a jumper, or using some other means.

DISK

A magnetically encoded storage medium in the form of a plate (also called a platter). The following types of disks are used with personal computers.

> **Hard disks** use a metallic base and are usually installed within a computer or disk subsystem. (Some hard disks are removable.)

> **Floppy disks** (also called *diskettes*) use a polyester base and are removable.

> **CD-ROM** (Compact Disc Read Only Memory) is a small plastic optical disk that isn't erasable or writable.

> **Optical disks** are either erasable and writable or write-once, read-many (WORM).

DISK CONTROLLER

A hardware device that controls how data is written to and retrieved from the disk drive. The disk controller sends signals to the disk drive's logic board to regulate the movement of the head as it reads data from or writes data to the disk.

DISK COPROCESSOR BOARD (DCB)

An intelligent board that acts as an interface between the host microprocessor and the disk controller. See *DCB*.

DISK DRIVER

An NLM that forms the interface between the NetWare operating system and the hard disks. The disk driver talks to an adapter that is connected by an internal cable to the disk drives. Depending on the type of disk controller, one or more drives can be connected.

The driver is loaded into the operating system at the command line.

DISK DUPLEXING

A means of duplicating data to provide data protection. Disk duplexing consists of copying data onto two hard disks, each on a separate disk channel. This protects data against the failure of a hard disk or failure of the hard-disk channel between the disk and the file server. (The hard-disk channel includes the disk controller and interface cable.)

If any component on one channel fails, the other disk can continue to operate without data loss or interruption, because it is on a different channel.

DISK FORMATTING

The preparation of a disk by dividing it into sectors so that it can receive data from the computer's operating system. A NetWare file server works with two kinds of hard disk formatting: DOS and NetWare.

DOS format

The DOS format allows you to boot the file server from a DOS partition. (This is optional, since a file server running NetWare 3.12 can also be booted from a diskette.)

NetWare format

NetWare partitions do not need to be formatted initially, unless a large percentage of the disk has bad blocks.

If you need to check for bad blocks, use the NetWare surface test rather than the NetWare format program. Use the nondestructive surface test if you have data already saved to the hard disk.

DISK INTERFACE BOARD

An add-on board that acts as an interface between the host microprocessor and the disk controller.

DISK MIRRORING

The duplication of data from the NetWare partition on one hard disk to the NetWare partition on another hard disk.

When you mirror disks, two or more hard disks on the same channel are paired. Blocks of data written to the original (primary) disk are also written to the duplicate (secondary) disk.

The disks operate in tandem, constantly storing and updating the same files. Should one of the disks fail, the other disk can continue to operate without data loss or interruption.

DISK SUBSYSTEM

An external unit that attaches to the file server and contains hard disk drives, a tape drive, optical drives, or any combination of these. The disk subsystem gives the server more storage capacity.

DMA (DIRECT MEMORY ACCESS)

A method used to reduce the burden on the processor in sending data to or receiving data from external devices.

The DMA controller chip moves data directly from a device to random access memory (RAM). When the data transfer is complete, the controller signals the processor that the job is complete.

Since the processor handles many tasks and the DMA handles only data delivery to and from RAM, the DMA chip is usually faster than the processor.

DOS BOOT RECORD

A record containing information that ROM-BIOS uses to determine which device to boot from. The boot record can be on either a floppy diskette, a local hard disk, or a remote boot chip.

ROM-BIOS then runs a short program from the boot record to determine disk format and location of system files and directories. Using this information, ROM-BIOS loads the system files (including two hidden files) and the command processor (COMMAND.COM).

DOS DEVICE

A storage unit compatible with the DOS disk format—usually a disk drive or tape backup unit.

DOS DIRECTORIES

NetWare directories that you create for DOS files.

DOS is an operating system used by individual workstations. You can access it from local drives; but it is more convenient to copy DOS program files and utilities to the network.

You must create one or more network directories for DOS and then copy the DOS files to the directories.

DOS SETUP ROUTINE

The routine that sets up the system configuration of your DOS client or file server. The setup routine records the system's built-in features (add-on boards, hard drives, disk drives, ports, math coprocessor) and available system memory. It also lets you set date and time, password, and keyboard speed.

The system configuration is accessed from the reference diskette (for IBM PS/2 systems) or from the setup or user diagnostics diskette (for most other systems).

DOS VERSION

The version number and name of the kind of DOS you are using (DR DOS 6.0, MS-DOS 3.3, etc.). Different machine types use different versions of DOS that are generally not compatible.

Since all DOS versions have identically named utilities and command interpreters, you can't place the files of different DOS versions in the same directory. Create a DOS directory for each workstation type or DOS version you use and load the DOS files into it.

DRIVE

Physical drive

A storage device that data is written to and read from, such as a disk drive or tape drive. A drive that is physically contained in or attached to a workstation is called a local drive.

Logical drive

An identification for a specific directory located on a disk drive. For example, network drives point to a directory on the network, rather than to a local disk.

DRIVE MAPPING

A pointer to a location in the directory structure, represented as a letter assigned to a directory path on a volume.

To locate a file, you follow a path that includes the volume, directory, and any subdirectories leading to the file. You create drive mappings to follow these paths for you. You assign a letter to the path, and then use the letter in place of the complete path name.

NetWare recognizes three types of drive mappings: local drive mappings, network drive mappings, and search-drive mappings.

Local drive mappings

Local drive mappings are paths to local media such as hard disk drives and floppy disk drives.

In DOS 3.0 and later, drives A: through E: are reserved for local mappings. To change this default, use the DOS LASTDRIVE command in your workstation's CONFIG.SYS file.

Network drive mappings

Network drive mappings point to volumes and directories on the network. Drives F: through Z: can be used for network mappings. Each user can map drive letters to different directories.

Search-drive mappings

Search-drive mappings are pointers to directories containing applications, DOS files, etc. Search-drive mappings let you execute a program even if it isn't located in the directory you're working in by enabling the system to search for the program.

When you request a file and the system can't find it in your current directory, the system looks in every directory a search drive is mapped to. The system searches, following the numerical order of the search drives, until either the program file is found or can't be located.

(Search-drive mappings aren't supported on OS/2 workstations. The search functionality is provided with the OS/2 PATH, LIBPATH, and DPATH commands.)

DRIVER

An NLM that forms the interface between the NetWare operating system and devices such as hard disks or network boards.

DYNAMIC CONFIGURATION

A means of allowing the file server to allocate resources according to need and availability. When the server boots, all free memory is assigned to file caching. As demand increases for other resources (directory cache buffers, for example), the number of available file cache buffers decreases.

The operating system doesn't immediately allocate new resources when a request is received. It waits a specified amount of time to see if existing resources become available to service the demand. If resources become available, no new resources are allocated. If they don't become available within the time limit, new resources are allocated.

The time limit ensures that sudden, infrequent peaks of server activity don't permanently allocate unneeded resources.

DYNAMIC MEMORY

The most common form of memory, used for RAM. Dynamic memory requires a continual rewriting of all stored information to preserve data.

If dynamic memory is too slow for a computer's microprocessor, overall performance will suffer while the CPU waits for requested information to arrive from memory.

A continuous electrical current is necessary to maintain dynamic memory. All data is lost from dynamic memory when the power is turned off.

E

EFFECTIVE RIGHTS

The rights that a user can actually exercise in a given directory or file.

Directory effective rights

These are determined by trustee assignments, if they exist. Otherwise the effective rights of the current directory are determined by the intersection of the effective rights of the parent directory and the current directory's Inherited Rights Mask.

No effective rights exist in a volume's root directory until you assign trustee rights.

File effective rights

These are determined by trustee assignments to the file if they exist. Otherwise they are the same as the directory effective rights.

ELEVATOR SEEKING

A method of organizing the way data is read from hard disk storage devices. Elevator seeking logically organizes disk operations as they arrive at the server for processing.

A queue is maintained for each disk driver in the server. As read and write requests are queued for a specific drive, the operating system sorts incoming requests into an order of priority based on the drive's current head position.

Elevator seeking, therefore, improves disk channel performance by significantly reducing rapid back-and-forth movements of the disk head and by minimizing head seek times.

EMBEDDED SCSI

A hard disk that has a SCSI and a hard disk controller built into the hard disk unit.

ENABLE

1 · To turn on, especially to restore a feature that has been disabled.

2 · To place in a state that will allow certain interrupts to occur in a processing unit (such as a network board). Interrupts are usually enabled by setting a switch or a jumper.

ENCRYPTED PASSWORD

A password that is scrambled before it is stored at the file server, to prevent an intruder from viewing or copying it.

Some encryption schemes encrypt the password at the workstation before it is transmitted to the file server. This prevents monitoring of the password over the transmission lines.

ERASE RIGHT

A file-system right that grants the right to delete directories, subdirectories, or files.

ETHERNET CONFIGURATION

The setup that allows communication using an Ethernet environment. In an Ethernet environment, stations communicate with each other by sending data in frames along an Ethernet cabling system.

Different Ethernet standards use different frame formats. NetWare 3.12 uses the IEEE 802.2 standard by default. However, you can configure file servers, workstations, and routers to use the Ethernet II standard or Ethernet 802.3 as well.

EVERYONE

A system-created group that includes all users created on the file server. Users are automatically added as members of EVERYONE when they are created. When all users need the same rights, you can grant those rights to the group EVERYONE.

EVERYONE is assigned Read and File Scan rights in SYS:PUBLIC. These rights allow all users to run NetWare utilities, execute DOS commands, and access application programs residing in that directory.

EVERYONE is also automatically assigned Create rights in SYS:MAIL. These rights allow any user to create and send mail to any other user.

The network supervisor can delete any user from the group EVERYONE or change EVERYONE's trustee rights in any directory.

EXECUTE ONLY ATTRIBUTE

A file-system attribute that prevents a file from being copied.

F

FAKE ROOT

A subdirectory that functions as a root directory. NetWare allows you to map a drive to a fake root (a directory where rights can be assigned to users).

Some applications can't be run from subdirectories because they read files from and write files to the root directory. But for security reasons, you shouldn't assign users rights at the root or volume directory level. Instead, load the files in a subdirectory and designate it as a fake root directory in the login script.

FAT (FILE ALLOCATION TABLE)

An index table that points to the disk areas where a file is located. Because one file may be in any number of blocks spread over the disk, the FAT links the file together.

In NetWare, the FAT is accessed from the directory table. The FAT is cached in server memory, allowing the server to quickly access the data.

Each volume contains a FAT. NetWare divides each volume into disk allocation blocks that can be configured to 4, 8, 16, 32, or 64K. (All blocks on one volume are the same size.) NetWare stores files on the volume in these blocks. If a file consists of one or more blocks, the file may be stored in blocks that aren't adjacent.

When a file exceeds 64 blocks (and the corresponding number of FAT entries), NetWare creates a turbo FAT index to group together all FAT entries for that file. A turbo FAT index enables a large file to be accessed quickly.

The first entry in a turbo FAT index table consists of the first FAT number of the file. The second entry consists of the second FAT number, etc.

FILE CACHING

The use of file server RAM to improve file access time.

NetWare file servers use cache memory located in the file server's RAM to speed up access time from the file server.

Cache memory allocates space for the hash table, the FAT, the turbo FAT, the directory cache, a temporary data storage area for files and NetWare loadable modules, and an open space for other functions.

If the cache memory uses the default block size (4 KB) and a file takes more than one block, the file is placed in a second 4KB noncontiguous block both in cache memory and on the volume (on the fixed disks).

Reading Files from Cache

Workstations can access the file server's cache memory up to 100 times faster than the file server's fixed disks.

When a workstation makes a read request from the file server, the file server executes a hash algorithm to predict a file address from a hash table. Hashing is a quick way of predicting the file's address in the directory table.

Writing Files to Cache

When a workstation writes a file to the file server, the file server performs the hash algorithm to find the file's cache buffer. It writes the file to the designated location and updates the directory table in the directory cache. Since the file has changed, its cache buffer becomes "dirty."

"Dirty" cache buffers indicate the file in cache memory is different from the file on disk. Since writes to disk take longer to perform than writes to cache, the file server keeps the "dirty buffer" designation on the file in cache until the disk receives the file.

Once the file is written to disk, the file server checks the data in memory against the data on disk. If there is a match, the buffer is no longer dirty.

As the cache memory fills up, buffers containing least-used files and directories are eliminated.

FILE INDEXING

The method of indexing FAT entries for faster access to large files. For example, to go to block 128 of a file, file indexing allows you to go right to the block instead of scanning through the 127 previous blocks.

NetWare 3.12 supports automatic file indexing above 64 blocks. The two levels of file indexing in NetWare 3.12 refer to the size of the table it uses to index the FAT. The first level indexes 64 to 1,023 blocks; the second level, 1,024 or more blocks.

FILE LOCKING

The means of ensuring that a file is updated correctly before another user, application, or process can access the file. For example, without file locking, if two users attempted to update the same word-processing file simultaneously, one user could overwrite the file update of the other user.

FILE RIGHTS

Rights that control what a trustee can do with a file.

FILE SCAN RIGHT

A file-system right that grants the right to see the directory and file with the DIR or NDIR directory command.

FILE SERVER

A computer that runs NetWare operating system software. The NetWare operating system enables the file server to regulate communications among the personal computers attached to it and to manage any shared resources (such as printers).

FILE SERVER CONSOLE OPERATOR

A user or a member of a group to whom SUPERVISOR delegates certain rights in managing the file server.

A Console Operator has rights to use the FCONSOLE utility. This utility allows the Console Operator to do the following:

- ▶ broadcast messages to users

- ▶ change file servers

- ▶ access connection information

- ▶ view NetWare version information

- ▶ change the system date and time

- ▶ enable or disable login for additional users

- ▶ enable or disable TTS

FILE SHARING

A feature of networking that allows more than one user to access the same file at the same time.

FILENAME EXTENSION

The extension used after the period in filenames. Under the File Allocation Table (FAT) system used by DOS and OS/2, filename extensions can be up to three characters. Under the High Performance File System (HPFS) used by OS/2, filename extensions aren't restricted to three characters.

FLAG

See *Attributes* under the entry *security*.

FORM

In a NetWare printer command, the name and size of the paper used for a print job.

FRAME

I · A variation of a protocol, such as Ethernet 802.2, Ethernet 802.3, Ethernet II, Ethernet SNAP, Token Ring, or Token Ring SNAP.

2 · A packet.

G

GATEWAY

A link between two networks. A gateway allows communication between dissimilar protocols (for example, NetWare and nonNetWare networks) using industry-standard protocols such as TCP/IP, X.25, or SNA.

GROUPS

A network convention that allows you to deal with users collectively rather than individually.

When users are created, they automatically become members of the group EVERYONE and have the rights assigned to that group. You can use SYSCON to create other groups based on who uses the same applications, printers, or print queues, who performs similar tasks, or who has similar needs for information.

You can use groups to simplify trustee assignments and login scripts.

GUEST

A username for anyone who needs temporary and restricted access to the file server.

NetWare creates the user GUEST automatically. You should evaluate the security needs of the network and determine whether to retain GUEST. You must also determine what rights temporary users can exercise and what information they can access.

GUEST is automatically a member of the group EVERYONE, and GUEST's rights flow from membership in that group. Any trustee assignments you make to the group EVERYONE will apply to GUEST as well.

The GUEST account has no initial password, but you can require a password on GUEST's account. We suggest you assign GUEST a password and change it frequently. Do not allow GUEST to change the password.

H

HANDSHAKING

The initial exchange between two data communication systems prior to and during data transmission to ensure proper data transmission. A handshake method (such as XON/XOFF) is part of the complete transmission protocol.

A serial (asynchronous) transmission protocol might include the handshake method (XON/XOFF), baud rate, parity setting, number of data bits, and number of stop bits.

HARD DISK

A high-capacity magnetic storage device that allows a user to write and read data. Hard disks can be network or local workstation disks. Internal disks use channel 0 and external hard disks use channels 1 through 4.

HASHING

A process that facilitates access to a file in a large volume by calculating the file's address both in cache memory and on the hard disk.

When a workstation wants to read a file from the file server, the server performs a hash algorithm which predicts an address on a hash table. In NetWare 3.12, it is common to find the file on the first try 95 percent of the time. This method is much more efficient than searching for a file sequentially.

HEXADECIMAL

A base-16 alphanumeric numbering system used to specify addresses in computer memory. In hexadecimal notation, the decimal numbers 0 through 15 are represented by the decimal digits 0 through 9 and the alphabetic digits A through F (A = decimal 10, B = decimal 11, etc.).

HIDDEN ATTRIBUTE

A DOS and OS/2 attribute that hides a directory or file from the DOS or OS/2 DIR command and prevents the directory or file from being deleted or copied.

HOME DIRECTORY

A private network directory that the network supervisor can create for a user. The user's login script should contain a drive mapping to his or her home directory.

HOP COUNT

The number of network boards a message packet passes through on the way to its destination on an internetwork. The destination network can be no more than 16 hops (file server or router interface boards) from the source.

HOT FIX

A method NetWare uses to ensure that data is stored safely. Data blocks are redirected from faulty blocks on the server's disk to a small portion of disk space set aside as the Hot Fix redirection area. Once the operating system records the address of the defective block in a section of the Hot Fix area reserved for that purpose, the server won't attempt to store data in defective blocks.

By default, 2 percent of a disk partition's space is set aside as the Hot Fix redirection area.

HUB

A device that modifies transmission signals, allowing the network to be lengthened or expanded with additional workstations. There are two kinds of hubs:

- ▸ Active hubs
- ▸ Passive hubs

Active hubs

An active hub amplifies transmission signals in network topologies. Use an active hub to add workstations to a network or to extend the cable distance between stations and the server.

Passive hubs

A device used in certain network topologies to split a transmission signal, allowing additional workstations to be added. A passive hub can't amplify the signal, so it must be cabled directly to a station or to an active hub.

I

IDENTIFIER VARIABLES

Variables used in login scripts that allow you to enter a variable (such as LOGIN_NAME) in a login script command, rather than a specific name (such as RICHARD).

INDEXED ATTRIBUTE

A status flag set when a file exceeds a set size, indicating that the file is indexed for fast access.

INHERITED RIGHTS MASK

A list of rights that can be created for any file and directory. When the Inherited Rights Mask is created, it controls which rights users can inherit. The Inherited Rights Mask for any file or directory is modified by revoking rights.

The *directory's* Inherited Rights Mask controls which parent directory effective rights can be exercised in the current directory. The *file's* Inherited Rights Mask controls which of the current directory's rights can be exercised in the file.

INTERLEAVE FACTOR

A method of adjusting the speed of the controller to match the speed of the hard disk.

Typically, a hard disk spins faster than a controller can perform a read/write. If the controller is not fast enough to read or write consecutive sectors on a hard disk track, then the controller can be programmed to skip one or more sectors of the hard disk before the next read/write is performed.

If the controller reads or writes one sector and then skips a sector, the interleave factor is 2 (one out of every two sectors is used). The interleave factor can be written as 2:1.

INTERNETWORK

Two or more networks connected by an internal or external router. Users on an internetwork can use the resources (files, printers, hard disks) of all connected networks, provided they have security clearance.

INTERRUPT

A signal or call to a specific routine. The microprocessor suspends the current program until the routine is completed. The processor continues with the original program after the routine is completed.

Interrupts are divided into two general types: hardware and software. A *hardware interrupt* is caused by a signal from a hardware device, such as a printer. A *software interrupt* is created by instructions from within a software program.

IPX INTERNAL NETWORK NUMBER

A logical network number that identifies an individual file server. The IPX internal network number for each server must be unique, hexadecimal, and from one to eight digits long (1 to FFFFFFFE), and is assigned to the server during installation.

J

JUMPER BLOCK

A group of jumper pins that can be connected (jumpered) or left unconnected to make hardware configuration settings on a circuit board.

L

LAN DRIVER

Software routines that understand, and control, the physical structure of a network board. A LAN driver serves as a link between a station's operating system and the physical network parts.

LAN drivers are specific to a particular network board, but when you run WSGEN and adapt the driver to the IPX protocol, you allow the operating system to communicate on a network regardless of the type of network board.

LINK SUPPORT LAYER (LSL)

An implementation of the Open Data-Link Interface (ODI) specification that serves as an intermediary between the workstation's LAN drivers and communication protocols, such as IPX, AFP, or TCP/IP. The LSL allows one or more network boards to service one or more similar or dissimilar protocol stacks.

LOADABLE MODULE (NLM)

A program you can load and unload from file server memory while the server is running. NLMs link disk drivers, LAN drivers, name space, and other file server management and enhancement utilities to the operating system.

The file server allocates a portion of memory to the loadable module when it is loaded. The module uses the memory to perform a task and then returns control of the memory back to the operating system when the module is unloaded.

NetWare 3.12 has four types of loadable modules:

- ► disk drivers

- ► LAN drivers

- ► Management utilities and server applications modules

- ► Name space modules

Disk drivers

These control communication between the operating system and the hard disks. These loadable modules have a .DSK extension.

LAN drivers

These control communication between the operating system and the network boards. These loadable modules have an .LAN extension.

Management utilities and server applications modules

These allow you to monitor and change configuration options. These loadable modules have an .NLM extension.

Name space modules

These allow non-DOS naming conventions to be stored in the directory and file naming system. These loadable modules have an .NAM extension.

LOADING AND UNLOADING

The process of linking and unlinking NLMs to the NetWare operating system. NLMs can be loaded and unloaded while NetWare is running.

LOG IN

To initialize the user's security rights and the user's environment by using the LOGIN command.

When a user initiates a login request, the operating system scans the bindery and reads the user's bindery information into memory. The user is then asked for a password.

All security information is then placed into the file server's connection list and the user is said to be "logged in."

At this point, the login program executes the login script to initialize environmental variables, map network drives, and control the user's program execution.

LOG OUT

To break the file server/workstation connection and delete any drives mapped to that server by using the LOGOUT utility.

LOGIN DIRECTORY

The SYS:LOGIN directory, created during network installation, that contains the LOGIN and SLIST utilities. Users can use these utilities to log in and view a list of available file servers.

LOGIN RESTRICTIONS

Limitations on a user account that control access to the network, including requiring a password, setting account limits, limiting disk space, specifying the number of connections, and setting time restrictions.

When a user violates login restrictions, NetWare disables the account and no one can log in using that user name. This prevents unauthorized users from logging in.

LOGIN SCRIPT

A file containing commands that set up your users' workstation environments whenever they log in. Login scripts are similar to configurable batch files and are executed by the LOGIN utility.

You can use login scripts to map drives and search drives to directories, display messages, set environment variables, and execute programs or menus.

Types of login scripts

NetWare uses two kinds of login scripts:

- ▶ System login scripts
- ▶ User login scripts

System login scripts   These allow the network supervisor to set network drive mappings and search drive mappings for all users. It includes commands that should be executed for every user.

User login scripts   These specify the users' individual drive mappings and environment variables. A user login script is created for each user in SYSCON and saved in an ID subdirectory for that user in the SYS:MAIL directory.

LONG MACHINE TYPE

A six-letter name representing a DOS workstation brand. (This doesn't apply to OS/2 workstations.) Use the long machine type in system login scripts (using the MACHINE identifier variable) to automatically map a drive to the correct version of DOS assigned to the station.

IBM computers use the long machine type IBM_PC. If the station is not an IBM computer, create a long machine type for the station in a NET.CFG file. Use the six-letter name for the long machine type as the subdirectory name when you use more than one brand of workstation. Example: COMPAQ.

LPT1

The primary parallel printer port of a personal computer.

LSL

See *Link Support Layer.*

M

MACINTOSH FILES

Files used on Macintosh computers. A Macintosh file contains two parts, the data fork and the resource fork:

> ► The *data fork* contains information (data) specified by the user.

> ▸ The *resource fork* contains file resources, including Macintosh-specific information such as the windows and icons used with the file.

When a Macintosh client accesses the file stored on the server, it accesses both the data and resource forks; both of these are required for the Macintosh to use the file. When a non-Macintosh client accesses the file stored on the server, only the data fork is used.

MAIL DIRECTORY

The SYS:MAIL directory, created during network installation, used by mail programs that are compatible with NetWare.

When network users are created, they are assigned a User ID number. Users are also assigned a subdirectory, or mailbox, in the MAIL directory. The User ID number is used as the mailbox name.

Each user's login script is stored in his or her mailbox, allowing the login script to be accessed each time the user logs in.

MAJOR RESOURCE

A category of data defined by the Target Service Agent, and recognized by SBACKUP. A major resource contains data that can be backed up as a group—for example, server, volume, etc.

MAP

For DOS and OS/2 clients, to assign a drive letter to a directory path on a volume. Example: If you map drive F: to the directory SYS:ACCTS/RECEIVE, you access that directory every time you change to drive F:.

MEMORY

The internal dynamic storage of a computer that can be addressed by the computer's operating system; referred to frequently as RAM (random-access memory).

Memory accepts and holds binary data. To be effective, a computer must store the data that will be operated on as well as the program that directs the operations to be performed.

Memory stores information and rapidly accesses any part of the information upon request.

MEMORY BOARD

An add-on board that increases the amount of RAM within a personal computer.

MEMORY POOLS

NetWare 3.12 uses memory for many functions. To initialize the operating system, DOS must be booted and loaded into low memory. Then the operating system is booted and loaded into high memory (memory above 1 MB).

The memory that is not used for the OS or DOS is given to three main memory pools:

- ▸ the file cache buffer pool
- ▸ the permanent pool
- ▸ the alloc memory pool

File cache buffer pool

This is used to store the most frequently used files. It is the pool from which all other pools obtain additional memory.

Permanent pool

This is used for long-term memory needs, such as directory cache buffers and packet receive buffers.

Alloc memory pool

This stores the following information:.

- ▸ drive mappings
- ▸ service request buffers
- ▸ open and locked files
- ▸ server advertising
- ▸ user connection information
- ▸ messages waiting to be broadcast
- ▸ loadable module tables
- ▸ queue manager tables

MESSAGE PACKET

A unit of information used in network communication. Messages sent between network devices (workstations, file servers, etc.) are formed into packets at the source device. The packets are reassembled, if necessary, into complete messages when they reach their destination.

A message packet might contain a request for service, information on how to handle the request, and the data that will be serviced.

MESSAGE SYSTEM

A communications protocol that runs on top of IPX. It provides an engine that allows a node on the network to send messages to other nodes. A set of APIs (application program interfaces) gives programs access to the message system.

MINOR RESOURCE

A category of data defined by the Target Service Agent and recognized by SBACKUP. A minor resource might be located in the directory structure below the selected major resource—for example, directories, subdirectories, or files.

MODIFY BIT

A bit set by the operating system, when a file is changed, to indicate that data has been modified. When a backup is performed, SBACKUP can check to see whether Modify bits are set, and can back up only those files that have their Modify bit set.

MODIFY RIGHT

A directory or file right that grants the right to change the attributes or name of a directory or file.

MULTIPLE NAME-SPACE SUPPORT

The method that allows various workstations running different operating systems to create their own familiar naming conventions. In other words, the file system can present multiple client views for any given file.

Each file stored on a given volume has a name that any workstation can recognize. This name is stored in a file entry in the volume's directory table.

Different operating systems (DOS, OS/2, Macintosh, Windows, and UNIX) have different conventions for naming files. These conventions include name length, allowable characters, case-sensitivity, data and resource forks, length of extensions, multiple extensions, etc.

MULTISERVER NETWORK

A single network that has two or more file servers operating. On a multiserver network, users can access files from any file server they have access rights to.

A multiserver network isn't the same as an internetwork, where two or more networks are linked through a router.

N

NAME SPACE

A loadable module that allows you to store non-DOS files on a NetWare 3.12 server. Files appear in native mode to users at different workstations.

DOS name space is always provided by the operating system. Any other file types, such as Macintosh or OS/2, must have a name space loadable module linked with the operating system before the file server can store such files.

These modules have a .NAM extension. Once the module is loaded, you must use ADD NAME SPACE to configure the volumes so that you can store the other types of files.

When the name space support is added to the volume, the volume creates another entry in the directory table for the directory and file naming conventions of that file system.

NETBIOS.EXE

NetWare's NetBIOS emulator program that allows workstations to run applications written for peer-to-peer communication or distributed processing. The INT2F.COM file is used with NETBIOS.EXE.

NETWARE EXPRESS

Novell's private electronic information service that provides access to Novell's Network Support Encyclopedia. NetWare Express uses the GE Information Services network and software and requires a connection through an asynchronous modem.

NETWARE LOADABLE MODULE (NLM)

See *Loadable Module (NLM)*.

NETWARE OPERATING SYSTEM

The network operating system developed by Novell, Inc. The NetWare operating system runs in the file server and controls system resources and information processing on the entire network or internetwork.

NETWARE PARTITION

A partition created on each network hard disk, from which volumes are created. See *partition*.

NETWIRE

Novell's online information service, which provides access to Novell product information, Novell services information, and time-sensitive technical information for NetWare users.

NetWire is accessed through the CompuServe Information Service. It requires a PC or compatible workstation, a modem, and a communications program.

NETWORK

A group of computers that can communicate with each other, share peripherals (such as hard disks and printers), and access remote hosts or other networks.

A NetWare network consists of workstations, peripherals, and one or more file servers. NetWare network users can share the same files (both data and program files), send messages directly between workstations, and protect files with an extensive security system.

NETWORK BACKBONE

A cabling system that file servers and routers are attached to. If your network has three or more file servers, this may be an efficient way to improve network performance. The central cable handles all network traffic, decreasing packet transmission time and traffic on the network.

NETWORK BOARD

A circuit board installed in each workstation to allow stations to communicate with each other and with the file server. Some printers contain their own network board to allow them to attach directly to the network cabling.

NETWORK COMMUNICATION

Data transmission between workstations. Requests for services and data pass from one workstation to another through a communication medium such as cabling.

NETWORK INTERFACE CONTROLLER (NIC)

A circuit board installed in each workstation to allow stations to communicate with each other and with the file server. NetWare documentation uses the term *Network board* instead of *Network Interface Controller.*

NETWORK NODE

A personal computer or other device connected to a network by a network board and a communication medium. A network node can be a server, workstation, router, printer, or fax machine.

NETWORK NUMBERING

The system of numbers that identifies servers, network boards, and cable segments. These network numbers include the following:

- ▸ *IPX external network number.* A number that uniquely identifies a network cable segment.

- ▸ *IPX internal network number.* A number that identifies an individual file server.

▸ *Node number.* A number that identifies a network board (in a server, workstation, or router).

NETWORK PRINTER

A printer shared in a network environment.

NETWORK SUPERVISOR

See *SUPERVISOR.*

NETWORK SUPPORT ENCYCLOPEDIA (NSE)

Novell's electronic information database containing comprehensive information about network technology.

The NSE includes downloadable NetWare patches, fixes, drivers, and utilities as well as Novell technical bulletins and manuals. NSE contains NetWare Application Notes (with graphics), the NetWare Buyer's Guide, Novell press releases, and additional product information. The NSE also includes Novell Labs' hardware- and software-compatibility test results.

NETX

The NetWare workstation shell that runs in real-mode memory. In NetWare 3.12, it is still available, but the use of VLMs is preferred.

A VLM (NETX.VLM) under the NetWare DOS Requester that provides backward compatibility with NETX and other older versions of the shell.

NIC

See *Network Interface Controller.*

NLM

See *Loadable Module (NLM).*

NODE NUMBER

A number that uniquely identifies a network board (in a server, workstation, or router). Every station on a network has a unique node number to distinguish it from other stations.

O

OBJECT

An entity defined on the network and thus given access to the file server. Object types include users, groups, file servers, print servers, and archive servers and are defined in the file server's bindery.

OPEN DATA-LINK INTERFACE (ODI)

An architecture that allows multiple LAN drivers and protocols to coexist on network systems.

ODI supports media- and protocol-independent communications by providing a standard interface that allows transport protocols to share a single network board without conflict.

P

PACKET

See *Message packet.*

PACKET RECEIVE BUFFER

An area in the file server's memory set aside to temporarily hold data packets arriving from the various workstations. The packets remain in this buffer until the server is ready to process them and send them to their destination. This ensures the smooth flow of data into the server, even during times of particularly heavy input/output operations.

PARALLEL PORT
A printer interface that allows data to be transmitted a byte at a time, all eight bits moving in parallel.

PARENT DIRECTORY
The directory immediately above any subdirectory. For example, the parent directory of the subdirectory SYS:ACCTS/RECEIVE would be SYS:ACCTS.

PARITY
A method of checking for errors in transmitted data.

PARTITION
A logical unit that file server hard disks can be divided into. One of the server's internal hard disks can contain both an active, primary DOS partition and a NetWare partition. When the server boot files are copied to the DOS partition and included in the AUTOEXEC.BAT file, the NetWare operating system boots automatically.

You need only one DOS partition; the other hard disks need to contain only a NetWare partition. A NetWare partition consists of a Hot Fix redirection area plus a large data area. The logical sector 0 of a NetWare partition is the first sector of the data area.

PASSIVE HUB
A device used in some network topologies to split a transmission signal, allowing additional workstations to be added. See *hub*.

PASSWORD

The characters a user must type to log in with. NetWare allows the supervisor to specify whether passwords are required and, if so, to assign a login password to each user on the network.

In NetWare 3.12, login passwords are encrypted at the workstation and put into a format that only the file server can decode. This format helps prevent intruders from accessing network files.

PATH

The location of a file or directory in the directory structure. For example, the path for file REPORT.FIL in subdirectory ACCTG in directory CORP on vol SYS: of server ADMIN is

ADMIN\SYS:CORP\ACCTG\REPORT.FIL

PORT

Hardware port

A connecting component that allows a microprocessor to communicate with a compatible peripheral.

Software port

A memory address that identifies the physical circuit used to transfer information between a microprocessor and a peripheral.

POWER CONDITIONING

Methods of protecting sensitive network hardware components against power disturbances. Power disturbances can be categorized in several ways:

▸ *A transient* (sometimes called a *spike* or *surge*)—a very short, but extreme, burst of voltage.

▸ *Noise or static*—a smaller change in voltage.

▸ *Blackouts and brownouts*—the temporary drop in or loss of electrical power.

Three types of protection are available:

▸ *Suppression.* Protects against transients. The most common suppression devices are surge protectors, which usually include circuitry to prevent excess voltage.

▸ *Isolation.* Protects against noise, using ferro-resonant isolation transformers to control voltage irregularities.

▸ *Regulation.* Protects against brownouts and blackouts. The uninterruptible power supply (UPS) is the most commonly used form of regulation.

PRINT DEVICE
A printer, plotter, or other peripheral that prints from the network.

PRINT FUNCTION
A printer command that determines the characteristics of a print job. For example, a print function can specify the style of typeface.

PRINT JOB
A file stored in a print queue directory waiting to be printed. As soon as a print server sends a print job to the printer, the print job is deleted from the queue directory.

PRINT JOB CONFIGURATION
A group of characteristics that determine how a job is printed. The characteristics may include the following:

▸ the printer the print job will be printed on

▸ the print queue the print job is sent through

- the number of copies to print

- the use of a banner page

- the printer form number

- the print-device mode

PRINT QUEUE

A network directory that stores print jobs. When the printer assigned to a print queue is ready, the print server takes the print job out of the print queue and sends it to the printer. The print queue can hold as many print jobs as disk space allows.

PRINT-QUEUE OPERATOR

A user who can edit other users' print jobs, delete print jobs from the print queue, or modify the print queue status by changing the operator flags. Print-queue operators can also change the order in which print jobs are serviced. They can also change the service mode.

PRINT SERVER

A server that takes print jobs out of a print queue and sends them to a network printer.

PRINT SERVER OPERATOR

A printing supervisor with rights to manage the print server. A Print Server operator has rights to control notify lists, printers, and queue assignments.

SUPERVISOR is a print queue operator by default; however, SUPERVISOR can delegate this responsibility to another user using the PCONSOLE utility.

PRINTER DEFINITION

A set of printer control characters used to interpret commands to bold, italicize, and center text. Printer definitions are specific to a printer brand and model.

PRINTER FORM

A print option designed to prevent print jobs from being printed on the wrong paper. NetWare print services allow you to send print jobs that will not print until you make sure that the correct paper is in the printer.

For each type of paper (such as regular, letterhead, and bond paper), you can create a printer form. Each form has a unique name and number (between 0 and 255). If you specify this form in a print-job configuration or in NPRINT or CAPTURE with the form option, the print job won't print unless the mounted form matches the number required by the print job.

PRINTING

The ability to transfer data from computer files to paper.

Network and Stand-alone Printing

When a user at a stand-alone workstation sends a print job to a local printer, the job is sent directly to the printer for processing.

However, when a user on a network workstation sends a print job to a network printer, the job is routed first through the file server and then delivered to the printer by the print server.

When a print job leaves a network workstation, it is stored temporarily in a print queue on the file server before being sent to a printer. Print queues, which are basically subdirectories, are created when the print server is installed.

NetWare Printing Services

The NetWare printing services control the network printing process at different stages.

When the print job is ready to be sent from the workstation to the queue, users can use NetWare printing utilities to control and monitor their print jobs. Once the print job is in the queue, the NetWare print server takes the job and sends it to the printer that has been mapped to that particular queue.

NetWare printing services consist of the following:

> The **NetWare print server** allows you to increase the number of printers on your network. It also allows you to locate printers where you need them in the workplace, not just next to the file server.

> The **remote printer software** allows the print server to use a printer attached directly to your workstation as a remote network printer.

> The **NetWare printing utilities** allow you to set up, control, and monitor the network print process.

PROMPT

A character or message that appears on the display screen and requires a response (such as a command or a utility name) from the user.

Standard types of prompts include:

- ▸ *The DOS prompt,* which, by default, displays the current drive letter followed by a > symbol: **F>**

- ▸ *The OS/2 prompt,* which, by default, displays the current drive mapping in brackets: [**C:**]

- ▸ *The file server console prompt,* which displays : (a colon)

PROPERTY

A descriptive feature of a bindery object such as a password, account restriction, account balance, internetwork address, or list of authorized clients.

PROTECTED MODE

The mode that 80286, 80386, and 80486 processors run in by default. When running in protected mode, these processors aren't subject to the same memory constraints as 8086 processors.

The 80286 processor uses a 24-bit address bus, and can address up to 16 MB of memory. The 80386 and 80486 processors use a 32-bit address bus, and can address up to 4 GB of memory.

Protected-mode operating provides the capability of multitasking (running more than one application or process at a time). Protected mode allocates memory to various processes running concurrently so that memory used by one process doesn't overlap memory used by another process.

By contrast, 8086 processors can address only 1 MB of memory, and can run only one application or process at a time. 80286, 80386, and 80486 processors can be set to run in *real mode*, in which case they emulate an 8086 processor (and are subject to its memory constraints).

PUBLIC ACCESS

A security condition that gives all NetWare users access rights to a particular directory.

For example, all NetWare users must be able to access NetWare utilities. Therefore, NetWare utilities are usually placed in a directory (named SYS:PUBLIC) that has public access rights; in other words, all users have rights to Open, Read, and Search for files in that directory.

PUBLIC DIRECTORY

The SYS:PUBLIC directory, created during network installation, that allows general access to the network and contains NetWare utilities and programs for network users.

PUBLIC FILES

Files that must be accessed by all NetWare users, including NetWare utilities, help files, and some message and data files. By convention, the files are located in the SYS:PUBLIC directory.

All NetWare users have Read, Open, and Search rights to the files.

PURGE ATTRIBUTE

A file-system attribute that causes NetWare to purge the directory or file when it is deleted.

R

RAM (RANDOM ACCESS MEMORY)

The internal dynamic storage of a computer that can be addressed by the computer's operating system.

READ-AFTER-WRITE VERIFICATION

A means of assuring that data written to the hard disk matches the original data still in memory.

If the data from the disk matches the data in memory, the data in memory is released. If the data doesn't match, the block location is recognized as "bad," and Hot Fix redirects the data to a good block location within the Hot Fix redirection area.

READ-ONLY ATTRIBUTE

A file-system attribute that indicates that no one can write to the file.

READ RIGHT

A file-system right that grants the right to open and read files.

Also, a property right that grants the right to read the values of the property.

READ-WRITE ATTRIBUTE

A file-system attribute that indicates that the file can be read and written to.

REAL MODE

The mode that allows 80286, 80386, and 80486 processors to emulate an 8086 processor and run as though they actually were an 8086 processor.

The 8086 processor uses a 20-bit address bus, and can address up to 1 MB of memory. The 8086 processor is also limited to running only one application or process at a time.

When running in protected mode, the 80286, 80386, and 80486 processors are capable of multitasking and addressing much more than 1 MB of memory.

When running in real mode, these processors are subject to the same 1 MB memory constraint as the 8086 processor, and they can run only one application or process at a time. However, the 80286, 80386, and 80486 processors running in real mode perform more efficiently than the 8086 processor, because they operate at a faster clock rate.

RECORD LOCKING

A feature of NetWare that prevents different users from gaining simultaneous access to the same record in a shared file, preventing overlapping disk writes and ensuring data integrity.

RECURSIVE COPYING

The process of copying a specified source directory to a destination directory until all files and subdirectories in and below the specified source directory are copied.

Recursive copying copies all directories and files of a logical drive to the destination, keeping them exactly as they were in the source directory. Whether a trustee's rights are copied with the files and directories depends on what rights are assigned in the destination directory.

The DOS and OS/2 XCOPY and BACKUP utilities use recursive copying, as does the NetWare NCOPY command.

REMOTE BOOT

A method that allows a user to boot a workstation from remote boot image files on a file server rather than from a boot diskette in the workstation's local drive.

When a workstation is booted, the Remote Reset PROM (installed on the workstation's network board) directs the nearest (default) file server to run the remote boot image file commands contained in the default server's LOGIN directory.

REMOTE CONNECTION

A connection between a LAN on one end and a workstation or network on the other, often using telephone lines and modems. A remote connection allows data to be sent and received across greater distances than those allowed by normal cabling.

REMOTE CONSOLE

Software that allows network supervisors to manage servers from a DOS workstation or from a PC using a modem. Remote Console gives you greater server security since you can lock servers in a safe place and remove the keyboards and monitors.

From a remote console, supervisors can

- ▶ Use console commands as if they were at the server console.

- ▶ Scan directories and edit text files in both NetWare and DOS partitions on a server.

- ▶ Transfer files to (but not from) a server.

- ▶ Bring down or reboot a server.

- ▶ Install or upgrade NetWare on a remote server.

REMOTE RESET

Software that allows you to boot a DOS workstation (including a diskless workstation) from a remote boot image file on a file server, rather than from a boot diskette in the workstation's local drive.

To use Remote Reset to boot a workstation, install a Remote Reset PROM on the station's network board and run the DOSGEN utility. DOSGEN uploads the station's boot files into a remote boot image file, NET$DOS.SYS, in the server's LOGIN directory.

The remote boot image file includes the station's AUTOEXEC.BAT file, used by the station as if the file were present on a local boot diskette. Copy the workstation's AUTOEXEC.BAT file to the remote boot image file, to the LOGIN directory, and to any default directory named in the workstation's login script.

Using Remote Reset with multiple servers

If you have multiple file servers on your network, copy the remote boot image files onto each server that may come up as the remote boot workstation's default server. Then, if the first default server isn't available, the station can boot from the next available server.

Using multiple remote boot image files

For more than one workstation to use Remote Reset, upload multiple remote boot image files for each station into SYS:LOGIN.

Instead of the single NET$DOS.SYS file, upload a separate remote boot image file for each workstation. Name the image files for each user (FRED.SYS for user FRED, JANE.SYS for user JANE, etc.). Then, in the LOGIN directory, create a BOOTCONF.SYS file, which is a DOS text file that, for each station's network board, identifies the

- ▸ IPX external network number
- ▸ node number
- ▸ remote boot image filename (FRED.SYS, JANE.SYS, etc.)

REMOTE WORKSTATION

A terminal or personal computer connected to the LAN by a router or through a remote asynchronous connection. A remote workstation can be either a stand-alone computer or a workstation on another network.

RENAME INHIBIT ATTRIBUTE

A file-system attribute that prevents any user from renaming the directory or file.

RESOURCE FORK

The part of a Macintosh file that contains file resources, including Macintosh-specific information such as the windows and icons used with the file. See *Macintosh files*.

RESOURCE TAGS

Operating system tags that keep track of file server resources such as screens and allocated memory.

NLMs request a resource from the file server for each kind of resource they use and give it a resource tag name. NLMs return resources when they no longer need them. When the NLM is unloaded, the resources are returned to the file server.

Resource tags ensure that allocated resources are properly returned to the operating system upon termination of an NLM.

RESOURCES

The manageable components of a network, including:

- ▸ Networking components—cabling, hubs, concentrators, adapters, and network boards.

- ▸ Hardware components—servers, workstations, hard disks, printers, etc.

> ▸ Major software components—the NetWare operating system and resulting network services such as file, mail, queue, communication, etc.

> ▸ Minor software components that are controlled by the operating system of its subsystems—protocols, gateways, LAN and disk drivers, etc.

> ▸ Data structures and other network resources that don't easily fit into one of the above categories, or are created by a combination of network components—volumes, queues, users, processes, security, etc.

RESTORE

A retrieval of data previously copied and backed up to a storage media. Perform a restore if data has been lost or corrupted since the backup.

RIBBON CABLE

A cable in which the wires are placed side by side in the insulation material instead of being bunched or twisted together in a circle inside the insulation material. Typically, ribbon cables are used for connecting internal disk or tape drives.

RIGHTS

Qualities assigned to users and groups that control what the user or group can do with directories or files.

Eight rights can be granted at either the directory or file level: Access Control, Create, Erase, File Scan, Modify, Read, Supervisory, and Write.

Rights granted at the directory level can be redefined for a file by making new trustee assignments or revoking rights from the Inherited Rights Masks.

SUPERVISOR has all rights and grants trustee assignments to users and groups.

When users are created, they are made a member of the group EVERYONE and obtain any rights granted to that group. All other rights must be individually granted.

Users are automatically granted the right to search to the root of a directory whenever they are granted any rights to a directory or file. They cannot see any subdirectories unless they are granted rights to the subdirectories or to files in the subdirectories.

ROOT DIRECTORY

The highest directory level in a hierarchical directory structure. With NetWare, the root directory is the volume; all other directories are subdirectories of the volume.

ROUTER

A workstation or file server running software that manages the exchange of information (in the form of data packets) between network cabling systems.

NetWare router vs. traditional bridge

A NetWare router, unlike a traditional bridge, does more than just transfer data packets between networks that use the same communications protocol. A NetWare router is intelligent. It not only passes packets of data between different cabling systems, but also routes the packets through the most efficient path.

A NetWare router can also connect cabling systems that use different kinds of transmission media and different addressing systems. For example, a NetWare router can connect a network using the Ethernet addressing structure and RG/58 coaxial cable to another network using the ARCnet addressing structure and RG/62 coaxial cable.

Local vs. remote

When a router is used within the cable length limitations for its LAN drivers, it is a local router. If the router is connected beyond its driver limitations or through a modem, it is a remote router.

ROUTING BUFFERS

Portions of memory reserved in a router's RAM. Routing buffers are used to temporarily store and queue the message packets sent between communicating stations when the network bus is busy.

S

SALVAGEABLE FILES

Files saved by NetWare, after being deleted by users, that can be salvaged (recovered). Salvageable files are usually stored in the directory they were deleted from. If the user deletes that directory, the file is saved in a DELETED.SAV directory located in the volume's root directory.

The user can view a list of deleted files in a directory and recover files by using the SALVAGE or FILER utilities. Recovered files contain information about who deleted the files and when they were deleted.

Deleted files are saved until the user deliberately purges them or until the file server runs out of disk allocation blocks on the volume. When the file server runs out of blocks, it purges deleted files on a first-deleted, first-purged basis.

SCSI (SMALL COMPUTER SYSTEM INTERFACE)

Commonly pronounced *scuzzy*. An industry standard that sets guidelines for connecting peripheral devices and their controllers to a microprocessor. The SCSI interface defines both hardware and software standards for communication between a host computer and a peripheral.

Computers and peripheral devices designed to meet SCSI specifications have a large degree of compatibility.

SCSI BUS

An interface that connects additional disk coprocessor boards to controllers and hard disks. (If you are using a SCSI bus, make sure connected peripherals are properly terminated and addressed.)

SEARCH DRIVE

A drive that is searched by the operating system when a requested file isn't found in the current directory. Search drives are supported only from DOS workstations.

A search drive allows a user working in one directory to access an application or data file located in another directory.

SEARCH MODES

Methods of operation that specify how a program will use search drives when looking for a data file.

When an .EXE or .COM file requires an auxiliary file, it makes an open request through the operating system. The request may or may not specify the path to that file.

If a path is specified, the operating system searches that path. Otherwise, it only searches the default directory. If the file isn't found, the NetWare shell uses the search mode of the executable file to determine if it should continue looking for the file in the search drives.

SECURITY

Elements that control access to the network or to specific information on the network. NetWare security controls:

- ► Who can access the networks
- ► What resources (directories and files) users can access

> ► What users can do with those resources (for example, read or modify a file)

> ► Who can perform tasks at the file server console

Login security

Login security controls access to the network. It determines:

> ► Which users can work on the file server

> ► When users can work

> ► What workstations users can work from

> ► Which resources they can use

The network supervisor establishes login security by assigning usernames, requiring passwords, and setting up restrictions.

Rights

Rights security controls which directories, subdirectories, and files a user can access and what the user is allowed to do with them.

Rights security is controlled by trustee assignments and by the Inherited Rights Mask.

> ► Trustee assignments grant rights to specific users (or groups) that specify how they can use a file or directory (for example, only for reading).

> ► Inherited Rights Masks are given to each file and directory when they are created. The only rights the user can "inherit" for a file or subdirectory are rights that are allowed by the Inherited Rights Mask.

Attributes

Attribute security assigns special properties to individual directories or files. Attributes override rights granted with trustee assignments and can prevent tasks that effective rights would allow.

For example, attributes can be used to prevent the following:

- deleting a file or a directory
- copying a file
- viewing a file or a directory
- writing to a file

Attributes are also used for the following:

- Controlling whether files can be shared, so that only one or many can access the file at the same time
- Marking files as modified so that backup utilities can select only the files that have been modified
- Protecting files from data corruption by ensuring that either all changes are made or no changes are made when a file is being modified

SECURITY EQUIVALENCE

An assignment that allows one user or group to have the same rights as another.

Use security equivalence when you need to give a user access to the same information as another user. You thus avoid having to review the directory structure and determine which rights need to be assigned in which directories or to which files.

SEMAPHORE

A flag that coordinates activities of both programs and processes to prevent data corruption in multiprocess environments.

Semaphores with byte value 0 allow a file to be shared. Byte value 1 locks the file while in use, thereby preventing another user from accessing or altering the shared file.

Semaphores can lock resources so that only one user or process has access to the resource. Semaphores can also allow a limited number of users access to a resource, such as to network applications with limited-user licenses. When the specified number is reached, the semaphore denies access to additional users.

SEQUENCED PACKET EXCHANGE (SPX)

A Novell communication protocol that monitors network transmissions to ensure successful delivery. SPX verifies and acknowledges successful packet delivery to any network destination by requesting a verification from the destination that the data was received.

The SPX verification must include a value that matches the value calculated from the data before transmission. By comparing these values, SPX ensures not only that the data packet made it to the destination, but that it arrived intact.

SERIAL COMMUNICATION

The transmission of data between devices over a single line, one bit at a time.

NetWare uses the RS-232 serial communication standard to send information to serial printers, remote workstations, remote routers, and asynchronous communication servers. The RS-232 standard, developed by the Electronic Industries Association (EIA), enhances the delivery of information from one system to another.

A system can be any device or group of devices that can handle and process the data received. For example, a printer can be thought of as a system that transforms the binary data it receives from the computer into printed text.

Parameters

The RS-232 standard uses several parameters that must match on both systems for valid information to be transferred:

- ▸ *Baud rate.* The signal modulation rate, or the speed with which a signal changes.

- ▸ *Character length.* The number of data bits used to form a character.

- ▸ *Parity.* A method of checking for errors in transmitted data. You can set parity to even or odd, or not use parity at all.

- ▸ *Stop bit.* A special signal that indicates the end of that character. Today's modems are fast enough that the stop bit is always set to 1. Slower modems formerly required two stop bits.

- ▸ *XON/XOFF.* One of many methods that prevents the sending system from transmitting data faster than the receiving system can accept it.

SERIAL PORT

A port that allows data to be transmitted asynchronously, one bit at a time. Typically, serial ports are used for modems or serial printers.

On IBM PC compatible computers, COM1 and COM2 are asynchronous serial ports.

SERIALIZATION

The process of serializing software to prevent unlawful software duplication.

Each NetWare operating system has a unique serial number. If two NetWare operating systems with the same serial number exist on the same internetwork, each file server displays a copyright violation warning at the server console and at each logged-in workstation.

SERVER

File server
A computer running the NetWare operating system software. See *file server.*

Print server
A computer that takes print jobs out of a print queue and sends them to a network printer. See *print server.*

SERVER CONSOLE
See *console.*

SERVICE ADVERTISING PROTOCOL (SAP)
A protocol that provides a way for servers to advertise their services on a NetWare internetwork.

Servers advertise their services with SAP, allowing routers to create and maintain a database of current internetwork server information.

Routers send periodic SAP broadcasts to keep all routers on the internetwork synchronized. Routers also send SAP update broadcasts whenever they detect a change in the internetwork configuration.

Workstations can query the network to find a server by broadcasting SAP request packets. When a workstation logs in to a network, it broadcasts a "Get Nearest Server" SAP request and attaches to the first server that replies.

SFT
See *System Fault Tolerance.*

SHAREABLE ATTRIBUTE
A file-system attribute that allows a file to be accessed by more than one user at a time.

SHORT MACHINE TYPE

A four-letter (or less) name representing a DOS workstation brand. The short machine type is similar to the long machine type, except the short machine type is used specifically with overlay files.

Files using the short machine type include the IBM$RUN.OVL file for windowing utilities and the CMPQ$RUN.OVL file that uses a default black-and-white color palette for NetWare menus.

The short machine type is set in the NET.CFG file, using the SHORT MACHINE TYPE parameter. The default is IBM.

SMS

See *Storage Management Services.*

SOURCE ROUTING

IBM's method of routing data across source-routing bridges. NetWare source routing programs allow an IBM Token Ring network bridge to forward NetWare packets (or frames).

IBM bridges can be configured as either single-route broadcast or all-routes broadcast. The default is single-route broadcast.

Single-route broadcasting

Only designated single-route bridges pass the packet and only one copy of the packet arrives on each ring in the network. Single-route bridges can transmit single-route, all-routes, and specifically routed packets.

All-routes broadcasting

Sends the packet across every possible route in the network, resulting in as many copies of the frame at the destination as there are bridges in the network. All-routes bridges pass both all-routes broadcasts and specifically routed packets.

SPARSE FILE

A file with at least one empty block. (NetWare won't write any block that is completely empty.)

Databases often create sparse files. For example, suppose the disk allocation block size for volume VOL1: is 4K. Also suppose that a database opens a new file, seeks out the 1,048,576th byte, writes five bytes, and closes the file.

An inefficient operating system would save the entire file to disk. The file would be comprised of 256 zero-filled disk allocation blocks (the first 1 MB) and one more disk allocation block with five bytes of data and 4,091 zeros. This method would waste 1 MB of disk space.

However, NetWare writes only the last block to disk, saving time and disk space.

The NetWare NCOPY command doesn't write to sparse files automatically. NCOPY has a /f option that forces the operating system to write to sparse files.

SPOOL

To transfer data that was intended for a peripheral device (such as a printer) into temporary storage. From there the data can be transferred to the peripheral later, without affecting or delaying the operating system as it performs other operations.

SPX

See *Sequenced Packet Exchange.*

STARTUP.NCF

A file server boot file that loads the file server's disk driver and name spaces and some SET parameters.

STATION

Usually a shortened form for *workstation*, but can also be a server, router, printer, fax machine, or any computer device connected to a network by a network board and a communication medium.

STOP BIT

In serial communication, a signal that indicates the end of a character.

STORAGE MANAGEMENT SERVICES (SMS)

Services that allow data to be stored and retrieved. SMS is independent of backup/restore hardware and file systems (such as DOS, OS/2, Macintosh, Windows, or UNIX).

SMS architecture

SMS provides NLMs and other software modules that run on file servers. Modules used in SMS are

- ► *SBACKUP.* Provides backup and restore capabilities.

- ► *SMDR (Storage Management Data Requester).* Passes commands and information between SBACKUP and Target Service Agents (TSAs).

- ► *Device drivers.* Acting on commands passed through the Storage Device Interface from SBACKUP, device drivers control the mechanical operation of storage devices and media.

- ► *File-server TSAs (Target Service Agents).* Pass requests for data (generated within SBACKUP) to the file server where the data resides, then return requested data through the SMDR to SBACKUP.

- ► *Database TSAs.* Pass commands and data between the host server (where SBACKUP resides) and the database where the data to be backed up resides, then return the requested data through the SMDR to SBACKUP.

- ► *Workstation TSAs.* Pass commands and data between the host server (where SBACKUP resides) and the station where the data to be backed up resides, then return the requested data through the SMDR to SBACKUP.

▶ *Workstation Manager.* Receives "I am here" messages from stations available to be backed up. It keeps the names of these stations in an internal list.

STREAMS

NLMs that provide a common interface between NetWare and transport protocols such as IPX/SPX, TCP/IP, SNA, and OSI that need to deliver data and requests to NetWare for processing. By making the transport protocol transparent to the network operating system, STREAMS allows services to be provided across the network, regardless of the transport protocols used.

If the applications support multiple protocols, Network managers can install the protocols of their choice or change the protocols used without affecting the level of services delivered to the user.

NetWare 3.12 implements STREAMS as the following NLMs:

▶ *STREAMS.NLM* includes the STREAMS application interface routines, the utility routines for STREAMS modules, the log device, and a driver for the Open Data-Link Interface (ODI).

▶ *SPXS.NLM* provides access to the SPX protocol from STREAMS.

▶ *IPXS.NLM* provides access to the IPX protocol from STREAMS.

▶ *CLIB.NLM* is a library of functions that some NLMs use.

▶ *TLI.NLM* is an application programming interface that sits between STREAMS and applications, allowing interface with transport-level protocols such as IPX/SPX or TCP/IP.

SUBDIRECTORY

A directory below another in the file-system structure. For example, in SYS:ACCTS\RECEIVE, RECEIVE is a subdirectory of SYS:ACCTS.

SUPERVISOR

The username for the network supervisor or system administrator present in the bindery as a bindery object when the file server is first brought up.

SUPERVISOR:

- ▶ Is assigned ID Number 1 and cannot be deleted or renamed.

- ▶ Has all rights in all directories; these rights cannot be revoked.

- ▶ Has no initial password so that the network supervisor can log in to the file server to set up the network environment.

SUPERVISORY RIGHT

A file-system right that grants all rights to the respective directory and files.

SURFACE TEST

A test in the NetWare INSTALL program that lets you test the NetWare partition on a hard disk for bad blocks. The surface test can run in the background on one or more dismounted hard disks so that you (or other users) can work on mounted volumes on other hard disks.

You can choose either a destructive or a nondestructive surface test:

- ▶ *Destructive test.* Acts like a disk format—it destroys data as it makes several passes over the disk surface, reading and writing test patterns.

- ▶ *Nondestructive test.* Prereads and saves existing data while it reads and writes test patterns to the hard disk. Then the program writes the data back to the disk.

SWITCH BLOCK

A set of switches mounted to form a single component.

In some file servers, a switch block is used to control system configuration data, such as type of monitor, amount of memory, and number of drives. Network boards often use switch blocks to set system addresses (such as station, base I/O, and base memory addresses).

SYSTEM ATTRIBUTE

A file-system attribute that marks directories or files for use only by the operating system.

SYSTEM DIRECTORY

The SYS:SYSTEM directory, created during network installation, that contains NetWare operating-system files as well as NLMs and NetWare utilities for managing the network.

SYSTEM FAULT TOLERANCE (SFT)

A means of protecting data by providing data duplication on multiple storage devices; if one storage device fails, the data is available from another device.

There are several levels of hardware and software system fault tolerance; each level of redundancy (duplication) decreases the possibility of data loss.

T

TAPE BACKUP UNIT

Typically, an external tape drive that backs up data from hard disks.

TARGET

A server from which you back up data or to which you restore data. Any file server, workstation, or service on the network can be a target, as long as the Target Service Agent (TSA) files are loaded.

A target can be either a different server than the host or the same server as the host. If you are backing up and restoring on the same server, the target and the host are the same.

TARGET SERVICE AGENT (TSA)

A program that processes data moving between a specific target and SBACKUP. SBACKUP, running on the host, sends requests to the TSA, which:

1 · Receives the commands from SBACKUP and processes them so that the target operating system can handle the request for data.

2 · Passes the data request from SBACKUP to the target.

3 · Receives the requested data from the target and returns it to SBACKUP in standard SMS format.

Servers and workstations running different software releases, or having different operating systems, require NetWare-compatible TSAs to communicate with SBACKUP.

TERMINATION

Placing a terminating resistor at the end of a bus, line, chain, or cable to prevent signals from being reflected or echoed.

Data signals travel along a cable or bus that is in many ways analogous to a pipe. You must terminate the end components to ensure that the signal doesn't echo back along the cable or bus and cause corruption.

TOPOLOGY

The physical layout of network components (cables, stations, gateways, hubs, and so on). There are three basic topologies:

- ▶ Star
- ▶ Ring
- ▶ Bus

Star network

Workstations are connected directly to a file server but not to each other.

Ring network

The file server and workstations are cabled in a ring; a workstation's messages may have to pass through several other workstations before reaching the file server.

Bus network

All workstations and the file server are connected to a central cable (called a trunk or bus).

TRANSACTION TRACKING SYSTEM (TTS)

A system that protects database applications from corruption by "backing out" incomplete transactions that result from a failure in a network component. When a transaction is backed out, data and index information in the database are returned to the state they were in before the transaction began.

TTS is a standard feature on NetWare 3.12 servers. This function can be turned on and off.

TTS protection

TTS protects data from failure in certain situations (see below) by making a copy of the original data before it is overwritten by new data. If a failure occurs during the transaction, TTS can "back out" the transaction and restore the original data.

A transaction on a network can be saved improperly in any of the following situations:

- ▸ Power to a server or a station is interrupted during a transaction.

- ▸ Server or station hardware fails during a transaction (for example, a parity error or a network board failure).

- ▸ A server or a station "hangs" (a software failure) during a transaction.

- ▸ A network transmission component (such as a hub, a repeater, or a cable) fails during a transaction.

How TTS operates

TTS guarantees that all changes to a file are either wholly completed or aren't made at all. To track transactions on a given file with TTS, flag the file as Transactional.

When a workstation begins a transaction in a database file, TTS follows four basic steps to maintain the integrity of the file:

1 · TTS makes a copy of the original data so that the original data can be restored if the transaction fails. The copy is placed in a file external to the database file. This external file contains all transaction backout information; only the operating system uses it.

2 · TTS writes the changed data to the database file after the copy of the original has been written to the backout file.

3 · TTS repeats Steps 1 and 2 for additional transactions. (A single transaction can consist of a sequence of changes.)

4 · When all changed data has been written to disk, TTS writes a record to the backout file, indicating that the transaction is complete. Completed transactions won't be backed out if the file server, workstation, or network transmission components fail.

TRANSACTIONAL ATTRIBUTE
A file-system attribute that indicates the file is protected by TTS.

TRUSTEE RIGHTS
Permissions that control which directories and files a user or group can access and what a user or group is allowed to do in them.

A trustee assignment consists of the rights assigned to a user or group. A user or group that has been assigned rights to work in a directory or file is known as a "trustee" of that directory or file.

If you make a trustee assignment in a directory, the trustee has access to the directory, its files, and its subdirectories (unless the rights are redefined at the file or subdirectory level). In other words, trustee rights "flow down" through the structure unless

▸ Other trustee assignments are granted at a lower level of the directory structure;

▸ The Inherited Rights Mask of a subdirectory or file revokes rights assigned in a trustee assigment.

TSA
See *Target Service Agent*.

TSA RESOURCES
Categories of data, referred to as *major resources* and *minor resources*, created by each TSA (Target Service Agent). Because these resources vary with each TSA, SBACKUP processes these resources in different ways.

TTS

See *Transaction Tracking System.*

TURBO FAT INDEX TABLE

A special FAT (File Allocation Table) index table used when a file exceeds 64 blocks (and the corresponding number of FAT entries). NetWare creates a turbo FAT index to group together all FAT entries for that file. The turbo FAT index enables a large file to be accessed quickly.

See also *File Allocation Table (FAT).*

U

UNBINDING

The process of removing a communication protocol from network boards and LAN drivers. See *binding and unbinding.*

UNINTERRUPTIBLE POWER SUPPLY (UPS)

A backup power unit that supplies uninterrupted power if a commercial power outage occurs.

Types of UPS are *online* and *offline.* Attaching a UPS to a server enables the server to properly close files and rewrite the system directory to disk.

Online UPS

Actively modifies the power as it moves through the unit. If a power outage occurs, the unit is already active and continues to provide power. An online UPS is usually more expensive than an offline UPS, but provides a nearly constant source of energy during power outages.

Offline UPS

Monitors the power line. When power drops, the UPS is activated. The drawback to this method is the slight lag before the offline UPS becomes active. However, most offline UPS systems are fast enough to offset this lag.

UNLOADING

The process of unlinking NLMs from the NetWare operating system. See *loading and unloading*.

UPS

See *uninterruptible power supply*.

UPS MONITORING

The process a file server uses to ensure that an attached UPS (uninterruptible power supply) is functioning properly.

A Novell-certified UPS is attached to a server to provide backup power. (You can also attach a UPS to workstations without installing UPS monitoring hardware on the stations.) When a power failure occurs, NetWare notifies users. After a timeout specified in SERVER.CFG, the server logs out remaining users, closes open files, and shuts itself down.

USER

An identity created on the network that represents a person with access to the network.

Once a username exists as an object in the file server bindery, the user can then log in to the file server with that username and access the network.

Although any number of users can be created, only 250 users can be logged in simultaneously to a file server running NetWare 3.12.

USER ACCOUNT

A set of restrictions, privileges, and rights that, with the username, comprise a user's identity on the network. Each user has a user account. User accounts are part of network security and also control the user environment.

User accounts include the features described below. Some features of user accounts are automatically assigned to each user, some must be created or assigned, and some are optional.

Usernames

The username is also the login name and must be supplied when logging in.

Usernames can be up to 47 characters long and usually consist of the user's given name, surname, or initials and surname.

Group membership

Users are automatically assigned to the group EVERYONE and inherit the rights assigned to the group EVERYONE.

Other groups are created in SYSCON as empty sets and then users are assigned or added. Group members inherit the rights assigned to groups.

Home or username directories

The home or username directory serves as personal "workspace." These directories are optional.

Trustee assignments

Trustee assignments allow users to have access to specific directories and files. You can assign users trustee rights to specified directories and files.

Security Equivalences

With a security equivalence, a user can exercise rights equivalent to those of another user. Assigning a security equivalence is convenient when you need to give a user access to the same information another user has access to.

ID numbers

ID numbers are random, hexadecimal numbers assigned by the file server to each bindery object (including users).

Mailboxes

Mailboxes in the SYS:MAIL directory contain user login scripts and print job configurations. Each user automatically gets a mailbox directory named with the user's ID number. Users receive all but the Supervisory right in this directory.

User Login Scripts

Login scripts are configurable batch files that customize the network environment for individual users by initializing environment variables, mapping drives, and executing other commands.

Print Job Configurations

Print job configurations define how a print job is printed. Each user can use printing defaults, or you can create print job configurations in PRINTCON and copy them from one user to another. Print job configurations are stored in each user's mailbox directory in SYS:MAIL.

Account Management

SUPERVISOR manages the accounts of all users.

If users are created by a Workgroup Manager, then the Workgroup Manager can manage these user accounts.

You can assign existing users to a User Account Manager, who can be either a Workgroup Manager or any other user. You can also have more than one manager for a user account.

Account Restrictions

Login restrictions are assigned at the account level to make it difficult for unauthorized users to access the file server. When certain limits are exceeded, an account is disabled.

When an account is disabled, no one can log in to the file server under that username.

You can restrict logins in the ways described below.

Account balance   If you have installed Accounting to monitor or limit network resources, you can assign initial account balances for users and specify credit limits. When the account balance is depleted, the account is disabled.

Expiration   You can specify an expiration date for a user account. Any attempt to log in after the account expires disables the account.

Password   You can require a password. You can also specify minimum password lengths, how often the password must be changed, whether the password must be unique, whether the user can change the password, and the number of grace logins allowed.

Disk space restrictions   You can limit the amount of disk space for each user by specifying the maximum number of blocks available for each user per volume.

Connection restrictions   You can limit the number of workstations a user can log in from concurrently. You can specify the maximum number of concurrent connections permitted.

Time restrictions   You can restrict the hours during which users can log in.

Station restrictions   You can restrict the physical locations that a user can log in from by specifying the network and node addresses of the workstation the user is permitted to log in from.

USER ACCOUNT MANAGER

A user or group that has rights to manage certain user accounts and groups.

Existing users can be assigned to a Workgroup Manager or to any other user or group for account management. Workgroup Managers automatically become User Account Managers for users they create. Even though account management is delegated, SUPERVISOR still has all rights to manage user accounts.

UTILITIES

Programs that add functionality to the NetWare operating system. NetWare utilities are divided into groups according to where the commands to enter the utilities are executed: file server utilities, workstation utilities, and router utilities.

File server utilities

File server utilities consist of two types: console commands and NetWare loadable modules (NLMs).

Console commands   These are part of the SERVER.EXE file server program that you run to install a NetWare 3.12 file server.

After you run this file server program, you can perform various installation and maintenance tasks by typing these commands at the file server console. You can also issue screen commands and see file server configuration information.

NetWare loadable modules (NLMs)   NLMs are code modules that can be linked to and unlinked from the file server while it is still running.

Loadable modules reside in file server memory with the NetWare operating system and can access a large number of file server functions directly.

Workstation utilities

NetWare workstation utilities are designed to change the network after initial installation or to perform network tasks. The two types of workstation utilities are command line utilities and menu utilities.

Command-line utilities   These are executed at the DOS prompt. You can use these utilities to manipulate rights and attributes, copy and print files, log in and out of file servers, view file server information, and map network drives.

Menu utilities   These allow you to perform network tasks by choosing options from menus. You can complete some tasks, such as creating print queues, only in a menu utility.

Router utilities

Router utilities are executed at the router console to monitor and regulate the router's resources.

V

VALUE-ADDED PROCESS (VAP)

A process that ties enhanced operating system features to a NetWare 2.x operating system without interfering with the network's normal operation. VAPs run on top of the operating system in much the same way a word processing or spreadsheet application runs on top of DOS.

NLMs provide this type of enhancement for NetWare 3.x. (See *NetWare Loadable Module (NLM)*.

VALUE-ADDED SERVER

A separate, specialized, dedicated computer (such as a print server or a database server) that fulfills a specific function for network users.

VAP

See *Value-Added Process.*

VOLUME

A physical amount of hard disk storage space, fixed in size.

A NetWare volume is the highest level in the NetWare directory structure (on the same level as a DOS root directory). A NetWare file server supports up to 64 volumes.

The first network volume is named SYS:, and contains the SYSTEM, PUBLIC, LOGIN, MAIL, and DELETED.SAV directories. Additional volumes can be defined with INSTALL, and are assigned volume names between 2 and 15 characters long.

When a volume is used as part of a directory path, either in NetWare documentation or on the screen, the volume name is followed by a colon (:), as in SYS:PUBLIC.

VOLUME DEFINITION TABLE

A table that keeps track of volume segment information such as volume name, volume size, and where volume segments are located on various network hard disks. Each NetWare volume contains a volume definition table in its NetWare partition.

VOLUME SEGMENT

A physical division of a volume. A volume can have up to 32 volume segments. The maximum number of volume segments on a NetWare disk partition is 8.

A volume can have multiple physical segments spanning multiple hard disks, allowing you to create large volumes. NetWare maintains a volume definition table that maps the segments on the hard disk to the volume.

W

WAIT STATE

A period of time when the processor does nothing; it simply waits. A wait state is used to synchronize circuitry or devices operating at different speeds. For example, wait states used in memory access slow down the CPU so all components seem to be running at the same speed.

WAIT TIME

In a NetWare UPS system, the number of seconds the UPS will wait before signaling to the file server that the normal power supply is off. The file server then alerts attached workstations to log out.

WAN

See *wide area network.*

WIDE AREA NETWORK (WAN)

A network that communicates over a long distance, such as across a city or around the world.

A local area network becomes a part of a wide area network when a link is established (using modems, remote routers, phone lines, satellites, or a microwave connection) to a mainframe system, a public data network, or another local area network.

WORKGROUP MANAGER

An assistant network supervisor with rights to create and delete bindery objects (such as users, groups, or print queues) and to manage user accounts.

A Workgroup Manager has supervisory privileges over a part of the bindery. When several groups share a file server, use Workgroup Managers over groups that want autonomous control over their own users and data.

Workgroup Managers supplement, but do not replace, the network SUPERVISOR. SUPERVISOR retains absolute control over the network. Workgroup Managers do not automatically acquire rights to the directory structure and file system. These rights must be granted by SUPERVISOR.

WORKSTATION

A personal computer connected to a NetWare network and used to perform tasks through application programs or utilities. Also referred to as a *client* or, simply, a *station*.

WRITE RIGHT

A file-system right that grants the right to open and write to files.

X

XON/XOFF

A handshake protocol that prevents a sending system from transmitting data faster than a receiving system can accept it.

Index

· ·

About This Index: Page numbers shown in **boldface** indicate principal discussions of primary topics and subtopics. Page numbers shown in *italics* denote illustrations.

Q

T

A Network Administrator's Checklist

TASK	AS NEEDED	DAILY	WEEKLY	MONTHLY	CHAPTER
USER SUPPORT					
Provide user support		●			12
Provide user training				●	12
User accounts—setup	●				8, 9, 10, 12, 13, 18
User accounts—maintenance	●				12, 13
User accounts—removal	●				8, 10, 12
DISK SPACE MANAGEMENT					
Review user disk space usage				●	15
Clean out "common" areas				●	15
Remove unnecessary files from volume roots			●		10, 15
FILE/DIRECTORY MANAGEMENT					
Check for duplicate files		●			15
Archive unused files				●	17
Maintain naming scheme for data files		●			8, 16
Maintain logical directory structure	●				8, 16
Separate data/applications files	●				8, 13, 16
SECURITY					
Password checks			●		10, 15
Trustee rights review			●		10, 15
Anti-viral scans (network)				●	10, 16
Anti-viral scans (workstations)		●			10, 12

13. On what computer-related subject(s) would you like to see more books?

_____

_____

_____

14. Do you have any other comments about this book? (Please feel free to use a separate piece of paper if you need more room)

_____

_____

_____

_____

PLEASE FOLD, SEAL, AND MAIL TO SYBEX

SYBEX INC.
Department M
2021 Challenger Drive
Alameda, CA
94501

GET A FREE CATALOG JUST FOR EXPRESSING YOUR OPINION.

Help us improve our books and get a *FREE* full-color catalog in the bargain. Please complete this form, pull out this page and send it in today. The address is on the reverse side.

Name _____   Company _____

Address _____   City _____ State ____ Zip _____

Phone (___) _____

1. How would you rate the overall quality of this book?

❑ Excellent
❑ Very Good
❑ Good
❑ Fair
❑ Below Average
❑ Poor

2. What were the things you liked most about the book? (Check all that apply)

❑ Pace
❑ Format
❑ Writing Style
❑ Examples
❑ Table of Contents
❑ Index
❑ Price
❑ Illustrations
❑ Type Style
❑ Cover
❑ Depth of Coverage
❑ Fast Track Notes

3. What were the things you liked *least* about the book? (Check all that apply)

❑ Pace
❑ Format
❑ Writing Style
❑ Examples
❑ Table of Contents
❑ Index
❑ Price
❑ Illustrations
❑ Type Style
❑ Cover
❑ Depth of Coverage
❑ Fast Track Notes

4. Where did you buy this book?

❑ Bookstore chain
❑ Small independent bookstore
❑ Computer store
❑ Wholesale club
❑ College bookstore
❑ Technical bookstore
❑ Other _____

5. How did you decide to buy this particular book?

❑ Recommended by friend
❑ Recommended by store personnel
❑ Author's reputation
❑ Sybex's reputation
❑ Read book review in _____
❑ Other _____

6. How did you pay for this book?

❑ Used own funds
❑ Reimbursed by company
❑ Received book as a gift

7. What is your level of experience with the subject covered in this book?

❑ Beginner
❑ Intermediate
❑ Advanced

8. How long have you been using a computer?

years _____
months _____

9. Where do you most often use your computer?

❑ Home
❑ Work

❑ Both
❑ Other _____

10. What kind of computer equipment do you have? (Check all that apply)

❑ PC Compatible Desktop Computer
❑ PC Compatible Laptop Computer
❑ Apple/Mac Computer
❑ Apple/Mac Laptop Computer
❑ CD ROM
❑ Fax Modem
❑ Data Modem
❑ Scanner
❑ Sound Card
❑ Other _____

11. What other kinds of software packages do you ordinarily use?

❑ Accounting
❑ Databases
❑ Networks
❑ Apple/Mac
❑ Desktop Publishing
❑ Spreadsheets
❑ CAD
❑ Games
❑ Word Processing
❑ Communications
❑ Money Management
❑ Other _____

12. What operating systems do you ordinarily use?

❑ DOS
❑ OS/2
❑ Windows
❑ Apple/Mac
❑ Windows NT
❑ Other _____